COMPUTER ORGANIZATION AND ARCHITECTURE
DESIGNING FOR PERFORMANCE
NINTH EDITION

William Stallings

PEARSON

Boston   Columbus   Indianapolis   New York   San Francisco   Upper Saddle River
Amsterdam   Cape Town   Dubai   London   Madrid   Milan   Munich   Paris   Montréal   Toronto
Delhi   Mexico City   São Paulo   Sydney   Hong Kong   Seoul   Singapore   Taipei   Tokyo

Editorial Director: Marcia Horton
Executive Editor: Tracy Dunkelberger
Associate Editor: Carole Snyder
Director of Marketing: Patrice Jones
Marketing Manager: Yez Alayan
Marketing Coordinator: Kathryn Ferranti
Marketing Assistant: Emma Snider
Director of Production: Vince O'Brien
Managing Editor: Jeff Holcomb
Production Project Manager: Kayla Smith-Tarbox
Production Editor: Pat Brown
Manufacturing Buyer: Pat Brown
Creative Director: Jayne Conte

Designer: Bruce Kenselaar
Manager, Visual Research: Karen Sanatar
Manager, Rights and Permissions: Mike Joyce
Text Permission Coordinator: Jen Roach
Cover Art: Charles Bowman/Robert Harding
Lead Media Project Manager: Daniel Sandin
Full-Service Project Management: Shiny Rajesh/
   Integra Software Services Pvt. Ltd.
Composition: Integra Software Services Pvt. Ltd.
Printer/Binder: Edward Brothers
Cover Printer: Lehigh-Phoenix Color/Hagerstown
Text Font: Times Ten-Roman

Credits: Figure 2.14: reprinted with permission from The Computer Language Company, Inc. Figure 17.10: Buyya, Rajkumar, High-Performance Cluster Computing: Architectures and Systems, Vol I, 1st edition, ©1999. Reprinted and Electronically reproduced by permission of Pearson Education, Inc. Upper Saddle River, New Jersey. Figure 17.11: Reprinted with permission from Ethernet Alliance.

Credits and acknowledgments borrowed from other sources and reproduced, with permission, in this textbook appear on the appropriate page within text.

Library of Congress Cataloging-in-Publication Data available upon request

10 9 8 7 6 5 4 3 2 1

ISBN 10:   0-13-293633-X
ISBN 13: 978-0-13-293633-0

To Tricia (ATS),
my loving wife, the kindest
and gentlest person

CONTENTS

ONLINE CHAPTERS[1]

ONLINE APPENDICES

---

[1]Online chapters, appendices, and other documents are Premium Content, available via the access card at the front of this book.

ONLINE RESOURCES

Site	Location	Description
Companion Website	WilliamStallings.com/ ComputerOrganization	*Student Resources* link: Useful links and documents for students. *Instructor Resources* link: Useful links and documents for instructors.
Premium Content	Click on *Premium Content* link at Companion Website or at pearsonhighered.com/stallings and enter the student access code found on the card in the front of the book.	Online chapters, appendices, and other documents that supplement the book.
Instructor Resource Center (IRC)	Click on *Pearson Resources for Instructors* link at Companion Website or on *Instructor Resource* link at pearsonhighered.com/stallings.	Solutions manual, projects manual, slides, and other useful documents.
Computer Science Student Resource Site	ComputerScienceStudent.com	Useful links and documents for computer science students.

PREFACE

WHAT'S NEW IN THE NINTH EDITION

In the four years since the eighth edition of this book was published, the field has seen continued innovations and improvements. In this new edition, I try to capture these changes while maintaining a broad and comprehensive coverage of the entire field. To begin this process of revision, the eighth edition of this book was extensively reviewed by a number of professors who teach the subject and by professionals working in the field. The result is that, in many places, the narrative has been clarified and tightened, and illustrations have been improved.

Beyond these refinements to improve pedagogy and user-friendliness, there have been substantive changes throughout the book. Roughly the same chapter organization has been retained, but much of the material has been revised and new material has been added. The most noteworthy changes are as follows:

- **Point-to-point interconnect:** The traditional bus architecture has increasingly been replaced with high-speed point-to-point interconnect schemes. A new section explores this technology, using Intel's QuickPath Interconnect (QPI) as an example.

- **PCI Express:** PCI Express (PCIe) has become a standard peripheral interconnect architecture, replacing PCI and other bus-based architectures. A new section covers PCIe.

- **Solid state drive and flash memory:** Solid state drives are increasingly displacing hard disk drives over a range of computers. A new section covers SSDs and the underlying flash memory technology.

- **IEEE 754 Floating-Point Standard:** The coverage of IEEE 754 has been updated to reflect the 2008 standard.

- **Contemporary mainframe organization:** Chapters 7 and 18 include sections on the zEnterprise 196, IBM's latest mainframe computer offering (at the time of this writing), introduced in 2010.

- **I/O standards:** The book has been updated to reflect the latest developments, including Thunderbolt.

- **Multicore architecture:** The material on multicore architecture has been expanded significantly.

- **Student study aids:** Each chapter now begins with a list of learning objectives.

- **Sample syllabus:** The text contains more material than can be conveniently covered in one semester. Accordingly, instructors are provided with several sample syllabi that guide the use of the text within limited time (e.g., 16 weeks or 12 weeks). These samples are based on real-world experience by professors with the eighth edition.
- **Test bank:** A set of review questions, including yes/no, multiple choice, and fill in the blank is provided for each chapter.

With each new edition it is a struggle to maintain a reasonable page count while adding new material. In part this objective is realized by eliminating obsolete material and tightening the narrative. For this edition, chapters and appendices that are of less general interest have been moved online, as individual PDF files. This has allowed an expansion of material without the corresponding increase in size and price.

OBJECTIVES

This book is about the structure and function of computers. Its purpose is to present, as clearly and completely as possible, the nature and characteristics of modern-day computer systems.

This task is challenging for several reasons. First, there is a tremendous variety of products that can rightly claim the name of computer, from single-chip microprocessors costing a few dollars to supercomputers costing tens of millions of dollars. Variety is exhibited not only in cost but also in size, performance, and application. Second, the rapid pace of change that has always characterized computer technology continues with no letup. These changes cover all aspects of computer technology, from the underlying integrated circuit technology used to construct computer components to the increasing use of parallel organization concepts in combining those components.

In spite of the variety and pace of change in the computer field, certain fundamental concepts apply consistently throughout. The application of these concepts depends on the current state of the technology and the price/performance objectives of the designer. The intent of this book is to provide a thorough discussion of the fundamentals of computer organization and architecture and to relate these to contemporary design issues.

The subtitle suggests the theme and the approach taken in this book. It has always been important to design computer systems to achieve high performance, but never has this requirement been stronger or more difficult to satisfy than today. All of the basic performance characteristics of computer systems, including processor speed, memory speed, memory capacity, and interconnection data rates, are increasing rapidly. Moreover, they are increasing at different rates. This makes it difficult to design a balanced system that maximizes the performance and utilization of all elements. Thus, computer design increasingly becomes a game of changing the structure or function in one area to compensate for a performance mismatch in another area. We will see this game played out in numerous design decisions throughout the book.

A computer system, like any system, consists of an interrelated set of components. The system is best characterized in terms of structure—the way in which components are interconnected, and function—the operation of the individual components. Furthermore, a computer's organization is hierarchical. Each major component can be further described by decomposing it into its major subcomponents and describing their structure and function.

For clarity and ease of understanding, this hierarchical organization is described in this book from the top down:

- **Computer system:** Major components are processor, memory, I/O.
- **Processor:** Major components are control unit, registers, ALU, and instruction execution unit.
- **Control unit:** Provides control signals for the operation and coordination of all processor components. Traditionally, a microprogramming implementation has been used, in which major components are control memory, microinstruction sequencing logic, and registers. More recently, microprogramming has been less prominent but remains an important implementation technique.

The objective is to present the material in a fashion that keeps new material in a clear context. This should minimize the chance that the reader will get lost and should provide better motivation than a bottom-up approach.

Throughout the discussion, aspects of the system are viewed from the points of view of both architecture (those attributes of a system visible to a machine language programmer) and organization (the operational units and their interconnections that realize the architecture).

EXAMPLE SYSTEMS

This text is intended to acquaint the reader with the design principles and implementation issues of contemporary operating systems. Accordingly, a purely conceptual or theoretical treatment would be inadequate. To illustrate the concepts and to tie them to real-world design choices that must be made, two processor families have been chosen as running examples:

- **Intel x86 architecture:** The x86 architecture is the most widely used for nonembedded computer systems. The x86 is essentially a complex instruction set computer (CISC) with some RISC features. Recent members of the x86 family make use of superscalar and multicore design principles. The evolution of features in the x86 architecture provides a unique case study of the evolution of most of the design principles in computer architecture.
- **ARM:** The ARM architecture is arguably the most widely used embedded processor, used in cell phones, iPods, remote sensor equipment, and many other devices. The ARM is essentially a reduced instruction set computer (RISC). Recent members of the ARM family make use of superscalar and multicore design principles.

Many, but by no means all, of the examples in this book are drawn from these two computer families. Numerous other systems, both contemporary and historical, provide examples of important computer architecture design features.

PLAN OF THE TEXT

The book is organized into six parts (see Chapter 0 for an overview):

- Overview
- The computer system

- Arithmetic and logic
- The central processing unit
- Parallel organization, including multicore
- The control unit

The book includes a number of pedagogic features, including the use of interactive simulations and numerous figures and tables to clarify the discussion. Each chapter includes a list of key words, review questions, homework problems, and suggestions for further reading. The book also includes an extensive glossary, a list of frequently used acronyms, and a bibliography.

INTENDED AUDIENCE

The book is intended for both an academic and a professional audience. As a textbook, it is intended as a one- or two-semester undergraduate course for computer science, computer engineering, and electrical engineering majors. It covers all the core topics in the body of knowledge category, *Architecture and Organization*, in the *IEEE/ACM Computer Curriculum 2008: An Interim Revision to CS 2001*. This book also covers the core area *CE-CAO Computer Architecture and Organization* from the *IEEE/ACM Computer Engineering Curriculum Guidelines 2004*.

For the professional interested in this field, the book serves as a basic reference volume and is suitable for self-study.

INSTRUCTOR SUPPORT MATERIALS

Support materials for instructors are available at the **Instructor Resource Center (IRC)** for this textbook, which can be reached through the Publisher's Website www.pearsonhighered .com/stallings or by clicking on the link labeled "Pearson Resources for Instructors" at this book's Companion Website at WilliamStallings.com/ComputerOrganization. To gain access to the IRC, please contact your local Pearson sales representative via pearsonhighered .com/educator/replocator/requestSalesRep.page or call Pearson Faculty Services at 1-800-526-0485. The IRC provides the following materials:

- **Projects manual:** Project resources including documents and portable software, plus suggested project assignments for all of the project categories listed subsequently in this Preface.
- **Solutions manual:** Solutions to end-of-chapter Review Questions and Problems.
- **PowerPoint slides:** A set of slides covering all chapters, suitable for use in lecturing.
- **PDF files:** Copies of all figures and tables from the book.
- **Test bank:** A chapter-by-chapter set of questions.
- **Sample syllabuses:** The text contains more material than can be conveniently covered in one semester. Accordingly, instructors are provided with several sample syllabuses that guide the use of the text within limited time. These samples are based on real-world experience by professors with the first edition.

The **Companion Website**, at WilliamStallings.com/ComputerOrganization (click on Instructor Resources link) includes the following:

- Links to Websites for other courses being taught using this book.
- Sign-up information for an Internet mailing list for instructors using this book to exchange information, suggestions, and questions with each other and with the author.

STUDENT RESOURCES

For this new edition, a tremendous amount of original supporting material for students has been made available online, at two Web locations. The **Companion Website**, at WilliamStallings.com/ComputerOrganization (click on Student Resources link), includes a list of relevant links organized by chapter and an errata sheet for the book.

Purchasing this textbook new grants the reader six months of access to the **Premium Content Site**, which includes the following materials:

- **Online chapters:** To limit the size and cost of the book, two chapters of the book are provided in PDF format. The chapters are listed in this book's table of contents.
- **Online appendices:** There are numerous interesting topics that support material found in the text but whose inclusion is not warranted in the printed text. A total of 13 appendices cover these topics for the interested student. The appendices are listed in this book's table of contents.
- **Homework problems and solutions:** To aid the student in understanding the material, a separate set of homework problems with solutions are available. Students can enhance their understanding of the material by working out the solutions to these problems and then checking their answers.
- **Key papers:** Several dozen papers from the professional literature, many hard to find, are provided for further reading.
- **Supporting documents:** A variety of other useful documents are referenced in the text and provided online.

Finally, I maintain the Computer Science Student Resource Site at **WilliamStallings .com/StudentSupport.html**.

PROJECTS AND OTHER STUDENT EXERCISES

For many instructors, an important component of a computer organization and architecture course is a project or set of projects by which the student gets hands-on experience to reinforce concepts from the text. This book provides an unparalleled degree of support for including a projects component in the course. The instructor's support materials available through Prentice Hall not only includes guidance on how to assign and structure the projects but also includes a set of user's manuals for various project types plus specific assignments, all written especially for this book. Instructors can assign work in the following areas:

- **Interactive simulation assignments:** Described subsequently.

- **Research projects:** A series of research assignments that instruct the student to research a particular topic on the Internet and write a report.
- **Simulation projects:** The IRC provides support for the use of the two simulation packages: SimpleScalar can be used to explore computer organization and architecture design issues. SMPCache provides a powerful educational tool for examining cache design issues for symmetric multiprocessors.
- **Assembly language projects:** A simplified assembly language, CodeBlue, is used and assignments based on the popular Core Wars concept are provided.
- **Reading/report assignments:** A list of papers in the literature, one or more for each chapter, that can be assigned for the student to read and then write a short report.
- **Writing assignments:** A list of writing assignments to facilitate learning the material.
- **Test bank:** Includes T/F, multiple choice, and fill-in-the-blanks questions and answers.

   This diverse set of projects and other student exercises enables the instructor to use the book as one component in a rich and varied learning experience and to tailor a course plan to meet the specific needs of the instructor and students. See Appendix A in this book for details.

INTERACTIVE SIMULATIONS

An important feature in this edition is the incorporation of interactive simulations. These simulations provide a powerful tool for understanding the complex design features of a modern computer system. A total of 20 interactive simulations are used to illustrate key functions and algorithms in computer organization and architecture design. At the relevant point in the book, an icon indicates that a relevant interactive simulation is available online for student use. Because the animations enable the user to set initial conditions, they can serve as the basis for student assignments. The instructor's supplement includes a set of assignments, one for each of the animations. Each assignment includes several specific problems that can be assigned to students. For access to the animations, click on the rotating globe at this book's Website at http://williamstallings.com/ComputerOrganization.

ACKNOWLEDGMENTS

This new edition has benefited from review by a number of people, who gave generously of their time and expertise. The following professors and instructors reviewed all or a large part of the manuscript: Branson Murrill (Virginia Commonwealth University), Pan Deng (Florida International University), Bob Broeg (Western Oregon University), Curtis Meadow (University of Maine, Orono), Charles Weems (University of Massachusetts), and Mike Jochen (East Stroudsberg University).

   Thanks also to the many people who provided detailed technical reviews of one or more chapters: Kauser Johar, Todd Bezenek (Quantum), Moustafa Mohamed (University of Colorado at Boulder), Dharmesh Parikh, Qigang Wang, Rajiv Dasmohapatra (WIPRO Ltd), Anup Holey (University of Minnesota, Twin Cities), Alexandre Keunecke Ignacio de Mendonca, Douglas Tiedt, Kursad Albayraktaroglu (Advanced Micro Device), Nilanjan Goswami (University of Florida, Gainesville), Adnan Khaleel (Cray, Inc.), Geri Lamble,

Liu Han, Mafijul Islam (Volvo Technology, Sweden), Roger Kahn, Brian Case, Mani Srinivasan, Abhishek Deb, Sushil Menon (University of Pennsylvania), Jigar Savla (Georgia Institute of Technology), Madhu Mutyam, Karl Stevens, Vineet Chadha (Intel Labs), Xingxing Jin (University of Saskatchewan), Jan Hoogerbrugge (NXP Semiconductors), Ninad Laxman Sawant, Aziz Eker (TOBB University of Economics and Technology, Ankara, Turkey), Bhupati Shukla, Niket Choudhary (North Carolina State University), and Oguz Ergin (TOBB University of Economics and Technology, Ankara, Turkey).

Professor Cindy Norris of Appalachian State University, Professor Bin Mu of the University of New Brunswick, and Professor Kenrick Mock of the University of Alaska kindly supplied homework problems.

Aswin Sreedhar of the University of Massachusetts developed the interactive simulation assignments and also wrote the test bank.

Professor Miguel Angel Vega Rodriguez, Professor Dr. Juan Manuel Sánchez Pérez, and Professor Dr. Juan Antonio Gómez Pulido, all of University of Extremadura, Spain, prepared the SMPCache problems in the instructor's manual and authored the SMPCache User's Guide.

Todd Bezenek of the University of Wisconsin and James Stine of Lehigh University prepared the SimpleScalar problems in the instructor's manual, and Todd also authored the SimpleScalar User's Guide.

Finally, I would like to thank the many people responsible for the publication of the book, all of whom did their usual excellent job. This includes the staff at Pearson Education, particularly my editor Tracy Dunkelberger, her assistant Carole Snyder, and production managers Kayla Smith-Tarbox and Pat Brown. I also thank Shiny Rajesh and the production staff at Integra for another excellent and rapid job. Thanks also to the marketing and sales staffs at Pearson, without whose efforts this book would not be in your hands.

ABOUT THE AUTHOR

Dr. William Stallings has made a unique contribution to understanding the broad sweep of technical developments in computer security, computer networking and computer architecture. He has authored 17 titles, and counting revised editions, a total of 42 books on various aspects of these subjects. His writings have appeared in numerous ACM and IEEE publications, including the *Proceedings of the IEEE* and *ACM Computing Reviews*.

He has 10 times received the award for the best Computer Science textbook of the year from the Text and Academic Authors Association.

In over 30 years in the field, he has been a technical contributor, technical manager, and an executive with several high-technology firms. He has designed and implemented both TCP/IP-based and OSI-based protocol suites on a variety of computers and operating systems, ranging from microcomputers to mainframes. As a consultant, he has advised government agencies, computer and software vendors, and major users on the design, selection, and use of networking software and products.

He created and maintains the **Computer Science Student Resource Site** at WilliamStallings.com/StudentSupport.html. This site provides documents and links on a variety of subjects of general interest to computer science students (and professionals). He is a member of the editorial board of Cryptologia, a scholarly journal devoted to all aspects of cryptology.

Dr. Stallings holds a PhD from M.I.T. in Computer Science and a B.S. from Notre Dame in electrical engineering.

CHAPTER 0

READER'S AND INSTRUCTOR'S GUIDE

This book, with its accompanying Web sites, covers a lot of material. In this chapter, we give the reader an overview.

0.1 OUTLINE OF THE BOOK

The book is organized into five parts:

Part One Overview: Provides an overview of computer organization and architecture and looks at how computer design has evolved.

Part Two The Computer System: Examines the major components of a computer and their interconnections, both with each other and the outside world. This part also includes a detailed discussion of internal and external memory and of input/output (I/O). Finally, the relationship between a computer's architecture and the operating system running on that architecture is examined.

Part Three Arithmetic and Logic: This part begins with a chapter that reviews number systems. Chapter 10 is an extended discussion of computer arithmetic. Chapter 11 is a survey of digital logic.

Part Four The Central Processing Unit: Examines the internal architecture and organization of the processor. This part looks at the instruction set architecture. The remainder of the part deals with the structure and function of the processor, including a discussion of reduced instruction set computer (RISC) and superscalar approaches.

Part Five Parallel Organization: Deals with parallel organization, including symmetric multiprocessing, clusters, and multicore architecture.

Part Six The Control Unit: Discusses the internal structure of the processor's control unit and the use of microprogramming.

A number of online chapters and appendices at this book's Web site cover additional topics relevant to the book.

This text is intended to acquaint you with the design principles and implementation issues of contemporary computer organization and architecture. Accordingly, a purely conceptual or theoretical treatment would be inadequate. This book uses examples from a number of different machines to clarify and reinforce the concepts being presented. Many, but by no means all, of the examples are drawn from two computer families: the Intel x86 family and the ARM family. These two systems together encompass most of the current computer design trends. The Intel x86 architecture is essentially a complex instruction set computer (CISC) with some RISC features, while the ARM is essentially a RISC. Both systems make use of superscalar design principles, and both support multiple processor and multicore configurations.

0.2 A ROADMAP FOR READERS AND INSTRUCTORS

This book follows a top–down approach to the presentation of the material. As we discuss in more detail in Section 1.2, a computer system can be viewed as a hierarchical structure. At a top level, we are concerned with the major components of the computers: processor, I/O, memory, and peripheral devices. Part Two examines these components and looks in some detail at each component except the processor. This approach allows us to see the external functional requirements that drive the processor design, setting the stage for Parts Three and Four. Part Three looks at the arithmetic and logic component of the processor in detail. Then Part Four examine the processor in great detail. Because we have the context provided by Part Two, we are able, in Part Four, to see the design decisions that must be made so that the processor supports the overall function of the computer system. Next, in Part Five, we examine systems with multiple processors, including clusters, multiprocessor computers, and multicore computers. Finally, Part Six looks at the control unit, which is at the heart of the processor. Again, the design of the control unit can best be explained in the context of the function it performs within the context of the processor.

0.3 WHY STUDY COMPUTER ORGANIZATION AND ARCHITECTURE?

The *IEEE/ACM Computer Science Curriculum 2008*, prepared by the Joint Task Force on Computing Curricula of the IEEE (Institute of Electrical and Electronics Engineers) Computer Society and ACM (Association for Computing Machinery), lists computer architecture as one of the core subjects that should be in the curriculum of all students in computer science and computer engineering. The report says the following:

> The computer lies at the heart of computing. Without it most of the computing disciplines today would be a branch of theoretical mathematics. A professional in any field of computing should not regard the computer as just a black box that executes programs by magic. All students of computing should acquire some understanding and appreciation of a computer system's functional components, their characteristics, their performance, and their interactions. Students need to understand computer architecture in order to make best use of the software tools and computer languages they use to create programs. In this introduction the term architecture is taken to include instruction set architecture (the programmer's abstraction of a computer), organization or microarchitecture (the internal implementation of a computer at the register and functional unit level), and system architecture (the organization of the computer at the cache and bus level). Students should also understand the complex trade-offs between CPU clock speed, cache size, bus organization, number of core processors, and so on. Computer architecture also underpins other areas of the computing curriculum such as operating systems (input/output, memory technology) and high-level languages (pointers, parameter passing).

Another publication of the task force, *Computer Engineering 2004 Curriculum Guidelines*, emphasized the importance of Computer Architecture and Organization as follows:

> Computer architecture is a key component of computer engineering and the practicing computer engineer should have a practical understanding of this topic. It is concerned with all aspects of the design and organization of the central processing unit and the integration of the CPU into the computer system itself. Architecture extends upward into computer software because a processor's architecture must cooperate with the operating system and system software. It is difficult to design an operating system well without knowledge of the underlying architecture. Moreover, the computer designer must have an understanding of software in order to implement the optimum architecture.
>
> The computer architecture curriculum has to achieve multiple objectives. It must provide an overview of computer architecture and teach students the operation of a typical computing machine. It must cover basic principles, while acknowledging the complexity of existing commercial systems. Ideally, it should reinforce topics that are common to other areas of computer engineering; for example, teaching register indirect addressing reinforces the concept of pointers in C. Finally, students must understand how various peripheral devices interact with, and how they are interfaced to a CPU.

[CLEM00] gives the following examples as reasons for studying computer architecture:

1. Suppose a graduate enters the industry and is asked to select the most cost-effective computer for use throughout a large organization. An understanding of the implications of spending more for various alternatives, such as a larger cache or a higher processor clock rate, is essential to making the decision.

2. Many processors are not used in PCs or servers but in embedded systems. A designer may program a processor in C that is embedded in some real-time or larger system, such as an intelligent automobile electronics controller. Debugging the system may require the use of a logic analyzer that displays the relationship between interrupt requests from engine sensors and machine-level code.

3. Concepts used in computer architecture find application in other courses. In particular, the way in which the computer provides architectural support for programming languages and operating system facilities reinforces concepts from those areas.

As can be seen by perusing the table of contents of this book, computer organization and architecture encompasses a broad range of design issues and concepts. A good overall understanding of these concepts will be useful both in other areas of study and in future work after graduation.

0.4 INTERNET AND WEB RESOURCES

There are a number of resources available on the Internet and the Web that support this book and help readers keep up with developments in this field.

Web Sites for This Book

Three Web sites provide additional resources for students and instructors.

We maintain a **Companion Web site** for this book at http://williamstallings.com/ComputerOrganization. For students, this Web site includes a list of relevant links, organized by chapter, and an errata list for the book. For instructors, this Web site provides links to course pages by professors teaching from this book.

There is also an access-controlled **Premium Content Web site** that provides a wealth of supporting material, including additional online chapters, additional online appendices, a set of homework problems with solutions, copies of a number of key papers in this field, and a number of other supporting documents. See the card at the front of this book for access information.

Finally, additional material for instructors is available at the **Instructor Resource Center (IRC)** for this book. See Preface for details and access information.

Computer Science Student Resource Site

I also maintain the Computer Science Student Resource Site, at ComputerScienceStudent.com. The purpose of this site is to provide documents, information, and links for computer science students and professionals. Links and documents are organized into six categories:

- **Math:** Includes a basic math refresher, a queuing analysis primer, a number system primer, and links to numerous math sites.
- **How-to:** Advice and guidance for solving homework problems, writing technical reports, and preparing technical presentations.
- **Research resources:** Links to important collections of papers, technical reports, and bibliographies.
- **Miscellaneous:** A variety of other useful documents and links.
- **Computer science careers:** Useful links and documents for those considering a career in computer science.
- **Humor and other diversions:** You have to take your mind off your work once in a while.

Other Web Sites

Numerous Web sites provide information related to the topics of this book. The Companion Web site provides links to these sites, organized by chapter.

CHAPTER 1

INTRODUCTION

This book is about the structure and function of computers. Its purpose is to present, as clearly and completely as possible, the nature and characteristics of modern-day computers. This task is a challenging one for two reasons.

First, there is a tremendous variety of products, from single-chip microcomputers costing a few dollars to supercomputers costing tens of millions of dollars, that can rightly claim the name *computer*. Variety is exhibited not only in cost, but also in size, performance, and application. Second, the rapid pace of change that has always characterized computer technology continues with no letup. These changes cover all aspects of computer technology, from the underlying integrated circuit technology used to construct computer components to the increasing use of parallel organization concepts in combining those components.

In spite of the variety and pace of change in the computer field, certain fundamental concepts apply consistently throughout. To be sure, the application of these concepts depends on the current state of technology and the price/performance objectives of the designer. The intent of this book is to provide a thorough discussion of the fundamentals of computer organization and architecture and to relate these to contemporary computer design issues. This chapter introduces the descriptive approach to be taken.

1.1 ORGANIZATION AND ARCHITECTURE

In describing computers, a distinction is often made between *computer architecture* and *computer organization*. Although it is difficult to give precise definitions for these terms, a consensus exists about the general areas covered by each (e.g., see [VRAN80], [SIEW82], and [BELL78a]); an interesting alternative view is presented in [REDD76].

Computer architecture refers to those attributes of a system visible to a programmer or, put another way, those attributes that have a direct impact on the logical execution of a program. **Computer organization** refers to the operational units and their interconnections that realize the architectural specifications. Examples of architectural attributes include the instruction set, the number of bits used to represent various data types (e.g., numbers, characters), I/O mechanisms, and techniques for addressing memory. Organizational attributes include those hardware details transparent to the programmer, such as control signals; interfaces between the computer and peripherals; and the memory technology used.

For example, it is an architectural design issue whether a computer will have a multiply instruction. It is an organizational issue whether that instruction will be implemented by a special multiply unit or by a mechanism that makes repeated use of the add unit of the system. The organizational decision may be based on the anticipated frequency of use of the multiply instruction, the relative speed of the two approaches, and the cost and physical size of a special multiply unit.

Historically, and still today, the distinction between architecture and organization has been an important one. Many computer manufacturers offer a family of computer models, all with the same architecture but with differences in organization. Consequently, the different models in the family have different price and performance characteristics. Furthermore, a particular architecture may span many years and encompass a number of different computer models, its organization changing with changing technology. A prominent example of both these phenomena is the IBM System/370 architecture. This architecture was first introduced in 1970 and included a number of models. The customer with modest requirements could buy a cheaper, slower model and, if demand increased, later upgrade to a more expensive, faster model without having to abandon software that had already been developed. Over the years, IBM has introduced many new models with improved technology to replace older models, offering the customer greater speed, lower cost, or both. These newer models retained the same architecture so that the customer's software investment was protected. Remarkably, the System/370 architecture, with a few enhancements, has survived to this day as the architecture of IBM's mainframe product line.

In a class of computers called microcomputers, the relationship between architecture and organization is very close. Changes in technology not only influence organization but also result in the introduction of more powerful and more complex architectures. Generally, there is less of a requirement for generation-to-generation compatibility for these smaller machines. Thus, there is more interplay between organizational and architectural design decisions. An intriguing example of this is the reduced instruction set computer (RISC), which we examine in Chapter 15.

This book examines both computer organization and computer architecture. The emphasis is perhaps more on the side of organization. However, because a computer organization must be designed to implement a particular architectural specification, a thorough treatment of organization requires a detailed examination of architecture as well.

1.2 STRUCTURE AND FUNCTION

A computer is a complex system; contemporary computers contain millions of elementary electronic components. How, then, can one clearly describe them? The key is to recognize the hierarchical nature of most complex systems, including the computer [SIMO96]. A hierarchical system is a set of interrelated subsystems, each of the latter, in turn, hierarchical in structure until we reach some lowest level of elementary subsystem.

The hierarchical nature of complex systems is essential to both their design and their description. The designer need only deal with a particular level of the system at a time. At each level, the system consists of a set of components and their interrelationships. The behavior at each level depends only on a simplified, abstracted characterization of the system at the next lower level. At each level, the designer is concerned with structure and function:

- **Structure:** The way in which the components are interrelated.
- **Function:** The operation of each individual component as part of the structure.

In terms of description, we have two choices: starting at the bottom and building up to a complete description, or beginning with a top view and decomposing the system into its subparts. Evidence from a number of fields suggests that the top-down approach is the clearest and most effective [WEIN75].

The approach taken in this book follows from this viewpoint. The computer system will be described from the top down. We begin with the major components of a computer, describing their structure and function, and proceed to successively lower layers of the hierarchy. The remainder of this section provides a very brief overview of this plan of attack.

Function

Both the structure and functioning of a computer are, in essence, simple. Figure 1.1 depicts the basic functions that a computer can perform. In general terms, there are only four:

- Data processing
- Data storage
- Data movement
- Control

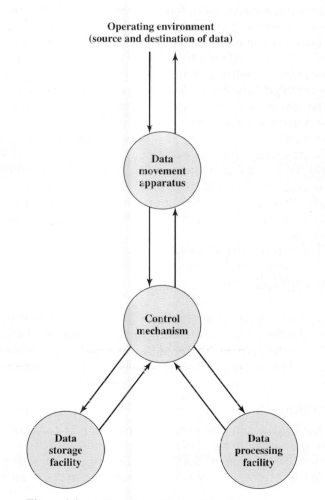

Figure 1.1   A Functional View of the Computer

The computer, of course, must be able to **process data**. The data may take a wide variety of forms, and the range of processing requirements is broad. However, we shall see that there are only a few fundamental methods or types of data processing.

It is also essential that a computer **store data**. Even if the computer is processing data on the fly (i.e., data come in and get processed, and the results go out immediately), the computer must temporarily store at least those pieces of data that are being worked on at any given moment. Thus, there is at least a short-term data storage function. Equally important, the computer performs a long-term data storage function. Files of data are stored on the computer for subsequent retrieval and update.

The computer must be able to **move data** between itself and the outside world. The computer's operating environment consists of devices that serve as either sources or destinations of data. When data are received from or delivered to a device that is directly connected to the computer, the process is known as *input–output* (I/O), and the device is referred to as a *peripheral*. When data are moved over longer distances, to or from a remote device, the process is known as *data communications*.

Finally, there must be **control** of these three functions. Ultimately, this control is exercised by the individual(s) who provides the computer with instructions. Within the computer, a control unit manages the computer's resources and orchestrates the performance of its functional parts in response to those instructions.

At this general level of discussion, the number of possible operations that can be performed is few. Figure 1.2 depicts the four possible types of operations. The computer can function as a data movement device (Figure 1.2a), simply transferring data from one peripheral or communication line to another. It can also function as a data storage device (Figure 1.2b), with data transferred from the external environment to computer storage (read) and vice versa (write). The final two diagrams show operations involving data processing, on data either in storage (Figure 1.2c) or en route between storage and the external environment (Figure 1.2d).

The preceding discussion may seem absurdly generalized. It is certainly possible, even at a top level of computer structure, to differentiate a variety of functions, but, to quote [SIEW82],

> There is remarkably little shaping of computer structure to fit the function to be performed. At the root of this lies the general-purpose nature of computers, in which all the functional specialization occurs at the time of programming and not at the time of design.

Structure

Figure 1.3 is the simplest possible depiction of a computer. The computer interacts in some fashion with its external environment. In general, all of its linkages to the external environment can be classified as peripheral devices or communication lines. We will have something to say about both types of linkages.

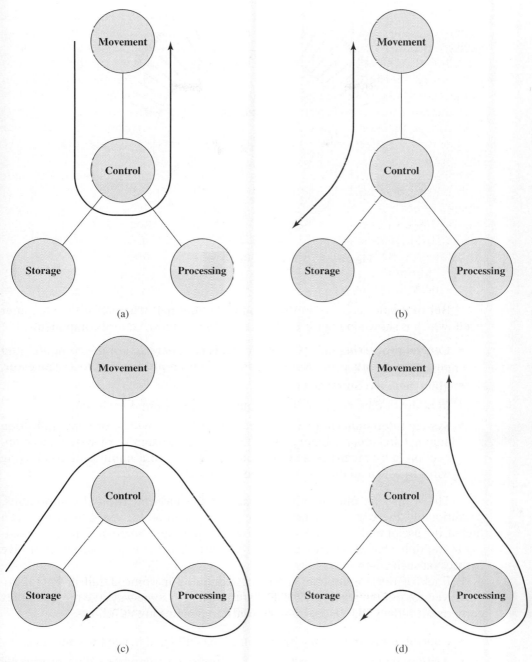

(a)

(b)

(c)

(d)

Figure 1.2   Possible Computer Operations

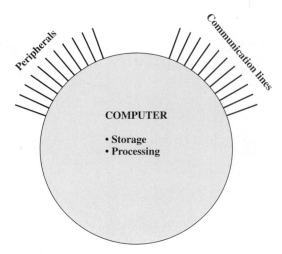

Figure 1.3 The Computer

But of greater concern in this book is the internal structure of the computer itself, which is shown in Figure 1.4. There are four main structural components:

- **Central processing unit (CPU):** Controls the operation of the computer and performs its data processing functions; often simply referred to as **processor**.
- **Main memory:** Stores data.
- **I/O:** Moves data between the computer and its external environment.
- **System interconnection:** Some mechanism that provides for communication among CPU, main memory, and I/O. A common example of system interconnection is by means of a **system bus**, consisting of a number of conducting wires to which all the other components attach.

There may be one or more of each of the aforementioned components. Traditionally, there has been just a single processor. In recent years, there has been increasing use of multiple processors in a single computer. Some design issues relating to multiple processors crop up and are discussed as the text proceeds; Part Five focuses on such computers.

Each of these components will be examined in some detail in Part Two. However, for our purposes, the most interesting and in some ways the most complex component is the CPU. Its major structural components are as follows:

- **Control unit:** Controls the operation of the CPU and hence the computer.
- **Arithmetic and logic unit (ALU):** Performs the computer's data processing functions.
- **Registers:** Provides storage internal to the CPU.
- **CPU interconnection:** Some mechanism that provides for communication among the control unit, ALU, and registers.

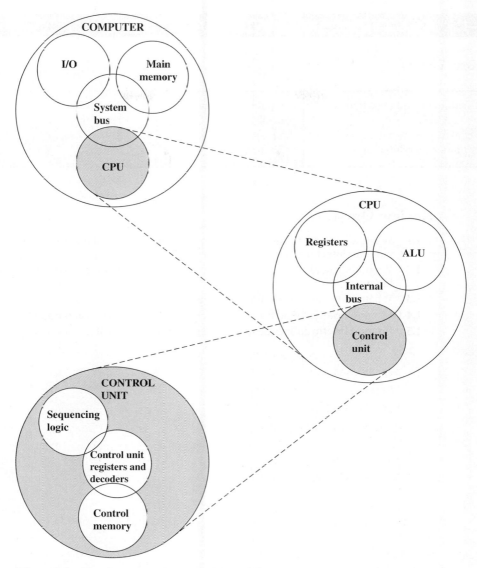

Figure 1.4   The Computer: Top-Level Structure

Each of these components will be examined in some detail in Part Three, where we will see that complexity is added by the use of parallel and pipelined organizational techniques. Finally, there are several approaches to the implementation of the control unit; one common approach is a *microprogrammed* implementation. In essence, a microprogrammed control unit operates by executing microinstructions that define the functionality of the control unit. With this approach, the structure of the control unit can be depicted, as in Figure 1.4. This structure will be examined in Part Four.

1.3   KEY TERMS AND REVIEW QUESTIONS

Key Terms

arithmetic and logic unit (ALU)	computer organization	processor
central processing unit (CPU)	control unit	registers
computer architecture	input–output (I/O)	system bus
	main memory	

Review Questions

1.1   What, in general terms, is the distinction between computer organization and computer architecture?

1.2   What, in general terms, is the distinction between computer structure and computer function?

1.3   What are the four main functions of a computer?

1.4   List and briefly define the main structural components of a computer.

1.5   List and briefly define the main structural components of a processor.

CHAPTER 2

COMPUTER EVOLUTION AND PERFORMANCE

LEARNING OBJECTIVES

After studying this chapter, you should be able to:

◆ Present an overview of the evolution of computer technology from early digital computers to the latest microprocessors.

◆ Understand the key performance issues that relate to computer design.

◆ Explain the reasons for the move to multicore organization, and understand the trade-off between cache and processor resources on a single chip.

◆ Distinguish among multicore, MIC, and GPGPU organizations.

◆ Present an overview of the evolution of the x86 architecture.

◆ Define embedded systems and list some of the requirements and constraints that various embedded systems must meet.

◆ Summarize some of the issues in computer performance assessment.

We begin our study of computers with a brief history. This history is itself interesting and also serves the purpose of providing an overview of computer structure and function. Next, we address the issue of performance. A consideration of the need for balanced utilization of computer resources provides a context that is useful throughout the book. Finally, we look briefly at the evolution of the two systems that serve as key examples throughout the book: the Intel x86 and ARM processor families.

2.1 A BRIEF HISTORY OF COMPUTERS[1]

The First Generation: Vacuum Tubes

ENIAC The ENIAC (Electronic Numerical Integrator And Computer), designed and constructed at the University of Pennsylvania, was the world's first general-purpose electronic digital computer. The project was a response to U.S. needs during World War II. The Army's Ballistics Research Laboratory (BRL), an agency responsible for developing range and trajectory tables for new weapons, was having difficulty supplying these tables accurately and within a reasonable time frame. Without these firing tables, the new weapons and artillery were useless to gunners. The BRL employed more than 200 people who, using desktop calculators, solved the necessary ballistics equations. Preparation of the tables for a single weapon would take one person many hours, even days.

John Mauchly, a professor of electrical engineering at the University of Pennsylvania, and John Eckert, one of his graduate students, proposed to build a general-purpose computer using vacuum tubes for the BRL's application. In 1943, the Army accepted this proposal, and work began on the ENIAC. The resulting

---

[1]This book's Companion Web site contains several links to sites that provide photographs of many of the devices and components discussed in this section.

machine was enormous, weighing 30 tons, occupying 1500 square feet of floor space, and containing more than 18,000 vacuum tubes. When operating, it consumed 140 kilowatts of power. It was also substantially faster than any electromechanical computer, capable of 5000 additions per second.

The ENIAC was a decimal rather than a binary machine. That is, numbers were represented in decimal form, and arithmetic was performed in the decimal system. Its memory consisted of 20 *accumulators*, each capable of holding a 10-digit decimal number. A ring of 10 vacuum tubes represented each digit. At any time, only one vacuum tube was in the ON state, representing one of the 10 digits. The major drawback of the ENIAC was that it had to be programmed manually by setting switches and plugging and unplugging cables.

The ENIAC was completed in 1946, too late to be used in the war effort. Instead, its first task was to perform a series of complex calculations that were used to help determine the feasibility of the hydrogen bomb. The use of the ENIAC for a purpose other than that for which it was built demonstrated its general-purpose nature. The ENIAC continued to operate under BRL management until 1955, when it was disassembled.

THE VON NEUMANN MACHINE The task of entering and altering programs for the ENIAC was extremely tedious. But suppose a program could be represented in a form suitable for storing in memory alongside the data. Then, a computer could get its instructions by reading them from memory, and a program could be set or altered by setting the values of a portion of memory.

This idea, known as the **stored-program concept**, is usually attributed to the ENIAC designers, most notably the mathematician John von Neumann, who was a consultant on the ENIAC project. Alan Turing developed the idea at about the same time. The first publication of the idea was in a 1945 proposal by von Neumann for a new computer, the EDVAC (Electronic Discrete Variable Computer).[2]

In 1946, von Neumann and his colleagues began the design of a new stored-program computer, referred to as the IAS computer, at the Princeton Institute for Advanced Studies. The IAS computer, although not completed until 1952, is the prototype of all subsequent general-purpose computers.[3]

Figure 2.1 shows the general structure of the IAS computer (compare to middle portion of Figure 1.4). It consists of

- A **main memory**, which stores both data and instructions[4]
- An **arithmetic and logic unit (ALU)** capable of operating on binary data
- A **control unit**, which interprets the instructions in memory and causes them to be executed
- **Input/output (I/O)** equipment operated by the control unit

---

[2]The 1945 report on EDVAC is in the Premium Content section of this book's Web site.

[3]A 1954 report [GOLD54] describes the implemented IAS machine and lists the final instruction set. It is provided in the Premium Content section of this book's Web site.

[4]In this book, unless otherwise noted, the term *instruction* refers to a machine instruction that is directly interpreted and executed by the processor, in contrast to an instruction in a high-level language, such as Ada or C++, which must first be compiled into a series of machine instructions before being executed.

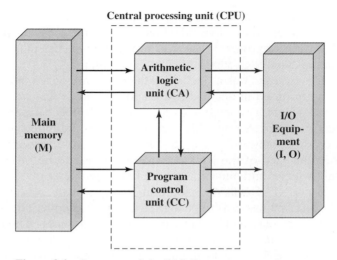

Figure 2.1 Structure of the IAS Computer

This structure was outlined in von Neumann's earlier proposal, which is worth quoting in part at this point [VONN45]:

> 2.2 **First:** Since the device is primarily a computer, it will have to perform the elementary operations of arithmetic most frequently. These are addition, subtraction, multiplication, and division. It is therefore reasonable that it should contain specialized organs for just these operations.
>
> It must be observed, however, that while this principle as such is probably sound, the specific way in which it is realized requires close scrutiny. At any rate a *central arithmetical* part of the device will probably have to exist, and this constitutes *the first specific part: CA*.
>
> 2.3 **Second:** The logical control of the device, that is, the proper sequencing of its operations, can be most efficiently carried out by a central control organ. If the device is to be *elastic,* that is, as nearly as possible *all purpose,* then a distinction must be made between the specific instructions given for and defining a particular problem, and the general control organs that see to it that these instructions—no matter what they are—are carried out. The former must be stored in some way; the latter are represented by definite operating parts of the device. By the *central control* we mean this latter function only, and the organs that perform it form *the second specific part: CC*.
>
> 2.4 **Third:** Any device that is to carry out long and complicated sequences of operations (specifically of calculations) must have a considerable memory...

The instructions which govern a complicated problem may constitute considerable material, particularly so, if the code is circumstantial (which it is in most arrangements). This material must be remembered.

At any rate, the total *memory* constitutes *the third specific part of the device: M.*

2.6 The three specific parts CA, CC (together C), and M correspond to the *associative* neurons in the human nervous system. It remains to discuss the equivalents of the *sensory* or *afferent* and the *motor* or *efferent* neurons. These are the *input* and *output* organs of the device.

The device must be endowed with the ability to maintain input and output (sensory and motor) contact with some specific medium of this type. The medium will be called the *outside recording medium of the device: R.*

2.7 **Fourth:** The device must have organs to transfer... information from R into its specific parts C and M. These organs form its *input, the fourth specific part: I.* It will be seen that it is best to make all transfers from R (by I) into M and never directly from C.

2.8 **Fifth:** The device must have organs to transfer... from its specific parts C and M into R. These organs form its *output, the fifth specific part: O.* It will be seen that it is again best to make all transfers from M (by O) into R, and never directly from C.

With rare exceptions, all of today's computers have this same general structure and function and are thus referred to as **von Neumann machines**. Thus, it is worthwhile at this point to describe briefly the operation of the IAS computer [BURK46]. Following [HAYE98], the terminology and notation of von Neumann are changed in the following to conform more closely to modern usage; the examples and illustrations accompanying this discussion are based on that latter text.

The memory of the IAS consists of 1000 storage locations, called **words**, of 40 binary digits (bits) each.[5] Both data and instructions are stored there. Numbers are represented in binary form, and each instruction is a binary code. Figure 2.2 illustrates these formats. Each number is represented by a sign bit and a 39-bit value. A word may also contain two 20-bit instructions, with each instruction consisting of an 8-bit operation code **(opcode)** specifying the operation to be performed and a 12-bit address designating one of the words in memory (numbered from 0 to 999).

The control unit operates the IAS by fetching instructions from memory and executing them one at a time. To explain this, a more detailed structure diagram is

---

[5]There is no universal definition of the term *word*. In general, a word is an ordered set of bytes or bits that is the normal unit in which information may be stored, transmitted, or operated on within a given computer. Typically, if a processor has a fixed-length instruction set, then the instruction length equals the word length.

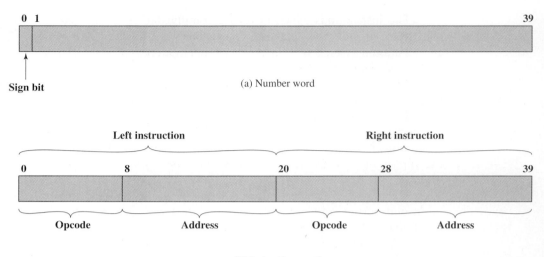

Figure 2.2 IAS Memory Formats

needed, as indicated in Figure 2.3. This figure reveals that both the control unit and the ALU contain storage locations, called *registers*, defined as follows:

- **Memory buffer register (MBR):** Contains a word to be stored in memory or sent to the I/O unit, or is used to receive a word from memory or from the I/O unit.
- **Memory address register (MAR):** Specifies the address in memory of the word to be written from or read into the MBR.
- **Instruction register (IR):** Contains the 8-bit opcode instruction being executed.
- **Instruction buffer register (IBR):** Employed to hold temporarily the right-hand instruction from a word in memory.
- **Program counter (PC):** Contains the address of the next instruction pair to be fetched from memory.
- **Accumulator (AC) and multiplier quotient (MQ):** Employed to hold temporarily operands and results of ALU operations. For example, the result of multiplying two 40-bit numbers is an 80-bit number; the most significant 40 bits are stored in the AC and the least significant in the MQ.

The IAS operates by repetitively performing an **instruction cycle**, as shown in Figure 2.4. Each instruction cycle consists of two subcycles. During the **fetch cycle**, the opcode of the next instruction is loaded into the IR and the address portion is loaded into the MAR. This instruction may be taken from the IBR, or it can be obtained from memory by loading a word into the MBR, and then down to the IBR, IR, and MAR.

Why the indirection? These operations are controlled by electronic circuitry and result in the use of data paths. To simplify the electronics, there is only one register that is used to specify the address in memory for a read or write and only one register used for the source or destination.

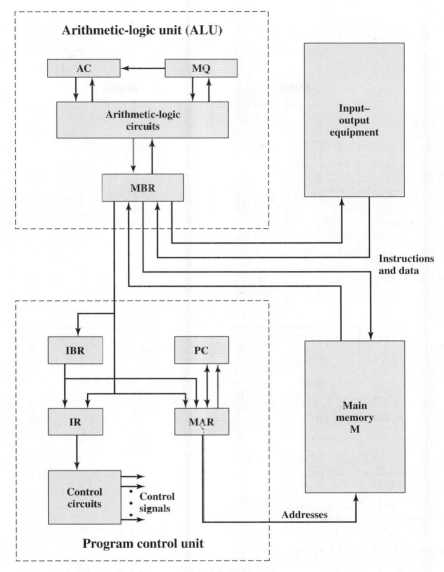

Figure 2.3 Expanded Structure of IAS Computer

Once the opcode is in the IR, the **execute cycle** is performed. Control circuitry interprets the opcode and executes the instruction by sending out the appropriate control signals to cause data to be moved or an operation to be performed by the ALU.

The IAS computer had a total of 21 instructions, which are listed in Table 2.1. These can be grouped as follows:

- **Data transfer:** Move data between memory and ALU registers or between two ALU registers.

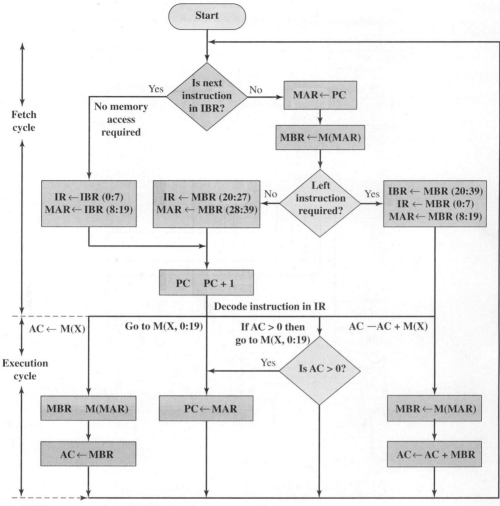

Figure 2.4 Partial Flowchart of IAS Operation

- **Unconditional branch:** Normally, the control unit executes instructions in sequence from memory. This sequence can be changed by a branch instruction, which facilitates repetitive operations.

- **Conditional branch:** The branch can be made dependent on a condition, thus allowing decision points.

- **Arithmetic:** Operations performed by the ALU.

- **Address modify:** Permits addresses to be computed in the ALU and then inserted into instructions stored in memory. This allows a program considerable addressing flexibility.

Table 2.1 The IAS Instruction Set

Instruction Type	Opcode	Symbolic Representation	Description
Data transfer	00001010	LOAD MQ	Transfer contents of register MQ to the accumulator AC
	00001001	LOAD MQ,M(X)	Transfer contents of memory location X to MQ
	00100001	STOR M(X)	Transfer contents of accumulator to memory location X
	00000001	LOAD M(X)	Transfer M(X) to the accumulator
	00000010	LOAD – M(X)	Transfer –M(X) to the accumulator
	00000011	LOAD |M(X)|	Transfer absolute value of M(X) to the accumulator
	00000100	LOAD – |M(X)|	Transfer –|M(X)| to the accumulator
Unconditional branch	00001101	JUMP M(X,0:19)	Take next instruction from left half of M(X)
	00001110	JUMP M(X,20:39)	Take next instruction from right half of M(X)
Conditional branch	00001111	JUMP + M(X,0:19)	If number in the accumulator is nonnegative, take next instruction from left half of M(X)
	00010000	JUMP + M(X,20:39)	If number in the accumulator is nonnegative, take next instruction from right half of M(X)
Arithmetic	00000101	ADD M(X)	Add M(X) to AC; put the result in AC
	00000111	ADD |M(X)|	Add |M(X)| to AC; put the result in AC
	00000110	SUB M(X)	Subtract M(X) from AC; put the result in AC
	00001000	SUB |M(X)|	Subtract |M(X)| from AC; put the remainder in AC
	00001011	MUL M(X)	Multiply M(X) by MQ; put most significant bits of result in AC, put least significant bits in MQ
	00001100	DIV M(X)	Divide AC by M(X); put the quotient in MQ and the remainder in AC
	00010100	LSH	Multiply accumulator by 2; that is, shift left one bit position
	00010101	RSH	Divide accumulator by 2; that is, shift right one position
Address modify	00010010	STOR M(X,8:19)	Replace left address field at M(X) by 12 rightmost bits of AC
	00010011	STOR M(X,28:39)	Replace right address field at M(X) by 12 rightmost bits of AC

Table 2.1 presents instructions in a symbolic, easy-to-read form. Actually, each instruction must conform to the format of Figure 2.2b. The opcode portion (first 8 bits) specifies which of the 21 instructions is to be executed. The address portion (remaining 12 bits) specifies which of the 1000 memory locations is to be involved in the execution of the instruction.

Figure 2.4 shows several examples of instruction execution by the control unit. Note that each operation requires several steps. Some of these are quite elaborate. The multiplication operation requires 39 suboperations, one for each bit position except that of the sign bit.

COMMERCIAL COMPUTERS The 1950s saw the birth of the computer industry with two companies, Sperry and IBM, dominating the marketplace.

In 1947, Eckert and Mauchly formed the Eckert-Mauchly Computer Corporation to manufacture computers commercially. Their first successful machine was the UNIVAC I (Universal Automatic Computer), which was commissioned by the Bureau of the Census for the 1950 calculations. The Eckert-Mauchly Computer Corporation became part of the UNIVAC division of Sperry-Rand Corporation, which went on to build a series of successor machines.

The UNIVAC I was the first successful commercial computer. It was intended for both scientific and commercial applications. The first paper describing the system listed matrix algebraic computations, statistical problems, premium billings for a life insurance company, and logistical problems as a sample of the tasks it could perform.

The UNIVAC II, which had greater memory capacity and higher performance than the UNIVAC I, was delivered in the late 1950s and illustrates several trends that have remained characteristic of the computer industry. First, advances in technology allow companies to continue to build larger, more powerful computers. Second, each company tries to make its new machines *backward compatible*[6] with the older machines. This means that the programs written for the older machines can be executed on the new machine. This strategy is adopted in the hopes of retaining the customer base; that is, when a customer decides to buy a newer machine, he or she is likely to get it from the same company to avoid losing the investment in programs.

The UNIVAC division also began development of the 1100 series of computers, which was to be its major source of revenue. This series illustrates a distinction that existed at one time. The first model, the UNIVAC 1103, and its successors for many years were primarily intended for scientific applications, involving long and complex calculations. Other companies concentrated on business applications, which involved processing large amounts of text data. This split has largely disappeared, but it was evident for a number of years.

IBM, then the major manufacturer of punched-card processing equipment, delivered its first electronic stored-program computer, the 701, in 1953. The 701 was intended primarily for scientific applications [BASH81]. In 1955, IBM introduced the companion 702 product, which had a number of hardware features that suited it to business applications. These were the first of a long series of 700/7000 computers that established IBM as the overwhelmingly dominant computer manufacturer.

The Second Generation: Transistors

The first major change in the electronic computer came with the replacement of the vacuum tube by the transistor. The transistor is smaller, cheaper, and dissipates less heat than a vacuum tube but can be used in the same way as a vacuum tube to construct computers. Unlike the vacuum tube, which requires wires, metal plates, a glass capsule, and a vacuum, the transistor is a *solid-state device*, made from silicon.

The transistor was invented at Bell Labs in 1947 and by the 1950s had launched an electronic revolution. It was not until the late 1950s, however, that fully transistorized computers were commercially available. IBM again was not the

---

[6]Also called *downward compatible*. The same concept, from the point of view of the older system, is referred to as **upward compatible**, or *forward compatible*.

Table 2.2   Computer Generations

Generation	Approximate Dates	Technology	Typical Speed (operations per second)
1	1946–1957	Vacuum tube	40,000
2	1958–1964	Transistor	200,000
3	1965–1971	Small- and medium-scale integration	1,000,000
4	1972–1977	Large-scale integration	10,000,000
5	1978–1991	Very-large-scale integration	100,000,000
6	1991–	Ultra-large-scale integration	1,000,000,000

first company to deliver the new technology. NCR and, more successfully, RCA were the front-runners with some small transistor machines. IBM followed shortly with the 7000 series.

The use of the transistor defines the *second generation* of computers. It has become widely accepted to classify computers into generations based on the fundamental hardware technology employed (Table 2.2). Each new generation is characterized by greater processing performance, larger memory capacity, and smaller size than the previous one.

But there are other changes as well. The second generation saw the introduction of more complex arithmetic and logic units and control units, the use of high-level programming languages, and the provision of *system software* with the computer. In broad terms, system software provided the ability to load programs, move data to peripherals, and libraries to perform common computations, similar to what modern OSes like Windows and Linux do.

The second generation is noteworthy also for the appearance of the Digital Equipment Corporation (DEC). DEC was founded in 1957 and, in that year, delivered its first computer, the PDP-1. This computer and this company began the minicomputer phenomenon that would become so prominent in the third generation.

THE IBM 7094 From the introduction of the 700 series in 1952 to the introduction of the last member of the 7000 series in 1964, this IBM product line underwent an evolution that is typical of computer products. Successive members of the product line show increased performance, increased capacity, and/or lower cost.

Table 2.3 illustrates this trend. The size of main memory, in multiples of 2^{10} 36-bit words, grew from 2K ($1K = 2^{10}$) to 32K words,[7] while the time to access one word of memory, the *memory cycle time*, fell from 30 μs to 1.4 μs. The number of opcodes grew from a modest 24 to 185.

The final column indicates the relative execution speed of the central processing unit (CPU). Speed improvements are achieved by improved electronics (e.g., a transistor implementation is faster than a vacuum tube implementation) and more complex circuitry. For example, the IBM 7094 includes an Instruction Backup

---

[7]A discussion of the uses of numerical prefixes, such as kilo and giga, is contained in a supporting document at the Computer Science Student Resource Site at ComputerScienceStudent.com.

Table 2.3 Example members of the IBM 700/7000 Series

Model Number	First Delivery	CPU Tech-nology	Memory Tech-nology	Cycle Time (μs)	Memory Size (K)	Number of Opcodes	Number of Index Registers	Hardwired Floating-Point	I/O Overlap (Channels)	Instruc-tion Fetch Overlap	Speed (relative to 701)
701	1952	Vacuum tubes	Electrostatic tubes	30	2–4	24	0	no	no	no	1
704	1955	Vacuum tubes	Core	12	4–32	80	3	yes	no	no	2.5
709	1958	Vacuum tubes	Core	12	32	140	3	yes	yes	no	4
7090	1960	Transistor	Core	2.18	32	169	3	yes	yes	no	25
7094 I	1962	Transistor	Core	2	32	185	7	yes (double precision)	yes	yes	30
7094 II	1964	Transistor	Core	1.4	32	185	7	yes (double precision)	yes	yes	50

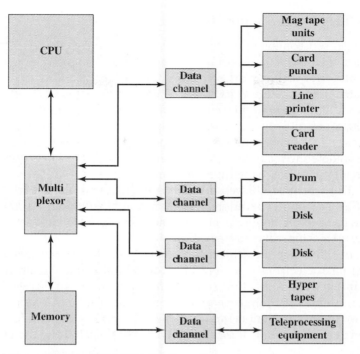

Figure 2.5 An IBM 7094 Configuration

Register, used to buffer the next instruction. The control unit fetches two adjacent words from memory for an instruction fetch. Except for the occurrence of a branching instruction, which is relatively infrequent (perhaps 10 to 15%), this means that the control unit has to access memory for an instruction on only half the instruction cycles. This prefetching significantly reduces the average instruction cycle time.

The remainder of the columns of Table 2.3 will become clear as the text proceeds.

Figure 2.5 shows a large (many peripherals) configuration for an IBM 7094, which is representative of second-generation computers [BELL71]. Several differences from the IAS computer are worth noting. The most important of these is the use of **data channels**. A data channel is an independent I/O module with its own processor and instruction set. In a computer system with such devices, the CPU does not execute detailed I/O instructions. Such instructions are stored in a main memory to be executed by a special-purpose processor in the data channel itself. The CPU initiates an I/O transfer by sending a control signal to the data channel, instructing it to execute a sequence of instructions in memory. The data channel performs its task independently of the CPU and signals the CPU when the operation is complete. This arrangement relieves the CPU of a considerable processing burden.

Another new feature is the **multiplexor**, which is the central termination point for data channels, the CPU, and memory. The multiplexor schedules access to the memory from the CPU and data channels, allowing these devices to act independently.

The Third Generation: Integrated Circuits

A single, self-contained transistor is called a *discrete component*. Throughout the 1950s and early 1960s, electronic equipment was composed largely of discrete components—transistors, resistors, capacitors, and so on. Discrete components were manufactured separately, packaged in their own containers, and soldered or wired together onto masonite-like circuit boards, which were then installed in computers, oscilloscopes, and other electronic equipment. Whenever an electronic device called for a transistor, a little tube of metal containing a pinhead-sized piece of silicon had to be soldered to a circuit board. The entire manufacturing process, from transistor to circuit board, was expensive and cumbersome.

These facts of life were beginning to create problems in the computer industry. Early second-generation computers contained about 10,000 transistors. This figure grew to the hundreds of thousands, making the manufacture of newer, more powerful machines increasingly difficult.

In 1958 came the achievement that revolutionized electronics and started the era of microelectronics: the invention of the integrated circuit. It is the **integrated circuit** that defines the third generation of computers. In this section, we provide a brief introduction to the technology of integrated circuits. Then we look at perhaps the two most important members of the third generation, both of which were introduced at the beginning of that era: the IBM System/360 and the DEC PDP-8.

MICROELECTRONICS Microelectronics means, literally, "small electronics." Since the beginnings of digital electronics and the computer industry, there has been a persistent and consistent trend toward the reduction in size of digital electronic circuits. Before examining the implications and benefits of this trend, we need to say something about the nature of digital electronics. A more detailed discussion is found in Chapter 11.

The basic elements of a digital computer, as we know, must perform storage, movement, processing, and control functions. Only two fundamental types of components are required (Figure 2.6): gates and memory cells. A gate is a device that implements a simple Boolean or logical function, such as IF *A* AND *B* ARE TRUE THEN *C* IS TRUE (AND gate). Such devices are called gates because they control data flow in much the same way that canal gates control the flow of water. The memory cell is a device that can store one bit of data; that is, the device can be in one of two stable states at any time. By interconnecting large numbers of these

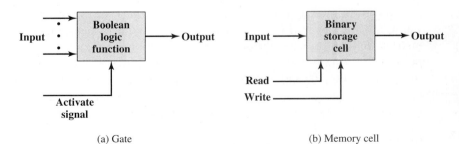

(a) Gate (b) Memory cell

Figure 2.6 Fundamental Computer Elements

fundamental devices, we can construct a computer. We can relate this to our four basic functions as follows:

- **Data storage:** Provided by memory cells.
- **Data processing:** Provided by gates.
- **Data movement:** The paths among components are used to move data from memory to memory and from memory through gates to memory.
- **Control:** The paths among components can carry control signals. For example, a gate will have one or two data inputs plus a control signal input that activates the gate. When the control signal is ON, the gate performs its function on the data inputs and produces a data output. Similarly, the memory cell will store the bit that is on its input lead when the WRITE control signal is ON and will place the bit that is in the cell on its output lead when the READ control signal is ON.

Thus, a computer consists of gates, memory cells, and interconnections among these elements. The gates and memory cells are, in turn, constructed of simple digital electronic components.

The integrated circuit exploits the fact that such components as transistors, resistors, and conductors can be fabricated from a semiconductor such as silicon. It is merely an extension of the solid-state art to fabricate an entire circuit in a tiny piece of silicon rather than assemble discrete components made from separate pieces of silicon into the same circuit. Many transistors can be produced at the same time on a single wafer of silicon. Equally important, these transistors can be connected with a process of metallization to form circuits.

Figure 2.7 depicts the key concepts in an integrated circuit. A thin **wafer** of silicon is divided into a matrix of small areas, each a few millimeters square. The identical circuit pattern is fabricated in each area, and the wafer is broken up into **chips**. Each chip consists of many gates and/or memory cells plus a number of input and output attachment points. This chip is then packaged in housing that protects it and provides pins for attachment to devices beyond the chip. A number of these packages can then be interconnected on a printed circuit board to produce larger and more complex circuits.

Initially, only a few gates or memory cells could be reliably manufactured and packaged together. These early integrated circuits are referred to as *small-scale integration* (SSI). As time went on, it became possible to pack more and more components on the same chip. This growth in density is illustrated in Figure 2.8; it is one of the most remarkable technological trends ever recorded.[8] This figure reflects the famous Moore's law, which was propounded by Gordon Moore, cofounder of Intel, in 1965 [MOOR65]. Moore observed that the number of transistors that could be put on a single chip was doubling every year and correctly predicted that this pace would continue into the near future. To the surprise of many, including Moore, the pace continued year after year and decade after decade. The pace slowed to a doubling every 18 months in the 1970s but has sustained that rate ever since.

---

[8]Note that the vertical axis uses a log scale. A basic review of log scales is in the math refresher document at the Computer Science Student Resource Site at ComputerScienceStudent.com.

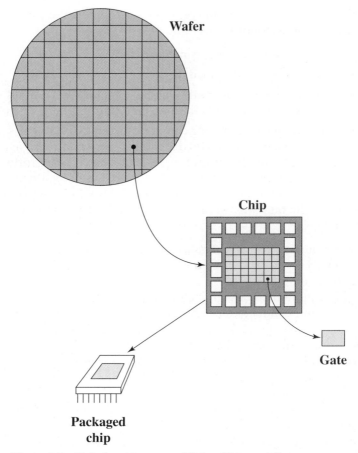

Figure 2.7 Relationship among Wafer, Chip, and Gate

The consequences of Moore's law are profound:

1. The cost of a chip has remained virtually unchanged during this period of rapid growth in density. This means that the cost of computer logic and memory circuitry has fallen at a dramatic rate.

2. Because logic and memory elements are placed closer together on more densely packed chips, the electrical path length is shortened, increasing operating speed.

3. The computer becomes smaller, making it more convenient to place in a variety of environments.

4. There is a reduction in power and cooling requirements.

5. The interconnections on the integrated circuit are much more reliable than solder connections. With more circuitry on each chip, there are fewer inter-chip connections.

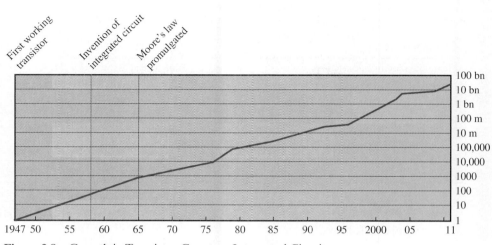

Figure 2.8   Growth in Transistor Count on Integrated Circuits

IBM SYSTEM/360 By 1964, IBM had a firm grip on the computer market with its 7000 series of machines. In that year, IBM announced the System/360, a new family of computer products. Although the announcement itself was no surprise, it contained some unpleasant news for current IBM customers: the 360 product line was incompatible with older IBM machines. Thus, the transition to the 360 would be difficult for the current customer base. This was a bold step by IBM, but one IBM felt was necessary to break out of some of the constraints of the 7000 architecture and to produce a system capable of evolving with the new integrated circuit technology [PADE81, GIFF87]. The strategy paid off both financially and technically. The 360 was the success of the decade and cemented IBM as the overwhelmingly dominant computer vendor, with a market share above 70%. And, with some modifications and extensions, the architecture of the 360 remains to this day the architecture of IBM's mainframe[9] computers. Examples using this architecture can be found throughout this text.

The System/360 was the industry's first planned family of computers. The family covered a wide range of performance and cost. Table 2.4 indicates some of the key characteristics of the various models in 1965 (each member of the family is distinguished by a model number). The models were compatible in the sense that a program written for one model should be capable of being executed by another model in the series, with only a difference in the time it takes to execute.

The concept of a family of compatible computers was both novel and extremely successful. A customer with modest requirements and a budget to match could start with the relatively inexpensive Model 30. Later, if the customer's needs grew, it was possible to upgrade to a faster machine with more memory without

---

[9]The term *mainframe* is used for the larger, most powerful computers other than supercomputers. Typical characteristics of a mainframe are that it supports a large database, has elaborate I/O hardware, and is used in a central data processing facility.

Table 2.4   Key Characteristics of the System/360 Family

Characteristic	Model 30	Model 40	Model 50	Model 65	Model 75
Maximum memory size (bytes)	64K	256K	256K	512K	512K
Data rate from memory (Mbytes/s)	0.5	0.8	2.0	8.0	16.0
Processor cycle time (μs)	1.0	0.625	0.5	0.25	0.2
Relative speed	1	3.5	10	21	50
Maximum number of data channels	3	3	4	6	6
Maximum data rate on one channel (Kbytes/s)	250	400	800	1250	1250

sacrificing the investment in already-developed software. The characteristics of a family are as follows:

- **Similar or identical instruction set:** In many cases, the exact same set of machine instructions is supported on all members of the family. Thus, a program that executes on one machine will also execute on any other. In some cases, the lower end of the family has an instruction set that is a subset of that of the top end of the family. This means that programs can move up but not down.
- **Similar or identical operating system:** The same basic operating system is available for all family members. In some cases, additional features are added to the higher-end members.
- **Increasing speed:** The rate of instruction execution increases in going from lower to higher family members.
- **Increasing number of I/O ports:** The number of I/O ports increases in going from lower to higher family members.
- **Increasing memory size:** The size of main memory increases in going from lower to higher family members.
- **Increasing cost:** At a given point in time, the cost of a system increases in going from lower to higher family members.

How could such a family concept be implemented? Differences were achieved based on three factors: basic speed, size, and degree of simultaneity [STEV64]. For example, greater speed in the execution of a given instruction could be gained by the use of more complex circuitry in the ALU, allowing suboperations to be carried out in parallel. Another way of increasing speed was to increase the width of the data path between main memory and the CPU. On the Model 30, only 1 byte (8 bits) could be fetched from main memory at a time, whereas 8 bytes could be fetched at a time on the Model 75.

The System/360 not only dictated the future course of IBM but also had a profound impact on the entire industry. Many of its features have become standard on other large computers.

DEC PDP-8   In the same year that IBM shipped its first System/360, another momentous first shipment occurred: PDP-8 from Digital Equipment

Corporation (DEC). At a time when the average computer required an air-conditioned room, the PDP-8 (dubbed a minicomputer by the industry, after the miniskirt of the day) was small enough that it could be placed on top of a lab bench or be built into other equipment. It could not do everything the mainframe could, but at $16,000, it was cheap enough for each lab technician to have one. In contrast, the System/360 series of mainframe computers introduced just a few months before cost hundreds of thousands of dollars.

The low cost and small size of the PDP-8 enabled another manufacturer to purchase a PDP-8 and integrate it into a total system for resale. These other manufacturers came to be known as **original equipment manufacturers (OEMs)**, and the OEM market became and remains a major segment of the computer marketplace.

The PDP-8 was an immediate hit and made DEC's fortune. This machine and other members of the PDP-8 family that followed it (see Table 2.5) achieved a production status formerly reserved for IBM computers, with about 50,000 machines sold over the next dozen years. As DEC's official history puts it, the PDP-8 "established the concept of minicomputers, leading the way to a multibillion dollar industry." It also established DEC as the number one minicomputer vendor, and, by the time the PDP-8 had reached the end of its useful life, DEC was the number two computer manufacturer, behind IBM.

In contrast to the central-switched architecture (Figure 2.5) used by IBM on its 700/7000 and 360 systems, later models of the PDP-8 used a structure that is now virtually universal for microcomputers: the bus structure. This is illustrated in Figure 2.9. The PDP-8 bus, called the Omnibus, consists of 96 separate signal paths, used to carry control, address, and data signals. Because all system components share a common set of signal paths, their use can be controlled by the CPU. This architecture is highly flexible, allowing modules to be plugged into the bus to create various configurations.

Later Generations

Beyond the third generation there is less general agreement on defining generations of computers. Table 2.2 suggests that there have been a number of later generations, based on advances in integrated circuit technology. With the introduction of large-scale integration (LSI), more than 1000 components can be placed on a single integrated circuit chip. Very-large-scale integration (VLSI) achieved more than 10,000 components per chip, while current ultra-large-scale integration (ULSI) chips can contain more than one billion components.

With the rapid pace of technology, the high rate of introduction of new products, and the importance of software and communications as well as hardware, the classification by generation becomes less clear and less meaningful. It could be said that the commercial application of new developments resulted in a major change in the early 1970s and that the results of these changes are still being worked out. In this section, we mention two of the most important of these results.

SEMICONDUCTOR MEMORY The first application of integrated circuit technology to computers was construction of the processor (the control unit and the arithmetic and logic unit) out of integrated circuit chips. But it was also found that this same technology could be used to construct memories.

Table 2.5 Evolution of the PDP-8

Model	First Shipped	Cost of Processor + 4K 12-bit Words of Memory ($1000s)	Data Rate from Memory (words/μs)	Volume (cubic feet)	Innovations and Improvements
PDP-8	4/65	16.2	1.26	8.0	Automatic wire-wrapping production
PDP-8/5	9/66	8.79	0.08	3.2	Serial instruction implementation
PDP-8/1	4/68	11.6	1.34	8.0	Medium-scale integrated circuits
PDP-8/L	11/68	7.0	1.26	2.0	Smaller cabinet
PDP-8/E	3/71	4.99	1.52	2.2	Omnibus
PDP-8/M	6/72	3.69	1.52	1.8	Half-size cabinet with fewer slots than 8/E
PDP-8/A	1/75	2.6	1.34	1.2	Semiconductor memory; floating-point processor

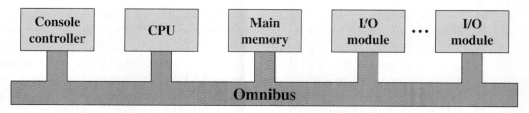

Figure 2.9 PDP-8 Bus Structure

In the 1950s and 1960s, most computer memory was constructed from tiny rings of ferromagnetic material, each about a sixteenth of an inch in diameter. These rings were strung up on grids of fine wires suspended on small screens inside the computer. Magnetized one way, a ring (called a *core*) represented a one; magnetized the other way, it stood for a zero. Magnetic-core memory was rather fast; it took as little as a millionth of a second to read a bit stored in memory. But it was expensive, bulky, and used destructive readout: The simple act of reading a core erased the data stored in it. It was therefore necessary to install circuits to restore the data as soon as it had been extracted.

Then, in 1970, Fairchild produced the first relatively capacious semiconductor memory. This chip, about the size of a single core, could hold 256 bits of memory. It was nondestructive and much faster than core. It took only 70 billionths of a second to read a bit. However, the cost per bit was higher than for that of core.

In 1974, a seminal event occurred: The price per bit of semiconductor memory dropped below the price per bit of core memory. Following this, there has been a continuing and rapid decline in memory cost accompanied by a corresponding increase in physical memory density. This has led the way to smaller, faster machines with memory sizes of larger and more expensive machines from just a few years earlier. Developments in memory technology, together with developments in processor technology to be discussed next, changed the nature of computers in less than a decade. Although bulky, expensive computers remain a part of the landscape, the computer has also been brought out to the "end user," with office machines and personal computers.

Since 1970, semiconductor memory has been through 13 generations: 1K, 4K, 16K, 64K, 256K, 1M, 4M, 16M, 64M, 256M, 1G, 4G, and, as of this writing, 16 Gbits on a single chip ($1K = 2^{10}$, $1M = 2^{20}$, $1G = 2^{30}$). Each generation has provided four times the storage density of the previous generation, accompanied by declining cost per bit and declining access time.

MICROPROCESSORS Just as the density of elements on memory chips has continued to rise, so has the density of elements on processor chips. As time went on, more and more elements were placed on each chip, so that fewer and fewer chips were needed to construct a single computer processor.

A breakthrough was achieved in 1971, when Intel developed its 4004. The 4004 was the first chip to contain *all* of the components of a CPU on a single chip: The microprocessor was born.

The 4004 can add two 4-bit numbers and can multiply only by repeated addition. By today's standards, the 4004 is hopelessly primitive, but it marked the beginning of a continuing evolution of microprocessor capability and power.

This evolution can be seen most easily in the number of bits that the processor deals with at a time. There is no clear-cut measure of this, but perhaps the best measure is the data bus width: the number of bits of data that can be brought into or sent out of the processor at a time. Another measure is the number of bits in the accumulator or in the set of general-purpose registers. Often, these measures coincide, but not always. For example, a number of microprocessors were developed that operate on 16-bit numbers in registers but can only read and write 8 bits at a time.

The next major step in the evolution of the microprocessor was the introduction in 1972 of the Intel 8008. This was the first 8-bit microprocessor and was almost twice as complex as the 4004.

Neither of these steps was to have the impact of the next major event: the introduction in 1974 of the Intel 8080. This was the first general-purpose microprocessor. Whereas the 4004 and the 8008 had been designed for specific applications, the 8080 was designed to be the CPU of a general-purpose microcomputer. Like the 8008, the 8080 is an 8-bit microprocessor. The 8080, however, is faster, has a richer instruction set, and has a large addressing capability.

About the same time, 16-bit microprocessors began to be developed. However, it was not until the end of the 1970s that powerful, general-purpose 16-bit microprocessors appeared. One of these was the 8086. The next step in this trend occurred in 1981, when both Bell Labs and Hewlett-Packard developed 32-bit, single-chip microprocessors. Intel introduced its own 32-bit microprocessor, the 80386, in 1985 (Table 2.6).

Table 2.6 Evolution of Intel Microprocessors

(a) 1970s Processors

	4004	8008	8080	8086	8088
Introduced	1971	1972	1974	1978	1979
Clock speeds	108 kHz	108 kHz	2 MHz	5 MHz, 8 MHz, 10 MHz	5 MHz, 8 MHz
Bus width	4 bits	8 bits	8 bits	16 bits	8 bits
Number of transistors	2300	3500	6000	29,000	29,000
Feature size (μm)	10		6	3	6
Addressable memory	640 Bytes	16 kB	64 kB	1 MB	1 MB

(b) 1980s Processors

	80286	386TM DX	386TM SX	486TM DX CPU
Introduced	1982	1985	1988	1989
Clock speeds	6 MHz–12.5 MHz	16 MHz–33 MHz	16 MHz–33 MHz	25 MHz–50 MHz
Bus width	16 bits	32 bits	16 bits	32 bits
Number of transistors	134,000	275,000	275,000	1.2 million
Feature size (μm)	1.5	1	1	0.8–1
Addressable memory	16 MB	4 GB	16 MB	4 GB
Virtual memory	1 GB	64 TB	64 TB	64 TB
Cache	—	—	—	8 kB

Table 2.6 Continued

(c) 1990s Processors

	486TM SX	**Pentium**	**Pentium Pro**	**Pentium II**
Introduced	1991	1993	1995	1997
Clock speeds	16 MHz–33 MHz	60 MHz–166 MHz,	150 MHz–200 MHz	200 MHz–300 MHz
Bus width	32 bits	32 bits	64 bits	64 bits
Number of transistors	1.185 million	3.1 million	5.5 million	7.5 million
Feature size (μm)	1	0.8	0.6	0.35
Addressable memory	4 GB	4 GB	64 GB	64 GB
Virtual memory	64 TB	64 TB	64 TB	64 TB
Cache	8 kB	8 kB	512 kB L1 and 1 MB L2	512 kB L2

(d) Recent Processors

	Pentium III	**Pentium 4**	**Core 2 Duo**	**Core i7 EE 990**
Introduced	1999	2000	2006	2011
Clock speeds	450–660 MHz	1.3–1.8 GHz	1.06–1.2 GHz	3.5 GHz
Bus width	64 bits	64 bits	64 bits	64 bits
Number of transistors	9.5 million	42 million	167 million	1170 million
Feature size (nm)	250	180	65	32
Addressable memory	64 GB	64 GB	64 GB	64 GB
Virtual memory	64 TB	64 TB	64 TB	64 TB
Cache	512 kB L2	256 kB L2	2 MB L2	1.5 MB L2/12 MB L3

2.2 DESIGNING FOR PERFORMANCE

Year by year, the cost of computer systems continues to drop dramatically, while the performance and capacity of those systems continue to rise equally dramatically. Today's laptops have the computing power of an IBM mainframe from 10 or 15 years ago. Thus, we have virtually "free" computer power. Processors are so inexpensive that we now have microprocessors we throw away. The digital pregnancy test as an example (used once and then thrown away). And this continuing technological revolution has enabled the development of applications of astounding complexity and power. For example, desktop applications that require the great power of today's microprocessor-based systems include

- Image processing
- Speech recognition
- Videoconferencing
- Multimedia authoring
- Voice and video annotation of files
- Simulation modeling

Workstation systems now support highly sophisticated engineering and scientific applications, as well as simulation systems, and have the ability to support image and video applications. In addition, businesses are relying on increasingly powerful servers to handle transaction and database processing and to support massive client/server networks that have replaced the huge mainframe computer centers of yesteryear.

What is fascinating about all this from the perspective of computer organization and architecture is that, on the one hand, the basic building blocks for today's computer miracles are virtually the same as those of the IAS computer from over 50 years ago, while on the other hand, the techniques for squeezing the last iota of performance out of the materials at hand have become increasingly sophisticated.

This observation serves as a guiding principle for the presentation in this book. As we progress through the various elements and components of a computer, two objectives are pursued. First, the book explains the fundamental functionality in each area under consideration, and second, the book explores those techniques required to achieve maximum performance. In the remainder of this section, we highlight some of the driving factors behind the need to design for performance.

Microprocessor Speed

What gives Intel x86 processors or IBM mainframe computers such mind-boggling power is the relentless pursuit of speed by processor chip manufacturers. The evolution of these machines continues to bear out Moore's law, mentioned previously. So long as this law holds, chipmakers can unleash a new generation of chips every three years—with four times as many transistors. In memory chips, this has quadrupled the capacity of dynamic random-access memory (DRAM), still the basic technology for computer main memory, every three years. In microprocessors, the addition of new circuits, and the speed boost that comes from reducing the distances between them, has improved performance four- or fivefold every three years or so since Intel launched its x86 family in 1978.

But the raw speed of the microprocessor will not achieve its potential unless it is fed a constant stream of work to do in the form of computer instructions. Anything that gets in the way of that smooth flow undermines the power of the processor. Accordingly, while the chipmakers have been busy learning how to fabricate chips of greater and greater density, the processor designers must come up with ever more elaborate techniques for feeding the monster. Among the techniques built into contemporary processors are the following:

- **Pipelining:** With pipelining, a processor can simultaneously work on multiple instructions. The processor overlaps operations by moving data or instructions into a conceptual pipe with all stages of the pipe processing simultaneously. For example, while one instruction is being executed, the computer is decoding the next instruction.
- **Branch prediction:** The processor looks ahead in the instruction code fetched from memory and predicts which branches, or groups of instructions, are likely to be processed next. If the processor guesses right most of the time, it can prefetch the correct instructions and buffer them so that the processor is kept busy. The more sophisticated examples of this strategy predict not just the

next branch but multiple branches ahead. Thus, branch prediction increases the amount of work available for the processor to execute.

- **Data flow analysis:** The processor analyzes which instructions are dependent on each other's results, or data, to create an optimized schedule of instructions. In fact, instructions are scheduled to be executed when ready, independent of the original program order. This prevents unnecessary delay.

- **Speculative execution:** Using branch prediction and data flow analysis, some processors speculatively execute instructions ahead of their actual appearance in the program execution, holding the results in temporary locations. This enables the processor to keep its execution engines as busy as possible by executing instructions that are likely to be needed.

These and other sophisticated techniques are made necessary by the sheer power of the processor. They make it possible to exploit the raw speed of the processor.

Performance Balance

While processor power has raced ahead at breakneck speed, other critical components of the computer have not kept up. The result is a need to look for performance balance: an adjusting of the organization and architecture to compensate for the mismatch among the capabilities of the various components.

Nowhere is the problem created by such mismatches more critical than in the interface between processor and main memory. While processor speed has grown rapidly, the speed with which data can be transferred between main memory and the processor has lagged badly. The interface between processor and main memory is the most crucial pathway in the entire computer because it is responsible for carrying a constant flow of program instructions and data between memory chips and the processor. If memory or the pathway fails to keep pace with the processor's insistent demands, the processor stalls in a wait state, and valuable processing time is lost.

A system architect can attack this problem in a number of ways, all of which are reflected in contemporary computer designs. Consider the following examples:

- Increase the number of bits that are retrieved at one time by making DRAMs "wider" rather than "deeper" and by using wide bus data paths.

- Change the DRAM interface to make it more efficient by including a cache[10] or other buffering scheme on the DRAM chip.

- Reduce the frequency of memory access by incorporating increasingly complex and efficient cache structures between the processor and main memory. This includes the incorporation of one or more caches on the processor chip as well as on an off-chip cache close to the processor chip.

- Increase the interconnect bandwidth between processors and memory by using higher-speed buses and a hierarchy of buses to buffer and structure data flow.

---

[10]A cache is a relatively small fast memory interposed between a larger, slower memory and the logic that accesses the larger memory. The cache holds recently accessed data and is designed to speed up subsequent access to the same data. Caches are discussed in Chapter 4.

Another area of design focus is the handling of I/O devices. As computers become faster and more capable, more sophisticated applications are developed that support the use of peripherals with intensive I/O demands. Figure 2.10 gives some examples of typical peripheral devices in use on personal computers and workstations. These devices create tremendous data throughput demands. While the current generation of processors can handle the data pumped out by these devices, there remains the problem of getting that data moved between processor and peripheral. Strategies here include caching and buffering schemes plus the use of higher-speed interconnection buses and more elaborate structures of buses. In addition, the use of multiple-processor configurations can aid in satisfying I/O demands.

The key in all this is balance. Designers constantly strive to balance the throughput and processing demands of the processor components, main memory, I/O devices, and the interconnection structures. This design must constantly be rethought to cope with two constantly evolving factors:

- The rate at which performance is changing in the various technology areas (processor, buses, memory, peripherals) differs greatly from one type of element to another.

- New applications and new peripheral devices constantly change the nature of the demand on the system in terms of typical instruction profile and the data access patterns.

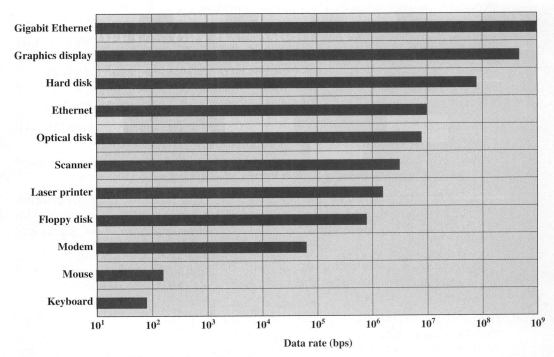

Figure 2.10   Typical I/O Device Data Rates'

Thus, computer design is a constantly evolving art form. This book attempts to present the fundamentals on which this art form is based and to present a survey of the current state of that art.

Improvements in Chip Organization and Architecture

As designers wrestle with the challenge of balancing processor performance with that of main memory and other computer components, the need to increase processor speed remains. There are three approaches to achieving increased processor speed:

- Increase the hardware speed of the processor. This increase is fundamentally due to shrinking the size of the logic gates on the processor chip, so that more gates can be packed together more tightly and to increasing the clock rate. With gates closer together, the propagation time for signals is significantly reduced, enabling a speeding up of the processor. An increase in clock rate means that individual operations are executed more rapidly.

- Increase the size and speed of caches that are interposed between the processor and main memory. In particular, by dedicating a portion of the processor chip itself to the cache, cache access times drop significantly.

- Make changes to the processor organization and architecture that increase the effective speed of instruction execution. Typically, this involves using parallelism in one form or another.

Traditionally, the dominant factor in performance gains has been in increases in clock speed due and logic density. However, as clock speed and logic density increase, a number of obstacles become more significant [INTE04b]:

- **Power:** As the density of logic and the clock speed on a chip increase, so does the power density (Watts/cm^2). The difficulty of dissipating the heat generated on high-density, high-speed chips is becoming a serious design issue [GIBB04, BORK03].

- **RC delay:** The speed at which electrons can flow on a chip between transistors is limited by the resistance and capacitance of the metal wires connecting them; specifically, delay increases as the RC product increases. As components on the chip decrease in size, the wire interconnects become thinner, increasing resistance. Also, the wires are closer together, increasing capacitance.

- **Memory latency:** Memory speeds lag processor speeds, as previously discussed.

Thus, there will be more emphasis on organization and architectural approaches to improving performance. These techniques are discussed in later chapters of the book.

Beginning in the late 1980s, and continuing for about 15 years, two main strategies have been used to increase performance beyond what can be achieved simply by increasing clock speed. First, there has been an increase in cache capacity. There are now typically two or three levels of cache between the processor and main memory. As chip density has increased, more of the cache memory has been incorporated on the chip, enabling faster cache access. For example, the original Pentium chip devoted about 10% of on-chip area to a cache. Contemporary chips devote over half of the chip area to caches.

Second, the instruction execution logic within a processor has become increasingly complex to enable parallel execution of instructions within the processor. Two noteworthy design approaches have been pipelining and superscalar. A pipeline works much as an assembly line in a manufacturing plant enabling different stages of execution of different instructions to occur at the same time along the pipeline. A superscalar approach in essence allows multiple pipelines within a single processor so that instructions that do not depend on one another can be executed in parallel.

By the mid to late 90s, both of these approaches were reaching a point of diminishing returns. The internal organization of contemporary processors is exceedingly complex and is able to squeeze a great deal of parallelism out of the instruction stream. It seems likely that further significant increases in this direction will be relatively modest [GIBB04]. With three levels of cache on the processor chip, each level providing substantial capacity, it also seems that the benefits from the cache are reaching a limit.

However, simply relying on increasing clock rate for increased performance runs into the power dissipation problem already referred to. The faster the clock rate, the greater the amount of power to be dissipated, and some fundamental physical limits are being reached.

Figure 2.11 illustrates the concepts we have been discussing.[11] The top line shows that, as per Moore's Law, the number of transistors on a single chip continues to grow exponentially.[12] Meanwhile, the clock speed has leveled off, in order

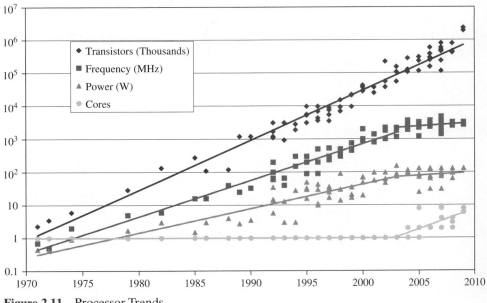

Figure 2.11   Processor Trends

[11]I am grateful to Professor Kathy Yelick of UC Berkeley, who provided this graph.
[12]The observant reader will note that the transistor count values in this figure are significantly less than those of Figure 2.8. That latter figure shows the transistor count for a form of main memory known as DRAM (discussed in Chapter 5), which supports higher transistor density than processor chips.

to prevent a further rise in power. To continue to increase performance, designers have had to find ways of exploiting the growing number of transistors other than simply building a more complex processor. The response in recent years has been the development of the multicore computer chip.

2.3 MULTICORE, MICS, AND GPGPUS

With all of the difficulties cited in the preceding paragraphs in mind, designers have turned to a fundamentally new approach to improving performance: placing multiple processors on the same chip, with a large shared cache. The use of multiple processors on the same chip, also referred to as multiple cores, or **multicore**, provides the potential to increase performance without increasing the clock rate. Studies indicate that, within a processor, the increase in performance is roughly proportional to the square root of the increase in complexity [BORK03]. But if the software can support the effective use of multiple processors, then doubling the number of processors almost doubles performance. Thus, the strategy is to use two simpler processors on the chip rather than one more complex processor.

In addition, with two processors, larger caches are justified. This is important because the power consumption of memory logic on a chip is much less than that of processing logic.

As the logic density on chips continues to rise, the trend to both more cores and more cache on a single chip continues. Two-core chips were quickly followed by four-core chips, then 8, then 16, and so on. As the caches became larger, it made performance sense to create two and then three levels of cache on a chip, with the first-level cache dedicated to an individual processor and levels two and three being shared by all the processors.

Chip manufacturers are now in the process of making a huge leap forward in the number of cores per chip, with more than 50 cores per chip. The leap in performance as well as the challenges in developing software to exploit such a large number of cores have led to the introduction of a new term: **many integrated core (MIC)**.

The multicore and MIC strategy involves a homogeneous collection of general-purpose processors on a single chip. At the same time, chip manufacturers are pursuing another design option: a chip with multiple general-purpose processors plus **graphics processing units (GPUs)** and specialized cores for video processing and other tasks. In broad terms, a GPU is a core designed to perform parallel operations on graphics data. Traditionally found on a plug-in graphics card (display adapter), it is used to encode and render 2D and 3D graphics as well as process video.

Since GPUs perform parallel operations on multiple sets of data, they are increasingly being used as vector processors for a variety of applications that require repetitive computations. This blurs the line between the GPU and the CPU [FATA08, PROP11]. When a broad range of applications are supported by such a processor, the term **general-purpose computing on GPUs (GPGPU)** is used.

We explore design characteristics of multicore computers in Chapter 18.

2.4 THE EVOLUTION OF THE INTEL x86 ARCHITECTURE

Throughout this book, we rely on many concrete examples of computer design and implementation to illustrate concepts and to illuminate trade-offs. Numerous systems, both contemporary and historical, provide examples of important computer architecture design features. But the book relies on examples from two processor families: the Intel x86 and the ARM architecture. The current x86 offerings represent the results of decades of design effort on complex instruction set computers (CISCs). The x86 incorporates the sophisticated design principles once found only on mainframes and supercomputers and serves as an excellent example of CISC design. An alternative approach to processor design in the reduced instruction set computer (RISC). The ARM architecture is used in a wide variety of embedded systems and is one of the most powerful and best-designed RISC-based systems on the market.

In this section and the next, we provide a brief overview of these two systems.

In terms of market share, Intel has ranked as the number one maker of microprocessors for nonembedded systems for decades, a position it seems unlikely to yield. The evolution of its flagship microprocessor product serves as a good indicator of the evolution of computer technology in general.

Table 2.6 shows that evolution. Interestingly, as microprocessors have grown faster and much more complex, Intel has actually picked up the pace. Intel used to develop microprocessors one after another, every four years. But Intel hopes to keep rivals at bay by trimming a year or two off this development time, and has done so with the most recent x86 generations.[13]

It is worthwhile to list some of the highlights of the evolution of the Intel product line:

- **8080:** The world's first general-purpose microprocessor. This was an 8-bit machine, with an 8-bit data path to memory. The 8080 was used in the first personal computer, the Altair.

- **8086:** A far more powerful, 16-bit machine. In addition to a wider data path and larger registers, the 8086 sported an instruction cache, or queue, that prefetches a few instructions before they are executed. A variant of this processor, the 8088, was used in IBM's first personal computer, securing the success of Intel. The 8086 is the first appearance of the x86 architecture.

- **80286:** This extension of the 8086 enabled addressing a 16-MByte memory instead of just 1 MByte.

- **80386:** Intel's first 32-bit machine, and a major overhaul of the product. With a 32-bit architecture, the 80386 rivaled the complexity and power of minicomputers and mainframes introduced just a few years earlier. This was the first Intel processor to support multitasking, meaning it could run multiple programs at the same time.

- **80486:** The 80486 introduced the use of much more sophisticated and powerful cache technology and sophisticated instruction pipelining. The 80486 also

---

[13]Intel refers to this as the *tick-tock model.* Using this model, Intel has successfully delivered next-generation silicon technology as well as new processor microarchitecture on alternating years for the past several years. See http://www.intel.com/content/www/us/en/silicon-innovations/intel-tick-tock-model-general.html

offered a built-in math coprocessor, offloading complex math operations from the main CPU.

- **Pentium:** With the Pentium, Intel introduced the use of superscalar techniques, which allow multiple instructions to execute in parallel.
- **Pentium Pro:** The Pentium Pro continued the move into superscalar organization begun with the Pentium, with aggressive use of register renaming, branch prediction, data flow analysis, and speculative execution.
- **Pentium II:** The Pentium II incorporated Intel MMX technology, which is designed specifically to process video, audio, and graphics data efficiently.
- **Pentium III:** The Pentium III incorporates additional floating-point instructions to support 3D graphics software.
- **Pentium 4:** The Pentium 4 includes additional floating-point and other enhancements for multimedia.[14]
- **Core:** This is the first Intel x86 microprocessor with a dual core, referring to the implementation of two processors on a single chip.
- **Core 2:** The Core 2 extends the architecture to 64 bits. The Core 2 Quad provides four processors on a single chip. More recent Core offerings have up to 10 processors per chip.

Over 30 years after its introduction in 1978, the x86 architecture continues to dominate the processor market outside of embedded systems. Although the organization and technology of the x86 machines have changed dramatically over the decades, the instruction set architecture has evolved to remain backward compatible with earlier versions. Thus, any program written on an older version of the x86 architecture can execute on newer versions. All changes to the instruction set architecture have involved additions to the instruction set, with no subtractions. The rate of change has been the addition of roughly one instruction per month added to the architecture over the 30 years [ANTH08], so that there are now over 500 instructions in the instruction set.

The x86 provides an excellent illustration of the advances in computer hardware over the past 30 years. The 1978 8086 was introduced with a clock speed of 5 MHz and had 29,000 transistors. A quad-core Intel Core 2 introduced in 2008 operates at 3 GHz, a speedup of a factor of 600, and has 820 million transistors, about 28,000 times as many s the 8086. Yet the Core 2 is in only a slightly larger package than the 8086 and has a comparable cost.

2.5 EMBEDDED SYSTEMS AND THE ARM

The ARM architecture refers to a processor architecture that has evolved from RISC design principles and is used in embedded systems. Chapter 15 examines RISC design principles in detail. In this section, we give a brief overview of the concept of embedded systems and then look at the evolution of the ARM.

---

[14]With the Pentium 4, Intel switched from Roman numerals to Arabic numerals for model numbers.

Embedded Systems

The term *embedded system* refers to the use of electronics and software within a product, as opposed to a general-purpose computer, such as a laptop or desktop system. The following is a good general definition:[15]

> **Embedded system.**   A combination of computer hardware and software, and perhaps additional mechanical or other parts, designed to perform a dedicated function. In many cases, embedded systems are part of a larger system or product, as in the case of an antilock braking system in a car.

Embedded systems far outnumber general-purpose computer systems, encompassing a broad range of applications (Table 2.7). These systems have widely varying requirements and constraints, such as the following [GRIM05]:

- Small to large systems, implying very different cost constraints, thus different needs for optimization and reuse

Table 2.7   Examples of Embedded Systems and Their Markets

Market	Embedded Device
Automotive	Ignition system Engine control Brake system
Consumer electronics	Digital and analog televisions Set-top boxes (DVDs, VCRs, Cable boxes) Personal digital assistants (PDAs) Kitchen appliances (refrigerators, toasters, microwave ovens) Automobiles Toys/games Telephones/cell phones/pagers Cameras Global positioning systems
Industrial control	Robotics and controls systems for manufacturing Sensors
Medical	Infusion pumps Dialysis machines Prosthetic devices Cardiac monitors
Office automation	Fax machine Photocopier Printers Monitors Scanners

---

[15]Michael Barr, *Embedded Systems Glossary*. Netrino Technical Library. http://www.netrino.com/Embedded-Systems/Glossary

- Relaxed to very strict requirements and combinations of different quality requirements, for example, with respect to safety, reliability, real-time, and flexibility
- Short to long life times
- Different environmental conditions in terms of, for example, radiation, vibrations, and humidity
- Different application characteristics resulting in static versus dynamic loads, slow to fast speed, compute versus interface intensive tasks, and/or combinations thereof
- Different models of computation ranging from discrete-event systems to those involving continuous time dynamics (usually referred to as hybrid systems)

Often, embedded systems are tightly coupled to their environment. This can give rise to real-time constraints imposed by the need to interact with the environment. Constraints, such as required speeds of motion, required precision of measurement, and required time durations, dictate the timing of software operations. If multiple activities must be managed simultaneously, this imposes more complex real-time constraints.

Figure 2.12, based on [KOOP96], shows in general terms an embedded system organization. In addition to the processor and memory, there are a number of elements that differ from the typical desktop or laptop computer:

- There may be a variety of interfaces that enable the system to measure, manipulate, and otherwise interact with the external environment.
- The human interface may be as simple as a flashing light or as complicated as real-time robotic vision.

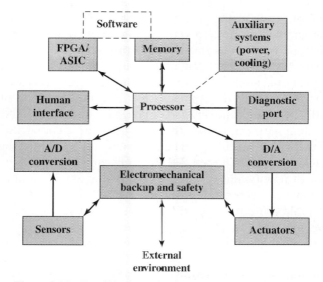

Figure 2.12 Possible Organization of an Embedded System

- The diagnostic port may be used for diagnosing the system that is being controlled—not just for diagnosing the computer.
- Special-purpose field programmable (FPGA), application specific (ASIC), or even nondigital hardware may be used to increase performance or safety.
- Software often has a fixed function and is specific to the application.

ARM Evolution

ARM is a family of RISC-based microprocessors and microcontrollers designed by ARM Inc., Cambridge, England. The company doesn't make processors but instead designs microprocessor and multicore architectures and licenses them to manufacturers. ARM chips are high-speed processors that are known for their small die size and low power requirements. They are widely used in PDAs and other handheld devices, including games and phones as well as a large variety of consumer products. ARM chips are the processors in Apple's popular iPod and iPhone devices. ARM is probably the most widely used embedded processor architecture and indeed the most widely used processor architecture of any kind in the world.

The origins of ARM technology can be traced back to the British-based Acorn Computers company. In the early 1980s, Acorn was awarded a contract by the British Broadcasting Corporation (BBC) to develop a new microcomputer architecture for the BBC Computer Literacy Project. The success of this contract enabled Acorn to go on to develop the first commercial RISC processor, the Acorn RISC Machine (ARM). The first version, ARM1, became operational in 1985 and was used for internal research and development as well as being used as a coprocessor in the BBC machine. Also in 1985, Acorn released the ARM2, which had greater functionality and speed within the same physical space. Further improvements were achieved with the release in 1989 of the ARM3.

Throughout this period, Acorn used the company VLSI Technology to do the actual fabrication of the processor chips. VLSI was licensed to market the chip on its own and had some success in getting other companies to use the ARM in their products, particularly as an embedded processor.

The ARM design matched a growing commercial need for a high-performance, low-power-consumption, small-size, and low-cost processor for embedded applications. But further development was beyond the scope of Acorn's capabilities. Accordingly, a new company was organized, with Acorn, VLSI, and Apple Computer as founding partners, known as ARM Ltd. The Acorn RISC Machine became the Advanced RISC Machine.[16] The new company's first offering, an improvement on the ARM3, was designated ARM6. Subsequently, the company has introduced a number of new families, with increasing functionality and performance. Table 2.8 shows some characteristics of the various ARM architecture families. The numbers in this table are only approximate guides; actual values vary widely for different implementations.

---

[16]The company dropped the designation *Advanced RISC Machine* in the late 1990s. It is now simply known as the ARM architecture.

Table 2.8 ARM Evolution

Family	Notable Features	Cache	Typical MIPS @ MHz
ARM1	32-bit RISC	None	
ARM2	Multiply and swap instructions; Integrated memory management unit, graphics and I/O processor	None	7 MIPS @ 12 MHz
ARM3	First use of processor cache	4 kB unified	12 MIPS @ 25 MHz
ARM6	First to support 32-bit addresses; floating-point unit	4 kB unified	28 MIPS @ 33 MHz
ARM7	Integrated SoC	8 kB unified	60 MIPS @ 60 MHz
ARM8	5-stage pipeline; static branch prediction	8 kB unified	84 MIPS @ 72 MHz
ARM9		16 kB/16 kB	300 MIPS @ 300 MHz
ARM9E	Enhanced DSP instructions	16 kB/16 kB	220 MIPS @ 200 MHz
ARM10E	6-stage pipeline	32 kB/32 kB	
ARM11	9-stage pipeline	Variable	740 MIPS @ 665 MHz
Cortex	13-stage superscalar pipeline	Variable	2000 MIPS @ 1 GHz
XScale	Applications processor; 7-stage pipeline	32 kB/32 kB L1 512 kB L2	1000 MIPS @ 1.25 GHz

DSP = digital signal processor
SoC = system on a chip

According to the ARM Web site arm.com, ARM processors are designed to meet the needs of three system categories:

- **Embedded real-time systems:** Systems for storage, automotive body and power-train, industrial, and networking applications
- **Application platforms:** Devices running open operating systems including Linux, Palm OS, Symbian OS, and Windows CE in wireless, consumer entertainment and digital imaging applications
- **Secure applications:** Smart cards, SIM cards, and payment terminals

2.6 PERFORMANCE ASSESSMENT

In evaluating processor hardware and setting requirements for new systems, performance is one of the key parameters to consider, along with cost, size, security, reliability, and, in some cases, power consumption.

It is difficult to make meaningful performance comparisons among different processors, even among processors in the same family. Raw speed is far less important than how a processor performs when executing a given application. Unfortunately, application performance depends not just on the raw speed of the processor but also on the instruction set, choice of implementation language, efficiency of the compiler, and skill of the programming done to implement the application.

We begin this section with a look at some traditional measures of processor speed. Then we examine the most common approach to assessing processor and computer system performance. We follow this with a discussion of how to average results from multiple tests. Finally, we look at the insights produced by considering **Amdahl's law**.

Clock Speed and Instructions per Second

THE SYSTEM CLOCK Operations performed by a processor, such as fetching an instruction, decoding the instruction, performing an arithmetic operation, and so on, are governed by a system clock. Typically, all operations begin with the pulse of the clock. Thus, at the most fundamental level, the speed of a processor is dictated by the pulse frequency produced by the clock, measured in cycles per second, or Hertz (Hz).

Typically, clock signals are generated by a quartz crystal, which generates a constant signal wave while power is applied. This wave is converted into a digital voltage pulse stream that is provided in a constant flow to the processor circuitry (Figure 2.13). For example, a 1-GHz processor receives 1 billion pulses per second. The rate of pulses is known as the **clock rate**, or **clock speed**. One increment, or pulse, of the clock is referred to as a **clock cycle**, or a **clock tick**. The time between pulses is the **cycle time**.

The clock rate is not arbitrary, but must be appropriate for the physical layout of the processor. Actions in the processor require signals to be sent from one processor element to another. When a signal is placed on a line inside the processor, it takes some finite amount of time for the voltage levels to settle down so that an accurate value (1 or 0) is available. Furthermore, depending on the physical layout of the processor circuits, some signals may change more rapidly than others. Thus, operations must be synchronized and paced so that the proper electrical signal (voltage) values are available for each operation.

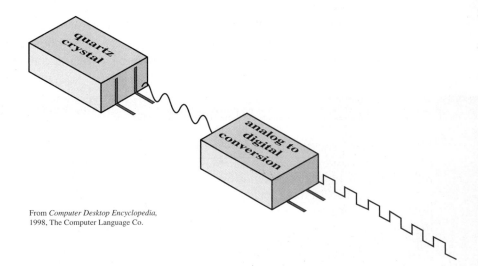

From *Computer Desktop Encyclopedia,*
1998, The Computer Language Co.

Figure 2.13   System Clock

The execution of an instruction involves a number of discrete steps, such as fetching the instruction from memory, decoding the various portions of the instruction, loading and storing data, and performing arithmetic and logical operations. Thus, most instructions on most processors require multiple clock cycles to complete. Some instructions may take only a few cycles, while others require dozens. In addition, when pipelining is used, multiple instructions are being executed simultaneously. Thus, a straight comparison of clock speeds on different processors does not tell the whole story about performance.

INSTRUCTION EXECUTION RATE A processor is driven by a clock with a constant frequency f or, equivalently, a constant cycle time τ, where $\tau = 1/f$. Define the instruction count, I_c, for a program as the number of machine instructions executed for that program until it runs to completion or for some defined time interval. Note that this is the number of instruction executions, not the number of instructions in the object code of the program. An important parameter is the average cycles per instruction (*CPI*) for a program. If all instructions required the same number of clock cycles, then *CPI* would be a constant value for a processor. However, on any give processor, the number of clock cycles required varies for different types of instructions, such as load, store, branch, and so on. Let CPI_i be the number of cycles required for instruction type i and I_i be the number of executed instructions of type i for a given program. Then we can calculate an overall *CPI* as follows:

$$CPI = \frac{\sum_{i=1}^{n}(CPI_i \times I_i)}{I_c} \tag{2.1}$$

The processor time T needed to execute a given program can be expressed as

$$T = I_c \times CPI \times \tau$$

We can refine this formulation by recognizing that during the execution of an instruction, part of the work is done by the processor, and part of the time a word is being transferred to or from memory. In this latter case, the time to transfer depends on the memory cycle time, which may be greater than the processor cycle time. We can rewrite the preceding equation as

$$T = I_c \times [p + (m \times k)] \times \tau$$

where p is the number of processor cycles needed to decode and execute the instruction, m is the number of memory references needed, and k is the ratio between memory cycle time and processor cycle time. The five performance factors in the preceding equation (I_c, p, m, k, τ) are influenced by four system attributes: the design of the instruction set (known as *instruction set architecture*), compiler technology (how effective the compiler is in producing an efficient machine language program from a high-level language program), processor implementation, and cache and memory hierarchy. Table 2.9 is a matrix in which one dimension shows the five performance factors and the other dimension shows the four system attributes. An X in a cell indicates a system attribute that affects a performance factor.

A common measure of performance for a processor is the rate at which instructions are executed, expressed as millions of instructions per second (MIPS),

Table 2.9 Performance Factors and System Attributes

	I_c	p	m	k	τ
Instruction set architecture	X	X			
Compiler technology	X	X	X		
Processor implementation		X			X
Cache and memory hierarchy				X	X

referred to as the **MIPS rate**. We can express the MIPS rate in terms of the clock rate and *CPI* as follows:

$$\text{MIPS rate} = \frac{I_c}{T \times 10^6} = \frac{f}{CPI \times 10^6} \tag{2.2}$$

For example, consider the execution of a program that results in the execution of 2 million instructions on a 400-MHz processor. The program consists of four major types of instructions. The instruction mix and the CPI for each instruction type are given below based on the result of a program trace experiment:

Instruction Type	CPI	Instruction Mix (%)
Arithmetic and logic	1	60
Load/store with cache hit	2	18
Branch	4	12
Memory reference with cache miss	8	10

The average CPI when the program is executed on a uniprocessor with the above trace results is $CPI = 0.6 + (2 \times 0.18) + (4 \times 0.12) + (8 \times 0.1) = 2.24$. The corresponding MIPS rate is $(400 \times 10^6)/(2.24 \times 10^6) \approx 178$.

Another common performance measure deals only with floating-point instructions. These are common in many scientific and game applications. Floating-point performance is expressed as millions of floating-point operations per second (MFLOPS), defined as follows:

$$\text{MFLOPS rate} = \frac{\text{Number of executed floating-point operations in a program}}{\text{Execution time} \times 10^6}$$

Benchmarks

Measures such as MIPS and MFLOPS have proven inadequate to evaluating the performance of processors. Because of differences in instruction sets, the instruction execution rate is not a valid means of comparing the performance of different architectures. For example, consider this high-level language statement:

```
A = B + C    /* assume all quantities in main memory */
```

With a traditional instruction set architecture, referred to as a complex instruction set computer (CISC), this instruction can be compiled into one processor instruction:

```
add     mem(B), mem(C), mem (A)
```

On a typical RISC machine, the compilation would look something like this:

```
load    mem(B), reg(1);
load    mem(C), reg(2);
add     reg(1), reg(2), reg(3);
store   reg(3), mem (A)
```

Because of the nature of the RISC architecture (discussed in Chapter 15), both machines may execute the original high-level language instruction in about the same time. If this example is representative of the two machines, then if the CISC machine is rated at 1 MIPS, the RISC machine would be rated at 4 MIPS. But both do the same amount of high-level language work in the same amount of time.

Further, the performance of a given processor on a given program may not be useful in determining how that processor will perform on a very different type of application. Accordingly, beginning in the late 1980s and early 1990s, industry and academic interest shifted to measuring the performance of systems using a set of benchmark programs. The same set of programs can be run on different machines and the execution times compared.

[WEIC90] lists the following as desirable characteristics of a benchmark program:

1. It is written in a high-level language, making it portable across different machines.
2. It is representative of a particular kind of programming style, such as systems programming, numerical programming, or commercial programming.
3. It can be measured easily.
4. It has wide distribution.

SPEC *BENCHMARKS* The common need in industry and academic and research communities for generally accepted computer performance measurements has led to the development of standardized benchmark suites. A benchmark suite is a collection of programs, defined in a high-level language, that together attempt to provide a representative test of a computer in a particular application or system programming area. The best known such collection of benchmark suites is defined and maintained by the System Performance Evaluation Corporation (SPEC), an industry consortium. SPEC performance measurements are widely used for comparison and research purposes.

The best known of the SPEC benchmark suites is SPEC CPU2006. This is the industry standard suite for processor-intensive applications. That is, SPEC CPU2006 is appropriate for measuring performance for applications that spend most of their time doing computation rather than I/O. The CPU2006 suite is based on existing applications that have already been ported to a wide variety of platforms by SPEC industry members. It consists of 17 floating-point programs written in C, C++, and Fortran; and 12 integer programs written in C and C++. The suite contains over 3 million lines of code. This is the fifth generation of processor-intensive suites from SPEC, replacing SPEC CPU2000, SPEC CPU95, SPEC CPU92, and SPEC CPU89 [HENN07].

Other SPEC suites include the following:

- **SPECjvm98:** Intended to evaluate performance of the combined hardware and software aspects of the Java Virtual Machine (JVM) client platform
- **SPECjbb2000 (Java Business Benchmark):** A benchmark for evaluating server-side Java-based electronic commerce applications
- **SPECweb99:** Evaluates the performance of World Wide Web (WWW) servers
- **SPECmail2001:** Designed to measure a system's performance acting as a mail server

AVERAGING RESULTS To obtain a reliable comparison of the performance of various computers, it is preferable to run a number of different benchmark programs on each machine and then average the results. For example, if there are m different benchmark programs, then a simple **arithmetic mean** can be calculated as follows:

$$R_A = \frac{1}{m} \sum_{i=1}^{m} R_i \qquad (2.3)$$

where R_i is the high-level language instruction execution rate for the ith benchmark program.

An alternative is to take the **harmonic mean**:

$$R_H = \frac{m}{\sum_{i=1}^{m} \frac{1}{R_i}} \qquad (2.4)$$

Ultimately, the user is concerned with the execution time of a system, not its execution rate. If we take arithmetic mean of the instruction rates of various benchmark programs, we get a result that is proportional to the sum of the inverses of execution times. But this is not inversely proportional to the sum of execution times. In other words, the arithmetic mean of the instruction rate does not cleanly relate to execution time. On the other hand, the harmonic mean instruction rate is the inverse of the average execution time.

SPEC benchmarks do not concern themselves with instruction execution rates. Rather, two fundamental metrics are of interest: a speed metric and a rate metric. The **speed metric** measures the ability of a computer to complete a single task. SPEC defines a base runtime for each benchmark program using a reference machine. Results for a system under test are reported as the **ratio** of the reference run time to the system run time. The ratio is calculated as follows:

$$r_i = \frac{Tref_i}{Tsut_i} \qquad (2.5)$$

where $Tref_i$ is the execution time of benchmark program i on the reference system and $Tsut_i$ is the execution time of benchmark program i on the system under test.

As an example of the calculation and reporting, consider the Sun Blade 6250, which consists of two chips with four cores, or processors, per chip. One of the SPEC CPU2006 integer benchmark is 464.h264ref. This is a reference implementation of H.264/AVC (Advanced Video Coding), the latest state-of-the-art video compression standard. The Sun system executes this program in 934 seconds. The reference implementation requires 22,135 seconds. The ratio is calculated as: 22136/934 = 23.7.

Because the time for the system under test is in the denominator, the larger the ratio, the higher the speed. An overall performance measure for the system under test is calculated by averaging the values for the ratios for all 12 integer benchmarks. SPEC specifies the use of a **geometric mean** defined as follows:

$$r_G = \left(\prod_{i=1}^{n} r_i \right)^{1/n} \tag{2.6}$$

where r_i is the ratio for the ith benchmark program. For the Sun Blade 6250, the SPEC integer speed ratios were reported as follows:

The speed metric is calculated by taking the twelfth root of the product of the ratios:

Benchmark	Ratio		Benchmark	Ratio
400.perlbench	17.5		458.sjeng	17.0
401.bzip2	14.0		462.libquantum	31.3
403.gcc	13.7		464.h264ref	23.7
429.mcf	17.6		471.omnetpp	9.23
445.gobmk	14.7		473.astar	10.9
456.hmmer	18.6		483.xalancbmk	14.7

$$(17.5 \times 14 \times 13.7 \times 17.6 \times 14.7 \times 18.6 \times 17 \times 31.3 \times 23.7 \times 9.23 \times 10.9 \times 14.7)^{1/12} = 18.5$$

The **rate metric** measures the throughput or rate of a machine carrying out a number of tasks. For the rate metrics, multiple copies of the benchmarks are run simultaneously. Typically, the number of copies is the same as the number of processors on the machine. Again, a ratio is used to report results, although the calculation is more complex. The ratio is calculated as follows:

$$r_i = \frac{N \times Tref_i}{Tsut_i} \tag{2.7}$$

where $Tref_i$ is the reference execution time for benchmark i, N is the number of copies of the program that are run simultaneously, and $Tsut_i$ is the elapsed time from the start of the execution of the program on all N processors of the system under test until the completion of all the copies of the program. Again, a geometric mean is calculated to determine the overall performance measure.

SPEC chose to use a geometric mean because it is the most appropriate for normalized numbers, such as ratios. [FLEM86] demonstrates that the geometric mean has the property of performance relationships consistently maintained regardless of the computer that is used as the basis for normalization.

Amdahl's Law

When considering system performance, computer system designers look for ways to improve performance by improvement in technology or change in design. Examples include the use of parallel processors, the use of a memory cache hierarchy, and speedup in memory access time and I/O transfer rate due to technology improvements. In all of these cases, it is important to note that a speedup in one aspect of the technology or design does not result in a corresponding improvement in performance. This limitation is succinctly expressed by Amdahl's law.

Amdahl's law was first proposed by Gene Amdahl in [AMDA67] and deals with the potential speedup of a program using multiple processors compared to a single processor. Consider a program running on a single processor such that a fraction $(1 - f)$ of the execution time involves code that is inherently serial and a fraction f that involves code that is infinitely parallelizable with no scheduling overhead. Let T be the total execution time of the program using a single processor. Then the speedup using a parallel processor with N processors that fully exploits the parallel portion of the program is as follows:

$$\text{Speedup} = \frac{\text{Time to execute program on a single processor}}{\text{Time to execute program on } N \text{ parallel processors}}$$

$$= \frac{T(1 - f) + Tf}{T(1 - f) + \dfrac{Tf}{N}} = \frac{1}{(1 - f) + \dfrac{f}{N}}$$

This equation is illustrated in Figure 2.14. Two important conclusions can be drawn:

1. When f is small, the use of parallel processors has little effect.
2. As N approaches infinity, speedup is bound by $1/(1 - f)$, so that there are diminishing returns for using more processors.

These conclusions are too pessimistic, an assertion first put forward in [GUST88]. For example, a server can maintain multiple threads or multiple tasks to handle multiple clients and execute the threads or tasks in parallel up to the limit of the number of processors. Many database applications involve computations on massive amounts of data that can be split up into multiple parallel tasks. Nevertheless, Amdahl's law illustrates the problems facing industry in the development of multicore machines with an ever-growing number of cores: The software that runs on such machines must be adapted to a highly parallel execution environment to exploit the power of parallel processing.

Amdahl's law can be generalized to evaluate any design or technical improvement in a computer system. Consider any enhancement to a feature of a system that results in a speedup. The speedup can be expressed as

$$\text{Speedup} = \frac{\text{Performance after enhancement}}{\text{Performance before enhancement}} = \frac{\text{Execution time before enhancement}}{\text{Execution time after enhancement}}$$

$$(2.8)$$

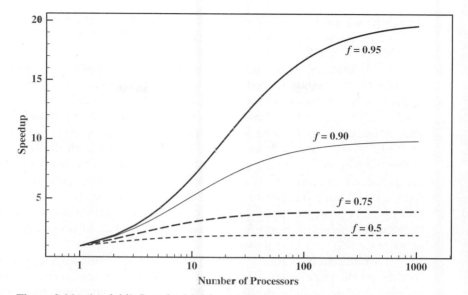

Figure 2.14   Amdahl's Law for Multiprocessors

Suppose that a feature of the system is used during execution a fraction of the time f, before enhancement, and that the speedup of that feature after enhancement is SU_f. Then the overall speedup of the system is

$$\text{Speedup} = \frac{1}{(1 - f) + \dfrac{f}{SU_f}}$$

For example, suppose that a task makes extensive use of floating-point operations, with 40% of the time is consumed by floating-point operations. With a new hardware design, the floating-point module is speeded up by a factor of K. Then the overall speedup is as follows:

$$\text{Speedup} = \frac{1}{0.6 + \dfrac{0.4}{K}}$$

Thus, independent of K, the maximum speedup is 1.67.

Little's Law

A fundamental and simple relation with broad applications is Little's Law [LITT61, LITT11].[17] We can apply it to almost any system that is statistically in steady state, and in which there is no leakage. The general setup is that we have a steady state system to which items arrive at an average rate of λ items per unit

---

[17]The second reference is a retrospective article on his law that Little wrote 50 years after his original paper. That must be unique in the history of the technical literature.

time. The items stay in the system an average of W units of time. Finally, there is an average of L units in the system at any one time. Little's Law relates these three variables as $L = \lambda W$.

Using queuing theory terminology, Little's Law applies to a queuing system. The central element of the system is a server, which provides some service to items. Items from some population of items arrive at the system to be served. If the server is idle, an item is served immediately. Otherwise, an arriving item joins a waiting line, or queue. There can be a single queue for a single server, a single queue for multiple servers, or multiples queues, one for each of multiple servers. When a server has completed serving an item, the item departs. If there are items waiting in the queue, one is immediately dispatched to the server. The server in this model can represent anything that performs some function or service for a collection of items. Examples: A processor provides service to processes; a transmission line provides a transmission service to packets or frames of data; and an I/O device provides a read or write service for I/O requests.

To understand Little's formula, consider the following argument, which focuses on the experience of a single item. When the item arrives, it will find on average w items waiting ahead of it. When the item leaves the queue behind it to be serviced, it will leave behind on average the same number of items in the queue, namely w. To see this, note that while the item is waiting, the line in front of it shrinks until the item is at the front of the line; meanwhile, additional items arrive and get in line behind this item. When the item leaves the queue to be serviced, the number of items behind it, on average, is w, because w is defined as the average number of items waiting. Further, the average time that the item was waiting for service is T_w. Since items arrive at a rate of λ, we can reason that in the time T_w, a total of λT_w items must have arrived. Thus, $w = \lambda T_w$.

To summarize, under steady state conditions, the average number of items in a queuing system equals the average rate at which items arrive multiplied by the average time that an item spends in the system. This relationship requires very few assumptions. We do not need to know what the service time distribution is, what the distribution of arrival times is, or the order or priority in which items are served. Because of its simplicity and generality, Little's Law is extremely useful and has experienced somewhat of a revival due to the interest in performance problems related to multicore computers.

A very simple example, from [LITT11], illustrates how Little's Law might be applied. Consider a multicore system, with each core supporting multiple threads of execution. At some level, the cores share a common memory. The cores share a common main memory and typically share a common cache memory as well. In any case, when a thread is executing, it may arrive at a point at which it must retrieve a piece of data from the common memory. The thread stops and sends out a request for that data. All such stopped threads are in a queue. If the system is being used as a server, an analyst can determine the demand on the system in terms of the rate of user requests, and then translate that into the rate of requests for data from the threads generated to respond to an individual user request. For this purpose, each user request is broken down into subtasks that are implemented as threads. We then have λ = the average rate of total thread processing required after all members' requests have been broken down into whatever detailed subtasks are required. Define L as the average number of stopped threads waiting during some relevant time. Then W = average response time. This simple model can serve as a guide to designers as to whether user requirements are being met and, if not, provide a quantitative measure of the amount of improvement needed.

2.7 RECOMMENDED READING

A description of the IBM 7000 series can be found in [BELL71]. There is good coverage of the IBM 360 in [SIEW82] and of the PDP-8 and other DEC machines in [BELL78a]. These three books also contain numerous detailed examples of other computers spanning the history of computers through the early 1980s. [BLAA97] includes an excellent set of case studies of historical machines. A good history of the microprocessor is [BETK97].

[OLUK96], [HAMM97], and [SAKA02] discuss the motivation for multiple processors on a single chip.

[BREY09] provides a good survey of the Intel microprocessor line. The Intel documentation itself is also good [INTE11]. [SING11] is an interesting short history of the x86.

The most thorough documentation available for the ARM architecture is [SEAL00].[18] [FURB00] is another excellent source of information. [SMIT08] is an interesting comparison of the ARM and x86 approaches to embedding processors in mobile wireless devices.

For interesting discussions of Moore's law and its consequences, see [FULL11], [HUTC96], [SCHA97], and [BOHR98].

[HENN06] provides a detailed description of each of the benchmarks in CPU2006. [SMIT88] discusses the relative merits of arithmetic, harmonic, and geometric means.

BELL71 Bell, C., and Newell, A. *Computer Structures: Readings and Examples.* New York: McGraw-Hill, 1971.

BELL78a Bell, C.; Mudge, J.; and McNamara, J. *Computer Engineering: A DEC View of Hardware Systems Design.* Bedford, MA: Digital Press, 1978.

BETK97 Betker, M.; Fernando, J.; and Whalen, S. "The History of the Microprocessor." *Bell Labs Technical Journal,* Autumn 1997.

BLAA97 Blaauw, G., and Brooks, F. *Computer Architecture: Concepts and Evolution.* Reading, MA: Addison-Wesley, 1997.

BOHR98 Bohr, M. "Silicon Trends and Limits for Advanced Microprocessors." *Communications of the ACM,* March 1998.

BREY09 Brey, B. *The Intel Microprocessors: 8086/8066, 80186/80188, 80286, 80386, 80486, Pentium, Pentium Pro Processor, Pentium II, Pentium III, Pentium 4 and Core2 with 64-bit Extensions.* Upper Saddle River, NJ: Prentice Hall, 2009.

---

[18]Known in the ARM community as the "ARM ARM."

FULL11   Fuller, S., and Millet, L., eds. *The Future of Computing Performance: Game Over or Next Level?* Washington, DC: National Academies Press, 2011. www.nap.edu

FURB00   Furber, S. *ARM System-On-Chip Architecture.* Reading, MA: Addison-Wesley, 2000.

HAMM97   Hammond, L.; Nayfay, B.; and Olukotun, K. "A Single-Chip Multiprocessor." *Computer*, September 1997.

HENN06   Henning, J. "SPEC CPU2006 Benchmark Descriptions." *Computer Architecture News*, September 2006.

HUTC96   Hutcheson, G., and Hutcheson, J. "Technology and Economics in the Semiconductor Industry." *Scientific American*, January 1996.

INTE11   Intel Corp. Intel ® 64 and *IA-32 Intel Architectures Software Developer's Manual (3 volumes).* Denver, CO, 2011.

OLUK96   Olukotun, K., et al. "The Case for a Single-Chip Multiprocessor." *Proceedings, Seventh International Conference on Architectural Support for Programming Languages and Operating Systems*, 1996.

SAKA02   Sakai, S. "CMP on SoC: Architect's View." *Proceedings of the 15th International Symposium on System Synthesis*, 2002.

SCHA97   Schaller, R. "Moore's Law: Past, Present, and Future." *IEEE Spectrum*, June 1997.

SEAL00   Seal, D., ed. *ARM Architecture Reference Manual.* Reading, MA: Addison-Wesley, 2000.

SIEW82   Siewiorek, D.; Bell, C.; and Newell, A. *Computer Structures: Principles and Examples.* New York: McGraw-Hill, 1982.

SING11   Singh, G. "The IBM PC: The Silicon Story." *Computer*, August 2011.

SMIT88   Smith, J. "Characterizing Computer Performance with a Single Number." *Communications of the ACM*, October 1988.

SMIT08   Smith, B. "ARM and Intel Battle over the Mobile Chip's Future." *Computer*, May 2008.

2.8   KEY TERMS, REVIEW QUESTIONS, AND PROBLEMS

Key Terms

accumulator (AC)	clock tick	graphics processing unit (GPU)
Amdahl's law	control unit	harmonic mean
arithmetic and logic unit (ALU)	cycle time	input-output (I/O)
arithmetic mean	data channel	instruction buffer register (IBR)
benchmark	embedded system	instruction cycle
chip	execute cycle	instruction register (IR)
clock cycle	fetch cycle	instruction set
clock rate	geometric mean	integrated circuit (IC)
clock speed	general-purpose computing on GPUs (GPGPU)	

main memory	multicore	SPEC
many integrated core (MIC)	multiplexor	speed metric
MIPS rate	opcode	stored-program concept
memory address register	original equipment	upward compatible
(MAR)	manufacturer (OEM)	von Neumann machine
memory buffer register	program counter (PC)	wafer
(MBR)	rate metric	word
microprocessor	ratio	

Review Questions

2.1 What is a stored program computer?

2.2 What are the four main components of any general-purpose computer?

2.3 At the integrated circuit level, what are the three principal constituents of a computer system?

2.4 Explain Moore's law.

2.5 List and explain the key characteristics of a computer family.

2.6 What is the key distinguishing feature of a microprocessor?

Problems

2.1 You are to write an IAS program to compute the results of the following equation.

$$Y = \sum_{X=1}^{N} X$$

Assume that the result of the computation does not arithmetic overflow and that X, Y, and N are positive integers with $N \, n \, 1$. *Note*: The IAS did not have assembly language only machine language.

    a. Use the equation Sum$(Y) = N(N+1)/2$ when writing the IAS program.

    b. Do it the "hard way," without using the equation from part (a).

2.2 **a.** On the IAS, what would the machine code instruction look like to load the contents of memory address 2 to the accumulator?

    b. How many trips to memory does the CPU need to make to complete this instruction during the instruction cycle?

2.3 On the IAS, describe in English the process that the CPU must undertake to read a value from memory and to write a value to memory in terms of what is put into the MAR, MBR, address bus, data bus, and control bus.

2.4 Given the memory contents of the IAS computer shown below,

Address	Contents
08A	010FA210FB
08B	010FA0F08D
08C	020FA210FB

show the assembly language code for the program, starting at address 08A. Explain what this program does.

2.5 In Figure 2.3, indicate the width, in bits, of each data path (e.g., between AC and ALU).

2.6 In the IBM 360 Models 65 and 75, addresses are staggered in two separate main memory units (e.g., all even-numbered words in one unit and all odd-numbered words in another). What might be the purpose of this technique?

2.7 With reference to Table 2.4, we see that the relative performance of the IBM 360 Model 75 is 50 times that of the 360 Model 30, yet the instruction cycle time is only 5 times as fast. How do you account for this discrepancy?

2.8 While browsing at Billy Bob's computer store, you overhear a customer asking Billy Bob what is the fastest computer in the store that he can buy. Billy Bob replies, "You're looking at our Macintoshes. The fastest Mac we have runs at a clock speed of 1.2 GHz. If you really want the fastest machine, you should buy our 2.4-GHz Intel Pentium IV instead." Is Billy Bob correct? What would you say to help this customer?

2.9 The ENIAC was a decimal machine, where a register was represented by a ring of 10 vacuum tubes. At any time, only one vacuum tube was in the ON state, representing one of the 10 digits. Assuming that ENIAC had the capability to have multiple vacuum tubes in the ON and OFF state simultaneously, why is this representation "wasteful" and what range of integer values could we represent using the 10 vacuum tubes?

2.10 A benchmark program is run on a 40 MHz processor. The executed program consists of 100,000 instruction executions, with the following instruction mix and clock cycle count:

Instruction Type	Instruction Count	Cycles per Instruction
Integer arithmetic	45,000	1
Data transfer	32,000	2
Floating point	15,000	2
Control transfer	8000	2

Determine the effective CPI, MIPS rate, and execution time for this program.

2.11 Consider two different machines, with two different instruction sets, both of which have a clock rate of 200 MHz. The following measurements are recorded on the two machines running a given set of benchmark programs:

Instruction Type	Instruction Count (millions)	Cycles Per Instruction
Machine A		
Arithmetic and logic	8	1
Load and store	4	3
Branch	2	4
Others	4	3
Machine A		
Arithmetic and logic	10	1
Load and store	8	2
Branch	2	4
Others	4	3

a. Determine the effective CPI, MIPS rate, and execution time for each machine.
b. Comment on the results.

2.12 Early examples of CISC and RISC design are the VAX 11/780 and the IBM RS/6000, respectively. Using a typical benchmark program, the following machine characteristics result:

Processor	Clock Frequency (MHz)	Performance (MIPS)	CPU Time (seconds)
VAX 11/780	5	1	$12x$
IBM RS/6000	25	18	x

The final column shows that the VAX required 12 times longer than the IBM measured in CPU time.

a. What is the relative size of the instruction count of the machine code for this benchmark program running on the two machines?

b. What are the *CPI* values for the two machines?

2.13 Four benchmark programs are executed on three computers with the following results:

	Computer A	Computer B	Computer C
Program 1	1	10	20
Program 2	1000	100	20
Program 3	500	1000	50
Program 4	100	800	100

The table shows the execution time in seconds, with 100.000,000 instructions executed in each of the four programs. Calculate the MIPS values for each computer for each program. Then calculate the arithmetic and harmonic means assuming equal weights for the four programs, and rank the computers based on arithmetic mean and harmonic mean.

2.14 The following table, based on data reported in the literature [HEAT84], shows the execution times, in seconds, for five different benchmark programs on three machines.

Benchmark	Processor		
	R	M	Z
E	417	244	134
F	83	70	70
H	66	153	135
I	39,449	35,527	66,000
K	772	368	369

a. Compute the speed metric for each processor for each benchmark, normalized to machine R. That is, the ratio values for R are all 1.0. Other ratios are calculated using Equation (2.5) with R treated as the reference system. Then compute the arithmetic mean value for each system using Equation (2.3). This is the approach taken in [HEAT84].

b. Repeat part (a) using M as the reference machine. This calculation was not tried in [HEAT84].

c. Which machine is the slowest based on each of the preceding two calculations?

d. Repeat the calculations of parts (a) and (b) using the geometric mean, defined in Equation (2.6). Which machine is the slowest based on the two calculations?

2.15 To clarify the results of the preceding problem, we look at a simpler example.

Benchmark	Processor		
	X	Y	Z
1	20	10	40
2	40	80	20

    a. Compute the arithmetic mean value for each system using X as the reference machine and then using Y as the reference machine. Argue that intuitively the three machines have roughly equivalent performance and that the arithmetic mean gives misleading results.

    b. Compute the geometric mean value for each system using X as the reference machine and then using Y as the reference machine. Argue that the results are more realistic than with the arithmetic mean.

2.16 Consider the example in Section 2.5 for the calculation of average CPI and MIPS rate, which yielded the result of CPI = 2.24 and MIPS rate = 178. Now assume that the program can be executed in eight parallel tasks or threads with roughly equal number of instructions executed in each task. Execution is on an 8-core system with each core (processor) having the same performance as the single processor originally used. Coordination and synchronization between the parts adds an extra 25,000 instruction executions to each task. Assume the same instruction mix as in the example for each task, but increase the CPI for memory reference with cache miss to 12 cycles due to contention for memory.

    a. Determine the average CPI.

    b. Determine the corresponding MIPS rate.

    c. Calculate the speedup factor.

    d. Compare the actual speedup factor with the theoretical speedup factor determined by Amdhal's law.

2.17 A processor accesses main memory with an average access time of T_2. A smaller cache memory is interposed between the processor and main memory. The cache has a significantly faster access time of $T_1 < T_2$. The cache holds, at any time, copies of some main memory words and is designed so that the words more likely to be accessed in the near future are in the cache. Assume that the probability that the next word accessed by the processor is in the cache is H, known as the hit ratio.

    a. For any single memory access, what is the theoretical speedup of accessing the word in the cache rather than in main memory?

    b. Let T be the average access time. Express T as a function of T_1, T_2, and H. What is the overall speedup as a function of H?

    c. In practice, a system may be designed so that the processor must first access the cache to determine if the word is in the cache and, if it is not, then access main memory, so that on a miss (opposite of a hit), memory access time is $T_1 + T_2$. Express T as a function of T_1, T_2, and H. Now calculate the speedup and compare to the result produced in part (b).

2.18 The owner of a shop observes that on average 18 customers per hour arrive and there are typically 8 customers in the shop. What is the average length of time each customer spends in the shop?

A Top-Level View of Computer Function and Interconnection

LEARNING OBJECTIVES

After studying this chapter, you should be able to:

◆ Understand the basic elements of an instruction cycle and the role of interrupts.

◆ Describe the concept of interconnection within a computer system.

◆ Understand the difference between synchronous and asynchronous bus timing.

◆ Explain the need for multiple buses arranged in a hierarchy.

◆ Assess the relative advantages of point-to-point interconnection compared to bus interconnection.

◆ Present an overview of QPI.

◆ Present an overview of PCIe.

At a top level, a computer consists of CPU (central processing unit), memory, and I/O components, with one or more modules of each type. These components are interconnected in some fashion to achieve the basic function of the computer, which is to execute programs. Thus, at a top level, we can characterize a computer system by describing (1) the external behavior of each component, that is, the data and control signals that it exchanges with other components and (2) the interconnection structure and the controls required to manage the use of the interconnection structure.

This top-level view of structure and function is important because of its explanatory power in understanding the nature of a computer. Equally important is its use to understand the increasingly complex issues of performance evaluation. A grasp of the top-level structure and function offers insight into system bottlenecks, alternate pathways, the magnitude of system failures if a component fails, and the ease of adding performance enhancements. In many cases, requirements for greater system power and fail-safe capabilities are being met by changing the design rather than merely increasing the speed and reliability of individual components.

This chapter focuses on the basic structures used for computer component interconnection. As background, the chapter begins with a brief examination of the basic components and their interface requirements. Then a functional overview is provided. We are then prepared to examine the use of buses to interconnect system components.

3.1 COMPUTER COMPONENTS

As discussed in Chapter 2, virtually all contemporary computer designs are based on concepts developed by John von Neumann at the Institute for Advanced Studies, Princeton. Such a design is referred to as the *von Neumann architecture* and is based on three key concepts:

- Data and instructions are stored in a single read–write memory.
- The contents of this memory are addressable by location, without regard to the type of data contained there.
- Execution occurs in a sequential fashion (unless explicitly modified) from one instruction to the next.

The reasoning behind these concepts was discussed in Chapter 2 but is worth summarizing here. There is a small set of basic logic components that can be combined in various ways to store binary data and perform arithmetic and logical operations on that data. If there is a particular computation to be performed, a configuration of logic components designed specifically for that computation could be constructed. We can think of the process of connecting the various components in the desired configuration as a form of programming. The resulting "program" is in the form of hardware and is termed a *hardwired program*.

Now consider this alternative. Suppose we construct a general-purpose configuration of arithmetic and logic functions. This set of hardware will perform various functions on data depending on control signals applied to the hardware. In the original case of customized hardware, the system accepts data and produces results (Figure 3.1a). With general-purpose hardware, the system accepts data and control signals and produces results. Thus, instead of rewiring the hardware for each new program, the programmer merely needs to supply a new set of control signals.

How shall control signals be supplied? The answer is simple but subtle. The entire program is actually a sequence of steps. At each step, some arithmetic or

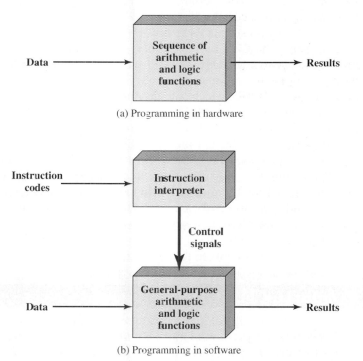

(a) Programming in hardware

(b) Programming in software

Figure 3.1 Hardware and Software Approaches

logical operation is performed on some data. For each step, a new set of control signals is needed. Let us provide a unique code for each possible set of control signals, and let us add to the general-purpose hardware a segment that can accept a code and generate control signals (Figure 3.1b).

Programming is now much easier. Instead of rewiring the hardware for each new program, all we need to do is provide a new sequence of codes. Each code is, in effect, an instruction, and part of the hardware interprets each instruction and generates control signals. To distinguish this new method of programming, a sequence of codes or instructions is called *software*.

Figure 3.1b indicates two major components of the system: an instruction interpreter and a module of general-purpose arithmetic and logic functions. These two constitute the CPU. Several other components are needed to yield a functioning computer. Data and instructions must be put into the system. For this we need some sort of input module. This module contains basic components for accepting data and instructions in some form and converting them into an internal form of signals usable by the system. A means of reporting results is needed, and this is in the form of an output module. Taken together, these are referred to as *I/O components*.

One more component is needed. An input device will bring instructions and data in sequentially. But a program is not invariably executed sequentially; it may jump around (e.g., the IAS jump instruction). Similarly, operations on data may require access to more than just one element at a time in a predetermined sequence. Thus, there must be a place to store temporarily both instructions and data. That module is called *memory*, or *main memory*, to distinguish it from external storage or peripheral devices. Von Neumann pointed out that the same memory could be used to store both instructions and data.

Figure 3.2 illustrates these top-level components and suggests the interactions among them. The CPU exchanges data with memory. For this purpose, it typically makes use of two internal (to the CPU) registers: a **memory address register (MAR)**, which specifies the address in memory for the next read or write, and a **memory buffer register (MBR)**, which contains the data to be written into memory or receives the data read from memory. Similarly, an I/O address register (I/OAR) specifies a particular I/O device. An I/O buffer (I/OBR) register is used for the exchange of data between an I/O module and the CPU.

A memory module consists of a set of locations, defined by sequentially numbered addresses. Each location contains a binary number that can be interpreted as either an instruction or data. An I/O module transfers data from external devices to CPU and memory, and vice versa. It contains internal buffers for temporarily holding these data until they can be sent on.

Having looked briefly at these major components, we now turn to an overview of how these components function together to execute programs.

3.2   COMPUTER FUNCTION

The basic function performed by a computer is execution of a program, which consists of a set of instructions stored in memory. The processor does the actual work by executing instructions specified in the program. This section provides an overview of

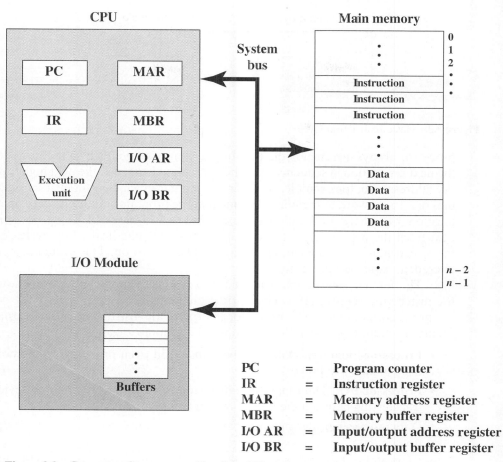

Figure 3.2 Computer Components: Top-Level View

the key elements of program execution. In its simplest form, instruction processing consists of two steps: The processor reads (*fetches*) instructions from memory one at a time and executes each instruction. Program execution consists of repeating the process of instruction fetch and instruction execution. The instruction execution may involve several operations and depends on the nature of the instruction (see, for example, the lower portion of Figure 2.4).

The processing required for a single instruction is called an **instruction cycle**. Using the simplified two-step description given previously, the instruction cycle is depicted in Figure 3.3. The two steps are referred to as the **fetch cycle** and the **execute cycle**. Program execution halts only if the machine is turned off, some sort of unrecoverable error occurs, or a program instruction that halts the computer is encountered.

Instruction Fetch and Execute

At the beginning of each instruction cycle, the processor fetches an instruction from memory. In a typical processor, a register called the program counter (PC) holds the address of the instruction to be fetched next. Unless told otherwise, the

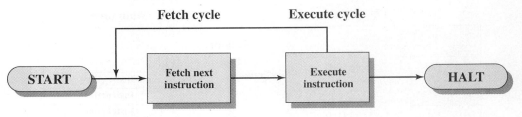

Figure 3.3   Basic Instruction Cycle

processor always increments the PC after each instruction fetch so that it will fetch the next instruction in sequence (i.e., the instruction located at the next higher memory address). So, for example, consider a computer in which each instruction occupies one 16-bit word of memory. Assume that the program counter is set to memory location 300, where the location address refers to a 16-bit word. The processor will next fetch the instruction at location 300. On succeeding instruction cycles, it will fetch instructions from locations 301, 302, 303, and so on. This sequence may be altered, as explained presently.

The fetched instruction is loaded into a register in the processor known as the instruction register (IR). The instruction contains bits that specify the action the processor is to take. The processor interprets the instruction and performs the required action. In general, these actions fall into four categories:

- **Processor-memory:** Data may be transferred from processor to memory or from memory to processor.
- **Processor-I/O:** Data may be transferred to or from a peripheral device by transferring between the processor and an I/O module.
- **Data processing:** The processor may perform some arithmetic or logic operation on data.
- **Control:** An instruction may specify that the sequence of execution be altered. For example, the processor may fetch an instruction from location 149, which specifies that the next instruction be from location 182. The processor will remember this fact by setting the program counter to 182. Thus, on the next fetch cycle, the instruction will be fetched from location 182 rather than 150.

An instruction's execution may involve a combination of these actions.

Consider a simple example using a hypothetical machine that includes the characteristics listed in Figure 3.4. The processor contains a single data register, called an accumulator (AC). Both instructions and data are 16 bits long. Thus, it is convenient to organize memory using 16-bit words. The instruction format provides 4 bits for the opcode, so that there can be as many as $2^4 = 16$ different opcodes, and up to $2^{12} = 4096$ (4K) words of memory can be directly addressed.

Figure 3.5 illustrates a partial program execution, showing the relevant portions of memory and processor registers.[1] The program fragment shown adds the contents of the memory word at address 940 to the contents of the memory

---

[1]Hexadecimal notation is used, in which each digit represents 4 bits. This is the most convenient notation for representing the contents of memory and registers when the word length is a multiple of 4. See Chapter 9 for a basic refresher on number systems (decimal, binary, hexadecimal).

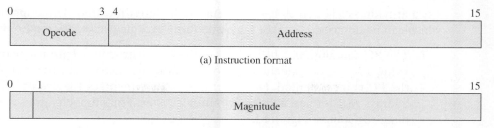

(a) Instruction format

(b) Integer format

Program counter (PC) = Address of instruction
Instruction register (IR) = Instruction being executed
Accumulator (AC) = Temporary storage

(c) Internal CPU registers

0001 = Load AC from memory
0010 = Store AC to memory
0101 = Add to AC from memory

(d) Partial list of opcodes

Figure 3.4 Characteristics of a Hypothetical Machine

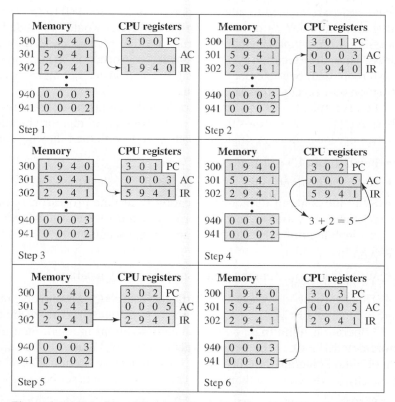

Figure 3.5 Example of Program Execution (contents of memory and registers in hexadecimal)

word at address 941 and stores the result in the latter location. Three instructions, which can be described as three fetch and three execute cycles, are required:

1. The PC contains 300, the address of the first instruction. This instruction (the value 1940 in hexadecimal) is loaded into the instruction register IR, and the PC is incremented. Note that this process involves the use of a memory address register and a memory buffer register. For simplicity, these intermediate registers are ignored.

2. The first 4 bits (first hexadecimal digit) in the IR indicate that the AC is to be loaded. The remaining 12 bits (three hexadecimal digits) specify the address (940) from which data are to be loaded.

3. The next instruction (5941) is fetched from location 301, and the PC is incremented.

4. The old contents of the AC and the contents of location 941 are added, and the result is stored in the AC.

5. The next instruction (2941) is fetched from location 302, and the PC is incremented.

6. The contents of the AC are stored in location 941.

In this example, three instruction cycles, each consisting of a fetch cycle and an execute cycle, are needed to add the contents of location 940 to the contents of 941. With a more complex set of instructions, fewer cycles would be needed. Some older processors, for example, included instructions that contain more than one memory address. Thus, the execution cycle for a particular instruction on such processors could involve more than one reference to memory. Also, instead of memory references, an instruction may specify an I/O operation.

For example, the PDP-11 processor includes an instruction, expressed symbolically as ADD B,A, that stores the sum of the contents of memory locations B and A into memory location A. A single instruction cycle with the following steps occurs:

- Fetch the ADD instruction.
- Read the contents of memory location A into the processor.
- Read the contents of memory location B into the processor. In order that the contents of A are not lost, the processor must have at least two registers for storing memory values, rather than a single accumulator.
- Add the two values.
- Write the result from the processor to memory location A.

Thus, the execution cycle for a particular instruction may involve more than one reference to memory. Also, instead of memory references, an instruction may specify an I/O operation. With these additional considerations in mind, Figure 3.6 provides a more detailed look at the basic instruction cycle of Figure 3.3. The figure is in the form of a state diagram. For any given instruction cycle, some states may be null and others may be visited more than once. The states can be described as follows:

- **Instruction address calculation (iac):** Determine the address of the next instruction to be executed. Usually, this involves adding a fixed number to

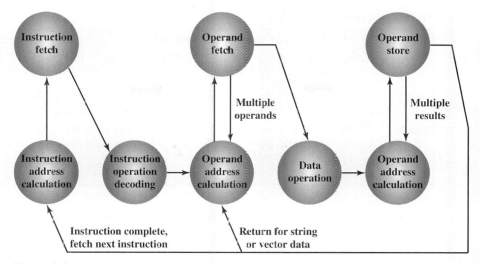

Figure 3.6   Instruction Cycle State Diagram

the address of the previous instruction. For example, if each instruction is 16 bits long and memory is organized into 16-bit words, then add 1 to the previous address. If, instead, memory is organized as individually addressable 8-bit bytes, then add 2 to the previous address.

- **Instruction fetch (if):**   Read instruction from its memory location into the processor.
- **Instruction operation decoding (iod):**   Analyze instruction to determine type of operation to be performed and operand(s) to be used.
- **Operand address calculation (oac):**   If the operation involves reference to an operand in memory or available via I/O, then determine the address of the operand.
- **Operand fetch (of):**   Fetch the operand from memory or read it in from I/O.
- **Data operation (do):**   Perform the operation indicated in the instruction.
- **Operand store (os):**   Write the result into memory or out to I/O.

States in the upper part of Figure 3.6 involve an exchange between the processor and either memory or an I/O module. States in the lower part of the diagram involve only internal processor operations. The oac state appears twice, because an instruction may involve a read, a write, or both. However, the action performed during that state is fundamentally the same in both cases, and so only a single state identifier is needed.

Also note that the diagram allows for multiple operands and multiple results, because some instructions on some machines require this. For example, the PDP-11 instruction ADD A,B results in the following sequence of states: iac, if, iod, oac, of, oac, of, do, oac, os.

Finally, on some machines, a single instruction can specify an operation to be performed on a vector (one-dimensional array) of numbers or a string (one-dimensional

Table 3.1 Classes of Interrupts

Program	Generated by some condition that occurs as a result of an instruction execution, such as arithmetic overflow, division by zero, attempt to execute an illegal machine instruction, or reference outside a user's allowed memory space.
Timer	Generated by a timer within the processor. This allows the operating system to perform certain functions on a regular basis.
I/O	Generated by an I/O controller, to signal normal completion of an operation, request service from the processor, or to signal a variety of error conditions.
Hardware Failure	Generated by a failure such as power failure or memory parity error.

array) of characters. As Figure 3.6 indicates, this would involve repetitive operand fetch and/or store operations.

Interrupts

Virtually all computers provide a mechanism by which other modules (I/O, memory) may **interrupt** the normal processing of the processor. Table 3.1 lists the most common classes of interrupts. The specific nature of these interrupts is examined later in this book, especially in Chapters 7 and 14. However, we need to introduce the concept now to understand more clearly the nature of the instruction cycle and the implications of interrupts on the interconnection structure. The reader need not be concerned at this stage about the details of the generation and processing of interrupts, but only focus on the communication between modules that results from interrupts.

Interrupts are provided primarily as a way to improve processing efficiency. For example, most external devices are much slower than the processor. Suppose that the processor is transferring data to a printer using the instruction cycle scheme of Figure 3.3. After each write operation, the processor must pause and remain idle until the printer catches up. The length of this pause may be on the order of many hundreds or even thousands of instruction cycles that do not involve memory. Clearly, this is a very wasteful use of the processor.

Figure 3.7a illustrates this state of affairs. The user program performs a series of WRITE calls interleaved with processing. Code segments 1, 2, and 3 refer to sequences of instructions that do not involve I/O. The WRITE calls are to an I/O program that is a system utility and that will perform the actual I/O operation. The I/O program consists of three sections:

- A sequence of instructions, labeled 4 in the figure, to prepare for the actual I/O operation. This may include copying the data to be output into a special buffer and preparing the parameters for a device command.

- The actual I/O command. Without the use of interrupts, once this command is issued, the program must wait for the I/O device to perform the requested function (or periodically poll the device). The program might wait by simply repeatedly performing a test operation to determine if the I/O operation is done.

- A sequence of instructions, labeled 5 in the figure, to complete the operation. This may include setting a flag indicating the success or failure of the operation.

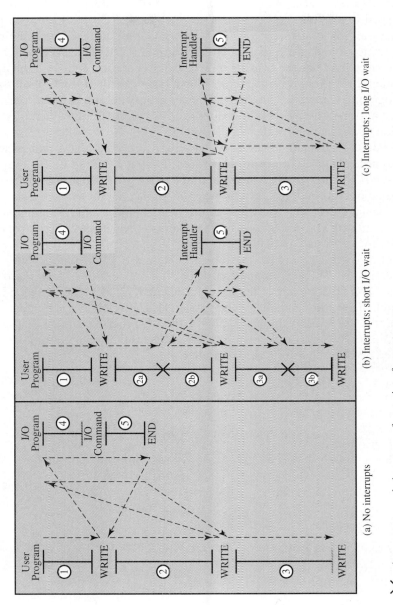

X = interrupt occurs during course of execution of user program

Figure 3.7 Program Flow of Control without and with Interrupts

(a) No interrupts

(b) Interrupts; short I/O wait

(c) Interrupts; long I/O wait

Because the I/O operation may take a relatively long time to complete, the I/O program is hung up waiting for the operation to complete; hence, the user program is stopped at the point of the WRITE call for some considerable period of time.

INTERRUPTS AND THE INSTRUCTION CYCLE With interrupts, the processor can be engaged in executing other instructions while an I/O operation is in progress. Consider the flow of control in Figure 3.7b. As before, the user program reaches a point at which it makes a system call in the form of a WRITE call. The I/O program that is invoked in this case consists only of the preparation code and the actual I/O command. After these few instructions have been executed, control returns to the user program. Meanwhile, the external device is busy accepting data from computer memory and printing it. This I/O operation is conducted concurrently with the execution of instructions in the user program.

When the external device becomes ready to be serviced—that is, when it is ready to accept more data from the processor—the I/O module for that external device sends an *interrupt request* signal to the processor. The processor responds by suspending operation of the current program, branching off to a program to service that particular I/O device, known as an **interrupt handler**, and resuming the original execution after the device is serviced. The points at which such interrupts occur are indicated by an asterisk in Figure 3.7b.

Let us try to clarify what is happening in Figure 3.7. We have a user program that contains two WRITE commands. There is a segment of code at the beginning, then one WRITE command, then a second segment of code, then a second WRITE command, then a third and final segment of code. The WRITE command invokes the I/O program provided by the OS. Similarly, the I/O program consists of a segment of code, followed by an I/O command, followed by another segment of code. The I/O command invokes a hardware I/O operation.

USER PROGRAM

```
⟨statement⟩ ⎫
⟨statement⟩ ⎬  Code segment 1
     ⋮      
⟨statement⟩ ⎭

WRITE

⟨statement⟩ ⎫
⟨statement⟩ ⎬  Code segment 2
     ⋮      
⟨statement⟩ ⎭

WRITE

⟨statement⟩ ⎫
⟨statement⟩ ⎬  Code segment 3
     ⋮      
⟨statement⟩ ⎭
```

I/O PROGRAM

```
⟨statement⟩ ⎫
⟨statement⟩ ⎬  Code segment 4
     ⋮      
⟨statement⟩ ⎭

I/O command

⟨statement⟩ ⎫
⟨statement⟩ ⎬  Code segment 5
     ⋮      
⟨statement⟩ ⎭
```

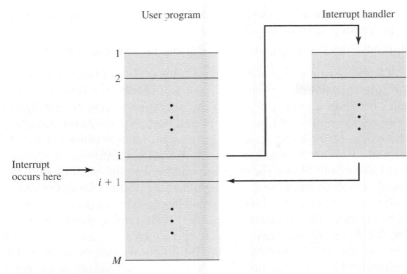

Figure 3.8 Transfer of Control via Interrupts

From the point of view of the user program, an interrupt is just that: an interruption of the normal sequence of execution. When the interrupt processing is completed, execution resumes (Figure 3.8). Thus, the user program does not have to contain any special code to accommodate interrupts; the processor and the operating system are responsible for suspending the user program and then resuming it at the same point.

To accommodate interrupts, an *interrupt cycle* is added to the instruction cycle, as shown in Figure 3.9. In the interrupt cycle, the processor checks to see if any interrupts have occurred, indicated by the presence of an interrupt signal. If no interrupts are pending, the processor proceeds to the fetch cycle and fetches the next instruction of the current program. If an interrupt is pending, the processor does the following:

- It suspends execution of the current program being executed and saves its context. This means saving the address of the next instruction to be executed

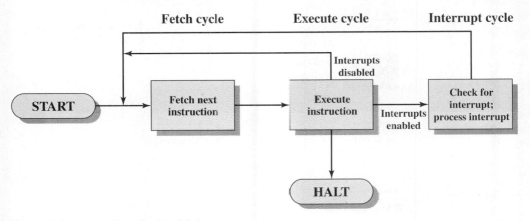

Figure 3.9 Instruction Cycle with Interrupts

(current contents of the program counter) and any other data relevant to the processor's current activity.

- It sets the program counter to the starting address of an *interrupt handler* routine.

The processor now proceeds to the fetch cycle and fetches the first instruction in the interrupt handler program, which will service the interrupt. The interrupt handler program is generally part of the operating system. Typically, this program determines the nature of the interrupt and performs whatever actions are needed. In the example we have been using, the handler determines which I/O module generated the interrupt and may branch to a program that will write more data out to that I/O module. When the interrupt handler routine is completed, the processor can resume execution of the user program at the point of interruption.

It is clear that there is some overhead involved in this process. Extra instructions must be executed (in the interrupt handler) to determine the nature of the interrupt and to decide on the appropriate action. Nevertheless, because of the relatively large amount of time that would be wasted by simply waiting on an I/O operation, the processor can be employed much more efficiently with the use of interrupts.

To appreciate the gain in efficiency, consider Figure 3.10, which is a timing diagram based on the flow of control in Figures 3.7a and 3.7b. In this figure, user program code segments are shaded green, and I/O program code segments are shaded

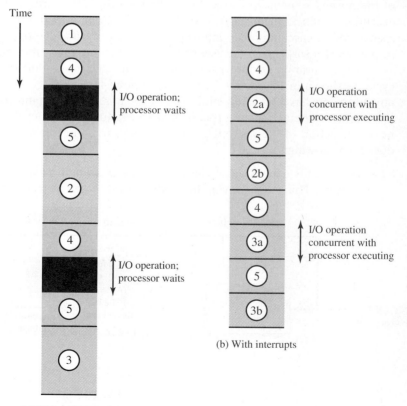

(a) Without interrupts

(b) With interrupts

Figure 3.10 Program Timing: Short I/O Wait

gray. Figure 3.10a shows the case in which interrupts are not used. The processor must wait while an I/O operation is performed.

Figures 3.7b and 3.10b assume that the time required for the I/O operation is relatively short: less than the time to complete the execution of instructions between write operations in the user program. In this case, the segment of code labeled code segment 2 is interrupted. A portion of the code (2a) executes (while the I/O operation is performed) and then the interrupt occurs (upon the completion of the I/O operation). After the interrupt is serviced, execution resumes with the remainder of code segment 2 (2b).

The more typical case, especially for a slow device such as a printer, is that the I/O operation will take much more time than executing a sequence of user instructions. Figure 3.7c indicates this state of affairs. In this case, the user program reaches the second WRITE call before the I/O operation spawned by the first call is complete. The result is that the user program is hung up at that point. When the preceding I/O operation is completed, this new WRITE call may be processed, and a new I/O operation may be started. Figure 3.11 shows the timing for this situation with

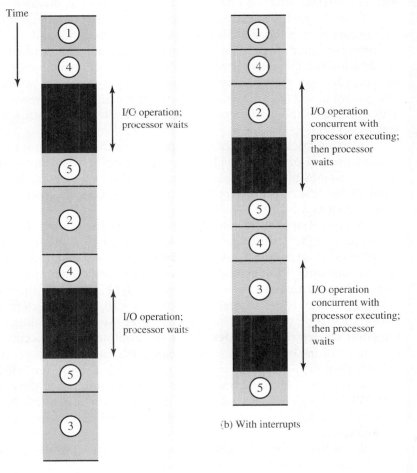

(a) Without interrupts

Figure 3.11   Program Timing: Long I/O Wait

and without the use of interrupts. We can see that there is still a gain in efficiency because part of the time during which the I/O operation is under way overlaps with the execution of user instructions.

Figure 3.12 shows a revised instruction cycle state diagram that includes interrupt cycle processing.

MULTIPLE INTERRUPTS The discussion so far has focused only on the occurrence of a single interrupt. Suppose, however, that multiple interrupts can occur. For example, a program may be receiving data from a communications line and printing results. The printer will generate an interrupt every time it completes a print operation. The communication line controller will generate an interrupt every time a unit of data arrives. The unit could either be a single character or a block, depending on the nature of the communications discipline. In any case, it is possible for a communications interrupt to occur while a printer interrupt is being processed.

Two approaches can be taken to dealing with multiple interrupts. The first is to disable interrupts while an interrupt is being processed. A **disabled interrupt** simply means that the processor can and will ignore that interrupt request signal. If an interrupt occurs during this time, it generally remains pending and will be checked by the processor after the processor has enabled interrupts. Thus, when a user program is executing and an interrupt occurs, interrupts are disabled immediately. After the interrupt handler routine completes, interrupts are enabled before resuming the user program, and the processor checks to see if additional interrupts have occurred. This approach is nice and simple, as interrupts are handled in strict sequential order (Figure 3.13a).

The drawback to the preceding approach is that it does not take into account relative priority or time-critical needs. For example, when input arrives from the communications line, it may need to be absorbed rapidly to make room for more input. If the first batch of input has not been processed before the second batch arrives, data may be lost.

A second approach is to define priorities for interrupts and to allow an interrupt of higher priority to cause a lower-priority interrupt handler to be itself interrupted (Figure 3.13b). As an example of this second approach, consider a system with three I/O devices: a printer, a disk, and a communications line, with increasing priorities of 2, 4, and 5, respectively. Figure 3.14 illustrates a possible sequence. A user program begins at $t = 0$. At $t = 10$, a printer interrupt occurs; user information is placed on the system stack and execution continues at the printer **interrupt service routine (ISR)**. While this routine is still executing, at $t = 15$, a communications interrupt occurs. Because the communications line has higher priority than the printer, the interrupt is honored. The printer ISR is interrupted, its state is pushed onto the stack, and execution continues at the communications ISR. While this routine is executing, a disk interrupt occurs ($t = 20$). Because this interrupt is of lower priority, it is simply held, and the communications ISR runs to completion.

When the communications ISR is complete ($t = 25$), the previous processor state is restored, which is the execution of the printer ISR. However, before even a single instruction in that routine can be executed, the processor honors the higher-priority disk interrupt and control transfers to the disk ISR. Only when that routine

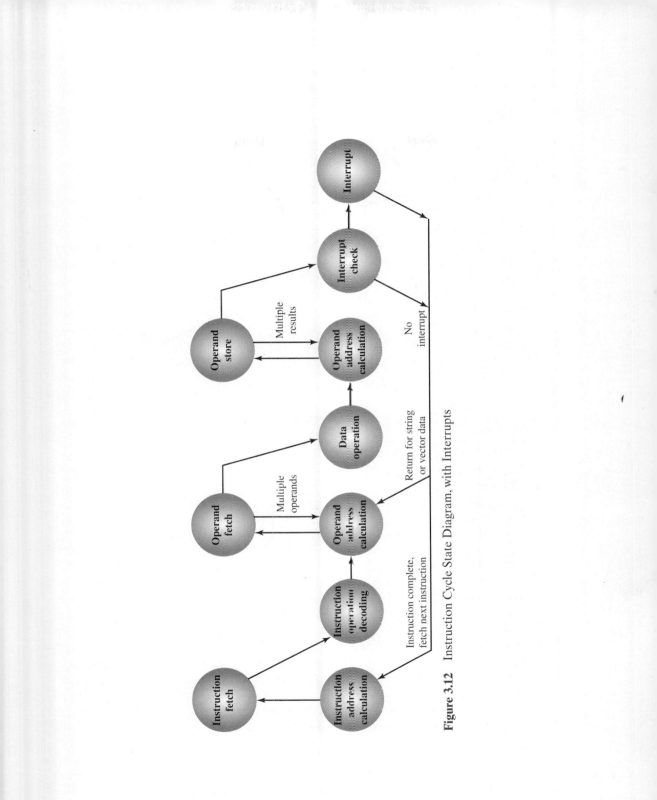

Figure 3.12 Instruction Cycle State Diagram, with Interrupts

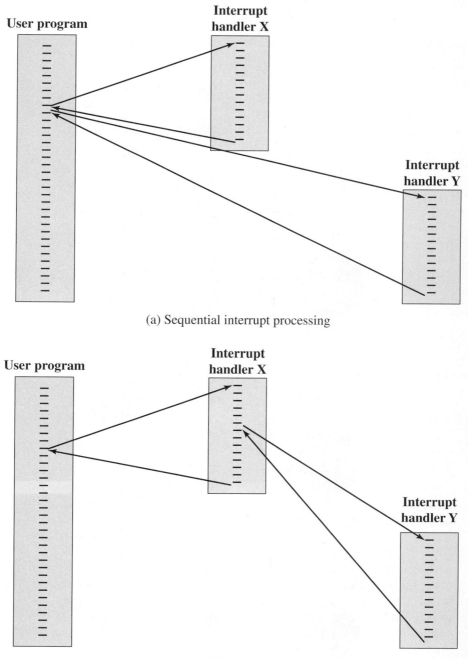

(a) Sequential interrupt processing

(b) Nested interrupt processing

Figure 3.13   Transfer of Control with Multiple Interrupts

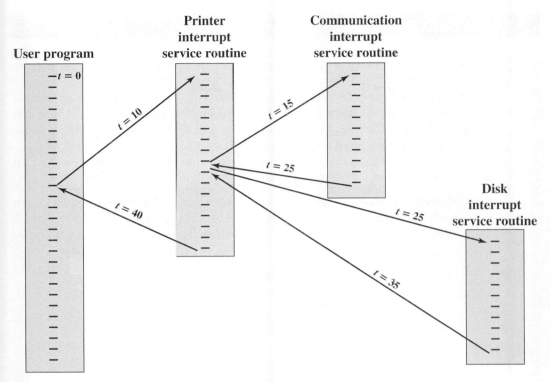

Figure 3.14 Example Time Sequence of Multiple Interrupts

is complete ($t = 35$) is the printer ISR resumed. When that routine completes ($t = 40$), control finally returns to the user program.

I/O Function

Thus far, we have discussed the operation of the computer as controlled by the processor, and we have looked primarily at the interaction of processor and memory. The discussion has only alluded to the role of the I/O component. This role is discussed in detail in Chapter 7, but a brief summary is in order here.

An I/O module (e.g., a disk controller) can exchange data directly with the processor. Just as the processor can initiate a read or write with memory, designating the address of a specific location, the processor can also read data from or write data to an I/O module. In this latter case, the processor identifies a specific device that is controlled by a particular I/O module. Thus, an instruction sequence similar in form to that of Figure 3.5 could occur, with I/O instructions rather than memory-referencing instructions.

In some cases, it is desirable to allow I/O exchanges to occur directly with memory. In such a case, the processor grants to an I/O module the authority to read from or write to memory, so that the I/O-memory transfer can occur without tying up the processor. During such a transfer, the I/O module issues read or write commands to memory, relieving the processor of responsibility for the exchange. This operation is known as direct memory access (DMA) and is examined in Chapter 7.

3.3 INTERCONNECTION STRUCTURES

A computer consists of a set of components or modules of three basic types (processor, memory, I/O) that communicate with each other. In effect, a computer is a network of basic modules. Thus, there must be paths for connecting the modules.

The collection of paths connecting the various modules is called the *interconnection structure*. The design of this structure will depend on the exchanges that must be made among modules.

Figure 3.15 suggests the types of exchanges that are needed by indicating the major forms of input and output for each module type[2]:

- **Memory:** Typically, a memory module will consist of N words of equal length. Each word is assigned a unique numerical address $(0, 1, ..., N-1)$. A word of data can be read from or written into the memory. The nature of the operation

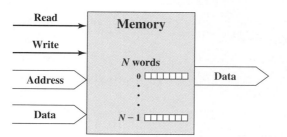

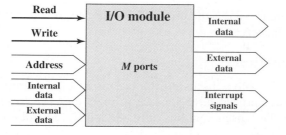

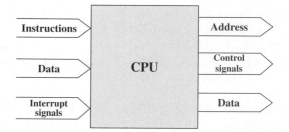

Figure 3.15 Computer Modules

---

[2]The wide arrows represent multiple signal lines carrying multiple bits of information in parallel. Each narrow arrow represents a single signal line.

is indicated by read and write control signals. The location for the operation is specified by an address.

- **I/O module:** From an internal (to the computer system) point of view, I/O is functionally similar to memory. There are two operations, read and write. Further, an I/O module may control more than one external device. We can refer to each of the interfaces to an external device as a *port* and give each a unique address (e.g., 0, 1, ..., $M - 1$). In addition, there are external data paths for the input and output of data with an external device. Finally, an I/O module may be able to send interrupt signals to the processor.

- **Processor:** The processor reads in instructions and data, writes out data after processing, and uses control signals to control the overall operation of the system. It also receives interrupt signals.

The preceding list defines the data to be exchanged. The interconnection structure must support the following types of transfers:

- **Memory to processor:** The processor reads an instruction or a unit of data from memory.
- **Processor to memory:** The processor writes a unit of data to memory.
- **I/O to processor:** The processor reads data from an I/O device via an I/O module.
- **Processor to I/O:** The processor sends data to the I/O device.
- **I/O to or from memory:** For these two cases, an I/O module is allowed to exchange data directly with memory, without going through the processor, using direct memory access.

Over the years, a number of interconnection structures have been tried. By far the most common are (1) the bus and various multiple-bus structures, and (2) point-to-point interconnection structures with packetized data transfer. We devote the remainder of this chapter for a discussion of these structures.

3.4 BUS INTERCONNECTION

A bus is a communication pathway connecting two or more devices. A key characteristic of a bus is that it is a shared transmission medium. Multiple devices connect to the bus, and a signal transmitted by any one device is available for reception by all other devices attached to the bus. If two devices transmit during the same time period, their signals will overlap and become garbled. Thus, only one device at a time can successfully transmit.

Typically, a bus consists of multiple communication pathways, or lines. Each line is capable of transmitting signals representing binary 1 and binary 0. Over time, a sequence of binary digits can be transmitted across a single line. Taken together, several lines of a bus can be used to transmit binary digits simultaneously (in parallel). For example, an 8-bit unit of data can be transmitted over eight bus lines.

Computer systems contain a number of different buses that provide pathways between components at various levels of the computer system hierarchy. A bus that connects major computer components (processor, memory, I/O) is called a **system bus**. The most common computer interconnection structures are based on the use of one or more system buses.

Bus Structure

A system bus consists, typically, of from about fifty to hundreds of separate lines. Each line is assigned a particular meaning or function. Although there are many different bus designs, on any bus the lines can be classified into three functional groups (Figure 3.16): data, address, and control lines. In addition, there may be power distribution lines that supply power to the attached modules.

The **data lines** provide a path for moving data among system modules. These lines, collectively, are called the **data bus**. The data bus may consist of 32, 64, 128, or even more separate lines, the number of lines being referred to as the *width* of the data bus. Because each line can carry only 1 bit at a time, the number of lines determines how many bits can be transferred at a time. The width of the data bus is a key factor in determining overall system performance. For example, if the data bus is 32 bits wide and each instruction is 64 bits long, then the processor must access the memory module twice during each instruction cycle.

The **address lines** are used to designate the source or destination of the data on the data bus. For example, if the processor wishes to read a word (8, 16, or 32 bits) of data from memory, it puts the address of the desired word on the address lines. Clearly, the width of the **address bus** determines the maximum possible memory capacity of the system. Furthermore, the address lines are generally also used to address I/O ports. Typically, the higher-order bits are used to select a particular module on the bus, and the lower-order bits select a memory location or I/O port within the module. For example, on an 8-bit address bus, address 01111111 and below might reference locations in a memory module (module 0) with 128 words of memory, and address 10000000 and above refer to devices attached to an I/O module (module 1).

The **control lines** are used to control the access to and the use of the data and address lines. Because the data and address lines are shared by all components, there must be a means of controlling their use. Control signals transmit both command and timing information among system modules. Timing signals indicate the validity of data and address information. Command signals specify operations to be performed. Typical control lines include:

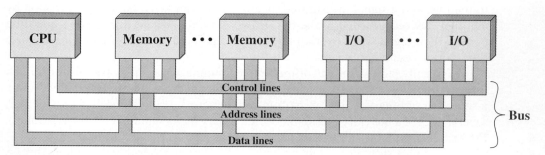

Figure 3.16   Bus Interconnection Scheme

- **Memory write:** causes data on the bus to be written into the addressed location
- **Memory read:** causes data from the addressed location to be placed on the bus
- **I/O write:** causes data on the bus to be output to the addressed I/O port
- **I/O read:** causes data from the addressed I/O port to be placed on the bus
- **Transfer ACK:** indicates that data have been accepted from or placed on the bus
- **Bus request:** indicates that a module needs to gain control of the bus
- **Bus grant:** indicates that a requesting module has been granted control of the bus
- **Interrupt request:** indicates that an interrupt is pending
- **Interrupt ACK:** acknowledges that the pending interrupt has been recognized
- **Clock:** is used to synchronize operations
- **Reset:** initializes all modules.

The operation of the bus is as follows. If one module wishes to send data to another, it must do two things: (1) obtain the use of the bus, and (2) transfer data via the bus. If one module wishes to request data from another module, it must (1) obtain the use of the bus, and (2) transfer a request to the other module over the appropriate control and address lines. It must then wait for that second module to send the data.

Multiple-Bus Hierarchies

If a great number of devices are connected to the bus, performance will suffer. There are two main causes:

1. In general, the more devices attached to the bus, the greater the bus length and hence the greater the propagation delay. This delay determines the time it takes for devices to coordinate the use of the bus. When control of the bus passes from one device to another frequently, these propagation delays can noticeably affect performance.
2. The bus may become a bottleneck as the aggregate data transfer demand approaches the capacity of the bus. This problem can be countered to some extent by increasing the data rate that the bus can carry and by using wider buses (e.g., increasing the data bus from 32 to 64 bits). However, because the data rates generated by attached devices (e.g., graphics and video controllers, network interfaces) are growing rapidly, this is a race that a single bus is ultimately destined to lose.

Accordingly, most bus-based computer systems use multiple buses, generally laid out in a hierarchy. A typical traditional structure is shown in Figure 3.17a. There is a local bus that connects the processor to a cache memory and that may support one or more local devices. The cache memory controller connects the cache not only to this local bus, but to a system bus to which are attached all of the main memory modules. In contemporary systems, the cache is in the same chip as the processor, and

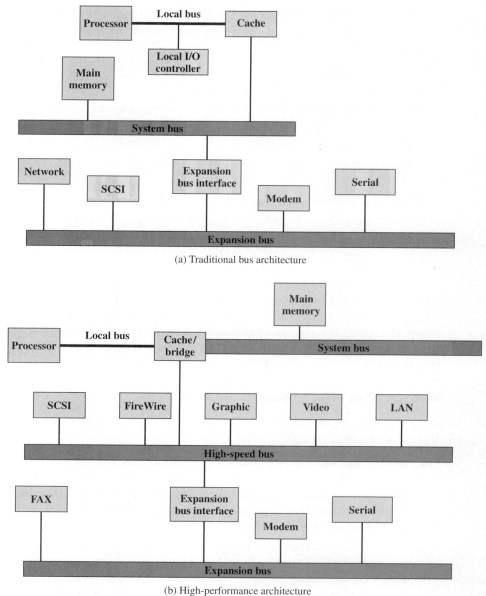

(a) Traditional bus architecture

(b) High-performance architecture

Figure 3.17 Example Bus Configurations

so an external bus or other interconnect scheme is not needed, although there may also be an external cache. As will be discussed in Chapter 4, the use of a cache structure insulates the processor from a requirement to access main memory frequently. Hence, main memory can be moved off of the local bus onto a system bus. In this way, I/O transfers to and from the main memory across the system bus do not interfere with the processor's activity.

It is possible to connect I/O controllers directly onto the system bus. A more efficient solution is to make use of one or more expansion buses for this purpose. An expansion bus interface buffers data transfers between the system bus and the I/O controllers on the expansion bus. This arrangement allows the system to support a wide variety of I/O devices and at the same time insulate memory-to-processor traffic from I/O traffic.

Figure 3.17a shows some typical examples of I/O devices that might be attached to the expansion bus. Network connections include local area networks (LANs) such as a 10-Mbps Ethernet and connections to wide area networks (WANs) such as a packet-switching network. SCSI (small computer system interface) is itself a type of bus used to support local disk drives and other peripherals. A serial port could be used to support a printer or scanner.

This traditional bus architecture is reasonably efficient but begins to break down as higher and higher performance is seen in the I/O devices. In response to these growing demands, a common approach taken by industry is to build a high-speed bus that is closely integrated with the rest of the system, requiring only a bridge between the processor's bus and the high-speed bus. This arrangement is sometimes known as a mezzanine architecture.

Figure 3.17b shows a typical realization of this approach. Again, there is a local bus that connects the processor to a cache controller, which is in turn connected to a system bus that supports main memory. The cache controller is integrated into a bridge, or buffering device, that connects to the high-speed bus. This bus supports connections to high-speed LANs, such as Fast Ethernet at 100 Mbps, video and graphics workstation controllers, as well as interface controllers to local peripheral buses, including SCSI and FireWire. The latter is a high-speed bus arrangement specifically designed to support high-capacity I/O devices. Lower-speed devices are still supported off an expansion bus, with an interface buffering traffic between the expansion bus and the high-speed bus.

The advantage of this arrangement is that the high-speed bus brings high-demand devices into closer integration with the processor and at the same time is independent of the processor. Thus, differences in processor and high-speed bus speeds and signal line definitions are tolerated. Changes in processor architecture do not affect the high-speed bus, and vice versa.

Elements of Bus Design

Although a variety of different bus implementations exist, there are a few basic parameters or design elements that serve to classify and differentiate buses. Table 3.2 lists key elements.

BUS TYPES Bus lines can be separated into two generic types: dedicated and multiplexed. A dedicated bus line is permanently assigned either to one function or to a physical subset of computer components.

An example of functional dedication is the use of separate dedicated address and data lines, which is common on many buses. However, it is not essential. For example, address and data information may be transmitted over the same set of lines using an Address Valid control line. At the beginning of a data transfer, the address is placed on the bus and the Address Valid line is activated. At this point,

Table 3.2   Elements of Bus Design

Type	Bus Width
Dedicated	Address
Multiplexed	Data
Method of Arbitration	**Data Transfer Type**
Centralized	Read
Distributed	Write
Timing	Read-modify-write
	Read-after-write
Synchronous	Block
Asynchronous	

each module has a specified period of time to copy the address and determine if it is the addressed module. The address is then removed from the bus, and the same bus connections are used for the subsequent read or write data transfer. This method of using the same lines for multiple purposes is known as *time multiplexing*.

The advantage of time multiplexing is the use of fewer lines, which saves space and, usually, cost. The disadvantage is that more complex circuitry is needed within each module. Also, there is a potential reduction in performance because certain events that share the same lines cannot take place in parallel.

Physical dedication refers to the use of multiple buses, each of which connects only a subset of modules. A typical example is the use of an I/O bus to interconnect all I/O modules; this bus is then connected to the main bus through some type of I/O adapter module. The potential advantage of physical dedication is high throughput, because there is less bus contention. A disadvantage is the increased size and cost of the system.

METHOD OF ARBITRATION In all but the simplest systems, more than one module may need control of the bus. For example, an I/O module may need to read or write directly to memory, without sending the data to the processor. Because only one unit at a time can successfully transmit over the bus, some method of **arbitration** is needed. The various methods can be roughly classified as being either **centralized arbitration** or **distributed arbitration**. In a centralized scheme, a single hardware device, referred to as a *bus controller* or *arbiter*, is responsible for allocating time on the bus. The device may be a separate module or part of the processor. In a distributed scheme, there is no central controller. Rather, each module contains access control logic and the modules act together to share the bus. With both methods of arbitration, the purpose is to designate one device, either the processor or an I/O module, as master. The master may then initiate a data transfer (e.g., read or write) with some other device, which acts as slave for this particular exchange.

TIMING Timing refers to the way in which events are coordinated on the bus. Buses use either synchronous timing or asynchronous timing.

With **synchronous timing**, the occurrence of events on the bus is determined by a clock. The bus includes a clock line upon which a clock transmits a regular sequence of alternating 1s and 0s of equal duration. A single 1–0 transmission is referred to as a *clock cycle* or *bus cycle* and defines a time slot. All other devices on the bus can read the clock line, and all events start at the beginning of a clock cycle. Figure 3.18 shows a typical, but simplified, timing diagram for synchronous read and write operations (see Appendix N for a description of timing diagrams). Other bus signals may change at the leading edge of the clock signal (with a slight reaction delay). Most events occupy a single clock cycle. In this simple example, the processor places a memory address on the address lines during the first clock cycle and may assert various status lines. Once the address lines have stabilized, the processor issues an address enable signal. For a read operation, the processor issues a read command at the start of the second cycle. A memory module recognizes the address and, after a delay of one cycle, places the data on the data lines. The processor reads the data from the data lines and drops the read signal. For a write operation, the processor puts the data on the data lines at the start of the second cycle and issues a write command after the data lines have stabilized. The memory module copies the information from the data lines during the third clock cycle.

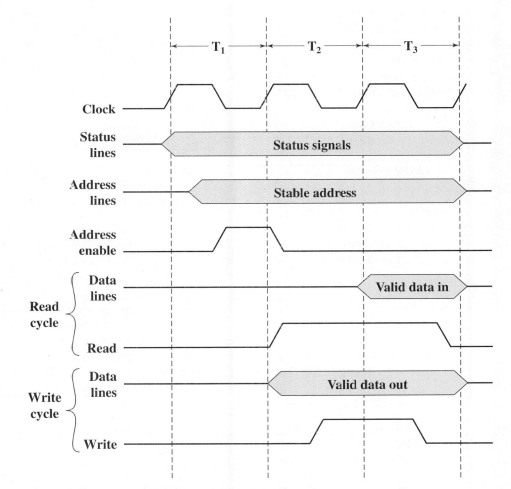

Figure 3.18   Timing of Synchronous Bus Operations

With **asynchronous timing**, the occurrence of one event on a bus follows and depends on the occurrence of a previous event. In the simple read example of Figure 3.19a, the processor places address and status signals on the bus. After pausing for these signals to stabilize, it issues a read command, indicating the presence of valid address and control signals. The appropriate memory decodes the address and responds by placing the data on the data line. Once the data lines have stabilized, the memory module asserts the acknowledged line to signal the processor that the data are available. Once the master has read the data from the data lines, it deasserts the read signal. This causes the memory module to drop the data and acknowledge lines. Finally, once the acknowledge line is dropped, the master removes the address information.

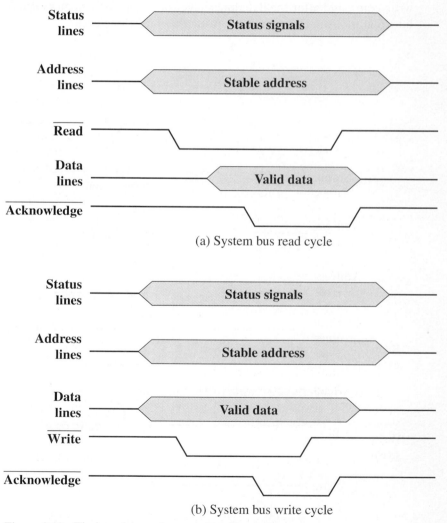

(a) System bus read cycle

(b) System bus write cycle

Figure 3.19 Timing of Asynchronous Bus Operations

Figure 3.19b shows a simple asynchronous write operation. In this case, the master places the data on the data line at the same time that it puts signals on the status and address lines. The memory module responds to the write command by copying the data from the data lines and then asserting the acknowledge line. The master then drops the write signal and the memory module drops the acknowledge signal.

Synchronous timing is simpler to implement and test. However, it is less flexible than asynchronous timing. Because all devices on a synchronous bus are tied to a fixed clock rate, the system cannot take advantage of advances in device performance. With asynchronous timing, a mixture of slow and fast devices, using older and newer technology, can share a bus.

3.5 POINT-TO-POINT INTERCONNECT

The shared bus architecture was the standard approach to interconnection between the processor and other components (memory, I/O, and so on) for decades. But contemporary systems increasingly rely on point-to-point interconnection rather than shared buses.

The principal reason driving the change from bus to point-to-point interconnect was the electrical constraints encountered with increasing the frequency of wide synchronous buses. At higher and higher data rates, it becomes increasingly difficult to perform the synchronization and arbitration functions in a timely fashion. Further, with the advent of multicore chips, with multiple processors and significant memory on a single chip, it was found that the use of a conventional shared bus on the same chip magnified the difficulties of increasing bus data rate and reducing bus latency to keep up with the processors. Compared to the shared bus, the point-to-point interconnect has lower latency, higher data rate, and better scalability.

In this section, we look at an important and representative example of the point-to-point interconnect approach: Intel's **QuickPath Interconnect (QPI)**, which was introduced in 2008.

The following are significant characteristics of QPI and other point-to-point interconnect schemes:

- **Multiple direct connections:** Multiple components within the system enjoy direct pairwise connections to other components. This eliminates the need for arbitration found in shared transmission systems.

- **Layered protocol architecture:** As found in network environments, such as TCP/IP-based data networks, these processor-level interconnects use a layered protocol architecture, rather than the simple use of control signals found in shared bus arrangements.

- **Packetized data transfer:** Data are not sent as a raw bit stream. Rather, data are sent as a sequence of packets, each of which includes control headers and error control codes.

Figure 3.20 illustrates a typical use of QPI on a multicore computer. The QPI links (indicated by the green arrow pairs in the figure) form a switching fabric

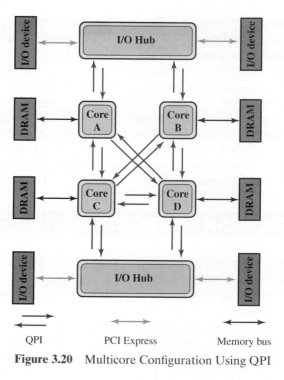

Figure 3.20 Multicore Configuration Using QPI

that enables data to move throughout the network. Direct QPI connections can be established between each pair of core processors. If core A in Figure 3.20 needs to access the memory controller in core D, it sends its request through either cores B or C, which must in turn forward that request on to the memory controller in core D. Similarly, larger systems with eight or more processors can be built using processors with three links and routing traffic through intermediate processors.

In addition, QPI is used to connect to an I/O module, called an I/O hub (IOH). The IOH acts as a switch directing traffic to and from I/O devices. Typically in newer systems, the link from the IOH to the I/O device controller uses an interconnect technology called PCI Express (PCIe), described later in this chapter. The IOH translates between the QPI protocols and formats and the PCIe protocols and formats. A core also links to a main memory module (typically the memory uses dynamic access random memory (DRAM) technology) using a dedicated memory bus.

QPI is defined as a four-layer protocol architecture,[3] encompassing the following layers (Figure 3.21):

- **Physical:** Consists of the actual wires carrying the signals, as well as circuitry and logic to support ancillary features required in the transmission and receipt of the 1s and 0s. The unit of transfer at the Physical layer is 20 bits, which is called a **Phit** (physical unit).

---

[3]The reader unfamiliar with the concept of a protocol architecture will find a brief overview in Appendix L.

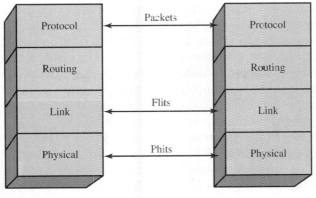

Figure 3.21   QPI Layers

- **Link:** Responsible for reliable transmission and flow control. The Link layer's unit of transfer is an 80-bit **Flit** (flow control unit).
- **Routing:** Provides the framework for directing packets through the fabric.
- **Protocol:** The high-level set of rules for exchanging **packets** of data between devices. A packet is comprised of an integral number of Flits.

QPI Physical Layer

Figure 3.22 shows the physical architecture of a QPI port. The QPI port consists of 84 individual links grouped as follows. Each data path consists of a pair of wires that transmits data one bit at a time; the pair is referred to as a **lane**. There are 20 data lanes

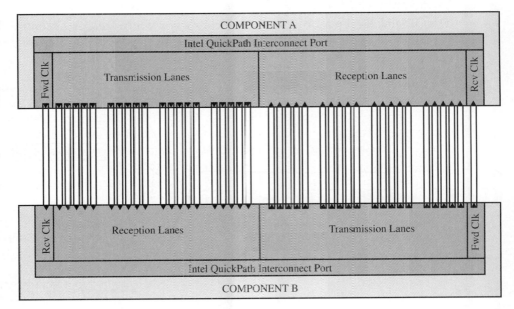

Figure 3.22   Physical Interface of the Intel QPI Interconnect

in each direction (transmit and receive), plus a clock lane in each direction. Thus, QPI is capable of transmitting 20 bits in parallel in each direction. The 20-bit unit is referred to as a *phit*. Typical signaling speeds of the link in current products calls for operation at 6.4 GT/s (transfers per second). At 20 bits per transfer, that adds up to 16 GB/s, and since QPI links involve dedicated bidirectional pairs, the total capacity is 32 GB/s.

The lanes in each direction are grouped into four quadrants of 5 lanes each. In some applications, the link can also operate at half or quarter widths in order to reduce power consumption or work around failures.

The form of transmission on each lane is known as **differential signaling**, or **balanced transmission**. With balanced transmission, signals are transmitted as a current that travels down one conductor and returns on the other. The binary value depends on the voltage difference. Typically, one line has a positive voltage value and the other line has zero voltage, and one line is associated with binary 1 and one line is associated with binary 0. Specifically, the technique used by QPI is known as *low-voltage differential signaling* (LVDS). In a typical implementation, the transmitter injects a small current into one wire or the other, depending on the logic level to be sent. The current passes through a resistor at the receiving end, and then returns in the opposite direction along the other wire. The receiver senses the polarity of the voltage across the resistor to determine the logic level.

Another function performed by the physical layer is that it manages the translation between 80-bit flits and 20-bit phits using a technique known as **multilane distribution**. The flits can be considered as a bit stream that is distributed across the data lanes in a round-robin fashion (first bit to first lane, second bit to second lane, etc.), as illustrated in Figure 3.23. This approach enables QPI to achieve very high data rates by implementing the physical link between two ports as multiple parallel channels.

QPI Link Layer

The QPI link layer performs two key functions: flow control and error control. These functions are performed as part of the QPI link layer protocol, and operate on the

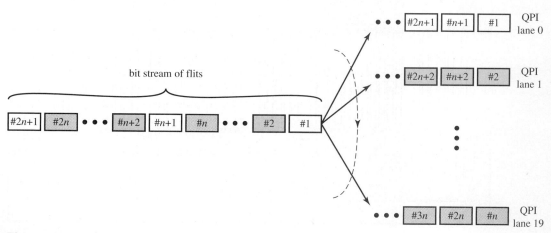

Figure 3.23 QPI Multilane Distribution

level of the flit (flow control unit). Each flit consists of a 72-bit message payload and an 8-bit error control code called a cyclic redundancy check (CRC). We discuss error control codes in Chapter 5.

A flit payload may consist of data or message information. The data flits transfer the actual bits of data between cores or between a core and an IOH. The message flits are used for such functions as flow control, error control, and cache coherence. We discuss cache coherence in Chapters 5 and 17.

The **flow control function** is needed to ensure that a sending QPI entity does not overwhelm a receiving QPI entity by sending data faster than the receiver can process the data and clear buffers for more incoming data. To control the flow of data, QPI makes use of a credit scheme. During initialization, a sender is given a set number of credits to send flits to a receiver. Whenever a flit is sent to the receiver, the sender decrements its credit counters by one credit. Whenever a buffer is freed at the receiver, a credit is returned to the sender for that buffer. Thus, the receiver controls that pace at which data is transmitted over a QPI link.

Occasionally, a bit transmitted at the physical layer is changed during transmission, due to noise or some other phenomenon. The **error control function** at the link layer detects and recovers from such bit errors, and so isolates higher layers from experiencing bit errors. The procedure works as follows for a flow of data from system A to system B:

1. As mentioned, each 80-bit flit includes an 8-bit CRC field. The CRC is a function of the value of the remaining 72 bits. On transmission, A calculates a CRC value for each flit and inserts that value into the flit.

2. When a flit is received, B calculates a CRC value for the 72-bit payload and compares this value with the value of the incoming CRC value in the flit. If the two CRC values do not match, an error has been detected.

3. When B detects an error, it sends a request to A to retransmit the flit that is in error. However, because A may have had sufficient credit to send a stream of flits, so that additional flits have been transmitted after the flit in error and before A receives the request to retransmit. Therefore, the request is for A to back up and retransmit the damaged flit plus all subsequent flits.

QPI Routing Layer

The Routing layer is used to determine the course that a packet will traverse across the available system interconnects. Routing tables are defined by firmware and describe the possible paths that a packet can follow. In small configurations, such as a two-socket platform, the routing options are limited and the routing tables quite simple. For larger systems, the routing table options are more complex, giving the flexibility of routing and rerouting traffic depending on how (1) devices are populated in the platform, (2) system resources are partitioned, and (3) reliability events result in mapping around a failing resource.

QPI Protocol Layer

In this layer, the packet is defined as the unit of transfer. The packet contents definition is standardized with some flexibility allowed to meet differing market segment requirements. One key function performed at this level is a cache coherency protocol, which deals with making sure that main memory values held in multiple caches are consistent. A typical data packet payload is a block of data being sent to or from a cache.

3.6 PCI EXPRESS

The **peripheral component interconnect (PCI)** is a popular high-bandwidth, processor-independent bus that can function as a mezzanine or peripheral bus. Compared with other common bus specifications, PCI delivers better system performance for high-speed I/O subsystems (e.g., graphic display adapters, network interface controllers, and disk controllers).

Intel began work on PCI in 1990 for its Pentium-based systems. Intel soon released all the patents to the public domain and promoted the creation of an industry association, the PCI Special Interest Group (SIG), to develop further and maintain the compatibility of the PCI specifications. The result is that PCI has been widely adopted and is finding increasing use in personal computer, workstation, and server systems. Because the specification is in the public domain and is supported by a broad cross section of the microprocessor and peripheral industry, PCI products built by different vendors are compatible.

As with the system bus discussed in the preceding sections, the bus-based PCI scheme has not been able to keep pace with the data rate demands of attached devices. Accordingly, a new version, known as **PCI Express (PCIe)** has been developed. PCIe, as with QPI, is a point-to-point interconnect scheme intended to replace bus-based schemes such as PCI.

A key requirement for PCIe is high capacity to support the needs of higher data rate I/O devices, such as Gigabit Ethernet. Another requirement deals with the need to support time-dependent data streams. Applications such as video-on-demand and audio redistribution are putting real-time constraints on servers too. Many communications applications and embedded PC control systems also process data in real-time. Today's platforms must also deal with multiple concurrent transfers at ever-increasing data rates. It is no longer acceptable to treat all data as equal—it is more important, for example, to process streaming data first since late real-time data is as useless as no data. Data needs to be tagged so that an I/O system can prioritize its flow throughout the platform.

PCI Physical and Logical Architecture

Figure 3.24 shows a typical configuration that supports the use of PCIe. A **root complex** device, also referred to as a *chipset* or a *host bridge,* connects the processor and memory subsystem to the PCI Express switch fabric comprising one or more PCIe and PCIe switch devices. The root complex acts as a buffering device, to deal with difference in data rates between I/O controllers and memory and processor components. The root complex also translates between PCIe transaction formats and the processor and memory signal and control requirements. The chipset will typically support multiple PCIe ports, some of which attach directly to a PCIe

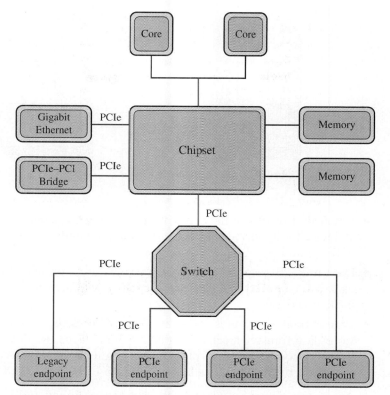

Figure 3.24   Typical Configuration Using PCIe

device and one or more that attach to a switch that manages multiple PCIe streams. PCIe links from the chipset may attach to the following kinds of devices that implement PCIe:

- **Switch:** The switch manages multiple PCIe streams.
- **PCIe endpoint:** An I/O device or controller that implements PCIe, such as a Gigabit Ethernet switch, a graphics or video controller, disk interface, or a communications controller.
- **Legacy endpoint:** Legacy endpoint category is intended for existing designs that have been migrated to PCI Express, and it allows legacy behaviors such as use of I/O space and locked transactions. PCI Express endpoints are not permitted to require the use of I/O space at runtime and must not use locked transactions. By distinguishing these categories, it is possible for a system designer to restrict or eliminate legacy behaviors that have negative impacts on system performance and robustness.
- **PCIe/PCI bridge:** Allows older PCI devices to be connected to PCIe-based systems.

As with QPI, PCIe interactions are defined using a protocol architecture. The PCIe protocol architecture encompasses the following layers (Figure 3.25):

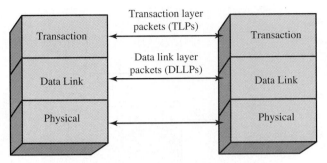

Figure 3.25   PCIe Protocol Layers

- **Physical:** Consists of the actual wires carrying the signals, as well as circuitry and logic to support ancillary features required in the transmission and receipt of the 1s and 0s.
- **Data link:** Is responsible for reliable transmission and flow control. Data packets generated and consumed by the DLL are called Data Link Layer Packets (DLLPs).
- **Transaction:** Generates and consumes data packets used to implement load/ store data transfer mechanisms and also manages the flow control of those packets between the two components on a link. Data packets generated and consumed by the TL are called Transaction Layer Packets (TLPs).

Above the TL are software layers that generate read and write requests that are transported by the transaction layer to the I/O devices using a packet-based transaction protocol.

PCIe Physical Layer

Similar to QPI, PCIe is a point-to-point architecture. Each PCIe port consists of a number of bidirectional lanes (note that in QPI, the lane refers to transfer in one direction only). Transfer in each direction in a lane is by means of differential signaling over a pair of wires. A PCI port can provide 1, 4, 6, 16, or 32 lanes. In what follows, we refer to the PCIe 3.0 specification, introduced in late 2010.

As with QPI, PCIe uses a multilane distribution technique. Figure 3.26 shows an example for a PCIe port consisting of four lanes. Data are distributed to the four lanes 1 byte at a time using a simple round-robin scheme. At each physical lane, data are buffered and processed 16 bytes (128 bits) at a time. Each block of 128 bits is encoded into a unique 130-bit codeword for transmission; this is referred to as 128b/130b encoding. Thus, the effective data rate of an individual lane is reduced by a factor of 128/130.

To understand the rationale for the 128b/130b encoding, note that unlike QPI, PCIe does not use its clock line to synchronize the bit stream. That is, the clock line is not used to determine the start and end point of each incoming bit; it is used for other signaling purposes only. However, it is necessary for the receiver to be synchronized with the transmitter, so that the receiver knows when each bit begins and ends. If there is any drift between the clocks used for bit transmission

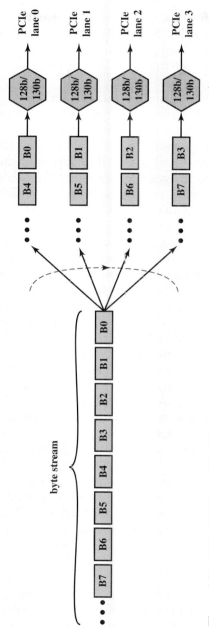

Figure 3.26 PCIe Multilane Distribution

and reception of the transmitter and receiver, errors may occur. To compensate for the possibility of drift, PCIe relies on the receiver synchronizing with the transmitter based on the transmitted signal. As with QPI, PCIe uses differential signaling over a pair of wires. Synchronization can be achieved by the receiver looking for transitions in the data and synchronizing its clock to the transition. However, consider that with a long string of 1s or 0s using differential signaling, the output is a constant voltage over a long period of time. Under these circumstances, any drift between the clocks of transmitter and receiver will result in loss of synchronization between the two.

A common approach, and the one used in PCIe 3.0, to overcoming the problem of a long string of bits of one value is scrambling. Scrambling, which does not increase the number of bits to be transmitted, is a mapping technique that tends to make the data appear more random. The scrambling tends to spread out the number of transitions so that they appear at the receiver more uniformly spaced, which is good for synchronization. Also, other transmission properties, such as spectral properties, are enhanced if the data are more nearly of a random nature rather than constant or repetitive. For more discussion of scrambling, see Appendix M.

Another technique that can aid in synchronization is encoding, in which additional bits are inserted into the bit stream to force transitions. For PCIe 3.0, each group of 128 bits of input is mapped into a 130-bit block by adding a 2-bit block sync header. The value of the header is 10 for a data block and 01 for what is called an *ordered set block*, which refers to a link-level information block.

Figure 3.27 illustrates the use of scrambling and encoding. Data to be transmitted are fed into a scrambler. The scrambled output is then fed into a 128b/130b encoder, which buffers 128 bits and then maps the 128-bit block into a 130-bit block. This block then passes through a parallel-to-serial converter and transmitted one bit at a time using differential signaling.

At the receiver, a clock is synchronized to the incoming data to recover the bit stream. This then passes through a serial-to-parallel converter to produce a stream of 130-bit blocks. Each block is passed through a 128b/130b decoder to recover the original scrambled bit pattern, which is then descrambled to produce the original bit stream.

Using these techniques, a data rate of 16 GB/s can be achieved. One final detail to mention. Each transmission of a block of data over a PCI link begins and ends with an 8-bit framing sequence intended to give the receiver time to synchronize with the incoming physical layer bit stream.

PCIe Transaction Layer

The transaction layer (TL) receives read and write requests from the software above the TL and creates request packets for transmission to a destination via the link layer. Most transactions use a *split transaction* technique, which works in the following fashion. A request packet is sent out by a source PCIe device, which then waits for a response, called a *completion* packet. The completion following a request is initiated by the completer only when it has the data and/or status ready for delivery. Each packet has a unique identifier that enables completion packets to be directed

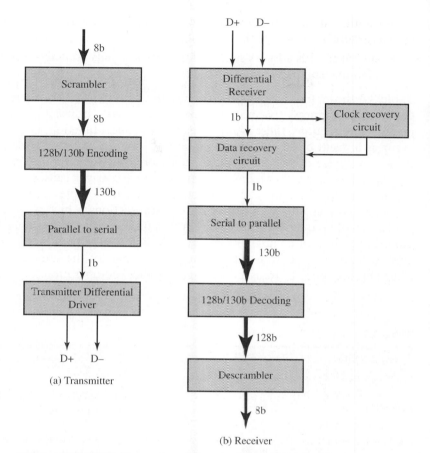

Figure 3.27   PCIe Transmit and Receive Block Diagrams

to the correct originator. With the split transaction technique, the completion is separated in time from the request, in contrast to a typical bus operation in which both sides of a transaction must be available to seize and use the bus. Between the request and the completion, other PCIe traffic may use the link.

TL messages and some write transactions are *posted transactions*, meaning that no response is expected.

The TL packet format supports 32-bit memory addressing and extended 64-bit memory addressing. Packets also have attributes such as "no-snoop," "relaxedordering," and "priority," which may be used to optimally route these packets through the I/O subsystem.

ADDRESS SPACES AND TRANSACTION TYPES The TL supports four address spaces:

- **Memory:** The memory space includes system main memory. It also includes PCIe I/O devices. Certain ranges of memory addresses map into I/O devices.
- **I/O:** This address space is used for legacy PCI devices, with reserved memory address ranges used to address legacy I/O devices.

- **Configuration:** This address space enables the TL to read/write configuration registers associated with I/O devices.
- **Message:** This address space is for control signals related to interrupts, error handling, and power management.

Table 3.3 shows the transaction types provided by the TL. For memory, I/O, and configuration address spaces, there are read and write transactions. In the case of memory transactions, there is also a read lock request function. Locked operations occur as a result of device drivers requesting atomic access to registers on a PCIe device. A device driver, for example, can atomically read, modify, and then write to a device register. To accomplish this, the device driver causes the processor to execute an instruction or set of instructions. The root complex converts these processor instructions into a sequence of PCIe transactions, which perform individual read and write requests for the device driver. If these transactions must be executed atomically, the root complex locks the PCIe link while executing the transactions. This locking prevents transactions that are not part of the sequence from occurring. This sequence of transactions is called a locked operation. The particular set

Table 3.3   PCIe TLP Transaction Types

Address Space	TLP Type	Purpose
Memory	Memory Read Request	Transfer data to or from a location in the system memory map.
	Memory Read Lock Request	
	Memory Write Request	
I/O	I/O Read Request	Transfer data to or from a location in the system memory map for legacy devices.
	I/O Write Request	
Configuration	Config Type 0 Read Request	Transfer data to or from a location in the configuration space of a PCIe device.
	Config Type 0 Write Request	
	Config Type 1 Read Request	
	Config Type 1 Write Request	
Message	Message Request	Provides in-band messaging and event reporting.
	Message Request with Data	
Memory, I/O, Configuration	Completion	Returned for certain requests.
	Completion with Data	
	Completion Locked	
	Completion Locked with Data	

of processor instructions that can cause a locked operation to occur depends on the system chip set and processor architecture.

To maintain compatibility with PCI, PCIe supports both Type 0 and Type 1 configuration cycles. A Type 1 cycle propagates downstream until it reaches the bridge interface hosting the bus (link) that the target device resides on. The configuration transaction is converted on the destination link from Type 1 to Type 0 by the bridge.

Finally, completion messages are used with split transactions for memory, I/O, and configuration transactions.

TLP PACKET ASSEMBLY PCIe transactions are conveyed using transaction layer packets, which are illustrated in Figure 3.28a. A TLP originates in the

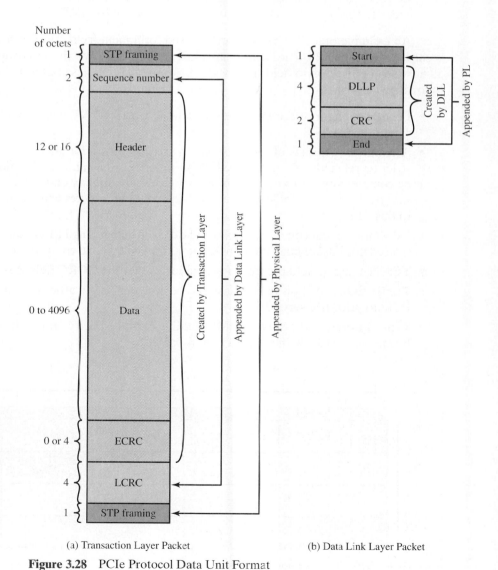

(a) Transaction Layer Packet   (b) Data Link Layer Packet

Figure 3.28   PCIe Protocol Data Unit Format

transaction layer of the sending device and terminates at the transaction layer of the receiving device.

Upper layer software sends to the TL the information needed for the TL to create the core of the TLP, which consists of the following fields:

- **Header:** The Header describes the type of packet and includes information needed by the receiver to process the packet, including any needed routing information. The internal header format is discussed subsequently.
- **Data:** A Data field of up to 4096 bytes may be included in the TLP. Some TLPs do not contain a Data field.
- **ECRC:** An optional end-to-end CRC field enables the destination TL layer to check for errors in the Header and Data portions of the TLP.

An example of a TLP header format, used for a memory request transaction, is shown in Figure 3.29. The fields shaded green indicate fields that are present in all headers. In addition to fields reserved for future use (R), these fields include the following:

- **Length:** Length of the Data field in double words (DW), where one DW = 4 bytes.
- **Attributes:** Consists of two bits. The *relaxed ordering bit* indicates whether strict or relaxed ordering is used. With relaxed ordering, a transaction may be completed prior to other transactions that were already enqueued. The *no snoop bit*, when set, indicates that no cache coherency issues exist with respect to this TLP.
- **EP:** Poisoned data bit. If set, this bit indicates the data in this TLP should be considered invalid, although the transaction is being allowed to complete normally.
- **TE:** TLP digest field present. If set, indicates that the ECRC field is present.
- **Traffic Class:** A 3-bit traffic class can be assigned to a traffic flow to enable PCIe to prioritize service.
- **Type, Format:** These two fields, totaling 7 bits, specify transaction type, header size, and whether a data field is present.

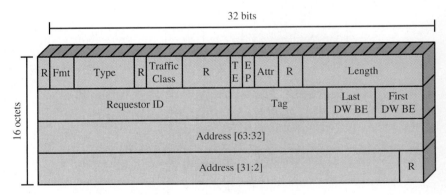

Figure 3.29 TLP Memory Request Format

- **First DW Byte Enables:** These four bits indicate, respectively, whether the corresponding byte in the first DW is valid.
- **Last DW Byte Enables:** These four bits indicate, respectively, whether the corresponding byte in the last DW is valid. This and the preceding field have the effect of allowing smaller transfers that a full DW and offsetting the start and end addresses from the DW boundary.

Figure 3.29 shows a TLP header for a memory request transaction. The Requestor ID identifies the memory requestor, telling the completer where to send its response. The Tag is a number assigned to this transaction by the requestor; the completer must include this Tag in its response so that the requestor can match request and response. The Address field indicates the starting memory address to be read from.

PCIe Data Link Layer

The purpose of the PCIe data link layer is to ensure reliable delivery of packets across the PCIe link. The DLL participates in the formation of TLPs and also transmits DLLPs.

DATA LINK LAYER PACKETS Data link layer packets originate at the data link layer of a transmitting device and terminate at the DLL of the device on the other end of the link. Figure 3.29b shows the format of a DLLP. There are three important groups of DLLPs used in managing a link: flow control packets, power management packets, and TLP ACK and NAK packets. Power management packets are used in managing power platform budgeting. Flow control packets regulate the rate at which TLPs and DLLPs can be transmitted across a link. The ACK and NAK packets are used in TLP processing, discussed in the following paragraphs.

TRANSACTION LAYER PACKET PROCESSING The DLL adds two fields to the core of the TLP created by the TL (Figure 3.29a): a 16-bit sequence number and a 32-bit link-layer CRC (LCRC). Whereas the core fields created at the TL are only used at the destination TL, the two fields added by the DLL are processed at each intermediate node on the way from source to destination.

When a TLP arrives at a device, the DLL strips off the sequence number and LCRC fields and checks the LCRC. There are two possibilities:

1. If no errors are detected, the core portion of the TLP is handed up to the local transaction layer. If this receiving device is the intended destination, then the TL processes the TLP. Otherwise, the TL determines a route for the TLP and passes it back down to the DLL for transmission over the next link on the way to the destination.

2. If an error is detected, the DLL schedules an NAK DLL packet to return back to the remote transmitter. The TLP is eliminated.

When the DLL transmits a TLP, it retains a copy of the TLP. If it receives an NAK for the TLP with this sequence number, it retransmits the TLP. When it receives an ACK, it discards the buffered TLP.

3.7 RECOMMENDED READING

[SING10] provides a good overview of QPI. For a thorough discussion, see [MADD09]. [KOLB05] is a good overview of PCIe. The clearest book-length description of PCIe is [WILE03].

KOLB05 Kolbehdari, M., et al. "The Emergence of PCI Express* in the Next Generation of Mobile Platforms." *Intel Technology Journal*, February 2005.

MADD09 Maddox, R., et al. *Weaving High Performance Multiprocessor Fabric: Architectural Insights to the Intel QuickPath Interconnect.* Hillsboro, OR: Intel Press, 2009.

SING10 Singh, G., et al. "The Feeding of High-Performance Processor Cores—Quickpath Interconnects and the New I/O Hubs." *Intel Technology Journal*, September 2010.

WILE03 Wilen, A.; Schade, J.; and Thronburg, R. *Introduction to PCI Express—A Hardware and Software Developers Guide.* Hillsboro, OR: Intel Press, 2003.

3.8 KEY TERMS, REVIEW QUESTIONS, AND PROBLEMS

Key Terms

address bus	distributed arbitration	memory buffer register (MBR)
address lines	error control function	multilane distribution
arbitration	execute cycle	Packets
asynchronous timing	fetch cycle	PCI Express (PCIe)
balanced transmission	flit	peripheral component
bus	flow control function	interconnect (PCI)
bus width	instruction cycle	phit
centralized arbitration	interrupt	QuickPath Interconnect
control lines	interrupt handler	(QPI)
data bus	interrupt service routine (ISR)	root complex
data lines	lane	synchronous timing
differential signaling	memory address register	system bus
disabled interrupt	(MAR)	

Review Questions

3.1 What general categories of functions are specified by computer instructions?

3.2 List and briefly define the possible states that define an instruction execution.

3.3 List and briefly define two approaches to dealing with multiple interrupts.

3.4 What types of transfers must a computer's interconnection structure (e.g., bus) support?

3.5 What is the benefit of using a multiple-bus architecture compared to a single-bus architecture?

3.6 List and briefly define the QPI protocol layers.

3.7 List and briefly define the PCIe protocol layers.

Problems

3.1   The hypothetical machine of Figure 3.4 also has two I/O instructions:

$$0011 = \text{Load AC from I/O}$$
$$0111 = \text{Store AC to I/O}$$

In these cases, the 12-bit address identifies a particular I/O device. Show the program execution (using the format of Figure 3.5) for the following program:

1. Load AC from device 5.
2. Add contents of memory location 940.
3. Store AC to device 6.

Assume that the next value retrieved from device 5 is 3 and that location 940 contains a value of 2.

3.2   The program execution of Figure 3.5 is described in the text using six steps. Expand this description to show the use of the MAR and MBR.

3.3   Consider a hypothetical 32-bit microprocessor having 32-bit instructions composed of two fields: the first byte contains the opcode and the remainder the immediate operand or an operand address.
  a.   What is the maximum directly addressable memory capacity (in bytes)?
  b.   Discuss the impact on the system speed if the microprocessor bus has
    1. a 32-bit local address bus and a 16-bit local data bus, or
    2. a 16-bit local address bus and a 16-bit local data bus.
  c.   How many bits are needed for the program counter and the instruction register?

3.4   Consider a hypothetical microprocessor generating a 16-bit address (for example, assume that the program counter and the address registers are 16 bits wide) and having a 16-bit data bus.
  a.   What is the maximum memory address space that the processor can access directly if it is connected to a "16-bit memory"?
  b.   What is the maximum memory address space that the processor can access directly if it is connected to an "8-bit memory"?
  c.   What architectural features will allow this microprocessor to access a separate "I/O space"?
  d.   If an input and an output instruction can specify an 8-bit I/O port number, how many 8-bit I/O ports can the microprocessor support? How many 16-bit I/O ports? Explain.

3.5   Consider a 32-bit microprocessor, with a 16-bit external data bus, driven by an 8-MHz input clock. Assume that this microprocessor has a bus cycle whose minimum duration equals four input clock cycles. What is the maximum data transfer rate across the bus that this microprocessor can sustain, in bytes/s? To increase its performance, would it be better to make its external data bus 32 bits or to double the external clock frequency supplied to the microprocessor? State any other assumptions you make, and explain. *Hint:* Determine the number of bytes that can be transferred per bus cycle.

3.6   Consider a computer system that contains an I/O module controlling a simple keyboard/printer teletype. The following registers are contained in the processor and connected directly to the system bus:

INPR: Input Register, 8 bits
OUTR: Output Register, 8 bits
FGI: Input Flag, 1 bit
FGO: Output Flag, 1 bit
IEN: Interrupt Enable, 1 bit

Keystroke input from the teletype and printer output to the teletype are controlled by the I/O module. The teletype is able to encode an alphanumeric symbol to an 8-bit word and decode an 8-bit word into an alphanumeric symbol.

     a. Describe how the processor, using the first four registers listed in this problem, can achieve I/O with the teletype.

     b. Describe how the function can be performed more efficiently by also employing IEN.

3.7 Consider two microprocessors having 8- and 16-bit-wide external data buses, respectively. The two processors are identical otherwise and their bus cycles take just as long.

     a. Suppose all instructions and operands are two bytes long. By what factor do the maximum data transfer rates differ?

     b. Repeat assuming that half of the operands and instructions are one byte long.

3.8 Figure 3.30 indicates a distributed arbitration scheme that can be used with an obsolete bus scheme known as Multibus I. Agents are daisy-chained physically in priority order. The left-most agent in the diagram receives a constant *bus priority in* (BPRN) signal indicating that no higher-priority agent desires the bus. If the agent does not require the bus, it asserts its *bus priority out* (BPRO) line. At the beginning of a clock cycle, any agent can request control of the bus by lowering its BPRO line. This lowers the BPRN line of the next agent in the chain, which is in turn required to lower its BPRO line. Thus, the signal is propagated the length of the chain. At the end of this chain reaction, there should be only one agent whose BPRN is asserted and whose BPRO is not. This agent has priority. If, at the beginning of a bus cycle, the bus is not busy (BUSY inactive), the agent that has priority may seize control of the bus by asserting the BUSY line.

     It takes a certain amount of time for the BPR signal to propagate from the highest-priority agent to the lowest. Must this time be less than the clock cycle? Explain.

3.9 The VAX SBI bus uses a distributed, synchronous arbitration scheme. Each SBI device (i.e., processor, memory, I/O module) has a unique priority and is assigned a unique transfer request (TR) line. The SBI has 16 such lines (TR0, TR1, ..., TR15), with TR0 having the highest priority. When a device wants to use the bus, it places a reservation for a future time slot by asserting its TR line during the current time slot. At the end of the current time slot, each device with a pending reservation examines the TR lines; the highest-priority device with a reservation uses the next time slot.

     A maximum of 17 devices can be attached to the bus. The device with priority 16 has no TR line. Why not?

3.10 On the VAX SBI, the lowest-priority device usually has the lowest average wait time. For this reason, the processor is usually given the lowest priority on the SBI. Why does the priority 16 device usually have the lowest average wait time? Under what circumstances would this not be true?

3.11 For a synchronous read operation (Figure 3.18), the memory module must place the data on the bus sufficiently ahead of the falling edge of the Read signal to allow for

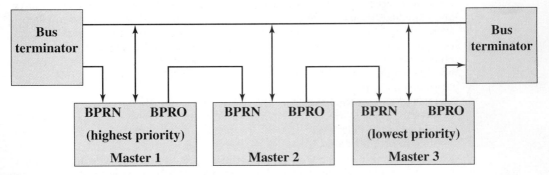

Figure 3.30 Multibus I Distributed Arbitration

signal settling. Assume a microprocessor bus is clocked at 10 MHz and that the Read signal begins to fall in the middle of the second half of T_3.

  a. Determine the length of the memory read instruction cycle.

  b. When, at the latest, should memory data be placed on the bus? Allow 20 ns for the settling of data lines.

3.12 Consider a microprocessor that has a memory read timing as shown in Figure 3.18. After some analysis, a designer determines that the memory falls short of providing read data on time by about 180 ns.

  a. How many wait states (clock cycles) need to be inserted for proper system operation if the bus clocking rate is 8 MHz?

  b. To enforce the wait states, a Ready status line is employed. Once the processor has issued a Read command, it must wait until the Ready line is asserted before attempting to read data. At what time interval must we keep the Ready line low in order to force the processor to insert the required number of wait states?

3.13 A microprocessor has a memory write timing as shown in Figure 3.18. Its manufacturer specifies that the width of the Write signal can be determined by $T - 50$, where T is the clock period in ns.

  a. What width should we expect for the Write signal if bus clocking rate is 5 MHz?

  b. The data sheet for the microprocessor specifies that the data remain valid for 20 ns after the falling edge of the Write signal. What is the total duration of valid data presentation to memory?

  c. How many wait states should we insert if memory requires valid data presentation for at least 190 ns?

3.14 A microprocessor has an increment memory direct instruction, which adds 1 to the value in a memory location. The instruction has five stages: fetch opcode (four bus clock cycles), fetch operand address (three cycles), fetch operand (three cycles), add 1 to operand (three cycles), and store operand (three cycles).

  a. By what amount (in percent) will the duration of the instruction increase if we have to insert two bus wait states in each memory read and memory write operation?

  b. Repeat assuming that the increment operation takes 13 cycles instead of 3 cycles.

3.15 The Intel 8088 microprocessor has a read bus timing similar to that of Figure 3.18, but requires four processor clock cycles. The valid data is on the bus for an amount of time that extends into the fourth processor clock cycle. Assume a processor clock rate of 8 MHz.

  a. What is the maximum data transfer rate?

  b. Repeat but assume the need to insert one wait state per byte transferred.

3.16 The Intel 8086 is a 16-bit processor similar in many ways to the 8-bit 8088. The 8086 uses a 16-bit bus that can transfer 2 bytes at a time, provided that the lower-order byte has an even address. However, the 8086 allows both even- and odd-aligned word operands. If an odd-aligned word is referenced, two memory cycles, each consisting of four bus cycles, are required to transfer the word. Consider an instruction on the 8086 that involves two 16-bit operands. How long does it take to fetch the operands? Give the range of possible answers. Assume a clocking rate of 4 MHz and no wait states.

3.17 Consider a 32-bit microprocessor whose bus cycle is the same duration as that of a 16-bit microprocessor. Assume that, on average, 20% of the operands and instructions are 32 bits long, 40% are 16 bits long, and 40% are only 8 bits long. Calculate the improvement achieved when fetching instructions and operands with the 32-bit microprocessor.

3.18 The microprocessor of Problem 3.14 initiates the fetch operand stage of the increment memory direct instruction at the same time that a keyboard actives an interrupt request line. After how long does the processor enter the interrupt processing cycle? Assume a bus clocking rate of 10 MHz.

CHAPTER 4

CACHE MEMORY

> **LEARNING OBJECTIVES**
>
> After studying this chapter, you should be able to:
>
> ◆ Present an overview of the main characteristics of computer memory systems and the use of a memory hierarchy.
> ◆ Describe the basic concepts and intent of cache memory.
> ◆ Discuss the key elements of cache design.
> ◆ Distinguish among direct mapping. associative mapping, and set-associative mapping.
> ◆ Explain the reasons for using multiple levels of cache.
> ◆ Understand the performance implications of multiple levels of memory.

Although seemingly simple in concept, computer memory exhibits perhaps the widest range of type, technology, organization, performance, and cost of any feature of a computer system. No single technology is optimal in satisfying the memory requirements for a computer system. As a consequence, the typical computer system is equipped with a hierarchy of memory subsystems, some internal to the system (directly accessible by the processor) and some external (accessible by the processor via an I/O module).

This chapter and the next focus on internal memory elements. while Chapter 6 is devoted to external memory. To begin, the first section examines key characteristics of computer memories. The remainder of the chapter examines an essential element of all modern computer systems: cache memory.

4.1   COMPUTER MEMORY SYSTEM OVERVIEW

Characteristics of Memory Systems

The complex subject of computer memory is made more manageable if we classify memory systems according to their key characteristics. The most important of these are listed in Table 4.1.

The term **location** in Table 4.1 refers to whether memory is internal and external to the computer. Internal memory is often equated with main memory. But there are other forms of internal memory. The processor requires its own local memory, in the form of registers (e.g., see Figure 2.3). Further, as we shall see, the control unit portion of the processor may also require its own internal memory. We will defer discussion of these latter two types of internal memory to later chapters. Cache is another form of internal memory. External memory consists of peripheral storage devices, such as disk and tape, that are accessible to the processor via I/O controllers.

An obvious characteristic of memory is its **capacity**. For internal memory, this is typically expressed in terms of bytes (1 byte = 8 bits) or words. Common word lengths are 8, 16, and 32 bits. External memory capacity is typically expressed in terms of bytes.

A related concept is the **unit of transfer**. For internal memory, the unit of transfer is equal to the number of electrical lines into and out of the memory

Table 4.1   Key Characteristics of Computer Memory Systems

Location	Performance
Internal (e.g., processor registers, cache, main memory)	Access time
	Cycle time
External (e.g., optical disks, magnetic disks, tapes)	Transfer rate
Capacity	**Physical Type**
Number of words	Semiconductor
Number of bytes	Magnetic
Unit of Transfer	Optical
Word	Magneto-optical
Block	**Physical Characteristics**
Access Method	Volatile/nonvolatile
Sequential	Erasable/nonerasable
Direct	**Organization**
Random	Memory modules
Associative	

module. This may be equal to the word length, but is often larger, such as 64, 128, or 256 bits. To clarify this point, consider three related concepts for internal memory:

- **Word:** The "natural" unit of organization of memory. The size of a word is typically equal to the number of bits used to represent an integer and to the instruction length. Unfortunately, there are many exceptions. For example, the CRAY C90 (an older model CRAY supercomputer) has a 64-bit word length but uses a 46-bit integer representation. The Intel x86 architecture has a wide variety of instruction lengths, expressed as multiples of bytes, and a word size of 32 bits.

- **Addressable units:** In some systems, the addressable unit is the word. However, many systems allow addressing at the byte level. In any case, the relationship between the length in bits A of an address and the number N of addressable units is $2^A = N$.

- **Unit of transfer:** For main memory, this is the number of bits read out of or written into memory at a time. The unit of transfer need not equal a word or an addressable unit. For external memory, data are often transferred in much larger units than a word, and these are referred to as blocks.

Another distinction among memory types is the **method of accessing** units of data. These include the following:

- **Sequential access:** Memory is organized into units of data, called records. Access must be made in a specific linear sequence. Stored addressing information is used to separate records and assist in the retrieval process. A shared read–write mechanism is used, and this must be moved from its current location to the desired location, passing and rejecting each intermediate record. Thus, the time to access an arbitrary record is highly variable. Tape units, discussed in Chapter 6, are sequential access.

- **Direct access:** As with sequential access, direct access involves a shared read–write mechanism. However, individual blocks or records have a unique address based on physical location. Access is accomplished by direct access to reach a general vicinity plus sequential searching, counting, or waiting to reach the final location. Again, access time is variable. Disk units, discussed in Chapter 6, are direct access.
- **Random access:** Each addressable location in memory has a unique, physically wired-in addressing mechanism. The time to access a given location is independent of the sequence of prior accesses and is constant. Thus, any location can be selected at random and directly addressed and accessed. Main memory and some cache systems are random access.
- **Associative:** This is a random access type of memory that enables one to make a comparison of desired bit locations within a word for a specified match, and to do this for all words simultaneously. Thus, a word is retrieved based on a portion of its contents rather than its address. As with ordinary random-access memory, each location has its own addressing mechanism, and retrieval time is constant independent of location or prior access patterns. Cache memories may employ associative access.

From a user's point of view, the two most important characteristics of memory are capacity and **performance**. Three performance parameters are used:

- **Access time (latency):** For random-access memory, this is the time it takes to perform a read or write operation, that is, the time from the instant that an address is presented to the memory to the instant that data have been stored or made available for use. For non-random-access memory, access time is the time it takes to position the read–write mechanism at the desired location.
- **Memory cycle time:** This concept is primarily applied to random-access memory and consists of the access time plus any additional time required before a second access can commence. This additional time may be required for transients to die out on signal lines or to regenerate data if they are read destructively. Note that memory cycle time is concerned with the system bus, not the processor.
- **Transfer rate:** This is the rate at which data can be transferred into or out of a memory unit. For random-access memory, it is equal to 1/(cycle time).

For non-random-access memory, the following relationship holds:

$$T_n = T_A + \frac{n}{R} \tag{4.1}$$

where

T_n = Average time to read or write n bits

T_A = Average access time

n = Number of bits

R = Transfer rate, in bits per second (bps)

A variety of **physical types** of memory have been employed. The most common today are semiconductor memory, magnetic surface memory, used for disk and tape, and optical and magneto-optical.

Several **physical characteristics** of data storage are important. In a volatile memory, information decays naturally or is lost when electrical power is switched off. In a nonvolatile memory, information once recorded remains without deterioration until deliberately changed; no electrical power is needed to retain information. Magnetic-surface memories are nonvolatile. Semiconductor memory (memory on integrated circuits) may be either volatile or nonvolatile. Nonerasable memory cannot be altered, except by destroying the storage unit. Semiconductor memory of this type is known as *read-only memory* (ROM). Of necessity, a practical nonerasable memory must also be nonvolatile.

For random-access memory, the **organization** is a key design issue. In this context, *organization* refers to the physical arrangement of bits to form words. The obvious arrangement is not always used, as is explained in Chapter 5.

The Memory Hierarchy

The design constraints on a computer's memory can be summed up by three questions: How much? How fast? How expensive?

The question of how much is somewhat open ended. If the capacity is there, applications will likely be developed to use it. The question of how fast is, in a sense, easier to answer. To achieve greatest performance, the memory must be able to keep up with the processor. That is, as the processor is executing instructions, we would not want it to have to pause waiting for instructions or operands. The final question must also be considered. For a practical system, the cost of memory must be reasonable in relationship to other components.

As might be expected, there is a trade-off among the three key characteristics of memory: capacity, access time, and cost. A variety of technologies are used to implement memory systems, and across this spectrum of technologies, the following relationships hold:

- Faster access time, greater cost per bit
- Greater capacity, smaller cost per bit
- Greater capacity, slower access time

The dilemma facing the designer is clear. The designer would like to use memory technologies that provide for large-capacity memory, both because the capacity is needed and because the cost per bit is low. However, to meet performance requirements, the designer needs to use expensive, relatively lower-capacity memories with short access times.

The way out of this dilemma is not to rely on a single memory component or technology, but to employ a **memory hierarchy**. A typical hierarchy is illustrated in Figure 4.1. As one goes down the hierarchy, the following occur:

a. Decreasing cost per bit

b. Increasing capacity

c. Increasing access time

d. Decreasing frequency of access of the memory by the processor

Thus, smaller, more expensive, faster memories are supplemented by larger, cheaper, slower memories. The key to the success of this organization is item (d):

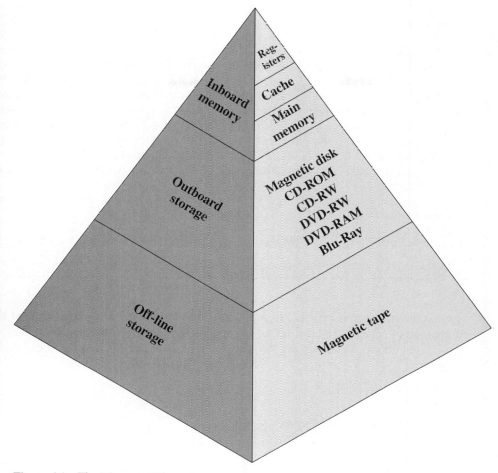

Figure 4.1   The Memory Hierarchy

decreasing frequency of access. We examine this concept in greater detail when we discuss the cache, later in this chapter, and virtual memory in Chapter 8. A brief explanation is provided at this point.

The use of two levels of memory to reduce average access time works in principle, but only if conditions (a) through (d) apply. By employing a variety of technologies, a spectrum of memory systems exists that satisfies conditions (a) through (c). Fortunately, condition (d) is also generally valid.

The basis for the validity of condition (d) is a principle known as **locality of reference** [DENN68]. During the course of execution of a program, memory references by the processor, for both instructions and data, tend to cluster. Programs typically contain a number of iterative loops and subroutines. Once a loop or subroutine is entered, there are repeated references to a small set of instructions. Similarly, operations on tables and arrays involve access to a clustered set of data words. Over a long period of time, the clusters in use change, but over a short period of time, the processor is primarily working with fixed clusters of memory references.

> **Example 4.1** Suppose that the processor has access to two levels of memory. Level 1 contains 1000 words and has an access time of 0.01 μs; level 2 contains 100,000 words and has an access time of 0.1 μs. Assume that if a word to be accessed is in level 1, then the processor accesses it directly. If it is in level 2, then the word is first transferred to level 1 and then accessed by the processor. For simplicity, we ignore the time required for the processor to determine whether the word is in level 1 or level 2. Figure 4.2 shows the general shape of the curve that covers this situation. The figure shows the average access time to a two-level memory as a function of the hit ratio H, where H is defined as the fraction of all memory accesses that are found in the faster memory (e.g., the cache), T_1 is the access time to level 1, and T_2 is the access time to level 2.[1] As can be seen, for high percentages of level 1 access, the average total access time is much closer to that of level 1 than that of level 2.
>
> In our example, suppose 95% of the memory accesses are found in level 1. Then the average time to access a word can be expressed as
>
> $$(0.95)(0.01\,\mu s) + (0.05)(0.01\,\mu s + 0.1\,\mu s) = 0.0095 + 0.0055 = 0.015\,\mu s$$
>
> The average access time is much closer to 0.01 μs than to 0.1 μs, as desired.

Accordingly, it is possible to organize data across the hierarchy such that the percentage of accesses to each successively lower level is substantially less than that of the level above. Consider the two-level example already presented. Let level 2

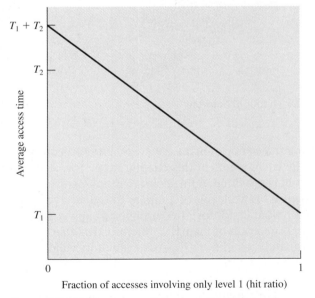

Fraction of accesses involving only level 1 (hit ratio)

Figure 4.2 Performance of Accesses Involving only Level 1 (hit ratio)

---

[1]If the accessed word is found in the faster memory, that is defined as a **hit**. A **miss** occurs if the accessed word is not found in the faster memory.

memory contains all program instructions and data. The current clusters can be temporarily placed in level 1. From time to time, one of the clusters in level 1 will have to be swapped back to level 2 to make room for a new cluster coming in to level 1. On average, however, most references will be to instructions and data contained in level 1.

This principle can be applied across more than two levels of memory, as suggested by the hierarchy shown in Figure 4.1. The fastest, smallest, and most expensive type of memory consists of the registers internal to the processor. Typically, a processor will contain a few dozen such registers, although some machines contain hundreds of registers. Main memory is the principal internal memory system of the computer. Each location in main memory has a unique address. Main memory is usually extended with a higher-speed, smaller cache. The cache is not usually visible to the programmer or, indeed, to the processor. It is a device for staging the movement of data between main memory and processor registers to improve performance.

The three forms of memory just described are, typically, volatile and employ semiconductor technology. The use of three levels exploits the fact that semiconductor memory comes in a variety of types, which differ in speed and cost. Data are stored more permanently on external mass storage devices, of which the most common are hard disk and removable media, such as removable magnetic disk, tape, and optical storage. External, nonvolatile memory is also referred to as **secondary memory** or **auxiliary memory**. These are used to store program and data files and are usually visible to the programmer only in terms of files and records, as opposed to individual bytes or words. Disk is also used to provide an extension to main memory known as virtual memory, which is discussed in Chapter 8.

Other forms of memory may be included in the hierarchy. For example, large IBM mainframes include a form of internal memory known as expanded storage. This uses a semiconductor technology that is slower and less expensive than that of main memory. Strictly speaking, this memory does not fit into the hierarchy but is a side branch: Data can be moved between main memory and expanded storage but not between expanded storage and external memory. Other forms of secondary memory include optical and magneto-optical disks. Finally, additional levels can be effectively added to the hierarchy in software. A portion of main memory can be used as a buffer to hold data temporarily that is to be read out to disk. Such a technique, sometimes referred to as a disk cache,[2] improves performance in two ways:

- Disk writes are clustered. Instead of many small transfers of data, we have a few large transfers of data. This improves disk performance and minimizes processor involvement.

- Some data destined for write-out may be referenced by a program before the next dump to disk. In that case, the data are retrieved rapidly from the software cache rather than slowly from the disk.

Appendix 4A examines the performance implications of multilevel memory structures.

---

[2]Disk cache is generally a purely software technique and is not examined in this book. See [STAL12] for a discussion.

4.2 CACHE MEMORY PRINCIPLES

Cache memory is designed to combine the memory access time of expensive, high-speed memory combined with the large memory size of less expensive, lower-speed memory. The concept is illustrated in Figure 4.3a. There is a relatively large and slow main memory together with a smaller, faster cache memory. The cache contains a copy of portions of main memory. When the processor attempts to read a word of memory, a check is made to determine if the word is in the cache. If so, the word is delivered to the processor. If not, a block of main memory, consisting of some fixed number of words, is read into the cache and then the word is delivered to the processor. Because of the phenomenon of locality of reference, when a block of data is fetched into the cache to satisfy a single memory reference, it is likely that there will be future references to that same memory location or to other words in the block.

Figure 4.3b depicts the use of multiple levels of cache. The L2 cache is slower and typically larger than the L1 cache, and the L3 cache is slower and typically larger than the L2 cache.

Figure 4.4 depicts the structure of a cache/main-memory system. Main memory consists of up to 2^n addressable words, with each word having a unique n-bit address. For mapping purposes, this memory is considered to consist of a number of fixed-length blocks of K words each. That is, there are $M = 2^n/K$ blocks in main memory. The cache consists of m blocks, called **lines**.[3] Each line contains K words,

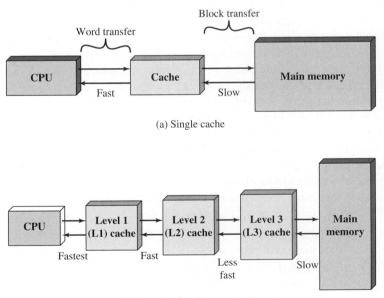

(a) Single cache

(b) Three-level cache organization

Figure 4.3 Cache and Main Memory

---

[3]In referring to the basic unit of the cache, the term *line* is used, rather than the term *block*, for two reasons: (1) to avoid confusion with a main memory block, which contains the same number of data words as a cache line; and (2) because a cache line includes not only K words of data, just as a main memory block, but also includes tag and control bits.

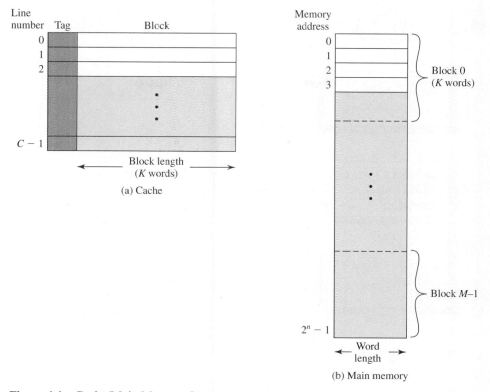

Figure 4.4   Cache/Main Memory Structure

plus a tag of a few bits. Each line also includes control bits (not shown), such as a bit to indicate whether the line has been modified since being loaded into the cache. The length of a line, not including tag and control bits, is the **line size**. The line size may be as small as 32 bits, with each "word" being a single byte; in this case the line size is 4 bytes. The number of lines is considerably less than the number of main memory blocks ($m \ll M$). At any time, some subset of the blocks of memory resides in lines in the cache. If a word in a block of memory is read, that block is transferred to one of the lines of the cache. Because there are more blocks than lines, an individual line cannot be uniquely and permanently dedicated to a particular block. Thus, each line includes a **tag** that identifies which particular block is currently being stored. The tag is usually a portion of the main memory address, as described later in this section.

Figure 4.5 illustrates the read operation. The processor generates the read address (RA) of a word to be read. If the word is contained in the cache, it is delivered to the processor. Otherwise, the block containing that word is loaded into the cache, and the word is delivered to the processor. Figure 4.5 shows these last two operations occurring in parallel and reflects the organization shown in Figure 4.6, which is typical of contemporary cache organizations. In this organization, the cache connects to the processor via data, control, and address lines. The data and address lines also attach to data and address buffers, which attach to a system bus from

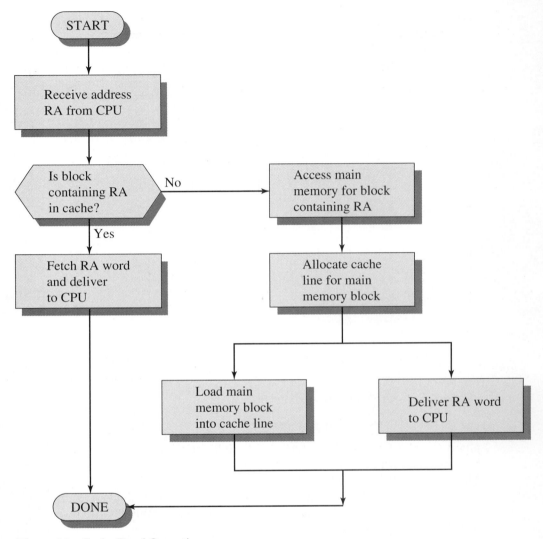

Figure 4.5 Cache Read Operation

which main memory is reached. When a cache hit occurs, the data and address buffers are disabled and communication is only between processor and cache, with no system bus traffic. When a cache miss occurs, the desired address is loaded onto the system bus and the data are returned through the data buffer to both the cache and the processor. In other organizations, the cache is physically interposed between the processor and the main memory for all data, address, and control lines. In this latter case, for a cache miss, the desired word is first read into the cache and then transferred from cache to processor.

A discussion of the performance parameters related to cache use is contained in Appendix 4A.

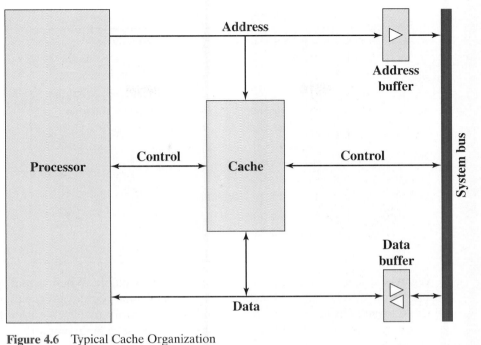

Figure 4.6   Typical Cache Organization

4.3   ELEMENTS OF CACHE DESIGN

This section provides an overview of cache design parameters and reports some typical results. We occasionally refer to the use of caches in high-performance computing (HPC). HPC deals with supercomputers and their software, especially for scientific applications that involve large amounts of data, vector and matrix computation, and the use of parallel algorithms. Cache design for HPC is quite different than for other hardware platforms and applications. Indeed, many researchers have found that HPC applications perform poorly on computer architectures that employ caches [BAIL93]. Other researchers have since shown that a cache hierarchy can be useful in improving performance if the application software is tuned to exploit the cache [WANG99, PRES01].[4]

Although there are a large number of cache implementations, there are a few basic design elements that serve to classify and differentiate cache architectures. Table 4.2 lists key elements.

Cache Addresses

Almost all nonembedded processors, and many embedded processors, support virtual memory, a concept discussed in Chapter 8. In essence, virtual memory is a facility that allows programs to address memory from a logical point of view, without

---

[4]For a general discussion of HPC, see [DOWD98].

Table 4.2 Elements of Cache Design

Cache Addresses	Write Policy
Logical	Write through
Physical	Write back
Cache Size	**Line Size**
Mapping Function	**Number of Caches**
Direct	Single or two level
Associative	Unified or split
Set associative	
Replacement Algorithm	
Least recently used (LRU)	
First in first out (FIFO)	
Least frequently used (LFU)	
Random	

regard to the amount of main memory physically available. When virtual memory is used, the address fields of machine instructions contain virtual addresses. For reads to and writes from main memory, a hardware memory management unit (MMU) translates each virtual address into a physical address in main memory.

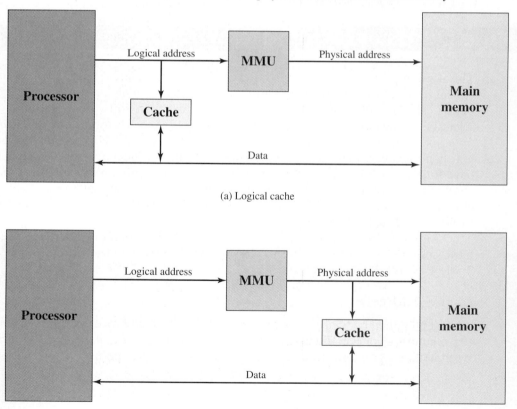

(a) Logical cache

(b) Physical cache

Figure 4.7 Logical and Physical Caches

When virtual addresses are used, the system designer may choose to place the cache between the processor and the MMU or between the MMU and main memory (Figure 4.7). A **logical cache**, also known as a **virtual cache**, stores data using **virtual addresses**. The processor accesses the cache directly, without going through the MMU. A physical cache stores data using main memory **physical addresses**.

One obvious advantage of the logical cache is that cache access speed is faster than for a physical cache, because the cache can respond before the MMU performs an address translation. The disadvantage has to do with the fact that most virtual memory systems supply each application with the same virtual memory address space. That is, each application sees a virtual memory that starts at address 0. Thus, the same virtual address in two different applications refers to two different physical addresses. The cache memory must therefore be completely flushed with each application context switch, or extra bits must be added to each line of the cache to identify which virtual address space this address refers to.

The subject of logical versus physical cache is a complex one, and beyond the scope of this book. For a more in-depth discussion, see [CEKL97] and [JACO08].

Cache Size

The first item in Table 4.2, cache size, has already been discussed. We would like the size of the cache to be small enough so that the overall average cost per bit is close to that of main memory alone and large enough so that the overall average access time is close to that of the cache alone. There are several other motivations for minimizing cache size. The larger the cache, the larger the number of gates involved in addressing the cache. The result is that large caches tend to be slightly slower than small ones—even when built with the same integrated circuit technology and put in the same place on chip and circuit board. The available chip and board area also limits cache size. Because the performance of the cache is very sensitive to the nature of the workload, it is impossible to arrive at a single "optimum" cache size. Table 4.3 lists the cache sizes of some current and past processors.

Mapping Function

Because there are fewer cache lines than main memory blocks, an algorithm is needed for mapping main memory blocks into cache lines. Further, a means is needed for determining which main memory block currently occupies a cache line. The choice of the mapping function dictates how the cache is organized. Three techniques can be used: direct, associative, and set associative. We examine each of these in turn. In each case, we look at the general structure and then a specific example.

Example 4.2 For all three cases, the example includes the following elements:

- The cache can hold 64 Kbytes.
- Data are transferred between main memory and the cache in blocks of 4 bytes each. This means that the cache is organized as $16K = 2^{14}$ lines of 4 bytes each.
- The main memory consists of 16 Mbytes, with each byte directly addressable by a 24-bit address ($2^{24} = 16M$). Thus, for mapping purposes, we can consider main memory to consist of 4M blocks of 4 bytes each.

Table 4.3 Cache Sizes of Some Processors

Processor	Type	Year of Introduction	L1 Cache[a]	L2 Cache	L3 Cache
IBM 360/85	Mainframe	1968	16–32 kB	—	—
PDP-11/70	Minicomputer	1975	1 kB	—	—
VAX 11/780	Minicomputer	1978	16 kB	—	—
IBM 3033	Mainframe	1978	64 kB	—	—
IBM 3090	Mainframe	1985	128–256 kB	—	—
Intel 80486	PC	1989	8 kB	—	—
Pentium	PC	1993	8 kB/8 kB	256–512 kB	—
PowerPC 601	PC	1993	32 kB	—	—
PowerPC 620	PC	1996	32 kB/32 kB	—	—
PowerPC G4	PC/server	1999	32 kB/32 kB	256 kB to 1 MB	2 MB
IBM S/390 G6	Mainframe	1999	256 kB	8 MB	—
Pentium 4	PC/server	2000	8 kB/8 kB	256 kB	—
IBM SP	High-end server/ supercomputer	2000	64 kB/32 kB	8 MB	—
CRAY MTA[b]	Supercomputer	2000	8 kB	2 MB	—
Itanium	PC/server	2001	16 kB/16 kB	96 kB	4 MB
Itanium 2	PC/server	2002	32 kB	256 kB	6 MB
IBM POWER5	High-end server	2003	64 kB	1.9 MB	36 MB
CRAY XD-1	Supercomputer	2004	64 kB/64 kB	1 MB	—
IBM POWER6	PC/server	2007	64 kB/64 kB	4 MB	32 MB
IBM z10	Mainframe	2008	64 kB/128 kB	3 MB	24–48 MB
Intel Core i7 EE 990	Workstation/ server	2011	6 × 32 kB/ 32 kB	1.5 MB	12 MB
IBM zEnterprise 196	Mainframe/ server	2011	24 × 64 kB/ 128 kB	24 × 1.5 MB	24 MB L3 192 MB L4

Notes:

[a] Two values separated by a slash refer to instruction and data caches.

[b] Both caches are instruction only; no data caches.

DIRECT MAPPING The simplest technique, known as direct mapping, maps each block of main memory into only one possible cache line. The mapping is expressed as

$$i = j \bmod m$$

where

i = cache line number

j = main memory block number

m = number of lines in the cache

Figure 4.8a shows the mapping for the first m blocks of main memory. Each block of main memory maps into one unique line of the cache. The next m blocks

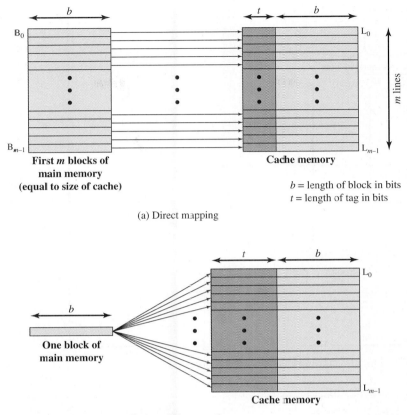

(a) Direct mapping

(b) Associative mapping

Figure 4.8   Mapping from Main Memory to Cache: Direct and Associative

of main memory map into the cache in the same fashion; that is, block B_m of main memory maps into line L_0 of cache, block B_{m+1} maps into line L_1, and so on.

The mapping function is easily implemented using the main memory address. Figure 4.9 illustrates the general mechanism. For purposes of cache access, each main memory address can be viewed as consisting of three fields. The least significant w bits identify a unique word or byte within a block of main memory; in most contemporary machines, the address is at the byte level. The remaining s bits specify one of the 2^s blocks of main memory. The cache logic interprets these s bits as a tag of $s - r$ bits (most significant portion) and a line field of r bits. This latter field identifies one of the $m = 2^r$ lines of the cache. To summarize,

- Address length = $(s + w)$ bits
- Number of addressable units = 2^{s+w} words or bytes
- Block size = line size = $2w$ words or bytes
- Number of blocks in main memory = $\dfrac{2^{s+w}}{2^w} = 2^s$
- Number of lines in cache = $m = 2r$
- Size of cache = 2^{r+w} words or bytes
- Size of tag = $(s - r)$ bits

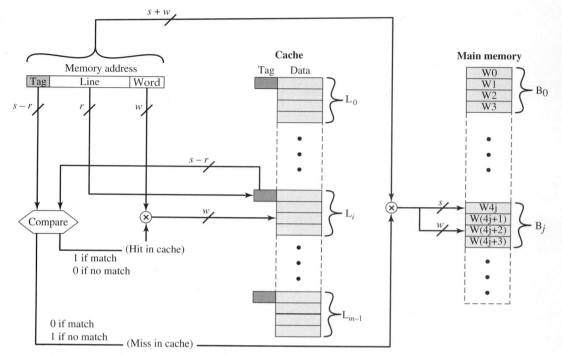

Figure 4.9 Direct-Mapping Cache Organization

Example 4.2a Figure 4.10 shows our example system using direct mapping.[5] In the example, $m = 16K = 2^{14}$ and $i = j$ modulo 2^{14}. The mapping becomes

Cache Line	Starting Memory Address of Block
0	000000, 010000, ..., FF0000
1	000004, 010004, ..., FF0004
⋮	⋮
$2^{14} - 1$	00FFFC, 01FFFC, ..., FFFFFC

Note that no two blocks that map into the same line number have the same tag number. Thus, blocks with starting addresses 000000, 010000, ..., FF0000 have tag numbers 00, 01, ..., FF, respectively.

Referring back to Figure 4.5, a read operation works as follows. The cache system is presented with a 24-bit address. The 14-bit line number is used as an index into the cache to access a particular line. If the 8-bit tag number matches the tag number currently stored in that line, then the 2-bit word number is used to select one of the 4 bytes in that line. Otherwise, the 22-bit tag-plus-line field is used to fetch a block from main memory. The actual address that is used for the fetch is the 22-bit tag-plus-line concatenated with two 0 bits, so that 4 bytes are fetched starting on a block boundary.

---

[5]In this and subsequent figures, memory values are represented in hexadecimal notation. See Chapter 9 for a basic refresher on number systems (decimal, binary, hexadecimal).

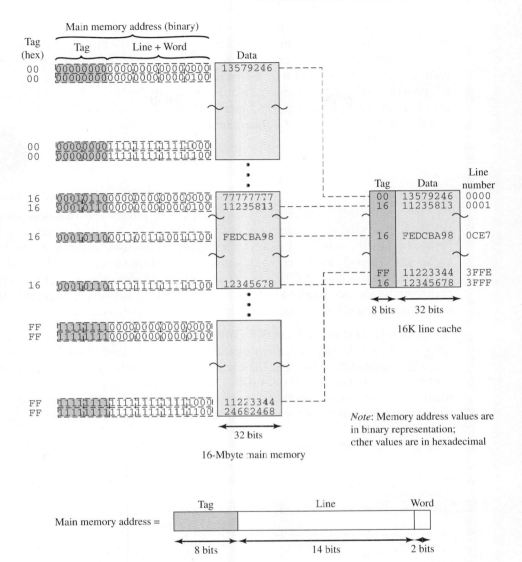

Figure 4.10 Direct Mapping Example

The effect of this mapping is that blocks of main memory are assigned to lines of the cache as follows:

Cache line	Main memory blocks assigned
0	$0, m, 2m, \ldots, 2^s - m$
1	$1, m + 1, 2m + 1, \ldots, 2^s - m + 1$
⋮	⋮
$m - 1$	$m - 1, 2m - 1, 3m - 1, \ldots, 2^s - 1$

Thus, the use of a portion of the address as a line number provides a unique mapping of each block of main memory into the cache. When a block is actually read into its assigned line, it is necessary to tag the data to distinguish it from other blocks that can fit into that line. The most significant $s - r$ bits serve this purpose.

The direct mapping technique is simple and inexpensive to implement. Its main disadvantage is that there is a fixed cache location for any given block. Thus, if a program happens to reference words repeatedly from two different blocks that map into the same line, then the blocks will be continually swapped in the cache, and the hit ratio will be low (a phenomenon known as *thrashing*).

Selective Victim Cache Simulator

One approach to lower the miss penalty is to remember what was discarded in case it is needed again. Since the discarded data has already been fetched, it can be used again at a small cost. Such recycling is possible using a victim cache. Victim cache was originally proposed as an approach to reduce the conflict misses of direct mapped caches without affecting its fast access time. Victim cache is a fully associative cache, whose size is typically 4 to 16 cache lines, residing between a direct mapped L1 cache and the next level of memory. This concept is explored in Appendix D.

ASSOCIATIVE MAPPING Associative mapping overcomes the disadvantage of direct mapping by permitting each main memory block to be loaded into any line of the cache (Figure 4.8b). In this case, the cache control logic interprets a memory address simply as a Tag and a Word field. The Tag field uniquely identifies a block of main memory. To determine whether a block is in the cache, the cache control logic must simultaneously examine every line's tag for a match. Figure 4.11 illustrates the logic.

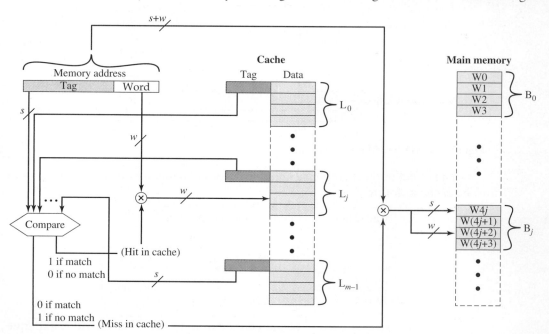

Figure 4.11 Fully Associative Cache Organization

Example 4.2b Figure 4.12 shows our example using associative mapping. A main memory address consists of a 22-bit tag and a 2-bit byte number. The 22-bit tag must be stored with the 32-bit block of data for each line in the cache. Note that it is the leftmost (most significant) 22 bits of the address that form the tag. Thus, the 24-bit hexadecimal address 16339C has the 22-bit tag 058CE7. This is easily seen in binary notation:

memory address	0001	0110	0011	0011	1001	1100	(binary)
	1	6	3	3	9	C	(hex)
tag (leftmost 22 bits)	00	0101	1000	1100	1110	0111	(binary)
	0	5	8	C	E	7	(hex)

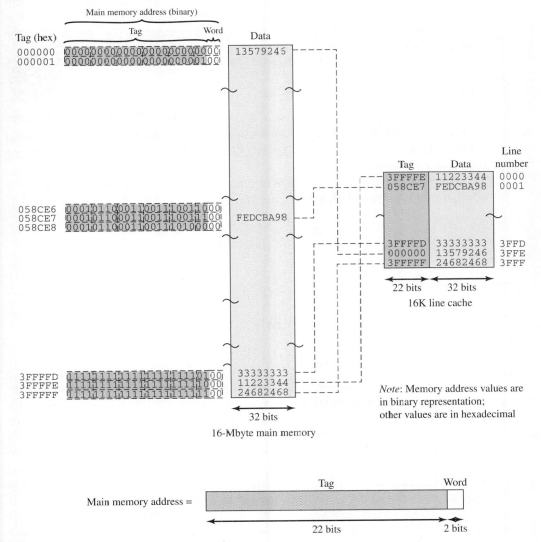

Figure 4.12 Associative Mapping Example

Note that no field in the address corresponds to the line number, so that the number of lines in the cache is not determined by the address format. To summarize,

- Address length $= (s + w)$ bits
- Number of addressable units $= 2^{s+w}$ words or bytes
- Block size $=$ line size $= 2w$ words or bytes
- Number of blocks in main memory $= \dfrac{2^{s+w}}{2^w} = 2^s$
- Number of lines in cache $=$ undetermined
- Size of tag $= s$ bits

With associative mapping, there is flexibility as to which block to replace when a new block is read into the cache. Replacement algorithms, discussed later in this section, are designed to maximize the hit ratio. The principal disadvantage of associative mapping is the complex circuitry required to examine the tags of all cache lines in parallel.

Cache Time Analysis Simulator

SET–ASSOCIATIVE MAPPING Set-associative mapping is a compromise that exhibits the strengths of both the direct and associative approaches while reducing their disadvantages.

In this case, the cache consists of a number sets, each of which consists of a number of lines. The relationships are

$$m = v \times k$$
$$i = j \bmod v$$

where

$\quad i =$ cache set number
$\quad j =$ main memory block number
$\quad m =$ number of lines in the cache
$\quad v =$ number of sets
$\quad k =$ number of lines in each set

This is referred to as k-way set-associative mapping. With set-associative mapping, block B_j can be mapped into any of the lines of set j. Figure 4.13a illustrates this mapping for the first v blocks of main memory. As with associative mapping, each word maps into multiple cache lines. For set-associative mapping, each word maps into all the cache lines in a specific set, so that main memory block B_0 maps into set 0, and so on. Thus, the set-associative cache can be physically implemented as v associative caches. It is also possible to implement the set-associative cache as k direct mapping caches, as shown in Figure 4.13b. Each direct-mapped cache is referred to as a *way*, consisting of v lines. The first v lines of main memory are direct mapped into the v lines of each way; the next group of v lines of main memory are similarly mapped, and so on. The direct-mapped implementation is typically used

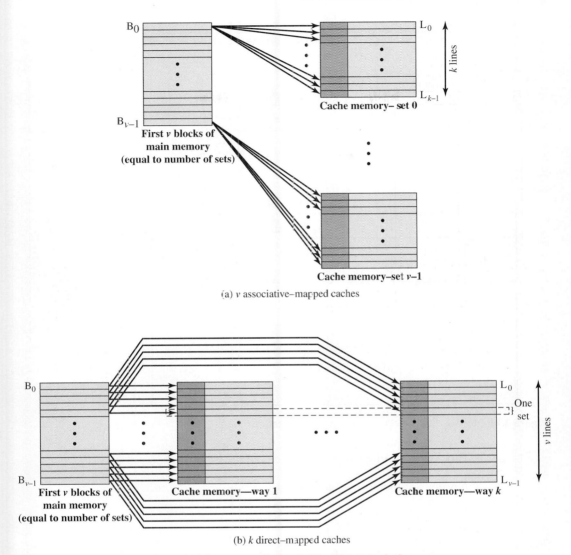

(a) *v* associative–mapped caches

(b) *k* direct–mapped caches

Figure 4.13 Mapping from Main Memory to Cache: *k*-Way Set Associative

for small degrees of associativity (small values of *k*) while the associative-mapped implementation is typically used for higher degrees of associativity [JACO08].

For set-associative mapping, the cache control logic interprets a memory address as three fields: Tag, Set, and Word. The *d* set bits specify one of $v = 2^d$ sets. The *s* bits of the Tag and Set fields specify one of the 2^s blocks of main memory. Figure 4.14 illustrates the cache control logic. With fully associative mapping, the tag in a memory address is quite large and must be compared to the tag of every line in the cache. With *k*-way set-associative mapping, the tag in a memory address is much smaller and is only compared to the *k* tags within a single set. To summarize,

- Address length = $(s + w)$ bits
- Number of addressable units = 2^{s+w} words or bytes

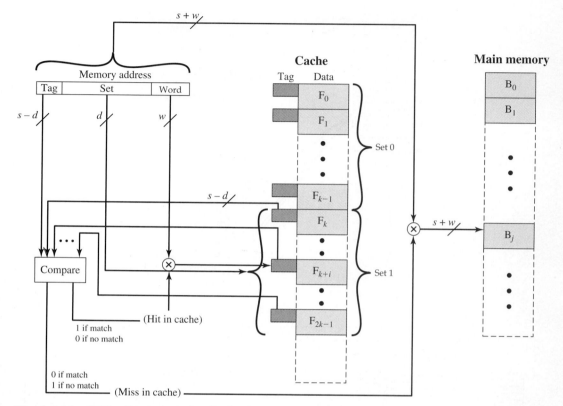

Figure 4.14 *K*-Way Set Associative Cache Organization

- Block size = line size = 2^w words or bytes
- Number of blocks in main memory = $\dfrac{2^{s+w}}{2^w} = 2^s$
- Number of lines in set = k
- Number of sets = $\nu = 2^d$
- Number of lines in cache = $m = k\nu = k \times 2^d$
- Size of cache = $k \times 2^{d+w}$ words or bytes
- Size of tag = $(s - d)$ bits

Example 4.2c Figure 4.15 shows our example using set-associative mapping with two lines in each set, referred to as two-way set-associative. The 13-bit set number identifies a unique set of two lines within the cache. It also gives the number of the block in main memory, modulo 2^{13}. This determines the mapping of blocks into lines. Thus, blocks 000000, 008000, ..., FF8000 of main memory map into cache set 0. Any of those blocks can be loaded into either of the two lines in the set. Note that no two blocks that map into the same cache set have the same tag number. For a read operation, the 13-bit set number is used to determine which set of two lines is to be examined. Both lines in the set are examined for a match with the tag number of the address to be accessed.

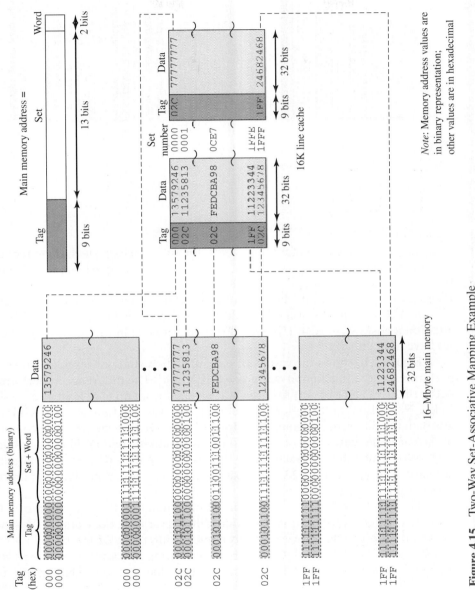

Figure 4.15 Two-Way Set-Associative Mapping Example

135

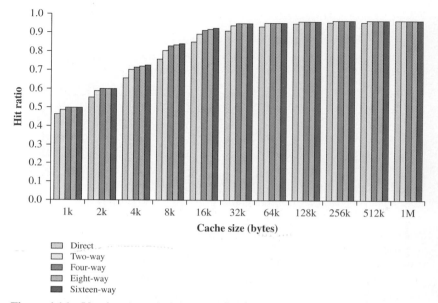

Figure 4.16   Varying Associativity over Cache Size

In the extreme case of $\nu = m$, $k = 1$, the set-associative technique reduces to direct mapping, and for $\nu = 1$, $k = m$, it reduces to associative mapping. The use of two lines per set ($\nu = m/2$, $k = 2$) is the most common set-associative organization. It significantly improves the hit ratio over direct mapping. Four-way set associative ($\nu = m/4$, $k = 4$) makes a modest additional improvement for a relatively small additional cost [MAYB84, HILL89]. Further increases in the number of lines per set have little effect.

Figure 4.16 shows the results of one simulation study of set-associative cache performance as a function of cache size [GENU04]. The difference in performance between direct and two-way set associative is significant up to at least a cache size of 64 kB. Note also that the difference between two-way and four-way at 4 kB is much less than the difference in going from for 4 kB to 8 kB in cache size. The complexity of the cache increases in proportion to the associativity, and in this case would not be justifiable against increasing cache size to 8 or even 16 Kbytes. A final point to note is that beyond about 32 kB, increase in cache size brings no significant increase in performance.

The results of Figure 4.16 are based on simulating the execution of a GCC compiler. Different applications may yield different results. For example, [CANT01] reports on the results for cache performance using many of the CPU2000 SPEC benchmarks. The results of [CANT01] in comparing hit ratio to cache size follow the same pattern as Figure 4.16, but the specific values are somewhat different.

Cache Simulator
Multitask Cache Simulator

Replacement Algorithms

Once the cache has been filled, when a new block is brought into the cache, one of the existing blocks must be replaced. For direct mapping, there is only one possible line for any particular block, and no choice is possible. For the associative and set-associative techniques, a replacement algorithm is needed. To achieve high speed, such an algorithm must be implemented in hardware. A number of algorithms have been tried. We mention four of the most common. Probably the most effective is least recently used (LRU): Replace that block in the set that has been in the cache longest with no reference to it. For two-way set associative, this is easily implemented. Each line includes a USE bit. When a line is referenced, its USE bit is set to 1 and the USE bit of the other line in that set is set to 0. When a block is to be read into the set, the line whose USE bit is 0 is used. Because we are assuming that more recently used memory locations are more likely to be referenced, LRU should give the best hit ratio. LRU is also relatively easy to implement for a fully associative cache. The cache mechanism maintains a separate list of indexes to all the lines in the cache. When a line is referenced, it moves to the front of the list. For replacement, the line at the back of the list is used. Because of its simplicity of implementation, LRU is the most popular replacement algorithm.

Another possibility is first-in-first-out (FIFO): Replace that block in the set that has been in the cache longest. FIFO is easily implemented as a round-robin or circular buffer technique. Still another possibility is least frequently used (LFU): Replace that block in the set that has experienced the fewest references. LFU could be implemented by associating a counter with each line. A technique not based on usage (i.e., not LRU, LFU, FIFO, or some variant) is to pick a line at random from among the candidate lines. Simulation studies have shown that random replacement provides only slightly inferior performance to an algorithm based on usage [SMIT82].

Write Policy

When a block that is resident in the cache is to be replaced, there are two cases to consider. If the old block in the cache has not been altered, then it may be overwritten with a new block without first writing out the old block. If at least one write operation has been performed on a word in that line of the cache, then main memory must be updated by writing the line of cache out to the block of memory before bringing in the new block. A variety of write policies, with performance and economic trade-offs, is possible. There are two problems to contend with. First, more than one device may have access to main memory. For example, an I/O module may be able to read-write directly to memory. If a word has been altered only in the cache, then the corresponding memory word is invalid. Further, if the I/O device has altered main memory, then the cache word is invalid. A more complex problem occurs when multiple processors are attached to the same bus and each processor has its own local cache. Then, if a word is altered in one cache, it could conceivably invalidate a word in other caches.

The simplest technique is called **write through.** Using this technique, all write operations are made to main memory as well as to the cache, ensuring that main memory is always valid. Any other processor-cache module can monitor traffic to main memory to maintain consistency within its own cache. The main disadvantage of this technique is that it generates substantial memory traffic and may create a bottleneck. An alternative technique, known as **write back,** minimizes memory writes. With write back, updates are made only in the cache. When an update occurs, a **dirty bit**, or **use bit**, associated with the line is set. Then, when a block is replaced, it is written back to main memory if and only if the dirty bit is set. The problem with write back is that portions of main memory are invalid, and hence accesses by I/O modules can be allowed only through the cache. This makes for complex circuitry and a potential bottleneck. Experience has shown that the percentage of memory references that are writes is on the order of 15% [SMIT82]. However, for HPC applications, this number may approach 33% (vector-vector multiplication) and can go as high as 50% (matrix transposition).

Example 4.3   Consider a cache with a line size of 32 bytes and a main memory that requires 30 ns to transfer a 4-byte word. For any line that is written at least once before being swapped out of the cache, what is the average number of times that the line must be written before being swapped out for a write-back cache to be more efficient that a write-through cache?

For the write-back case, each dirty line is written back once, at swap-out time, taking $8 \times 30 = 240$ ns. For the write-through case, each update of the line requires that one word be written out to main memory, taking 30 ns. Therefore, if the average line that gets written at least once gets written more than 8 times before swap out, then write back is more efficient.

In a bus organization in which more than one device (typically a processor) has a cache and main memory is shared, a new problem is introduced. If data in one cache are altered, this invalidates not only the corresponding word in main memory, but also that same word in other caches (if any other cache happens to have that same word). Even if a write-through policy is used, the other caches may contain invalid data. A system that prevents this problem is said to maintain cache coherency. Possible approaches to cache coherency include the following:

- **Bus watching with write through:** Each cache controller monitors the address lines to detect write operations to memory by other bus masters. If another master writes to a location in shared memory that also resides in the cache memory, the cache controller invalidates that cache entry. This strategy depends on the use of a write-through policy by all cache controllers.

- **Hardware transparency:** Additional hardware is used to ensure that all updates to main memory via cache are reflected in all caches. Thus, if one processor modifies a word in its cache, this update is written to main memory. In addition, any matching words in other caches are similarly updated.

- **Noncacheable memory:** Only a portion of main memory is shared by more than one processor, and this is designated as noncacheable. In such a system, all accesses to shared memory are cache misses, because the shared memory is never copied into the cache. The noncacheable memory can be identified using chip-select logic or high-address bits.

Cache coherency is an active field of research. This topic is explored further in Part Five.

Line Size

Another design element is the line size. When a block of data is retrieved and placed in the cache, not only the desired word but also some number of adjacent words are retrieved. As the block size increases from very small to larger sizes, the hit ratio will at first increase because of the principle of locality, which states that data in the vicinity of a referenced word are likely to be referenced in the near future. As the block size increases, more useful data are brought into the cache. The hit ratio will begin to decrease, however, as the block becomes even bigger and the probability of using the newly fetched information becomes less than the probability of reusing the information that has to be replaced. Two specific effects come into play:

- Larger blocks reduce the number of blocks that fit into a cache. Because each block fetch overwrites older cache contents, a small number of blocks results in data being overwritten shortly after they are fetched.
- As a block becomes larger, each additional word is farther from the requested word and therefore less likely to be needed in the near future.

The relationship between block size and hit ratio is complex, depending on the locality characteristics of a particular program, and no definitive optimum value has been found. A size of from 8 to 64 bytes seems reasonably close to optimum [SMIT87, PRZY88, PRZY90, HAND98]. For HPC systems, 64- and 128-byte cache line sizes are most frequently used.

Number of Caches

When caches were originally introduced, the typical system had a single cache. More recently, the use of multiple caches has become the norm. Two aspects of this design issue concern the number of levels of caches and the use of unified versus split caches.

MULTILEVEL CACHES As logic density has increased, it has become possible to have a cache on the same chip as the processor: the on-chip cache. Compared with a cache reachable via an external bus, the on-chip cache reduces the processor's external bus activity and therefore speeds up execution times and increases overall system performance. When the requested instruction or data is found in the on-chip cache, the bus access is eliminated. Because of the short data paths internal to the processor, compared with bus lengths, on-chip cache accesses will complete appreciably faster than would even zero-wait state bus cycles. Furthermore, during this period the bus is free to support other transfers.

The inclusion of an on-chip cache leaves open the question of whether an off-chip, or external, cache is still desirable. Typically, the answer is yes, and most contemporary designs include both on-chip and external caches. The simplest such organization is known as a two-level cache, with the internal cache designated as level 1 (L1) and the external cache designated as level 2 (L2). The reason for including an L2 cache is the following: If there is no L2 cache and the processor makes an access request for a memory location not in the L1 cache, then the processor must access DRAM or

ROM memory across the bus. Due to the typically slow bus speed and slow memory access time, this results in poor performance. On the other hand, if an L2 SRAM (static RAM) cache is used, then frequently the missing information can be quickly retrieved. If the SRAM is fast enough to match the bus speed, then the data can be accessed using a zero-wait state transaction, the fastest type of bus transfer.

Two features of contemporary cache design for multilevel caches are noteworthy. First, for an off-chip L2 cache, many designs do not use the system bus as the path for transfer between the L2 cache and the processor, but use a separate data path, so as to reduce the burden on the system bus. Second, with the continued shrinkage of processor components, a number of processors now incorporate the L2 cache on the processor chip, improving performance.

The potential savings due to the use of an L2 cache depends on the hit rates in both the L1 and L2 caches. Several studies have shown that, in general, the use of a second-level cache does improve performance (e.g., see [AZIM92], [NOVI93], [HAND98]). However, the use of multilevel caches does complicate all of the design issues related to caches, including size, replacement algorithm, and write policy; see [HAND98] and [PEIR99] for discussions.

Figure 4.17 shows the results of one simulation study of two-level cache performance as a function of cache size [GENU04]. The figure assumes that both caches have the same line size and shows the total hit ratio. That is, a hit is counted if the desired data appears in either the L1 or the L2 cache. The figure shows the impact of L2 on total hits with respect to L1 size. L2 has little effect on the total number of cache hits until it is at least double the L1 cache size. Note that the steepest part of the slope for an L1 cache of 8 Kbytes is for an L2 cache of 16 Kbytes. Again for an L1 cache of 16 Kbytes, the steepest part of the curve is for an L2 cache size of 32 Kbytes. Prior to that point, the L2 cache has little, if any, impact on total cache performance. The need for the L2 cache to be larger than the L1 cache to

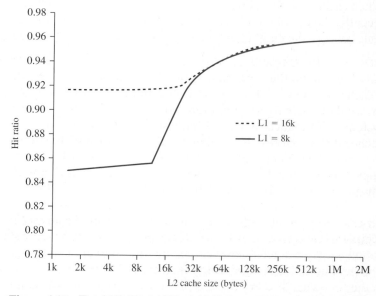

Figure 4.17 Total Hit Ratio (L1 and L2) for 8-Kbyte and 16-Kbyte L1

affect performance makes sense. If the L2 cache has the same line size and capacity as the L1 cache, its contents will more or less mirror those of the L1 cache.

With the increasing availability of on-chip area available for cache, most contemporary microprocessors have moved the L2 cache onto the processor chip and added an L3 cache. Originally, the L3 cache was accessible over the external bus. More recently, most microprocessors have incorporated an on-chip L3 cache. In either case, there appears to be a performance advantage to adding the third level (e.g., see [GHAI98]). Further, large systems, such as the IBM mainframe zEnterprise systems, now incorporate 3 on-chip cache levels and a fourth level of cache shared across multiple chips [CURR11]

UNIFIED VERSUS SPLIT CACHES When the on-chip cache first made an appearance, many of the designs consisted of a single cache used to store references to both data and instructions. More recently, it has become common to split the cache into two: one dedicated to instructions and one dedicated to data. These two caches both exist at the same level, typically as two L1 caches. When the processor attempts to fetch an instruction from main memory, it first consults the instruction L1 cache, and when the processor attempts to fetch data from main memory, it first consults the data L1 cache.

There are two potential advantages of a unified cache:

- For a given cache size, a unified cache has a higher hit rate than split caches because it balances the load between instruction and data fetches automatically. That is, if an execution pattern involves many more instruction fetches than data fetches, then the cache will tend to fill up with instructions, and if an execution pattern involves relatively more data fetches, the opposite will occur.
- Only one cache needs to be designed and implemented.

The trend is toward split caches at the L1 and unified caches for higher levels, particularly for superscalar machines, which emphasize parallel instruction execution and the prefetching of predicted future instructions. The key advantage of the split cache design is that it eliminates contention for the cache between the instruction fetch/decode unit and the execution unit. This is important in any design that relies on the pipelining of instructions. Typically, the processor will fetch instructions ahead of time and fill a buffer, or pipeline, with instructions to be executed. Suppose now that we have a unified instruction/data cache. When the execution unit performs a memory access to load and store data, the request is submitted to the unified cache. If, at the same time, the instruction prefetcher issues a read request to the cache for an instruction, that request will be temporarily blocked so that the cache can service the execution unit first, enabling it to complete the currently executing instruction. This cache contention can degrade performance by interfering with efficient use of the instruction pipeline. The split cache structure overcomes this difficulty.

4.4 PENTIUM 4 CACHE ORGANIZATION

The evolution of cache organization is seen clearly in the evolution of Intel microprocessors (Table 4.4). The 80386 does not include an on-chip cache. The 80486 includes a single on-chip cache of 8 Kbytes, using a line size of 16 bytes and a

Table 4.4 Intel Cache Evolution

Problem	Solution	Processor on Which Feature First Appears
External memory slower than the system bus.	Add external cache using faster memory technology.	386
Increased processor speed results in external bus becoming a bottleneck for cache access.	Move external cache on-chip, operating at the same speed as the processor.	486
Internal cache is rather small, due to limited space on chip.	Add external L2 cache using faster technology than main memory.	486
Contention occurs when both the Instruction Prefetcher and the Execution Unit simultaneously require access to the cache. In that case, the Prefetcher is stalled while the Execution Unit's data access takes place.	Create separate data and instruction caches.	Pentium
Increased processor speed results in external bus becoming a bottleneck for L2 cache access.	Create separate back-side bus that runs at higher speed than the main (front-side) external bus. The BSB is dedicated to the L2 cache.	Pentium Pro
	Move L2 cache on to the processor chip.	Pentium II
Some applications deal with massive databases and must have rapid access to large amounts of data. The on-chip caches are too small.	Add external L3 cache.	Pentium III
	Move L3 cache on-chip.	Pentium 4

four-way set-associative organization. All of the Pentium processors include two on-chip L1 caches, one for data and one for instructions. For the Pentium 4, the L1 data cache is 16 Kbytes, using a line size of 64 bytes and a four-way set-associative organization. The Pentium 4 instruction cache is described subsequently. The Pentium II also includes an L2 cache that feeds both of the L1 caches. The L2 cache is eight-way set associative with a size of 512 kB and a line size of 128 bytes. An L3 cache was added for the Pentium III and became on-chip with high-end versions of the Pentium 4.

Figure 4.18 provides a simplified view of the Pentium 4 organization, highlighting the placement of the three caches. The processor core consists of four major components:

- **Fetch/decode unit:** Fetches program instructions in order from the L2 cache, decodes these into a series of micro-operations, and stores the results in the L1 instruction cache.

- **Out-of-order execution logic:** Schedules execution of the micro-operations subject to data dependencies and resource availability; thus, micro-operations may be scheduled for execution in a different order than they were fetched from the instruction stream. As time permits, this unit schedules speculative execution of micro-operations that may be required in the future.

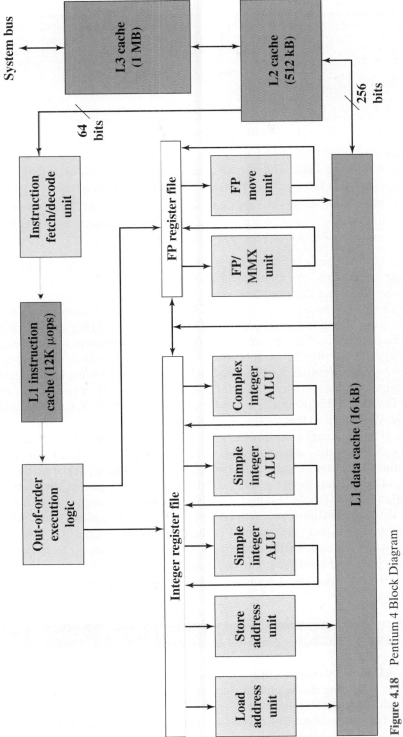

Figure 4.18 Pentium 4 Block Diagram

143

Table 4.5 Pentium 4 Cache Operating Modes

Control Bits		Operating Mode		
CD	**NW**	**Cache Fills**	**Write Throughs**	**Invalidates**
0	0	Enabled	Enabled	Enabled
1	0	Disabled	Enabled	Enabled
1	1	Disabled	Disabled	Disabled

Note: CD = 0; NW = 1 is an invalid combination.

- **Execution units:** These units executes micro-operations, fetching the required data from the L1 data cache and temporarily storing results in registers.
- **Memory subsystem:** This unit includes the L2 and L3 caches and the system bus, which is used to access main memory when the L1 and L2 caches have a cache miss and to access the system I/O resources.

Unlike the organization used in all previous Pentium models, and in most other processors, the Pentium 4 instruction cache sits between the instruction decode logic and the execution core. The reasoning behind this design decision is as follows: As discussed more fully in Chapter 16, the Pentium process decodes, or translates, Pentium machine instructions into simple RISC-like instructions called micro-operations. The use of simple, fixed-length micro-operations enables the use of superscalar pipelining and scheduling techniques that enhance performance. However, the Pentium machine instructions are cumbersome to decode; they have a variable number of bytes and many different options. It turns out that performance is enhanced if this decoding is done independently of the scheduling and pipelining logic. We return to this topic in Chapter 16.

The data cache employs a write-back policy: Data are written to main memory only when they are removed from the cache and there has been an update. The Pentium 4 processor can be dynamically configured to support write-through caching.

The L1 data cache is controlled by two bits in one of the control registers, labeled the CD (cache disable) and NW (not write-through) bits (Table 4.5). There are also two Pentium 4 instructions that can be used to control the data cache: INVD invalidates (flushes) the internal cache memory and signals the external cache (if any) to invalidate. WBINVD writes back and invalidates internal cache and then writes back and invalidates external cache.

Both the L2 and L3 caches are eight-way setassociative with a line size of 128 bytes.

4.5 ARM CACHE ORGANIZATION

The ARM cache organization has evolved with the overall architecture of the ARM family, reflecting the relentless pursuit of performance that is the driving force for all microprocessor designers.

Table 4.6 shows this evolution. The ARM7 models used a unified L1 cache, while all subsequent models use a split instruction/data cache. All of the ARM

Table 4.6 ARM Cache Features

Core	Cache Type	Cache Size (kB)	Cache Line Size (words)	Associativity	Location	Write Buffer Size (words)
ARM720T	Unified	8	4	4-way	Logical	8
ARM920T	Split	16/16 D/I	8	64-way	Logical	16
ARM926EJ-S	Split	4-128/4-128 D/I	8	4-way	Logical	16
ARM1022E	Split	16/16 D/I	8	64-way	Logical	16
ARM1026EJ-S	Split	4-128/4-128 D/I	8	4-way	Logical	8
Intel StrongARM	Split	16/16 D/I	4	32-way	Logical	32
Intel Xscale	Split	32/32 D/I	8	32-way	Logical	32
ARM1136-JF-S	Split	4-64/4-64 D/I	8	4-way	Physical	32

designs use a set-associative cache, with the degree of associativity and the line size varying. ARM cached cores with an MMU use a logical cache for processor families ARM7 through ARM10, including the Intel StongARM and Intel Xscale processors. The ARM11 family uses a physical cache. The distinction between logical and physical cache is discussed earlier in this chapter (Figure 4.7).

An interesting feature of the ARM architecture is the use of a small first-in-first out (FIFO) write buffer to enhance memory write performance. The write buffer is interposed between the cache and main memory and consists of a set of addresses and a set of data words. The write buffer is small compared to the cache, and may hold up to four independent addresses. Typically, the write buffer is enabled for all of main memory, although it may be selectively disabled at the page level. Figure 4.19, taken from [SLOS04], shows the relationship among the write buffer, cache, and main memory.

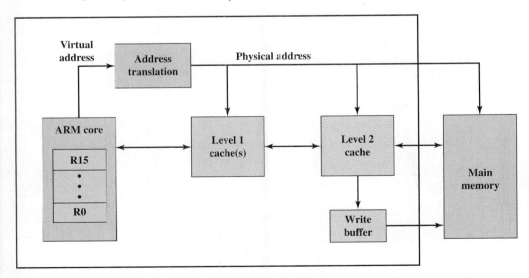

Figure 4.19 ARM Cache and Write Buffer Organization

The write buffer operates as follows: When the processor performs a write to a bufferable area, the data are placed in the write buffer at processor clock speed and the processor continues execution. A write occurs when data in the cache are written back to main memory. Thus, the data to be written are transferred from the cache to the write buffer. The write buffer then performs the external write in parallel. If, however, the write buffer is full (either because there are already the maximum number of words of data in the buffer or because there is no slot for the new address) then the processor is stalled until there is sufficient space in the buffer. As non-write operations proceed, the write buffer continues to write to main memory until the buffer is completely empty.

Data written to the write buffer are not available for reading back into the cache until the data have transferred from the write buffer to main memory. This is the principal reason that the write buffer is quite small. Even so, unless there is a high proportion of writes in an executing program, the write buffer improves performance.

4.6 RECOMMENDED READING

[JACO08] is an excellent, up-to-date treatment of cache design. Another thorough treatment is [HAND98]. A classic paper that is still well worth reading is [SMIT82]; it surveys the various elements of cache design and presents the results of an extensive set of analyses. Another interesting classic is [WILK65], which is probably the first paper to introduce the concept of the cache. [GOOD83] also provides a useful analysis of cache behavior. Another worthwhile analysis is [BELL74]. [AGAR89] presents a detailed examination of a variety of cache design issues related to multiprogramming and multiprocessing. [HIGB90] provides a set of simple formulas that can be used to estimate cache performance as a function of various cache parameters.

AGAR89 Agarwal, A. *Analysis of Cache Performance for Operating Systems and Multiprogramming.* Boston: Kluwer Academic Publishers, 1989.

BELL74 Bell, J.; Casasent, D.; and Bell, C. "An Investigation into Alternative Cache Organizations." *IEEE Transactions on Computers*, April 1974.

GOOD83 Goodman, J. "Using Cache Memory to Reduce Processor-Memory Bandwidth." *Proceedings, 10th Annual International Symposium on Computer Architecture*, 1983. Reprinted in [HILL00].

HAND98 Handy, J. *The Cache Memory Book.* San Diego: Academic Press, 1998.

HIGB90 Higbie, L. "Quick and Easy Cache Performance Analysis." *Computer Architecture News*, June 1990.

JACO08 Jacob, B.; Ng, S.; and Wang, D. *Memory Systems: Cache, DRAM, Disk.* Boston: Morgan Kaufmann, 2008.

SMIT82 Smith, A. "Cache Memories." *ACM Computing Surveys*, September 1982.

WILK65 Wilkes, M. "Slave Memories and Dynamic Storage Allocation," *IEEE Transactions on Electronic Computers*, April 1965. Reprinted in [HILL00].

4.7 KEY TERMS, REVIEW QUESTIONS, AND PROBLEMS

Key Terms

access time	hit ratio	replacement algorithm
associative mapping	instruction cache	secondary memory
secondary memory	L1 cache	sequential access
cache hit	L2 cache	set-associative mapping
cache line	L3 cache	spatial locality
cache memory	line	split cache
cache miss	locality	tag
cache set	logical cache	temporal locality
data cache	memory hierarchy	unified cache
direct access	miss	virtual address
direct mapping	multilevel cache	virtual cache
high-performance computing	physical address	write back
(HPC)	physical cache	write through
hit	random access	

Review Questions

4.1   What are the differences among sequential access, direct access, and random access?

4.2   What is the general relationship among access time, memory cost, and capacity?

4.3   How does the principle of locality relate to the use of multiple memory levels?

4.4   What are the differences among direct mapping, associative mapping, and set-associative mapping?

4.5   For a direct-mapped cache, a main memory address is viewed as consisting of three fields. List and define the three fields.

4.6   For an associative cache, a main memory address is viewed as consisting of two fields. List and define the two fields.

4.7   For a set-associative cache, a main memory address is viewed as consisting of three fields. List and define the three fields.

4.8   What is the distinction between spatial locality and temporal locality?

4.9   In general, what are the strategies for exploiting spatial locality and temporal locality?

Problems

4.1   A set-associative cache consists of 64 lines, or slots, divided into four-line sets. Main memory contains 4K blocks of 128 words each. Show the format of main memory addresses.

4.2   A two-way set-associative cache has lines of 16 bytes and a total size of 8 Kbytes. The 64-Mbyte main memory is byte addressable. Show the format of main memory addresses.

4.3   For the hexadecimal main memory addresses 111111, 666666, BBBBBB, show the following information, in hexadecimal format:

  a. Tag, Line, and Word values for a direct-mapped cache, using the format of Figure 4.10

  b. Tag and Word values for an associative cache, using the format of Figure 4.12

  c. Tag, Set, and Word values for a two-way set-associative cache, using the format of Figure 4.15

4.4 List the following values:

    a. For the direct cache example of Figure 4.10: address length, number of addressable units, block size, number of blocks in main memory, number of lines in cache, size of tag

    b. For the associative cache example of Figure 4.12: address length, number of addressable units, block size, number of blocks in main memory, number of lines in cache, size of tag

    c. For the two-way set-associative cache example of Figure 4.15: address length, number of addressable units, block size, number of blocks in main memory, number of lines in set, number of sets, number of lines in cache, size of tag

4.5 Consider a 32-bit microprocessor that has an on-chip 16-Kbyte four-way set-associative cache. Assume that the cache has a line size of four 32-bit words. Draw a block diagram of this cache showing its organization and how the different address fields are used to determine a cache hit/miss. Where in the cache is the word from memory location ABCDE8F8 mapped?

4.6 Given the following specifications for an external cache memory: four-way set associative; line size of two 16-bit words; able to accommodate a total of 4K 32-bit words from main memory; used with a 16-bit processor that issues 24-bit addresses. Design the cache structure with all pertinent information and show how it interprets the processor's addresses.

4.7 The Intel 80486 has an on-chip, unified cache. It contains 8 Kbytes and has a four-way set-associative organization and a block length of four 32-bit words. The cache is organized into 128 sets. There is a single "line valid bit" and three bits, B0, B1, and B2 (the "LRU" bits), per line. On a cache miss, the 80486 reads a 16-byte line from main memory in a bus memory read burst. Draw a simplified diagram of the cache and show how the different fields of the address are interpreted.

4.8 Consider a machine with a byte addressable main memory of 2^{16} bytes and block size of 8 bytes. Assume that a direct mapped cache consisting of 32 lines is used with this machine.

    a. How is a 16-bit memory address divided into tag, line number, and byte number?

    b. Into what line would bytes with each of the following addresses be stored?

        0001 0001 0001 1011

        1100 0011 0011 0100

        1101 0000 0001 1101

        1010 1010 1010 1010

    c. Suppose the byte with address 0001 1010 0001 1010 is stored in the cache. What are the addresses of the other bytes stored along with it?

    d. How many total bytes of memory can be stored in the cache?

    e. Why is the tag also stored in the cache?

4.9 For its on-chip cache, the Intel 80486 uses a replacement algorithm referred to as **pseudo least recently used**. Associated with each of the 128 sets of four lines (labeled L0, L1, L2, L3) are three bits B0, B1, and B2. The replacement algorithm works as follows: When a line must be replaced, the cache will first determine whether the most recent use was from L0 and L1 or L2 and L3. Then the cache will determine which of the pair of blocks was least recently used and mark it for replacement. Figure 4.20 illustrates the logic.

    a. Specify how the bits B0, B1, and B2 are set and then describe in words how they are used in the replacement algorithm depicted in Figure 4.20.

    b. Show that the 80486 algorithm approximates a true LRU algorithm. *Hint:* Consider the case in which the most recent order of usage is L0, L2, L3, L1.

    c. Demonstrate that a true LRU algorithm would require 6 bits per set.

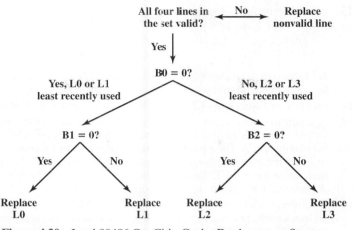

Figure 4.20 Intel 80486 On-Chip Cache Replacement Strategy

4.10 A set-associative cache has a block size of four 16-bit words and a set size of 2. The cache can accommodate a total of 4096 words. The main memory size that is cacheable is 64K $\times$ 32 bits. Design the cache structure and show how the processor's addresses are interpreted.

4.11 Consider a memory system that uses a 32-bit address to address at the byte level, plus a cache that uses a 64-byte line size.

    a. Assume a direct mapped cache with a tag field in the address of 20 bits. Show the address format and determine the following parameters: number of addressable units, number of blocks in main memory, number of lines in cache, size of tag.

    b. Assume an associative cache. Show the address format and determine the following parameters: number of addressable units, number of blocks in main memory, number of lines in cache, size of tag.

    c. Assume a four-way set-associative cache with a tag field in the address of 9 bits. Show the address format and determine the following parameters: number of addressable units, number of blocks in main memory, number of lines in set, number of sets in cache, number of lines in cache, size of tag.

4.12 Consider a computer with the following characteristics: total of 1Mbyte of main memory; word size of 1 byte; block size of 16 bytes; and cache size of 64 Kbytes.

    a. For the main memory addresses of F0010, 01234, and CABBE, give the corresponding tag, cache line address, and word offsets for a direct-mapped cache.

    b. Give any two main memory addresses with different tags that map to the same cache slot for a direct-mapped cache.

    c. For the main memory addresses of F0010 and CABBE, give the corresponding tag and offset values for a fully-associative cache.

    d. For the main memory addresses of F0010 and CABBE, give the corresponding tag, cache set, and offset values for a two-way set-associative cache.

4.13 Describe a simple technique for implementing an LRU replacement algorithm in a four-way set-associative cache.

4.14 Consider again Example 4.3. How does the answer change if the main memory uses a block transfer capability that has a first-word access time of 30 ns and an access time of 5 ns for each word thereafter?

4.15   Consider the following code:

```
for (i = 0; i < 20; i++)
    for (j = 0; j < 10; j++)
        a[i] = a[i]* j
```

    a. Give one example of the spatial locality in the code.
    b. Give one example of the temporal locality in the code.

4.16   Generalize Equations (4.2) and (4.3), in Appendix 4A, to N-level memory hierarchies.

4.17   A computer system contains a main memory of 32K 16-bit words. It also has a 4K-word cache divided into four-line sets with 64 words per line. Assume that the cache is initially empty. The processor fetches words from locations $0, 1, 2, \ldots, 4351$ in that order. It then repeats this fetch sequence nine more times. The cache is 10 times faster than main memory. Estimate the improvement resulting from the use of the cache. Assume an LRU policy for block replacement.

4.18   Consider a cache of 4 lines of 16 bytes each. Main memory is divided into blocks of 16 bytes each. That is, block 0 has bytes with addresses 0 through 15, and so on. Now consider a program that accesses memory in the following sequence of addresses:

Once: 63 through 70

Loop ten times: 15 through 32; 80 through 95

    a. Suppose the cache is organized as direct mapped. Memory blocks 0, 4, and so on are assigned to line 1; blocks 1, 5, and so on to line 2; and so on. Compute the hit ratio.
    b. Suppose the cache is organized as two-way set associative, with two sets of two lines each. Even-numbered blocks are assigned to set 0 and odd-numbered blocks are assigned to set 1. Compute the hit ratio for the two-way set-associative cache using the least recently used replacement scheme.

4.19   Consider a memory system with the following parameters:

$$T_c = 100 \text{ ns} \qquad C_c = 10^{-4} \text{ \$/bit}$$
$$T_m = 1200 \text{ ns} \qquad C_m = 10^{-5} \text{ \$/bit}$$

    a. What is the cost of 1 Mbyte of main memory?
    b. What is the cost of 1 Mbyte of main memory using cache memory technology?
    c. If the effective access time is 10% greater than the cache access time, what is the hit ratio H?

4.20   **a.** Consider an L1 cache with an access time of 1 ns and a hit ratio of $H = 0.95$. Suppose that we can change the cache design (size of cache, cache organization) such that we increase H to 0.97, but increase access time to 1.5 ns. What conditions must be met for this change to result in improved performance?
    b. Explain why this result makes intuitive sense.

4.21   Consider a single-level cache with an access time of 2.5 ns, a line size of 64 bytes, and a hit ratio of $H = 0.95$. Main memory uses a block transfer capability that has a first-word (4 bytes) access time of 50 ns and an access time of 5 ns for each word thereafter.
    a. What is the access time when there is a cache miss? Assume that the cache waits until the line has been fetched from main memory and then re-executes for a hit.
    b. Suppose that increasing the line size to 128 bytes increases the H to 0.97. Does this reduce the average memory access time?

4.22   A computer has a cache, main memory, and a disk used for virtual memory. If a referenced word is in the cache, 20 ns are required to access it. If it is in main memory but not in the cache, 60 ns are needed to load it into the cache, and then the reference is started again. If the word is not in main memory, 12 ms are required to fetch the word from disk, followed by 60 ns to copy it to the cache, and then the reference is started again. The cache hit ratio is 0.9 and the main memory hit ratio is 0.6. What is the average time in nanoseconds required to access a referenced word on this system?

4.23 Consider a cache with a line size of 64 bytes. Assume that on average 30% of the lines in the cache are dirty. A word consists of 8 bytes.
  a. Assume there is a 3% miss rate (0.97 hit ratio). Compute the amount of main memory traffic, in terms of bytes per instruction for both write-through and write-back policies. Memory is read into cache one line at a time. However, for write back, a single word can be written from cache to main memory.
  b. Repeat part a for a 5% rate.
  c. Repeat part a for a 7% rate.
  d. What conclusion can you draw from these results?

4.24 On the Motorola 68020 microprocessor, a cache access takes two clock cycles. Data access from main memory over the bus to the processor takes three clock cycles in the case of no wait state insertion; the data are delivered to the processor in parallel with delivery to the cache.
  a. Calculate the effective length of a memory cycle given a hit ratio of 0.9 and a clocking rate of 16.67 MHz.
  b. Repeat the calculations assuming insertion of two wait states of one cycle each per memory cycle. What conclusion can you draw from the results?

4.25 Assume a processor having a memory cycle time of 300 ns and an instruction processing rate of 1 MIPS. On average, each instruction requires one bus memory cycle for instruction fetch and one for the operand it involves.
  a. Calculate the utilization of the bus by the processor.
  b. Suppose the processor is equipped with an instruction cache and the associated hit ratio is 0.5. Determine the impact on bus utilization.

4.26 The performance of a single-level cache system for a read operation can be characterized by the following equation:

$$T_a = T_c + (1 - H)T_m$$

where T_a is the average access time, T_c is the cache access time, T_m is the memory access time (memory to processor register), and H is the hit ratio. For simplicity, we assume that the word in question is loaded into the cache in parallel with the load to processor register. This is the same form as Equation (4.2).
  a. Define T_b = time to transfer a line between cache and main memory, and W = fraction of write references. Revise the preceding equation to account for writes as well as reads, using a write-through policy.
  b. Define W_b as the probability that a line in the cache has been altered. Provide an equation for T_a for the write-back policy.

4.27 For a system with two levels of cache, define T_{c_1} = first-level cache access time; T_{c_2} = second-level cache access time; T_m = memory access time; H_1 = first-level cache hit ratio; H_2 = combined first/second level cache hit ratio. Provide an equation for T_a for a read operation.

4.28 Assume the following performance characteristics on a cache read miss: one clock cycle to send an address to main memory and four clock cycles to access a 32-bit word from main memory and transfer it to the processor and cache.
  a. If the cache line size is one word, what is the miss penalty (i.e., additional time required for a read in the event of a read miss)?
  b. What is the miss penalty if the cache line size is four words and a multiple, non-burst transfer is executed?
  c. What is the miss penalty if the cache line size is four words and a transfer is executed, with one clock cycle per word transfer?

4.29 For the cache design of the preceding problem, suppose that increasing the line size from one word to four words results in a decrease of the read miss rate from 3.2% to 1.1%. For both the nonburst transfer and the burst transfer case, what is the average miss penalty, averaged over all reads, for the two different line sizes?

APPENDIX 4A PERFORMANCE CHARACTERISTICS OF TWO-LEVEL MEMORIES

In this chapter, reference is made to a cache that acts as a buffer between main memory and processor, creating a two-level internal memory. This two-level architecture exploits a property known as locality to provide improved performance over a comparable one-level memory.

The main memory cache mechanism is part of the computer architecture, implemented in hardware and typically invisible to the operating system. There are two other instances of a two-level memory approach that also exploit locality and that are, at least partially, implemented in the operating system: virtual memory and the disk cache (Table 4.7). Virtual memory is explored in Chapter 8; disk cache is beyond the scope of this book but is examined in [STAL12]. In this appendix, we look at some of the performance characteristics of two-level memories that are common to all three approaches.

Locality

The basis for the performance advantage of a two-level memory is a principle known as **locality of reference** [DENN68]. This principle states that memory references tend to cluster. Over a long period of time, the clusters in use change, but over a short period of time, the processor is primarily working with fixed clusters of memory references.

Intuitively, the principle of locality makes sense. Consider the following line of reasoning:

1. Except for branch and call instructions, which constitute only a small fraction of all program instructions, program execution is sequential. Hence, in most cases, the next instruction to be fetched immediately follows the last instruction fetched.

2. It is rare to have a long uninterrupted sequence of procedure calls followed by the corresponding sequence of returns. Rather, a program remains confined to a rather narrow window of procedure-invocation depth. Thus, over a short period of time references to instructions tend to be localized to a few procedures.

Table 4.7 Characteristics of Two-Level Memories

	Main Memory Cache	Virtual Memory (paging)	Disk Cache
Typical access time ratios	5 : 1 (main memory vs. cache)	10^6 : 1 (main memory vs. disk)	10^6 : 1 (main memory vs. disk)
Memory management system	Implemented by special hardware	Combination of hardware and system software	System software
Typical block or page size	4 to 128 bytes (cache block)	64 to 4096 bytes (virtual memory page)	64 to 4096 bytes (disk block or pages)
Access of processor to second level	Direct access	Indirect access	Indirect access

Table 4.8   Relative Dynamic Frequency of High-Level Language Operations

Study Language Workload	[HUCK83] Pascal Scientific	[KNUT71] FORTRAN Student	[PATT82a] Pascal System	[PATT82a] C System	[TANE78] SAL System
Assign	74	67	45	38	42
Loop	4	3	5	3	4
Call	1	3	15	12	12
IF	20	11	29	43	36
GOTO	2	9	—	3	—
Other	—	7	6	1	6

3. Most iterative constructs consist of a relatively small number of instructions repeated many times. For the duration of the iteration, computation is therefore confined to a small contiguous portion of a program.

4. In many programs, much of the computation involves processing data structures, such as arrays or sequences of records. In many cases, successive references to these data structures will be to closely located data items.

This line of reasoning has been confirmed in many studies. With reference to point 1, a variety of studies have analyzed the behavior of high-level language programs. Table 4.8 includes key results, measuring the appearance of various statement types during execution, from the following studies. The earliest study of programming language behavior, performed by Knuth [KNUT71], examined a collection of FORTRAN programs used as student exercises. Tanenbaum [TANE78] published measurements collected from over 300 procedures used in operating-system programs and written in a language that supports structured programming (SAL). Patterson and Sequein [PATT82a] analyzed a set of measurements taken from compilers and programs for typesetting, computer-aided design (CAD), sorting, and file comparison. The programming languages C and Pascal were studied. Huck [HUCK83] analyzed four programs intended to represent a mix of general-purpose scientific computing, including fast Fourier transform and the integration of systems of differential equations. There is good agreement in the results of this mixture of languages and applications that branching and call instructions represent only a fraction of statements executed during the lifetime of a program. Thus, these studies confirm assertion 1.

With respect to assertion 2, studies reported in [PATT85a] provide confirmation. This is illustrated in Figure 4.21, which shows call-return behavior. Each call is represented by the line moving down and to the right, and each return by the line moving up and to the right. In the figure, a *window* with depth equal to 5 is defined. Only a sequence of calls and returns with a net movement of 6 in either direction causes the window to move. As can be seen, the executing program can remain within a stationary window for long periods of time. A study by the same analysts of C and Pascal programs showed that a window of depth 8 will need to shift only on less than 1% of the calls or returns [TAMI83].

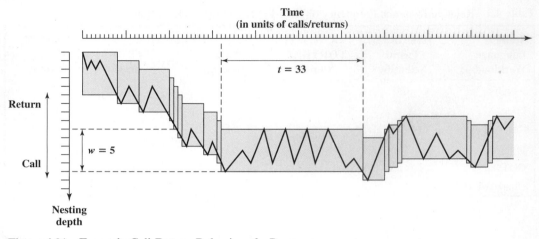

Figure 4.21 Example Call-Return Behavior of a Program

A distinction is made in the literature between spatial locality and temporal locality. **Spatial locality** refers to the tendency of execution to involve a number of memory locations that are clustered. This reflects the tendency of a processor to access instructions sequentially. Spatial location also reflects the tendency of a program to access data locations sequentially, such as when processing a table of data. **Temporal locality** refers to the tendency for a processor to access memory locations that have been used recently. For example, when an iteration loop is executed, the processor executes the same set of instructions repeatedly.

Traditionally, temporal locality is exploited by keeping recently used instruction and data values in cache memory and by exploiting a cache hierarchy. Spatial locality is generally exploited by using larger cache blocks and by incorporating prefetching mechanisms (fetching items of anticipated use) into the cache control logic. Recently, there has been considerable research on refining these techniques to achieve greater performance, but the basic strategies remain the same.

Operation of Two-Level Memory

The locality property can be exploited in the formation of a two-level memory. The upper-level memory (M1) is smaller, faster, and more expensive (per bit) than the lower-level memory (M2). M1 is used as a temporary store for part of the contents of the larger M2. When a memory reference is made, an attempt is made to access the item in M1. If this succeeds, then a quick access is made. If not, then a block of memory locations is copied from M2 to M1 and the access then takes place via M1. Because of locality, once a block is brought into M1, there should be a number of accesses to locations in that block, resulting in fast overall service.

To express the average time to access an item, we must consider not only the speeds of the two levels of memory, but also the probability that a given reference can be found in M1. We have

$$T_s = H \times T_1 + (1 - H) \times (T_1 + T_2)$$
$$= T_1 + (1 - H) \times T_2 \qquad\qquad \textbf{(4.2)}$$

where

T_s = average (system) access time
T_1 = access time of M1 (e.g., cache, disk cache)
T_2 = access time of M2 (e.g., main memory, disk)
H = hit ratio (fraction of time reference is found in M1)

Figure 4.2 shows average access time as a function of hit ratio. As can be seen, for a high percentage of hits, the average total access time is much closer to that of M1 than M2.

Performance

Let us look at some of the parameters relevant to an assessment of a two-level memory mechanism. First consider cost. We have

$$C_s = \frac{C_1 S_1 + C_2 S_2}{S_1 + S_2} \tag{4.3}$$

where

C_s = average cost per bit for the combined two-level memory
C_1 = average cost per bit of upper-level memory M1
C_2 = average cost per bit of lower-level memory M2
S_1 = size of M1
S_2 = size of M2

We would like $C_s \approx C_2$. Given that $C_1 \gg C_2$, this requires $S_1 < S_2$. Figure 4.22 shows the relationship.

Next, consider access time. For a two-level memory to provide a significant performance improvement, we need to have T_s approximately equal to T_1 ($T_s \approx T_1$). Given that T_1 is much less than T_2 ($T_1 \ll T_2$), a hit ratio of close to 1 is needed.

So we would like M1 to be small to hold down cost, and large to improve the hit ratio and therefore the performance. Is there a size of M1 that satisfies both requirements to a reasonable extent? We can answer this question with a series of subquestions:

- What value of hit ratio is needed so that $T_s \approx T_1$?
- What size of M1 will assure the needed hit ratio?
- Does this size satisfy the cost requirement?

To get at this, consider the quantity T_1/T_s, which is referred to as the *access efficiency*. It is a measure of how close average access time (T_s) is to M1 access time (T_1). From Equation (4.2),

$$\frac{T_1}{T_s} = \frac{1}{1 + (1 - H)\dfrac{T_2}{T_1}} \tag{4.4}$$

Figure 4.23 plots T_1/T_s as a function of the hit ratio H, with the quantity T_2/T_1 as a parameter. Typically, on-chip cache access time is about 25 to 50 times faster than main memory access time (i.e., T_2/T_1 is 25 to 50), off-chip cache access time is about 5 to 15 times faster than main memory access time (i.e., T_2/T_1 is 5 to 15), and main

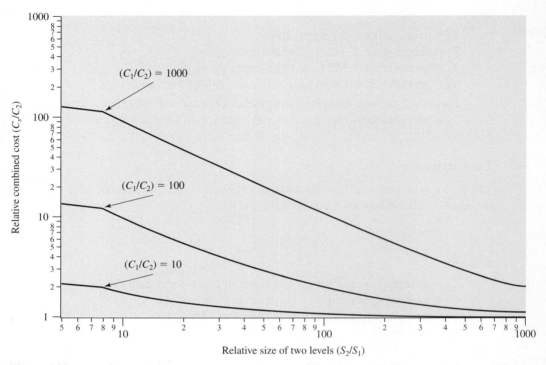

Figure 4.22 Relationship of Average Memory Cost to Relative Memory Size for a Two-Level Memory

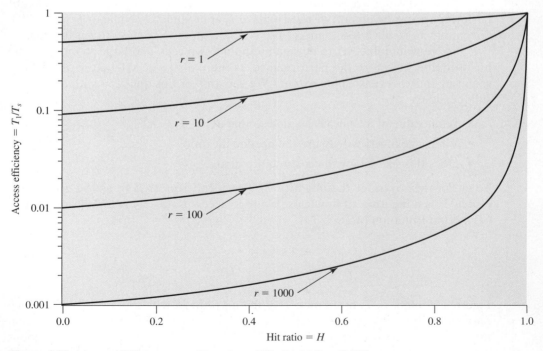

Figure 4.23 Access Efficiency as a Function of Hit Ratio ($r = T_2/T_1$)

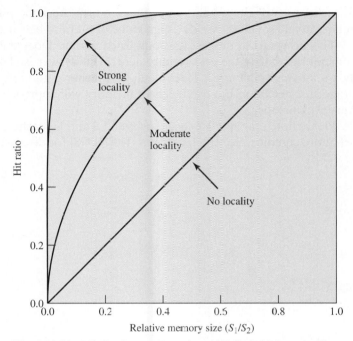

Figure 4.24   Hit Ratio as a Function of Relative Memory Size

memory access time is about 1000 times faster than disk access time ($T_2/T_1 = 1000$). Thus, a hit ratio in the range of near 0.9 would seem to be needed to satisfy the performance requirement.

We can now phrase the question about relative memory size more exactly. Is a hit ratio of, say, 0.8 or better reasonable for $S_1 \ll S_2$? This will depend on a number of factors, including the nature of the software being executed and the details of the design of the two-level memory. The main determinant is, of course, the degree of locality. Figure 4.24 suggests the effect that locality has on the hit ratio. Clearly, if M1 is the same size as M2, then the hit ratio will be 1.0: All of the items in M2 are always stored also in M1. Now suppose that there is no locality; that is, references are completely random. In that case the hit ratio should be a strictly linear function of the relative memory size. For example, if M1 is half the size of M2, then at any time half of the items from M2 are also in M1 and the hit ratio will be 0.5. In practice, however, there is some degree of locality in the references. The effects of moderate and strong locality are indicated in the figure. Note that Figure 4.24 is not derived from any specific data or model; the figure suggests the type of performance that is seen with various degrees of locality.

So if there is strong locality, it is possible to achieve high values of hit ratio even with relatively small upper-level memory size. For example, numerous studies have shown that rather small cache sizes will yield a hit ratio above 0.75 *regardless of the size of main memory* (e.g., [AGAR89], [PRZY88], [STRE83], and [SMIT82]). A cache in the range of 1K to 128K words is generally adequate, whereas main memory is now typically in the gigabyte range. When we consider virtual memory and disk cache, we will cite other studies that confirm the same phenomenon, namely that a relatively small M1 yields a high value of hit ratio because of locality.

This brings us to the last question listed earlier: Does the relative size of the two memories satisfy the cost requirement? The answer is clearly yes. If we need only a relatively small upper-level memory to achieve good performance, then the average cost per bit of the two levels of memory will approach that of the cheaper lower-level memory.

Please note that with L2 cache, or even L2 and L3 caches, involved, analysis is much more complex. See [PEIR99] and [HAND98] for discussions.

CHAPTER 5

INTERNAL MEMORY

LEARNING OBJECTIVES

After studying this chapter, you should be able to:

◆ Present an overview of the principle types of semiconductor main memory.

◆ Understand the operation of a basic code that can detect and correct single-bit errors in 8-bit words.

◆ Summarize the properties of contemporary advanced DRAM organizations.

We begin this chapter with a survey of semiconductor main memory subsystems, including ROM, DRAM, and SRAM memories. Then we look at error control techniques used to enhance memory reliability. Following this, we look at more advanced DRAM architectures.

5.1 SEMICONDUCTOR MAIN MEMORY

In earlier computers, the most common form of random-access storage for computer main memory employed an array of doughnut-shaped ferromagnetic loops referred to as *cores*. Hence, main memory was often referred to as *core,* a term that persists to this day. The advent of, and advantages of, microelectronics has long since vanquished the magnetic core memory. Today, the use of semiconductor chips for main memory is almost universal. Key aspects of this technology are explored in this section.

Organization

The basic element of a **semiconductor memory** is the memory cell. Although a variety of electronic technologies are used, all semiconductor memory cells share certain properties:

- They exhibit two stable (or semistable) states, which can be used to represent binary 1 and 0.
- They are capable of being written into (at least once), to set the state.
- They are capable of being read to sense the state.

Figure 5.1 depicts the operation of a memory cell. Most commonly, the cell has three functional terminals capable of carrying an electrical signal. The select terminal, as the name suggests, selects a memory cell for a read or write operation. The control terminal indicates read or write. For writing, the other terminal provides an electrical signal that sets the state of the cell to 1 or 0. For reading, that terminal is used for output of the cell's state. The details of the internal organization, functioning, and timing of the memory cell depend on the specific integrated circuit technology used and are beyond the scope of this book, except for a brief summary. For our purposes, we will take it as given that individual cells can be selected for reading and writing operations.

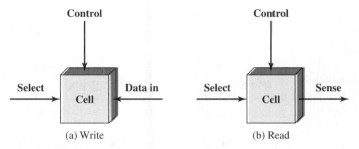

Figure 5.1 Memory Cell Operation

DRAM and SRAM

All of the memory types that we will explore in this chapter are random access. That is, individual words of memory are directly accessed through wired-in addressing logic.

Table 5.1 lists the major types of semiconductor memory. The most common is referred to as *random-access memory* (RAM). This is, in fact, a misuse of the term, because all of the types listed in the table are random access. One distinguishing characteristic of memory that is designated as RAM is that it is possible both to read data from the memory and to write new data into the memory easily and rapidly. Both the reading and writing are accomplished through the use of electrical signals.

The other distinguishing characteristic of RAM is that it is volatile. A RAM must be provided with a constant power supply. If the power is interrupted, then the data are lost. Thus, RAM can be used only as temporary storage. The two traditional forms of RAM used in computers are DRAM and SRAM.

DYNAMIC RAM RAM technology is divided into two technologies: dynamic and static. A **dynamic RAM (DRAM)** is made with cells that store data as charge on capacitors. The presence or absence of charge in a capacitor is interpreted as a binary 1 or 0. Because capacitors have a natural tendency to discharge, dynamic

Table 5.1 Semiconductor Memory Types

Memory Type	Category	Erasure	Write Mechanism	Volatility
Random-access memory (RAM)	Read-write memory	Electrically, byte-level	Electrically	Volatile
Read-only memory (ROM)	Read-only memory	Not possible	Masks	Nonvolatile
Programmable ROM (PROM)				
Erasable PROM (EPROM)	Read-mostly memory	UV light, chip-level	Electrically	
Electrically Erasable PROM (EEPROM)		Electrically, byte-level		
Flash memory		Electrically, block-level		

RAMs require periodic charge refreshing to maintain data storage. The term *dynamic* refers to this tendency of the stored charge to leak away, even with power continuously applied.

Figure 5.2a is a typical DRAM structure for an individual cell that stores 1 bit. The address line is activated when the bit value from this cell is to be read or written. The transistor acts as a switch that is closed (allowing current to flow) if a voltage is applied to the address line and open (no current flows) if no voltage is present on the address line.

For the write operation, a voltage signal is applied to the bit line; a high voltage represents 1, and a low voltage represents 0. A signal is then applied to the address line, allowing a charge to be transferred to the capacitor.

For the read operation, when the address line is selected, the transistor turns on and the charge stored on the capacitor is fed out onto a bit line and to a sense amplifier. The sense amplifier compares the capacitor voltage to a reference value and determines if the cell contains a logic 1 or a logic 0. The readout from the cell discharges the capacitor, which must be restored to complete the operation.

Although the DRAM cell is used to store a single bit (0 or 1), it is essentially an analog device. The capacitor can store any charge value within a range; a threshold value determines whether the charge is interpreted as 1 or 0.

STATIC RAM In contrast, a **static RAM (SRAM)** is a digital device that uses the same logic elements used in the processor. In a SRAM, binary values are stored using traditional flip-flop logic-gate configurations (see Chapter 11 for a description of flip-flops). A static RAM will hold its data as long as power is supplied to it.

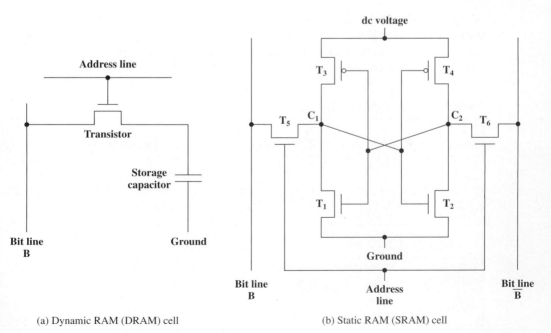

(a) Dynamic RAM (DRAM) cell   (b) Static RAM (SRAM) cell

Figure 5.2 Typical Memory Cell Structures

Figure 5.2b is a typical SRAM structure for an individual cell. Four transistors (T_1, T_2, T_3, T_4) are cross connected in an arrangement that produces a stable logic state. In logic state 1, point C_1 is high and point C_2 is low; in this state, T_1 and T_4 are off and T_2 and T_3 are on.[1] In logic state 0, point C_1 is low and point C_2 is high; in this state, T_1 and T_4 are on and T_2 and T_3 are off. Both states are stable as long as the direct current (dc) voltage is applied. Unlike the DRAM, no refresh is needed to retain data.

As in the DRAM, the SRAM address line is used to open or close a switch. The address line controls two transistors (T_5 and T_6). When a signal is applied to this line, the two transistors are switched on, allowing a read or write operation. For a write operation, the desired bit value is applied to line B, while its complement is applied to line $\overline{B}$. This forces the four transistors (T_1, T_2, T_3, T_4) into the proper state. For a read operation, the bit value is read from line B.

SRAM VERSUS DRAM Both static and dynamic RAMs are volatile; that is, power must be continuously supplied to the memory to preserve the bit values. A dynamic memory cell is simpler and smaller than a static memory cell. Thus, a DRAM is more dense (smaller cells = more cells per unit area) and less expensive than a corresponding SRAM. On the other hand, a DRAM requires the supporting refresh circuitry. For larger memories, the fixed cost of the refresh circuitry is more than compensated for by the smaller variable cost of DRAM cells. Thus, DRAMs tend to be favored for large memory requirements. A final point is that SRAMs are somewhat faster than DRAMs. Because of these relative characteristics, SRAM is used for cache memory (both on and off chip), and DRAM is used for main memory.

Types of ROM

As the name suggests, a **read-only memory** (ROM) contains a permanent pattern of data that cannot be changed. A ROM is nonvolatile; that is, no power source is required to maintain the bit values in memory. While it is possible to read a ROM, it is not possible to write new data into it. An important application of ROMs is microprogramming, discussed in Part Four. Other potential applications include

- Library subroutines for frequently wanted functions
- System programs
- Function tables

For a modest-sized requirement, the advantage of ROM is that the data or program is permanently in main memory and need never be loaded from a secondary storage device.

A ROM is created like any other integrated circuit chip, with the data actually wired into the chip as part of the fabrication process. This presents two problems:

- The data insertion step includes a relatively large fixed cost, whether one or thousands of copies of a particular ROM are fabricated.
- There is no room for error. If one bit is wrong, the whole batch of ROMs must be thrown out.

---

[1] The circles associated with T_3 and T_4 in Figure 5.2b indicate signal negation.

When only a small number of ROMs with a particular memory content is needed, a less expensive alternative is the **programmable ROM (PROM)**. Like the ROM, the PROM is **nonvolatile** and may be written into only once. For the PROM, the writing process is performed electrically and may be performed by a supplier or customer at a time later than the original chip fabrication. Special equipment is required for the writing or "programming" process. PROMs provide flexibility and convenience. The ROM remains attractive for high-volume production runs.

Another variation on read-only memory is the **read-mostly memory**, which is useful for applications in which read operations are far more frequent than write operations but for which nonvolatile storage is required. There are three common forms of read-mostly memory: EPROM, EEPROM, and flash memory.

The optically **erasable programmable read-only memory (EPROM)** is read and written electrically, as with PROM. However, before a write operation, all the storage cells must be erased to the same initial state by exposure of the packaged chip to ultraviolet radiation. Erasure is performed by shining an intense ultraviolet light through a window that is designed into the memory chip. This erasure process can be performed repeatedly; each erasure can take as much as 20 minutes to perform. Thus, the EPROM can be altered multiple times and, like the ROM and PROM, holds its data virtually indefinitely. For comparable amounts of storage, the EPROM is more expensive than PROM, but it has the advantage of the multiple update capability.

A more attractive form of read-mostly memory is **electrically erasable programmable read-only memory (EEPROM)**. This is a read-mostly memory that can be written into at any time without erasing prior contents; only the byte or bytes addressed are updated. The write operation takes considerably longer than the read operation, on the order of several hundred microseconds per byte. The EEPROM combines the advantage of nonvolatility with the flexibility of being updatable in place, using ordinary bus control, address, and data lines. EEPROM is more expensive than EPROM and also is less dense, supporting fewer bits per chip.

Another form of semiconductor memory is **flash memory** (so named because of the speed with which it can be reprogrammed). First introduced in the mid-1980s, flash memory is intermediate between EPROM and EEPROM in both cost and functionality. Like EEPROM, flash memory uses an electrical erasing technology. An entire flash memory can be erased in one or a few seconds, which is much faster than EPROM. In addition, it is possible to erase just blocks of memory rather than an entire chip. Flash memory gets its name because the microchip is organized so that a section of memory cells are erased in a single action or "flash." However, flash memory does not provide byte-level erasure. Like EPROM, flash memory uses only one transistor per bit, and so achieves the high density (compared with EEPROM) of EPROM.

Chip Logic

As with other integrated circuit products, semiconductor memory comes in packaged chips (Figure 2.7). Each chip contains an array of memory cells.

In the memory hierarchy as a whole, we saw that there are trade-offs among speed, capacity, and cost. These trade-offs also exist when we consider the organization of memory cells and functional logic on a chip. For semiconductor memories, one of the key design issues is the number of bits of data that may be read/written at a time. At one extreme is an organization in which the physical arrangement of cells in the array is the same as the logical arrangement (as perceived by the processor) of words in memory. The array is organized into W words of B bits each. For example, a 16-Mbit chip could be organized as 1M 16-bit words. At the other extreme is the so-called 1-bit-per-chip organization, in which data are read/written 1 bit at a time. We will illustrate memory chip organization with a DRAM; ROM organization is similar, though simpler.

Figure 5.3 shows a typical organization of a 16-Mbit DRAM. In this case, 4 bits are read or written at a time. Logically, the memory array is organized as four square arrays of 2048 by 2048 elements. Various physical arrangements are possible. In any case, the elements of the array are connected by both horizontal (row) and vertical (column) lines. Each horizontal line connects to the Select terminal of each cell in its row; each vertical line connects to the Data-In/Sense terminal of each cell in its column.

Address lines supply the address of the word to be selected. A total of $\log_2 W$ lines are needed. In our example, 11 address lines are needed to select one of 2048 rows. These 11 lines are fed into a row decoder, which has 11 lines of input and 2048 lines for output. The logic of the decoder activates a single one of the 2048 outputs depending on the bit pattern on the 11 input lines ($2^{11} = 2048$).

An additional 11 address lines select one of 2048 columns of 4 bits per column. Four data lines are used for the input and output of 4 bits to and from a data buffer. On input (write), the bit driver of each bit line is activated for a 1 or 0 according to the value of the corresponding data line. On output (read), the value of each bit line is passed through a sense amplifier and presented to the data lines. The row line selects which row of cells is used for reading or writing.

Because only 4 bits are read/written to this DRAM, there must be multiple DRAMs connected to the memory controller to read/write a word of data to the bus.

Note that there are only 11 address lines (A0–A10), half the number you would expect for a 2048 $\times$ 2048 array. This is done to save on the number of pins. The 22 required address lines are passed through select logic external to the chip and multiplexed onto the 11 address lines. First, 11 address signals are passed to the chip to define the row address of the array, and then the other 11 address signals are presented for the column address. These signals are accompanied by row address select ($\overline{\text{RAS}}$) and column address select ($\overline{\text{CAS}}$) signals to provide timing to the chip.

The write enable ($\overline{\text{WE}}$) and output enable ($\overline{\text{OE}}$) pins determine whether a write or read operation is performed. Two other pins, not shown in Figure 5.3, are ground (Vss) and a voltage source (Vcc).

As an aside, multiplexed addressing plus the use of square arrays result in a quadrupling of memory size with each new generation of memory chips. One more pin devoted to addressing doubles the number of rows and columns, and so the size of the chip memory grows by a factor of 4.

Figure 5.3 also indicates the inclusion of refresh circuitry. All DRAMs require a refresh operation. A simple technique for refreshing is, in effect, to disable the DRAM chip while all data cells are refreshed. The refresh counter steps through all of the row values. For each row, the output lines from the refresh counter are supplied to the row decoder and the RAS line is activated. The data are read out and written back into the same location. This causes each cell in the row to be refreshed.

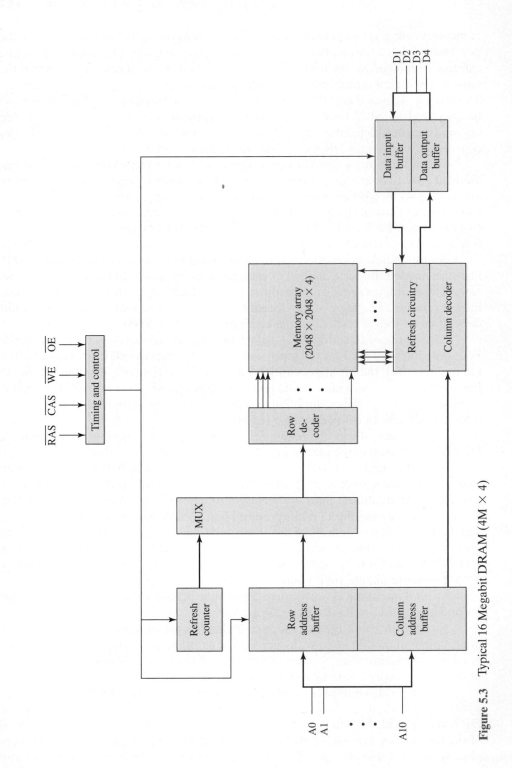

Figure 5.3 Typical 16 Megabit DRAM (4M × 4)

Chip Packaging

As was mentioned in Chapter 2, an integrated circuit is mounted on a package that contains pins for connection to the outside world.

Figure 5.4a shows an example EPROM package, which is an 8-Mbit chip organized as 1M × 8. In this case, the organization is treated as a one-word-per-chip package. The package includes 32 pins, which is one of the standard chip package sizes. The pins support the following signal lines:

- The address of the word being accessed. For 1M words, a total of 20 ($2^{20} = 1M$) pins are needed (A0–A19).
- The data to be read out, consisting of 8 lines (D0–D7).
- The power supply to the chip (V_{cc}).
- A ground pin (V_{ss}).
- A chip enable (CE) pin. Because there may be more than one memory chip, each of which is connected to the same address bus, the CE pin is used to indicate whether or not the address is valid for this chip. The CE pin is activated by logic connected to the higher-order bits of the address bus (i.e., address bits above A19). The use of this signal is illustrated presently.
- A program voltage (V_{pp}) that is supplied during programming (write operations).

A typical DRAM pin configuration is shown in Figure 5.4b, for a 16-Mbit chip organized as 4M × 4. There are several differences from a ROM chip. Because a RAM can be updated, the data pins are input/output. The write enable (WE) and output enable (OE) pins indicate whether this is a write or read operation.

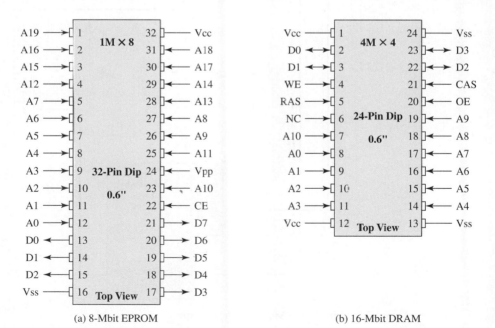

(a) 8-Mbit EPROM

(b) 16-Mbit DRAM

Figure 5.4 Typical Memory Package Pins and Signals

Because the DRAM is accessed by row and column, and the address is multiplexed, only 11 address pins are needed to specify the 4M row/column combinations ($2^{11} \times 2^{11} = 2^{22} = 4M$). The functions of the row address select (RAS) and column address select (CAS) pins were discussed previously. Finally, the no connect (NC) pin is provided so that there are an even number of pins.

Module Organization

If a RAM chip contains only 1 bit per word, then clearly we will need at least a number of chips equal to the number of bits per word. As an example, Figure 5.5 shows how a memory module consisting of 256K 8-bit words could be organized. For 256K words, an 18-bit address is needed and is supplied to the module from some external source (e.g., the address lines of a bus to which the module is attached). The address is presented to 8 256K $\times$ 1-bit chips, each of which provides the input/output of 1 bit.

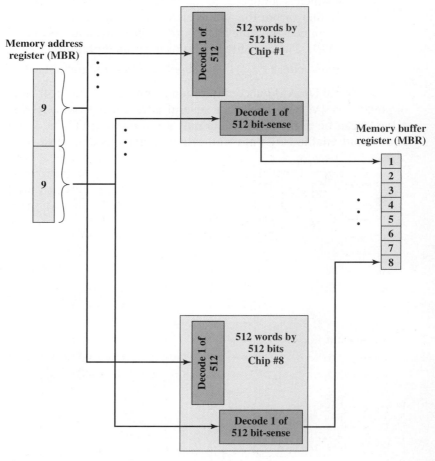

Figure 5.5   256-KByte Memory Organization

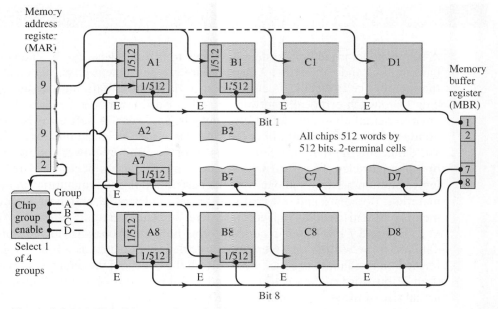

Figure 5.6   1-Mbyte Memory Organization

This organization works as long as the size of memory equals the number of bits per chip. In the case in which larger memory is required, an array of chips is needed. Figure 5.6 shows the possible organization of a memory consisting of 1M word by 8 bits per word. In this case, we have four columns of chips, each column containing 256K words arranged as in Figure 5.5. For 1M word, 20 address lines are needed. The 18 least significant bits are routed to all 32 modules. The high-order 2 bits are input to a group select logic module that sends a chip enable signal to one of the four columns of modules.

Interleaved Memory Simulator

Interleaved Memory

Main memory is composed of a collection of DRAM memory chips. A number of chips can be grouped together to form a *memory bank*. It is possible to organize the memory banks in a way known as interleaved memory. Each bank is independently able to service a memory read or write request, so that a system with K banks can service K requests simultaneously, increasing memory read or write rates by a factor of K. If consecutive words of memory are stored in different banks, then the transfer of a block of memory is speeded up. Appendix E explores the topic of interleaved memory.

5.2 ERROR CORRECTION

A semiconductor memory system is subject to errors. These can be categorized as hard failures and soft errors. A **hard failure** is a permanent physical defect so that the memory cell or cells affected cannot reliably store data but become stuck at 0 or 1 or switch erratically between 0 and 1. Hard errors can be caused by harsh environmental abuse, manufacturing defects, and wear. A **soft error** is a random, nondestructive event that alters the contents of one or more memory cells without damaging the memory. Soft errors can be caused by power supply problems or alpha particles. These particles result from radioactive decay and are distressingly common because radioactive nuclei are found in small quantities in nearly all materials. Both hard and soft errors are clearly undesirable, and most modern main memory systems include logic for both detecting and correcting errors.

Figure 5.7 illustrates in general terms how the process is carried out. When data are to be written into memory, a calculation, depicted as a function f, is performed on the data to produce a code. Both the code and the data are stored. Thus, if an M-bit word of data is to be stored and the code is of length K bits, then the actual size of the stored word is $M + K$ bits.

When the previously stored word is read out, the code is used to detect and possibly correct errors. A new set of K code bits is generated from the M data bits and compared with the fetched code bits. The comparison yields one of three results:

- No errors are detected. The fetched data bits are sent out.
- An error is detected, and it is possible to correct the error. The data bits plus **error correction** bits are fed into a corrector, which produces a corrected set of M bits to be sent out.
- An error is detected, but it is not possible to correct it. This condition is reported.

Codes that operate in this fashion are referred to as **error-correcting codes**. A code is characterized by the number of bit errors in a word that it can correct and detect.

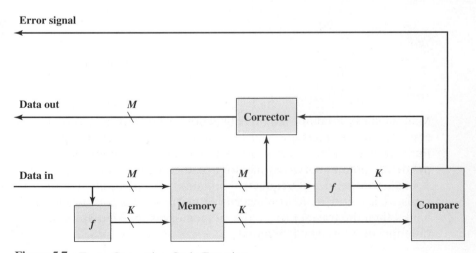

Figure 5.7 Error-Correcting Code Function

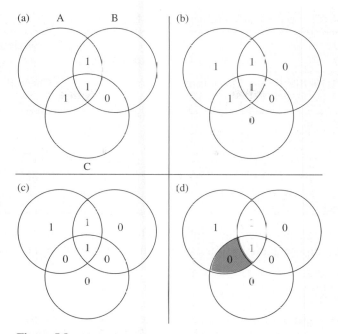

Figure 5.8 Hamming Error-Correcting Code

The simplest of the error-correcting codes is the **Hamming code** devised by Richard Hamming at Bell Laboratories. Figure 5.8 uses Venn diagrams to illustrate the use of this code on 4-bit words ($M = 4$). With three intersecting circles, there are seven compartments. We assign the 4 data bits to the inner compartments (Figure5.8a). The remaining compartments are filled with what are called *parity bits*. Each parity bit is chosen so that the total number of 1s in its circle is even (Figure5.8b). Thus, because circle A includes three data 1s, the parity bit in that circle is set to 1. Now, if an error changes one of the data bits (Figure 5.8c), it is easily found. By checking the parity bits, discrepancies are found in circle A and circle C but not in circle B. Only one of the seven compartments is in A and C but not B. The error can therefore be corrected by changing that bit.

To clarify the concepts involved, we will develop a code that can detect and correct single-bit errors in 8-bit words.

To start, let us determine how long the code must be. Referring to Figure 5.7, the comparison logic receives as input two K-bit values. A bit-by-bit comparison is done by taking the exclusive-OR of the two inputs. The result is called the *syndrome word*. Thus, each bit of the **syndrome** is 0 or 1 according to if there is or is not a match in that bit position for the two inputs.

The syndrome word is therefore K bits wide and has a range between 0 and $2^K - 1$. The value 0 indicates that no error was detected, leaving $2^K - 1$ values to indicate, if there is an error, which bit was in error. Now, because an error could occur on any of the M data bits or K check bits, we must have

$$2^K - 1 \geq M + K$$

Table 5.2 Increase in Word Length with Error Correction

Data Bits	Single-Error Correction		Single-Error Correction/ Double-Error Detection	
	Check Bits	% Increase	Check Bits	% Increase
8	4	50	5	62.5
16	5	31.25	6	37.5
32	6	18.75	7	21.875
64	7	10.94	8	12.5
128	8	6.25	9	7.03
256	9	3.52	10	3.91

This inequality gives the number of bits needed to correct a single bit error in a word containing M data bits. For example, for a word of 8 data bits ($M = 8$), we have

- $K = 3: 2^3 - 1 < 8 + 3$
- $K = 4: 2^4 - 1 > 8 + 4$

Thus, eight data bits require four check bits. The first three columns of Table 5.2 lists the number of check bits required for various data word lengths.

For convenience, we would like to generate a 4-bit syndrome for an 8-bit data word with the following characteristics:

- If the syndrome contains all 0s, no error has been detected.
- If the syndrome contains one and only one bit set to 1, then an error has occurred in one of the 4 check bits. No correction is needed.
- If the syndrome contains more than one bit set to 1, then the numerical value of the syndrome indicates the position of the data bit in error. This data bit is inverted for correction.

To achieve these characteristics, the data and check bits are arranged into a 12-bit word as depicted in Figure 5.9. The bit positions are numbered from 1 to 12. Those bit positions whose position numbers are powers of 2 are designated as check bits. The check bits are calculated as follows, where the symbol $\oplus$ designates the exclusive-OR operation:

$$C1 = D1 \oplus D2 \oplus \quad\quad D4 \oplus D5 \oplus \quad\quad\quad D7$$
$$C2 = D1 \oplus \quad\quad D3 \oplus D4 \oplus \quad\quad D6 \oplus D7$$
$$C4 = \quad\quad D2 \oplus D3 \oplus D4 \oplus \quad\quad\quad\quad D8$$
$$C8 = \quad\quad\quad\quad\quad\quad D5 \oplus D6 \oplus D7 \oplus D8$$

Bit position	12	11	10	9	8	7	6	5	4	3	2	1
Position number	1100	1011	1010	1001	1000	0111	0110	0101	0100	0011	0010	0001
Data bit	D8	D7	D6	D5		D4	D3	D2		D1		
Check bit					C8				C4		C2	C1

Figure 5.9 Layout of Data Bits and Check Bits

Each check bit operates on every data bit whose position number contains a 1 in the same bit position as the position number of that check bit. Thus, data bit positions 3, 5, 7, 9, and 11 (D1, D2, D4, D5, D7) all contain a 1 in the least significant bit of their position number as does C1; bit positions 3, 6, 7, 10, and 11 all contain a 1 in the second bit position, as does C2; and so on. Looked at another way, bit position n is checked by those bits C_i such that $\sum_i = n$. For example, position 7 is checked by bits in position 4, 2, and 1; and $7 = 4 + 2 + 1$.

Let us verify that this scheme works with an example. Assume that the 8-bit input word is 00111001, with data bit D1 in the rightmost position. The calculations are as follows:

$$C1 = 1 \oplus 0 \oplus 1 \oplus 1 \oplus 0 = 1$$
$$C2 = 1 \oplus 0 \oplus 1 \oplus 1 \oplus 0 = 1$$
$$C4 = 0 \oplus 0 \oplus 1 \oplus 0 = 1$$
$$C8 = 1 \oplus 1 \oplus 0 \oplus 0 = 0$$

Suppose now that data bit 3 sustains an error and is changed from 0 to 1. When the check bits are recalculated, we have

$$C1 = 1 \oplus 0 \oplus 1 \oplus 1 \oplus 0 = 1$$
$$C2 = 1 \oplus 1 \oplus 1 \oplus 1 \oplus 0 = 0$$
$$C4 = 0 \oplus 1 \oplus 1 \oplus 0 = 0$$
$$C8 = 1 \oplus 1 \oplus 0 \oplus 0 = 0$$

When the new check bits are compared with the old check bits, the syndrome word is formed:

	C8	C4	C2	C1
	0	1	1	1
$\oplus$	0	0	0	1
	0	1	1	0

The result is 0110, indicating that bit position 6, which contains data bit 3, is in error.

Figure 5.10 illustrates the preceding calculation. The data and check bits are positioned properly in the 12-bit word. Four of the data bits have a value 1 (shaded in the table), and their bit position values are XORed to produce the Hamming code 0111, which forms the four check digits. The entire block that is stored is

Bit position	12	11	10	9	8	7	6	5	4	3	2	1
Position number	1100	1011	1010	1001	1000	0111	0110	0101	0100	0011	0010	0001
Data bit	D8	D7	D6	D5		D4	D3	D2		D1		
Check bit					C8				C4		C2	C1
Word stored as	0	0	1	1	0	1	0	0	1	1	1	1
Word fetched as	0	0	1	1	0	1	1	0	1	1	1	1
Position number	1100	1011	1010	1001	1000	0111	0110	0101	0100	0011	0010	0001
Check bit					0				0		0	1

Figure 5.10 Check Bit Calculation

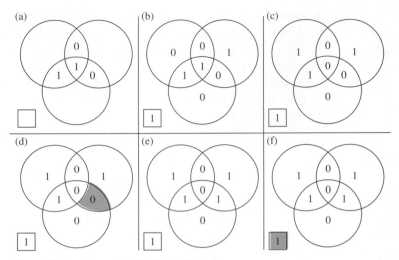

Figure 5.11 Hamming SEC-DEC Code

001101001111. Suppose now that data bit 3, in bit position 6, sustains an error and is changed from 0 to 1. The resulting block is 001101101111, with a Hamming code of 0111. An XOR of the Hamming code and all of the bit position values for nonzero data bits results in 0110. The nonzero result detects an error and indicates that the error is in bit position 6.

The code just described is known as a **single-error-correcting (SEC) code**. More commonly, semiconductor memory is equipped with a **single-error-correcting, double-error-detecting (SEC-DED) code**. As Table 5.2 shows, such codes require one additional bit compared with SEC codes.

Figure 5.11 illustrates how such a code works, again with a 4-bit data word. The sequence shows that if two errors occur (Figure 5.11c), the checking procedure goes astray (d) and worsens the problem by creating a third error (e). To overcome the problem, an eighth bit is added that is set so that the total number of 1s in the diagram is even. The extra parity bit catches the error (f).

An error-correcting code enhances the reliability of the memory at the cost of added complexity. With a 1-bit-per-chip organization, an SEC-DED code is generally considered adequate. For example, the IBM 30xx implementations used an 8-bit SEC-DED code for each 64 bits of data in main memory. Thus, the size of main memory is actually about 12% larger than is apparent to the user. The VAX computers used a 7-bit SEC-DED for each 32 bits of memory, for a 22% overhead. A number of contemporary DRAMs use 9 check bits for each 128 bits of data, for a 7% overhead [SHAR97].

5.3 ADVANCED DRAM ORGANIZATION

As discussed in Chapter 2, one of the most critical system bottlenecks when using high-performance processors is the interface to main internal memory. This interface is the most important pathway in the entire computer system. The basic building block of main memory remains the DRAM chip, as it has for decades; until

Table 5.3 Performance Comparison of Some DRAM Alternatives

	Clock Frequency (MHz)	Transfer Rate (GB/s)	Access Time (ns)	Pin Count
SDRAM	166	1.3	18	168
DDR	200	3.2	12.5	184
RDRAM	600	4.8	12	162

recently, there had been no significant changes in DRAM architecture since the early 1970s. The traditional DRAM chip is constrained both by its internal architecture and by its interface to the processor's memory bus.

We have seen that one attack on the performance problem of DRAM main memory has been to insert one or more levels of high-speed SRAM cache between the DRAM main memory and the processor. But SRAM is much costlier than DRAM, and expanding cache size beyond a certain point yields diminishing returns.

In recent years, a number of enhancements to the basic DRAM architecture have been explored, and some of these are now on the market. The schemes that currently dominate the market are SDRAM, DDR-DRAM, and RDRAM. Table 5.3 provides a performance comparison. CDRAM has also received considerable attention. We examine each of these approaches in this section.

Synchronous DRAM

One of the most widely used forms of DRAM is the **synchronous DRAM (SDRAM)** [VOGL94]. Unlike the traditional DRAM, which is asynchronous, the SDRAM exchanges data with the processor synchronized to an external clock signal and running at the full speed of the processor/memory bus without imposing wait states.

In a typical DRAM, the processor presents addresses and control levels to the memory, indicating that a set of data at a particular location in memory should be either read from or written into the DRAM. After a delay, the access time, the DRAM either writes or reads the data. During the access-time delay, the DRAM performs various internal functions, such as activating the high capacitance of the row and column lines, sensing the data, and routing the data out through the output buffers. The processor must simply wait through this delay, slowing system performance.

With synchronous access, the DRAM moves data in and out under control of the system clock. The processor or other master issues the instruction and address information, which is latched by the DRAM. The DRAM then responds after a set number of clock cycles. Meanwhile, the master can safely do other tasks while the SDRAM is processing the request.

Figure 5.12 shows the internal logic of IBM's 64-Mb SDRAM [IBM01], which is typical of SDRAM organization, and Table 5.4 defines the various pin assignments. The SDRAM employs a burst mode to eliminate the address setup time and row and column line precharge time after the first access. In burst mode, a series of

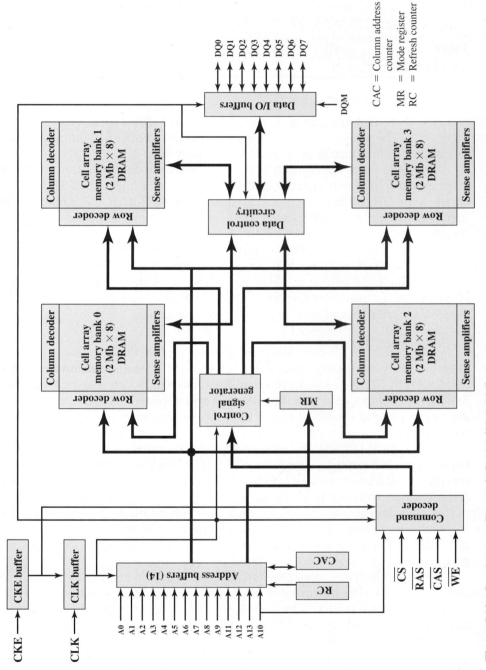

Figure 5.12 Synchronous Dynamic RAM (SDRAM)

Table 5.4 SDRAM Pin Assignments

A0 to A13	Address inputs
CLK	Clock input
CKE	Clock enable
$\overline{CS}$	Chip select
$\overline{RAS}$	Row address strobe
$\overline{CAS}$	Column address strobe
$\overline{WE}$	Write enable
DQ0 to DQ7	Data input/output
DQM	Data mask

data bits can be clocked out rapidly after the first bit has been accessed. This mode is useful when all the bits to be accessed are in sequence and in the same row of the array as the initial access. In addition, the SDRAM has a multiple-bank internal architecture that improves opportunities for on-chip parallelism.

The mode register and associated control logic is another key feature differentiating SDRAMs from conventional DRAMs. It provides a mechanism to customize the SDRAM to suit specific system needs. The mode register specifies the burst length, which is the number of separate units of data synchronously fed onto the bus. The register also allows the programmer to adjust the latency between receipt of a read request and the beginning of data transfer.

The SDRAM performs best when it is transferring large blocks of data serially, such as for applications like word processing, spreadsheets, and multimedia.

Figure 5.13 shows an example of SDRAM operation. In this case, the burst length is 4 and the latency is 2. The burst read command is initiated by having $\overline{CS}$ and $\overline{CAS}$ low while holding $\overline{RAS}$ and $\overline{WE}$ high at the rising edge of the clock. The address inputs determine the starting column address for the burst, and the mode register sets the type of burst (sequential or interleave) and the burst length (1, 2, 4, 8, full page). The delay from the start of the command to when the data from the first cell appears on the outputs is equal to the value of the $\overline{CAS}$ latency that is set in the mode register.

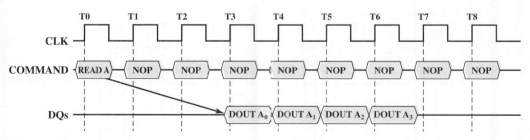

Figure 5.13 SDRAM Read Timing (burst length = 4, $\overline{CAS}$ latency = 2)

There is now an enhanced version of SDRAM, known as double data rate SDRAM (DDR-SDRAM) that overcomes the once-per-cycle limitation. DDR-SDRAM can send data to the processor twice per clock cycle.

Rambus DRAM

RDRAM, developed by Rambus [FARM92, CRIS97], has been adopted by Intel for its Pentium and Itanium processors. It has become the main competitor to SDRAM. RDRAM chips are vertical packages, with all pins on one side. The chip exchanges data with the processor over 28 wires no more than 12 centimeters long. The bus can address up to 320 RDRAM chips and is rated at 1.6 GBps.

The special RDRAM bus delivers address and control information using an asynchronous block-oriented protocol. After an initial 480 ns access time, this produces the 1.6 GBps data rate. What makes this speed possible is the bus itself, which defines impedances, clocking, and signals very precisely. Rather than being controlled by the explicit RAS, CAS, R/W, and CE signals used in conventional DRAMs, an RDRAM gets a memory request over the high-speed bus. This request contains the desired address, the type of operation, and the number of bytes in the operation.

Figure 5.14 illustrates the RDRAM layout. The configuration consists of a controller and a number of RDRAM modules connected via a common bus. The controller is at one end of the configuration, and the far end of the bus is a parallel termination of the bus lines. The bus includes 18 data lines (16 actual data, two parity) cycling at twice the clock rate; that is, 1 bit is sent at the leading and following edge of each clock signal. This results in a signal rate on each data line of 800 Mbps. There is a separate set of 8 lines (RC) used for address and control signals. There is also a clock signal that starts at the far end from the controller propagates to the controller end and then loops back. A RDRAM module sends data to the controller synchronously to the clock to master, and the controller sends data to an RDRAM synchronously with the clock signal in the opposite direction. The remaining bus lines include a reference voltage, ground, and power source.

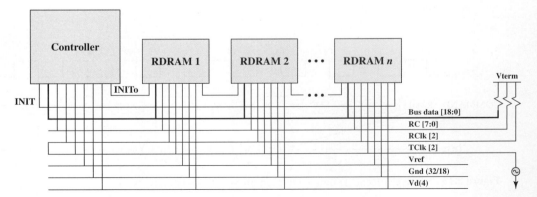

Figure 5.14 RDRAM Structure

DDR SDRAM

SDRAM is limited by the fact that it can only send data to the processor once per bus clock cycle. A new version of SDRAM, referred to as double-data-rate SDRAM can send data twice per clock cycle, once on the rising edge of the clock pulse and once on the falling edge.

DDR DRAM was developed by the JEDEC Solid State Technology Association, the Electronic Industries Alliance's semiconductor-engineering-standardization body. Numerous companies make DDR chips, which are widely used in desktop computers and servers.

Figure 5.15 shows the basic timing for a DDR read. The data transfer is synchronized to both the rising and falling edge of the clock. It is also synchronized to a bidirectional data strobe (DQS) signal that is provided by the memory controller during a read and by the DRAM during a write. In typical implementations the

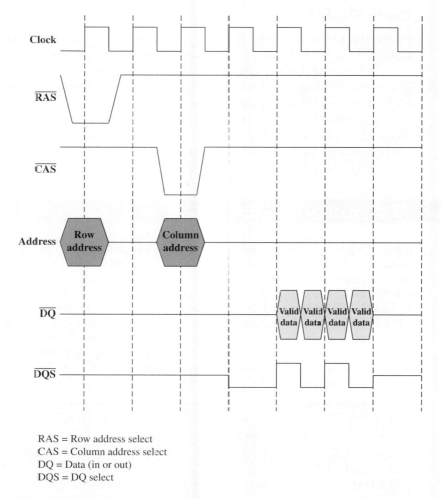

RAS = Row address select
CAS = Column address select
DQ = Data (in or out)
DQS = DQ select

Figure 5.15 DDR SDRAM Road Timing

DQS is ignored during the read. An explanation of the use of DQS on writes is beyond our scope; see [JACO08] for details.

There have been two generations of improvement to the DDR technology. DDR2 increases the data transfer rate by increasing the operational frequency of the RAM chip and by increasing the prefetch buffer from 2 bits to 4 bits per chip. The prefetch buffer is a memory cache located on the RAM chip. The buffer enables theRAM chip to preposition bits to be placed on the data bus as rapidly as possible. DDR3, introduced in 2007, increases the prefetch buffer size to 8 bits.

Theoretically, a DDR module can transfer data at a clock rate in the range of 200 to 600 MHz; a DDR2 module transfers at a clock rate of 400 to 1066 MHz; and a DDR3 module transfers at a clock rate of 800 to 1600 MHz. In practice, somewhat smaller rates are achieved.

Appendix K provides more detail on DDR technology.

Cache DRAM

Cache DRAM (CDRAM), developed by Mitsubishi [HIDA90, ZHAN01], integrates a small SRAM cache (16 Kb) onto a generic DRAM chip.

The SRAM on the CDRAM can be used in two ways. First, it can be used as a true cache, consisting of a number of 64-bit lines. The cache mode of the CDRAM is effective for ordinary random access to memory.

The SRAM on the CDRAM can also be used as a buffer to support the serial access of a block of data. For example, to refresh a bit-mapped screen, the CDRAM can prefetch the data from the DRAM into the SRAM buffer. Subsequent accesses to the chip result in accesses solely to the SRAM.

5.4 RECOMMENDED READING

[PRIN97] provides a comprehensive treatment of semiconductor memory technologies, including SRAM, DRAM, and flash memories. [SHAR97] covers the same material, with more emphasis on testing and reliability issues. [SHAR03] and [PRIN02] focus on advanced DRAM and SRAM architectures. For an in-depth look at DRAM, see [JACO08] and [KEET01]. [CUPP01] provides an interesting performance comparison of various DRAM schemes. [BEZ03] is a comprehensive introduction to flash memory technology.

A good explanation of error-correcting codes is contained in [MCEL85]. For a deeper study, worthwhile book-length treatments are [ADAM91] and [BLAH83]. A readable theoretical and mathematical treatment of error-correcting codes is [ASH90]. [SHAR97] contains a good survey of codes used in contemporary main memories.

ADAM91   Adamek, J. *Foundations of Coding.* New York: Wiley, 1991.

ASH90   Ash, R. *Information Theory.* New York: Dover, 1990.

BEZ03   Bez, R.; et al. Introduction to Flash Memory. *Proceedings of the IEEE,* April 2003.

BLAH83   Blahut, R. *Theory and Practice of Error Control Codes.* Reading, MA: Addison-Wesley, 1983.

CUPP01 Cuppu, V., et al. "High Performance DRAMS in Workstation Environments." *IEEE Transactions on Computers*, November 2001.

JACO08 Jacob, B.; Ng, S.; and Wang, D. *Memory Systems: Cache, DRAM, Disk.* Boston: Morgan Kaufmann, 2008.

KEET01 Keeth, B., and Baker, R. *DRAM Circuit Design: A Tutorial.* Piscataway, NJ: IEEE Press, 2001.

MCEL85 McEliece, R. "The Reliability of Computer Memories." *Scientific American*, January 1985.

PRIN97 Prince, B. *Semiconductor Memories.* New York: Wiley, 1997.

PRIN02 Prince, B. *Emerging Memories: Technologies and Trends.* Norwell, MA: Kluwer, 2002.

SHAR97 Sharma, A. *Semiconductor Memories: Technology, Testing, and Reliability.* New York: IEEE Press, 1997.

SHAR03 Sharma, A. *Advanced Semiconductor Memories: Architectures, Designs, and Applications.* New York: IEEE Press, 2003.

5.5 KEY TERMS, REVIEW QUESTIONS, AND PROBLEMS

Key Terms

cache DRAM (CDRAM)	Hamming code	single-error-correcting (SEC) code
dynamic RAM (DRAM)	hard failure	single-error-correcting, double-error-detecting (SEC-DED) code
electrically erasable programmable ROM (EEPROM)	nonvolatile memory	
	programmable ROM (PROM)	
erasable programmable ROM (EPROM)	RamBus DRAM (RDRAM)	soft error
error correcting code (ECC)	read-mostly memory	static RAM (SRAM)
	read-only memory (ROM)	synchronous DRAM (SDRAM)
error correction		syndrome
flash memory	semiconductor memory	volatile memory

Review Questions

5.1 What are the key properties of semiconductor memory?

5.2 What are two interpretations of the term *random-access memory*?

5.3 What is the difference between DRAM and SRAM in terms of application?

5.4 What is the difference between DRAM and SRAM in terms of characteristics such as speed, size, and cost?

5.5 Explain why one type of RAM is considered to be analog and the other digital.

5.6 What are some applications for ROM?

5.7 What are the differences among EPROM, EEPROM, and flash memory?

5.8 Explain the function of each pin in Figure 5.4b.

5.9   What is a parity bit?

5.10 How is the syndrome for the Hamming code interpreted?

5.11 How does SDRAM differ from ordinary DRAM?

Problems

5.1   Suggest reasons why RAMs traditionally have been organized as only 1 bit per chip whereas ROMs are usually organized with multiple bits per chip.

5.2   Consider a dynamic RAM that must be given a refresh cycle 64 times per ms. Each refresh operation requires 150 ns; a memory cycle requires 250 ns. What percentage of the memory's total operating time must be given to refreshes?

5.3   Figure 5.16 shows a simplified timing diagram for a DRAM read operation over a bus. The access time is considered to last from t_1 to t_2. Then there is a recharge time, lasting from t_2 to t_3, during which the DRAM chips will have to recharge before the processor can access them again.

  a.   Assume that the access time is 60 ns and the recharge time is 40 ns. What is the memory cycle time? What is the maximum data rate this DRAM can sustain, assuming a 1-bit output?

  b.   Constructing a 32-bit wide memory system using these chips yields what data transfer rate?

5.4   Figure 5.6 indicates how to construct a module of chips that can store 1 MByte based on a group of four 256-Kbyte chips. Let's say this module of chips is packaged as a single 1-Mbyte chip, where the word size is 1 byte. Give a high-level chip diagram of how to construct an 8-Mbyte computer memory using eight 1-Mbyte chips. Be sure to show the address lines in your diagram and what the address lines are used for.

5.5   On a typical Intel 8086-based system, connected via system bus to DRAM memory, for a read operation, $\overline{RAS}$ is activated by the trailing edge of the Address Enable signal (Figure 3.19). However, due to propagation and other delays, $\overline{RAS}$ does not go active until 50 ns after Address Enable returns to a low. Assume the latter occurs in the middle of the second half of state T_1 (somewhat earlier than in Figure 3.19). Data are read by the processor at the end of T_3. For timely presentation to the processor, however, data must be provided 60 ns earlier by memory. This interval accounts for

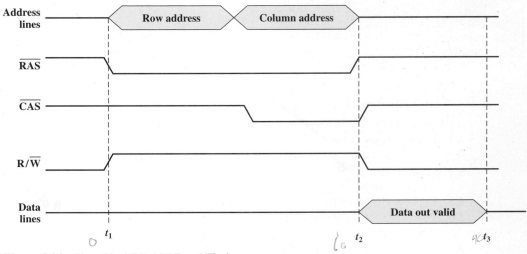

Figure 5.16   Simplified DRAM Read Timing

propagation delays along the data paths (from memory to processor) and processor data hold time requirements. Assume a clocking rate of 10 MHz.

    a. How fast (access time) should the DRAMs be if no wait states are to be inserted?

    b. How many wait states do we have to insert per memory read operation if the access time of the DRAMs is 150 ns?

5.6 The memory of a particular microcomputer is built from 64K $\times$ 1 DRAMs. According to the data sheet, the cell array of the DRAM is organized into 256 rows. Each row must be refreshed at least once every 4 ms. Suppose we refresh the memory on a strictly periodic basis.

    a. What is the time period between successive refresh requests?

    b. How long a refresh address counter do we need?

5.7 Figure 5.17 shows one of the early SRAMs, the 16 $\times$ 4 Signetics 7489 chip, which stores 16 4-bit words.

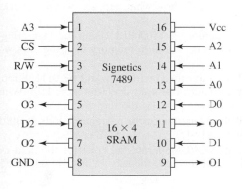

(a) Pin layout

Operating Mode	Inputs			Outputs
	$\overline{CS}$	$R/\overline{W}$	Dn	On
Write	L	L	L	L
	L	L	H	H
Read	L	H	X	Data
Inhibit writing	H	L	L	H
	H	L	H	L
Store - disable outputs	H	H	X	H

H = high voltage level
L = low voltage level
X = don't care

(b) Truth table

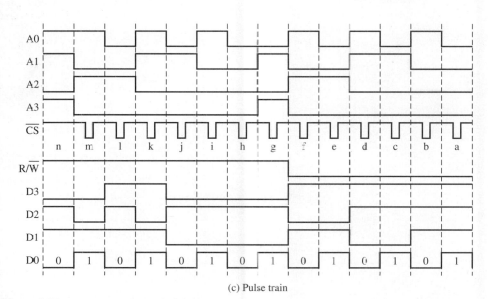

(c) Pulse train

Figure 5.17   The Signetics 7489 SRAM

    a. List the mode of operation of the chip for each $\overline{CS}$ input pulse shown in Figure 5.17c.

    b. List the memory contents of word locations 0 through 6 after pulse n.

    c. What is the state of the output data leads for the input pulses h through m?

5.8 Design a 16-bit memory of total capacity 8192 bits using SRAM chips of size 64 × 1 bit. Give the array configuration of the chips on the memory board showing all required input and output signals for assigning this memory to the lowest address space. The design should allow for both byte and 16-bit word accesses.

5.9 A common unit of measure for failure rates of electronic components is the **Failure unIT** (FIT), expressed as a rate of failures per billion device hours. Another well known but less used measure is **mean time between failures** (MTBF), which is the average time of operation of a particular component until it fails. Consider a 1 MB memory of a 16-bit microprocessor with 256K × 1 DRAMs. Calculate its MTBF assuming 2000 FITS for each DRAM.

5.10 For the Hamming code shown in Figure 5.10, show what happens when a check bit rather than a data bit is in error?

5.11 Suppose an 8-bit data word stored in memory is 11000010. Using the Hamming algorithm, determine what check bits would be stored in memory with the data word. Show how you got your answer.

5.12 For the 8-bit word 00111001, the check bits stored with it would be 0111. Suppose when the word is read from memory, the check bits are calculated to be 1101. What is the data word that was read from memory?

5.13 How many check bits are needed if the Hamming error correction code is used to detect single bit errors in a 1024-bit data word?

5.14 Develop an SEC code for a 16-bit data word. Generate the code for the data word 0101000000111001. Show that the code will correctly identify an error in data bit 5.

CHAPTER 6

EXTERNAL MEMORY

LEARNING OBJECTIVES

After studying this chapter, you should be able to:

◆ Understand the key properties of magnetic disks.

◆ Understand the performance issues involved in **magnetic disk** access.

◆ Explain the concept of **RAID** and describe the various levels.

◆ Compare and contrast hard disk drives and solid disk drives.

◆ Describe in general terms the operation of **flash memory**.

◆ Understand the differences among the different optical disk storage media.

◆ Present an overview of **magnetic tape** storage technology.

This chapter examines a range of external memory devices and systems. We begin with the most important device, the magnetic disk. Magnetic disks are the foundation of external memory on virtually all computer systems. The next section examines the use of disk arrays to achieve greater performance, looking specifically at the family of systems known as RAID (Redundant Array of Independent Disks). An increasingly important component of many computer systems is the solid state disk, which is discussed next. Then, external **optical memory** is examined. Finally, magnetic tape is described.

6.1 MAGNETIC DISK

A disk is a circular **platter** constructed of nonmagnetic material, called the **substrate**, coated with a magnetizable material. Traditionally, the substrate has been an aluminum or aluminum alloy material. More recently, glass substrates have been introduced. The glass substrate has a number of benefits, including the following:

- Improvement in the uniformity of the magnetic film surface to increase disk reliability
- A significant reduction in overall surface defects to help reduce read-write errors
- Ability to support lower fly heights (described subsequently)
- Better stiffness to reduce disk dynamics
- Greater ability to withstand shock and damage

Magnetic Read and Write Mechanisms

Data are recorded on and later retrieved from the disk via a conducting coil named the **head**; in many systems, there are two heads, a read head and a write head. During a read or write operation, the head is stationary while the platter rotates beneath it.

The write mechanism exploits the fact that electricity flowing through a coil produces a magnetic field. Electric pulses are sent to the write head, and the resulting magnetic patterns are recorded on the surface below, with different patterns for positive and negative currents. The write head itself is made of easily magnetizable

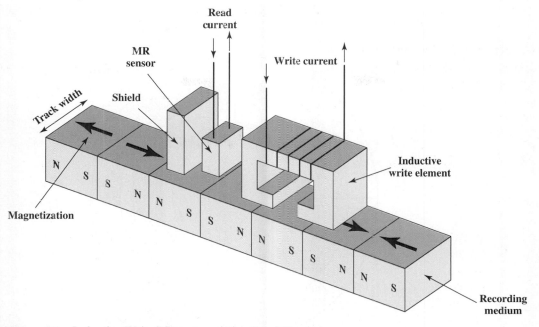

Figure 6.1   Inductive Write/Magnetoresistive Read Head

material and is in the shape of a rectangular doughnut with a gap along one side and a few turns of conducting wire along the opposite side (Figure 6.1). An electric current in the wire induces a magnetic field across the gap, which in turn magnetizes a small area of the recording medium. Reversing the direction of the current reverses the direction of the magnetization on the recording medium.

The traditional read mechanism exploits the fact that a magnetic field moving relative to a coil produces an electrical current in the coil. When the surface of the disk passes under the head, it generates a current of the same polarity as the one already recorded. The structure of the head for reading is in this case essentially the same as for writing and therefore the same head can be used for both. Such single heads are used in floppy disk systems and in older rigid disk systems.

Contemporary rigid disk systems use a different read mechanism, requiring a separate read head, positioned for convenience close to the write head. The read head consists of a partially shielded **magnetoresistive** (MR) sensor. The MR material has an electrical resistance that depends on the direction of the magnetization of the medium moving under it. By passing a current through the MR sensor, resistance changes are detected as voltage signals. The MR design allows higher-frequency operation, which equates to greater storage densities and operating speeds.

Data Organization and Formatting

The head is a relatively small device capable of reading from or writing to a portion of the platter rotating beneath it. This gives rise to the organization of data on the platter in a concentric set of rings, called **tracks**. Each track is the same width as the head. There are thousands of tracks per surface.

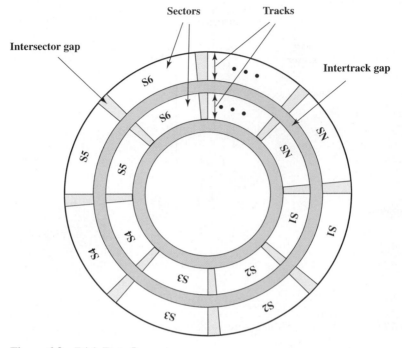

Figure 6.2   Disk Data Layout

Figure 6.2 depicts this data layout. Adjacent tracks are separated by **gaps**. This prevents, or at least minimizes, errors due to misalignment of the head or simply interference of magnetic fields.

Data are transferred to and from the disk in **sectors** (Figure 6.2). There are typically hundreds of sectors per track, and these may be of either fixed or variable length. In most contemporary systems, fixed-length sectors are used, with 512 bytes being the nearly universal sector size. To avoid imposing unreasonable precision requirements on the system, adjacent sectors are separated by intratrack (intersector) gaps.

A bit near the center of a rotating disk travels past a fixed point (such as a read–write head) slower than a bit on the outside. Therefore, some way must be found to compensate for the variation in speed so that the head can read all the bits at the same rate. This can be done by increasing the spacing between bits of information recorded in segments of the disk. The information can then be scanned at the same rate by rotating the disk at a fixed speed, known as the **constant angular velocity** (CAV). Figure 6.3a shows the layout of a disk using CAV. The disk is divided into a number of pie-shaped sectors and into a series of concentric tracks. The advantage of using CAV is that individual blocks of data can be directly addressed by track and sector. To move the head from its current location to a specific address, it only takes a short movement of the head to a specific track and a short wait for the proper sector to spin under the head. The disadvantage of CAV is that the amount of data that can be stored on the long outer tracks is the only same as what can be stored on the short inner tracks.

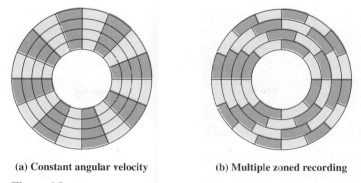

(a) Constant angular velocity   **(b) Multiple zoned recording**

Figure 6.3   Comparison of Disk Layout Methods

Because the **density**, in bits per linear inch, increases in moving from the outermost track to the innermost track, disk storage capacity in a straightforward CAV system is limited by the maximum recording density that can be achieved on the innermost track. To increase density, modern hard disk systems use a technique known as **multiple zone recording**, in which the surface is divided into a number of concentric zones (16 is typical). Within a zone, the number of bits per track is constant. Zones farther from the center contain more bits (more sectors) than zones closer to the center. This allows for greater overall storage capacity at the expense of somewhat more complex circuitry. As the disk head moves from one zone to another, the length (along the track) of individual bits changes, causing a change in the timing for reads and writes. Figure 6.3b suggests the nature of multiple zone recording; in this illustration, each zone is only a single track wide.

Some means is needed to locate sector positions within a track. Clearly, there must be some starting point on the track and a way of identifying the start and end of each sector. These requirements are handled by means of control data recorded on the disk. Thus, the disk is formatted with some extra data used only by the disk drive and not accessible to the user.

An example of disk formatting is shown in Figure 6.4. In this case, each track contains 30 fixed-length sectors of 600 bytes each. Each sector holds 512 bytes of

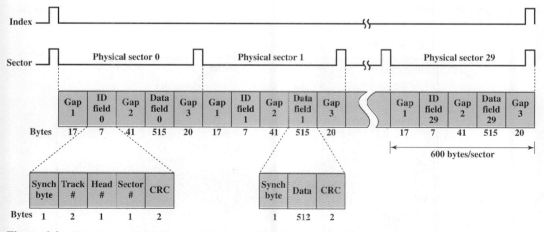

Figure 6.4   Winchester Disk Format (Seagate ST506)

data plus control information useful to the disk controller. The ID field is a unique identifier or address used to locate a particular sector. The SYNCH byte is a special bit pattern that delimits the beginning of the field. The track number identifies a track on a surface. The head number identifies a head, because this disk has multiple surfaces (explained presently). The ID and data fields each contain an error-detecting code.

Physical Characteristics

Table 6.1 lists the major characteristics that differentiate among the various types of magnetic disks. First, the head may either be fixed or movable with respect to the radial direction of the platter. In a **fixed-head disk**, there is one read-write head per track. All of the heads are mounted on a rigid arm that extends across all tracks; such systems are rare today. In a **movable-head disk**, there is only one read-write head. Again, the head is mounted on an arm. Because the head must be able to be positioned above any track, the arm can be extended or retracted for this purpose.

The disk itself is mounted in a disk drive, which consists of the arm, a spindle that rotates the disk, and the electronics needed for input and output of binary data. A **nonremovable disk** is permanently mounted in the disk drive; the hard disk in a personal computer is a nonremovable disk. A **removable disk** can be removed and replaced with another disk. The advantage of the latter type is that unlimited amounts of data are available with a limited number of disk systems. Furthermore, such a disk may be moved from one computer system to another. Floppy disks and ZIP cartridge disks are examples of removable disks.

For most disks, the magnetizable coating is applied to both sides of the platter, which is then referred to as **double sided**. Some less expensive disk systems use **single-sided** disks.

Some disk drives accommodate **multiple platters** stacked vertically a fraction of an inch apart. Multiple arms are provided (Figure 6.5). Multiple–platter disks employ a movable head, with one read-write head per platter surface. All of the heads are mechanically fixed so that all are at the same distance from the center of the disk and move together. Thus, at any time, all of the heads are positioned over

Table 6.1   Physical Characteristics of Disk Systems

Head Motion		**Platters**
Fixed head (one per track)		Single platter
Movable head (one per surface)		Multiple platter
Disk Portability		**Head Mechanism**
Nonremovable disk		Contact (floppy)
Removable disk		Fixed gap
		Aerodynamic gap (Winchester)
Sides		
Single sided		
Double sided		

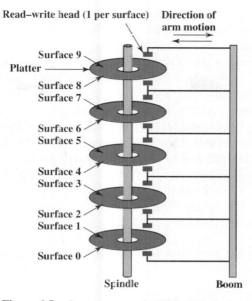

Figure 6.5   Components of a Disk Drive

tracks that are of equal distance from the center of the disk. The set of all the tracks in the same relative position on the platter is referred to as a **cylinder**. For example, all of the shaded tracks in Figure 6.6 are part of one cylinder.

Finally, the head mechanism provides a classification of disks into three types. Traditionally, the read-write head has been positioned a fixed distance above the platter, allowing an air gap. At the other extreme is a head mechanism that actually comes into physical contact with the medium during a read or write operation. This mechanism is used with the **floppy disk**, which is a small, flexible platter and the least expensive type of disk.

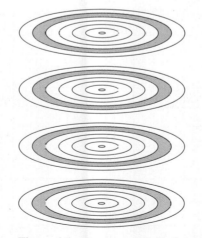

Figure 6.6   Tracks and Cylinders

To understand the third type of disk, we need to comment on the relationship between data density and the size of the air gap. The head must generate or sense an electromagnetic field of sufficient magnitude to write and read properly. The narrower the head is, the closer it must be to the platter surface to function. A narrower head means narrower tracks and therefore greater data density, which is desirable. However, the closer the head is to the disk, the greater the risk of error from impurities or imperfections. To push the technology further, the Winchester disk was developed. Winchester heads are used in sealed drive assemblies that are almost free of contaminants. They are designed to operate closer to the disk's surface than conventional rigid disk heads, thus allowing greater data density. The head is actually an aerodynamic foil that rests lightly on the platter's surface when the disk is motionless. The air pressure generated by a spinning disk is enough to make the foil rise above the surface. The resulting noncontact system can be engineered to use narrower heads that operate closer to the platter's surface than conventional rigid disk heads.

Table 6.2 gives disk parameters for typical contemporary high-performance disks.

Disk Performance Parameters

The actual details of disk I/O operation depend on the computer system, the operating system, and the nature of the I/O channel and disk controller hardware. A general timing diagram of disk I/O transfer is shown in Figure 6.7.

When the disk drive is operating, the disk is rotating at constant speed. To read or write, the head must be positioned at the desired track and at the beginning of the desired sector on that track. Track selection involves moving the head in a

Table 6.2 Typical Hard Disk Drive Parameters

Characteristics	Constellation ES.2	Seagate Barracuda XT	Cheetah NS	Momentus
Application	Enterprise	Desktop	Network attached storage, application servers	Laptop
Capacity	3 TB	3 TB	400 GB	640 GB
Average seek time	8.5 ms read 9.5 ms write	N/A	3.9 ms read 4.2 ms write	13 ms
Spindle speed	7200 rpm	7200 rpm	10, 075 rpm	5400 rpm
Average latency	4.16 ms	4.16 ms	2.98	5.6 ms
Maximum sustained transfer rate	155 MB/s	149 MB/s	97 MB/s	300 MB/s
Bytes per sector	512	512	512	4096
Tracks per cylinder (number of platter surfaces)	8	10	8	4
Cache	64 MB	64 MB	16 MB	8 MB

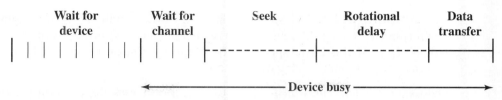

Figure 6.7 Timing of a Disk I/O Transfer

movable-head system or electronically selecting one head on a fixed-head system. On a movable-head system, the time it takes to position the head at the track is known as **seek time**. In either case, once the track is selected, the disk controller waits until the appropriate sector rotates to line up with the head. The time it takes for the beginning of the sector to reach the head is known as **rotational delay**, or *rotational latency*. The sum of the seek time, if any, and the rotational delay equals the **access time**, which is the time it takes to get into position to read or write. Once the head is in position, the read or write operation is then performed as the sector moves under the head; this is the data transfer portion of the operation; the time required for the transfer is the **transfer time**.

In addition to the access time and transfer time, there are several queuing delays normally associated with a disk I/O operation. When a process issues an I/O request, it must first wait in a queue for the device to be available. At that time, the device is assigned to the process. If the device shares a single I/O channel or a set of I/O channels with other disk drives, then there may be an additional wait for the channel to be available. At that point, the seek is performed to begin disk access.

In some high-end systems for servers, a technique known as rotational positional sensing (RPS) is used. This works as follows: When the seek command has been issued, the channel is released to handle other I/O operations. When the seek is completed, the device determines when the data will rotate under the head. As that sector approaches the head, the device tries to reestablish the communication path back to the host. If either the control unit or the channel is busy with another I/O, then the reconnection attempt fails and the device must rotate one whole revolution before it can attempt to reconnect, which is called an RPS miss. This is an extra delay element that must be added to the timeline of Figure 6.7.

SEEK TIME Seek time is the time required to move the disk arm to the required track. It turns out that this is a difficult quantity to pin down. The seek time consists of two key components: the initial startup time, and the time taken to traverse the tracks that have to be crossed once the access arm is up to speed. Unfortunately, the traversal time is not a linear function of the number of tracks, but includes a settling time (time after positioning the head over the target track until track identification is confirmed).

Much improvement comes from smaller and lighter disk components. Some years ago, a typical disk was 14 inches (36 cm) in diameter, whereas the most common size today is 3.5 inches (8.9 cm), reducing the distance that the arm has to travel. A typical average seek time on contemporary hard disks is under 10 ms.

ROTATIONAL DELAY Disks, other than floppy disks, rotate at speeds ranging from 3600 rpm (for handheld devices such as digital cameras) up to, as of this writing, 20,000 rpm; at this latter speed, there is one revolution per 3 ms. Thus, on the average, the rotational delay will be 1.5 ms.

TRANSFER TIME The transfer time to or from the disk depends on the rotation speed of the disk in the following fashion:

$$T = \frac{b}{rN}$$

where

T = transfer time

b = number of bytes to be transferred

N = number of bytes on a track

r = rotation speed, in revolutions per second

Thus the total average access time can be expressed as

$$T_a = T_s + \frac{1}{2r} + \frac{b}{rN}$$

where T_s is the average seek time. Note that on a zoned drive, the number of bytes per track is variable, complicating the calculation.[1]

A TIMING COMPARISON With the foregoing parameters defined, let us look at two different I/O operations that illustrate the danger of relying on average values. Consider a disk with an advertised average seek time of 4 ms, rotation speed of 15,000 rpm, and 512-byte sectors with 500 sectors per track. Suppose that we wish to read a file consisting of 2500 sectors for a total of 1.28 Mbytes. We would like to estimate the total time for the transfer.

First, let us assume that the file is stored as compactly as possible on the disk. That is, the file occupies all of the sectors on 5 adjacent tracks (5 tracks × 500 sectors/ track = 2500 sectors). This is known as *sequential organization*. Now, the time to read the first track is as follows:

Average seek	4 ms
Average rotational delay	2 ms
Read 500 sectors	4 ms
	10 ms

Suppose that the remaining tracks can now be read with essentially no seek time. That is, the I/O operation can keep up with the flow from the disk. Then, at most, we need to deal with rotational delay for each succeeding track. Thus each successive track is read in 2 + 4 = 6 ms. To read the entire file,

Total time = 10 + (4 × 6) = 34 ms = 0.034 seconds

---

[1]Compare the two preceding equations to Equation (4.1).

Now let us calculate the time required to read the same data using random access rather than sequential access; that is, accesses to the sectors are distributed randomly over the disk. For each sector, we have

Average seek	4	ms
Rotational delay	2	ms
Read 1 sectors	0.008 ms	
	6.008 ms	

$$\text{Total time} = 2500 \times 6.008 = 15{,}020 \text{ ms} = 15.02 \text{ seconds}$$

It is clear that the order in which sectors are read from the disk has a tremendous effect on I/O performance. In the case of file access in which multiple sectors are read or written, we have some control over the way in which sectors of data are deployed. However, even in the case of a file access, in a multiprogramming environment, there will be I/O requests competing for the same disk. Thus, it is worthwhile to examine ways in which the performance of disk I/O can be improved over that achieved with purely random access to the disk. This leads to a consideration of disk scheduling algorithms, which is the province of the operating system and beyond the scope of this book (see [STAL12] for a discussion).

RAID Simulator

6.2 RAID

As discussed earlier, the rate in improvement in secondary storage performance has been considerably less than the rate for processors and main memory. This mismatch has made the disk storage system perhaps the main focus of concern in improving overall computer system performance.

As in other areas of computer performance, disk storage designers recognize that if one component can only be pushed so far, additional gains in performance are to be had by using multiple parallel components. In the case of disk storage, this leads to the development of arrays of disks that operate independently and in parallel. With multiple disks, separate I/O requests can be handled in parallel, as long as the data required reside on separate disks. Further, a single I/O request can be executed in parallel if the block of data to be accessed is distributed across multiple disks.

With the use of multiple disks, there is a wide variety of ways in which the data can be organized and in which redundancy can be added to improve reliability. This could make it difficult to develop database schemes that are usable on a number of platforms and operating systems. Fortunately, industry has agreed on a standardized scheme for multiple-disk database design, known as

RAID (Redundant Array of Independent Disks). The RAID scheme consists of seven levels,[2] zero through six. These levels do not imply a hierarchical relationship but designate different design architectures that share three common characteristics:

1. RAID is a set of physical disk drives viewed by the operating system as a single logical drive.

2. Data are distributed across the physical drives of an array in a scheme known as striping, described subsequently.

3. Redundant disk capacity is used to store parity information, which guarantees data recoverability in case of a disk failure.

The details of the second and third characteristics differ for the different RAID levels. RAID 0 and RAID 1 do not support the third characteristic.

The term *RAID* was originally coined in a paper by a group of researchers at the University of California at Berkeley [PATT88].[3] The paper outlined various RAID configurations and applications and introduced the definitions of the RAID levels that are still used. The RAID strategy employs multiple disk drives and distributes data in such a way as to enable simultaneous access to data from multiple drives, thereby improving I/O performance and allowing easier incremental increases in capacity.

The unique contribution of the RAID proposal is to address effectively the need for redundancy. Although allowing multiple heads and actuators to operate simultaneously achieves higher I/O and transfer rates, the use of multiple devices increases the probability of failure. To compensate for this decreased reliability, RAID makes use of stored parity information that enables the recovery of data lost due to a disk failure.

We now examine each of the RAID levels. Table 6.3 provides a rough guide to the seven levels. In the table, I/O performance is shown both in terms of data transfer capacity, or ability to move data, and I/O request rate, or ability to satisfy I/O requests, since these RAID levels inherently perform differently relative to these two metrics. Each RAID level's strong point is highlighted by darker shading. Figure 6.8 illustrates the use of the seven RAID schemes to support a data capacity requiring four disks with no redundancy. The figures highlight the layout of user data and redundant data and indicates the relative storage requirements of the various levels. We refer to these figures throughout the following discussion.

---

[2]Additional levels have been defined by some researchers and some companies, but the seven levels described in this section are the ones universally agreed on.

[3]In that paper, the acronym RAID stood for Redundant Array of Inexpensive Disks. The term *inexpensive* was used to contrast the small relatively inexpensive disks in the RAID array to the alternative, a single large expensive disk (SLED). The SLED is essentially a thing of the past, with similar disk technology being used for both RAID and non-RAID configurations. Accordingly, the industry has adopted the term *independent* to emphasize that the RAID array creates significant performance and reliability gains.

Table 6.3 RAID Levels

Category	Level	Description	Disks Required	Data Availability	Large I/O Data Transfer Capacity	Small I/O Request Rate
Striping	0	Nonredundant	N	Lower than single disk	Very high	Very high for both read and write
Mirroring	1	Mirrored	$2N$	Higher than RAID 2, 3, 4, or 5; lower than RAID 6	Higher than single disk for read; similar to single disk for write	Up to twice that of a single disk for read; similar to single disk for write
Parallel access	2	Redundant via Hamming code	$N + m$	Much higher than single disk; comparable to RAID 3, 4, or 5	Highest of all listed alternatives	Approximately twice that of a single disk
	3	Bit-interleaved parity	$N + 1$	Much higher than single disk; comparable to RAID 2, 4, or 5	Highest of all listed alternatives	Approximately twice that of a single disk
	4	Block-interleaved parity	$N + 1$	Much higher than single disk; comparable to RAID 2, 3, or 5	Similar to RAID 0 for read; significantly lower than single disk for write	Similar to RAID 0 for read; significantly lower than single disk for write
Independent access	5	Block-interleaved distributed parity	$N + 1$	Much higher than single disk; comparable to RAID 2, 3, or 4	Similar to RAID 0 for read; lower than single disk for write	Similar to RAID 0 for read; generally lower than single disk for write
	6	Block-interleaved dual distributed parity	$N + 2$	Highest of all listed alternatives	Similar to RAID 0 for read; lower than RAID 5 for write	Similar to RAID 0 for read; significantly lower than RAID 5 for write

Note: $N =$ number of data disks; m proportional to log N

197

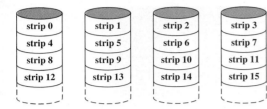

(a) RAID 0 (Nonredundant)

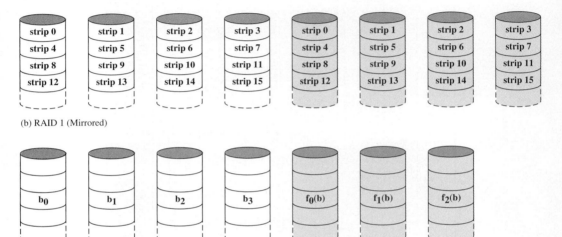

(b) RAID 1 (Mirrored)

(c) RAID 2 (Redundancy through Hamming code)

Figure 6.8 RAID Levels

RAID Level 0

RAID level 0 is not a true member of the RAID family because it does not include redundancy to improve performance. However, there are a few applications, such as some on supercomputers in which performance and capacity are primary concerns and low cost is more important than improved reliability.

For RAID 0, the user and system data are distributed across all of the disks in the array. This has a notable advantage over the use of a single large disk: If two -different I/O requests are pending for two different blocks of data, then there is a good chance that the requested blocks are on different disks. Thus, the two requests can be issued in parallel, reducing the I/O queuing time.

But RAID 0, as with all of the RAID levels, goes further than simply distributing the data across a disk array: The data are *striped* across the available disks. This is best understood by considering Figure 6.9. All of the user and system data are viewed as being stored on a logical disk. The logical disk is divided into strips; these strips may be physical blocks, sectors, or some other unit. The strips are mapped round robin to consecutive physical disks in the RAID array. A set of logically consecutive strips that maps exactly one strip to each array member is referred to as a **stripe.** In an *n*-disk array, the first *n* logical strips are physically stored as the first strip on each of the *n* disks, forming the first stripe; the second *n* strips are distributed as the

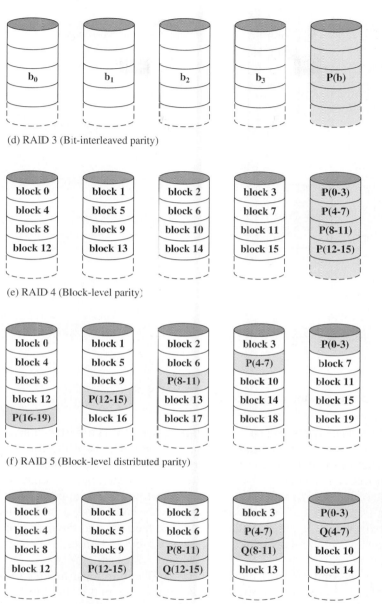

(d) RAID 3 (Bit-interleaved parity)

(e) RAID 4 (Block-level parity)

(f) RAID 5 (Block-level distributed parity)

(g) RAID 6 (Dual redundancy)

Figure 6.8 RAID Levels (*continued*)

second strips on each disk; and so on. The advantage of this layout is that if a single I/O request consists of multiple logically contiguous strips, then up to n strips for that request can be handled in parallel, greatly reducing the I/O transfer time.

Figure 6.9 indicates the use of array management software to map between logical and physical disk space. This software may execute either in the disk subsystem or in a host computer.

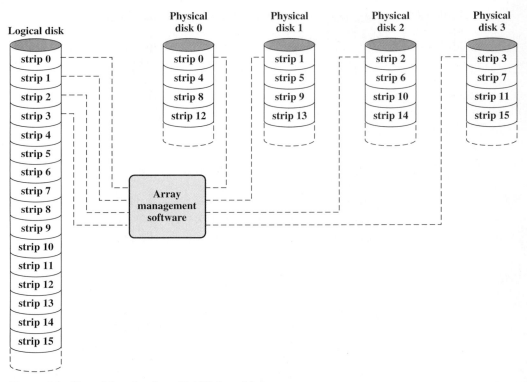

Figure 6.9 Data Mapping for a RAID Level 0 Array

RAID 0 FOR HIGH DATA TRANSFER CAPACITY The performance of any of the RAID levels depends critically on the request patterns of the host system and on the layout of the data. These issues can be most clearly addressed in RAID 0, where the impact of redundancy does not interfere with the analysis. First, let us consider the use of RAID 0 to achieve a high data transfer rate. For applications to experience a high transfer rate, two requirements must be met. First, a high transfer capacity must exist along the entire path between host memory and the individual disk drives. This includes internal controller buses, host system I/O buses, I/O adapters, and host memory buses.

The second requirement is that the application must make I/O requests that drive the disk array efficiently. This requirement is met if the typical request is for large amounts of logically contiguous data, compared to the size of a strip. In this case, a single I/O request involves the parallel transfer of data from multiple disks, increasing the effective transfer rate compared to a single-disk transfer.

RAID 0 FOR HIGH I/O REQUEST RATE In a transaction-oriented environment, the user is typically more concerned with response time than with transfer rate. For an individual I/O request for a small amount of data, the I/O time is dominated by the motion of the disk heads (seek time) and the movement of the disk (rotational latency).

In a transaction environment, there may be hundreds of I/O requests per second. A disk array can provide high I/O execution rates by balancing the I/O load across multiple disks. Effective load balancing is achieved only if there are typically multiple I/O requests outstanding. This, in turn, implies that there are multiple independent applications or a single transaction-oriented application that is capable of multiple asynchronous I/O requests. The performance will also be influenced by the strip size. If the strip size is relatively large, so that a single I/O request only involves a single disk access, then multiple waiting I/O requests can be handled in parallel, reducing the queuing time for each request.

RAID Level 1

RAID 1 differs from RAID levels 2 through 6 in the way in which redundancy is achieved. In these other RAID schemes, some form of parity calculation is used to introduce redundancy, whereas in RAID 1, redundancy is achieved by the simple expedient of duplicating all the data. As Figure 6.8b shows, data striping is used, as in RAID 0. But in this case, each logical strip is mapped to two separate physical disks so that every disk in the array has a mirror disk that contains the same data. RAID 1 can also be implemented without data striping, though this is less common.

There are a number of positive aspects to the RAID 1 organization:

1. A read request can be serviced by either of the two disks that contains the requested data, whichever one involves the minimum seek time plus rotational latency.
2. A write request requires that both corresponding strips be updated, but this can be done in parallel. Thus, the write performance is dictated by the slower of the two writes (i.e., the one that involves the larger seek time plus rotational latency). However, there is no "write penalty" with RAID 1. RAID levels 2 through 6 involve the use of parity bits. Therefore, when a single strip is updated, the array management software must first compute and update the parity bits as well as updating the actual strip in question.
3. Recovery from a failure is simple. When a drive fails, the data may still be accessed from the second drive.

The principal disadvantage of RAID 1 is the cost; it requires twice the disk space of the logical disk that it supports. Because of that, a RAID 1 configuration is likely to be limited to drives that store system software and data and other highly critical files. In these cases, RAID 1 provides real-time copy of all data so that in the event of a disk failure, all of the critical data are still immediately available.

In a transaction-oriented environment, RAID 1 can achieve high I/O request rates if the bulk of the requests are reads. In this situation, the performance of RAID 1 can approach double of that of RAID 0. However, if a substantial fraction of the I/O requests are write requests, then there may be no significant performance gain over RAID 0. RAID 1 may also provide improved performance over RAID 0 for data transfer intensive applications with a high percentage of reads. Improvement occurs if the application can split each read request so that both disk members participate.

RAID Level 2

RAID levels 2 and 3 make use of a parallel access technique. In a parallel access array, all member disks participate in the execution of every I/O request. Typically, the spindles of the individual drives are synchronized so that each disk head is in the same position on each disk at any given time.

As in the other RAID schemes, data striping is used. In the case of RAID 2 and 3, the strips are very small, often as small as a single byte or word. With RAID 2, an error-correcting code is calculated across corresponding bits on each data disk, and the bits of the code are stored in the corresponding bit positions on multiple parity disks. Typically, a Hamming code is used, which is able to correct single-bit errors and detect double-bit errors.

Although RAID 2 requires fewer disks than RAID 1, it is still rather costly. The number of redundant disks is proportional to the log of the number of data disks. On a single read, all disks are simultaneously accessed. The requested data and the associated error-correcting code are delivered to the array controller. If there is a single-bit error, the controller can recognize and correct the error instantly, so that the read access time is not slowed. On a single write, all data disks and parity disks must be accessed for the write operation.

RAID 2 would only be an effective choice in an environment in which many disk errors occur. Given the high reliability of individual disks and disk drives, RAID 2 is overkill and is not implemented.

RAID Level 3

RAID 3 is organized in a similar fashion to RAID 2. The difference is that RAID 3 requires only a single redundant disk, no matter how large the disk array. RAID 3 employs parallel access, with data distributed in small strips. Instead of an error-correcting code, a simple parity bit is computed for the set of individual bits in the same position on all of the data disks.

REDUNDANCY In the event of a drive failure, the parity drive is accessed and data is reconstructed from the remaining devices. Once the failed drive is replaced, the missing data can be restored on the new drive and operation resumed.

Data reconstruction is simple. Consider an array of five drives in which X0 through X3 contain data and X4 is the parity disk. The parity for the ith bit is calculated as follows:

$$X4(i) = X3(i) \oplus X2(i) \oplus X1(i) \oplus X0(i)$$

where $\oplus$ is exclusive-OR function.

Suppose that drive X1 has failed. If we add $X4(i) \oplus X1(i)$ to both sides of the preceding equation, we get

$$X1(i) = X4(i) \oplus X3(i) \oplus X2(i) \oplus X0(i)$$

Thus, the contents of each strip of data on X1 can be regenerated from the contents of the corresponding strips on the remaining disks in the array. This principle is true for RAID levels 3 through 6.

In the event of a disk failure, all of the data are still available in what is referred to as reduced mode. In this mode, for reads, the missing data are regenerated on the fly using the exclusive-OR calculation. When data are written to a reduced RAID 3 array, consistency of the parity must be maintained for later regeneration. Return to full operation requires that the failed disk be replaced and the entire contents of the failed disk be regenerated on the new disk.

PERFORMANCE Because data are striped in very small strips, RAID 3 can achieve very high data transfer rates. Any I/O request will involve the parallel transfer of data from all of the data disks. For large transfers, the performance improvement is especially noticeable. On the other hand, only one I/O request can be executed at a time. Thus, in a transaction-oriented environment, performance suffers.

RAID Level 4

RAID levels 4 through 6 make use of an independent access technique. In an independent access array, each member disk operates independently, so that separate I/O requests can be satisfied in parallel. Because of this, independent access arrays are more suitable for applications that require high I/O request rates and are relatively less suited for applications that require high data transfer rates.

As in the other RAID schemes, data striping is used. In the case of RAID 4 through 6, the strips are relatively large. With RAID 4, a bit-by-bit parity strip is calculated across corresponding strips on each data disk, and the parity bits are stored in the corresponding strip on the parity disk.

RAID 4 involves a write penalty when an I/O write request of small size is performed. Each time that a write occurs, the array management software must update not only the user data but also the corresponding parity bits. Consider an array of five drives in which X0 through X3 contain data and X4 is the parity disk. Suppose that a write is performed that only involves a strip on disk X1. Initially, for each bit i, we have the following relationship:

$$X4(i) = X3(i) \oplus X2(i) \oplus X1(i) \oplus X0(i) \tag{6.1}$$

After the update, with potentially altered bits indicated by a prime symbol:

$$\begin{aligned} X4'(i) &= X3(i) \oplus X2(i) \oplus X1'(i)X0(i) \\ &= X3(i) \oplus X2(i) \oplus X1'(i) \oplus X0(i) \oplus X1(i) \oplus X1(i) \\ &= X3(i) \oplus X2(i) \oplus X1(i) \oplus X0(i) \oplus X1(i) \oplus X1(i) \\ &= X4(i) \oplus X1(i) \oplus X1'(i) \end{aligned}$$

The preceding set of equations is derived as follows. The first line shows that a change in X1 will also affect the parity disk X4. In the second line, we add the terms $\oplus X1(i) \oplus X1(i)$]. Because the exclusive-OR of any quantity with itself is 0, this does not affect the equation. However, it is a convenience that is used to create the third line, by reordering. Finally, Equation (6.1) is used to replace the first four terms by $X4(i)$.

To calculate the new parity, the array management software must read the old user strip and the old parity strip. Then it can update these two strips with the new data and the newly calculated parity. Thus, each strip write involves two reads and two writes.

In the case of a larger size I/O write that involves strips on all disk drives, parity is easily computed by calculation using only the new data bits. Thus, the parity drive can be updated in parallel with the data drives and there are no extra reads or writes.

In any case, every write operation must involve the parity disk, which therefore can become a bottleneck.

RAID Level 5

RAID 5 is organized in a similar fashion to RAID 4. The difference is that RAID 5 distributes the parity strips across all disks. A typical allocation is a round-robin scheme, as illustrated in Figure 6.8f. For an n-disk array, the parity strip is on a different disk for the first n stripes, and the pattern then repeats.

The distribution of parity strips across all drives avoids the potential I/O bottle-neck found in RAID 4.

RAID Level 6

RAID 6 was introduced in a subsequent paper by the Berkeley researchers [KATZ89]. In the RAID 6 scheme, two different parity calculations are carried out and stored in separate blocks on different disks. Thus, a RAID 6 array whose user data require N disks consists of $N + 2$ disks.

Figure 6.8g illustrates the scheme. P and Q are two different data check algorithms. One of the two is the exclusive-OR calculation used in RAID 4 and 5. But the other is an independent data check algorithm. This makes it possible to regenerate data even if two disks containing user data fail.

The advantage of RAID 6 is that it provides extremely high data availability. Three disks would have to fail within the MTTR (mean time to repair) interval to cause data to be lost. On the other hand, RAID 6 incurs a substantial write penalty, because each write affects two parity blocks. Performance benchmarks [EISC07] show a RAID 6 controller can suffer more than a 30% drop in overall write performance compared with a RAID 5 implementation. RAID 5 and RAID 6 read performance is comparable.

Table 6.4 is a comparative summary of the seven levels.

Table 6.4 RAID Comparison

Level	Advantages	Disadvantages	Applications
0	I/O performance is greatly improved by spreading the I/O load across many channels and drives No parity calculation overhead is involved Very simple design Easy to implement	The failure of just one drive will result in all data in an array being lost	Video production and editing Image Editing Pre-press applications Any application requiring high bandwidth
1	100% redundancy of data means no rebuild is necessary in case of a disk failure, just a copy to the replacement disk Under certain circumstances, RAID 1 can sustain multiple simultaneous drive failures Simplest RAID storage subsystem design	Highest disk overhead of all RAID types (100%)—inefficient	Accounting Payroll Financial Any application requiring very high availability

(Continued)

Table 6.4   Continued

Level	Advantages	Disadvantages	Applications
2	Extremely high data transfer rates possible The higher the data transfer rate required, the better the ratio of data disks to ECC disks Relatively simple controller design compared to RAID levels 3, 4, & 5	Very high ratio of ECC disks to data disks with smaller word sizes—inefficient Entry level cost very high—requires very high transfer rate requirement to justify	No commercial implementations exist/ not commercially viable
3	Very high read data transfer rate Very high write data transfer rate Disk failure has an insignificant impact on throughput Low ratio of ECC (parity) disks to data disks means high efficiency	Transaction rate equal to that of a single disk drive at best (if spindles are synchronized) Controller design is fairly complex	Video production and live streaming Image editing Video editing Prepress applications Any application requiring high throughput
4	Very high Read data transaction rate Low ratio of ECC (parity) disks to data disks means high efficiency	Quite complex controller design Worst write transaction rate and Write aggregate transfer rate Difficult and inefficient data rebuild in the event of disk failure	No commercial implementations exist/ not commercially viable
5	Highest Read data transaction rate Low ratio of ECC (parity) disks to data disks means high efficiency Good aggregate transfer rate	Most complex controller design Difficult to rebuild in the event of a disk failure (as compared to RAID level 1)	File and application servers Database servers Web, e-mail, and news servers Intranet servers Most versatile RAID level
6	Provides for an extremely high data fault tolerance and can sustain multiple simultaneous drive failures	More complex controller design Controller overhead to compute parity addresses is extremely high	Perfect solution for mission critical applications

6.3   SOLID STATE DRIVES

One of the most significant developments in computer architecture in recent years is the increasing use of solid state drives (SSDs) to complement or even replace **hard disk drives (HDDs)**, both as internal and external secondary memory. The term *solid state* refers to electronic circuitry built with semiconductors. A **solid state drive** is a memory device made with solid state components that can be used as a replacement to a hard disk drive. The SSDs now on the market and coming on line use a type of semiconductor memory referred to as flash memory. In this section, we first provide an introduction to flash memory, and then look at its use in SSDs.

Flash Memory

Flash memory is a type of semiconductor memory that has been around for a number of years and is used in many consumer electronic products, including smart phones, GPS devices, MP3 players, digital cameras, and USB devices. In recent years, the cost and performance of flash memory has evolved to the point where it is feasible to use flash memory drives to replace HDDs.

Figure 6.10 illustrates the basic operation of a flash memory. For comparison, Figure 6.10a depicts the operation of a transistor. Transistors exploit the properties of semiconductors so that a small voltage applied to the gate can be used to control the flow of a large current between the source and the drain.

In a flash memory cell, a second gate—called a floating gate, because it is insulated by a thin oxide layer—is added to the transistor. Initially, the floating gate does not interfere with the operation of the transistor (Figure 6.10b). In this state, the cell is deemed to represent binary 1. Applying a large voltage across the oxide layer causes electrons to tunnel through it and become trapped on the floating gate, where they remain even if the power is disconnected (Figure 6.10c). In this state, the cell is deemed to represent binary 0. The state of the cell can be read by using external circuitry to test whether the transistor is working or not. Applying a large voltage in the opposite direction removes the electrons from the floating gate, returning to a state of binary 0.

There are two distinctive types of flash memory, designated as NOR and NAND. In **NOR flash memory**, the basic unit of access is a bit, and the logical organization resembles a NOR logic device.[4] For **NAND flash memory**, the basic unit is 16 or 32 bits, and the logical organization resembles NAND devices.

NOR flash memory provides high-speed random access. It can read and write data to specific locations, and can reference and retrieve a single byte. NOR

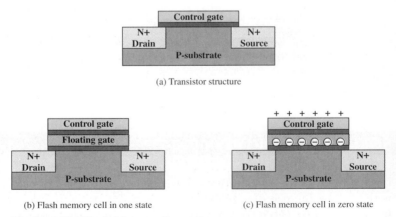

(a) Transistor structure

(b) Flash memory cell in one state   (c) Flash memory cell in zero state

Figure 6.10 Flash Memory Operation

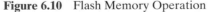

[4]See Chapter 11 for a discussion of NOR and NAND gates.

flash memory is used to store cell phone operating system code and on Windows computers for the BIOS program that runs at startup. NAND reads and writes in small blocks. It is used in USB flash drives, memory cards (in digital cameras, MP3 players, etc.), and in SSDs. NAND provides higher bit density than NOR and greater write speed. NAND flash does not provide a random-access external address bus so the data must be read on a blockwise basis (also known as page access), where each block holds hundreds to thousands of bits.

SSD Compared to HDD

As the cost of flash-based SSDs has dropped and the performance and bit density increased, SSDs have become increasingly competitive with HDDs. Table 6.5 shows typical measures of comparison at the time of this writing.

SSDs have the following advantages over HDDs:

- **High-performance input/output operations per second (IOPS):** Significantly increases performance I/O subsystems.
- **Durability:** Less susceptible to physical shock and vibration.
- **Longer lifespan:** SSDs are not susceptible to mechanical wear.
- **Lower power consumption:** SSDs use as little as 2.1 watts of power per drive, considerably less than comparable-size HDDs.
- **Quieter and cooler running capabilities:** Less floor space required, lower energy costs, and a greener enterprise.
- **Lower access times and latency rates:** Over 10 times faster than the spinning disks in an HDD.

Currently, HDDs enjoy a cost per bit advantage and a capacity advantage, but these differences are shrinking.

SSD Organization

Figure 6.11 illustrates a general view of the common architectural system component associated with any SDD system. On the host system, to operating system invokes file system software to access data on the disk. The file system, in turn, invokes I/O driver software. The I/O driver software provides host access to the particular SSD product. The interface component in Figure 6.11 refers to the physical and electrical interface between the host processor and the SSD peripheral device. If the device is

Table 6.5 Comparison of Solid State Drives and Disk Drives

	NAND Flash Drives	**Disk Drives**
I/O per second (sustained)	Read: 45,000 Write: 15,000	300
Throughput (MB/s)	Read: 200+ Write: 100+	up to 80
Random access time (ms)	0.1	4–10
Storage capacity	up to 256 GB	up to 4 TB

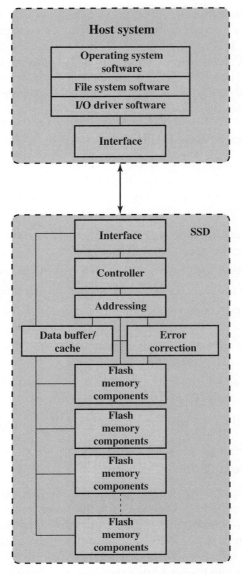

Figure 6.11 Solid State Drive Architecture

an internal hard drive, a common interface is PCIe. For external devices, one common interface is USB.

In addition to the interface to the host system, the SSD contains the following components:

- **Controller:** Provides SSD device level interfacing and firmware execution.
- **Addressing:** Logic that performs the selection function across the flash memory components.
- **Data buffer/cache:** High speed RAM memory components used for speed matching and to increased data throughput.

- **Error correction:** Logic for error detection and correction.
- **Flash memory components:** Individual NAND flash chips.

Practical Issues

There are two practical issues peculiar to SSDs that are not faced by HDDs. First, SDD performance has a tendency to slow down as the device is used. To understand the reason for this, you need to know that files are stored on disk as a set of pages, typically 4 KB in length. These pages are not necessarily, and indeed not typically, stored as a contiguous set of pages on the disk. The reason for this arrangement is explained in our discussion of virtual memory in Chapter 8. However, flash memory is accessed in blocks, with a typically block size of 512 KB, so that there are typically 128 pages per block. Now consider what must be done to write a page onto a flash memory.

1. The entire block must be read from the flash memory and placed in a RAM buffer. Then the appropriate page in the RAM buffer is updated.
2. Before the block can be written back to flash memory, the entire block of flash memory must be erased—it is not possible to erase just one page of the flash memory.
3. The entire block from the buffer is now written back to the flash memory.

Now, when a flash drive is relatively empty and a new file is created, the pages of that file are written on to the drive contiguously, so that one or only a few blocks are affected. However, over time, because of the way virtual memory works, files become fragmented, with pages scattered over multiple blocks. As the drive become more occupied, there is more fragmentation, so the writing of a new file can affect multiple blocks. Thus, the writing of multiple pages from one block becomes slower, the more fully occupied the disk is. Manufacturers have developed a variety of techniques to compensate for this property of flash memory, such as setting aside a substantial portion of the SSD as extra space for write operations (called over-provisioning), then to erase inactive pages during idle time used to defragment the disk. Another technique is the TRIM command, which allows an operating system to inform a solid state drive (SSD) which blocks of data are no longer considered in use and can be wiped internally.[5]

A second practical issue with flash memory drives is that a flash memory becomes unusable after a certain number of writes. As flash cells are stressed, they lose their ability to record and retain values. A typical limit is 100,000 writes [GSOE08]. Techniques for prolonging the life of an SSD drive include front-ending the flash with a cache to delay and group write operations, using wear-leveling algorithms that evenly distribute writes across block of cells, and sophisticated bad-block management techniques. In addition, vendors are deploying SSDs in RAID configurations to further reduce the probability of data loss. Most flash devices are also capable of estimating their own remaining lifetimes so systems can anticipate failure and take preemptive action.

---

[5]While TRIM is frequently spelled in capital letters, it is not an acronym; it is merely a command name.

6.4 OPTICAL MEMORY

In 1983, one of the most successful consumer products of all time was introduced: the compact disk (CD) digital audio system. The CD is a nonerasable disk that can store more than 60 minutes of audio information on one side. The huge commercial success of the CD enabled the development of low-cost optical-disk storage technology that has revolutionized computer data storage. A variety of optical-disk systems have been introduced (Table 6.6). We briefly review each of these.

Compact Disk

CD-ROM Both the audio CD and the **CD-ROM** (compact disk read-only memory) share a similar technology. The main difference is that CD-ROM players are more rugged and have error correction devices to ensure that data are properly transferred from disk to computer. Both types of disk are made the same way. The disk is formed from a resin, such as polycarbonate. Digitally recorded information (either music or computer data) is imprinted as a series of microscopic pits on the surface of the polycarbonate. This is done, first of all, with a finely focused, high-intensity laser to create a master disk. The master is used, in turn, to make a die to

Table 6.6 Optical Disk Products

CD
Compact Disk. A nonerasable disk that stores digitized audio information. The standard system uses 12-cm disks and can record more than 60 minutes of uninterrupted playing time.
CD-ROM
Compact Disk Read-Only Memory. A nonerasable disk used for storing computer data. The standard system uses 12-cm disks and can hold more than 650 Mbytes.
CD-R
CD Recordable. Similar to a CD-ROM. The user can write to the disk only once.
CD-RW
CD Rewritable. Similar to a CD-ROM. The user can erase and rewrite to the disk multiple times.
DVD
Digital Versatile Disk. A technology for producing digitized, compressed representation of video information, as well as large volumes of other digital data. Both 8 and 12 cm diameters are used, with a double-sided capacity of up to 17 Gbytes. The basic DVD is read-only (DVD-ROM).
DVD-R
DVD Recordable. Similar to a DVD-ROM. The user can write to the disk only once. Only one-sided disks can be used.
DVD-RW
DVD Rewritable. Similar to a DVD-ROM. The user can erase and rewrite to the disk multiple times. Only one-sided disks can be used.
Blu-ray DVD
High-definition video disk. Provides considerably greater data storage density than DVD, using a 405-nm (blue-violet) laser. A single layer on a single side can store 25 Gbytes.

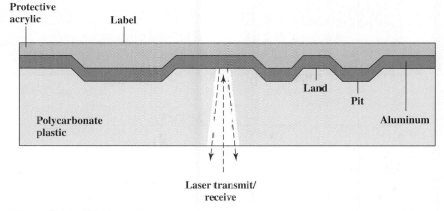

Figure 6.12   CD Operation

stamp out copies onto polycarbonate. The pitted surface is then coated with a highly reflective surface, usually aluminum or gold. This shiny surface is protected against dust and scratches by a top coat of clear acrylic. Finally, a label can be silkscreened onto the acrylic.

Information is retrieved from a CD or CD-ROM by a low-powered laser housed in an optical-disk player, or drive unit. The laser shines through the clear polycarbonate while a motor spins the disk past it (Figure 6.12). The intensity of the reflected light of the laser changes as it encounters a **pit**. Specifically, if the laser beam falls on a pit, which has a somewhat rough surface, the light scatters and a low intensity is reflected back to the source. The areas between pits are called **lands**. A land is a smooth surface, which reflects back at higher intensity. The change between pits and lands is detected by a photosensor and converted into a digital signal. The sensor tests the surface at regular intervals. The beginning or end of a pit represents a 1; when no change in elevation occurs between intervals, a 0 is recorded.

Recall that on a magnetic disk, information is recorded in concentric tracks. With the simplest constant angular velocity (CAV) system, the number of bits per track is constant. An increase in density is achieved with **multiple zoned recording**, in which the surface is divided into a number of zones, with zones farther from the center containing more bits than zones closer to the center. Although this technique increases capacity, it is still not optimal.

To achieve greater capacity, CDs and CD-ROMs do not organize information on concentric tracks. Instead, the disk contains a single spiral track, beginning near the center and spiraling out to the outer edge of the disk. Sectors near the outside of the disk are the same length as those near the inside. Thus, information is packed evenly across the disk in segments of the same size and these are scanned at the same rate by rotating the disk at a variable speed. The pits are then read by the laser at a **constant linear velocity (CLV)**. The disk rotates more slowly for accesses near the outer edge than for those near the center. Thus, the capacity of a track and the rotational delay both increase for positions nearer the outer edge of the disk. The data capacity for a CD-ROM is about 680 MB.

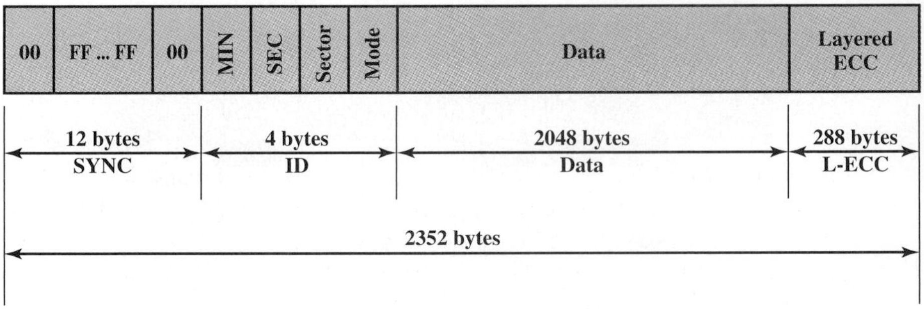

00	FF ... FF	00	MIN	SEC	Sector	Mode	Data	Layered ECC

12 bytes	4 bytes	2048 bytes	288 bytes
SYNC	ID	Data	L-ECC

2352 bytes

Figure 6.13   CD-ROM Block Format

Data on the CD-ROM are organized as a sequence of blocks. A typical block format is shown in Figure 6.13. It consists of the following fields:

- **Sync:** The sync field identifies the beginning of a block. It consists of a byte of all 0s, 10 bytes of all 1s, and a byte of all 0s.

- **Header:** The header contains the block address and the mode byte. Mode 0 specifies a blank data field; mode 1 specifies the use of an error-correcting code and 2048 bytes of data; mode 2 specifies 2336 bytes of user data with no error-correcting code.

- **Data:** User data.

- **Auxiliary:** Additional user data in mode 2. In mode 1, this is a 288-byte error-correcting code.

With the use of CLV, random access becomes more difficult. Locating a specific address involves moving the head to the general area, adjusting the rotation speed and reading the address, and then making minor adjustments to find and access the specific sector.

CD-ROM is appropriate for the distribution of large amounts of data to a large number of users. Because of the expense of the initial writing process, it is not appropriate for individualized applications. Compared with traditional magnetic disks, the CD-ROM has two advantages:

- The optical disk together with the information stored on it can be mass replicated inexpensively—unlike a magnetic disk. The database on a magnetic disk has to be reproduced by copying one disk at a time using two disk drives.

- The optical disk is removable, allowing the disk itself to be used for archival storage. Most magnetic disks are nonremovable. The information on nonremovable magnetic disks must first be copied to another storage medium before the disk drive/disk can be used to store new information.

The disadvantages of CD-ROM are as follows:

- It is read-only and cannot be updated.

- It has an access time much longer than that of a magnetic disk drive, as much as half a second.

CD RECORDABLE To accommodate applications in which only one or a small number of copies of a set of data is needed, the write-once read-many CD, known as the CD recordable (**CD-R**), has been developed. For CD-R, a disk is prepared in such a way that it can be subsequently written once with a laser beam of modest -intensity. Thus, with a some what more expensive disk controller than for CD-ROM, the customer can write once as well as read the disk.

The CD-R medium is similar to but not identical to that of a CD or CD-ROM. For CDs and CD-ROMs, information is recorded by the pitting of the surface of the medium, which changes reflectivity. For a CD-R, the medium includes a dye layer. The dye is used to change reflectivity and is activated by a high-intensity laser. The resulting disk can be read on a CD-R drive or a CD-ROM drive.

The CD-R optical disk is attractive for archival storage of documents and files. It provides a permanent record of large volumes of user data.

CD REWRITABLE The **CD-RW** optical disk can be repeatedly written and overwritten, as with a magnetic disk. Although a number of approaches have been tried, the only pure optical approach that has proved attractive is called **phase change**. The phase change disk uses a material that has two significantly different reflectivities in two different phase states. There is an amorphous state, in which the molecules exhibit a random orientation that reflects light poorly; and a crystalline state, which has a smooth surface that reflects light well. A beam of laser light can change the material from one phase to the other. The primary disadvantage of phase change optical disks is that the material eventually and permanently loses its desirable properties. Current materials can be used for between 500,000 and 1,000,000 erase cycles.

The CD-RW has the obvious advantage over CD-ROM and CD-R that it can be rewritten and thus used as a true secondary storage. As such, it competes with magnetic disk. A key advantage of the optical disk is that the engineering tolerances for optical disks are much less severe than for high-capacity magnetic disks. Thus, they exhibit higher reliability and longer life.

Digital Versatile Disk

With the capacious digital versatile disk (**DVD**), the electronics industry has at last found an acceptable replacement for the analog VHS video tape. The DVD has replaced the videotape used in video cassette recorders (VCRs) and, more important for this discussion, replace the CD-ROM in personal computers and servers. The DVD takes video into the digital age. It delivers movies with impressive picture quality, and it can be randomly accessed like audio CDs, which DVD machines can also play. Vast volumes of data can be crammed onto the disk, currently seven times as much as a CD-ROM. With DVD's huge storage capacity and vivid quality, PC games have become more realistic and educational software incorporates more video. Following in the wake of these developments has been a new crest of traffic over the Internet and corporate intranets, as this material is incorporated into Web sites.

The DVD's greater capacity is due to three differences from CDs (Figure 6.14):

1. Bits are packed more closely on a DVD. The spacing between loops of a spiral on a CD is 1.6 μm and the minimum distance between pits along the spiral is 0.834 μm.

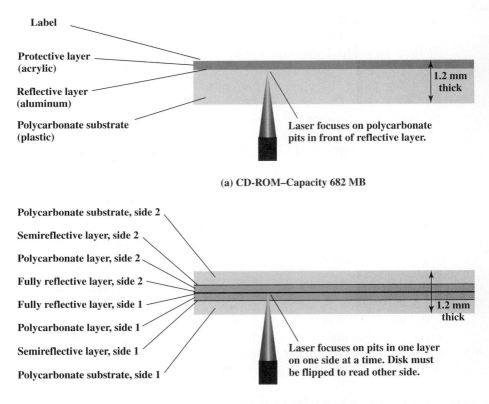

(a) CD-ROM–Capacity 682 MB

(b) DVD-ROM, double-sided, dual-layer–Capacity 17 GB

Figure 6.14 CD-ROM and DVD-ROM

The DVD uses a laser with shorter wavelength and achieves a loop spacing of 0.74 μm and a minimum distance between pits of 0.4 μm. The result of these two improvements is about a seven-fold increase in capacity, to about 4.7 GB.

2. The DVD employs a second layer of pits and lands on top of the first layer. A dual-layer DVD has a semireflective layer on top of the reflective layer, and by adjusting focus, the lasers in DVD drives can read each layer separately. This technique almost doubles the capacity of the disk, to about 8.5 GB. The lower reflectivity of the second layer limits its storage capacity so that a full doubling is not achieved.

3. The **DVD-ROM** can be two sided, whereas data are recorded on only one side of a CD. This brings total capacity up to 17 GB.

As with the CD, DVDs come in writeable as well as read-only versions (Table 6.6).

High-Definition Optical Disks

High-definition optical disks are designed to store high-definition videos and to provide significantly greater storage capacity compared to DVDs. The higher bit density is achieved by using a laser with a shorter wavelength, in the blue-violet

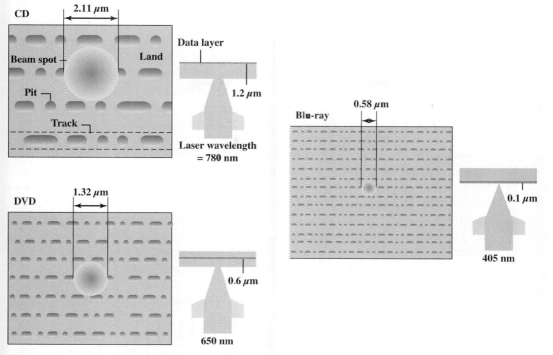

Figure 6.15   Optical Memory Characteristics

range. The data pits, which constitute the digital 1s and 0s, are smaller on the high-definition optical disks compared to DVD because of the shorter laser wavelength.

Two competing disk formats and technologies initially competed for market acceptance: HD DVD and **Blu-ray** DVD. The Blu-ray scheme ultimately achieved market dominance. The HD DVD scheme can store 15 GB on a single layer on a single side. Blu-ray positions the data layer on the disk closer to the laser (shown on the right-hand side of each diagram in Figure 6.15). This enables a tighter focus and less distortion and thus smaller pits and tracks. Blu-ray can store 25 GB on a single layer. Three versions are available: read only (BD-ROM), recordable once (BD-R), and rerecordable (BD-RE).

6.5 MAGNETIC TAPE

Tape systems use the same reading and recording techniques as disk systems. The medium is flexible polyester (similar to that used in some clothing) tape coated with magnetizable material. The coating may consist of particles of pure metal in special binders or vapor-plated metal films. The tape and the tape drive are analogous to a home tape recorder system. Tape widths vary from 0.38 cm (0.15 inch) to 1.27 cm (0.5 inch). Tapes used to be packaged as open reels that have to be threaded through a second spindle for use. Today, virtually all tapes are housed in cartridges.

Data on the tape are structured as a number of parallel tracks running lengthwise. Earlier tape systems typically used nine tracks. This made it possible to store data one byte at a time, with an additional parity bit as the ninth track. This was followed by tape systems using 18 or 36 tracks, corresponding to a digital word or double word. The recording of data in this form is referred to as **parallel recording**. Most modern systems instead use **serial recording**, in which data are laid out as a sequence of bits along each track, as is done with magnetic disks. As with the disk, data are read and written in contiguous blocks, called *physical records,* on a tape. Blocks on the tape are separated by gaps referred to as *interrecord* gaps. As with the disk, the tape is formatted to assist in locating physical records.

The typical recording technique used in serial tapes is referred to as **serpentine recording.** In this technique, when data are being recorded, the first set of bits is recorded along the whole length of the tape. When the end of the tape is reached, the heads are repositioned to record a new track, and the tape is again recorded on its whole length, this time in the opposite direction. That process continues, back and forth, until the tape is full (Figure 6.16a). To increase speed, the read-write head is capable of reading and writing a number of adjacent tracks simultaneously (typically two to eight tracks). Data are still recorded serially along individual tracks, but blocks in sequence are stored on adjacent tracks, as suggested by Figure 6.16b.

A tape drive is a *sequential-access* device. If the tape head is positioned at record 1, then to read record N, it is necessary to read physical records 1 through

(a) Serpentine reading and writing

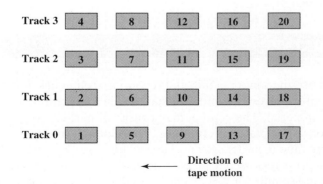

(b) Block layout for system that reads–writes four tracks simultaneously

Figure 6.16 Typical Magnetic Tape Features

Table 6.7   LTO Tape Drives

	LTO-1	LTO-2	LTO-3	LTO-4	LTO-5	LTO-6	LTO-7	LTO-8
Release date	2000	2003	2005	2007	2010	TBA	TBA	TBA
Compressed capacity	200 GB	400 GB	800 GB	1600 GB	3.2 TB	8 TB	16 TB	32 TB
Compressed transfer rate	40 MB/s	80 MB/s	160 MB/s	240 MB/s	280 MB/s	525 MB/s	788 MB/s	1.18 GB/s
Linear density (bits/mm)	4880	7398	9638	13250	15142			
Tape tracks	384	512	704	896	1280			
Tape length (m)	609	609	680	820	846			
Tape width (cm)	1.27	1.27	1.27	1.27	1.27			
Write elements	8	8	16	16	16			
WORM?	No	No	Yes	Yes	Yes	Yes	Yes	Yes
Encryption Capable?	No	No	No	Yes	Yes	Yes	Yes	Yes
Partitioning?	No	No	No	No	Yes	Yes	Yes	Yes

$N-1$, one at a time. If the head is currently positioned beyond the desired record, it is necessary to rewind the tape a certain distance and begin reading forward. Unlike the disk, the tape is in motion only during a read or write operation.

In contrast to the tape, the disk drive is referred to as a *direct-access* device. A disk drive need not read all the sectors on a disk sequentially to get to the desired one. It must only wait for the intervening sectors within one track and can make successive accesses to any track.

Magnetic tape was the first kind of secondary memory. It is still widely used as the lowest-cost, slowest-speed member of the memory hierarchy.

The dominant tape technology today is a cartridge system known as linear tape-open (LTO). LTO was developed in the late 1990s as an open-source alternative to the various proprietary systems on the market. Table 6.7 shows parameters for the various LTO generations. See Appendix J for details.

6.6   RECOMMENDED READING

[JACO08] provides good coverage of magnetic disks.

[GSOE08] is an introduction to solid state drives. For good technical descriptions of flash memory, see [PAVA97] and [OKLO08].

An excellent survey of RAID technology, written by the inventors of the RAID concept, is [CHEN94]. A good overview paper is [FRIE96]. A good performance comparison of the RAID architectures is [CHEN96].

A good survey of optical recording and reading technology is [MANS97].

[OSUN11] provides a detailed treatment of LTO.

CHEN94 Chen, P.; Lee, E.; Gibson, G.; Katz, R.; and Patterson, D. "RAID: High-Performance, Reliable Secondary Storage." *ACM Computing Surveys,* June 1994.

CHEN96 Chen, S., and Towsley, D. "A Performance Evaluation of RAID Architectures." *IEEE Transactions on Computers,* October 1996.

FRIE96 Friedman, M. "RAID Keeps Going and Going and…" *IEEE Spectrum*, April 1996.

HAUE08 Haeusser, B., et al. *IBM System Storage Tape Library Guide for Open Systems.* IBM Redbook SG24-5946-05, October 2007. ibm.com/redbooks

JACO08 Jacob, B.; Ng, S.; and Wang, D. *Memory Systems: Cache, DRAM, Disk.* Boston: Morgan Kaufmann, 2008.

MANS97 Mansuripur, M., and Sincerbox, G. "Principles and Techniques of Optical Data Storage." *Proceedings of the IEEE,* November 1997.

OKLO08 Oklobdzija, V., ed. *Digital Design and Fabrication.* Boca Raton, FL: CRC Press, 2008.

OSUN11 Osuna, A., et al. *IBM System Storage Tape Library Guide for Open Systems.* IBM Redbook SG24-5946-07, June 2011.

PAVA97 Pavan, P., et al. "Flash Memory Cells–An Overview." *Proceedings of the IEEE,* August 1997.

6.7 KEY TERMS, REVIEW QUESTIONS, AND PROBLEMS

Key Terms

access time	DVD-RW	optical memory
Blu-ray	fixed-head disk	pit
CD	flash memory	platter
CD-R	floppy disk	RAID
CD-ROM	gap	removable disk
CD-RW	hard disk drive (HDD)	rotational delay
constant angular velocity (CAV)	head	sector
	land	seek time
constant linear velocity (CLV)	magnetic disk	serpentine recording
	magnetic tape	solid state drive (SSD)
cylinder	magnetoresistive	striped data
DVD	movable-head disk	substrate
DVD-R	multiple zoned recording	track
DVD-ROM	nonremovable disk	transfer time

Review Questions

6.1 What are the advantages of using a glass substrate for a magnetic disk?

6.2 How are data written onto a magnetic disk?

6.3 How are data read from a magnetic disk?

6.4 Explain the difference between a simple CAV system and a multiple zoned recording system.

6.5 Define the terms *track, cylinder,* and *sector*.

6.6 What is the typical disk sector size?

6.7 Define the terms *seek time, rotational delay, access time,* and *transfer time.*

6.8 What common characteristics are shared by all RAID levels?

6.9 Briefly define the seven RAID levels.

6.10 Explain the term *striped data.*

6.11 How is redundancy achieved in a RAID system?

6.12 In the context of RAID, what is the distinction between parallel access and independent access?

6.13 What is the difference between CAV and CLV?

6.14 What differences between a CD and a DVD account for the larger capacity of the latter?

6.15 Explain serpentine recording.

Problems

6.1 Consider a disk with N tracks numbered from 0 to $(N-1)$ and assume that requested sectors are distributed randomly and evenly over the disk. We want to calculate the average number of tracks traversed by a seek.

    a. First, calculate the probability of a seek of length j when the head is currently positioned over track t. *Hint:* This is a matter of determining the total number of combinations, recognizing that all track positions for the destination of the seek are equally likely.

    b. Next, calculate the probability of a seek of length K. *Hint:* this involves the summing over all possible combinations of movements of K tracks.

    c. Calculate the average number of tracks traversed by a seek, using the formula for expected value

$$E[x] = \sum_{i=0}^{N-1} i \times \Pr[x = i]$$

    Hint: Use the equalities: $\sum_{i=1}^{n} i = \dfrac{n(n+1)}{2}$; $\sum_{i=1}^{n} i^2 = \dfrac{n(n+1)(2n+1)}{6}$.

    d. Show that for large values of N, the average number of tracks traversed by a seek approaches $N/3$.

6.2 Define the following for a disk system:

    t_s = seek time; average time to position head over track
    r = rotation speed of the disk, in revolutions per second
    n = number of bits per sector
    N = capacity of a track, in bits
    t_A = time to access a sector

    Develop a formula for t_A as a function of the other parameters.

6.3 Consider a magnetic disk drive with 8 surfaces, 512 tracks per surface, and 64 sectors per track. Sector size is 1 kB. The average seek time is 8 ms, the track-to-track access time is 1.5 ms, and the drive rotates at 3600 rpm. Successive tracks in a cylinder can be read without head movement.

    a. What is the disk capacity?

    b. What is the average access time? Assume this file is stored in successive sectors and tracks of successive cylinders, starting at sector 0, track 0, of cylinder i.

    c. Estimate the time required to transfer a 5-MB file.

    d. What is the burst transfer rate?

6.4 Consider a single-platter disk with the following parameters: rotation speed: 7200 rpm; number of tracks on one side of platter: 30,000; number of sectors per track: 600; seek time: one ms for every hundred tracks traversed. Let the disk receive a request to access a random sector on a random track and assume the disk head starts at track 0.

    a. What is the average seek time?

    b. What is the average rotational latency?

    c. What is the transfer time for a sector?

    d. What is the total average time to satisfy a request?

6.5 A distinction is made between physical records and logical records. A **logical record** is a collection of related data elements treated as a conceptual unit, independent of how or where the information is stored. A **physical record** is a contiguous area of storage space that is defined by the characteristics of the storage device and operating system. Assume a disk system in which each physical record contains thirty 120-byte logical records. Calculate how much disk space (in sectors, tracks, and surfaces) will be required to store 300,000 logical records if the disk is fixed-sector with 512 bytes/sector, with 96 sectors/track, 110 tracks per surface, and 8 usable surfaces. Ignore any file header record(s) and track indexes, and assume that records cannot span two sectors.

6.6 Consider a disk that rotates at 3600 rpm. The seek time to move the head between adjacent tracks is 2 ms. There are 32 sectors per track, which are stored in linear order from sector 0 through sector 31. The head sees the sectors in ascending order. Assume the read/write head is positioned at the start of sector 1 on track 8. There is a main memory buffer large enough to hold an entire track. Data is transferred between disk locations by reading from the source track into the main memory buffer and then writing the data from the buffer to the target track.

    a. How long will it take to transfer sector 1 on track 8 to sector 1 on track 9?

    b. How long will it take to transfer all the sectors of track 8 to the corresponding sectors of track 9?

6.7 It should be clear that disk striping can improve data transfer rate when the strip size is small compared to the I/O request size. It should also be clear that RAID 0 provides improved performance relative to a single large disk, because multiple I/O requests can be handled in parallel. However, in this latter case, is disk striping necessary? That is, does disk striping improve I/O request rate performance compared to a comparable disk array without striping?

6.8 Consider a 4-drive, 200GB-per-drive RAID array. What is the available data storage capacity for each of the RAID levels 0, 1, 3, 4, 5, and 6?

6.9 For a compact disk, audio is converted to digital with 16-bit samples, and is treated a stream of 8-bit bytes for storage. One simple scheme for storing this data, called direct recording, would be to represent a 1 by a land and a 0 by a pit. Instead, each byte is expanded into a 14-bit binary number. It turns out that exactly 256 (2^8) of the total of 16,134 (2^{14}) 14-bit numbers have at least two 0s between every pair of 1s, and these are the numbers selected for the expansion from 8 to 14 bits. The optical system detects the presence of 1s by detecting a transition for pit to land or land to pit. It detects 0s by measuring the distances between intensity changes. This scheme requires that there are no 1s in succession; hence the use of the 8-to-14 code.

    The advantage of this scheme is as follows. For a given laser beam diameter, there is a minimum-pit size, regardless of how the bits are represented. With this scheme, this minimum-pit size stores 3 bits, because at least two 0s follow every 1. With direct recording, the same pit would be able to store only one bit. Considering both the number of bits stored per pit and the 8-to-14 bit expansion, which scheme stores the most bits and by what factor?

6.10 Design a backup strategy for a computer system. One option is to use plug-in external disks, which cost $150 for each 500 GB drive. Another option is to buy a tape drive for $2500, and 400 GB tapes for $50 apiece. (These were realistic prices in 2008.) A typical backup strategy is to have two sets of backup media onsite, with backups alternately written on them so in case the system fails while making a backup, the previous version is still intact. There's also a third set kept offsite, with the offsite set periodically swapped with an on-site set.

    a. Assume you have 1 TB (1000 GB) of data to back up. How much would a disk backup system cost?

    b. How much would a tape backup system cost for 1 TB?

    c. How large would each backup have to be in order for a tape strategy to be less expensive?

    d. What kind of backup strategy favors tapes?

CHAPTER 7

INPUT/OUTPUT

221

LEARNING OBJECTIVES

After studying this chapter, you should be able to:

◆ Explain the use of I/O modules as part of a computer organization.

◆ Understand the difference between programmed I/O and interrupt-driven I/O and discuss their relative merits.

◆ Present an overview of the operation of direct memory access.

◆ Explain the function and use of I/O channels.

◆ Present an overview of Thunderbolt.

◆ Present an overview of InfiniBand.

I/O System Design Tool

In addition to the processor and a set of memory modules, the third key element of a computer system is a set of I/O modules. Each module interfaces to the system bus or central switch and controls one or more peripheral devices. An I/O module is not simply a set of mechanical connectors that wire a device into the system bus. Rather, the I/O module contains logic for performing a communication function between the peripheral and the bus.

The reader may wonder why one does not connect peripherals directly to the system bus. The reasons are as follows:

- There are a wide variety of peripherals with various methods of operation. It would be impractical to incorporate the necessary logic within the processor to control a range of devices.

- The data transfer rate of peripherals is often much slower than that of the memory or processor. Thus, it is impractical to use the high-speed system bus to communicate directly with a peripheral.

- On the other hand, the data transfer rate of some peripherals is faster than that of the memory or processor. Again, the mismatch would lead to inefficiencies if not managed properly.

- Peripherals often use different data formats and word lengths than the computer to which they are attached.

Thus, an I/O module is required. This module has two major functions (Figure 7.1):

- Interface to the processor and memory via the system bus or central switch

- Interface to one or more peripheral devices by tailored data links

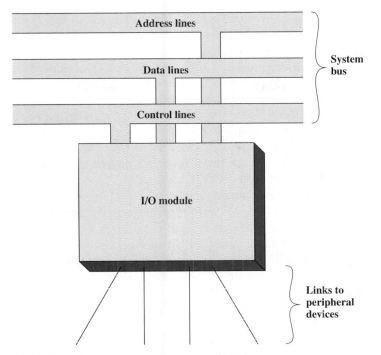

Figure 7.1 Generic Model of an I/O Module

We begin this chapter with a brief discussion of external devices, followed by an overview of the structure and function of an I/O module. Then we look at the various ways in which the I/O function can be performed in cooperation with the processor and memory: the internal I/O interface. Finally, we examine the external I/O interface, between the I/O module and the outside world.

7.1 EXTERNAL DEVICES

I/O operations are accomplished through a wide assortment of external devices that provide a means of exchanging data between the external environment and the computer. An external device attaches to the computer by a link to an I/O module (Figure 7.1). The link is used to exchange control, status, and data between the I/O module and the external device. An external device connected to an I/O module is often referred to as a *peripheral device* or, simply, a *peripheral.*

We can broadly classify external devices into three categories:

- **Human readable:** Suitable for communicating with the computer user
- **Machine readable:** Suitable for communicating with equipment
- **Communication:** Suitable for communicating with remote devices

Examples of human-readable devices are video display terminals (VDTs) and printers. Examples of machine-readable devices are magnetic disk and tape systems, and sensors and actuators, such as are used in a robotics application. Note that we are viewing disk and tape systems as I/O devices in this chapter, whereas in Chapter 6 we viewed them as memory devices. From a functional point of view, these devices are part of the memory hierarchy, and their use is appropriately discussed in Chapter 6. From a structural point of view, these devices are controlled by I/O modules and are hence to be considered in this chapter.

Communication devices allow a computer to exchange data with a remote device, which may be a human-readable device, such as a terminal, a machine-readable device, or even another computer.

In very general terms, the nature of an external device is indicated in Figure 7.2. The interface to the I/O module is in the form of control, data, and status signals. *Control signals* determine the function that the device will perform, such as send data to the I/O module (INPUT or READ), accept data from the I/O module (OUTPUT or WRITE), report status, or perform some control function particular to the device (e.g., position a disk head). *Data* are in the form of a set of bits to be sent to or received from the I/O module. *Status signals* indicate the state of the device. Examples are READY/NOT-READY to show whether the device is ready for data transfer.

Control logic associated with the device controls the device's operation in response to direction from the I/O module. The *transducer* converts data from electrical to other forms of energy during output and from other forms to electrical during input. Typically, a buffer is associated with the transducer to temporarily hold

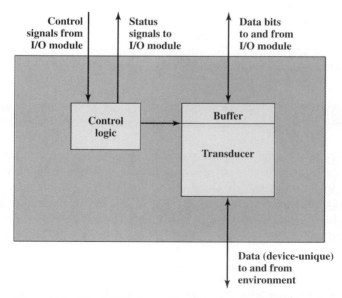

Figure 7.2   Block Diagram of an External Device

data being transferred between the I/O module and the external environment; a buffer size of 8 to 16 bits is common.

The interface between the I/O module and the external device will be examined in Section 7.7. The interface between the external device and the environment is beyond the scope of this book, but several brief examples are given here.

Keyboard/Monitor

The most common means of computer/user interaction is a keyboard/monitor arrangement. The user provides input through the keyboard. This input is then transmitted to the computer and may also be displayed on the monitor. In addition, the monitor displays data provided by the computer.

The basic unit of exchange is the character. Associated with each character is a code, typically 7 or 8 bits in length. The most commonly used text code is the International Reference Alphabet (IRA).[1] Each character in this code is represented by a unique 7-bit binary code; thus, 128 different characters can be represented. Characters are of two types: printable and control. Printable characters are the alphabetic, numeric, and special characters that can be printed on paper or displayed on a screen. Some of the control characters have to do with controlling the printing or displaying of characters; an example is carriage return. Other control characters are concerned with communications procedures. See Appendix F for details.

For keyboard input, when the user depresses a key, this generates an electronic signal that is interpreted by the transducer in the keyboard and translated into the bit pattern of the corresponding IRA code. This bit pattern is then transmitted to the I/O module in the computer. At the computer, the text can be stored in the same IRA code. On output, IRA code characters are transmitted to an external device from the I/O module. The transducer at the device interprets this code and sends the required electronic signals to the output device either to display the indicated character or perform the requested control function.

Disk Drive

A disk drive contains electronics for exchanging data, control, and status signals with an I/O module plus the electronics for controlling the disk read/write mechanism. In a fixed-head disk, the transducer is capable of converting between the magnetic patterns on the moving disk surface and bits in the device's buffer (Figure 7.2). A moving-head disk must also be able to cause the disk arm to move radially in and out across the disk's surface.

---

[1]IRA is defined in ITU-T Recommendation T.50 and was formerly known as International Alphabet Number 5 (IA5). The U.S. national version of IRA is referred to as the American Standard Code for Information Interchange (ASCII).

7.2 I/O MODULES

Module Function

The major functions or requirements for an I/O module fall into the following categories:

- Control and timing
- Processor communication
- Device communication
- Data buffering
- Error detection

During any period of time, the processor may communicate with one or more external devices in unpredictable patterns, depending on the program's need for I/O. The internal resources, such as main memory and the system bus, must be shared among a number of activities, including data I/O. Thus, the I/O function includes a **control and timing** requirement, to coordinate the flow of traffic between internal resources and external devices. For example, the control of the transfer of data from an external device to the processor might involve the following sequence of steps:

1. The processor interrogates the I/O module to check the status of the attached device.
2. The I/O module returns the device status.
3. If the device is operational and ready to transmit, the processor requests the transfer of data, by means of a command to the I/O module.
4. The I/O module obtains a unit of data (e.g., 8 or 16 bits) from the external device.
5. The data are transferred from the I/O module to the processor.

If the system employs a bus, then each of the interactions between the processor and the I/O module involves one or more bus arbitrations.

The preceding simplified scenario also illustrates that the I/O module must communicate with the processor and with the external device. **Processor communication** involves the following:

- **Command decoding:** The I/O module accepts commands from the processor, typically sent as signals on the control bus. For example, an I/O module for a disk drive might accept the following commands: READ SECTOR, WRITE SECTOR, SEEK track number, and SCAN record ID. The latter two commands each include a parameter that is sent on the data bus.
- **Data:** Data are exchanged between the processor and the I/O module over the data bus.
- **Status reporting:** Because peripherals are so slow, it is important to know the status of the I/O module. For example, if an I/O module is asked to send data to the processor (read), it may not be ready to do so because it is still working on the previous I/O command. This fact can be reported with a status signal.

Common status signals are BUSY and READY. There may also be signals to report various error conditions.

- **Address recognition:** Just as each word of memory has an address, so does each I/O device. Thus, an I/O module must recognize one unique address for each peripheral it controls.

On the other side, the I/O module must be able to perform **device communication**. This communication involves commands, status information, and data (Figure 7.2).

An essential task of an I/O module is **data buffering**. The need for this function is apparent from Figure 2.11. Whereas the transfer rate into and out of main memory or the processor is quite high, the rate is orders of magnitude lower for many peripheral devices and covers a wide range. Data coming from main memory are sent to an I/O module in a rapid burst. The data are buffered in the I/O module and then sent to the peripheral device at its data rate. In the opposite direction, data are buffered so as not to tie up the memory in a slow transfer operation. Thus, the I/O module must be able to operate at both device and memory speeds. Similarly, if the I/O device operates at a rate higher than the memory access rate, then the I/O module performs the needed buffering operation.

Finally, an I/O module is often responsible for **error detection** and for subsequently reporting errors to the processor. One class of errors includes mechanical and electrical malfunctions reported by the device (e.g., paper jam, bad disk track). Another class consists of unintentional changes to the bit pattern as it is transmitted from device to I/O module. Some form of error-detecting code is often used to detect transmission errors. A simple example is the use of a parity bit on each character of data. For example, the IRA character code occupies 7 bits of a byte. The eighth bit is set so that the total number of 1s in the byte is even (even parity) or odd (odd parity). When a byte is received, the I/O module checks the parity to determine whether an error has occurred.

I/O Module Structure

I/O modules vary considerably in complexity and the number of external devices that they control. We will attempt only a very general description here. (One specific device, the Intel 82C55A, is described in Section 7.4.) Figure 7.3 provides a general block diagram of an I/O module. The module connects to the rest of the computer through a set of signal lines (e.g., system bus lines). Data transferred to and from the module are buffered in one or more data registers. There may also be one or more status registers that provide current status information. A status register may also function as a control register, to accept detailed control information from the processor. The logic within the module interacts with the processor via a set of control lines. The processor uses the control lines to issue commands to the I/O module. Some of the control lines may be used by the I/O module (e.g., for arbitration and status signals). The module must also be able to recognize and generate addresses associated with the devices it controls. Each I/O module has a unique address or, if it controls more than one external device, a unique set of addresses. Finally, the I/O module contains logic specific to the interface with each device that it controls.

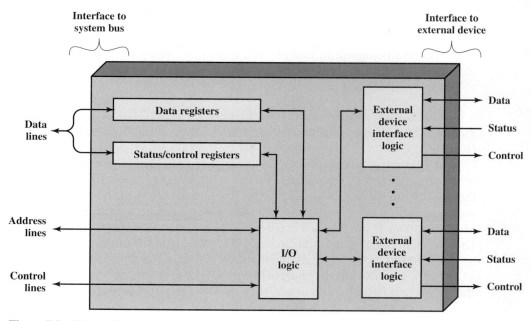

Figure 7.3 Block Diagram of an I/O Module

An I/O module functions to allow the processor to view a wide range of devices in a simple-minded way. There is a spectrum of capabilities that may be provided. The I/O module may hide the details of timing, formats, and the electromechanics of an external device so that the processor can function in terms of simple read and write commands, and possibly open and close file commands. In its simplest form, the I/O module may still leave much of the work of controlling a device (e.g., rewind a tape) visible to the processor.

An I/O module that takes on most of the detailed processing burden, presenting a high-level interface to the processor, is usually referred to as an *I/O channel* or *I/O processor*. An I/O module that is quite primitive and requires detailed control is usually referred to as an *I/O controller* or *device controller*. I/O controllers are commonly seen on microcomputers, whereas I/O channels are used on mainframes.

In what follows, we will use the generic term *I/O module* when no confusion results and will use more specific terms where necessary.

7.3 PROGRAMMED I/O

Three techniques are possible for I/O operations. With *programmed I/O*, data are exchanged between the processor and the I/O module. The processor executes a program that gives it direct control of the I/O operation, including sensing device status, sending a read or write command, and transferring the data. When the processor issues a command to the I/O module, it must wait until the I/O operation is complete. If the processor is faster than the I/O module, this is wasteful of processor time. With *interrupt-driven I/O*, the processor issues an *I/O command*, continues to execute

Table 7.1   I/O Techniques

	No Interrupts	Use of Interrupts
I/O-to-memory transfer through processor	Programmed I/O	Interrupt-driven I/O
Direct I/O-to-memory transfer		Direct memory access (DMA)

other instructions, and is interrupted by the I/O module when the latter has completed its work. With both programmed and *interrupt* I/O, the processor is responsible for extracting data from main memory for output and storing data in main memory for input. The alternative is known as *direct memory access* (DMA). In this mode, the I/O module and main memory exchange data directly, without processor involvement.

Table 7.1 indicates the relationship among these three techniques. In this section, we explore programmed I/O. Interrupt I/O and DMA are explored in the following two sections, respectively.

Overview of Programmed I/O

When the processor is executing a program and encounters an instruction relating to I/O, it executes that instruction by issuing a command to the appropriate I/O module. With programmed I/O, the I/O module will perform the requested action and then set the appropriate bits in the I/O status register (Figure 7.3). The I/O module takes no further action to alert the processor. In particular, it does not interrupt the processor. Thus, it is the responsibility of the processor periodically to check the status of the I/O module until it finds that the operation is complete.

To explain the programmed I/O technique, we view it first from the point of view of the I/O commands issued by the processor to the I/O module, and then from the point of view of the I/O instructions executed by the processor.

I/O Commands

To execute an I/O-related instruction, the processor issues an address, specifying the particular I/O module and external device, and an I/O command. There are four types of I/O commands that an I/O module may receive when it is addressed by a processor:

- **Control:** Used to activate a peripheral and tell it what to do. For example, a magnetic-tape unit may be instructed to rewind or to move forward one record. These commands are tailored to the particular type of peripheral device.
- **Test:** Used to test various status conditions associated with an I/O module and its peripherals. The processor will want to know that the peripheral of interest is powered on and available for use. It will also want to know if the most recent I/O operation is completed and if any errors occurred.
- **Read:** Causes the I/O module to obtain an item of data from the peripheral and place it in an internal buffer (depicted as a data register in Figure 7.3). The processor can then obtain the data item by requesting that the I/O module place it on the data bus.
- **Write:** Causes the I/O module to take an item of data (byte or word) from the data bus and subsequently transmit that data item to the peripheral.

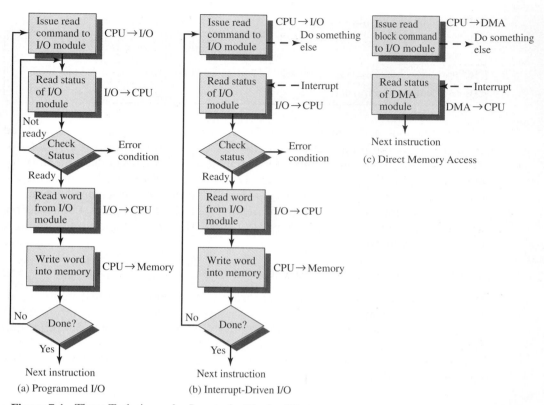

Figure 7.4   Three Techniques for Input of a Block of Data

Figure 7.4a gives an example of the use of programmed I/O to read in a block of data from a peripheral device (e.g., a record from tape) into memory. Data are read in one word (e.g., 16 bits) at a time. For each word that is read in, the processor must remain in a status-checking cycle until it determines that the word is available in the I/O module's data register. This flowchart highlights the main disadvantage of this technique: it is a time-consuming process that keeps the processor busy needlessly.

I/O Instructions

With programmed I/O, there is a close correspondence between the I/O-related instructions that the processor fetches from memory and the I/O commands that the processor issues to an I/O module to execute the instructions. That is, the instructions are easily mapped into I/O commands, and there is often a simple one-to-one relationship. The form of the instruction depends on the way in which external devices are addressed.

Typically, there will be many I/O devices connected through I/O modules to the system. Each device is given a unique identifier or address. When the processor issues an I/O command, the command contains the address of the desired device. Thus, each I/O module must interpret the address lines to determine if the command is for itself.

When the processor, main memory, and I/O share a common bus, two modes of addressing are possible: memory mapped and isolated. With **memory-mapped I/O**, there is a single address space for memory locations and I/O devices. The processor treats the status and data registers of I/O modules as memory locations and uses the same machine instructions to access both memory and I/O devices. So, for example, with 10 address lines, a combined total of $2^{10} = 1024$ memory locations and I/O addresses can be supported, in any combination.

With memory-mapped I/O, a single read line and a single write line are needed on the bus. Alternatively, the bus may be equipped with memory read and write plus input and output command lines. Now, the command line specifies whether the address refers to a memory location or an I/O device. The full range of addresses may be available for both. Again, with 10 address lines, the system may now support both 1024 memory locations and 1024 I/O addresses. Because the address space for I/O is isolated from that for memory, this is referred to as **isolated I/O**.

Figure 7.5 contrasts these two programmed I/O techniques. Figure 7.5a shows how the interface for a simple input device such as a terminal keyboard might appear to a programmer using memory-mapped I/O. Assume a 10-bit address, with a 512-bit memory (locations 0–511) and up to 512 I/O addresses (locations 512–1023). Two addresses are dedicated to keyboard input from a particular terminal. Address 516 refers to the data register and address 517 refers to the status register, which also functions as a control register for receiving processor commands. The program shown will read 1 byte of data from the keyboard into an accumulator register in the processor. Note that the processor loops until the data byte is available.

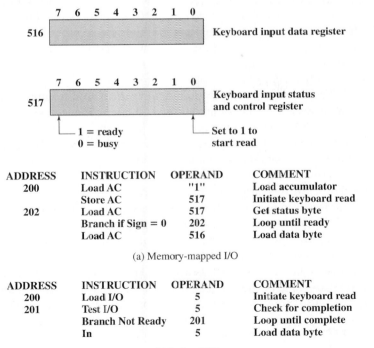

ADDRESS	INSTRUCTION	OPERAND	COMMENT
200	Load AC	"1"	Load accumulator
	Store AC	517	Initiate keyboard read
202	Load AC	517	Get status byte
	Branch if Sign = 0	202	Loop until ready
	Load AC	516	Load data byte

(a) Memory-mapped I/O

ADDRESS	INSTRUCTION	OPERAND	COMMENT
200	Load I/O	5	Initiate keyboard read
201	Test I/O	5	Check for completion
	Branch Not Ready	201	Loop until complete
	In	5	Load data byte

(b) Isolated I/O

Figure 7.5 Memory-Mapped and Isolated I/O

With isolated I/O (Figure 7.5b), the I/O ports are accessible only by special I/O commands, which activate the I/O command lines on the bus.

For most types of processors, there is a relatively large set of different instructions for referencing memory. If isolated I/O is used, there are only a few I/O instructions. Thus, an advantage of memory-mapped I/O is that this large repertoire of instructions can be used, allowing more efficient programming. A disadvantage is that valuable memory address space is used up. Both memory-mapped and isolated I/O are in common use.

7.4 INTERRUPT-DRIVEN I/O

The problem with programmed I/O is that the processor has to wait a long time for the I/O module of concern to be ready for either reception or transmission of data. The processor, while waiting, must repeatedly interrogate the status of the I/O module. As a result, the level of the performance of the entire system is severely degraded.

An alternative is for the processor to issue an I/O command to a module and then go on to do some other useful work. The I/O module will then interrupt the processor to request service when it is ready to exchange data with the processor. The processor then executes the data transfer, as before, and then resumes its former processing.

Let us consider how this works, first from the point of view of the I/O module. For input, the I/O module receives a READ command from the processor. The I/O module then proceeds to read data in from an associated peripheral. Once the data are in the module's data register, the module signals an interrupt to the processor over a control line. The module then waits until its data are requested by the processor. When the request is made, the module places its data on the data bus and is then ready for another I/O operation.

From the processor's point of view, the action for input is as follows. The processor issues a READ command. It then goes off and does something else (e.g., the processor may be working on several different programs at the same time). At the end of each instruction cycle, the processor checks for interrupts (Figure 3.9). When the interrupt from the I/O module occurs, the processor saves the context (e.g., program counter and processor registers) of the current program and processes the interrupt. In this case, the processor reads the word of data from the I/O module and stores it in memory. It then restores the context of the program it was working on (or some other program) and resumes execution.

Figure 7.4b shows the use of interrupt I/O for reading in a block of data. Compare this with Figure 7.4a. Interrupt I/O is more efficient than programmed I/O because it eliminates needless waiting. However, interrupt I/O still consumes a lot of processor time, because every word of data that goes from memory to I/O module or from I/O module to memory must pass through the processor.

Interrupt Processing

Let us consider the role of the processor in interrupt-driven I/O in more detail. The occurrence of an interrupt triggers a number of events, both in the processor hardware and in software. Figure 7.6 shows a typical sequence. When an I/O device completes an I/O operation, the following sequence of hardware events occurs:

1. The device issues an interrupt signal to the processor.
2. The processor finishes execution of the current instruction before responding to the interrupt, as indicated in Figure 3.9.
3. The processor tests for an interrupt, determines that there is one, and sends an acknowledgment signal to the device that issued the interrupt. The acknowledgment allows the device to remove its interrupt signal.
4. The processor now needs to prepare to transfer control to the interrupt routine. To begin, it needs to save information needed to resume the current program at the point of interrupt. The minimum information required is (a) the status of the processor, which is contained in a register called the program status word (PSW), and (b) the location of the next instruction to be executed, which is contained in the program counter. These can be pushed onto the system control stack.[2]
5. The processor now loads the program counter with the entry location of the interrupt-handling program that will respond to this interrupt. Depending on the computer architecture and operating system design, there may be a single

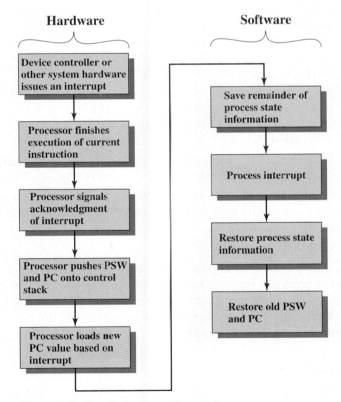

Figure 7.6 Simple Interrupt Processing

---

[2]See Appendix O for a discussion of stack operation.

program; one program for each type of interrupt; or one program for each device and each type of interrupt. If there is more than one interrupt-handling routine, the processor must determine which one to invoke. This information may have been included in the original interrupt signal, or the processor may have to issue a request to the device that issued the interrupt to get a response that contains the needed information.

Once the program counter has been loaded, the processor proceeds to the next instruction cycle, which begins with an instruction fetch. Because the instruction fetch is determined by the contents of the program counter, the result is that control is transferred to the interrupt-handler program. The execution of this program results in the following operations:

6. At this point, the program counter and PSW relating to the interrupted program have been saved on the system stack. However, there is other information that is considered part of the "state" of the executing program. In particular, the contents of the processor registers need to be saved, because these registers may be used by the interrupt handler. So, all of these values, plus any other state information, need to be saved. Typically, the interrupt handler will begin by saving the contents of all registers on the stack. Figure 7.7a shows a simple example. In this case, a user program is interrupted after the instruction at location N. The contents of all of the registers plus the address of the next instruction ($N + 1$) are pushed onto the stack. The stack pointer is updated to point to the new top of stack, and the program counter is updated to point to the beginning of the interrupt service routine.

7. The interrupt handler next processes the interrupt. This includes an examination of status information relating to the I/O operation or other event that caused an interrupt. It may also involve sending additional commands or acknowledgments to the I/O device.

8. When interrupt processing is complete, the saved register values are retrieved from the stack and restored to the registers (e.g., see Figure 7.7b).

9. The final act is to restore the PSW and program counter values from the stack. As a result, the next instruction to be executed will be from the previously interrupted program.

Note that it is important to save all the state information about the interrupted program for later resumption. This is because the interrupt is not a routine called from the program. Rather, the interrupt can occur at any time and therefore at any point in the execution of a user program. Its occurrence is unpredictable. Indeed, as we will see in the next chapter, the two programs may not have anything in common and may belong to two different users.

Design Issues

Two design issues arise in implementing interrupt I/O. First, because there will almost invariably be multiple I/O modules, how does the processor determine which device issued the interrupt? And second, if multiple interrupts have occurred, how does the processor decide which one to process?

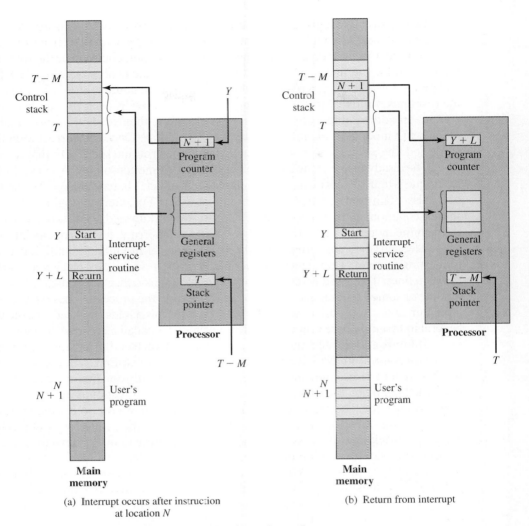

(a) Interrupt occurs after instruction
    at location N

(b) Return from interrupt

Figure 7.7   Changes in Memory and Registers for an Interrupt

Let us consider device identification first. Four general categories of techniques are in common use:

- Multiple interrupt lines
- Software poll
- Daisy chain (hardware poll, vectored)
- Bus arbitration (vectored)

The most straightforward approach to the problem is to provide **multiple interrupt lines** between the processor and the I/O modules. However, it is impractical to dedicate more than a few bus lines or processor pins to interrupt lines. Consequently, even if multiple lines are used, it is likely that each line will have multiple I/O modules attached to it. Thus, one of the other three techniques must be used on each line.

One alternative is the **software poll**. When the processor detects an interrupt, it branches to an interrupt-service routine whose job it is to poll each I/O module to determine which module caused the interrupt. The poll could be in the form of a separate command line (e.g., TESTI/O). In this case, the processor raises TESTI/O and places the address of a particular I/O module on the address lines. The I/O module responds positively if it sets the interrupt. Alternatively, each I/O module could contain an addressable status register. The processor then reads the status register of each I/O module to identify the interrupting module. Once the correct module is identified, the processor branches to a device-service routine specific to that device.

The disadvantage of the software poll is that it is time consuming. A more efficient technique is to use a **daisy chain**, which provides, in effect, a hardware poll. An example of a daisy-chain configuration is shown in Figure 3.30. For interrupts, all I/O modules share a common interrupt request line. The interrupt acknowledge line is daisy chained through the modules. When the processor senses an interrupt, it sends out an interrupt acknowledge. This signal propagates through a series of I/O modules until it gets to a requesting module. The requesting module typically responds by placing a word on the data lines. This word is referred to as a *vector* and is either the address of the I/O module or some other unique identifier. In either case, the processor uses the vector as a pointer to the appropriate device-service routine. This avoids the need to execute a general interrupt-service routine first. This technique is called a *vectored interrupt.*

There is another technique that makes use of vectored interrupts, and that is **bus arbitration**. With bus arbitration, an I/O module must first gain control of the bus before it can raise the interrupt request line. Thus, only one module can raise the line at a time. When the processor detects the interrupt, it responds on the interrupt acknowledge line. The requesting module then places its vector on the data lines.

The aforementioned techniques serve to identify the requesting I/O module. They also provide a way of assigning priorities when more than one device is requesting interrupt service. With multiple lines, the processor just picks the interrupt line with the highest priority. With software polling, the order in which modules are polled determines their priority. Similarly, the order of modules on a daisy chain determines their priority. Finally, bus arbitration can employ a priority scheme, as discussed in Section 3.4.

We now turn to two examples of interrupt structures.

Intel 82C59A Interrupt Controller

The Intel 80386 provides a single Interrupt Request (INTR) and a single Interrupt Acknowledge (INTA) line. To allow the 80386 to handle a variety of devices and priority structures, it is usually configured with an external interrupt arbiter, the 82C59A. External devices are connected to the 82C59A, which in turn connects to the 80386.

Figure 7.8 shows the use of the 82C59A to connect multiple I/O modules for the 80386. A single 82C59A can handle up to eight modules. If control for more than eight modules is required, a cascade arrangement can be used to handle up to 64 modules.

The 82C59A's sole responsibility is the management of interrupts. It accepts interrupt requests from attached modules, determines which interrupt has the highest priority, and then signals the processor by raising the INTR line. The processor acknowledges via the INTA line. This prompts the 82C59A to place the appropriate

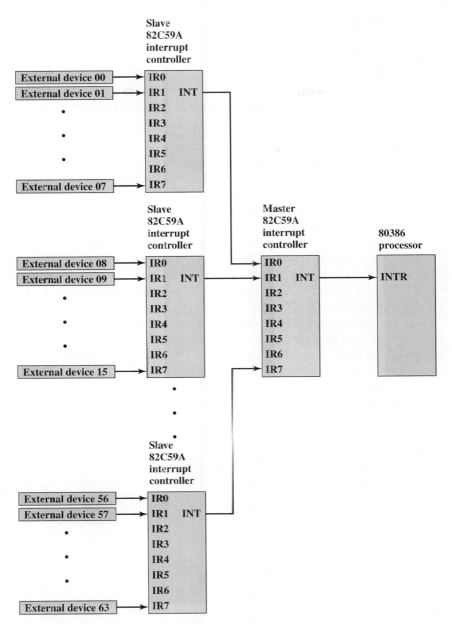

Figure 7.8 Use of the 82C59A Interrupt Controller

vector information on the data bus. The processor can then proceed to process the interrupt and to communicate directly with the I/O module to read or write data.

The 82C59A is programmable. The 80386 determines the priority scheme to be used by setting a control word in the 82C59A. The following interrupt modes are possible:

- **Fully nested:** The interrupt requests are ordered in priority from 0 (IR0) through 7 (IR7).

- **Rotating:** In some applications a number of interrupting devices are of equal priority. In this mode a device, after being serviced, receives the lowest priority in the group.

- **Special mask:** This allows the processor to inhibit interrupts from certain devices.

The Intel 82C55A Programmable Peripheral Interface

As an example of an I/O module used for programmed I/O and interrupt-driven I/O, we consider the Intel 82C55A Programmable Peripheral Interface. The 82C55A is a single-chip, general-purpose I/O module designed for use with the Intel 80386 processor. Figure 7.9 shows a general block diagram plus the pin assignment for the 40-pin package in which it is housed.

The right side of the block diagram is the external interface of the 82C55A. The 24 I/O lines are programmable by the 80386 by means of the control register. The 80386 can set the value of the control register to specify a variety of operating modes and configurations. The 24 lines are divided into three 8-bit groups (A, B, C). Each group can function as an 8-bit I/O port. In addition, group C is subdivided into 4-bit groups (C_A and C_B), which may be used in conjunction with the A and B I/O ports. Configured in this manner, group C lines carry control and status signals.

The left side of the block diagram is the internal interface to the 80386 bus. It includes an 8-bit bidirectional data bus (D0 through D7), used to transfer data to and from the I/O ports and to transfer control information to the control register. The two address lines specify one of the three I/O ports or the control register. A transfer takes place when the CHIP SELECT line is enabled together with either the READ or WRITE line. The RESET line is used to initialize the module.

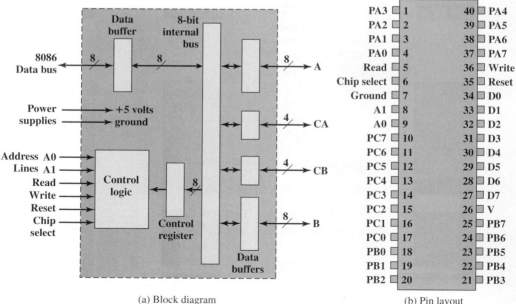

(a) Block diagram   (b) Pin layout

Figure 7.9   The Intel 82C55A Programmable Peripheral Interface

The control register is loaded by the processor to control the mode of operation and to define signals, if any. In Mode 0 operation, the three groups of eight external lines function as three 8-bit I/O ports. Each port can be designated as input or output. Otherwise, groups A and B function as I/O ports, and the lines of group C serve as control lines for A and B. The control signals serve two principal purposes: "handshaking" and interrupt request. Handshaking is a simple timing mechanism. One control line is used by the sender as a DATA READY line, to indicate when the data are present on the I/O data lines. Another line is used by the receiver as an ACKNOWLEDGE, indicating that the data have been read and the data lines may be cleared. Another line may be designated as an INTERRUPT REQUEST line and tied back to the system bus.

Because the 82C55A is programmable via the control register, it can be used to control a variety of simple peripheral devices. Figure 7.10 illustrates its use to control

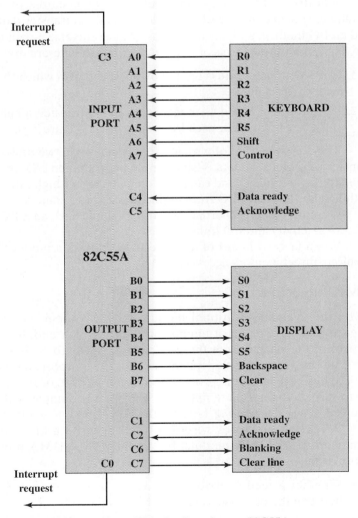

Figure 7.10 Keyboard/Display Interface to 82C55A

a keyboard/display terminal. The keyboard provides 8 bits of input. Two of these bits, SHIFT and CONTROL, have special meaning to the keyboard-handling program executing in the processor. However, this interpretation is transparent to the 82C55A, which simply accepts the 8 bits of data and presents them on the system data bus. Two handshaking control lines are provided for use with the keyboard.

The display is also linked by an 8-bit data port. Again, two of the bits have special meanings that are transparent to the 82C55A. In addition to two handshaking lines, two lines provide additional control functions.

7.5 DIRECT MEMORY ACCESS

Drawbacks of Programmed and Interrupt–Driven I/O

Interrupt-driven I/O, though more efficient than simple programmed I/O, still requires the active intervention of the processor to transfer data between memory and an I/O module, and any data transfer must traverse a path through the processor. Thus, both these forms of I/O suffer from two inherent drawbacks:

1. The I/O transfer rate is limited by the speed with which the processor can test and service a device.
2. The processor is tied up in managing an I/O transfer; a number of instructions must be executed for each I/O transfer (e.g., Figure 7.5).

There is somewhat of a trade-off between these two drawbacks. Consider the transfer of a block of data. Using simple programmed I/O, the processor is dedicated to the task of I/O and can move data at a rather high rate, at the cost of doing nothing else. Interrupt I/O frees up the processor to some extent at the expense of the I/O transfer rate. Nevertheless, both methods have an adverse impact on both processor activity and I/O transfer rate.

When large volumes of data are to be moved, a more efficient technique is required: direct memory access (DMA).

DMA Function

DMA involves an additional module on the system bus. The DMA module (Figure 7.11) is capable of mimicking the processor and, indeed, of taking over control of the system from the processor. It needs to do this to transfer data to and from memory over the system bus. For this purpose, the DMA module must use the bus only when the processor does not need it, or it must force the processor to suspend operation temporarily. The latter technique is more common and is referred to as *cycle stealing*, because the DMA module in effect steals a bus cycle.

When the processor wishes to read or write a block of data, it issues a command to the DMA module, by sending to the DMA module the following information:

- Whether a read or write is requested, using the read or write control line between the processor and the DMA module
- The address of the I/O device involved, communicated on the data lines

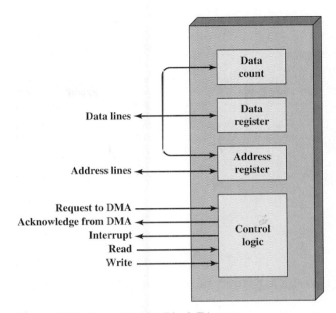

Figure 7.11 Typical DMA Block Diagram

- The starting location in memory to read from or write to, communicated on the data lines and stored by the DMA module in its address register
- The number of words to be read or written, again communicated via the data lines and stored in the data count register

The processor then continues with other work. It has delegated this I/O operation to the DMA module. The DMA module transfers the entire block of data, one word at a time, directly to or from memory, without going through the processor. When the transfer is complete, the DMA module sends an interrupt signal to the processor. Thus, the processor is involved only at the beginning and end of the transfer (Figure 7.4c).

Figure 7.12 shows where in the instruction cycle the processor may be suspended. In each case, the processor is suspended just before it needs to use the bus. The DMA module then transfers one word and returns control to the processor. Note that this is not an interrupt; the processor does not save a context and do something else. Rather, the processor pauses for one bus cycle. The overall effect is to cause the processor to execute more slowly. Nevertheless, for a multiple-word I/O transfer, DMA is far more efficient than interrupt-driven or programmed I/O.

The DMA mechanism can be configured in a variety of ways. Some possibilities are shown in Figure 7.13. In the first example, all modules share the same system bus. The DMA module, acting as a surrogate processor, uses programmed I/O to exchange data between memory and an I/O module through the DMA module. This configuration, while it may be inexpensive, is clearly inefficient. As with processor-controlled programmed I/O, each transfer of a word consumes two bus cycles.

The number of required bus cycles can be cut substantially by integrating the DMA and I/O functions. As Figure 7.13b indicates, this means that there is a path

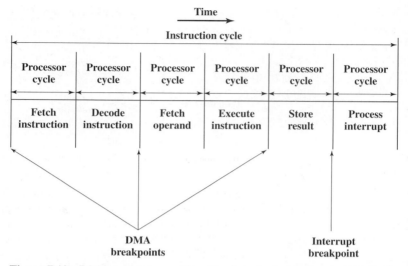

Figure 7.12 DMA and Interrupt Breakpoints during an Instruction Cycle

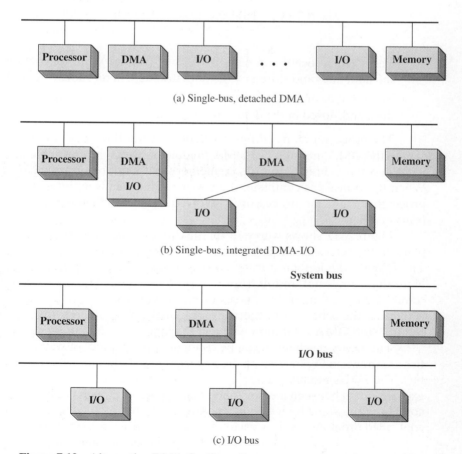

Figure 7.13 Alternative DMA Configurations

between the DMA module and one or more I/O modules that does not include the system bus. The DMA logic may actually be a part of an I/O module, or it may be a separate module that controls one or more I/O modules. This concept can be taken one step further by connecting I/O modules to the DMA module using an I/O bus (Figure 7.13c). This reduces the number of I/O interfaces in the DMA module to one and provides for an easily expandable configuration. In both of these cases (Figures 7.13b and c), the system bus that the DMA module shares with the processor and memory is used by the DMA module only to exchange data with memory. The exchange of data between the DMA and I/O modules takes place off the system bus.

Intel 8237A DMA Controller

The Intel 8237A DMA controller interfaces to the 80 x 86 family of processors and to DRAM memory to provide a DMA capability. Figure 7.14 indicates the location of the DMA module. When the DMA module needs to use the system buses (data, address, and control) to transfer data, it sends a signal called HOLD to the processor. The processor responds with the HLDA (hold acknowledge) signal, indicating that the DMA module can use the buses. For example, if the DMA module is to transfer a block of data from memory to disk, it will do the following:

1. The peripheral device (such as the disk controller) will request the service of DMA by pulling DREQ (DMA request) high.
2. The DMA will put a high on its HRQ (hold request), signaling the CPU through its HOLD pin that it needs to use the buses.

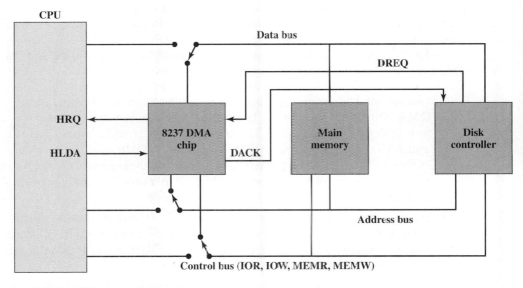

DACK = DMA acknowledge
DREQ = DMA request
HLDA = HOLD acknowledge
HRQ = HOLD request

Figure 7.14   8237 DMA Usage of System Bus

3. The CPU will finish the present bus cycle (not necessarily the present instruction) and respond to the DMA request by putting high on its HDLA (hold acknowledge), thus telling the 8237 DMA that it can go ahead and use the buses to perform its task. HOLD must remain active high as long as DMA is performing its task.

4. DMA will activate DACK (DMA acknowledge), which tells the peripheral device that it will start to transfer the data.

5. DMA starts to transfer the data from memory to peripheral by putting the address of the first byte of the block on the address bus and activating MEMR, thereby reading the byte from memory into the data bus; it then activates IOW to write it to the peripheral. Then DMA decrements the counter and increments the address pointer and repeats this process until the count reaches zero and the task is finished.

6. After the DMA has finished its job it will deactivate HRQ, signaling the CPU that it can regain control over its buses.

While the DMA is using the buses to transfer data, the processor is idle. Similarly, when the processor is using the bus, the DMA is idle. The 8237 DMA is known as a *fly-by* DMA controller. This means that the data being moved from one location to another does not pass through the DMA chip and is not stored in the DMA chip. Therefore, the DMA can only transfer data between an I/O port and a memory address, but not between two I/O ports or two memory locations. However, as explained subsequently, the DMA chip can perform a memory-to-memory transfer via a register.

The 8237 contains four DMA channels that can be programmed independently, and any one of the channels may be active at any moment. These channels are numbered 0, 1, 2, and 3.

The 8237 has a set of five control/command registers to program and control DMA operation over one of its channels (Table 7.2):

- **Command:** The processor loads this register to control the operation of the DMA. D0 enables a memory-to-memory transfer, in which channel 0 is used to transfer a byte into an 8237 temporary register and channel 1 is used to transfer the byte from the register to memory. When memory-to-memory is enabled, D1 can be used to disable increment/decrement on channel 0 so that a fixed value can be written into a block of memory. D2 enables or disables DMA.

- **Status:** The processor reads this register to determine DMA status. Bits D0–D3 are used to indicate if channels 0–3 have reached their TC (terminal count). Bits D4–D7 are used by the processor to determine if any channel has a DMA request pending.

- **Mode:** The processor sets this register to determine the mode of operation of the DMA. Bits D0 and D1 are used to select a channel. The other bits select various operation modes for the selected channel. Bits D2 and D3 determine if the transfer is from an I/O device to memory (write) or from memory to I/O (read), or a verify operation. If D4 is set, then the memory

Table 7.2 Intel 8237A Registers

Bit	Command	Status	Mode	Single Mask	All Mask
D0	Memory-to-memory E/D	Channel 0 has reached TC	Channel select	Select channel mask bit	Clear/set channel 0 mask bit
D1	Channel 0 address hold E/D	Channel 1 has reached TC			Clear/set channel 1 mask bit
D2	Controller E/D	Channel 2 has reached TC	Verify/write/ read transfer	Clear/set mask bit	Clear/set channel 2 mask bit
D3	Normal/compressed timing	Channel 3 has reached TC	Auto-initialization E/D		Clear/set channel 3 mask bit
D4	Fixed/rotating priority	Channel 0 request	Address increment/ decrement select	Not used	Not used
D5	Late/extended write selection	Channel 0 request			
D6	DREQ sense active high/low	Channel 0 request	Demand/single/block/ cascade mode select		
D7	DACK sense active high/low	Channel 0 request			

E/D = enable/disable

TC = terminal count

245

address register and the count register are reloaded with their original values at the end of a DMA data transfer. Bits D6 and D7 determine the way in which the 8237 is used. In single mode, a single byte of data is transferred. Block and demand modes are used for a block transfer, with the demand mode allowing for premature ending of the transfer. Cascade mode allows multiple 8237s to be cascaded to expand the number of channels to more than 4.

- **Single Mask:** The processor sets this register. Bits D0 and D1 select the channel. Bit D2 clears or sets the mask bit for that channel. It is through this register that the DREQ input of a specific channel can be masked (disabled) or unmasked (enabled). While the command register can be used to disable the whole DMA chip, the single mask register allows the programmer to disable or enable a specific channel.
- **All Mask:** This register is similar to the single mask register except that all four channels can be masked or unmasked with one write operation.

In addition, the 8237A has eight data registers: one memory address register and one count register for each channel. The processor sets these registers to indicate the location of size of main memory to be affected by the transfers.

7.6 I/O CHANNELS AND PROCESSORS

The Evolution of the I/O Function

As computer systems have evolved, there has been a pattern of increasing complexity and sophistication of individual components. Nowhere is this more evident than in the I/O function. We have already seen part of that evolution. The evolutionary steps can be summarized as follows:

1. The CPU directly controls a peripheral device. This is seen in simple microprocessor-controlled devices.
2. A controller or I/O module is added. The CPU uses programmed I/O without interrupts. With this step, the CPU becomes somewhat divorced from the specific details of external device interfaces.
3. The same configuration as in step 2 is used, but now interrupts are employed. The CPU need not spend time waiting for an I/O operation to be performed, thus increasing efficiency.
4. The I/O module is given direct access to memory via DMA. It can now move a block of data to or from memory without involving the CPU, except at the beginning and end of the transfer.
5. The I/O module is enhanced to become a processor in its own right, with a specialized instruction set tailored for I/O. The CPU directs the I/O processor

to execute an I/O program in memory. The I/O processor fetches and executes these instructions without CPU intervention. This allows the CPU to specify a sequence of I/O activities and to be interrupted only when the entire sequence has been performed.

6. The I/O module has a local memory of its own and is, in fact, a computer in its own right. With this architecture, a large set of I/O devices can be controlled, with minimal CPU involvement. A common use for such an architecture has been to control communication with interactive terminals. The I/O processor takes care of most of the tasks involved in controlling the terminals.

As one proceeds along this evolutionary path, more and more of the I/O function is performed without CPU involvement. The CPU is increasingly relieved of I/O-related tasks, improving performance. With the last two steps (5–6), a major change occurs with the introduction of the concept of an I/O module capable of executing a program. For step 5, the I/O module is often referred to as an *I/O channel*. For step 6, the term *I/O processor* is often used. However, both terms are on occasion applied to both situations. In what follows, we will use the term *I/O channel*.

Characteristics of I/O Channels

The I/O channel represents an extension of the DMA concept. An I/O channel has the ability to execute I/O instructions, which gives it complete control over I/O operations. In a computer system with such devices, the CPU does not execute I/O instructions. Such instructions are stored in main memory to be executed by a special-purpose processor in the I/O channel itself. Thus, the CPU initiates an I/O transfer by instructing the I/O channel to execute a program in memory. The program will specify the device or devices, the area or areas of memory for storage, priority, and actions to be taken for certain error conditions. The I/O channel follows these instructions and controls the data transfer.

Two types of I/O channels are common, as illustrated in Figure 7.15. A *selector channel* controls multiple high-speed devices and, at any one time, is dedicated to the transfer of data with one of those devices. Thus, the I/O channel selects one device and effects the data transfer. Each device, or a small set of devices, is handled by a *controller,* or I/O module, that is much like the I/O modules we have been discussing. Thus, the I/O channel serves in place of the CPU in controlling these I/O controllers. A *multiplexor channel* can handle I/O with multiple devices at the same time. For low-speed devices, a *byte multiplexor* accepts or transmits characters as fast as possible to multiple devices. For example, the resultant character stream from three devices with different rates and individual streams $A_1A_2A_3A_4 \ldots$, $B_1B_2B_3B_4 \ldots$, and $C_1C_2C_3C_4 \ldots$ might be $A_1B_1C_1A_2C_2A_3B_2C_3A_4$, and so on. For high-speed devices, a *block multiplexor* interleaves blocks of data from several devices.

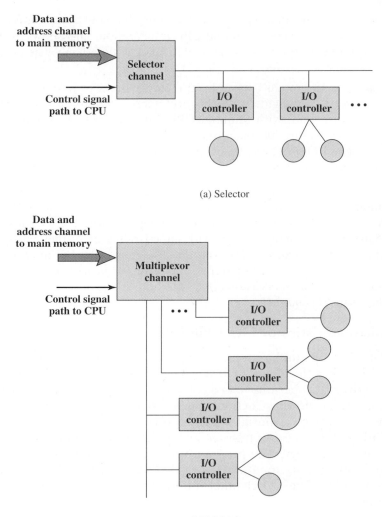

(a) Selector

(b) Multiplexor

Figure 7.15   I/O Channel Architecture

7.7   THE EXTERNAL INTERFACE: THUNDERBOLT AND INFINIBAND

Types of Interfaces

The interface to a peripheral from an I/O module must be tailored to the nature and operation of the peripheral. One major characteristic of the interface is whether it is serial or parallel (Figure 7.16). In a **parallel interface**, there are multiple lines connecting the I/O module and the peripheral, and multiple bits are transferred simultaneously, just as all of the bits of a word are transferred simultaneously over the data bus. In a **serial interface**, there is only one line used to transmit data, and bits must be transmitted one at a time. A parallel interface has traditionally been

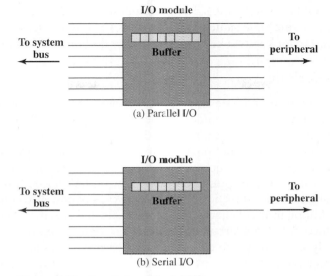

Figure 7.16 Parallel and Serial I/O

used for higher-speed peripherals, such as tape and disk, while the serial interface has traditionally been used for printers and terminals. With a new generation of high-speed serial interfaces, parallel interfaces are becoming much less common.

In either case, the I/O module must engage in a dialogue with the peripheral. In general terms, the dialogue for a write operation is as follows:

1. The I/O module sends a control signal requesting permission to send data.

2. The peripheral acknowledges the request.

3. The I/O module transfers data (one word or a block depending on the peripheral).

4. The peripheral acknowledges receipt of the data.

A read operation proceeds similarly.

Key to the operation of an I/O module is an internal buffer that can store data being passed between the peripheral and the rest of the system. This buffer allows the I/O module to compensate for the differences in speed between the system bus and its external lines.

Point-to-Point and Multipoint Configurations

The connection between an I/O module in a computer system and external devices can be either point-to-point or multipoint. A point-to-point interface provides a dedicated line between the I/O module and the external device. On small systems (PCs, workstations), typical point-to-point links include those to the keyboard, printer, and external modem. A typical example of such an interface is the EIA-232 specification (see [STAL11] for a description).

Of increasing importance are multipoint external interfaces, used to support external mass storage devices (disk and tape drives) and multimedia devices

(CD-ROMs, video, audio). These multipoint interfaces are in effect external buses, and they exhibit the same type of logic as the buses discussed in Chapter 3. In this section, we look at two key examples: Thunderbolt and InfiniBand.

Thunderbolt

The most recent, and fastest, peripheral connection technology to become available for general-purpose use is Thunderbolt, developed by Intel with collaboration from Apple. One Thunderbolt cable can manage the work previously required of multiple cables. The technology combines data, video, audio, and power into a single high-speed connection for peripherals such as hard drives, RAID (Redundant Array of Independent Disks) arrays, video-capture boxes, and network interfaces. It provides up to 10 Gbps throughput in each direction and up to 10 Watts of power to connected peripherals.

Although the technology and its associated specifications have stabilized, the introduction of Thunderbolt-equipped devices into the marketplace has, as of this writing, only slowly begun to develop. This is because a Thunderbolt-compatible peripheral interface is considerably more complex than that of a simple USB device. The first generation of Thunderbolt products are primarily aimed at the prosumer (professional-consumer) market such as audiovisual editors who want to be able to move large volumes of data quickly between storage devices and laptops. As the technology becomes cheaper, Thunderbolt will find mass consumer uses, such as enabling very high-speed data backups and editing high-definition photos. Thunderbolt is already a standard feature of Apple's MacBook Pro laptop and iMac desktop computers.

THUNDERBOLT CONFIGURATION Figure 7.17 shows a typical computer configuration that makes use of Thunderbolt. From the point of view of I/O, the central element in this configuration is the **Thunderbolt controller**, which is a high-performance, cross-bar switch. Unlike bus-based I/O architectures, each Thunderbolt port on a computer is capable of providing the full data transfer rate of the link in both directions with no sharing of data transmission capacity between ports or between upstream and downstream directions.

For communication internal to the computer, the Thunderbolt controller includes one or more **DisplayPort** protocol adapter ports. DisplayPort is a digital display interface standard now widely adopted for computer monitors, laptop displays, and other graphics and video interfaces. The controller also includes a **PCI Express switch** with up to four **PCI Express protocol adapter ports** for internal communication.

The Thunderbolt controller provides access to external devices through one or more **Thunderbolt connectors**. Each connector can provide one or two full-duplex channels, with each channel providing up to 10 Gbps in each direction. The same connector can be used for electrical or optical cables. The electrical cable can extend up to 3 meters, while the optical cable can extend into the tens of meters.

Users can connect high-performance peripherals to their PC over a cable, daisy chaining one after another, up to a total of 7 devices, 1 or 2 of which can be high-resolution DisplayPort displays (depending on the controller configuration in the host PC). Because Thunderbolt technology delivers two full-bandwidth channels, the user can realize high bandwidth not only on the first device attached but on downstream devices as well.

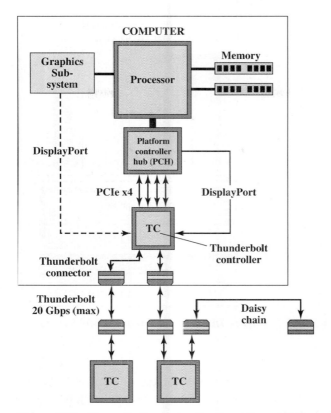

Figure 7.17 Example Computer Configuration with Thunderbolt

THUNDERBOLT PROTOCOL ARCHITECTURE Figure 7.18 illustrates the Thunderbolt protocol architecture. The **cable and connector layer** provides transmission medium access. This layer specifies the physical and electrical attributes of the connector port.

The Thunderbolt protocol **physical layer** is responsible for link maintenance including hot-plug[3] detection and data encoding to provide highly efficient data transfer. The physical layer has been designed to introduce very minimal overhead and provides full-duplex 10 Gbps of usable capacity to the upper layers.

The **common transport layer** is the key to the operation of Thunderbolt and what makes it attractive as a high-speed peripheral I/O technology. Some of the features include:

- A high-performance, low-power, switching architecture.
- A highly efficient, low-overhead packet format with flexible quality of service (QoS) support that allows multiplexing of bursty PCI Express transactions

---

[3]The term *hot plug* is defined as pulling out a component from a system and plugging in a new one while the main power is still on. It allows an external drive, network adapter, or other peripheral to be plugged in without having to power down the computer.

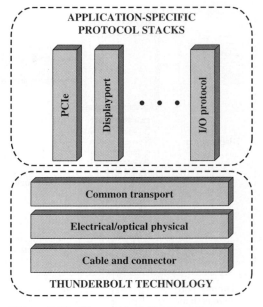

Figure 7.18 Thunderbolt Protocol Layers

with DisplayPort communication on the same link. The transport layer has the ability to flexibly allocate link bandwidth using priority and bandwidth reservation mechanisms.

- The use of small packet sizes to achieve low latency.
- The use of credit-based flow control to achieve small buffer sizes.
- A symmetric architecture that supports flexible topologies (star, tree, daisy chaining, etc.) and enables peer-to-peer communication (via software) between devices.
- A novel time synchronization protocol that allows all the Thunderbolt products connected in a domain to synchronize their time within 8ns of each other.

The **application layer** contains I/O protocols that are mapped onto the transport layer. Initially, Thunderbolt provides full support for PCIe and DisplayPort protocols. This function is provided by a protocol adapter, which is responsible for efficient encapsulation of the mapped protocol information into transport layer packets. Mapped protocol packets between a source device and a destination device may be routed over a path that may cross multiple Thunderbolt controllers. At the destination device, a protocol adapter re-creates the mapped protocol in a way that is indistinguishable from what was received by the source device. The advantage of doing protocol mapping in this way is that Thunderbolt technology–enabled product devices appear as PCIe or DisplayPort devices to the operating system of the host computer, thereby enabling the use of standard drivers that are available in many operating systems today.

InfiniBand

InfiniBand is a recent I/O specification aimed at the high-end server market.[4] The first version of the specification was released in early 2001 and has attracted numerous vendors. The standard describes an architecture and specifications for data flow among processors and intelligent I/O devices. InfiniBand has become a popular interface for storage area networking and other large storage configurations. In essence, InfiniBand enables servers, remote storage, and other network devices to be attached in a central fabric of switches and links. The switch-based architecture can connect up to 64,000 servers, storage systems, and networking devices.

INFINIBAND ARCHITECTURE Although PCI is a reliable interconnect method and continues to provide increased speeds, up to 4 Gbps, it is a limited architecture compared to InfiniBand. With InfiniBand, it is not necessary to have the basic I/O interface hardware inside the server chassis. With InfiniBand, remote storage, networking, and connections between servers are accomplished by attaching all devices to a central fabric of switches and links. Removing I/O from the server chassis allows greater server density and allows for a more flexible and scalable data center, as independent nodes may be added as needed.

Unlike PCI, which measures distances from a CPU motherboard in centimeters, InfiniBand's channel design enables I/O devices to be placed up to 17 meters away from the server using copper, up to 300 m using multimode optical fiber, and up to 10 km with single-mode optical fiber. Transmission rates has high as 30 Gbps can be achieved.

Figure 7.19 illustrates the InfiniBand architecture. The key elements are as follows:

- **Host channel adapter (HCA):** Instead of a number of PCI slots, a typical server needs a single interface to an HCA that links the server to an InfiniBand switch. The HCA attaches to the server at a memory controller, which has access to the system bus and controls traffic between the processor and memory and between the HCA and memory. The HCA uses direct-memory access (DMA) to read and write memory.

- **Target channel adapter (TCA):** A TCA is used to connect storage systems, routers, and other peripheral devices to an InfiniBand switch.

- **InfiniBand switch:** A switch provides point-to-point physical connections to a variety of devices and switches traffic from one link to another. Servers and devices communicate through their adapters, via the switch. The switch's intelligence manages the linkage without interrupting the servers' operation.

- **Links:** The link between a switch and a channel adapter, or between two switches.

- **Subnet:** A subnet consists of one or more interconnected switches plus the links that connect other devices to those switches. Figure 7.19 shows a subnet with

---

[4]InfiniBand is the result of the merger of two competing projects: Future I/O (backed by Cisco, HP, Compaq, and IBM) and Next Generation I/O (developed by Intel and backed by a number of other companies).

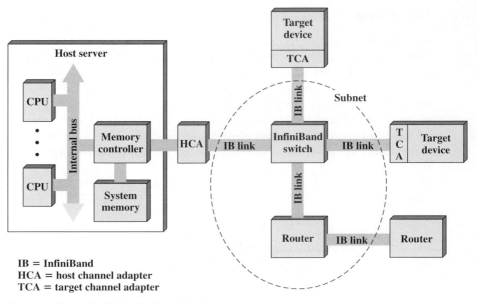

IB = InfiniBand
HCA = host channel adapter
TCA = target channel adapter

Figure 7.19   InfiniBand Switch Fabric

a single switch, but more complex subnets are required when a large number of devices are to be interconnected. Subnets allow administrators to confine broadcast and multicast transmissions within the subnet.

- **Router:** Connects InfiniBand subnets, or connects an InfiniBand switch to a network, such as a local area network, wide area network, or storage area network.

The channel adapters are intelligent devices that handle all I/O functions without the need to interrupt the server's processor. For example, there is a control protocol by which a switch discovers all TCAs and HCAs in the fabric and assigns logical addresses to each. This is done without processor involvement.

The InfiniBand switch temporarily opens up channels between the processor and devices with which it is communicating. The devices do not have to share a channel's capacity, as is the case with a bus-based design such as PCI, which requires that devices arbitrate for access to the processor. Additional devices are added to the configuration by hooking up each device's TCA to the switch.

INFINIBAND OPERATION   Each physical link between a switch and an attached interface (HCA or TCA) can be support up to 16 logical channels, called **virtual lanes**. One lane is reserved for fabric management and the other lanes for data transport. Data are sent in the form of a stream of packets, with each packet containing some portion of the total data to be transferred, plus addressing and control information. Thus, a set of communications protocols are used to manage the transfer of data. A virtual lane is temporarily dedicated to the transfer of data from one end node to another over the InfiniBand fabric. The InfiniBand switch maps traffic from an incoming lane to an outgoing lane to route the data between the desired end points.

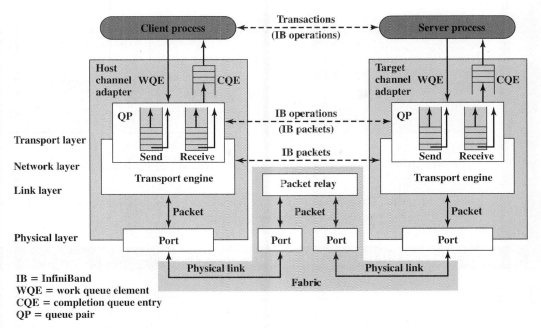

IB = InfiniBand
WQE = work queue element
CQE = completion queue entry
QP = queue pair

Figure 7.20   InfiniBand Communication Protocol Stack

Figure 7.20 indicates the logical structure used to support exchanges over InfiniBand. To account for the fact that some devices can send data faster than another destination device can receive it, a pair of queues at both ends of each link temporarily buffers excess outbound and inbound data. The queues can be located in the channel adapter or in the attached device's memory. A separate pair of queues is used for each virtual lane. The host uses these queues in the following fashion. The host places a transaction, called a work queue entry (WQE) into either the send or receive queue of the queue pair. The two most important WQEs are SEND and RECEIVE. For a SEND operation, the WQE specifies a block of data in the device's memory space for the hardware to send to the destination. A RECEIVE WQE specifies where the hardware is to place data received from another device when that consumer executes a SEND operation. The channel adapter processes each posted WQE in the proper prioritized order and generates a completion queue entry (CQE) to indicate the completion status.

Figure 7.20 also indicates that a layered protocol architecture is used, consisting of four layers:

- **Physical:** The physical-layer specification defines three link speeds (1X, 4X, and 12X) giving transmission rates of 2.5, 10, and 30 Gbps, respectively (Table 7.3). The physical layer also defines the physical media, including copper and optical fiber.

- **Link:** This layer defines the basic packet structure used to exchange data, including an addressing scheme that assigns a unique link address to every device in a subnet. This level includes the logic for setting up virtual lanes and for switching data through switches from source to destination within a subnet. The packet structure includes an error-detection code to provide reliability.

Table 7.3 InfiniBand Links and Data Throughput Rates

Link	Signal rate (unidirectional)	Usable capacity (80% of signal rate)	Effective data throughput (send + receive)
1-wide	2.5 Gbps	2 Gbps (250 MBps)	(250 + 250) MBps
4-wide	10 Gbps	8 Gbps (1 GBps)	(1 + 1) GBps
12-wide	30 Gbps	24 Gbps (3 GBps)	(3 + 3) Gbps

- **Network:** The network layer routes packets between different InfiniBand subnets.

- **Transport:** The transport layer provides reliability mechanism for end-to-end transfer of packets across one or more subnets.

7.8 IBM zENTERPRISE 196 I/O STRUCTURE

The zEnterprise 196 is IBM's latest mainframe computer offering (at the time of this writing), introduced in 2010. The system is based on the use of the z196 chip, which is a 5.2-GHz multicore chip with four cores. The z196 architecture can have a maximum of 24 processor chips for a total of 96 cores. In this section, we look at the I/O structure of the zEnterprise 196.

Channel Structure

The zEnterprise 196 has a dedicated I/O subsystem that manages all I/O operations, completely off-loading this processing and memory burden from the main processors. Figure 7.21 shows the logical structure of the I/O subsystem. Of the 96 core processors, up to 4 of these can be dedicated for I/O use, creating 4 **channel subsystems (CSS)**. Each CSS is made up of the following elements:

- **System assist processor (SAP):** The SAP is a core processor configured for I/O operation. Its role is to offload I/O operations and manage channels and the I/O operations queues. It relieves the other processors of all I/O tasks, allowing them to be dedicated to application logic.

- **Hardware system area (HSA):** The HSA is a reserved part of the system memory containing the I/O configuration. It is used by SAPs. A fixed amount of 16 GB is reserved, which is not part of the customer-purchased memory. This provides for greater configuration flexibility and higher availability by eliminating planned and preplanned outages.

- **Logical partitions:** A logical partition is a form of virtual machine, which is in essence, a logical processor defined at the operating system level.[5] Each CSS supports up to 16 logical partitions.

---

[5]A virtual machine is an instance of an operating system along with one or more applications running in an isolated memory partition within the computer. It enables different operating systems to run in the same computer at the same time as well as prevents applications from interfering with each other. See [STAL12] for a discussion of virtual machines.

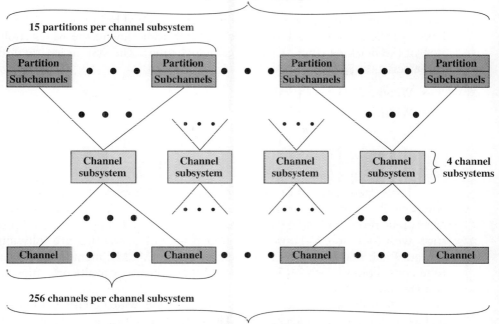

Figure 7.21   IBM z196 I/O Channel Subsystem Structure

- **Subchannels:** A subchannel appear to a program as a logical device and contain the information required to perform an I/O operation. One subchannel exists for each I/O device addressable by the CSS. A subchannel is used by the channel subsystem code running on a partition to pass an I/O request to the channel subsystem. A subchannel is assigned for each device defined to the logical partition. Up to 196k subchannels are supported per CSS.

- **Channel path:** A channel path is a single interface between a channel subsystem and one or more control units, via a channel. Commands and data are sent across a channel path to perform I/O requests. Each CSS can have up to 256 channel paths.

- **Channel:** Channels are small processors that communicate with the I/O control units (CUs). They manage the data transfer between memory and the external devices.

This elaborate structure enables the mainframe to manage a massive number of I/O devices and communication links. All I/O processing is offloaded from the application and server processors, enhancing performance. The channel subsystem processors are somewhat general in configuration, enabling them to manage a wide variety of I/O duties and to keep up with evolving requirements. The channel processors are specifically programmed for the I/O control units to which they interface.

I/O System Organization

To explain the I/O system organization, we need to first briefly explain the physical layout of the zEnterprise 196. Figure 7.22 is a front view of the water-cooled version of the machine (there is an air-cooled version). The system has the following characteristics:

- Weight: 2185 kg (4817 lbs)
- Width: 1.534 m (5 ft)
- Depth: 1.375 m (4.5 ft)
- Height: 2.012 m (6.6 ft)

Not exactly a laptop.

The system consists of two large bays, called frames, that house the various components of the zEnterprise 196. The right hand A frame includes two large cages, plus room for cabling and other components. The upper cage is a processor cage, with four slots to house up to four processor books that are fully interconnected. Each book contains a multichip module (MCM), memory cards, and I/O cage connections. Each MCM is a board that houses six multicore chips and two storage control chips.

The lower cage in the A frame is an I/O cage, which contains I/O hardware, including multiplexors and channels. The I/O cage is a fixed unit installed by IBM to the customer specifications at the factory.

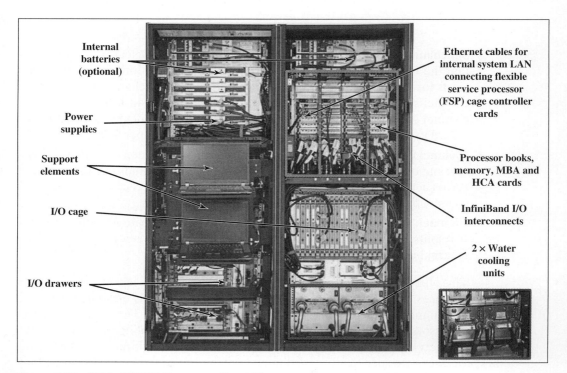

Figure 7.22   IBM z196 I/O Frames — Front View

The left hand Z frame contains internal batteries and power supplies and room for one or more support elements, which are used by a system manager for platform management. The Z frame also contains slots for two or more I/O drawers. An I/O drawer contains similar components to an I/O cage. The differences are that the drawer is smaller and easily swapped in and out at the customer site to meet changing requirements.

With this background, we now show a typical configuration of the zEnterprise 196 I/O system structure (Figure 7.23). The z196 processor book supports two internal (i.e., internal to the A and Z frames) I/O infrastructures: InfiniBand for I/O cages and I/O drawers, and PCI Express (PCIe) for I/O drawers. These channel controllers are referred to as **fanouts**.

The InfiniBand connections from the processor book to the I/O cages and I/O drawers are via a Host Channel Adapter (HCA) fanout, which has InfiniBand links to InfiniBand multiplexors in the I/O cage or drawer. The InfiniBand multiplexors are used to interconnect servers, communications infrastructure equipment, storage, and embedded systems. In addition to using InfiniBand to interconnect systems, all of which use InfiniBand, the InfiniBand multiplexor supports other I/O technologies. ESCON (Enterprise Systems Connection) supports connectivity to disks, tapes, and printer devices using a proprietary fiber-based technology. Ethernet connections provide 1-Gbps and 10-Gbps connections to a variety of devices that support this popular local area network technology. One noteworthy use of Ethernet is

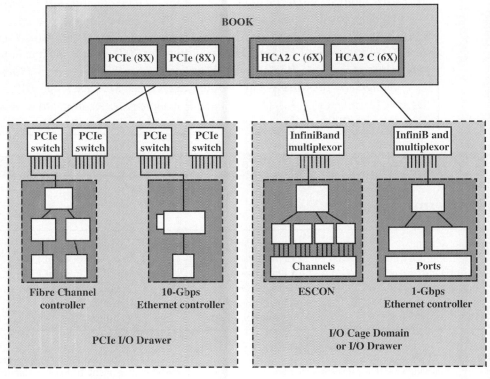

Figure 7.23   IBM z196 I/O System Structure

to construct large server farms, particularly to interconnect blade servers with each other and with other mainframes.[6]

The PCIe connections from the processor book to the I/O drawers are via a PCIe fanout to PCIe switches. The PCIe switches can connect to a number of I/O device controllers. Typical examples for zEnterprise 196 are 1-Gbps and 10-Gbps Ethernet and Fiber Channel.

Each book contains a combination of up to 8 InfiniBand HCA and PCIe fanouts. Each fanout supports up to 32 connections, for a total maximum of 256 connections per processor book, each connection controlled by a channel processor.

7.9 RECOMMENDED READING

A good discussion of Intel I/O modules and architecture, including the 82C59A, 82C55A, and 8237A, can be found in [BREY09] and [MAZI10].

InfiniBand is covered in great detail in [SHAN03] and [FUTR01]. [KAGA01] provides a concise overview.

BREY09   Brey, B. *The Intel Microprocessors: 8086/8066, 80186/80188, 80286, 80386, 80486, Pentium, Pentium Pro Processor, Pentium II, Pentium III, Pentium 4 and Core2 with 64-bit Extensions.* Upper Saddle River, NJ: Prentice Hall, 2009.

FUTR01   Futral, W. *InfiniBand Architecture: Development and Deployment.* Hillsboro, OR: Intel Press, 2001.

KAGA01   Kagan, M. "InfiniBand: Thinking Outside the Box Design." *Communications System Design*, September 2001. (www.csdmag.com)

MAZI10   Mazidi, M.; Mazidi, J.; and Causey, D. *The x86 PC: Assembly Language, Design and Interfacing.* Upper Saddle River, NJ: Prentice Hall, 2010.

SHAN03   Shanley, T. *InfinBand Network Architecture.* Reading, MA: Addison-Wesley, 2003.

7.10 KEY TERMS, REVIEW QUESTIONS, AND PROBLEMS

Key Terms

cycle stealing	I/O command	parallel I/O
direct memory access (DMA)	I/O module	peripheral device
InfiniBand	I/O processor	programmed I/O
interrupt	isolated I/O	selector channel
interrupt-driven I/O	memory-mapped I/O	serial I/O
I/O channel	multiplexor channel	Thunderbolt

---

[6]A blade server is a server architecture that houses multiple server modules (blades) in a single chassis. It is widely used in data centers to save space and improve system management. Either self-standing or rack mounted, the chassis provides the power supply, and each blade has its own CPU, memory, and hard disk.

Review Questions

7.1   List three broad classifications of external, or peripheral, devices.

7.2   What is the International Reference Alphabet?

7.3   What are the major functions of an I/O module?

7.4   List and briefly define three techniques for performing I/O.

7.5   What is the difference between memory-mapped I/O and isolated I/O?

7.6   When a device interrupt occurs, how does the processor determine which device issued the interrupt?

7.7   When a DMA module takes control of a bus, and while it retains control of the bus, what does the processor do?

Problems

7.1   On a typical microprocessor, a distinct I/O address is used to refer to the I/O data registers and a distinct address for the control and status registers in an I/O controller for a given device. Such registers are referred to as **ports**. In the Intel 8088, two I/O instruction formats are used. In one format, the 8-bit opcode specifies an I/O operation; this is followed by an 8-bit port address. Other I/O opcodes imply that the port address is in the 16-bit DX register. How many ports can the 8088 address in each I/O addressing mode? .

7.2   A similar instruction format is used in the Zilog Z8000 microprocessor family. In this case, there is a direct port addressing capability, in which a 16-bit port address is part of the instruction, and an indirect port addressing capability, in which the instruction references one of the 16-bit general purpose registers, which contains the port address. How many ports can the Z8000 address in each I/O addressing mode?

7.3   The Z8000 also includes a block I/O transfer capability that, unlike DMA, is under the direct control of the processor. The block transfer instructions specify a port address register (Rp), a count register (Rc), and a destination register (Rd). Rd contains the main memory address at which the first byte read from the input port is to be stored. Rc is any of the 16-bit general purpose registers. How large a data block can be transferred?

7.4   Consider a microprocessor that has a block I/O transfer instruction such as that found on the Z8000. Following its first execution, such an instruction takes five clock cycles to re-execute. However, if we employ a nonblocking I/O instruction, it takes a total of 20 clock cycles for fetching and execution. Calculate the increase in speed with the block I/O instruction when transferring blocks of 128 bytes.

7.5   A system is based on an 8-bit microprocessor and has two I/O devices. The I/O controllers for this system use separate control and status registers. Both devices handle data on a 1-byte-at-a-time basis. The first device has two status lines and three control lines. The second device has three status lines and four control lines.

  a.   How many 8-bit I/O control module registers do we need for status reading and control of each device?

  b.   What is the total number of needed control module registers given that the first device is an output-only device?

  c.   How many distinct addresses are needed to control the two devices?

7.6   For programmed I/O, Figure 7.5 indicates that the processor is stuck in a wait loop doing status checking of an I/O device. To increase efficiency, the I/O software could be written so that the processor periodically checks the status of the device. If the device is not ready, the processor can jump to other tasks. After some timed interval, the processor comes back to check status again.

  a.   Consider the above scheme for outputting data one character at a time to a printer that operates at 10 characters per second (cps). What will happen if its status is scanned every 200 ms?

b. Next consider a keyboard with a single character buffer. On average, characters are entered at a rate of 10 cps. However, the time interval between two consecutive key depressions can be as short as 60 ms. At what frequency should the keyboard be scanned by the I/O program?

7.7 A microprocessor scans the status of an output I/O device every 20 ms. This is accomplished by means of a timer alerting the processor every 20 ms. The interface of the device includes two ports: one for status and one for data output. How long does it take to scan and service the device given a clocking rate of 8 MHz? Assume for simplicity that all pertinent instruction cycles take 12 clock cycles.

7.8 In Section 7.3, one advantage and one disadvantage of memory-mapped I/O, compared with isolated I/O, were listed. List two more advantages and two more disadvantages.

7.9 A particular system is controlled by an operator through commands entered from a keyboard. The average number of commands entered in an 8-hour interval is 60.
a. Suppose the processor scans the keyboard every 100 ms. How many times will the keyboard be checked in an 8-hour period?
b. By what fraction would the number of processor visits to the keyboard be reduced if interrupt-driven I/O were used?

7.10 Consider a system employing interrupt-driven I/O for a particular device that transfers data at an average of 8 KB/s on a continuous basis.
a. Assume that interrupt processing takes about 100 μs (i.e., the time to jump to the interrupt service routine (ISR), execute it, and return to the main program). Determine what fraction of processor time is consumed by this I/O device if it interrupts for every byte.
b. Now assume that the device has two 16-byte buffers and interrupts the processor when one of the buffers is full. Naturally, interrupt processing takes longer, because the ISR must transfer 16 bytes. While executing the ISR, the processor takes about 8 μs for the transfer of each byte. Determine what fraction of processor time is consumed by this I/O device in this case.
c. Now assume that the processor is equipped with a block transfer I/O instruction such as that found on the Z8000. This permits the associated ISR to transfer each byte of a block in only 2 μs. Determine what fraction of processor time is consumed by this I/O device in this case.

7.11 In virtually all systems that include DMA modules, DMA access to main memory is given higher priority than CPU access to main memory. Why?

7.12 A DMA module is transferring characters to memory using cycle stealing, from a device transmitting at 9600 bps. The processor is fetching instructions at the rate of 1 million instructions per second (1 MIPS). By how much will the processor be slowed down due to the DMA activity?

7.13 Consider a system in which bus cycles takes 500 ns. Transfer of bus control in either direction, from processor to I/O device or vice versa, takes 250 ns. One of the I/O devices has a data transfer rate of 50 KB/s and employs DMA. Data are transferred 1 byte at a time.
a. Suppose we employ DMA in a burst mode. That is, the DMA interface gains bus mastership prior to the start of a block transfer and maintains control of the bus until the whole block is transferred. For how long would the device tie up the bus when transferring a block of 128 bytes?
b. Repeat the calculation for cycle-stealing mode.

7.14 Examination of the timing diagram of the 8237A indicates that once a block transfer begins, it takes three bus clock cycles per DMA cycle. During the DMA cycle, the 8237A transfers one byte of information between memory and I/O device.
a. Suppose we clock the 8237A at a rate of 5 MHz. How long does it take to transfer one byte?
b. What would be the maximum attainable data transfer rate?
c. Assume that the memory is not fast enough and we have to insert two wait states per DMA cycle. What will be the actual data transfer rate?

7.15 Assume that in the system of the preceding problem, a memory cycle takes 750 ns. To what value could we reduce the clocking rate of the bus without effect on the attainable data transfer rate?

7.16 A DMA controller serves four receive-only telecommunication links (one per DMA channel) having a speed of 64 Kbps each.
  a. Would you operate the controller in burst mode or in cycle-stealing mode?
  b. What priority scheme would you employ for service of the DMA channels?

7.17 A 32-bit computer has two selector channels and one multiplexor channel. Each selector channel supports two magnetic disk and two magnetic tape units. The multiplexor channel has two line printers, two card readers, and 10 VDT terminals connected to it. Assume the following transfer rates:

Disk drive	800 Kbytes/s
Magnetic tape drive	200 Kbytes/s
Line printer	6.6 Kbytes/s
Card reader	1.2 Kbytes/s
VDT	1 Kbyte/s

Estimate the maximum aggregate I/O transfer rate in this system.

7.18 A computer consists of a processor and an I/O device D connected to main memory M via a shared bus with a data bus width of one word. The processor can execute a maximum of 10^6 instructions per second. An average instruction requires five machine cycles, three of which use the memory bus. A memory read or write operation uses one machine cycle. Suppose that the processor is continuously executing "background" programs that require 95% of its instruction execution rate but not any I/O instructions. Assume that one processor cycle equals one bus cycle. Now suppose the I/O device is to be used to transfer very large blocks of data between M and D.
  a. If programmed I/O is used and each one-word I/O transfer requires the processor to execute two instructions, estimate the maximum I/O data-transfer rate, in words per second, possible through D.
  b. Estimate the same rate if DMA is used.

7.19 A data source produces 7-bit IRA characters, to each of which is appended a parity bit. Derive an expression for the maximum effective data rate (rate of IRA data bits) over an R-bps line for the following:
  a. Asynchronous transmission, with a 1.5-unit stop bit
  b. Bit-synchronous transmission, with a frame consisting of 48 control bits and 128 information bits
  c. Same as (b), with a 1024-bit information field
  d. Character-synchronous, with 9 control characters per frame and 16 information characters
  e. Same as (d), with 128 information characters

7.20 The following problem is based on a suggested illustration of I/O mechanisms in [ECKE90] (Figure 7.24):

Two women are on either side of a high fence. One of the women, named Apple-server, has a beautiful apple tree loaded with delicious apples growing on her side of the fence; she is happy to supply apples to the other woman whenever needed. The other woman, named Apple-eater, loves to eat apples but has none. In fact, she must eat her apples at a fixed rate (an apple a day keeps the doctor away). If she eats them faster than that rate, she will get sick. If she eats them slower, she will suffer malnutrition. Neither woman can talk, and so the problem is to get apples from Apple-server to Apple-eater at the correct rate.
  a. Assume that there is an alarm clock sitting on top of the fence and that the clock can have multiple alarm settings. How can the clock be used to solve the problem? Draw a timing diagram to illustrate the solution.

Figure 7.24   An Apple Problem

    b. Now assume that there is no alarm clock. Instead Apple-eater has a flag that she can wave whenever she needs an apple. Suggest a new solution. Would it be helpful for Apple-server also to have a flag? If so, incorporate this into the solution. Discuss the drawbacks of this approach.

    c. Now take away the flag and assume the existence of a long piece of string. Suggest a solution that is superior to that of (b) using the string.

7.21   Assume that one 16-bit and two 8-bit microprocessors are to be interfaced to a system bus. The following details are given:

    1. All microprocessors have the hardware features necessary for any type of data transfer: programmed I/O, interrupt-driven I/O, and DMA.

    2. All microprocessors have a 16-bit address bus.

    3. Two memory boards, each of 64-Kbytes capacity, are interfaced with the bus. The designer wishes to use a shared memory that is as large as possible.

    4. The system bus supports a maximum of four interrupt lines and one DMA line. Make any other assumptions necessary, and

    a. Give the system bus specifications in terms of number and types of lines.

    b. Describe a possible protocol for communicating on the bus (i.e., read-write, interrupt, and DMA sequences).

    c. Explain how the aforementioned devices are interfaced to the system bus.

CHAPTER 8

OPERATING SYSTEM SUPPORT

265

LEARNING OBJECTIVES

After studying this chapter, you should be able to:

◆ Summarize, at a top level, the key functions of an **operating system (OS)**.

◆ Discuss the evolution of operating systems for early simple batch systems to modern complex systems.

◆ Explain the differences among long-, medium-, and short-term scheduling.

◆ Understand the reason for memory **partitioning** and explain the various techniques that are used.

◆ Assess the relative advantages of paging and segmentation.

◆ Define virtual memory.

Although the focus of this text is computer hardware, there is one area of software that needs to be addressed: the computer's OS. The OS is a program that manages the computer's resources, provides services for programmers, and schedules the execution of other programs. Some understanding of operating systems is essential to appreciate the mechanisms by which the CPU controls the computer system. In particular, explanations of the effect of interrupts and of the management of the memory hierarchy are best explained in this context.

The chapter begins with an overview and brief history of operating systems. The bulk of the chapter looks at the two OS functions that are most relevant to the study of computer organization and architecture: scheduling and memory management.

8.1 OPERATING SYSTEM OVERVIEW

Operating System Objectives and Functions

An OS is a program that controls the execution of application programs and acts as an interface between applications and the computer hardware. It can be thought of as having two objectives:

- **Convenience:** An OS makes a computer more convenient to use.
- **Efficiency:** An OS allows the computer system resources to be used in an efficient manner.

Let us examine these two aspects of an OS in turn.

THE OPERATING SYSTEM AS A USER/COMPUTER INTERFACE The hardware and software used in providing applications to a user can be viewed in a layered or hierarchical fashion, as depicted in Figure 8.1. The user of those applications, the end user, generally is not concerned with the computer's architecture. Thus the end user views a computer system in terms of an application. That application can be expressed in a programming language and is developed by an application programmer. To develop an application program as a set of processor instructions

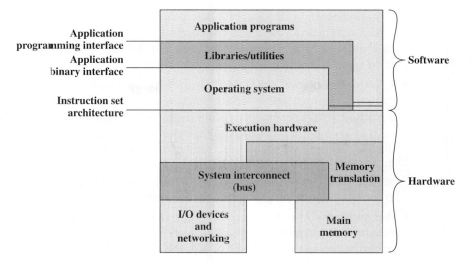

Figure 8.1   Computer Hardware and Software Structure

that is completely responsible for controlling the computer hardware would be an overwhelmingly complex task. To ease this task, a set of systems programs is provided. Some of these programs are referred to as **utilities.** These implement frequently used functions that assist in program creation, the management of files, and the control of I/O devices. A programmer makes use of these facilities in developing an application, and the application, while it is running, invokes the utilities to perform certain functions. The most important system program is the OS. The OS masks the details of the hardware from the programmer and provides the programmer with a convenient interface for using the system. It acts as mediator, making it easier for the programmer and for application programs to access and use those facilities and services.

Briefly, the OS typically provides services in the following areas:

- **Program creation:** The OS provides a variety of facilities and services, such as editors and debuggers, to assist the programmer in creating programs. Typically, these services are in the form of **utility** programs that are not actually part of the OS but are accessible through the OS.
- **Program execution:** A number of steps need to be performed to execute a program. Instructions and data must be loaded into main memory, I/O devices and files must be initialized, and other resources must be prepared. The OS handles all of this for the user.
- **Access to I/O devices:** Each I/O device requires its own specific set of instructions or control signals for operation. The OS takes care of the details so that the programmer can think in terms of simple reads and writes.
- **Controlled access to files:** In the case of files, control must include an understanding of not only the nature of the I/O device (disk drive, tape drive) but also the file format on the storage medium. Again, the OS worries about the details. Further, in the case of a system with multiple simultaneous users, the OS can provide protection mechanisms to control access to the files.

- **System access:** In the case of a shared or public system, the OS controls access to the system as a whole and to specific system resources. The access function must provide protection of resources and data from unauthorized users and must resolve conflicts for resource contention.

- **Error detection and response:** A variety of errors can occur while a computer system is running. These include internal and external hardware errors, such as a memory error, or a device failure or malfunction; and various software errors, such as arithmetic overflow, attempt to access forbidden memory location, and inability of the OS to grant the request of an application. In each case, the OS must make the response that clears the error condition with the least impact on running applications. The response may range from ending the program that caused the error, to retrying the operation, to simply reporting the error to the application.

- **Accounting:** A good OS collects usage statistics for various resources and monitor performance parameters such as response time. On any system, this information is useful in anticipating the need for future enhancements and in tuning the system to improve performance. On a multiuser system, the information can be used for billing purposes.

Figure 8.1 also indicates three key interfaces in a typical computer system:

- **Instruction set architecture (ISA):** The ISA defines the repertoire of machine language instructions that a computer can follow. This interface is the boundary between hardware and software. Note that both application programs and utilities may access the ISA directly. For these programs, a subset of the instruction repertoire is available (user ISA). The OS has access to additional machine language instructions that deal with managing system resources (system ISA).

- **Application binary interface (ABI):** The ABI defines a standard for binary portability across programs. The ABI defines the system call interface to the operating system and the hardware resources and services available in a system through the user ISA.

- **Application programming interface (API):** The API gives a program access to the hardware resources and services available in a system through the user ISA supplemented with high-level language (HLL) library calls. Any system calls are usually performed through libraries. Using an API enables application software to be ported easily, through recompilation, to other systems that support the same API.

THE OPERATING SYSTEM AS RESOURCE MANAGER A computer is a set of resources for the movement, storage, and processing of data and for the control of these functions. The OS is responsible for managing these resources.

Can we say that the OS controls the movement, storage, and processing of data? From one point of view, the answer is yes: By managing the computer's resources, the OS is in control of the computer's basic functions. But this control is exercised in a curious way. Normally, we think of a control mechanism as something external to that which is controlled, or at least as something that is a distinct and separate part of that which is controlled. (For example, a residential heating system is controlled by a thermostat, which is completely distinct from the heat-generation and heat-distribution apparatus.) This is not the case with the OS, which as a control mechanism is unusual in two respects:

- The OS functions in the same way as ordinary computer software; that is, it is a program executed by the processor.
- The OS frequently relinquishes control and must depend on the processor to allow it to regain control.

Like other computer programs, the OS provides instructions for the processor. The key difference is in the intent of the program. The OS directs the processor in the use of the other system resources and in the timing of its execution of other programs. But in order for the processor to do any of these things, it must cease executing the OS program and execute other programs. Thus, the OS relinquishes control for the processor to do some "useful" work and then resumes control long enough to prepare the processor to do the next piece of work. The mechanisms involved in all this should become clear as the chapter proceeds.

Figure 8.2 suggests the main resources that are managed by the OS. A portion of the OS is in main memory. This includes the **kernel,** or **nucleus,** which contains the most frequently used functions in the OS and, at a given time, other portions of the OS currently in use. The remainder of main memory contains user programs and data. The allocation of this resource (main memory) is controlled jointly by the OS and memory-management hardware in the processor, as we shall see. The OS decides when an I/O device can be used by a program in execution, and controls access to and

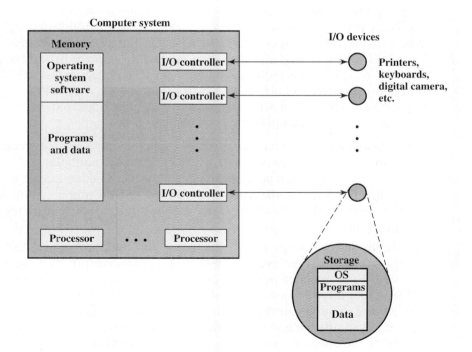

Figure 8.2 The Operating System as Resource Manager

use of files. The processor itself is a resource, and the OS must determine how much processor time is to be devoted to the execution of a particular user program. In the case of a multiple-processor system, this decision must span all of the processors.

Types of Operating Systems

Certain key characteristics serve to differentiate various types of operating systems. The characteristics fall along two independent dimensions. The first dimension specifies whether the system is batch or interactive. In an **interactive** system, the user/programmer interacts directly with the computer, usually through a keyboard/ display terminal, to request the execution of a job or to perform a transaction. Furthermore, the user may, depending on the nature of the application, communicate with the computer during the execution of the job. A **batch** system is the opposite of interactive. The user's program is batched together with programs from other users and submitted by a computer operator. After the program is completed, results are printed out for the user. Pure batch systems are rare today. However, it will be useful to the description of contemporary operating systems to examine batch systems briefly.

An independent dimension specifies whether the system employs **multiprogramming** or not. With multiprogramming, the attempt is made to keep the processor as busy as possible, by having it work on more than one program at a time. Several programs are loaded into memory, and the processor switches rapidly among them. The alternative is a **uniprogramming** system that works only one program at a time.

EARLY SYSTEMS With the earliest computers, from the late 1940s to the mid-1950s, the programmer interacted directly with the computer hardware; there was no OS. These processors were run from a console, consisting of display lights, toggle switches, some form of input device, and a printer. Programs in processor code were loaded via the input device (e.g., a card reader). If an error halted the program, the error condition was indicated by the lights. The programmer could proceed to examine registers and main memory to determine the cause of the error. If the program proceeded to a normal completion, the output appeared on the printer.

These early systems presented two main problems:

- **Scheduling:** Most installations used a sign-up sheet to reserve processor time. Typically, a user could sign up for a block of time in multiples of a half hour or so. A user might sign up for an hour and finish in 45 minutes; this would result in wasted computer idle time. On the other hand, the user might run into problems, not finish in the allotted time, and be forced to stop before resolving the problem.

- **Setup time:** A single program, called a **job**, could involve loading the compiler plus the high-level language program (source program) into memory, saving the compiled program (object program), and then loading and linking together the object program and common functions. Each of these steps could involve mounting or dismounting tapes, or setting up card decks. If an error occurred, the hapless user typically had to go back to the beginning of the setup sequence. Thus a considerable amount of time was spent just in setting up the program to run.

This mode of operation could be termed serial processing, reflecting the fact that users have access to the computer in series. Over time, various system software tools were developed to attempt to make serial processing more efficient. These include libraries of common functions, linkers, loaders, debuggers, and I/O driver routines that were available as common software for all users.

SIMPLE BATCH SYSTEMS Early processors were very expensive, and therefore it was important to maximize processor utilization. The wasted time due to scheduling and setup time was unacceptable.

To improve utilization, simple batch operating systems were developed. With such a system, also called a **monitor**, the user no longer has direct access to the processor. Rather, the user submits the job on cards or tape to a computer operator, who *batches* the jobs together sequentially and places the entire batch on an input device, for use by the monitor.

To understand how this scheme works, let us look at it from two points of view: that of the monitor and that of the processor. From the point of view of the monitor, the monitor controls the sequence of events. For this to be so, much of the monitor must always be in main memory and available for execution (Figure 8.3). That portion is referred to as the **resident monitor.** The rest of the monitor consists of utilities and common functions that are loaded as subroutines to the user program at the beginning of any job that requires them. The monitor reads in jobs one at a time from the input device (typically a card reader or magnetic tape drive). As it is read in, the current job is placed in the user program area, and control is passed to this job. When the job is completed, it returns control to the monitor, which immediately reads in the next job. The results of each job are printed out for delivery to the user.

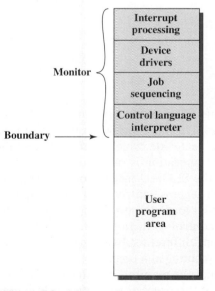

Figure 8.3 Memory Layout for a
Resident Monitor

Now consider this sequence from the point of view of the processor. At a certain point in time, the processor is executing instructions from the portion of main memory containing the monitor. These instructions cause the next job to be read in to another portion of main memory. Once a job has been read in, the processor will encounter in the monitor a branch instruction that instructs the processor to continue execution at the start of the user program. The processor will then execute the instruction in the user's program until it encounters an ending or error condition. Either event causes the processor to fetch its next instruction from the monitor program. Thus the phrase "control is passed to a job" simply means that the processor is now fetching and executing instructions in a user program, and "control is returned to the monitor" means that the processor is now fetching and executing instructions from the monitor program.

It should be clear that the monitor handles the scheduling problem. A batch of jobs is queued up, and jobs are executed as rapidly as possible, with no intervening idle time.

How about the job setup time? The monitor handles this as well. With each job, instructions are included in a **job control language (JCL)**. This is a special type of programming language used to provide instructions to the monitor. A simple example is that of a user submitting a program written in FORTRAN plus some data to be used by the program. Each FORTRAN instruction and each item of data is on a separate punched card or a separate record on tape. In addition to FORTRAN and data lines, the job includes job control instructions, which are denoted by the beginning "$". The overall format of the job looks like this:

```
$JOB
$FTN
  :          } FORTRAN instructions
  :
$LOAD
$RUN
  :          } Data
  :
$END
```

To execute this job, the monitor reads the $FTN line and loads the appropriate compiler from its mass storage (usually tape). The compiler translates the user's program into object code, which is stored in memory or mass storage. If it is stored in memory, the operation is referred to as "compile, load, and go." If it is stored on tape, then the $LOAD instruction is required. This instruction is read by the monitor, which regains control after the compile operation. The monitor invokes the loader, which loads the object program into memory in place of the compiler and transfers control to it. In this manner, a large segment of main memory can be shared among different subsystems, although only one such subsystem could be resident and executing at a time.

We see that the monitor, or batch OS, is simply a computer program. It relies on the ability of the processor to fetch instructions from various portions of main memory in order to seize and relinquish control alternately. Certain other hardware features are also desirable:

- **Memory protection:** While the user program is executing, it must not alter the memory area containing the monitor. If such an attempt is made, the processor hardware should detect an error and transfer control to the monitor. The monitor would then abort the job, print out an error message, and load the next job.
- **Timer:** A timer is used to prevent a single job from monopolizing the system. The timer is set at the beginning of each job. If the timer expires, an interrupt occurs, and control returns to the monitor.
- **Privileged instructions:** Certain instructions are designated privileged and can be executed only by the monitor. If the processor encounters such an instruction while executing a user program, an error interrupt occurs. Among the privileged instructions are I/O instructions, so that the monitor retains control of all I/O devices. This prevents, for example, a user program from accidentally reading job control instructions from the next job. If a user program wishes to perform I/O, it must request that the monitor perform the operation for it. If a privileged instruction is encountered by the processor while it is executing a user program, the processor hardware considers this an error and transfers control to the monitor.
- **Interrupts:** Early computer models did not have this capability. This feature gives the OS more flexibility in relinquishing control to and regaining control from user programs.

Processor time alternates between execution of user programs and execution of the monitor. There have been two sacrifices: Some main memory is now given over to the monitor and some processor time is consumed by the monitor. Both of these are forms of overhead. Even with this overhead, the simple batch system improves utilization of the computer.

MULTIPROGRAMMED BATCH SYSTEMS Even with the automatic job sequencing provided by a simple batch OS, the processor is often idle. The problem is that I/O devices are slow compared to the processor. Figure 8.4 details a representative calculation. The calculation concerns a program that processes a file of records and performs, on average, 100 processor instructions per record. In this example the computer spends over 96% of its time waiting for I/O devices to finish transferring data! Figure 8.5a illustrates this situation. The processor spends a certain amount of

Read one record from file	15 μs
Execute 100 instructions	1 μs
Write one record to file	15 μs
TOTAL	31 μs

Percent CPU utilization $= \dfrac{1}{31} = 0.032 = 3.2\%$

Figure 8.4   System Utilization Example

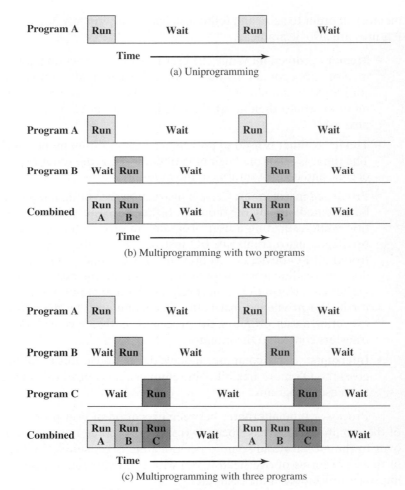

Figure 8.5   Multiprogramming Example

time executing, until it reaches an I/O instruction. It must then wait until that I/O instruction concludes before proceeding.

This inefficiency is not necessary. We know that there must be enough memory to hold the OS (resident monitor) and one user program. Suppose that there is room for the OS and two user programs. Now, when one job needs to wait for I/O, the processor can switch to the other job, which likely is not waiting for I/O (Figure 8.5b). Furthermore, we might expand memory to hold three, four, or more programs and switch among all of them (Figure 8.5c). This technique is known as **multiprogramming**, or **multitasking**.[1] It is the central theme of modern operating systems.

---

[1]The term *multitasking* is sometimes reserved to mean multiple tasks within the same program that may be handled concurrently by the OS, in contrast to *multiprogramming*, which would refer to multiple processes from multiple programs. However, it is more common to equate the terms *multitasking* and *multiprogramming*, as is done in most standards dictionaries (e.g., IEEE Std 100-1992, *The New IEEE Standard Dictionary of Electrical and Electronics Terms*).

Table 8.1   Sample Program Execution Attributes

	JOB1	JOB2	JOB3
Type of job	Heavy compute	Heavy I/O	Heavy I/O
Duration (min)	5	15	10
Memory required (M)	50	100	80
Need disk?	No	No	Yes
Need terminal?	No	Yes	No
Need printer?	No	No	Yes

Example 8.1   This example illustrates the benefit of multiprogramming. Consider a computer with 250 Mbytes of available memory (not used by the OS), a disk, a terminal, and a printer. Three programs, JOB1, JOB2, and JOB3, are submitted for execution at the same time, with the attributes listed in Table 8.1. We assume minimal processor requirements for JOB2 and JOB3 and continuous disk and printer use by JOB3. For a simple batch environment, these jobs will be executed in sequence. Thus, JOB1 completes in 5 minutes. JOB2 must wait until the 5 minutes is over and then completes 15 minutes after that. JOB3 begins after 20 minutes and completes at 30 minutes from the time it was initially submitted. The average resource utilization, throughput, and response times are shown in the uniprogramming column of Table 8.2. Device-by-device utilization is illustrated in Figure 8.6a. It is evident that there is gross underutilization for all resources when averaged over the required 30-minute time period.

Now suppose that the jobs are run concurrently under a multiprogramming OS. Because there is little resource contention between the jobs, all three can run in nearly minimum time while coexisting with the others in the computer (assuming that JOB2 and JOB3 are allotted enough processor time to keep their input and output operations active). JOB1 will still require 5 minutes to complete but at the end of that time, JOB2 will be one-third finished, and JOB3 will be half finished. All three jobs will have finished within 15 minutes. The improvement is evident when examining the multiprogramming column of Table 8.2, obtained from the histogram shown in Figure 8.6b.

As with a simple batch system, a multiprogramming batch system must rely on certain computer hardware features. The most notable additional feature that is useful for multiprogramming is the hardware that supports I/O interrupts and

Table 8.2   Effects of Multiprogramming on Resource Utilization

	Uniprogramming	Multiprogramming
Processor use (%)	20	40
Memory use (%)	33	67
Disk use (%)	33	67
Printer use (%)	33	67
Elapsed time (min)	30	15
Throughput rate (jobs/hr)	6	12
Mean response time (min)	18	10

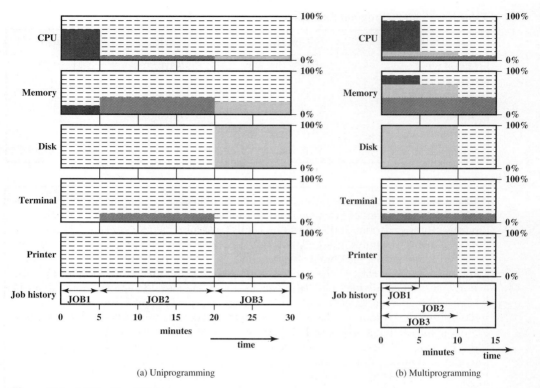

Figure 8.6 Utilization Histograms

DMA. With interrupt-driven I/O or DMA, the processor can issue an I/O command for one job and proceed with the execution of another job while the I/O is carried out by the device controller. When the I/O operation is complete, the processor is interrupted and control is passed to an interrupt-handling program in the OS. The OS will then pass control to another job.

Multiprogramming operating systems are fairly sophisticated compared to single-program, or **uniprogramming**, systems. To have several jobs ready to run, the jobs must be kept in main memory, requiring some form of **memory management.** In addition, if several jobs are ready to run, the processor must decide which one to run, which requires some algorithm for scheduling. These concepts are discussed later in this chapter.

TIME–SHARING SYSTEMS With the use of multiprogramming, batch processing can be quite efficient. However, for many jobs, it is desirable to provide a mode in which the user interacts directly with the computer. Indeed, for some jobs, such as transaction processing, an interactive mode is essential.

Today, the requirement for an interactive computing facility can be, and often is, met by the use of a dedicated microcomputer. That option was not available in the 1960s, when most computers were big and costly. Instead, time sharing was developed.

Just as multiprogramming allows the processor to handle multiple batch jobs at a time, multiprogramming can be used to handle multiple interactive jobs. In this latter case, the technique is referred to as time sharing, because the processor's time is shared among multiple users. In a **time-sharing system**, multiple users

Table 8.3 Batch Multiprogramming versus Time Sharing

	Batch Multiprogramming	**Time Sharing**
Principal objective	Maximize processor use	Minimize response time
Source of directives to operating system	Job control language commands provided with the job	Commands entered at the terminal

simultaneously access the system through terminals, with the OS interleaving the execution of each user program in a short burst or quantum of computation. Thus, if there are n users actively requesting service at one time, each user will only see on the average $1/n$ of the effective computer speed, not counting OS overhead. However, given the relatively slow human reaction time, the response time on a properly designed system should be comparable to that on a dedicated computer.

Both batch multiprogramming and time sharing use multiprogramming. The key differences are listed in Table 8.3.

8.2 SCHEDULING

The key to multiprogramming is scheduling. In fact, four types of scheduling are typically involved (Table 8.4). We will explore these presently. But first, we introduce the concept of **process.** This term was first used by the designers of the Multics OS in the 1960s. It is a somewhat more general term than *job.* Many definitions have been given for the term *process,* including

- A program in execution
- The "animated spirit" of a program
- That entity to which a processor is assigned

This concept should become clearer as we proceed.

Long-Term Scheduling

The long-term scheduler determines which programs are admitted to the system for processing. Thus, it controls the degree of multiprogramming (number of processes in memory). Once admitted, a job or user program becomes a process and is added to the queue for the short-term scheduler. In some systems, a newly created process begins in a swapped-out condition, in which case it is added to a queue for the medium-term scheduler.

Table 8.4 Types of Scheduling

Long-term scheduling	The decision to add to the pool of processes to be executed
Medium-term scheduling	The decision to add to the number of processes that are partially or fully in main memory
Short-term scheduling	The decision as to which available process will be executed by the processor
I/O scheduling	The decision as to which process's pending I/O request shall be handled by an available I/O device

In a batch system, or for the batch portion of a general-purpose OS, newly submitted jobs are routed to disk and held in a batch queue. The long-term scheduler creates processes from the queue when it can. There are two decisions involved here. First, the scheduler must decide that the OS can take on one or more additional processes. Second, the scheduler must decide which job or jobs to accept and turn into processes. The criteria used may include priority, expected execution time, and I/O requirements.

For interactive programs in a time-sharing system, a process request is generated when a user attempts to connect to the system. Time-sharing users are not simply queued up and kept waiting until the system can accept them. Rather, the OS will accept all authorized comers until the system is saturated, using some predefined measure of saturation. At that point, a connection request is met with a message indicating that the system is full and the user should try again later.

Medium–Term Scheduling

Medium-term scheduling is part of the swapping function, described in Section 8.3. Typically, the swapping-in decision is based on the need to manage the degree of multiprogramming. On a system that does not use virtual memory, memory management is also an issue. Thus, the swapping-in decision will consider the memory requirements of the swapped-out processes.

Short–Term Scheduling

The long-term scheduler executes relatively infrequently and makes the coarse-grained decision of whether or not to take on a new process, and which one to take. The short-term scheduler, also known as the **dispatcher**, executes frequently and makes the fine-grained decision of which job to execute next.

PROCESS STATES To understand the operation of the short-term scheduler, we need to consider the concept of a **process state.** During the lifetime of a process, its status will change a number of times. Its status at any point in time is referred to as a *state.* The term *state* is used because it connotes that certain information exists that defines the status at that point. At minimum, there are five defined states for a process (Figure 8.7):

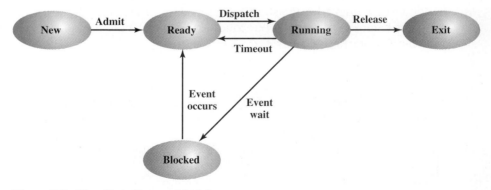

Figure 8.7   Five-State Process Model

- **New:** A program is admitted by the high-level scheduler but is not yet ready to execute. The OS will initialize the process, moving it to the ready state.
- **Ready:** The process is ready to execute and is awaiting access to the processor.
- **Running:** The process is being executed by the processor.
- **Waiting:** The process is suspended from execution waiting for some system resource, such as I/O.
- **Halted:** The process has terminated and will be destroyed by the OS.

For each process in the system, the OS must maintain information indicating the state of the process and other information necessary for process execution. For this purpose, each process is represented in the OS by a **process control block** (Figure 8.8), which typically contains

- **Identifier:** Each current process has a unique identifier.
- **State:** The current state of the process (new, ready, and so on).
- **Priority:** Relative priority level.
- **Program counter:** The address of the next instruction in the program to be executed.
- **Memory pointers:** The starting and ending locations of the process in memory.
- **Context data:** These are data that are present in registers in the processor while the process is executing, and they will be discussed in Part Three. For now, it is enough to say that these data represent the "context" of the process. The context data plus the program counter are saved when the process leaves the running state. They are retrieved by the processor when it resumes execution of the process.

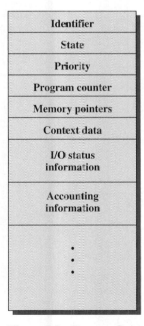

Figure 8.8 Process Control Block

- **I/O status information:** Includes outstanding I/O requests, I/O devices (e.g., tape drives) assigned to this process, a list of files assigned to the process, and so on.

- **Accounting information:** May include the amount of processor time and clock time used, time limits, account numbers, and so on.

When the scheduler accepts a new job or user request for execution, it creates a blank process control block and places the associated process in the new state. After the system has properly filled in the process control block, the process is transferred to the ready state.

SCHEDULING TECHNIQUES To understand how the OS manages the scheduling of the various jobs in memory, let us begin by considering the simple example in Figure 8.9. The figure shows how main memory is partitioned at a given point in time. The kernel of the OS is, of course, always resident. In addition, there are a number of active processes, including A and B, each of which is allocated a portion of memory.

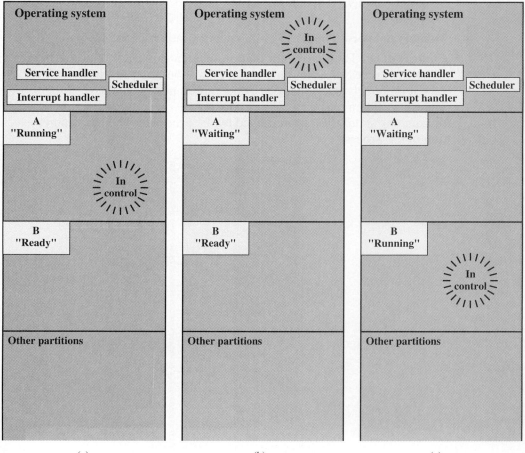

Figure 8.9 Scheduling Example

We begin at a point in time when process A is running. The processor is executing instructions from the program contained in A's memory partition. At some later point in time, the processor ceases to execute instructions in A and begins executing instructions in the OS area. This will happen for one of three reasons:

1. Process A issues a service call (e.g., an I/O request) to the OS. Execution of A is suspended until this call is satisfied by the OS.

2. Process A causes an *interrupt.* An interrupt is a hardware-generated signal to the processor. When this signal is detected, the processor ceases to execute A and transfers to the interrupt handler in the OS. A variety of events related to A will cause an interrupt. One example is an error, such as attempting to execute a privileged instruction. Another example is a timeout; to prevent any one process from monopolizing the processor, each process is only granted the processor for a short period at a time.

3. Some event unrelated to process A that requires attention causes an interrupt. An example is the completion of an I/O operation.

In any case, the result is the following. The processor saves the current context data and the program counter for A in A's process control block and then begins executing in the OS. The OS may perform some work, such as initiating an I/O operation. Then the short-term-scheduler portion of the OS decides which process should be executed next. In this example, B is chosen. The OS instructs the processor to restore B's context data and proceed with the execution of B where it left off.

This simple example highlights the basic functioning of the short-term scheduler. Figure 8.10 shows the major elements of the OS involved in the multiprogramming and scheduling of processes. The OS receives control of the processor at the

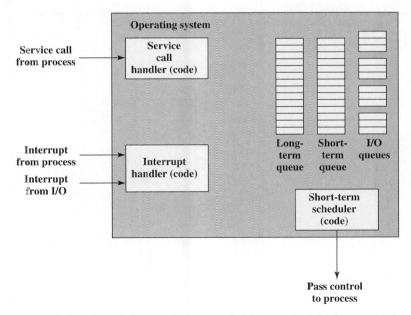

Figure 8.10   Key Elements of an Operating System for Multiprogramming

interrupt handler if an interrupt occurs and at the service-call handler if a service call occurs. Once the interrupt or service call is handled, the short-term scheduler is invoked to select a process for execution.

To do its job, the OS maintains a number of queues. Each queue is simply a waiting list of processes waiting for some resource. The **long-term queue** is a list of jobs waiting to use the system. As conditions permit, the high-level scheduler will allocate memory and create a process for one of the waiting items. The **short-term queue** consists of all processes in the ready state. Any one of these processes could use the processor next. It is up to the short-term scheduler to pick one. Generally, this is done with a round-robin algorithm, giving each process some time in turn. Priority levels may also be used. Finally, there is an **I/O queue** for each I/O device. More than one process may request the use of the same I/O device. All processes waiting to use each device are lined up in that device's queue.

Figure 8.11 suggests how processes progress through the computer under the control of the OS. Each process request (batch job, user-defined interactive job) is placed in the long-term queue. As resources become available, a process request becomes a process and is then placed in the ready state and put in the short-term queue. The processor alternates between executing OS instructions and executing user processes. While the OS is in control, it decides which process in the short-term queue should be executed next. When the OS has finished its immediate tasks, it turns the processor over to the chosen process.

As was mentioned earlier, a process being executed may be suspended for a variety of reasons. If it is suspended because the process requests I/O, then it

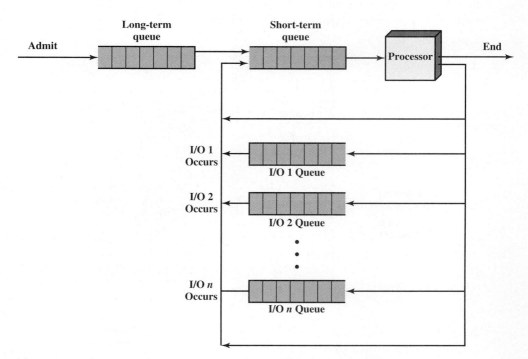

Figure 8.11   Queuing Diagram Representation of Processor Scheduling

is placed in the appropriate I/O queue. If it is suspended because of a timeout or because the OS must attend to pressing business, then it is placed in the ready state and put into the short-term queue.

Finally, we mention that the OS also manages the I/O queues. When an I/O operation is completed, the OS removes the satisfied process from that I/O queue and places it in the short-term queue. It then selects another waiting process (if any) and signals for the I/O device to satisfy that process's request.

8.3 MEMORY MANAGEMENT

In a uniprogramming system, main memory is divided into two parts: one part for the OS (resident monitor) and one part for the program currently being executed. In a multiprogramming system, the "user" part of memory is subdivided to accommodate multiple processes. The task of subdivision is carried out dynamically by the OS and is known as **memory management**.

Effective memory management is vital in a multiprogramming system. If only a few processes are in memory, then for much of the time all of the processes will be waiting for I/O and the processor will be idle. Thus, memory needs to be allocated efficiently to pack as many processes into memory as possible.

Swapping

Referring back to Figure 8.11, we have discussed three types of queues: the long-term queue of requests for new processes, the short-term queue of processes ready to use the processor, and the various I/O queues of processes that are not ready to use the processor. Recall that the reason for this elaborate machinery is that I/O activities are much slower than computation and therefore the processor in a uni-programming system is idle most of the time.

But the arrangement in Figure 8.11 does not entirely solve the problem. It is true that, in this case, memory holds multiple processes and that the processor can move to another process when one process is waiting. But the processor is so much faster than I/O that it will be common for *all* the processes in memory to be waiting on I/O. Thus, even with multiprogramming, a processor could be idle most of the time.

What to do? Main memory could be expanded, and so be able to accommodate more processes. But there are two flaws in this approach. First, main memory is expensive, even today. Second, the appetite of programs for memory has grown as fast as the cost of memory has dropped. So larger memory results in larger processes, not more processes.

Another solution is **swapping**, depicted in Figure 8.12. We have a long-term queue of process requests, typically stored on disk. These are brought in, one at a time, as space becomes available. As processes are completed, they are moved out of main memory. Now the situation will arise that none of the processes in memory are in the ready state (e.g., all are waiting on an I/O operation). Rather than remain idle, the processor *swaps* one of these processes back out to disk into an *intermediate queue*. This is a queue of existing processes that have been temporarily kicked out

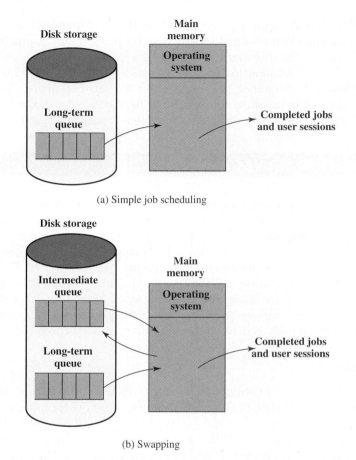

(a) Simple job scheduling

(b) Swapping

Figure 8.12 The Use of Swapping

of memory. The OS then brings in another process from the intermediate queue, or it honors a new process request from the long-term queue. Execution then continues with the newly arrived process.

Swapping, however, is an I/O operation, and therefore there is the potential for making the problem worse, not better. But because disk I/O is generally the fastest I/O on a system (e.g., compared with tape or printer I/O), swapping will usually enhance performance. A more sophisticated scheme, involving virtual memory, improves performance over simple swapping. This will be discussed shortly. But first, we must prepare the ground by explaining partitioning and paging.

Partitioning

The simplest scheme for partitioning available memory is to use *fixed-size partitions,* as shown in Figure 8.13. Note that, although the partitions are of fixed size, they need not be of equal size. When a process is brought into memory, it is placed in the smallest available partition that will hold it.

Even with the use of unequal fixed-size partitions, there will be wasted memory. In most cases, a process will not require exactly as much memory as provided by the

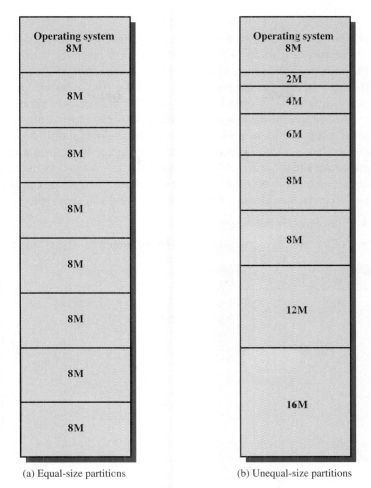

(a) Equal-size partitions   (b) Unequal-size partitions

Figure 8.13 Example of Fixed Partitioning of a 64-Mbyte Memory

partition. For example, a process that requires 3M bytes of memory would be placed in the 4M partition of Figure 8.13b, wasting 1M that could be used by another process.

A more efficient approach is to use *variable-size partitions*. When a process is brought into memory, it is allocated exactly as much memory as it requires and no more.

Example 8.2 An example, using 64 Mbytes of main memory, is shown in Figure 8.14. Initially, main memory is empty, except for the OS (a). The first three processes are loaded in, starting where the OS ends and occupying just enough space for each process (b, c, d). This leaves a "hole" at the end of memory that is too small for a fourth process. At some point, none of the processes in memory is ready. The OS swaps out process 2 (e), which leaves sufficient room to load a new process, process 4 (f). Because process 4 is smaller than process 2, another small hole is created. Later, a point is reached at which none of the processes in main memory is ready, but process 2, in the Ready-Suspend state, is available. Because there is insufficient room in memory for process 2, the OS swaps process 1 out (g) and swaps process 2 back in (h).

As this example shows, this method starts out well, but eventually it leads to a situation in which there are a lot of small holes in memory. As time goes on, memory becomes more and more fragmented, and memory utilization declines. One technique for overcoming this problem is **compaction**: From time to time, the OS shifts the processes in memory to place all the free memory together in one block. This is a time-consuming procedure, wasteful of processor time.

Before we consider ways of dealing with the shortcomings of partitioning, we must clear up one loose end. Consider Figure 8.14; it should be obvious that a process is not likely to be loaded into the same place in main memory each time it is swapped in. Furthermore, if compaction is used, a process may be shifted while in main memory. A process in memory consists of instructions plus data. The instructions will contain addresses for memory locations of two types:

- Addresses of data items
- Addresses of instructions, used for branching instructions

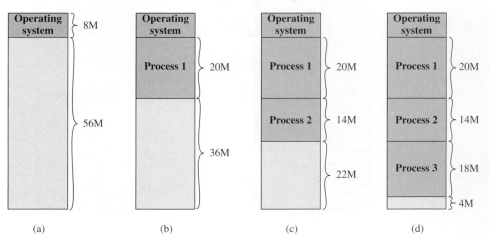

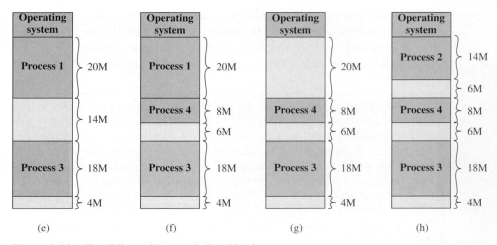

Figure 8.14   The Effect of Dynamic Partitioning

But these addresses are not fixed. They will change each time a process is swapped in. To solve this problem, a distinction is made between logical addresses and physical addresses. A **logical address** is expressed as a location relative to the beginning of the program. Instructions in the program contain only logical addresses. A **physical address** is an actual location in main memory. When the processor executes a process, it automatically converts from logical to physical address by adding the current starting location of the process, called its **base address**, to each logical address. This is another example of a processor hardware feature designed to meet an OS requirement. The exact nature of this hardware feature depends on the memory management strategy in use. We will see several examples later in this chapter.

Paging

Both unequal fixed-size and variable-size partitions are inefficient in the use of memory. Suppose, however, that memory is partitioned into equal fixed-size chunks that are relatively small, and that each process is also divided into small fixed-size chunks of some size. Then the chunks of a program, known as **pages**, could be assigned to available chunks of memory, known as **frames**, or page frames. At most, then, the wasted space in memory for that process is a fraction of the last page.

Figure 8.15 shows an example of the use of pages and frames. At a given point in time, some of the frames in memory are in use and some are free. The list of free frames is maintained by the OS. Process A, stored on disk, consists of four pages.

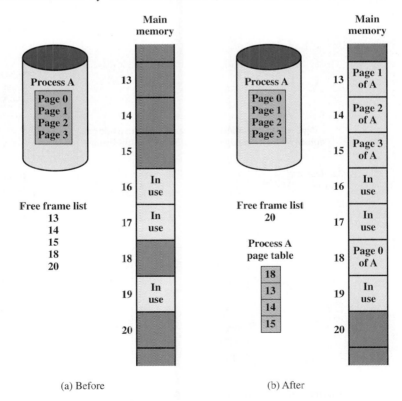

Figure 8.15 Allocation of Free Frames

When it comes time to load this process, the OS finds four free frames and loads the four pages of the process A into the four frames.

Now suppose, as in this example, that there are not sufficient unused contiguous frames to hold the process. Does this prevent the OS from loading A? The answer is no, because we can once again use the concept of logical address. A simple base address will no longer suffice. Rather, the OS maintains a **page table** for each process. The page table shows the frame location for each page of the process. Within the program, each logical address consists of a page number and a relative address within the page. Recall that in the case of simple partitioning, a logical address is the location of a word relative to the beginning of the program; the processor translates that into a physical address. With paging, the logical-to-physical address translation is still done by processor hardware. The processor must know how to access the page table of the current process. Presented with a logical address (page number, relative address), the processor uses the page table to produce a physical address (frame number, relative address). An example is shown in Figure 8.16.

This approach solves the problems raised earlier. Main memory is divided into many small equal-size frames. Each process is divided into frame-size pages: smaller processes require fewer pages, larger processes require more. When a process is brought in, its pages are loaded into available frames, and a page table is set up.

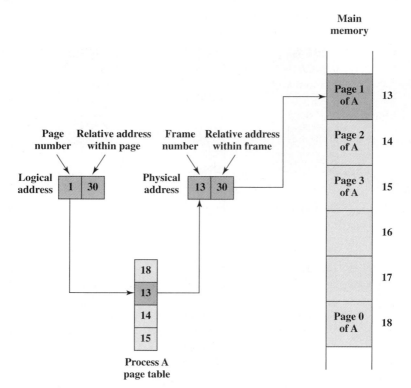

Figure 8.16 Logical and Physical Addresses

Virtual Memory

DEMAND PAGING With the use of paging, truly effective multiprogramming systems came into being. Furthermore, the simple tactic of breaking a process up into pages led to the development of another important concept: virtual memory.

To understand virtual memory, we must add a refinement to the paging scheme just discussed. That refinement is **demand paging**, which simply means that each page of a process is brought in only when it is needed, that is, on demand.

Consider a large process, consisting of a long program plus a number of arrays of data. Over any short period of time, execution may be confined to a small section of the program (e.g., a subroutine), and perhaps only one or two arrays of data are being used. This is the principle of locality, which we introduced in Appendix 4A. It would clearly be wasteful to load in dozens of pages for that process when only a few pages will be used before the program is suspended. We can make better use of memory by loading in just a few pages. Then, if the program branches to an instruction on a page not in main memory, or if the program references data on a page not in memory, a **page fault** is triggered. This tells the OS to bring in the desired page.

Thus, at any one time, only a few pages of any given process are in memory, and therefore more processes can be maintained in memory. Furthermore, time is saved because unused pages are not swapped in and out of memory. However, the OS must be clever about how it manages this scheme. When it brings one page in, it must throw another page out; this is known as **page replacement**. If it throws out a page just before it is about to be used, then it will just have to go get that page again almost immediately. Too much of this leads to a condition known as **thrashing**: the processor spends most of its time swapping pages rather than executing instructions. The avoidance of thrashing was a major research area in the 1970s and led to a variety of complex but effective algorithms. In essence, the OS tries to guess, based on recent history, which pages are least likely to be used in the near future.

Page Replacement Algorithm Simulators

A discussion of page replacement algorithms is beyond the scope of this chapter. A potentially effective technique is least recently used (LRU), the same algorithm discussed in Chapter 4 for cache replacement. In practice, LRU is difficult to implement for a virtual memory paging scheme. Several alternative approaches that seek to approximate the performance of LRU are in use; see Appendix F for details.

With demand paging, it is not necessary to load an entire process into main memory. This fact has a remarkable consequence: *It is possible for a process to be larger than all of main memory.* One of the most fundamental restrictions in programming has been lifted. Without demand paging, a programmer must be acutely aware of how much memory is available. If the program being written is too large, the programmer must devise ways to structure the program into pieces that can be loaded one at a time. With demand paging, that job is left to the OS and the hardware. As far as the programmer is concerned, he or she is dealing with a huge memory, the size associated with disk storage.

Because a process executes only in main memory, that memory is referred to as **real memory**. But a programmer or user perceives a much larger memory—that which is allocated on the disk. This latter is therefore referred to as **virtual memory**. Virtual memory allows for very effective multiprogramming and relieves the user of the unnecessarily tight constraints of main memory.

PAGE TABLE STRUCTURE The basic mechanism for reading a word from memory involves the translation of a virtual, or logical, address, consisting of page number and offset, into a physical address, consisting of frame number and offset, using a page table. Because the page table is of variable length, depending on the size of the process, we cannot expect to hold it in registers. Instead, it must be in main memory to be accessed. Figure 8.16 suggests a hardware implementation of this scheme. When a particular process is running, a register holds the starting address of the page table for that process. The page number of a virtual address is used to index that table and look up the corresponding frame number. This is combined with the offset portion of the virtual address to produce the desired real address.

In most systems, there is one page table per process. But each process can occupy huge amounts of virtual memory. For example, in the VAX architecture, each process can have up to $2^{31} = 2$ Gbytes of virtual memory. Using $2^9 = 512$-byte pages, that means that as many as 2^{22} page table entries are required *per process*. Clearly, the amount of memory devoted to page tables alone could be unacceptably high. To overcome this problem, most virtual memory schemes store page tables in virtual memory rather than real memory. This means that page tables are subject to paging just as other pages are. When a process is running, at least a part of its page table must be in main memory, including the page table entry of the currently executing page. Some processors make use of a two-level scheme to organize large page tables. In this scheme, there is a page directory, in which each entry points to a page table. Thus, if the length of the page directory is X, and if the maximum length of a page table is Y, then a process can consist of up to $X \times Y$ pages. Typically, the maximum length of a page table is restricted to be equal to one page. We will see an example of this two-level approach when we consider the Pentium II later in this chapter.

An alternative approach to the use of one- or two-level page tables is the use of an inverted page table structure (Figure 8.17). Variations on this approach are used on the PowerPC, UltraSPARC, and the IA-64 architecture. An implementation of the Mach OS on the RT-PC also uses this technique.

In this approach, the page number portion of a virtual address is mapped into a hash value using a simple hashing function.[2] The hash value is a pointer to the inverted page table, which contains the page table entries. There is one entry in the

---

[2]A hash function maps numbers in the range 0 through M into numbers in the range 0 through N, where $M > N$. The output of the hash function is used as an index into the hash table. Since more than one input maps into the same output, it is possible for an input item to map to a hash table entry that is already occupied. In that case, the new item must *overflow* into another hash table location. Typically, the new item is placed in the first succeeding empty space, and a pointer from the original location is provided to chain the entries together. See Appendix C for more information on hash functions.

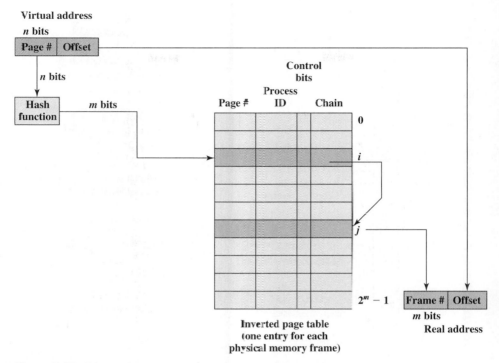

Figure 8.17   Inverted Page Table Structure

inverted page table for each real memory page frame rather than one per virtual page. Thus a fixed proportion of real memory is required for the tables regardless of the number of processes or virtual pages supported. Because more than one virtual address may map into the same hash table entry, a chaining technique is used for managing the overflow. The hashing technique results in chains that are typically short—between one and two entries. The page table's structure is called *inverted* because it indexes page table entries by frame number rather than by virtual page number.

Translation Lookaside Buffer

In principle, then, every virtual memory reference can cause two physical memory accesses: one to fetch the appropriate page table entry, and one to fetch the desired data. Thus, a straightforward virtual memory scheme would have the effect of doubling the memory access time. To overcome this problem, most virtual memory schemes make use of a special cache for page table entries, usually called a **translation lookaside buffer (TLB)**. This cache functions in the same way as a memory cache and contains those page table entries that have been most recently used. Figure 8.18 is a flowchart that shows the use of the TLB. By the principle of locality, most virtual memory references will be to locations in recently used pages. Therefore, most references will involve page table entries in the cache. Studies of the VAX TLB have shown that this scheme can significantly improve performance [CLAR85, SATY81].

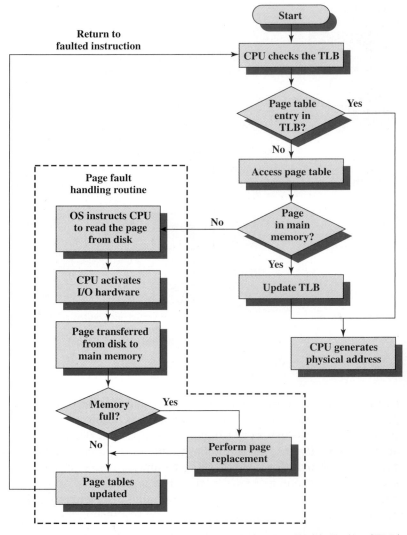

Figure 8.18 Operation of Paging and Translation Lookaside Buffer (TLB)

Note that the virtual memory mechanism must interact with the cache system (not the TLB cache, but the main memory cache). This is illustrated in Figure 8.19. A virtual address will generally be in the form of a page number, offset. First, the memory system consults the TLB to see if the matching page table entry is present. If it is, the real (physical) address is generated by combining the frame number with the offset. If not, the entry is accessed from a page table. Once the real address is generated, which is in the form of a tag and a remainder, the cache is consulted to see if the block containing that word is present (see Figure 4.5). If so, it is returned to the processor. If not, the word is retrieved from main memory.

The reader should be able to appreciate the complexity of the processor hardware involved in a single memory reference. The virtual address is translated into a real address. This involves reference to a page table, which may be in the TLB, in

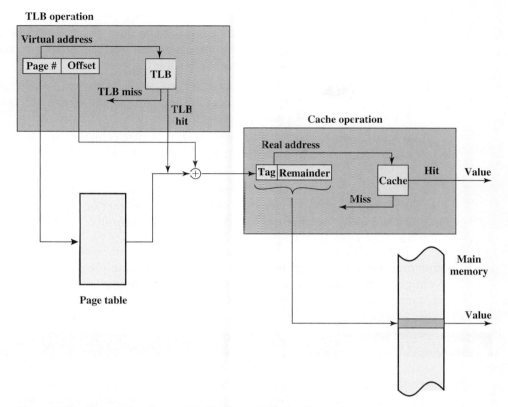

Figure 8.19   Translation Lookaside Buffer and Cache Operation

main memory, or on disk. The referenced word may be in cache, in main memory, or on disk. In the latter case, the page containing the word must be loaded into main memory and its block loaded into the cache. In addition, the page table entry for that page must be updated.

Segmentation

There is another way in which addressable memory can be subdivided, known as *segmentation*. Whereas paging is invisible to the programmer and serves the purpose of providing the programmer with a larger address space, segmentation is usually visible to the programmer and is provided as a convenience for organizing programs and data and as a means for associating privilege and protection attributes with instructions and data.

Segmentation allows the programmer to view memory as consisting of multiple address spaces or segments. Segments are of variable, indeed dynamic, size. Typically, the programmer or the OS will assign programs and data to different segments. There may be a number of program segments for various types of programs as well as a number of data segments. Each segment may be assigned access and usage rights. Memory references consist of a (segment number, offset) form of address.

This organization has a number of advantages to the programmer over a non-segmented address space:

1. It simplifies the handling of growing data structures. If the programmer does not know ahead of time how large a particular data structure will become, it is not necessary to guess. The data structure can be assigned its own segment, and the OS will expand or shrink the segment as needed.

2. It allows programs to be altered and recompiled independently without requiring that an entire set of programs be relinked and reloaded. Again, this is accomplished using multiple segments.

3. It lends itself to sharing among processes. A programmer can place a utility program or a useful table of data in a segment that can be addressed by other processes.

4. It lends itself to protection. Because a segment can be constructed to contain a well-defined set of programs or data, the programmer or a system administrator can assign access privileges in a convenient fashion.

These advantages are not available with paging, which is invisible to the programmer. On the other hand, we have seen that paging provides for an efficient form of memory management. To combine the advantages of both, some systems are equipped with the hardware and OS software to provide both.

8.4 PENTIUM MEMORY MANAGEMENT

Since the introduction of the 32-bit architecture, microprocessors have evolved sophisticated memory management schemes that build on the lessons learned with medium- and large-scale systems. In many cases, the microprocessor versions are superior to their larger-system antecedents. Because the schemes were developed by the microprocessor hardware vendor and may be employed with a variety of operating systems, they tend to be quite general purpose. A representative example is the scheme used on the Pentium II. The Pentium II memory management hardware is essentially the same as that used in the Intel 80386 and 80486 processors, with some refinements.

Address Spaces

The Pentium II includes hardware for both segmentation and paging. Both mechanisms can be disabled, allowing the user to choose from four distinct views of memory:

- **Unsegmented unpaged memory:** In this case, the virtual address is the same as the physical address. This is useful, for example, in low-complexity, high-performance controller applications.
- **Unsegmented paged memory:** Here memory is viewed as a paged linear address space. Protection and management of memory is done via paging. This is favored by some operating systems (e.g., Berkeley UNIX).
- **Segmented unpaged memory:** Here memory is viewed as a collection of logical address spaces. The advantage of this view over a paged approach is that it

affords protection down to the level of a single byte, if necessary. Furthermore, unlike paging, it guarantees that the translation table needed (the segment table) is on-chip when the segment is in memory. Hence, segmented unpaged memory results in predictable access times.

- **Segmented paged memory:** Segmentation is used to define logical memory partitions subject to access control, and paging is used to manage the allocation of memory within the partitions. Operating systems such as UNIX System V favor this view.

Segmentation

When segmentation is used, each virtual address (called a logical address in the Pentium II documentation) consists of a 16-bit segment reference and a 32-bit offset. Two bits of the segment reference deal with the protection mechanism, leaving 14 bits for specifying a particular segment. Thus, with unsegmented memory, the user's virtual memory is $2^{32} = 4$ Gbytes. With segmented memory, the total virtual memory space as seen by a user is $2^{46} = 64$ terabytes (Tbytes). The physical address space employs a 32-bit address for a maximum of 4 Gbytes.

The amount of virtual memory can actually be larger than the 64 Tbytes. This is because the processor's interpretation of a virtual address depends on which process is currently active. Virtual address space is divided into two parts. One-half of the virtual address space (8K segments $\times$ 4 Gbytes) is global, shared by all processes; the remainder is local and is distinct for each process.

Associated with each segment are two forms of protection: privilege level and access attribute. There are four privilege levels, from most protected (level 0) to least protected (level 3). The privilege level associated with a data segment is its "classification"; the privilege level associated with a program segment is its "clearance." An executing program may only access data segments for which its clearance level is lower than (more privileged) or equal to (same privilege) the privilege level of the data segment.

The hardware does not dictate how these privilege levels are to be used; this depends on the OS design and implementation. It was intended that privilege level 1 would be used for most of the OS, and level 0 would be used for that small portion of the OS devoted to memory management, protection, and access control. This leaves two levels for applications. In many systems, applications will reside at level 3, with level 2 being unused. Specialized application subsystems that must be protected because they implement their own security mechanisms are good candidates for level 2. Some examples are database management systems, office automation systems, and software engineering environments.

In addition to regulating access to data segments, the privilege mechanism limits the use of certain instructions. Some instructions, such as those dealing with memory-management registers, can only be executed in level 0. I/O instructions can only be executed up to a certain level that is designated by the OS; typically, this will be level 1.

The access attribute of a data segment specifies whether read/write or read-only accesses are permitted. For program segments, the access attribute specifies read/execute or read-only access.

The address translation mechanism for segmentation involves mapping a virtual address into what is referred to as a linear address (Figure 8.20b). A virtual address consists of the 32-bit offset and a 16-bit segment selector (Figure 8.20a). The segment selector consists of the following fields:

- **Table Indicator (TI):** Indicates whether the global segment table or a local segment table should be used for translation.
- **Segment Number:** The number of the segment. This serves as an index into the segment table.
- **Requested Privilege Level (RPL):** The privilege level requested for this access.

Each entry in a segment table consists of 64 bits, as shown in Figure 8.20c. The fields are defined in Table 8.5.

Paging

Segmentation is an optional feature and may be disabled. When segmentation is in use, addresses used in programs are virtual addresses and are converted into linear addresses, as just described. When segmentation is not in use, linear addresses are used in programs. In either case, the following step is to convert that linear address into a real 32-bit address.

To understand the structure of the linear address, you need to know that the Pentium II paging mechanism is actually a two-level table lookup operation. The first level is a page directory, which contains up to 1024 entries. This splits the 4-Gbyte linear memory space into 1024 page groups, each with its own page table, and each 4 Mbytes in length. Each page table contains up to 1024 entries; each entry corresponds to a single 4-Kbyte page. Memory management has the option of using one page directory for all processes, one page directory for each process, or some combination of the two. The page directory for the current task is always in main memory. Page tables may be in virtual memory.

Figure 8.20 shows the formats of entries in page directories and page tables, and the fields are defined in Table 8.5. Note that access control mechanisms can be provided on a page or page group basis.

The Pentium II also makes use of a translation lookaside buffer. The buffer can hold 32 page table entries. Each time that the page directory is changed, the buffer is cleared.

Figure 8.21 illustrates the combination of segmentation and paging mechanisms. For clarity, the translation lookaside buffer and memory cache mechanisms are not shown.

Finally, the Pentium II includes a new extension not found on the 80386 or 80486, the provision for two page sizes. If the PSE (page size extension) bit in control register 4 is set to 1, then the paging unit permits the OS programmer to define a page as either 4 Kbyte or 4 Mbyte in size.

When 4-Mbyte pages are used, there is only one level of table lookup for pages. When the hardware accesses the page directory, the page directory entry (Figure 8.20d) has the PS bit set to 1. In this case, bits 9 through 21 are ignored and bits 22 through 31 define the base address for a 4-Mbyte page in memory. Thus, there is a single page table.

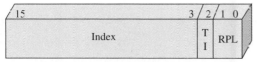

TI = Table indicator
RPL = Requestor privilege level

(a) Segment selector

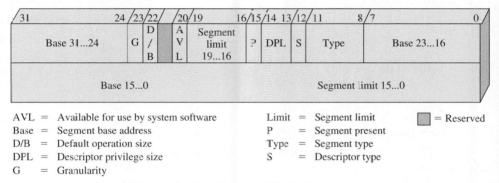

(b) Linear address

AVL = Available for use by system software   Limit = Segment limit   ▨ = Reserved
Base = Segment base address   P   = Segment present
D/B = Default operation size   Type   = Segment type
DPL = Descriptor privilege size   S   = Descriptor type
G   = Granularity

(c) Segment descriptor (segment table entry)

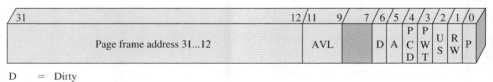

AVL = Available for systems programmer use   PWT = Write through
PS = Page size   US = User/supervisor
A   = Accessed   RW = Read-write
PCD = Cache disable   P   = Present

(d) Page directory entry

D   = Dirty

(e) Page table entry

Figure 8.20   Pentium Memory-Management Formats

Table 8.5   Pentium II Memory Management Parameters

Segment Descriptor (Segment Table Entry)

Base

Defines the starting address of the segment within the 4-Gbyte linear address space.

D/B bit

In a code segment, this is the D bit and indicates whether operands and addressing modes are 16 or 32 bits.

Descriptor Privilege Level (DPL)

Specifies the privilege level of the segment referred to by this segment descriptor.

Granularity bit (G)

Indicates whether the Limit field is to be interpreted in units by one byte or 4 Kbytes.

Limit

Defines the size of the segment. The processor interprets the limit field in one of two ways, depending on the granularity bit: in units of one byte, up to a segment size limit of 1 Mbyte, or in units of 4 Kbytes, up to a segment size limit of 4 Gbytes.

S bit

Determines whether a given segment is a system segment or a code or data segment.

Segment Present bit (P)

Used for nonpaged systems. It indicates whether the segment is present in main memory. For paged systems, this bit is always set to 1.

Type

Distinguishes between various kinds of segments and indicates the access attributes.

Page Directory Entry and Page Table Entry

Accessed bit (A)

This bit is set to 1 by the processor in both levels of page tables when a read or write operation to the corresponding page occurs.

Dirty bit (D)

This bit is set to 1 by the processor when a write operation to the corresponding page occurs.

Page Frame Address

Provides the physical address of the page in memory if the present bit is set. Since page frames are aligned on 4K boundaries, the bottom 12 bits are 0, and only the top 20 bits are included in the entry. In a page directory, the address is that of a page table.

Page Cache Disable bit (PCD)

Indicates whether data from page may be cached.

Page Size bit (PS)

Indicates whether page size is 4 Kbyte or 4 Mbyte.

Page Write Through bit (PWT)

Indicates whether write-through or write-back caching policy will be used for data in the corresponding page.

Present bit (P)

Indicates whether the page table or page is in main memory.

Read/Write bit (RW)

For user-level pages, indicates whether the page is read-only access or read/write access for user-level programs.

User/Supervisor bit (US)

Indicates whether the page is available only to the operating system (supervisor level) or is available to both operating system and applications (user level).

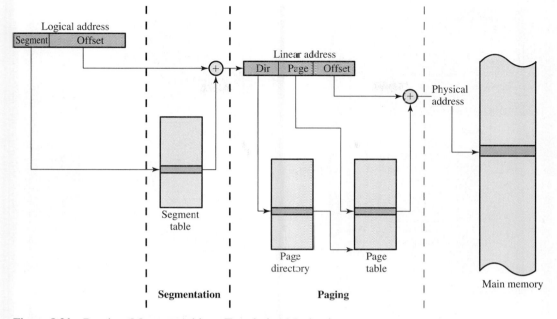

Figure 8.21   Pentium Memory Address Translation Mechanisms

The use of 4-Mbyte pages reduces the memory-management storage requirements for large main memories. With 4-Kbyte pages, a full 4-Gbyte main memory requires about 4 Mbytes of memory just for the page tables. With 4-Mbyte pages, a single table, 4 Kbytes in length, is sufficient for page memory management.

8.5   ARM MEMORY MANAGEMENT

ARM provides a versatile virtual memory system architecture that can be tailored to the needs of the embedded system designer.

Memory System Organization

Figure 8.22 provides an overview of the memory management hardware in the ARM for virtual memory. The virtual memory translation hardware uses one or two levels of tables for translation from virtual to physical addresses, as explained subsequently. The translation lookaside buffer (TLB) is a cache of recent page table entries. If an entry is available in the TLB, then the TLB directly sends a physical address to main memory for a read or write operation. As explained in Chapter 4, data is exchanged between the processor and main memory via the cache. If a logical cache organization is used (Figure 4.7a), then the ARM supplies that address directly to the cache as well as supplying it to the TLB when a cache miss occurs. If a physical cache organization is used (Figure 4.7b), then the TLB must supply the physical address to the cache.

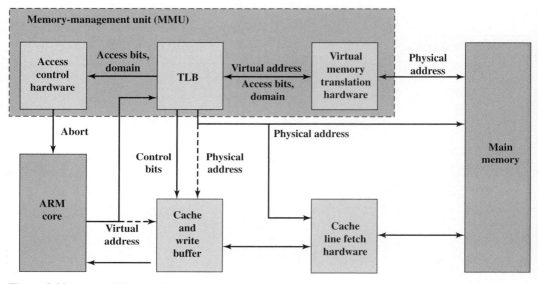

Figure 8.22 ARM Memory System Overview

Entries in the translation tables also include access control bits, which determine whether a given process may access a given portion of memory. If access is denied, access control hardware supplies an abort signal to the ARM processor.

Virtual Memory Address Translation

The ARM supports memory access based on either sections or pages:

- **Supersections (optional):** Consist of 16-MB blocks of main memory
- **Sections:** Consist of 1-MB blocks of main memory
- **Large pages:** Consist of 64-kB blocks of main memory
- **Small pages:** Consist of 4-kB blocks of main memory

Sections and supersections are supported to allow mapping of a large region of memory while using only a single entry in the TLB. Additional access control mechanisms are extended within small pages to 1kB subpages, and within large pages to 16kB subpages. The translation table held in main memory has two levels:

- **First-level table:** Holds section and supersection translations, and pointers to second-level tables
- **Second-level tables:** Hold both large and small page translations

The memory-management unit (MMU) translates virtual addresses generated by the processor into physical addresses to access main memory, and also derives and checks the access permission. Translations occur as the result of a TLB miss, and start with a first-level fetch. A section-mapped access only requires a first-level fetch, whereas a page-mapped access also requires a second-level fetch.

Figure 8.23 shows the two-level address translation process for small pages. There is a single level 1 (L1) page table with 4K 32-bit entries. Each L1 entry points to a level 2 (L2) page table with 255 32-bit entries. Each of the L2 entry points to a

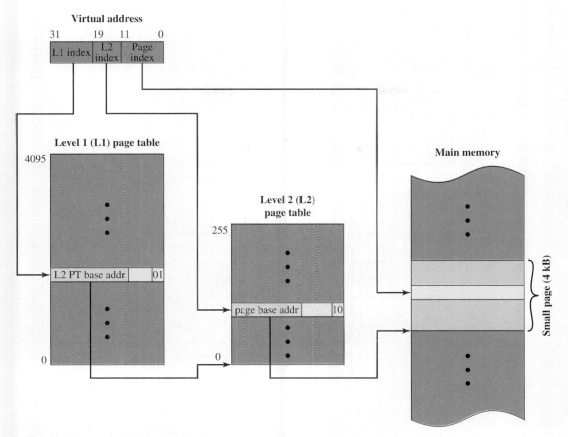

Figure 8.23   ARM Virtual Memory Address Translation for Small Pages

4-kB page in main memory. The 32-bit virtual address is interpreted as follows: The most significant 12 bits are an index into the L1 page table. The next 8 bits are an index into the relevant L2 page table. The least significant 12 bits index a byte in the relevant page in main memory.

A similar two-page lookup procedure is used for large pages. For sections and supersection, only the L1 page table lookup is required.

Memory–Management Formats

To get a better understanding of the ARM memory management scheme, we consider the key formats, as shown in Figure 8.24. The control bits shown in this figure are defined in Table 8.6.

For the L1 table, each entry is a descriptor of how its associated 1-MB virtual address range is mapped. Each entry has one of four alternative formats:

- **Bits [1:0] = 00:** The associated virtual addresses are unmapped, and attempts to access them generate a translation fault.
- **Bits [1:0] = 01:** The entry gives the physical address of an L2 page table, which specifies how the associated virtual address range is mapped.

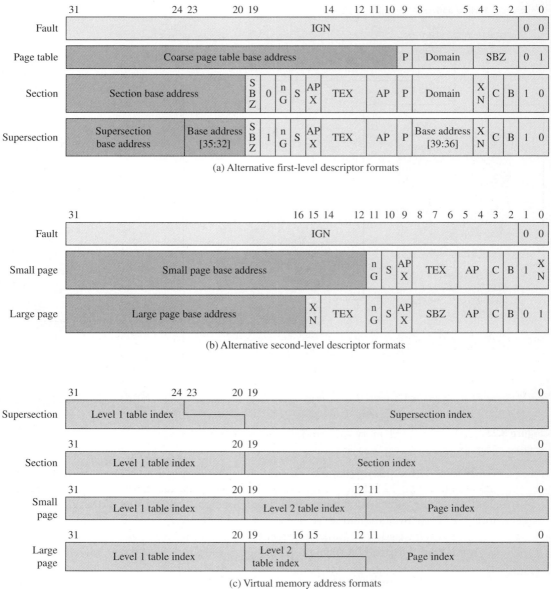

Figure 8.24 ARMv6 Memory-Management Formats

- **Bits [1:0] = 01 and bit 19 = 0:** The entry is a section descriptor for its associated virtual addresses.

- **Bits [1:0] = 01 and bit 19 = 1:** The entry is a supersection descriptor for its associated virtual addresses.

Entries with bits [1:0] = 11 are reserved.

For memory structured into pages, a two-level page table access is required. Bits [31:10] of the L1 page entry contain a pointer to a L1 page table. For small

Table 8.6   ARM Memory-Management Parameters

Access Permission (AP), Access Permission Extension (APX)
These bits control access to the corresponding memory region. If an access is made to an area of memory without the required permissions, a Permission Fault is raised.

Bufferable (B) bit
Determines, with the TEX bits, how the write buffer is used for cacheable memory.

Cacheable (C) bit
Determines whether this memory region can be mapped through the cache.

Domain
Collection of memory regions. Access control can be applied on the basis of domain.

not Global (nG)
Determines whether the translation should be marked as global (0), or process specific (1).

Shared (S)
Determines whether the translation is for not-shared (0), or shared (1) memory.

SBZ
Should be zero.

Type Extension (TEX)
These bits, together with the B and C bits, control accesses to the caches, how the write buffer is used, and if the memory region is shareable and therefore must be kept coherent.

Execute Never (XN)
Determines whether the region is executable (0) or not executable (1).

pages, the L2 entry contains a 20-bit pointer to the base address of a 4-kB page in main memory.

For large pages, the structure is more complex. As with virtual addresses for small pages, a virtual address for a large page structure includes a 12-bit index into the level one table and an 8-bit index into the L2 table. For the 64-kB large pages, the page index portion of the virtual address must be 16 bits. To accommodate all of these bits in a 32-bit format, there is a 4-bit overlap between the page index field and the L2 table index field. ARM accommodates this overlap by requiring that each page table entry in a L2 page table that supports large pages be replicated 16 times. In effect, the size of the L2 page table is reduced from 256 entries to 16 entries, if all of the entries refer to large pages. However, a given L2 page can service a mixture of large and small pages, hence the need for the replication for large page entries.

For memory structured into sections or supersections, a one-level page table access is required. For sections, bits [31:20] of the L1 entry contain a 12-bit pointer to the base of the 1-MB section in main memory.

For supersections, bits [31:24] of the L1 entry contain an 8-bit pointer to the base of the 16-MB section in main memory. As with large pages, a page table entry replication is required. In the case of supersections, the L1 table index portion of the virtual address overlaps by 4 bits with the supersection index portion of the virtual address Therefore, 16 identical L1 page table entries are required.

The range of physical address space can be expanded by up to eight additional address bits (bits [23:20] and [8:5]). The number of additional bits is implementation dependent. These additional bits can be interpreted as extending the size of physical memory by as much as a factor of $2^8 = 256$. Thus, physical memory may in fact be as much as 256 times as large as the memory space available to each individual process.

Access Control

The AP access control bits in each table entry control access to a region of memory by a given process. A region of memory can be designated as no access, read only, or read-write. Further, the region can be designated as privileged access only, reserved for use by the OS and not by applications.

ARM also employs the concept of a domain, which is a collection of sections and/or pages that have particular access permissions. The ARM architecture supports 16 domains. The domain feature allows multiple processes to use the same translation tables while maintaining some protection from each other.

Each page table entry and TLB entry contains a field that specifies which domain the entry is in. A 2-bit field in the Domain Access Control Register controls access to each domain. Each field allows the access to an entire domain to be enabled and disabled very quickly, so that whole memory areas can be swapped in and out of virtual memory very efficiently. Two kinds of domain access are supported:

- **Clients:** Users of domains (execute programs and access data) that must observe the access permissions of the individual sections and/or pages that make up that domain

- **Managers:** Control the behavior of the domain (the current sections and pages in the domain, and the domain access), and bypass the access permissions for table entries in that domain

One program can be a client of some domains, and a manager of some other domains, and have no access to the remaining domains. This allows very flexible memory protection for programs that access different memory resources.

8.6 RECOMMENDED READING

[STAL12] covers the topics of this chapter in detail.

> **STAL12** Stallings, W. *Operating Systems, Internals and Design Principles, Seventh Edition.* Upper Saddle River, NJ: Prentice Hall, 2012.

Systems and Applications: Includes an online newsletter and links to other sites

8.7 KEY TERMS, REVIEW QUESTIONS, AND PROBLEMS

Key Terms

batch system	job control language (JCL)	medium-term scheduling
demand paging	kernel	memory management
interactive operating system	logical address	memory protection
interrupt	long-term scheduling	multiprogramming

multitasking	process	thrashing
nucleus	process control block	time-sharing system
operating system (OS)	process state	translation lookaside buffer
paging	real memory	(TLB)
page table	resident monitor	utility
partitioning	segmentation	virtual memory
physical address	short-term scheduling	
privileged instruction	swapping	

Review Questions

8.1   What is an operating system?

8.2   List and briefly define the key services provided by an OS.

8.3   List and briefly define the major types of OS scheduling.

8.4   What is the difference between a process and a program?

8.5   What is the purpose of swapping?

8.6   If a process may be dynamically assigned to different locations in main memory, what is the implication for the addressing mechanism?

8.7   Is it necessary for all of the pages of a process to be in main memory while the process is executing?

8.8   Must the pages of a process in main memory be contiguous?

8.9   Is it necessary for the pages of a process in main memory to be in sequential order?

8.10   What is the purpose of a translation lookaside buffer?

Problems

8.1   Suppose that we have a multiprogrammed computer in which each job has identical characteristics. In one computation period, T, for a job, half the time is spent in I/O and the other half in processor activity. Each job runs for a total of N periods. Assume that a simple round-robin priority is used, and that I/O operations can overlap with processor operation. Define the following quantities:

- Turnaround time = actual to complete a job
- Throughput = average number of jobs completed per time period T
- Processor utilization = percentage of time that the processor is active (not waiting)

Compute these quantities for one, two, and four simultaneous jobs, assuming that the period T is distributed in each of the following ways:

a.   I/O first half, processor second half

b.   I/O first and fourth quarters, processor second and third quarters

8.2   An I/O-bound program is one that, if run alone, would spend more time waiting for I/O than using the processor. A processor-bound program is the opposite. Suppose a short-term scheduling algorithm favors those programs that have used little processor time in the recent past. Explain why this algorithm favors I/O-bound programs and yet does not permanently deny processor time to processor-bound programs.

8.3   A program computes the row sums

$$C_i = \sum_{j=1}^{n} a_{ij}$$

of an array A that is 100 by 100. Assume that the computer uses demand paging with a page size of 1000 words, and that the amount of main memory allotted for data is five page frames. Is there any difference in the page fault rate if A were stored in virtual memory by rows or columns? Explain.

8.4 Consider a fixed partitioning scheme with equal-size partitions of 2^{16} bytes and a total main memory size of 2^{24} bytes. A process table is maintained that includes a pointer to a partition for each resident process. How many bits are required for the pointer?

8.5 Consider a dynamic partitioning scheme. Show that, on average, the memory contains half as many holes as segments.

8.6 Suppose the page table for the process currently executing on the processor looks like the following. All numbers are decimal, everything is numbered starting from zero, and all addresses are memory byte addresses. The page size is 1024 bytes.

Virtual page number	Valid bit	Reference bit	Modify bit	Page frame number
0	1	1	0	4
1	1	1	1	7
2	0	0	0	—
3	1	0	0	2
4	0	0	0	—
5	1	0	1	0

a. Describe exactly how, in general, a virtual address generated by the CPU is translated into a physical main memory address.

b. What physical address, if any, would each of the following virtual addresses correspond to? (Do not try to handle any page faults, if any.)
(i) 1052
(ii) 2221
(iii) 5499

8.7 Give reasons that the page size in a virtual memory system should be neither very small nor very large.

8.8 A process references five pages, A, B, C, D, and E, in the following order:

A; B; C; D; A; B; E; A; B; C; D; E

Assume that the replacement algorithm is first-in-first-out and find the number of page transfers during this sequence of references starting with an empty main memory with three page frames. Repeat for four page frames.

8.9 The following sequence of virtual page numbers is encountered in the course of execution on a computer with virtual memory:

3 4 2 6 4 7 1 3 2 6 3 5 1 2 3

Assume that a least recently used page replacement policy is adopted. Plot a graph of page hit ratio (fraction of page references in which the page is in main memory) as a function of main-memory page capacity n for $1 \leq n \leq 8$. Assume that main memory is initially empty.

8.10 In the VAX computer, user page tables are located at virtual addresses in the system space. What is the advantage of having user page tables in virtual rather than main memory? What is the disadvantage?

8.11 Suppose the program statement

for $(i = 1; i <= n; i++)$
$a[i] = b[i] + c[i];$

is executed in a memory with page size of 1000 words. Let $n = 1000$. Using a machine that has a full range of register-to-register instructions and employs index registers, write a hypothetical program to implement the foregoing statement. Then show the sequence of page references during execution.

8.12 The IBM System/370 architecture uses a two-level memory structure and refers to the two levels as segments and pages, although the segmentation approach lacks many of the features described earlier in this chapter. For the basic 370 architecture, the page size may be either 2 Kbytes or 4 Kbytes, and the segment size is fixed at either 64 Kbytes or 1 Mbyte. For the 370/XA and 370/ESA architectures, the page size is 4 Kbytes and the segment size is 1 Mbyte. Which advantages of segmentation does this scheme lack? What is the benefit of segmentation for the 370?

8.13 Consider a computer system with both segmentation and paging. When a segment is in memory, some words are wasted on the last page. In addition, for a segment size s and a page size p, there are s/p page table entries. The smaller the page size, the less waste in the last page of the segment, but the larger the page table. What page size minimizes the total overhead?

8.14 A computer has a cache, main memory, and a disk used for virtual memory. If a referenced word is in the cache, 20 ns are required to access it. If it is in main memory but not in the cache, 60 ns are needed to load it into the cache, and then the reference is started again. If the word is not in main memory, 12 ms are required to fetch the word from disk, followed by 60 ns to copy it to the cache, and then the reference is started again. The cache hit ratio is 0.9 and the main-memory hit ratio is 0.6. What is the average time in ns required to access a referenced word on this system?

8.15 Assume a task is divided into four equal-sized segments and that the system builds an eight-entry page descriptor table for each segment. Thus, the system has a combination of segmentation and paging. Assume also that the page size is 2 Kbytes.
  a. What is the maximum size of each segment?
  b. What is the maximum logical address space for the task?
  c. Assume that an element in physical location 00021ABC is accessed by this task. What is the format of the logical address that the task generates for it? What is the maximum physical address space for the system?

8.16 Assume a microprocessor capable of accessing up to 2^{32} bytes of physical main memory. It implements one segmented logical address space of maximum size 2^{31} bytes. Each instruction contains the whole two-part address. External memory management units (MMUs) are used, whose management scheme assigns contiguous blocks of physical memory of fixed size 2^{22} bytes to segments. The starting physical address of a segment is always divisible by 1024. Show the detailed interconnection of the external mapping mechanism that converts logical addresses to physical addresses using the appropriate number of MMUs, and show the detailed internal structure of an MMU (assuming that each MMU contains a 128-entry directly mapped segment descriptor cache) and how each MMU is selected.

8.17 Consider a paged logical address space (composed of 32 pages of 2 Kbytes each) mapped into a 1-Mbyte physical memory space.
  a. What is the format of the processor's logical address?
  b. What is the length and width of the page table (disregarding the "access rights" bits)?
  c. What is the effect on the page table if the physical memory space is reduced by half?

8.18 In IBM's mainframe operating system, OS/390, one of the major modules in the kernel is the System Resource Manager (SRM). This module is responsible for the allocation of resources among address spaces (processes). The SRM gives OS/390 a degree of sophistication unique among operating systems. No other mainframe OS, and certainly no other type of OS, can match the functions performed by SRM. The concept of resource includes processor, real memory, and I/O channels. SRM accumulates statistics pertaining to utilization of processor, channel, and various key data structures. Its purpose is to provide optimum performance based on performance monitoring and analysis. The installation sets forth various performance objectives, and these serve as guidance to the SRM, which dynamically modifies installation and job performance characteristics based on system utilization. In turn, the SRM provides reports that enable the trained operator to refine the configuration and parameter settings to improve user service.

This problem concerns one example of SRM activity. Real memory is divided into equal-sized blocks called frames, of which there may be many thousands. Each frame can hold a block of virtual memory referred to as a page. SRM receives control approximately 20 times per second and inspects each and every page frame. If the page has not been referenced or changed, a counter is incremented by 1. Over time, SRM averages these numbers to determine the average number of seconds that a page frame in the system goes untouched. What might be the purpose of this and what action might SRM take?

8.19 For each of the ARM virtual address formats shown in Figure 8.24, show the physical address format.

8.20 Draw a figure similar to Figure 8.23 for ARM virtual memory translation when main memory is divided into sections.

CHAPTER **9**

NUMBER SYSTEMS

9.1 THE DECIMAL SYSTEM

In everyday life we use a system based on decimal digits (0, 1, 2, 3, 4, 5, 6, 7, 8, 9) to represent numbers, and refer to the system as the decimal system. Consider what the number 83 means. It means eight tens plus three:

$$83 = (8 \times 10) + 3$$

The number 4728 means four thousands, seven hundreds, two tens, plus eight:

$$4728 = (4 \times 1000) + (7 \times 100) + (2 \times 10) + 8$$

The decimal system is said to have a **base**, or **radix**, of 10. This means that each digit in the number is multiplied by 10 raised to a power corresponding to that digit's position:

$$83 = (8 \times 10^1) + (3 \times 10^0)$$
$$4728 = (4 \times 10^3) + (7 \times 10^2) + (2 \times 10^1) + (8 \times 10^0)$$

The same principle holds for decimal fractions, but negative powers of 10 are used. Thus, the decimal fraction 0.256 stands for 2 tenths plus 5 hundredths plus 6 thousandths:

$$0.256 = (2 \times 10^{-1}) + (5 \times 10^{-2}) + (6 \times 10^{-3})$$

A number with both an integer and fractional part has digits raised to both positive and negative powers of 10:

$$442.256 = (4 \times 10^2) + (4 + 10^1) + (2 \times 10^0) + (2 \times 10^{-1}) + (5 \times 10^{-2})$$
$$+ (6 \times 10^{-3})$$

In any number, the leftmost digit is referred to as the **most significant digit**, because it carries the highest value. The rightmost digit is called the **least significant digit**. In the preceding decimal number, the 4 on the left is the most significant digit and the 6 on the right is the least significant digit.

Table 9.1 shows the relationship between each digit position and the value assigned to that position. Each position is weighted 10 times the value of the position to the right and one-tenth the value of the position to the left. Thus, positions represent successive powers of 10. If we number the positions as indicated in Table 9.1, then position i is weighted by the value 10^i.

Table 9.1   Positional Interpretation of a Decimal Number

4	7	2	2	5	6
100s	10s	1s	tenths	hundredths	thousandths
10^2	10^1	10^9	10^{-1}	10^{-2}	10^{-3}
position 2	position 1	position 0	position –1	position –2	position –3

In general, for the decimal representation of $X = \{\ldots d_2 d_1 d_0.d_{-1}d_{-2}d_{-3}\ldots\}$, the value of X is

$$X = \sum_i (d_i \times 10^i) \tag{9.1}$$

One other observation is worth making. Consider the number 509 and ask how many tens are in the number. Because there is a 0 in the tens position, you might be tempted to say there are no tens. But there are in fact 50 tens. What the 0 in the tens position means is that there are no tens left over that cannot be lumped into the hundreds, or thousands, and so on. Therefore, because each position holds only the leftover numbers that cannot be lumped into higher positions, each digit position needs to have a value of no greater than 9. Nine is the maximum value that a position can hold before it flips over into the next higher position.

9.2   POSITIONAL NUMBER SYSTEMS

In a positional number system, each number is represented by a string of digits in which each digit position i has an associated weight r^i, where r is the radix, or base, of the number system. The general form of a number in such a system with radix r is

$$(\ldots a_3 a_2 a_1 a_0.a_{-1}a_{-2}a_{-3}\ldots)_r$$

where the value of any digit a_i is an integer in the range $0 \leq a_i < r$. The dot between a_0 and a_{-1} is called the **radix point**. The number is defined to have the value

$$\ldots + a_3 r^3 + a_2 r^2 + a_1 r^1 + a_0 r^0 + a_{-1} r^{-1} + a_{-2} r^{-2} + a_{-3} r^{-3} + \ldots$$
$$= \sum_i (a_i \times b^i) \tag{9.2}$$

The decimal system, then, is a special case of a positional number system with radix 10 and with digits in the range 0 through 9.

As an example of another positional system, consider the system with base 7. Table 9.2 shows the weighting value for positions –1 through 4. In each position, the digit value ranges from 0 through 6.

Table 9.2   Positional Interpretation of a Number in Base 7

Position	4	3	2	2	0	–1
Value in Exponential Form	7^4	7^3	7^2	7^1	7^0	7^{-1}
Decimal Value	2401	343	49	7	1	1/7

9.3 THE BINARY SYSTEM

In the decimal system, 10 different digits are used to represent numbers with a base of 10. In the binary system, we have only two digits, 1 and 0. Thus, numbers in the binary system are represented to the base 2.

To avoid confusion, we will sometimes put a subscript on a number to indicate its base. For example, 83_{10} and 4728_{10} are numbers represented in decimal notation or, more briefly, decimal numbers. The digits 1 and 0 in binary notation have the same meaning as in decimal notation:

$$0_2 = 0_{10}$$
$$1_2 = 1_{10}$$

To represent larger numbers, as with decimal notation, each digit in a binary number has a value depending on its position:

$$10_2 = (1 \times 2^1) + (0 \times 2^0) = 2_{10}$$
$$11_2 = (1 \times 2^1) + (1 \times 2^0) = 3_{10}$$
$$100_2 = (1 \times 2^2) + (0 \times 2^1) + (0 \times 2^0) = 4_{10}$$

and so on. Again, fractional values are represented with negative powers of the radix:

$$1001.101 = 2^3 + 2^0 + 2^{-1} + 2^{-3} = 9.625_{10}$$

In general, for the binary representation of $Y = \{\ldots b_2 b_1 b_0 . b_{-1} b_{-2} b_{-3} \ldots\}$, the value of Y is

$$Y = \sum_i (b_i \times 2^i) \tag{9.3}$$

9.4 CONVERTING BETWEEN BINARY AND DECIMAL

It is a simple matter to convert a number from binary notation to decimal notation. In fact, we showed several examples in the previous subsection. All that is required is to multiply each binary digit by the appropriate power of 2 and add the results.

To convert from decimal to binary, the integer and fractional parts are handled separately.

Integers

For the integer part, recall that in binary notation, an integer represented by

$$b_{m-1} b_{m-2} \ldots b_2 b_1 b_0 \qquad b_i = 0 \text{ or } 1$$

has the value

$$(b_{m-1} \times 2^{m-1}) + (b_{m-2} \times 2^{m-2}) + \ldots + (b_1 \times 2^1) + b_0$$

Suppose it is required to convert a decimal integer N into binary form. If we divide N by 2, in the decimal system, and obtain a quotient N_1 and a remainder R_0, we may write

$$N = 2 \times N_1 + R_0 \qquad R_0 = 0 \text{ or } 1$$

Next, we divide the quotient N_1 by 2. Assume that the new quotient is N_2 and the new remainder R_1. Then

$$N_1 = 2 \times N_2 + R_1 \qquad R_1 = 0 \text{ or } 1$$

so that

$$N = 2(2N_2 + R_1) + R_0 = (N_2 \times 2^2) + (R_1 \times 2^1) + R_0$$

If next

$$N_2 = 2N_3 + R_2$$

we have

$$N = (N_3 \times 2^3) + (R_2 \times 2^2) + (R_1 \times 2^1) + R_0$$

Because $N > N_1 > N_2 . . .$, continuing this sequence will eventually produce a quotient $N_{m-1} = 1$ (except for the decimal integers 0 and 1, whose binary equivalents are 0 and 1, respectively) and a remainder R_{m-2}, which is 0 or 1. Then

$$N = (1 \times 2^{m-1}) + (R_{m-2} \times 2^{m-2}) + \ldots + (R_2 \times 2^2) + (R_1 \times 2^1) + R_0$$

which is the binary form of N. Hence, we convert from base 10 to base 2 by repeated divisions by 2. The remainders and the final quotient, 1, give us, in order of increasing significance, the binary digits of N. Figure 9.1 shows two examples.

Fractions

For the fractional part, recall that in binary notation, a number with a value between 0 and 1 is represented by

$$0.b_{-1}b_{-2}b_{-3} \ldots \qquad b_i = 0 \text{ or } 1$$

and has the value

$$(b_{-1} \times 2^{-1}) + (b_{-2} \times 2^{-2}) + (b_{-3} \times 2^{-3}) \ldots$$

This can be rewritten as

$$2^{-1} \times (b_{-1} + 2^{-1} \times (b_{-2} + 2^{-1} \times (b_{-3} + \ldots) \ldots))$$

This expression suggests a technique for conversion. Suppose we want to convert the number F ($0 < F < 1$) from decimal to binary notation. We know that F can be expressed in the form

$$F = 2^{-1} \times (b_{-1} + 2^{-1} \times (b_{-2} + 2^{-1} \times (b_{-3} + \ldots) \ldots))$$

If we multiply F by 2, we obtain,

$$2 \times F = b_{-1} + 2^{-1} \times (b_{-2} + 2^{-1} \times (b_{-3} + \ldots) \ldots)$$

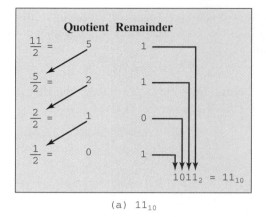

(a) 11_{10}

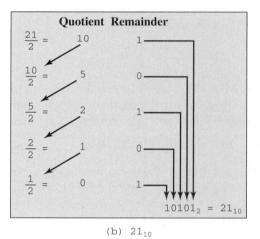

(b) 21_{10}

Figure 9.1 Examples of Converting from Decimal Notation to Binary Notation for Integers

From this equation, we see that the integer part of $(2 \times F)$, which must be either 0 or 1 because $0 < F < 1$, is simply b_{-1}. So we can say $(2 \times F) = b_{-1} + F_1$, where $0 < F_1 < 1$ and where

$$F_1 = 2^{-1} \times (b_{-2} + 2^{-1} \times (b_{-3} + 2^{-1} \times (b_{-4} + \ldots) \ldots))$$

To find b_{-2}, we repeat the process. Therefore, the conversion algorithm involves repeated multiplication by 2. At each step, the fractional part of the number from the previous step is multiplied by 2. The digit to the left of the decimal point in the product will be 0 or 1 and contributes to the binary representation, starting with the most significant digit. The fractional part of the product is used as the multiplicand in the next step. Figure 9.2 shows two examples.

This process is not necessarily exact; that is, a decimal fraction with a finite number of digits may require a binary fraction with an infinite number of digits. In such cases, the conversion algorithm is usually halted after a prespecified number of steps, depending on the desired accuracy.

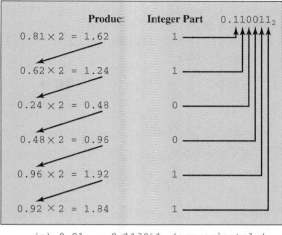

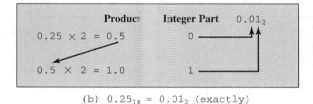

(a) $0.81_{10} = 0.110011_2$ (approximately)

(b) $0.25_{10} = 0.01_2$ (exactly)

Figure 9.2 Examples of Converting from Decimal
Notation to Binary Notation for Fractions

9.5 HEXADECIMAL NOTATION

Because of the inherent binary nature of digital computer components, all forms of
data within computers are represented by various binary codes. However, no matter
how convenient the binary system is for computers, it is exceedingly cumbersome
for human beings. Consequently, most computer professionals who must spend time
working with the actual raw data in the computer prefer a more compact notation.

What notation to use? One possibility is the decimal notation. This is certainly
more compact than binary notation, but it is awkward because of the tediousness of
converting between base 2 and base 10.

Instead, a notation known as hexadecimal has been adopted. Binary digits are
grouped into sets of four bits, called **a nibble.** Each possible combination of four
binary digits is given a symbol, as follows:

0000 = 0	0100 = 4	1000 = 8	1100 = C
0001 = 1	0101 = 5	1001 = 9	1101 = D
0010 = 2	0110 = 6	1010 = A	1110 = E
0011 = 3	0111 = 7	1011 = B	1111 = F

Because 16 symbols are used, the notation is called **hexadecimal,** and the 16 symbols are the **hexadecimal digits**.

A sequence of hexadecimal digits can be thought of as representing an integer in base 16 (Table 9.3). Thus,

$$2C_{16} = (2_{16} \times 16^1) + (C_{16} \times 16^0)$$
$$= (2_{10} \times 16^1) + (12_{10} \times 16^0) = 44$$

Thus, viewing hexadecimal numbers as numbers in the positional number system with base 16, we have

$$Z = \sum_i (h_i \times 16^i) \tag{9.4}$$

where 16 is the base and each hexadecimal digit h_i is in the decimal range $0 \le h_i < 15$, equivalent to the hexadecimal range $0 \le h_i \le F$.

Table 9.3 Decimal, Binary, and Hexadecimal

Decimal (base 10)	Binary (base 2)	Hexadecimal (base 16)
0	0000	0
1	0001	1
2	0010	2
3	0011	3
4	0100	4
5	0101	5
6	0110	6
7	0111	7
8	1000	8
9	1001	9
10	1010	A
11	1011	B
12	1100	C
13	1101	D
14	1110	E
15	1111	F
16	0001 0000	10
17	0001 0001	11
18	0001 0010	12
31	0001 1111	1F
100	0110 0100	64
255	1111 1111	FF
256	0001 0000 0000	100

Hexadecimal notation is not only used for representing integers but also used as a concise notation for representing any sequence of binary digits, whether they represent text, numbers, or some other type of data. The reasons for using hexadecimal notation are as follows:

1. It is more compact than binary notation.
2. In most computers, binary data occupy some multiple of 4 bits, and hence some multiple of a single hexadecimal digit.
3. It is extremely easy to convert between binary and hexadecimal notation.

As an example of the last point, consider the binary string 110111100001. This is equivalent to

$$1101 \quad 1110 \quad 0001 = DE1_{16}$$
$$D \qquad E \qquad 1$$

This process is performed so naturally that an experienced programmer can mentally convert visual representations of binary data to their hexadecimal equivalent without written effort.

9.6   RECOMMENDED READING

[KNUT98] provides an excellent discussion of positional number systems. [GREG98] also has a useful treatment of the subject.

GREG98   Gregg, J. *Ones and Zeros: Understanding Boolean Algebra, Digital Circuits, and the Logic of Sets.* Piscataway, NJ: IEEE Press, 1998.

KNUT98   Knuth, D. *The Art of Computer Programming, Volume 2: Seminumerical Algorithms.* Reading, MA: Addison-Wesley, 1998.

9.7   KEY TERMS AND PROBLEMS

Key Terms

base	hexadecimal	nibble
binary	integer	positional number system
decimal	least significant digit	radix
fraction	most significant digit	radix point

Problems

9.1   Count from 1 to 20_{10} in the following bases:
   a. 8   **b.** 6   **c.** 5   **d.** 3
9.2   Order the numbers $(1.1)_2$, $(1.4)_{10}$, and $(1.5)_{16}$ from smallest to largest.

9.3   Perform the indicated base conversions:
   a. 54_8 to base 5
   b. 312_4 to base 7
   c. 520_6 to base 7
   d. 12212_3 to base 9

9.4   What generalizations can you draw about converting a number from one base to a power of that base, e.g., from base 3 to base 9 (3^2) or from base 2 to base 4 (2^2) or base 8 (2^3)?

9.5   Convert the following binary numbers to their decimal equivalents:
   a. 001100   **b.** 000011   **c.** 011100   **d.** 111100   **e.** 101010

9.6   Convert the following binary numbers to their decimal equivalents:
   a. 11100.011   **b.** 110011.10011   **c.** 1010101010.1

9.7   Convert the following decimal numbers to their binary equivalents:
   a. 64   **b.** 100   **c.** 111   **d.** 145   **e.** 255

9.8   Convert the following decimal numbers to their binary equivalents:
   a. 34.75   **b.** 25.25   **c.** 27.1875

9.9   Prove that every real number with a terminating binary representation (finite number of digits to the right of the binary point) also has a terminating decimal representation (finite number of digits to the right of the decimal point).

9.10   Express the following octal numbers (number with radix 8) in hexadecimal notation:
   a. 12   **b.** 5655   **c.** 2550276   **d.** 76545336   **e.** 3726755

9.11   Convert the following hexadecimal numbers to their decimal equivalents:
   a. C   **b.** 9F   **c.** D52   **d.** 67E   **e.** ABCD

9.12   Convert the following hexadecimal numbers to their decimal equivalents:
   a. F.4   **b.** D3.E   **c.** 1111.1   **d.** 888.8   **e.** EBA.C

9.13   Convert the following decimal numbers to their hexadecimal equivalents:
   a. 16   **b.** 80   **c.** 2560   **d.** 3000   **e.** 62,500

9.14   Convert the following decimal numbers to their hexadecimal equivalents:
   a. 204.125   **b.** 255.875   **c.** 631.25   **d.** 10000.00390625

9.15   Convert the following hexadecimal numbers to their binary equivalents:
   a. E   **b.** 1C   **c.** A64   **d.** 1F.C   **e.** 239.4

9.16   Convert the following binary numbers to their hexadecimal equivalents:
   a. 1001.1111   **b.** 110101.011001   **c.** 10100111.111011

COMPUTER ARITHMETIC

LEARNING OBJECTIVES

After studying this chapter, you should be able to:

◆ Understand the distinction between the way in which numbers are represented (the binary format) and the algorithms used for the basic arithmetic operations.

◆ Explain twos complement representation.

◆ Present an overview of the techniques for doing basic arithmetic operation in two complement notation.

◆ Understand the use of significand, base, and exponent in the representation of floating-point numbers.

◆ Present an overview of the IEEE 754 standard for floating-point representation.

◆ Understand some of the key concepts related to floating-point arithmetic, including guard bits, rounding, subnormal numbers, underflow and overflow.

We begin our examination of the processor with an overview of the arithmetic and logic unit (ALU). The chapter then focuses on the most complex aspect of the ALU, computer arithmetic. The logic functions that are part of the ALU are described in Chapter 12, and implementations of simple logic and arithmetic functions in digital logic are described in Chapter 11.

Computer arithmetic is commonly performed on two very different types of numbers: integer and floating point. In both cases, the representation chosen is a crucial design issue and is treated first, followed by a discussion of arithmetic operations.

This chapter includes a number of examples, each of which is highlighted in a shaded box.

10.1 THE ARITHMETIC AND LOGIC UNIT

The ALU is that part of the computer that actually performs arithmetic and logical operations on data. All of the other elements of the computer system—control unit, registers, memory, I/O—are there mainly to bring data into the ALU for it to process and then to take the results back out. We have, in a sense, reached the core or essence of a computer when we consider the ALU.

An ALU and, indeed, all electronic components in the computer are based on the use of simple digital logic devices that can store binary digits and perform simple Boolean logic operations.

Figure 10.1 indicates, in general terms, how the ALU is interconnected with the rest of the processor. Operands for arithmetic and logic operations are presented to the ALU in registers, and the results of an operation are stored in registers. These registers are temporary storage locations within the processor that are connected by signal paths to the ALU (e.g., see Figure 2.3). The ALU may also set flags as the result of an operation. For example, an overflow flag is set to 1 if the result of a computation exceeds the length of the register into which it is to be stored.

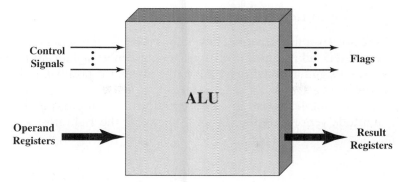

Figure 10.1   ALU Inputs and Outputs

The flag values are also stored in registers within the processor. The processor provides signals that control the operation of the ALU and the movement of the data into and out of the ALU.

10.2 INTEGER REPRESENTATION

In the binary number system,[1] arbitrary numbers can be represented with just the digits zero and one, the minus sign (for negative numbers), and the period, or **radix point** (for numbers with a fractional component).

$$-1101.0101_2 = -13.3125_{10}$$

For purposes of computer storage and processing, however, we do not have the benefit of special symbols for the minus sign and radix point. Only binary digits (0 and 1) may be used to represent numbers. If we are limited to nonnegative integers, the representation is straightforward.

An 8-bit word can represent the numbers from 0 to 255, such as

$$00000000 = 0$$
$$00000001 = 1$$
$$00101001 = 41$$
$$10000000 = 128$$
$$11111111 = 255$$

In general, if an n-bit sequence of binary digits $a_{n-1}a_{n-2} \ldots a_1a_0$ is interpreted as an unsigned integer A, its value is

$$A = \sum_{i=0}^{n-1} 2^i a_i$$

[1]See Chapter 9 for a basic refresher on number systems (decimal, binary, hexadecimal).

Sign–Magnitude Representation

There are several alternative conventions used to represent negative as well as positive integers, all of which involve treating the most significant (leftmost) bit in the word as a sign bit. If the sign bit is 0, the number is positive; if the sign bit is 1, the number is negative.

The simplest form of representation that employs a sign bit is the sign-magnitude representation. In an n-bit word, the rightmost $n - 1$ bits hold the magnitude of the integer.

$$
\begin{aligned}
+18 &= 00010010 \\
-18 &= 10010010 \quad \text{(sign magnitude)}
\end{aligned}
$$

The general case can be expressed as follows:

Sign Magnitude $\qquad A = \begin{cases} \displaystyle\sum_{i=0}^{n-2} 2^i a_i & \text{if } a_{n-1} = 0 \\ \displaystyle -\sum_{i=0}^{n-2} 2^i a_i & \text{if } a_{n-1} = 1 \end{cases}$ (10.1)

There are several drawbacks to sign-magnitude representation. One is that addition and subtraction require a consideration of both the signs of the numbers and their relative magnitudes to carry out the required operation. This should become clear in the discussion in Section 10.3. Another drawback is that there are two representations of 0:

$$
\begin{aligned}
+0_{10} &= 00000000 \\
-0_{10} &= 10000000 \quad \text{(sign magnitude)}
\end{aligned}
$$

This is inconvenient because it is slightly more difficult to test for 0 (an operation performed frequently on computers) than if there were a single representation.

Because of these drawbacks, sign-magnitude representation is rarely used in implementing the integer portion of the ALU. Instead, the most common scheme is twos complement representation.[2]

Twos Complement Representation

Like sign magnitude, twos complement representation uses the most significant bit as a sign bit, making it easy to test whether an integer is positive or negative. It differs from the use of the sign-magnitude representation in the way that the other bits are interpreted. Table 10.1 highlights key characteristics of twos complement representation and arithmetic, which are elaborated in this section and the next.

Most treatments of twos complement representation focus on the rules for producing negative numbers, with no formal proof that the scheme is valid. Instead,

---

[2]In the literature, the terms *two's complement* or *2's complement* are often used. Here we follow the practice used in standards documents and omit the apostrophe (e.g., IEEE Std 100-1992, *The New IEEE Standard Dictionary of Electrical and Electronics Terms*).

Table 10.1 Characteristics of Twos Complement Representation and Arithmetic

Range	-2^{n-1} through $2^{n-1} - 1$
Number of Representations of Zero	One
Negation	Take the Boolean complement of each bit of the corresponding positive number, then add 1 to the resulting bit pattern viewed as an unsigned integer.
Expansion of Bit Length	Add additional bit positions to the left and fill in with the value of the original sign bit.
Overflow Rule	If two numbers with the same sign (both positive or both negative) are added, then overflow occurs if and only if the result has the opposite sign.
Subtraction Rule	To subtract B from A, take the twos complement of B and add it to A.

our presentation of twos complement integers in this section and in Section 10.3 is based on [DATT93], which suggests that twos complement representation is best understood by defining it in terms of a weighted sum of bits, as we did previously for unsigned and sign-magnitude representations. The advantage of this treatment is that it does not leave any lingering doubt that the rules for arithmetic operations in twos complement notation may not work for some special cases.

Consider an n-bit integer A, in twos complement representation. If A is positive, then the sign bit, a_{n-1}, is zero. The remaining bits represent the magnitude of the number in the same fashion as for sign magnitude:

$$A = \sum_{i=0}^{n-2} 2^i a_i \qquad \text{for } A \geq 0$$

The number zero is identified as positive and therefore has a 0 sign bit and a magnitude of all 0s. We can see that the range of positive integers that may be represented is from 0 (all of the magnitude bits are 0) through $2^{n-1} - 1$ (all of the magnitude bits are 1). Any larger number would require more bits.

Now, for a negative number A ($A < 0$), the sign bit, a_{n-1}, is one. The remaining $n - 1$ bits can take on any one of 2^{n-1} values. Therefore, the range of negative integers that can be represented is from -1 to -2^{n-1}. We would like to assign the bit values to negative integers in such a way that arithmetic can be handled in a straightforward fashion, similar to unsigned integer arithmetic. In unsigned integer representation, to compute the value of an integer from the bit representation, the weight of the most significant bit is $+2^{n-1}$. For a representation with a sign bit, it turns out that the desired arithmetic properties are achieved, as we will see in Section 10.3, if the weight of the most significant bit is -2^{n-1}. This is the convention used in twos complement representation, yielding the following expression for negative numbers:

Twos Complement $\qquad A = -2^{n-1}a_{n-1} + \sum_{i=0}^{n-2} 2^i a_i$ **(10.2)**

Equation (10.2) defines the twos complement representation for both positive and negative numbers. For $a_{n-1} = 0$, the term $-2^{n-1}a_{n-1} = 0$ and the equation defines

Table 10.2 Alternative Representations for 4-Bit Integers

Decimal Representation	Sign-Magnitude Representation	Twos Complement Representation	Biased Representation
+8	—	—	1111
+7	0111	0111	1110
+6	0110	0110	1101
+5	0101	0101	1100
+4	0100	0100	1011
+3	0011	0011	1010
+2	0010	0010	1001
+1	0001	0001	1000
+0	0000	0000	0111
−0	1000	—	—
−1	1001	1111	0110
−2	1010	1110	0101
−3	1011	1101	0100
−4	1100	1100	0011
−5	1101	1011	0010
−6	1110	1010	0001
−7	1111	1001	0000
−8	—	1000	—

a nonnegative integer. When $a_{n-1} = 1$, the term 2^{n-1} is subtracted from the summation term, yielding a negative integer.

Table 10.2 compares the sign-magnitude and twos complement representations for 4-bit integers. Although twos complement is an awkward representation from the human point of view, we will see that it facilitates the most important arithmetic operations, addition and subtraction. For this reason, it is almost universally used as the processor representation for integers.

A useful illustration of the nature of twos complement representation is a value box, in which the value on the far right in the box is 1 (2^0) and each succeeding position to the left is double in value, until the leftmost position, which is negated. As you can see in Figure 10.2a, the most negative twos complement number that can be represented is -2^{n-1}; if any of the bits other than the sign bit is one, it adds a positive amount to the number. Also, it is clear that a negative number must have a 1 at its leftmost position and a positive number must have a 0 in that position. Thus, the largest positive number is a 0 followed by all 1s, which equals $2^{n-1} - 1$.

The rest of Figure 10.2 illustrates the use of the value box to convert from twos complement to decimal and from decimal to twos complement.

Range Extension

It is sometimes desirable to take an n-bit integer and store it in m bits, where $m > n$. This expansion of bit length is referred to as **range extension**, because the range of numbers that can be expressed is extended by increasing the bit length.

−128	64	32	16	8	4	2	1

(a) An eight-position twos complement value box

−128	64	32	16	8	4	2	1
1	0	0	0	0	0	1	1

−128   +2   +1   = −125

(b) Convert binary 10000011 to decimal

−128	64	32	16	8	4	2	1
1	0	0	0	1	0	0	0

−120 = −128   +8

(c) Convert decimal −120 to binary

Figure 10.2   Use of a Value Box for Conversion between Twos Complement Binary and Decimal

In sign-magnitude notation, this is easily accomplished: simply move the sign bit to the new leftmost position and fill in with zeros.

+18	=	00010010	(sign magnitude, 8 bits)
+18	=	0000000000010010	(sign magnitude, 16 bits)
−18	=	10010010	(sign magnitude, 8 bits)
−18	=	1000000000010010	(sign magnitude, 16 bits)

This procedure will not work for twos complement negative integers. Using the same example,

+18	=	00010010	(twos complement, 8 bits)
+18	=	0000000000010010	(twos complement, 16 bits)
−18	=	11101110	(twos complement, 8 bits)
−32,658	=	1000000001101110	(twos complement, 16 bits)

The next to last line is easily seen using the value box of Figure 10.2. The last line can be verified using Equation (10.2) or a 16-bit value box.

Instead, the rule for twos complement integers is to move the sign bit to the new leftmost position and fill in with copies of the sign bit. For positive numbers, fill in with zeros, and for negative numbers, fill in with ones. This is called sign extension.

−18	=	11101110	(twos complement, 8 bits)
−18	=	1111111111101110	(twos complement, 16 bits)

To see why this rule works, let us again consider an n-bit sequence of binary digits $a_{n-1}a_{n-2}\ldots a_1a_0$ interpreted as a twos complement integer A, so that its value is

$$A = -2^{n-1}a_{n-1} + \sum_{i=0}^{n-2} 2^i a_i$$

If A is a positive number, the rule clearly works. Now, if A is negative and we want to construct an m-bit representation, with $m > n$. Then

$$A = -2^{m-1}a_{m-1} + \sum_{i=0}^{m-2} 2^i a_i$$

The two values must be equal:

$$-2^{m-1} + \sum_{i=0}^{m-2} 2^i a_i = -2^{n-1} + \sum_{i=0}^{n-2} 2^i a_i$$

$$-2^{m-1} + \sum_{i=n-1}^{m-2} 2^i a_i = -2^{n-1}$$

$$-2^{n-1} + \sum_{i=n-1}^{m-2} 2^i a_i = 2^{m-1}$$

$$1 + \sum_{i=0}^{n-2} 2^i + \sum_{i=n-1}^{m-2} 2^i a_i = 1 + \sum_{i=0}^{m-2} 2^i$$

$$\sum_{i=n-1}^{m-2} 2^i a_i = \sum_{i=n-1}^{m-2} 2^i$$

$$\Rightarrow \quad a_{m-2} = \cdots = a_{n-2} = a_{n-1} = 1$$

In going from the first to the second equation, we require that the least significant $n-1$ bits do not change between the two representations. Then we get to the next to last equation, which is only true if all of the bits in positions $n-1$ through $m-2$ are 1. Therefore, the sign-extension rule works. The reader may find the rule easier to grasp after studying the discussion on twos complement negation at the beginning of Section 10.3.

Fixed–Point Representation

Finally, we mention that the representations discussed in this section are sometimes referred to as fixed point. This is because the radix point (binary point) is fixed and assumed to be to the right of the rightmost digit. The programmer can use the same representation for binary fractions by scaling the numbers so that the binary point is implicitly positioned at some other location.

10.3 INTEGER ARITHMETIC

This section examines common arithmetic functions on numbers in twos complement representation.

Negation

In sign-magnitude representation, the rule for forming the negation of an integer is simple: invert the sign bit. In twos complement notation, the negation of an integer can be formed with the following rules:

1. Take the Boolean complement of each bit of the integer (including the sign bit). That is, set each 1 to 0 and each 0 to 1.
2. Treating the result as an unsigned binary integer, add 1.

This two-step process is referred to as the **twos complement operation**, or the taking of the twos complement of an integer.

$$
\begin{array}{rcl}
+18 & = & 00010010 \quad \text{(twos complement)} \\
\text{bitwise complement} & = & 11101101 \\
& + & 1 \\
\hline
& & 11101110 = -18
\end{array}
$$

As expected, the negative of the negative of that number is itself:

$$
\begin{array}{rcl}
-18 & = & 11101110 \quad \text{(twos complement)} \\
\text{bitwise complement} & = & 00010001 \\
& + & 1 \\
\hline
& & 00010010 = +18
\end{array}
$$

We can demonstrate the validity of the operation just described using the definition of the twos complement representation in Equation (10.2). Again, interpret an n-bit sequence of binary digits $a_{n-1}a_{n-2}\ldots a_1a_0$ as a twos complement integer A, so that its value is

$$A = -2^{n-1}a_{n-1} + \sum_{i=0}^{n-2}2^i a_i$$

Now form the bitwise complement, $\overline{a_{n-1}a_{n-2}}\ldots\overline{a_0}$, and, treating this as an unsigned integer, add 1. Finally, interpret the resulting n-bit sequence of binary digits as a twos complement integer B, so that its value is

$$B = -2^{n-1}\overline{a_{n-1}} + 1 + \sum_{i=0}^{n-2}2^i\overline{a_i}$$

Now, we want $A = -B$, which means $A + B = 0$. This is easily shown to be true:

$$A + B = -(a_{n-1} + \overline{a_{n-1}})2^{n-1} + 1 + \left(\sum_{i=0}^{n-2}2^i(a_i + \overline{a_i})\right)$$

$$= -2^{n-1} + 1 + \left(\sum_{i=0}^{n-2}2^i\right)$$

$$= -2^{n-1} + 1 + (2^{n-1} - 1)$$

$$= -2^{n-1} + 2^{n-1} = 0$$

The preceding derivation assumes that we can first treat the bitwise complement of A as an unsigned integer for the purpose of adding 1, and then treat the result as a twos complement integer. There are two special cases to consider. First, consider $A = 0$. In that case, for an 8-bit representation:

$$
\begin{array}{rll}
0 & = & 00000000 \quad \text{(twos complement)} \\
\text{bitwise complement} & = & 11111111 \\
+ & & 1 \\
\hline
& & 100000000 = 0
\end{array}
$$

There is a *carry* out of the most significant bit position, which is ignored. The result is that the negation of 0 is 0, as it should be.

The second special case is more of a problem. If we take the negation of the bit pattern of 1 followed by $n - 1$ zeros, we get back the same number. For example, for 8-bit words,

$$
\begin{array}{rll}
-128 & = & 10000000 \quad \text{(twos complement)} \\
\text{bitwise complement} & = & 01111111 \\
+ & & 1 \\
\hline
& & 10000000 = -128
\end{array}
$$

Some such anomaly is unavoidable. The number of different bit patterns in an n-bit word is $2n$, which is an even number. We wish to represent positive and negative integers and 0. If an equal number of positive and negative integers are represented (sign magnitude), then there are two representations for 0. If there is only one representation of 0 (twos complement), then there must be an unequal number of negative and positive numbers represented. In the case of twos complement, for an n-bit length, there is a representation for -2^{n-1} but not for $+2^{n-1}$.

Addition and Subtraction

Addition in twos complement is illustrated in Figure 10.3. Addition proceeds as if the two numbers were unsigned integers. The first four examples illustrate successful operations. If the result of the operation is positive, we get a positive number in twos complement form, which is the same as in unsigned-integer form. If the result of the operation is negative, we get a negative number in twos complement form. Note that, in some instances, there is a carry bit beyond the end of the word (indicated by shading), which is ignored.

On any addition, the result may be larger than can be held in the word size being used. This condition is called **overflow**. When overflow occurs, the ALU must signal this fact so that no attempt is made to use the result. To detect overflow, the following rule is observed:

OVERFLOW RULE: If two numbers are added, and they are both positive or both negative, then overflow occurs if and only if the result has the opposite sign.

```
   1001  =  -7              1100  =  -4
  +0101  =   5             +0100  =   4
   1110  =  -2             10000  =   0

  (a) (-7) + (+5)          (b) (-4) + (+4)


   0011  =   3              1100  =  -4
  +0100  =   4             +1111  =  -1
   0111  =   7             11011  =  -5

  (c) (+3) + (+4)          (d) (-4) + (-1)


   0101  =   5              1001  =  -7
  +0100  =   4             +1010  =  -6
   1001  = Overflow        10011  = Overflow

  (e) (+5) + (+4)          (f) (-7) + (-6)
```

Figure 10.3   Addition of Numbers in Twos Complement Representation

Figures 10.3e and f show examples of overflow. Note that overflow can occur whether or not there is a carry.

Subtraction is easily handled with the following rule:

SUBTRACTION RULE: To subtract one number (subtrahend) from another (minuend), take the twos complement (negation) of the subtrahend and add it to the minuend.

Thus, subtraction is achieved using addition, as illustrated in Figure 10.4. The last two examples demonstrate that the overflow rule still applies.

```
      0010  =   2                  0101  =   5
     +1001  =  -7                 +1110  =  -2
      1011  =  -5                 10011  =   3

  (a) M = 2 = 0010            (b) M = 5 = 0101
      S = 7 = 0111                S = 2 = 0010
     -S =     1001               -S =     1110


      1011  =  -5                  0101  =   5
     +1110  =  -2                 +0010  =   2
     11001  =  -7                  0111  =   7

  (c) M = -5 = 1011            (d) M =  5 = 0101
      S =  2 = 0010                S = -2 = 1110
     -S =      1110               -S =     0010


      0111  =   7                  1010  =  -6
     +0111  =   7                 +1100  =  -4
      1110  = Overflow           10110  = Overflow

  (e) M =  7 = 0111            (f) M = -6 = 1010
      S = -7 = 1001                S =  4 = 0100
     -S =      0111               -S =     1100
```

Figure 10.4   Subtraction of Numbers in Twos Complement Representation (M − S)

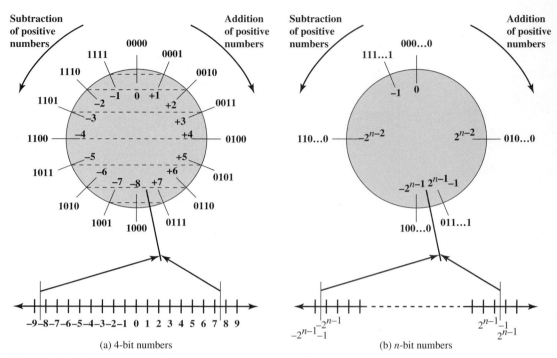

Figure 10.5 Geometric Depiction of Twos Complement Integers

Some insight into twos complement addition and subtraction can be gained by looking at a geometric depiction [BENH92], as shown in Figure 10.5. The circle in the upper half of each part of the figure is formed by selecting the appropriate segment of the number line and joining the endpoints. Note that when the numbers are laid out on a circle, the twos complement of any number is horizontally opposite that number (indicated by dashed horizontal lines). Starting at any number on the circle, we can add positive k (or subtract negative k) to that number by moving k positions clockwise, and we can subtract positive k (or add negative k) from that number by moving k positions counterclockwise. If an arithmetic operation results in traversal of the point where the endpoints are joined, an incorrect answer is given (overflow).

All of the examples of Figures 10.3 and 10.4 are easily traced in the circle of Figure 10.5.

Figure 10.6 suggests the data paths and hardware elements needed to accomplish addition and subtraction. The central element is a binary adder, which is presented two numbers for addition and produces a sum and an overflow indication. The binary adder treats the two numbers as unsigned integers. (A logic implementation of an adder is given in Chapter 11.) For addition, the two numbers are presented to the adder from two registers, designated in this case as A and B registers. The result may be stored in one of these registers or in a third. The overflow indication is stored in a 1-bit overflow flag (0 = no overflow; 1 = overflow). For subtraction, the subtrahend (B register) is passed through a twos complementer so that its twos complement is presented to the adder. Note that Figure 10.6 only

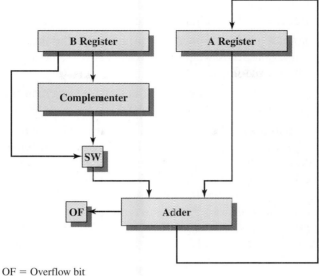

OF = Overflow bit
SW = Switch (select addition or subtraction)

Figure 10.6   Block Diagram of Hardware for Addition and Subtraction

shows the data paths. Control signals are needed to control whether or not the complementer is used, depending on whether the operation is addition or subtraction.

Multiplication

Compared with addition and subtraction, multiplication is a complex operation, whether performed in hardware or software. A wide variety of algorithms have been used in various computers. The purpose of this subsection is to give the reader some feel for the type of approach typically taken. We begin with the simpler problem of multiplying two unsigned (nonnegative) integers, and then we look at one of the most common techniques for multiplication of numbers in twos complement representation.

UNSIGNED INTEGERS Figure 10.7 illustrates the multiplication of unsigned binary integers, as might be carried out using paper and pencil. Several important observations can be made:

1. Multiplication involves the generation of partial products, one for each digit in the multiplier. These partial products are then summed to produce the final product.

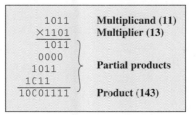

Figure 10.7   Multiplication of Unsigned Binary Integers

2. The partial products are easily defined. When the multiplier bit is 0, the partial product is 0. When the multiplier is 1, the partial product is the multiplicand.

3. The total product is produced by summing the partial products. For this operation, each successive partial product is shifted one position to the left relative to the preceding partial product.

4. The multiplication of two n-bit binary integers results in a product of up to $2n$ bits in length (e.g., $11 \times 11 = 1001$).

Compared with the pencil-and-paper approach, there are several things we can do to make computerized multiplication more efficient. First, we can perform a running addition on the partial products rather than waiting until the end. This eliminates the need for storage of all the partial products; fewer registers are needed. Second, we can save some time on the generation of partial products. For each 1 on the multiplier, an add and a shift operation are required; but for each 0, only a shift is required.

Figure 10.8a shows a possible implementation employing these measures. The multiplier and multiplicand are loaded into two registers (Q and M). A third register,

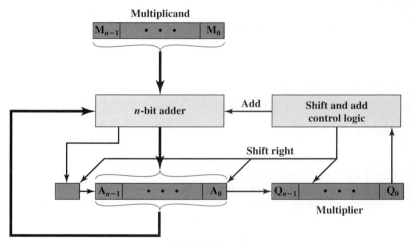

(a) Block diagram

C	A	Q	M		
0	0000	1101	1011	Initial values	
0	1011	1101	1011	Add	First
0	0101	1110	1011	Shift	cycle
0	0010	1111	1011	Shift	Second cycle
0	1101	1111	1011	Add	Third
0	0110	1111	1011	Shift	cycle
1	0001	1111	1011	Add	Fourth
0	1000	1111	1011	Shift	cycle

(b) Example from Figure 10.7 (product in A, Q)

Figure 10.8 Hardware Implementation of Unsigned Binary Multiplication

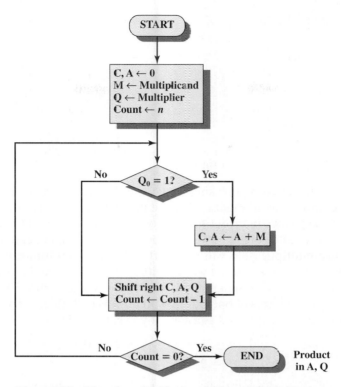

Figure 10.9 Flowchart for Unsigned Binary Multiplication

the A register, is also needed and is initially set to 0. There is also a 1-bit C register, initialized to 0, which holds a potential carry bit resulting from addition.

The operation of the multiplier is as follows. Control logic reads the bits of the multiplier one at a time. If Q_0 is 1, then the multiplicand is added to the A register and the result is stored in the A register, with the C bit used for overflow. Then all of the bits of the C, A, and Q registers are shifted to the right one bit, so that the C bit goes into A_{n-1}, A_0 goes into Q_{n-1} and Q_0 is lost. If Q_0 is 0, then no addition is performed, just the shift. This process is repeated for each bit of the original multiplier. The resulting $2n$-bit product is contained in the A and Q registers. A flowchart of the operation is shown in Figure 10.9, and an example is given in Figure 10.8b. Note that on the second cycle, when the multiplier bit is 0, there is no add operation.

TWOS COMPLEMENT MULTIPLICATION We have seen that addition and subtraction can be performed on numbers in twos complement notation by treating them as unsigned integers. Consider

$$
\begin{array}{r}
1001 \\
+0011 \\
\hline
1100
\end{array}
$$

If these numbers are considered to be unsigned integers, then we are adding 9 (1001) plus 3 (0011) to get 12 (1100). As twos complement integers, we are adding −7 (1001) to 3 (0011) to get −4 (1100).

```
        1011
      × 1101
    00001011   1011 × 1 × 2⁰
    00000000   1011 × 0 × 2¹
    00101100   1011 × 1 × 2²
    01011000   1011 × 1 × 2³
    10001111
```

Figure 10.10 Multiplication of Two Unsigned 4-Bit Integers Yielding an 8-Bit Result

Unfortunately, this simple scheme will not work for multiplication. To see this, consider again Figure 10.7. We multiplied 11 (1011) by 13 (1101) to get 143 (10001111). If we interpret these as twos complement numbers, we have −5 (1011) times −3 (1101) equals −113 (10001111). This example demonstrates that straightforward multiplication will not work if both the multiplicand and multiplier are negative. In fact, it will not work if either the multiplicand or the multiplier is negative. To justify this statement, we need to go back to Figure 10.7 and explain what is being done in terms of operations with powers of 2. Recall that any unsigned binary number can be expressed as a sum of powers of 2. Thus,

$$1101 = 1 \times 2^3 + 1 \times 2^2 + 0 \times 2^1 + 1 \times 2^0$$
$$= 2^3 + 2^2 + 2^0$$

Further, the multiplication of a binary number by 2^n is accomplished by shifting that number to the left n bits. With this in mind, Figure 10.10 recasts Figure 10.7 to make the generation of partial products by multiplication explicit. The only difference in Figure 10.10 is that it recognizes that the partial products should be viewed as $2n$-bit numbers generated from the n-bit multiplicand.

Thus, as an unsigned integer, the 4-bit multiplicand 1011 is stored in an 8-bit word as 00001011. Each partial product (other than that for 2^0) consists of this number shifted to the left, with the unoccupied positions on the right filled with zeros (e.g., a shift to the left of two places yields 00101100).

Now we can demonstrate that straightforward multiplication will not work if the multiplicand is negative. The problem is that each contribution of the negative multiplicand as a partial product must be a negative number on a $2n$-bit field; the sign bits of the partial products must line up. This is demonstrated in Figure 10.11, which shows that multiplication of 1001 by 0011. If these are treated as unsigned integers, the multiplication of $9 \times 3 = 27$ proceeds simply. However, if 1001 is interpreted

```
      1001  (9)                    1001  (−7)
    × 0011  (3)                  × 0011  (3)
    00001001  1001 × 2⁰          11111001  (−7) × 2⁰ = (−7)
    00010010  1001 × 2¹          11110010  (−7) × 2¹ = (−14)
    00011011  (27)               11101011  (−21)

    (a) Unsigned integers        (b) Twos complement integers
```

Figure 10.11 Comparison of Multiplication of Unsigned and Twos Complement Integers

as the twos complement value -7, then each partial product must be a negative twos complement number of $2n$ (8) bits, as shown in Figure 10.11b. Note that this is accomplished by padding out each partial product to the left with binary 1s.

If the multiplier is negative, straightforward multiplication also will not work. The reason is that the bits of the multiplier no longer correspond to the shifts or multiplications that must take place. For example, the 4-bit decimal number -3 is written 1101 in twos complement. If we simply took partial products based on each bit position, we would have the following correspondence:

$$1101 \longleftrightarrow \quad -(1 \times 2^3 + 1 \times 2^2 + 0 \times 2^1 + 1 \times 2^0) = -(2^3 + 2^2 + 2^0)$$

In fact, what is desired is $-(2^1 + 2^0)$. So this multiplier cannot be used directly in the manner we have been describing.

There are a number of ways out of this dilemma. One would be to convert both multiplier and multiplicand to positive numbers, perform the multiplication, and then take the twos complement of the result if and only if the sign of the two original numbers differed. Implementers have preferred to use techniques that do not require this final transformation step. One of the most common of these is Booth's algorithm. This algorithm also has the benefit of speeding up the multiplication process, relative to a more straightforward approach.

Booth's algorithm is depicted in Figure 10.12 and can be described as follows. As before, the multiplier and multiplicand are placed in the Q and M registers,

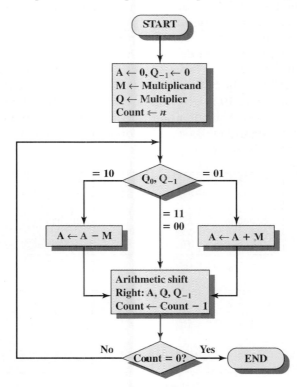

Figure 10.12   Booth's Algorithm for Twos Complement Multiplication

A	Q	Q_{-1}	M		
0000	0011	0	0111	Initial values	
1001	0011	0	0111	A ← A − M	First
1100	1001	1	0111	Shift	cycle
1110	0100	1	0111	Shift	Second cycle
0101	0100	1	0111	A ← A + M	Third
0010	1010	0	0111	Shift	cycle
0001	0101	0	0111	Shift	Fourth cycle

Figure 10.13 Example of Booth's Algorithm (7×3)

respectively. There is also a 1-bit register placed logically to the right of the least significant bit (Q_0) of the Q register and designated Q_{-1}; its use is explained shortly. The results of the multiplication will appear in the A and Q registers. A and Q_{-1} are initialized to 0. As before, control logic scans the bits of the multiplier one at a time. Now, as each bit is examined, the bit to its right is also examined. If the two bits are the same (1–1 or 0–0), then all of the bits of the A, Q, and Q_{-1} registers are shifted to the right 1 bit. If the two bits differ, then the multiplicand is added to or subtracted from the A register, depending on whether the two bits are 0–1 or 1–0. Following the addition or subtraction, the right shift occurs. In either case, the right shift is such that the leftmost bit of A, namely A_{n-1}, not only is shifted into A_{n-2}, but also remains in A_{n-1}. This is required to preserve the sign of the number in A and Q. It is known as an **arithmetic shift,** because it preserves the sign bit.

Figure 10.13 shows the sequence of events in Booth's algorithm for the multiplication of 7 by 3. More compactly, the same operation is depicted in Figure 10.14a. The rest of Figure 10.14 gives other examples of the algorithm. As can be seen, it works with any combination of positive and negative numbers. Note also the efficiency of the algorithm. Blocks of 1s or 0s are skipped over, with an average of only one addition or subtraction per block.

0111			0111		
× 0011	(0)		× 1101	(0)	
11111001	1–0		11111001	1–0	
0000000	1–1		0000111	0–1	
000111	0–1		111001	1–0	
00010101	(21)		11101011	(−21)	

       (a) $(7) \times (3) = (21)$ (b) $(7) \times (-3) = (-21)$

1001			1001		
× 0011	(0)		× 1101	(0)	
00000111	1–0		00000111	1–0	
0000000	1–1		1111001	0–1	
111001	0–1		000111	1–0	
11101011	(−21)		00010101	(21)	

       (c) $(-7) \times (3) = (-21)$ (d) $(-7) \times (-3) = (21)$

Figure 10.14 Examples Using Booth's Algorithm

Why does Booth's algorithm work? Consider first the case of a positive multiplier. In particular, consider a positive multiplier consisting of one block of 1s surrounded by 0s (e.g., 00011110). As we know, multiplication can be achieved by adding appropriately shifted copies of the multiplicand:

$$M \times (00011110) = M \times (2^4 + 2^3 + 2^2 - 2^1)$$
$$= M \times (16 + 8 + 4 + 2)$$
$$= M \times 30$$

The number of such operations can be reduced to two if we observe that

$$2^n + 2^{n-1} + \cdots + 2^{n-K} = 2^{n+1} - 2^{n-K} \qquad \textbf{(10.3)}$$

$$M \times (00011110) = M \times (2^5 - 2^1)$$
$$= M \times (32 - 2)$$
$$= M \times 30$$

So the product can be generated by one addition and one subtraction of the multiplicand. This scheme extends to any number of blocks of 1s in a multiplier, including the case in which a single 1 is treated as a block.

$$M \times (01111010) = M \times (2^6 + 2^5 + 2^4 + 2^3 - 2^1)$$
$$= M \times (2^7 - 2^3 + 2^2 - 2^1)$$

Booth's algorithm conforms to this scheme by performing a subtraction when the first 1 of the block is encountered (1–0) and an addition when the end of the block is encountered (0–1).

To show that the same scheme works for a negative multiplier, we need to observe the following. Let X be a negative number in twos complement notation:

$$\text{Representation of } X = \{1x_{n-2}x_{n-3} \ldots x_1x_0\}$$

Then the value of X can be expressed as follows:

$$X = -2^{n-1} + (x_{n-2} \times 2^{n-2}) + (x_{n-3} \times 2^{n-3}) + \cdots + (x_1 \times 2^1) + (x_0 \times 2^0) \quad \textbf{(10.4)}$$

The reader can verify this by applying the algorithm to the numbers in Table 10.2.

The leftmost bit of X is 1, because X is negative. Assume that the leftmost 0 is in the kth position. Thus, X is of the form

$$\text{Representation of } X = \{111 \ldots 10x_{k-1}x_{k-2} \ldots x_1x_0\} \qquad \textbf{(10.5)}$$

Then the value of X is

$$X = -2^{n-1} + 2^{n-2} + \cdots + 2^{k+1} + (x_{k-1} \times 2^{k-1}) + \cdots + (x_0 \times 2^0) \qquad \textbf{(10.6)}$$

From Equation (10.3), we can say that

$$2^{n-2} + 2^{n-3} + \cdots + 2^{k+1} = 2^{n-1} - 2^{k+1}$$

Rearranging

$$-2^{n-1} + 2^{n-2} + 2^{n-3} + \cdots + 2^{k+1} = -2^{k+1} \tag{10.7}$$

Substituting Equation (10.7) into Equation (10.6), we have

$$X = -2^{k+1} + (x_{k-1} \times 2^{k-1}) + \cdots + (x_0 \times 2^0) \tag{10.8}$$

At last we can return to Booth's algorithm. Remembering the representation of X [Equation (10.5)], it is clear that all of the bits from x_0 up to the leftmost 0 are handled properly because they produce all of the terms in Equation (10.8) but (-2^{k+1}) and thus are in the proper form. As the algorithm scans over the leftmost 0 and encounters the next 1 (2^{k+1}), a 1–0 transition occurs and a subtraction takes place (-2^{k+1}). This is the remaining term in Equation (10.8).

As an example, consider the multiplication of some multiplicand by (-6). In twos complement representation, using an 8-bit word, (-6) is represented as 11111010. By Equation (10.4), we know that

$$-6 = -2^7 + 2^6 + 2^5 + 2^4 + 2^3 + 2^1$$

which the reader can easily verify. Thus,

$$M \times (11111010) = M \times (-2^7 + 2^6 + 2^5 + 2^4 + 2^3 + 2^1)$$

Using Equation (10.7),

$$M \times (11111010) = M \times (-2^3 + 2^1)$$

which the reader can verify is still $M \times (-6)$. Finally, following our earlier line of reasoning,

$$M \times (11111010) = M \times (-2^3 + 2^2 - 2^1)$$

We can see that Booth's algorithm conforms to this scheme. It performs a subtraction when the first 1 is encountered (10), an addition when (01) is encountered, and finally another subtraction when the first 1 of the next block of 1s is encountered. Thus, Booth's algorithm performs fewer additions and subtractions than a more straightforward algorithm.

Division

Division is somewhat more complex than multiplication but is based on the same general principles. As before, the basis for the algorithm is the paper-and-pencil approach, and the operation involves repetitive shifting and addition or subtraction.

Figure 10.15 shows an example of the long division of unsigned binary integers. It is instructive to describe the process in detail. First, the bits of the dividend are examined from left to right, until the set of bits examined represents a number greater than or equal to the divisor; this is referred to as the divisor being able to divide the number. Until this event occurs, 0s are placed in the quotient from left to right. When the event occurs, a 1 is placed in the quotient and the divisor is subtracted from the partial dividend. The result is referred to as a *partial remainder*.

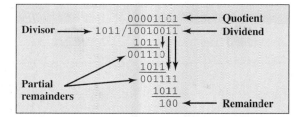

Figure 10.15 Example of Division of Unsigned Binary Integers

From this point on, the division follows a cyclic pattern. At each cycle, additional bits from the dividend are appended to the partial remainder until the result is greater than or equal to the divisor. As before, the divisor is subtracted from this number to produce a new partial remainder. The process continues until all the bits of the dividend are exhausted.

Figure 10.16 shows a machine algorithm that corresponds to the long division process. The divisor is placed in the M register, the dividend in the Q register. At each

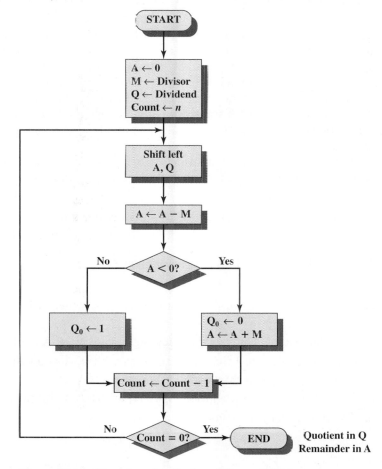

Figure 10.16 Flowchart for Unsigned Binary Division

A	Q	
0000	0111	Initial value
0000	1110	Shift
1101		Use twos complement of 0011 for subtraction
1101		Subtract
0000	1110	Restore, set $Q_0 = 0$
0001	1100	Shift
1101		
1110		Subtract
0001	1100	Restore, set $Q_0 = 0$
0011	1000	Shift
1101		
0000	1001	Subtract, set $Q_0 = 1$
0001	0010	Shift
1101		
1110		Subtract
0001	0010	Restore, set $Q_0 = 0$

Figure 10.17   Example of Restoring Twos Complement Division (7/3)

step, the A and Q registers together are shifted to the left 1 bit. M is subtracted from A to determine whether A divides the partial remainder.[3] If it does, then Q_0 gets a 1bit. Otherwise, Q_0 gets a 0 bit and M must be added back to A to restore the previous value. The count is then decremented, and the process continues for n steps. At the end, the quotient is in the Q register and the remainder is in the A register.

This process can, with some difficulty, be extended to negative numbers. We give here one approach for twos complement numbers. An example of this approach is shown in Figure 10.17.

The algorithm assumes that the divisor V and the dividend D are positive and that $|V| < |D|$. If $|V| = |D|$, then the quotient $Q = 1$ and the remainder $R = 0$. If $|V| > |D|$, then $Q = 0$ and $R = D$. The algorithm can be summarized as follows:

1. Load the twos complement of the divisor into the M register; that is, the M register contains the negative of the divisor. Load the dividend into the A, Q registers. The dividend must be expressed as a $2n$-bit positive number. Thus, for example, the 4-bit 0111 becomes 00000111.

2. Shift A, Q left 1 bit position.

3. Perform $A \leftarrow A - M$. This operation subtracts the divisor from the contents of A.

4. **a.** If the result is nonnegative (most significant bit of $A = 0$), then set $Q_0 \leftarrow 1$.
   b. If the result is negative (most significant bit of $A = 1$), then set $Q_0 \leftarrow 0$ and restore the previous value of A.

5. Repeat steps 2 through 4 as many times as there are bit positions in Q.

6. The remainder is in A and the quotient is in Q.

---

[3]This is subtraction of unsigned integers. A result that requires a borrow out of the most significant bit is a negative result.

To deal with negative numbers, we recognize that the remainder is defined by

$$D = Q \times V + R$$

That is, the remainder is the value of R needed for the preceding equation to be valid. Consider the following examples of integer division with all possible combinations of signs of D and V:

$$D = 7 \quad V = 3 \quad \Rightarrow \quad Q = 2 \quad R = 1$$
$$D = 7 \quad V = -3 \quad \Rightarrow \quad Q = -2 \quad R = 1$$
$$D = -7 \quad V = 3 \quad \Rightarrow \quad Q = -2 \quad R = -1$$
$$D = -7 \quad V = -3 \quad \Rightarrow \quad Q = 2 \quad R = -1$$

The reader will note from Figure 10.17 that $(-7)/(3)$ and $(7)/(-3)$ produce different remainders. We see that the magnitudes of Q and R are unaffected by the input signs and that the signs of Q and R are easily derivable from the signs of D and V. Specifically, $\text{sign}(R) = \text{sign}(D)$ and $\text{sign}(Q) = \text{sign}(D) \times \text{sign}(V)$. Hence, one way to do twos complement division is to convert the operands into unsigned values and, at the end, to account for the signs by complementation where needed. This is the method of choice for the restoring division algorithm [PARH10].

10.4 FLOATING-POINT REPRESENTATION

Principles

With a fixed-point notation (e.g., twos complement) it is possible to represent a range of positive and negative integers centered on or near 0. By assuming a fixed binary or radix point, this format allows the representation of numbers with a fractional component as well.

This approach has limitations. Very large numbers cannot be represented, nor can very small fractions. Furthermore, the fractional part of the quotient in a division of two large numbers could be lost.

For decimal numbers, we get around this limitation by using scientific notation. Thus, 976,000,000,000,000 can be represented as 9.76×10^{14}, and 0.0000000000000976 can be represented as 9.76×10^{-14}. What we have done, in effect, is dynamically to slide the decimal point to a convenient location and use the exponent of 10 to keep track of that decimal point. This allows a range of very large and very small numbers to be represented with only a few digits.

This same approach can be taken with binary numbers. We can represent a number in the form

$$\pm S \times B^{\pm E}$$

This number can be stored in a binary word with three fields:

- Sign: plus or minus
- Significand S
- Exponent E

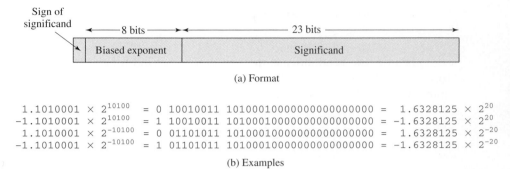

(a) Format

(b) Examples

Figure 10.18 Typical 32-Bit Floating-Point Format

The **base** B is implicit and need not be stored because it is the same for all numbers. Typically, it is assumed that the radix point is to the right of the leftmost, or most significant, bit of the significand. That is, there is one bit to the left of the radix point.

The principles used in representing binary floating-point numbers are best explained with an example. Figure 10.18a shows a typical 32-bit floating-point format. The leftmost bit stores the **sign** of the number (0 = positive, 1 = negative). The **exponent** value is stored in the next 8 bits. The representation used is known as a **biased representation**. A fixed value, called the bias, is subtracted from the field to get the true exponent value. Typically, the bias equals $(2^{k-1} - 1)$, where k is the number of bits in the binary exponent. In this case, the 8-bit field yields the numbers 0 through 255. With a bias of 127 $(2^7 - 1)$, the true exponent values are in the range -127 to $+128$. In this example, the base is assumed to be 2.

Table 10.2 shows the biased representation for 4-bit integers. Note that when the bits of a biased representation are treated as unsigned integers, the relative magnitudes of the numbers do not change. For example, in both biased and unsigned representations, the largest number is 1111 and the smallest number is 0000. This is not true of sign-magnitude or twos complement representation. An advantage of biased representation is that nonnegative floating-point numbers can be treated as integers for comparison purposes.

The final portion of the word (23 bits in this case) is the **significand**.[4]

Any floating-point number can be expressed in many ways.

The following are equivalent, where the significand is expressed in binary form:

$$0.110 \times 2^5$$
$$110 \times 2^2$$
$$0.0110 \times 2^6$$

To simplify operations on floating-point numbers, it is typically required that they be normalized. A **normal number** is one in which the most significant digit of the

---

[4]The term **mantissa**, sometimes used instead of *significand,* is considered obsolete. *Mantissa* also means "the fractional part of a logarithm," so is best avoided in this context.

significand is nonzero. For base 2 representation, a normal number is therefore one in which the most significant bit of the significand is one. As was mentioned, the typical convention is that there is one bit to the left of the radix point. Thus, a normal nonzero number is one in the form

$$\pm 1.bbb \ldots b \times 2^{\pm E}$$

where b is either binary digit (0 or 1). Because the most significant bit is always one, it is unnecessary to store this bit; rather, it is implicit. Thus, the 23-bit field is used to store a 24-bit significand with a value in the half open interval [1, 2). Given a number that is not normal, the number may be normalized by shifting the radix point to the right of the leftmost 1 bit and adjusting the exponent accordingly.

Figure 10.18b gives some examples of numbers stored in this format. For each example, on the left is the binary number; in the center is the corresponding bit pattern; on the right is the decimal value. Note the following features:

- The sign is stored in the first bit of the word.
- The first bit of the true significand is always 1 and need not be stored in the significand field.
- The value 127 is added to the true exponent to be stored in the exponent field.
- The base is 2.

For comparison, Figure 10.19 indicates the range of numbers that can be represented in a 32-bit word. Using twos complement integer representation, all of the integers from -2^{31} to $2^{31} - 1$ can be represented, for a total of 2^{32} different numbers. With the example floating-point format of Figure 10.18, the following ranges of numbers are possible:

- Negative numbers between $-(2 - 2^{-23}) \times 2^{128}$ and -2^{-127}
- Positive numbers between 2^{-127} and $(2 - 2^{-23}) \times 2^{128}$

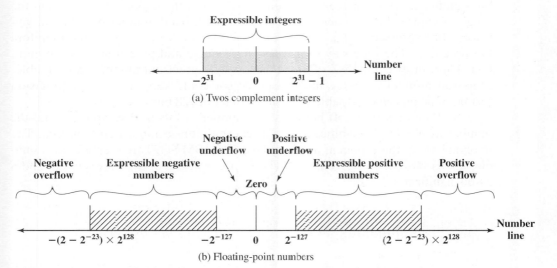

(a) Twos complement integers

(b) Floating-point numbers

Figure 10.19 Expressible Numbers in Typical 32-Bit Formats

Five regions on the number line are not included in these ranges:

- Negative numbers less than $-(2 - 2^{-23}) \times 2^{128}$, called **negative overflow**
- Negative numbers greater than 2^{-127}, called **negative underflow**
- Zero
- Positive numbers less than 2^{-127}, called **positive underflow**
- Positive numbers greater than $(2 - 2^{-23}) \times 2^{128}$, called **positive overflow**

The representation as presented will not accommodate a value of 0. However, as we shall see, actual floating-point representations include a special bit pattern to designate zero. Overflow occurs when an arithmetic operation results in an absolute value greater than can be expressed with an exponent of 128 (e.g., $2^{120} \times 2^{100} = 2^{220}$). Underflow occurs when the fractional magnitude is too small (e.g., $2^{-120} \times 2^{-100} = 2^{-220}$). Underflow is a less serious problem because the result can generally be satisfactorily approximated by 0.

It is important to note that we are not representing more individual values with floating-point notation. The maximum number of different values that can be represented with 32 bits is still 2^{32}. What we have done is to spread those numbers out in two ranges, one positive and one negative. In practice, most floating-point numbers that one would wish to represent are represented only approximately. However, for moderate sized integers, the representation is exact.

Also, note that the numbers represented in floating-point notation are not spaced evenly along the number line, as are fixed-point numbers. The possible values get closer together near the origin and farther apart as you move away, as shown in Figure 10.20. This is one of the trade-offs of floating-point math: Many calculations produce results that are not exact and have to be rounded to the nearest value that the notation can represent.

In the type of format depicted in Figure 10.18, there is a trade-off between range and precision. The example shows 8 bits devoted to the exponent and 23 to the significand. If we increase the number of bits in the exponent, we expand the range of expressible numbers. But because only a fixed number of different values can be expressed, we have reduced the density of those numbers and therefore the precision. The only way to increase both range and precision is to use more bits. Thus, most computers offer, at least, single-precision numbers and double-precision numbers. For example, a processor could support a single-precision format of 64 bits, and a double-precision format of 128 bits.

So there is a trade-off between the number of bits in the exponent and the number of bits in the significand. But it is even more complicated than that. The implied base of the exponent need not be 2. The IBM S/390 architecture, for example, uses a base of 16 [ANDE67b]. The format consists of a 7-bit exponent and a 24-bit significand.

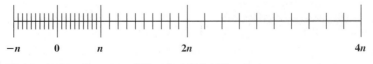

$-n$ 0 n $2n$ $4n$

Figure 10.20 Density of Floating-Point Numbers

In the IBM base-16 format,

$$0.11010001 \times 2^{10100} = 0.11010001 \times 16^{101}$$

and the exponent is stored to represent 5 rather than 20.

The advantage of using a larger exponent is that a greater range can be achieved for the same number of exponent bits. But remember, we have not increased the number of different values that can be represented. Thus, for a fixed format, a larger exponent base gives a greater range at the expense of less precision.

IEEE Standard for Binary Floating-Point Representation

The most important floating-point representation is defined in IEEE Standard 754, adopted in 1985 and revised in 2008. This standard was developed to facilitate the portability of programs from one processor to another and to encourage the development of sophisticated, numerically oriented programs. The standard has been widely adopted and is used on virtually all contemporary processors and arithmetic coprocessors. IEEE 754-2008 covers both binary and decimal floating-point representations. In this chapter, we deal only with binary representations.

IEEE 754-2008 defines the following different types of floating-point formats:

- **Arithmetic format:** All the mandatory operations defined by the standard are supported by the format. The format may be used to represent floating-point operands or results for the operations described in the standard.
- **Basic format:** This format covers five floating-point representations, three binary and two decimal, whose encodings are specified by the standard, and which can be used for arithmetic. At least one of the basic formats is implemented in any conforming implementation.
- **Interchange format:** A fully specified, fixed-length binary encoding that allows data interchange between different platforms and that can be used for storage.

The three basic binary formats have bit lengths of 32, 64, and 128 bits, with exponents of 8, 11, and 15 bits, respectively (Figure 10.21). Table 10.3 summarizes the characteristics of the three formats. The two basic decimal formats have bit lengths of 64 and 128 bits. All of the basic formats are also arithmetic format types (can be used for arithmetic operations) and interchange format types (platform independent).

Several other formats are specified in the standard. The binary16 format is only an interchange format and is intended for storage of values when higher precision is not required. The binary{k} format and the decimal{k} format are interchange formats with total length k bits and with defined lengths for the significand and exponent. The format must be a multiple of 32 bits; thus formats are defined for $k = 160$, 192, and so on. These two families of formats are also arithmetic formats.

In addition, the standard defines **extended precision formats**, which extend a supported basic format by providing additional bits in the exponent (extended range) and in the significand (extended precision). The exact format

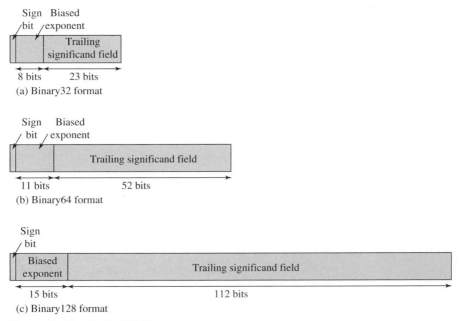

Figure 10.21 IEEE 754 Formats

is implementation dependent, but the standard places certain constraints on the length of the exponent and significand. These formats are arithmetic format types but not interchange format types. The extended formats are to be used for intermediate calculations. With their greater precision, the extended formats lessen the

Table 10.3 IEEE 754 Format Parameters

Parameter	Format		
	Binary32	Binary64	Binary128
Storage width (bits)	32	64	128
Exponent width (bits)	8	11	15
Exponent bias	127	1023	16383
Maximum exponent	127	1023	16383
Minimum exponent	-126	-1022	-16382
Approx normal number range (base 10)	$10^{-38}, 10^{+38}$	$10^{-308}, 10^{+308}$	$10^{-4932}, 10^{+4932}$
Trailing significand width (bits)*	23	52	112
Number of exponents	254	2046	32766
Number of fractions	2^{23}	2^{52}	2^{112}
Number of values	1.98×2^{31}	1.99×2^{63}	1.99×2^{128}
Smallest positive normal number	2^{-126}	2^{-1022}	2^{-16362}
Largest positive normal number	$2^{128} - 2^{104}$	$2^{1024} - 2^{971}$	$2^{16384} - 2^{16271}$
Smallest subnormal magnitude	2^{-149}	2^{-1074}	2^{-16494}

Note: *not including implied bit and not including sign bit

chance of a final result that has been contaminated by excessive roundoff error; with their greater range, they also lessen the chance of an intermediate overflow aborting a computation whose final result would have been representable in a basic format. An additional motivation for the extended format is that it affords some of the benefits of a larger basic format without incurring the time penalty usually associated with higher precision.

Finally, IEEE 754-2008 defines an **extendable precision format** as a format with a precision and range that are defined under user control. Again, these formats may be used for intermediate calculations, but the standard places no constraint or format or length.

Table 10.4 shows the relationship between defined formats and format types.

Not all bit patterns in the IEEE formats are interpreted in the usual way; instead, some bit patterns are used to represent special values. Table 10.5 indicates the values assigned to various bit patterns. The exponent values of all zeros (0 bits) and all ones (1 bits) define special values. The following classes of numbers are represented:

- For exponent values in the range of 1 through 254 for 32-bit format, 1 through 2046 for 64-bit format, and 1 through 16382, normal nonzero floating-point numbers are represented. The exponent is biased, so that the range of exponents is −126 through +127 for 32-bit format, and so on. A normal number requires a 1 bit to the left of the binary point; this bit is implied, giving an effective 24-bit, 53-bit, or 113-bit significand. Because one of the bits is implied, the corresponding field in the binary format is referred to as the **trailing significand field**.

- An exponent of zero together with a fraction of zero represents positive or negative zero, depending on the sign bit. As was mentioned, it is useful to have an exact value of 0 represented.

Table 10.4   IEEE Formats

Format	Format Type		
	Arithmetic Format	**Basic Format**	**Interchange Format**
binary16			X
binary32	X	X	X
binary64	X	X	X
binary128	X	X	X
binary{k} ($k = n \times 32$ for $n > 4$)	X		X
decimal64	X	X	X
decimal128	X	X	X
decimal{k} ($k = n \times 32$ for $n > 4$)	X		X
extended precision	X		
extendable precision	X		

Table 10.5 Interpretation of IEEE 754 Floating-Point Numbers

(a) binary32 format

	Sign	Biased Exponent	Fraction	Value
positive zero	0	0	0	0
negative zero	1	0	0	-0
plus infinity	0	all 1s	0	∞
minus infinity	1	all 1s	0	$-\infty$
quiet NaN	0 or 1	all 1s	$\neq 0$; first bit $= 1$	qNaN
signaling NaN	0 or 1	all 1s	$\neq 0$; first bit $= 0$	sNaN
positive normal nonzero	0	$0 < e < 255$	f	$2^{e-127}(1.f)$
negative normal nonzero	1	$0 < e < 255$	f	$-2^{e-127}(1.f)$
positive subnormal	0	0	$f \neq 0$	$2^{e-126}(0.f)$
negative subnormal	1	0	$f \neq 0$	$-2^{e-126}(0.f)$

(b) binary64 format

	Sign	Biased Exponent	Fraction	Value
positive zero	0	0	0	0
negative zero	1	0	0	-0
plus infinity	0	all 1s	0	∞
minus infinity	1	all 1s	0	$-\infty$
quiet NaN	0 or 1	all 1s	$\neq 0$; first bit $= 1$	qNaN
signaling NaN	0 or 1	all 1s	$\neq 0$; first bit $= 0$	sNaN
positive normal nonzero	0	$0 < e < 2047$	f	$2^{e-1023}(1.f)$
negative normal nonzero	1	$0 < e < 2047$	f	$-2^{e-1023}(1.f)$
positive subnormal	0	0	$f \neq 0$	$2^{e-1022}(0.f)$
negative subnormal	1	0	$f \neq 0$	$-2^{e-1022}(0.f)$

(c) binary128 format

	Sign	Biased Exponent	Fraction	Value
positive zero	0	0	0	0
negative zero	1	0	0	-0
plus infinity	0	all 1s	0	∞
minus infinity	1	all 1s	0	$-\infty$
quiet NaN	0 or 1	all 1s	$\neq 0$; first bit $= 1$	qNaN
signaling NaN	0 or 1	all 1s	$\neq 0$; first bit $= 0$	sNaN
positive normal nonzero	0	all 1s	f	$2^{e-16383}(1.f)$
negative normal nonzero	1	all 1s	f	$-2^{e-16383}(1.f)$
positive subnormal	0	0	$f \neq 0$	$2^{e-16383}(0.f)$
negative subnormal	1	0	$f \neq 0$	$-2^{e-16383}(0.f)$

- An exponent of all ones together with a fraction of zero represents positive or negative infinity, depending on the sign bit. It is also useful to have a representation of infinity. This leaves it up to the user to decide whether to treat overflow as an error condition or to carry the value ∞ and proceed with whatever program is being executed.

- An exponent of zero together with a nonzero fraction represents a subnormal number. In this case, the bit to the left of the binary point is zero and the true exponent is -126 or -1022. The number is positive or negative depending on the sign bit.

- An exponent of all ones together with a nonzero fraction is given the value NaN, which means *Not a Number*, and is used to signal various exception conditions.

The significance of subnormal numbers and NaNs is discussed in Section 10.5.

10.5 FLOATING-POINT ARITHMETIC

Table 10.6 summarizes the basic operations for floating-point arithmetic. For addition and subtraction, it is necessary to ensure that both operands have the same exponent value. This may require shifting the radix point on one of the operands to achieve alignment. Multiplication and division are more straightforward.

A floating-point operation may produce one of these conditions:

- **Exponent overflow:** A positive exponent exceeds the maximum possible exponent value. In some systems, this may be designated as $+\infty$ or $-\infty$.

- **Exponent underflow:** A negative exponent is less than the minimum possible exponent value (e.g., -200 is less than -127). This means that the number is too small to be represented, and it may be reported as 0.

Table 10.6 Floating-Point Numbers and Arithmetic Operations

Floating-Point Numbers	**Arithmetic Operations**
$X = X_S \times B^{X_E}$ $Y = Y_S \times B^{Y_E}$	$\left. \begin{array}{l} X + Y = (X_s \times B^{X_E - Y_E} + Y_s) \times B^{Y_E} \\ X - Y = (X_s \times B^{X_E - Y_E} - Y_s) \times B^{Y_E} \end{array} \right\} X_E \leq Y_E$ $X \times Y = (X_s \times Y_s) \times B^{X_E + Y_E}$ $\dfrac{X}{Y} = \left(\dfrac{X_s}{Y_s} \right) \times B^{X_E - Y_E}$

Examples:

$X = 0.3 \times 10^2 = 30$

$Y = 0.2 \times 10^3 = 200$

$X + Y = (0.3 \times 10^{2-3} + 0.2) \times 10^3 = 0.23 \times 10^3 = 230$

$X - Y = (0.3 \times 10^{2-3} - 0.2) \times 10^3 = (-0.17) \times 10^3 = -170$

$X \times Y = (0.3 \times 0.2) \times 10^{2+3} = 0.06 \times 10^5 = 6000$

$X \div Y = (0.3 \div 0.2) \times 10^{2-3} = 1.5 \times 10^{-1} = 0.15$

- **Significand underflow:** In the process of aligning significands, digits may flow off the right end of the significand. As we shall discuss, some form of rounding is required.

- **Significand overflow:** The addition of two significands of the same sign may result in a carry out of the most significant bit. This can be fixed by realignment, as we shall explain.

Addition and Subtraction

In floating-point arithmetic, addition and subtraction are more complex than multiplication and division. This is because of the need for alignment. There are four basic phases of the algorithm for addition and subtraction:

1. Check for zeros.
2. Align the significands.
3. Add or subtract the significands.
4. Normalize the result.

A typical flowchart is shown in Figure 10.22. A step-by-step narrative highlights the main functions required for floating-point addition and subtraction. We assume a format similar to those of Figure 10.21. For the addition or subtraction operation, the two operands must be transferred to registers that will be used by the ALU. If the floating-point format includes an implicit significand bit, that bit must be made explicit for the operation.

Phase 1: Zero check. Because addition and subtraction are identical except for a sign change, the process begins by changing the sign of the subtrahend if it is a subtract operation. Next, if either operand is 0, the other is reported as the result.

Phase 2: Significand alignment. The next phase is to manipulate the numbers so that the two exponents are equal.

To see the need for aligning exponents, consider the following decimal addition:

$$(123 \times 10^0) + (456 \times 10^{-2})$$

Clearly, we cannot just add the significands. The digits must first be set into equivalent positions, that is, the 4 of the second number must be aligned with the 3 of the first. Under these conditions, the two exponents will be equal, which is the mathematical condition under which two numbers in this form can be added. Thus,

$$(123 \times 10^0) + (456 \times 10^{-2}) = (123 \times 10^0) + (4.56 \times 10^0) = 127.56 \times 10^0$$

Alignment may be achieved by shifting either the smaller number to the right (increasing its exponent) or shifting the larger number to the left. Because either operation may result in the loss of digits, it is the smaller number that is shifted; any digits that are lost are therefore of relatively small significance. The

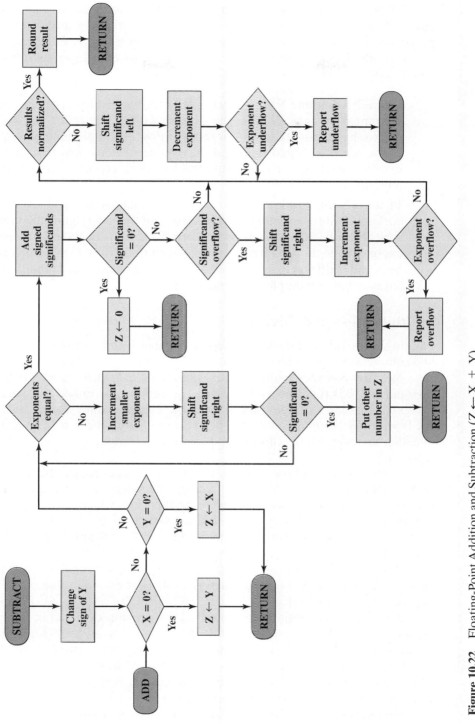

Figure 10.22 Floating-Point Addition and Subtraction $(Z \leftarrow X \pm Y)$

351

alignment is achieved by repeatedly shifting the magnitude portion of the significand right 1 digit and incrementing the exponent until the two exponents are equal. (Note that if the implied base is 16, a shift of 1 digit is a shift of 4 bits.) If this process results in a 0 value for the significand, then the other number is reported as the result. Thus, if two numbers have exponents that differ significantly, the lesser number is lost.

Phase 3: Addition. Next, the two significands are added together, taking into account their signs. Because the signs may differ, the result may be 0. There is also the possibility of significand overflow by 1 digit. If so, the significand of the result is shifted right and the exponent is incremented. An exponent overflow could occur as a result; this would be reported and the operation halted.

Phase 4: Normalization. The final phase normalizes the result. Normalization consists of shifting significand digits left until the most significant digit (bit, or 4 bits for base-16 exponent) is nonzero. Each shift causes a decrement of the exponent and thus could cause an exponent underflow. Finally, the result must be rounded off and then reported. We defer a discussion of rounding until after a discussion of multiplication and division.

Multiplication and Division

Floating-point multiplication and division are much simpler processes than addition and subtraction, as the following discussion indicates.

We first consider multiplication, illustrated in Figure 10.23. First, if either operand is 0, 0 is reported as the result. The next step is to add the exponents. If the exponents are stored in biased form, the exponent sum would have doubled the bias. Thus, the bias value must be subtracted from the sum. The result could be either an exponent overflow or underflow, which would be reported, ending the algorithm.

If the exponent of the product is within the proper range, the next step is to multiply the significands, taking into account their signs. The multiplication is performed in the same way as for integers. In this case, we are dealing with a sign-magnitude representation, but the details are similar to those for twos complement representation. The product will be double the length of the multiplier and multiplicand. The extra bits will be lost during rounding.

After the product is calculated, the result is then normalized and rounded, as was done for addition and subtraction. Note that normalization could result in exponent underflow.

Finally, let us consider the flowchart for division depicted in Figure 10.24. Again, the first step is testing for 0. If the divisor is 0, an error report is issued, or the result is set to infinity, depending on the implementation. A dividend of 0 results in 0. Next, the divisor exponent is subtracted from the dividend exponent. This removes the bias, which must be added back in. Tests are then made for exponent underflow or overflow.

The next step is to divide the significands. This is followed with the usual normalization and rounding.

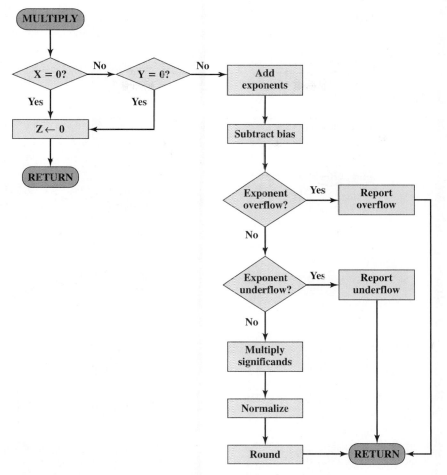

Figure 10.23   Floating-Point Multiplication (Z ← X × Y)

Precision Considerations

GUARD BITS We mentioned that, prior to a floating-point operation, the exponent and significand of each operand are loaded into ALU registers. In the case of the significand, the length of the register is almost always greater than the length of the significand plus an implied bit. The register contains additional bits, called guard bits, which are used to pad out the right end of the significand with 0s.

The reason for the use of guard bits is illustrated in Figure 10.25. Consider numbers in the IEEE format, which has a 24-bit significand, including an implied 1 bit to the left of the binary point. Two numbers that are very close in value are $x = 1.00 \cdots 00 \times 2^1$ and $y = 1.11 \cdots 11 \times 2^0$. If the smaller number is to be subtracted from the larger, it must be shifted right 1 bit to align the exponents. This is shown in Figure 10.25a. In the process, y loses 1 bit of significance; the

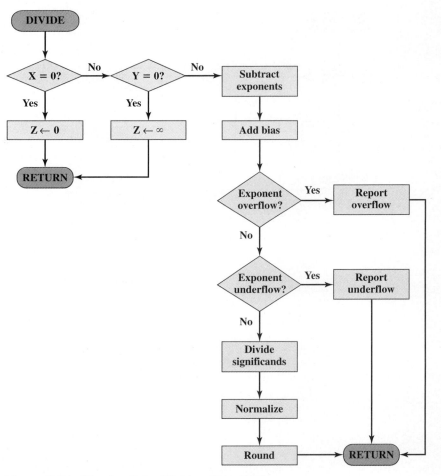

Figure 10.24 Floating-Point Division (Z ← X/Y)

x = 1.000.....00 × 2^1	x = .100000 × 16^1
$-y$ = 0.111.....11 × 2^1	$-y$ = .0FFFFF × 16^1
z = 0.000.....01 × 2^1	z = .000001 × 16^1
= 1.000.....00 × 2^{-22}	= .100000 × 16^{-4}

(a) Binary example, without guard bits   (c) Hexadecimal example, without guard bits

x = 1.000.....00 0000 × 2^1	x = .100000 00 × 16^1
$-y$ = 0.111.....11 1000 × 2^1	$-y$ = .0FFFFF F0 × 16^1
z = 0.000.....00 1000 × 2^1	z = .000000 10 × 16^1
= 1.000.....00 0000 × 2^{-23}	= .100000 00 × 16^{-5}

(b) Binary example, with guard bits   (d) Hexadecimal example, with guard bits

Figure 10.25 The Use of Guard Bits

result is 2^{-22}. The same operation is repeated in part (b) with the addition of guard bits. Now the least significant bit is not lost due to alignment, and the result is 2^{-23}, a difference of a factor of 2 from the previous answer. When the radix is 16, the loss of precision can be greater. As Figures 10.25c and d show, the difference can be a factor of 16.

ROUNDING Another detail that affects the precision of the result is the rounding policy. The result of any operation on the significands is generally stored in a longer register. When the result is put back into the floating-point format, the extra bits must be eliminated in such a way as to produce a result that is close to the exact result. This process is called **rounding**.

A number of techniques have been explored for performing rounding. In fact, the IEEE standard lists four alternative approaches:

- **Round to nearest:** The result is rounded to the nearest representable number.
- **Round toward $+\infty$:** The result is rounded up toward plus infinity.
- **Round toward $-\infty$:** The result is rounded down toward negative infinity.
- **Round toward 0:** The result is rounded toward zero.

Let us consider each of these policies in turn. **Round to nearest** is the default rounding mode listed in the standard and is defined as follows: The representable value nearest to the infinitely precise result shall be delivered.

If the extra bits, beyond the 23 bits that can be stored, are 10010, then the extra bits amount to more than one-half of the last representable bit position. In this case, the correct answer is to add binary 1 to the last representable bit, rounding up to the next representable number. Now consider that the extra bits are 01111. In this case, the extra bits amount to less than one-half of the last representable bit position. The correct answer is simply to drop the extra bits (truncate), which has the effect of rounding down to the next representable number.

The standard also addresses the special case of extra bits of the form 10000.... Here the result is exactly halfway between the two possible representable values. One possible technique here would be to always truncate, as this would be the simplest operation. However, the difficulty with this simple approach is that it introduces a small but cumulative bias into a sequence of computations. What is required is an unbiased method of rounding. One possible approach would be to round up or down on the basis of a random number so that, on average, the result would be unbiased. The argument against this approach is that it does not produce predictable, deterministic results. The approach taken by the IEEE standard is to force the result to be even: If the result of a computation is exactly midway between two representable numbers, the value is rounded up if the last representable bit is currently 1 and not rounded up if it is currently 0.

The next two options, **rounding to plus** and **minus infinity**, are useful in implementing a technique known as interval arithmetic. Interval arithmetic provides an efficient method for monitoring and controlling errors in floating-point computations by producing two values for each result. The two values correspond to the lower and upper endpoints of an interval that contains the true result. The width of the interval, which is the difference between the upper and lower endpoints, indicates the accuracy of the result. If the endpoints of an interval are not representable, then the interval endpoints are rounded down and up, respectively. Although the width of the interval may vary according to implementation, many algorithms have been designed to produce narrow intervals. If the range between the upper and lower bounds is sufficiently narrow, then a sufficiently accurate result has been obtained. If not, at least we know this and can perform additional analysis.

The final technique specified in the standard is **round toward zero**. This is, in fact, simple truncation: The extra bits are ignored. This is certainly the simplest technique. However, the result is that the magnitude of the truncated value is always less than or equal to the more precise original value, introducing a consistent bias toward zero in the operation. This is a serious bias because it affects every operation for which there are nonzero extra bits.

IEEE Standard for Binary Floating–Point Arithmetic

IEEE 754 goes beyond the simple definition of a format to lay down specific practices and procedures so that floating-point arithmetic produces uniform, predictable results independent of the hardware platform. One aspect of this has already been discussed, namely rounding. This subsection looks at three other topics: infinity, NaNs, and subnormal numbers.

INFINITY Infinity arithmetic is treated as the limiting case of real arithmetic, with the infinity values given the following interpretation:

$$-\infty < \text{(every finite number)} < +\infty$$

With the exception of the special cases discussed subsequently, any arithmetic operation involving infinity yields the obvious result.

For example:

$$5 + (+\infty) = +\infty \qquad 5 \div (+\infty) = +0$$
$$5 - (+\infty) = -\infty \qquad (+\infty) + (+\infty) = +\infty$$
$$5 + (-\infty) = -\infty \qquad (-\infty) + (-\infty) = -\infty$$
$$5 - (-\infty) = +\infty \qquad (-\infty) - (+\infty) = -\infty$$
$$5 \times (+\infty) = +\infty \qquad (+\infty) - (-\infty) = +\infty$$

QUIET AND SIGNALING NaNs A NaN is a symbolic entity encoded in floating-point format, of which there are two types: signaling and quiet. A signaling NaN signals an invalid operation exception whenever it appears as an operand. Signaling

Table 10.7   Operations that Produce a Quiet NaN

Operation	Quiet NaN Produced By
Any	Any operation on a signaling NaN
Add or subtract	Magnitude subtraction of infinities: $(+\infty) + (-\infty)$ $(-\infty) + (+\infty)$ $(+\infty) - (+\infty)$ $(-\infty) - (-\infty)$
Multiply	$0 \times \infty$
Division	$\dfrac{0}{0}$ or $\dfrac{\infty}{\infty}$
Remainder	x REM 0 or ∞ REM y
Square root	$\sqrt{x}$, where $x < 0$

NaNs afford values for uninitialized variables and arithmetic-like enhancements that are not the subject of the standard. A quiet NaN propagates through almost every arithmetic operation without signaling an exception. Table 10.7 indicates operations that will produce a quiet NaN.

Note that both types of NaNs have the same general format (Table 10.4): an exponent of all ones and a nonzero fraction. The actual bit pattern of the nonzero fraction is implementation dependent; the fraction values can be used to distinguish quiet NaNs from signaling NaNs and to specify particular exception conditions.

SUBNORMAL NUMBERS Subnormal numbers are included in IEEE 754 to handle cases of exponent underflow. When the exponent of the result becomes too small (a negative exponent with too large a magnitude), the result is subnormalized by right shifting the fraction and incrementing the exponent for each shift until the exponent is within a representable range.

Figure 10.26 illustrates the effect of including subnormal numbers. The representable numbers can be grouped into intervals of the form $[2^n, 2^{n+1}]$. Within each

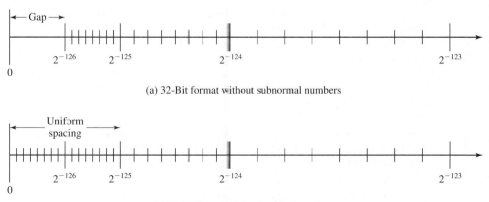

(a) 32-Bit format without subnormal numbers

(b) 32-Bit format with subnormal numbers

Figure 10.26   The Effect of IEEE 754 Subnormal Numbers

such interval, the exponent portion of the number remains constant while the fraction varies, producing a uniform spacing of representable numbers within the interval. As we get closer to zero, each successive interval is half the width of the preceding interval but contains the same number of representable numbers. Hence the density of representable numbers increases as we approach zero. However, if only normal numbers are used, there is a gap between the smallest normal number and 0. In the case of the 32-bit IEEE 754 format, there are 2^{23} representable numbers in each interval, and the smallest representable positive number is 2^{-126}. With the addition of subnormal numbers, an additional $2^{23} - 1$ numbers are uniformly added between 0 and 2^{-126}.

The use of subnormal numbers is referred to as *gradual underflow* [COON81]. Without subnormal numbers, the gap between the smallest representable nonzero number and zero is much wider than the gap between the smallest representable nonzero number and the next larger number. Gradual underflow fills in that gap and reduces the impact of exponent underflow to a level comparable with roundoff among the normal numbers.

10.6 RECOMMENDED READING

[ERCE04] and [PARH10] are excellent treatments of computer arithmetic, covering all of the topics in this chapter in detail. [FLYN01] is a useful discussion that focuses on practical design and implementation issues. For the serious student of computer arithmetic, a very useful reference is the two-volume [SWAR90]. Volume I was originally published in 1980 and provides key papers (some very difficult to obtain otherwise) on computer arithmetic fundamentals. Volume II contains more recent papers, covering theoretical, design, and implementation aspects of computer arithmetic.

For floating-point arithmetic, [GOLD91] is well named: "What Every Computer Scientist Should Know About Floating-Point Arithmetic." Another excellent treatment of the topic is contained in [KNUT98], which also covers integer computer arithmetic. The following more in-depth treatments are also worthwhile: [EVEN00a, OBER97a, OBER97b, SODE96]. [KUCK77] is a good discussion of rounding methods in floating-point arithmetic. [EVEN00b] examines rounding with respect to IEEE 754. For a thorough treatment of floating-point arithmetic, standards, and implementation, the book to read is [MULL10].

[SCHW99] describes the first IBM S/390 processor to integrate radix-16 and IEEE 754 floating-point arithmetic in the same floating-point unit.

William Kahan, the principal architect of the IEEE 754 standard, has written a series of documents that provide a deeper understanding of the standard, including a detailed set of lecture notes, a paper on the rationale for a floating-point standard, and a tutorial on gradual underflow. All of these documents are available in the premium content section of this book's Web site.

ERCE04   Ercegovac, M., and Lang, T. *Digital Arithmetic.* San Francisco: Morgan Kaufmann, 2004.

EVEN00a   Even, G., and Paul, W. "On the Design of IEEE Compliant Floating-Point Units." *IEEE Transactions on Computers,* May 2000.

EVEN00b Even, G., and Seidel, P. "A Comparison of Three Rounding Algorithms for IEEE Floating-Point Multiplication." *IEEE Transactions on Computers,* July 2000.

FLYN01 Flynn, M., and Oberman, S. *Advanced Computer Arithmetic Design.* New York: Wiley, 2001.

GOLD91 Goldberg, D. "What Every Computer Scientist Should Know About Floating-Point Arithmetic." *ACM Computing Surveys,* March 1991.

KNUT98 Knuth, D. *The Art of Computer Programming, Volume 2: Seminumerical Algorithms.* Reading, MA: Addison-Wesley, 1998.

KUCK77 Kuck, D.; Parker, D.; and Sameh, A. "An Analysis of Rounding Methods in Floating-Point Arithmetic." *IEEE Transactions on Computers,* July 1977.

MULL10 Muller, J., et al. *Handbook of Floating-Point Arithmetic.* Boston: Birkhauser, 2010.

OBER97a Oberman, S., and Flynn, M. "Design Issues in Division and Other Floating-Point Operations." *IEEE Transactions on Computers,* February 1997.

OBER97b Oberman, S., and Flynn, M. "Division Algorithms and Implementations." *IEEE Transactions on Computers,* August 1997.

PARH10 Parhami, B. *Computer Arithmetic: Algorithms and Hardware Design.* Oxford: Oxford University Press, 2010.

SCHW99 Schwarz, E., and Krygowski, C. "The S/390 G5 Floating-Point Unit." *IBM Journal of Research and Development,* September/November 1999.

SODE96 Soderquist, P., and Leeser, M. "Area and Performance Tradeoffs in Floating-Point Divide and Square-Root Implementations." *ACM Computing Surveys,* September 1996.

SWAR90 Swartzlander, E., ed. *Computer Arithmetic, Volumes I and II.* Los Alamitos, CA: IEEE Computer Society Press, 1990.

10.7 KEY TERMS, REVIEW QUESTIONS, AND PROBLEMS

Key Terms

arithmetic and logic unit (ALU)	mantissa	quotient
arithmetic shift	minuend	radix point
base	multiplicand	remainder
biased representation	multiplier	rounding
dividend	negative overflow	sign bit
divisor	negative underflow	significand
exponent	normal number	significand overflow
exponent overflow	ones complement representation	significand underflow
exponent underflow	overflow	sign-magnitude representation
fixed-point representation	partial product	subnormal number
floating-point representation	positive overflow	subtrahend
guard bits	positive underflow	twos complement representation
	product	

Review Questions

10.1 Briefly explain the following representations: sign magnitude, twos complement, biased.

10.2 Explain how to determine if a number is negative in the following representations: sign magnitude, twos complement, biased.

10.3 What is the sign-extension rule for twos complement numbers?

10.4 How can you form the negation of an integer in twos complement representation?

10.5 In general terms, when does the twos complement operation on an n-bit integer produce the same integer?

10.6 What is the difference between the twos complement representation of a number and the twos complement of a number?

10.7 If we treat 2 twos complement numbers as unsigned integers for purposes of addition, the result is correct if interpreted as a twos complement number. This is not true for multiplication. Why?

10.8 What are the four essential elements of a number in floating-point notation?

10.9 What is the benefit of using biased representation for the exponent portion of a floating-point number?

10.10 What are the differences among positive overflow, exponent overflow, and significand overflow?

10.11 What are the basic elements of floating-point addition and subtraction?

10.12 Give a reason for the use of guard bits.

10.13 List four alternative methods of rounding the result of a floating-point operation.

Problems

10.1 Represent the following decimal numbers in both binary sign/magnitude and twos complement using 16 bits: +512; −29.

10.2 Represent the following twos complement values in decimal: 1101011; 0101101.

10.3 Another representation of binary integers that is sometimes encountered is **ones complement.** Positive integers are represented in the same way as sign magnitude. A negative integer is represented by taking the Boolean complement of each bit of the corresponding positive number.
   a. Provide a definition of ones complement numbers using a weighted sum of bits, similar to Equations (10.1) and (10.2).
   b. What is the range of numbers that can be represented in ones complement?
   c. Define an algorithm for performing addition in ones complement arithmetic.
   Note: Ones complement arithmetic disappeared from hardware in the 1960s, but still survives checksum calculations for the Internet Protocol (IP) and the Transmission Control Protocol (TCP).

10.4 Add columns to Table 10.1 for sign magnitude and ones complement.

10.5 Consider the following operation on a binary word. Start with the least significant bit. Copy all bits that are 0 until the first bit is reached and copy that bit, too. Then take the complement of each bit thereafter. What is the result?

10.6 In Section 10.3, the twos complement operation is defined as follows. To find the twos complement of X, take the Boolean complement of each bit of X, and then add 1.
   a. Show that the following is an equivalent definition. For an n-bit integer X, the twos complement of X is formed by treating X as an unsigned integer and calculating $(2_n - X)$.
   b. Demonstrate that Figure 10.5 can be used to support graphically the claim in part (a), by showing how a clockwise movement is used to achieve subtraction.

10.7 The r's complement of an n-digit number N in base r is defined as $r^n - N$ for $N \neq 0$ and 0 for $N = 0$. Find the tens complement of the decimal number 13,250.

10.8 Calculate $(72,530 - 13,250)$ using tens complement arithmetic. Assume rules similar to those for twos complement arithmetic.

10.9 Consider the twos complement addition of two n-bit numbers:

$$z_{n-1}z_{n-2} \ldots z_0 = x_{n-1}x_{n-2} \ldots x_0 + y_{n-1}y_{n-2} \ldots y_0$$

Assume that bitwise addition is performed with a carry bit c_i generated by the addition of x_i, y_i, and c_{i-1}. Let ν be a binary variable indicating overflow when $\nu = 1$. Fill in the values in the table.

	x_{n-1}	0	0	0	0	1	1	1	1
Input	y_{n-1}	0	0	1	1	0	0	1	1
	c_{n-2}	0	1	0	1	0	1	0	1
Output	z_{n-1}								
	ν								

10.10 Assume numbers are represented in 8-bit twos complement representation. Show the calculation of the following:
    a. $5 + 13$ **b.** $-6 + 13$ **c.** $6 - 13$ **d.** $-6 - 13$

10.11 Find the following differences using twos complement arithmetic:
    a.   111000   **b.**   11001100   **c.**   111100001111   **d.**   11000011
        -110011 $-\ \ \ 101110$ -110011110011 -11101000

10.12 Is the following a valid alternative definition of overflow in twos complement arithmetic?

If the exclusive-OR of the carry bits into and out of the leftmost column is 1, then there is an overflow condition. Otherwise, there is not.

10.13 Compare Figures 10.9 and 10.12. Why is the C bit not used in the latter?

10.14 Given $x = 0101$ and $y = 1010$ in twos complement notation (i.e., $x = 5$, $y = -6$), compute the product $p = x \times y$ with Booth's algorithm.

10.15 Use the Booth algorithm to multiply 23 (multiplicand) by 29 (multiplier), where each number is represented using 6 bits.

10.16 Prove that the multiplication of two n-digit numbers in base B gives a product of no more than $2n$ digits.

10.17 Verify the validity of the unsigned binary division algorithm of Figure 10.16 by showing the steps involved in calculating the division depicted in Figure 10.15. Use a presentation similar to that of Figure 10.17.

10.18 The twos complement integer division algorithm described in Section 10.3 is known as the restoring method because the value in the A register must be restored following unsuccessful subtraction. A slightly more complex approach, known as nonrestoring, avoids the unnecessary subtraction and addition. Propose an algorithm for this latter approach.

10.19 Under computer integer arithmetic, the quotient J/K of two integers J and K is less than or equal to the usual quotient. True or false?

10.20 Divide -145 by 13 in binary twos complement notation, using 12-bit words. Use the algorithm described in Section 10.3.

10.21 **a.** Consider a fixed-point representation using decimal digits, in which the implied radix point can be in any position (to the right of the least significant digit, to the right of the most significant digit, and so on). How many decimal digits are needed to represent the approximations of both Planck's constant (6.63×10^{-27})

and Avogadro's number (6.02×10^{23})? The implied radix point must be in the same position for both numbers.

b. Now consider a decimal floating-point format with the exponent stored in a biased representation with a bias of 50. A normalized representation is assumed. How many decimal digits are needed to represent these constants in this floating-point format?

10.22 Assume that the exponent e is constrained to lie in the range $0 \leq e \leq X$, with a bias of q, that the base is b, and that the significand is p digits in length.

    a. What are the largest and smallest positive values that can be written?

    b. What are the largest and smallest positive values that can be written as normalized floating-point numbers?

10.23 Express the following numbers in IEEE 32-bit floating-point format:

    a. -5 **b.** -6 **c.** -1.5 **d.** 384   **e.** 1/16   **f.** $-1/32$

10.24 The following numbers use the IEEE 32-bit floating-point format. What is the equivalent decimal value?

    a. 1 10000011 11000000000000000000000

    b. 0 01111110 10100000000000000000000

    c. 0 10000000 00000000000000000000000

10.25 Consider a reduced 7-bit IEEE floating-point format, with 3 bits for the exponent and 3 bits for the significand. List all 127 values.

10.26 Express the following numbers in IBM's 32-bit floating-point format, which uses a 7-bit exponent with an implied base of 16 and an exponent bias of 64 (40 hexadecimal). A normalized floating-point number requires that the leftmost hexadecimal digit be nonzero; the implied radix point is to the left of that digit.

a. 1.0	**c.** 1/64	**e.** -15.0	**g.** 7.2×10^{75}
b. 0.5	**d.** 0.0	**f.** 5.4×10^{-79}	**h.** 65,535

10.27 Let 5BCA0000 be a floating-point number in IBM format, expressed in hexadecimal. What is the decimal value of the number?

10.28 What would be the bias value for

    a. A base-2 exponent (B = 2) in a 6-bit field?

    b. A base-8 exponent (B = 8) in a 7-bit field?

10.29 Draw a number line similar to that in Figure 10.19b for the floating-point format of Figure 10.21b.

10.30 Consider a floating-point format with 8 bits for the biased exponent and 23 bits for the significand. Show the bit pattern for the following numbers in this format:

    a. -720 **b.** 0.645

10.31 The text mentions that a 32-bit format can represent a maximum of 2^{32} different numbers. How many different numbers can be represented in the IEEE 32-bit format? Explain.

10.32 Any floating-point representation used in a computer can represent only certain real numbers exactly; all others must be approximated. If A' is the stored value approximating the real value A, then the relative error, r, is expressed as

$$r = \frac{A - A'}{A}$$

Represent the decimal quantity $+0.4$ in the following floating-point format: base = 2; exponent: biased, 4 bits; significand, 7 bits. What is the relative error?

10.33 If $A = 1.427$, find the relative error if A is truncated to 1.42 and if it is rounded to 1.43.

10.34 When people speak about inaccuracy in floating-point arithmetic, they often ascribe errors to cancellation that occurs during the subtraction of nearly equal quantities.

But when X and Y are approximately equal, the difference $X - Y$ is obtained exactly, with no error. What do these people really mean?

10.35 Numerical values A and B are stored in the computer as approximations A' and B'. Neglecting any further truncation or roundoff errors, show that the relative error of the product is approximately the sum of the relative errors in the factors.

10.36 One of the most serious errors in computer calculations occurs when two nearly equal numbers are subtracted. Consider $A = 0.22288$ and $B = 0.22211$. The computer truncates all values to four decimal digits. Thus $A' = 0.2228$ and $B' = 0.2221$.
   a. What are the relative errors for A' and B'?
   b. What is the relative error for $C' = A' - B'$?

10.37 To get some feel for the effects of denormalization and gradual underflow, consider a decimal system that provides 6 decimal digits for the significand and for which the smallest normalized number is 10^{-99}. A normalized number has one nonzero decimal digit to the left of the decimal point. Perform the following calculations and denormalize the results. Comment on the results.
   a. $(2.50000 \times 10^{-60}) \times (3.50000 \times 10^{-43})$
   b. $(2.50000 \times 10^{-60}) \times (3.50000 \times 10^{-60})$
   c. $(5.67834 \times 10^{-97}) - (5.67812 \times 10^{-97})$

10.38 Show how the following floating-point additions are performed (where significands are truncated to 4 decimal digits). Show the results in normalized form.
   a. $5.566 \times 10^2 + 7.777 \times 10^2$ **b.** $3.344 \times 10^1 + 8.877 \times 10^{-2}$

10.39 Show how the following floating-point subtractions are performed (where significands are truncated to 4 decimal digits). Show the results in normalized form.
   a. $7.744 \times 10^{-3} - 6.666 \times 10^{-3}$ **b.** $8.844 \times 10^{-3} - 2.233 \times 10^{-1}$

10.40 Show how the following floating-point calculations are performed (where significands are truncated to 4 decimal digits). Show the results in normalized form.
   a. $(2.255 \times 10^1) \times (1.234 \times 10^0)$ **b.** $(8.833 \times 10^2) \div (5.555 \times 10^4)$

DIGITAL LOGIC

The operation of the digital computer is based on the storage and processing of binary data. Throughout this book, we have assumed the existence of storage elements that can exist in one of two stable states and of circuits than can operate on binary data under the control of control signals to implement the various computer functions. In this chapter, we suggest how these storage elements and circuits can be implemented in digital logic, specifically with combinational and sequential circuits. The chapter begins with a brief review of Boolean algebra, which is the mathematical foundation of digital logic. Next, the concept of a gate is introduced. Finally, combinational and sequential circuits, which are constructed from **gates**, are described.

11.1 BOOLEAN ALGEBRA

The digital circuitry in digital computers and other digital systems is designed, and its behavior is analyzed, with the use of a mathematical discipline known as **Boolean algebra**. The name is in honor of an English mathematician George Boole, who proposed the basic principles of this algebra in 1854 in his treatise, *An Investigation of the Laws of Thought on Which to Found the Mathematical Theories of Logic and Probabilities.* In 1938, Claude Shannon, a research assistant in the Electrical Engineering Department at M.I.T., suggested that Boolean algebra could be used to solve problems in relay-switching circuit design [SHAN38].[1] Shannon's techniques were subsequently used in the analysis and design of electronic digital circuits. Boolean algebra turns out to be a convenient tool in two areas:

- **Analysis:** It is an economical way of describing the function of digital circuitry.
- **Design:** Given a desired function, Boolean algebra can be applied to develop a simplified implementation of that function.

As with any algebra, Boolean algebra makes use of variables and operations. In this case, the variables and operations are logical variables and operations. Thus, a variable may take on the value 1 (TRUE) or 0 (FALSE). The basic logical operations

---

[1]The paper is available at this book's Web site.

are AND, OR, and NOT, which are symbolically represented by dot, plus sign, and overbar[2]:

$$A \text{ AND } B = A \cdot B$$
$$A \text{ OR } B = A + B$$
$$\text{NOT } A = \overline{A}$$

The operation AND yields true (binary value 1) if and only if both of its operands are true. The operation OR yields true if either or both of its operands are true. The unary operation NOT inverts the value of its operand. For example, consider the equation

$$D = A + (\overline{B} \cdot C)$$

D is equal to 1 if A is 1 or if both B = 0 and C = 1. Otherwise D is equal to 0.

Several points concerning the notation are needed. In the absence of parentheses, the AND operation takes precedence over the OR operation. Also, when no ambiguity will occur, the AND operation is represented by simple concatenation instead of the dot operator. Thus,

$$A + B \cdot C = A + (B \cdot C) = A + BC$$

all mean: Take the AND of B and C; then take the OR of the result and A.

Table 11.1a defines the basic logical operations in a form known as a *truth table,* which lists the value of an operation for every possible combination of values of operands. The table also lists three other useful operators: XOR, NAND, and **NOR**. The exclusive-or (XOR) of two logical operands is 1 if and only if exactly one of the operands has the value 1. The NAND function is the complement (NOT) of the AND function, and the NOR is the complement of OR:

$$A \text{ NAND } B = \text{NOT}(A \text{ AND } B) = \overline{AB}$$
$$A \text{ NOR } B = \text{NOT}(A \text{ OR } B) = \overline{A + B}$$

As we shall see, these three new operations can be useful in implementing certain digital circuits.

The logical operations, with the exception of NOT, can be generalized to more than two variables, as shown in Table 11.1b.

Table 11.2 summarizes key identities of Boolean algebra. The equations have been arranged in two columns to show the complementary, or dual, nature of the AND and OR operations. There are two classes of identities: basic rules (or *postulates*), which are stated without proof, and other identities that can be derived from the basic postulates. The postulates define the way in which Boolean expressions are interpreted. One of the two distributive laws is worth noting because it differs from what we would find in ordinary algebra:

$$A + (B \cdot C) = (A + B) \cdot (A + C)$$

---

[2]Logical NOT is often indicated by an apostrophe: NOT A = A'.

Table 11.1   Boolean Operators

(a) Boolean Operators of Two Input Variables

P	Q	NOT P $(\overline{P})$	P AND Q $(P \cdot Q)$	P OR Q $(P + Q)$	P NAND Q $(\overline{P \cdot Q})$	P NOR Q $(\overline{P + Q})$	P XOR Q $(P \oplus Q)$
0	0	1	0	0	1	1	0
0	1	1	0	1	1	0	1
1	0	0	0	1	1	0	1
1	1	0	1	1	0	0	0

(b) Boolean Operators Extended to More than Two Inputs (A, B, . . .)

Operation	Expression	Output = 1 if
AND	$A \cdot B \cdot \ldots$	All of the set {A, B, ...} are 1.
OR	$A + B + \ldots$	Any of the set {A, B, ...} are 1.
NAND	$\overline{A \cdot B \cdot \ldots}$	Any of the set {A, B, ...} are 0.
NOR	$\overline{A + B + \ldots}$	All of the set {A, B, ...} are 0.
XOR	$A \oplus B \oplus \ldots$	The set {A, B, ...} contains an odd number of ones.

The two bottommost expressions are referred to as DeMorgan's theorem. We can restate them as follows:

$$A \text{ NOR } B = \overline{A} \text{ AND } \overline{B}$$
$$A \text{ NAND } B = \overline{A} \text{ OR } \overline{B}$$

The reader is invited to verify the expressions in Table 11.2 by substituting actual values (1s and 0s) for the variables A, B, and C.

Table 11.2   Basic Identities of Boolean Algebra

Basic Postulates		
$A \cdot B = B \cdot A$	$A + B = B + A$	Commutative Laws
$A \cdot (B + C) = (A \cdot B) + (A \cdot C)$	$A + (B \cdot C) = (A + B) \cdot (A + C)$	Distributive Laws
$1 \cdot A = A$	$0 + A = A$	Identity Elements
$A \cdot \overline{A} = 0$	$A + \overline{A} = 1$	Inverse Elements
Other Identities		
$0 \cdot A = 0$	$1 + A = 1$	
$A \cdot A = A$	$A + A = A$	
$A \cdot (B \cdot C) = (A \cdot B) \cdot C$	$A + (B + C) = (A + B) + C$	Associative Laws
$\overline{A \cdot B} = \overline{A} + \overline{B}$	$\overline{A + B} = \overline{A} \cdot \overline{B}$	DeMorgan's Theorem

11.2 GATES

The fundamental building block of all digital logic circuits is the gate. Logical functions are implemented by the interconnection of gates.

A gate is an electronic circuit that produces an output signal that is a simple Boolean operation on its input signals. The basic gates used in digital logic are AND, OR, NOT, NAND, NOR, and XOR. Figure 11.1 depicts these six gates. Each gate is defined in three ways: graphic symbol, algebraic notation, and truth table. The symbology used in this chapter is from the IEEE standard, IEEE Std 91. Note that the inversion (NOT) operation is indicated by a circle.

Each gate shown in Figure 11.1 has one or two inputs and one output. However, as indicated in Table 11.1b, all of the gates except NOT can have more than two inputs. Thus, $(X + Y + Z)$ can be implemented with a single **OR gate** with three inputs. When one or more of the values at the input are changed, the correct output signal appears almost instantaneously, delayed only by the propagation time of signals through the gate (known as the *gate delay*). The significance of this delay is discussed in Section 11.3. In some cases, a gate is implemented with two outputs, one output being the negation of the other output.

Name	Graphical Symbol	Algebraic Function	Truth Table
AND	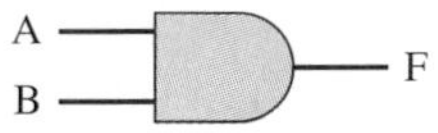 A, B → F	$F = A \cdot B$ or $F = AB$	A B | F 0 0 | 0 0 1 | 0 1 0 | 0 1 1 | 1
OR	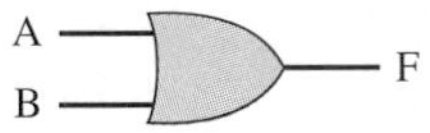 A, B → F	$F = A + B$	A B | F 0 0 | 0 0 1 | 1 1 0 | 1 1 1 | 1
NOT	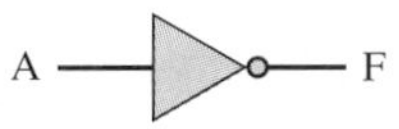 A → F	$F = \overline{A}$ or $F = A'$	A | F 0 | 1 1 | 0
NAND	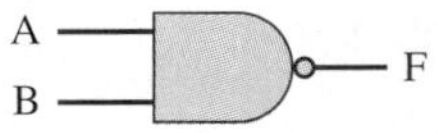 A, B → F	$F = \overline{AB}$	A B | F 0 0 | 1 0 1 | 1 1 0 | 1 1 1 | 0
NOR	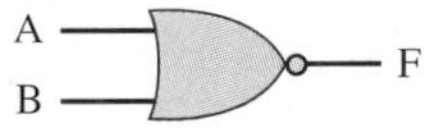 A, B → F	$F = \overline{A + B}$	A B | F 0 0 | 1 0 1 | 0 1 0 | 0 1 1 | 0
XOR	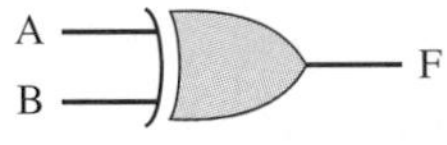 A, B → F	$F = A \oplus B$	A B | F 0 0 | 0 0 1 | 1 1 0 | 1 1 1 | 0

Figure 11.1 Basic Logic Gates

Here we introduce a common term: we say that to **assert** a signal is to cause a signal line to make a transition from its logically false (0) state to its logically true (1) state. The true (1) state is either a high or low voltage state, depending on the type of electronic circuitry.

Typically, not all gate types are used in implementation. Design and fabrication are simpler if only one or two types of gates are used. Thus, it is important to identify *functionally complete* sets of gates. This means that any Boolean function can be implemented using only the gates in the set. The following are functionally complete sets:

- AND, OR, NOT
- AND, NOT
- OR, NOT
- NAND
- NOR

It should be clear that AND, OR, and NOT gates constitute a functionally complete set, because they represent the three operations of Boolean algebra. For the AND and NOT gates to form a functionally complete set, there must be a way to synthesize the OR operation from the AND and NOT operations. This can be done by applying DeMorgan's theorem:

$$A + B = \overline{\overline{A} \cdot \overline{B}}$$

$$A \text{ OR } B = \text{NOT}((\text{NOT } A) \text{ AND } (\text{NOT } B))$$

Similarly, the OR and NOT operations are functionally complete because they can be used to synthesize the AND operation.

Figure 11.2 shows how the AND, OR, and NOT functions can be implemented solely with NAND gates, and Figure 11.3 shows the same thing for NOR gates. For this reason, digital circuits can be, and frequently are, implemented solely with NAND gates or solely with NOR gates.

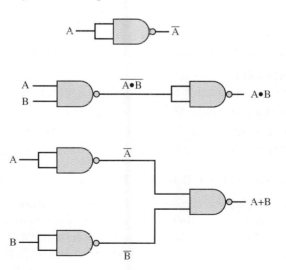

Figure 11.2 Some Uses of NAND Gates

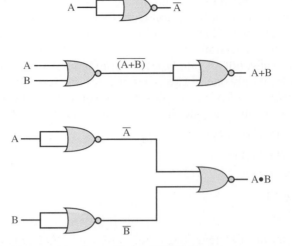

Figure 11.3 Some Uses of NOR Gates

With gates, we have reached the most primitive circuit level of computer hardware. An examination of the transistor combinations used to construct gates departs from that realm and enters the realm of electrical engineering. For our purposes, however, we are content to describe how gates can be used as building blocks to implement the essential logical circuits of a digital computer.

11.3 COMBINATIONAL CIRCUITS

A **combinational circuit** is an interconnected set of gates whose output at any time is a function only of the input at that time. As with a single gate, the appearance of the input is followed almost immediately by the appearance of the output, with only gate delays.

In general terms, a combinational circuit consists of n binary inputs and m binary outputs. As with a gate, a combinational circuit can be defined in three ways:

- **Truth table:** For each of the 2^n possible combinations of input signals, the binary value of each of the m output signals is listed.
- **Graphical symbols:** The interconnected layout of gates is depicted.
- **Boolean equations:** Each output signal is expressed as a Boolean function of its input signals.

Implementation of Boolean Functions

Any Boolean function can be implemented in electronic form as a network of gates. For any given function, there are a number of alternative realizations. Consider the Boolean function represented by the truth table in Table 11.3. We can express this function by simply itemizing the combinations of values of A, B, and C that cause F to be 1:

$$F + \overline{A}B\overline{C} + \overline{A}BC + AB\overline{C} \tag{11.1}$$

Table 11.3   A Boolean Function of Three Variables

A	B	C	F
0	0	0	0
0	0	1	0
0	1	0	1
0	1	1	1
1	0	0	0
1	0	1	0
1	1	0	1
1	1	1	0

There are three combinations of input values that cause F to be 1, and if any one of these combinations occurs, the result is 1. This form of expression, for self-evident reasons, is known as the **sum of products (SOP)** form. Figure 11.4 shows a straightforward implementation with AND, OR, and NOT gates.

Another form can also be derived from the truth table. The SOP form expresses that the output is 1 if any of the input combinations that produce 1 is true. We can also say that the output is 1 if none of the input combinations that produce 0 is true. Thus,

$$F = \overline{(\overline{A}\,\overline{B}\,\overline{C}) \cdot (\overline{A}\,\overline{B}\,C) \cdot (A\,\overline{B}\,\overline{C}) \cdot (A\,\overline{B}\,C) \cdot (A\,B\,C)}$$

This can be rewritten using a generalization of DeMorgan's theorem:

$$\overline{(X \cdot Y \cdot Z)} = \overline{X} - \overline{Y} + \overline{Z}$$

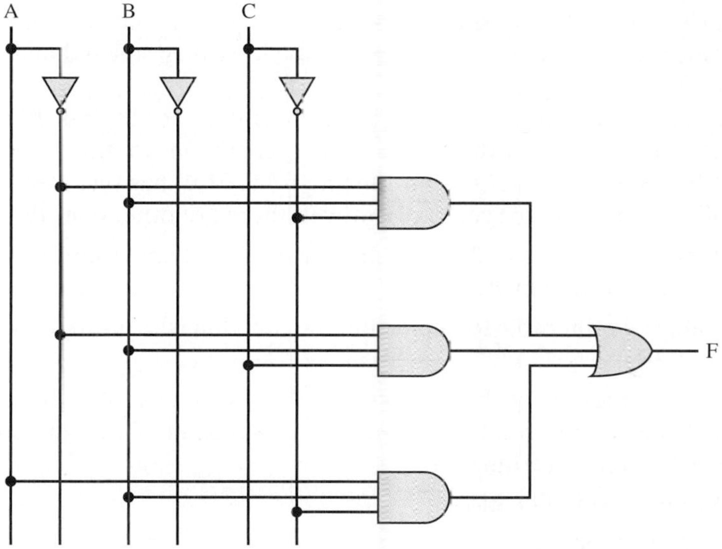

Figure 11.4   Sum-of-Products Implementation of Table 11.3

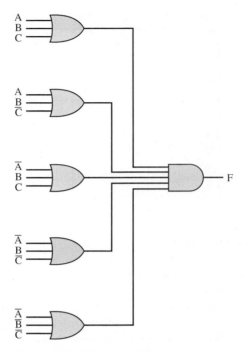

Figure 11.5   Product-of-Sums
Implementation of Table 11.3

Thus,

$$F = (\overline{\overline{A}} + \overline{\overline{B}} + \overline{\overline{C}}) \cdot (\overline{\overline{A}} + \overline{\overline{B}} + \overline{C}) \cdot (\overline{A} + \overline{\overline{B}} + \overline{\overline{C}}) \cdot (\overline{A} + \overline{\overline{B}} + \overline{C}) \cdot (\overline{A} + \overline{B} + \overline{C}) \quad \textbf{(11.2)}$$
$$= (A + B + C) \cdot (A + B + \overline{C}) \cdot (\overline{A} + B + C) \cdot (\overline{A} + B + \overline{C}) \cdot (\overline{A} + \overline{B} + \overline{C})$$

This is in the **product of sums (POS)** form, which is illustrated in Figure 11.5. For clarity, NOT gates are not shown. Rather, it is assumed that each input signal and its complement are available. This simplifies the logic diagram and makes the inputs to the gates more readily apparent.

Thus, a Boolean function can be realized in either SOP or POS form. At this point, it would seem that the choice would depend on whether the truth table contains more 1s or 0s for the output function: The SOP has one term for each 1, and the POS has one term for each 0. However, there are other considerations:

- It is often possible to derive a simpler Boolean expression from the truth table than either SOP or POS.

- It may be preferable to implement the function with a single gate type (NAND or NOR).

The significance of the first point is that, with a simpler Boolean expression, fewer gates will be needed to implement the function. Three methods that can be used to achieve simplification are

- Algebraic simplification
- Karnaugh maps
- Quine–McCluskey tables

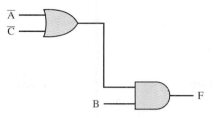

Figure 11.6   Simplified Implementation
of Table A.3

ALGEBRAIC SIMPLIFICATION Algebraic simplification involves the application of
the identities of Table 11.2 to reduce the Boolean expression to one with fewer
elements. For example, consider again Equation (11.1). Some thought should
convince the reader that an equivalent expression is

$$F = \overline{AB} - B\overline{C} \tag{11.3}$$

Or, even simpler,

$$F = B(\overline{A} + \overline{C})$$

This expression can be implemented as shown in Figure 11.6. The simplification
of Equation (11.1) was done essentially by observation. For more complex expressions, some more systematic approach is needed.

KARNAUGH MAPS For purposes of simplification, the **Karnaugh map** is a convenient
way of representing a Boolean function of a small number (up to four) of variables.
The map is an array of 2^n squares, representing all possible combinations of values
of n binary variables. Figure 11.7a shows the map of four squares for a function of
two variables. It is essential for later purposes to list the combinations in the order
00, 01, 11, 10. Because the squares corresponding to the combinations are to be
used for recording information, the combinations are customarily written above the
squares. In the case of three variables, the representation is an arrangement of eight
squares (Figure 11.7b), with the values for one of the variables to the left and for the
other two variables above the squares. For four variables, 16 squares are needed,
with the arrangement indicated in Figure 11.7c.

The map can be used to represent any Boolean function in the following way.
Each square corresponds to a unique product in the sum-of-products form, with a
1 value corresponding to the variable and a 0 value corresponding to the NOT of
that variable. Thus, the product $A\overline{B}$ corresponds to the fourth square in Figure
11.7a. For each such product in the function, 1 is placed in the corresponding square.
Thus, for the two-variable example, the map corresponds to $A\overline{B} + \overline{A}B$. Given the
truth table of a Boolean function, it is an easy matter to construct the map: for each
combination of values of variables that produce a result of 1 in the truth table, fill
in the corresponding square of the map with 1. Figure 11.7b shows the result for
the truth table of Table 11.3. To convert from a Boolean expression to a map, it
is first necessary to put the expression into what is referred to as *canonical* form:
each term in the expression must contain each variable. So, for example, if we have
Equation (11.3), we must first expand it into the full form of Equation (11.1) and
then convert this to a map.

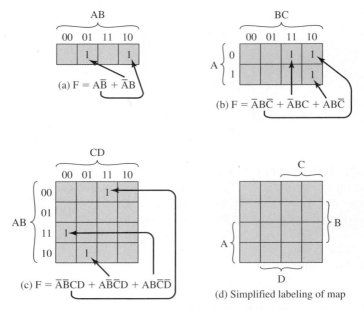

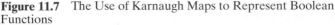

Figure 11.7 The Use of Karnaugh Maps to Represent Boolean Functions

The labeling used in Figure 11.7d emphasizes the relationship between variables and the rows and columns of the map. Here the two rows embraced by the symbol A are those in which the variable A has the value 1; the rows not embraced by the symbol A are those in which A is 0; similarly for B, C, and D.

Once the map of a function is created, we can often write a simple algebraic expression for it by noting the arrangement of the 1s on the map. The principle is as follows. Any two squares that are adjacent differ in only one of the variables. If two adjacent squares both have an entry of one, then the corresponding product terms differ in only one variable. In such a case, the two terms can be merged by eliminating that variable. For example, in Figure 11.8a, the two adjacent squares correspond to the two terms $\overline{A}B\overline{C}D$ and $\overline{A}BCD$. Thus, the function expressed is

$$\overline{A}B\overline{C}D + \overline{A}BCD = \overline{A}BD$$

This process can be extended in several ways. First, the concept of adjacency can be extended to include wrapping around the edge of the map. Thus, the top square of a column is adjacent to the bottom square, and the leftmost square of a row is adjacent to the rightmost square. These conditions are illustrated in Figures 11.8b and c. Second, we can group not just 2 squares but 2^n adjacent squares (i.e., 2, 4, 8, etc.). The next three examples in Figure 11.8 show groupings of 4 squares. Note that in this case, two of the variables can be eliminated. The last three examples show groupings of 8 squares, which allow three variables to be eliminated.

We can summarize the rules for simplification as follows:

1. Among the marked squares (squares with a 1), find those that belong to a unique largest block of 1, 2, 4, or 8 and circle those blocks.

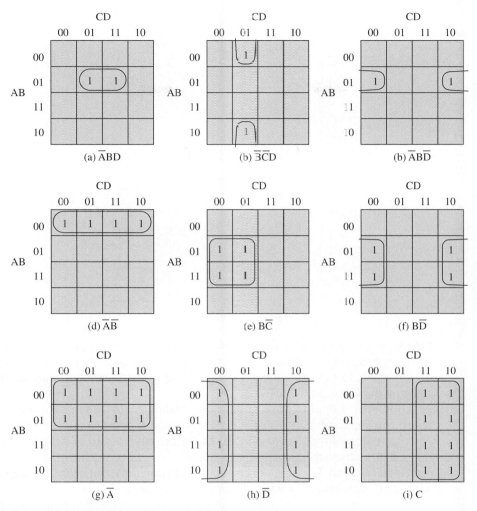

Figure 11.8 The Use of Karnaugh Maps

2. Select additional blocks of marked squares that are as large as possible and as few in number as possible, but include every marked square at least once. The results may not be unique in some cases. For example, if a marked square combines with exactly two other squares, and there is no fourth marked square to complete a larger group, then there is a choice to be made as two which of the two groupings to choose. When you are circling groups, you are allowed to use the same 1 value more than once.

3. Continue to draw loops around single marked squares, or pairs of adjacent marked squares, or groups of four, eight, and so on in such a way that every marked square belongs to at least one loop; then use as few of these blocks as possible to include all marked squares.

Figure 11.9a, based on Table 11.3, illustrates the simplification process. If any isolated 1s remain after the groupings, then each of these is circled as a group of 1s.

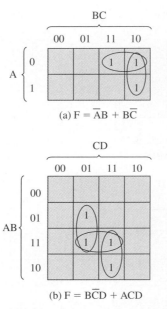

(a) $F = \overline{A}B + B\overline{C}$

(b) $F = B\overline{C}D + ACD$

Figure 11.9   Overlapping Groups

Finally, before going from the map to a simplified Boolean expression, any group of 1s that is completely overlapped by other groups can be eliminated. This is shown in Figure 11.9b. In this case, the horizontal group is redundant and may be ignored in creating the Boolean expression.

One additional feature of Karnaugh maps needs to be mentioned. In some cases, certain combinations of values of variables never occur, and therefore the corresponding output never occurs. These are referred to as "don't care" conditions. For each such condition, the letter "d" is entered into the corresponding square of the map. In doing the grouping and simplification, each "d" can be treated as a 1 or 0, whichever leads to the simplest expression.

An example, presented in [HAYE98], illustrates the points we have been discussing. We would like to develop the Boolean expressions for a circuit that adds 1 to a packed decimal digit. For packed decimal, each decimal digit is represented by a 4-bit code, in the obvious way. Thus, $0 = 0000, 1 = 0001, \ldots, 8 = 1000$, and $9 = 1001$. The remaining 4-bit values, from 1010 to 1111, are not used. This code is also referred to as Binary Coded Decimal (BCD).

Table 11.4 shows the truth table for producing a 4-bit result that is one more than a 4-bit BCD input. The addition is modulo 10. Thus, $9 + 1 = 0$. Also, note that six of the input codes produce "don't care" results, because those are not valid BCD inputs. Figure 11.10 shows the resulting Karnaugh maps for each of the output variables. The d squares are used to achieve the best possible groupings.

THE QUINE–MCCLUSKEY METHOD For more than four variables, the Karnaugh map method becomes increasingly cumbersome. With five variables, two 16×16 maps are needed, with one map considered to be on top of the other in three dimensions to achieve adjacency. Six variables require the use of four 16×16

Table 11.4   Truth Table for the One-Digit Packed Decimal Incrementer

	Input					Output			
Number	**A**	**B**	**C**	**D**	**Number**	**W**	**X**	**Y**	**Z**
0	0	0	0	0	1	0	0	0	1
1	0	0	0	1	2	0	0	1	0
2	0	0	1	0	3	0	0	1	1
3	0	0	1	1	4	0	1	0	0
4	0	1	0	0	5	0	1	0	1
5	0	1	0	1	6	0	1	1	0
6	0	1	1	0	7	0	1	1	1
7	0	1	1	1	8	1	0	0	0
8	1	0	0	0	9	1	0	0	1
9	1	0	0	1	0	0	0	0	0
Don't care condition	1	0	1	0		d	d	d	d
	1	0	1	1		d	d	d	d
	1	1	0	0		d	d	d	d
	1	1	0	1		d	d	d	d
	1	1	1	0		d	d	d	d
	1	1	1	1		d	d	d	d

tables in four dimensions! An alternative approach is a tabular technique, referred to as the Quine–McCluskey method. The method is suitable for programming on a computer to give an automatic tool for producing minimized Boolean expressions.

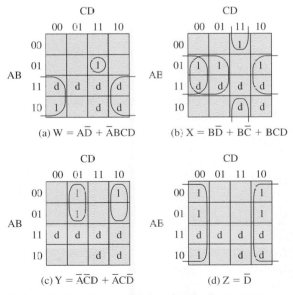

Figure 11.10   Karnaugh Maps for the Incrementer

The method is best explained by means of an example. Consider the following expression:

$$\mathrm{ABCD} + \mathrm{AB\overline{C}D} + \mathrm{AB\overline{C}\overline{D}} + \mathrm{A\overline{B}CD} + \mathrm{\overline{A}BCD} + \mathrm{\overline{A}BC\overline{D}} + \mathrm{\overline{A}B\overline{C}D} + \mathrm{\overline{A}\,\overline{B}CD}$$

Let us assume that this expression was derived from a truth table. We would like to produce a minimal expression suitable for implementation with gates.

The first step is to construct a table in which each row corresponds to one of the product terms of the expression. The terms are grouped according to the number of complemented variables. That is, we start with the term with no complements, if it exists, then all terms with one complement, and so on. Table 11.5 shows the list for our example expression, with horizontal lines used to indicate the grouping. For clarity, each term is represented by a 1 for each uncomplemented variable and a 0 for each complemented variable. Thus, we group terms according to the number of 1s they contain. The index column is simply the decimal equivalent and is useful in what follows.

The next step is to find all pairs of terms that differ in only one variable, that is, all pairs of terms that are the same except that one variable is 0 in one of the terms and 1 in the other. Because of the way in which we have grouped the terms, we can do this by starting with the first group and comparing each term of the first group with every term of the second group. Then compare each term of the second group with all of the terms of the third group, and so on. Whenever a match is found, place a check next to each term, combine the pair by eliminating the variable that differs in the two terms, and add that to a new list. Thus, for example, the terms $\mathrm{\overline{A}BC\overline{D}}$ and $\mathrm{\overline{A}BCD}$ are combined to produce $\mathrm{\overline{A}BC}$. This process continues until the entire original table has been examined. The result is a new table with the following entries:

$\mathrm{\overline{A}\,\overline{C}D}$	$\mathrm{AB\overline{C}}$	$\mathrm{ABD}\;\surd$
	$\mathrm{B\overline{C}D}\;\surd$	ACD
	$\mathrm{\overline{A}BC}$	$\mathrm{BCD}\;\surd$
	$\mathrm{\overline{A}BD}\;\surd$	

Table 11.5 First Stage of **Quine–McCluskey Method**
(for $\mathrm{F} = \mathrm{ABCD} + \mathrm{AB\overline{C}D} + \mathrm{AB\overline{C}\overline{D}} + \mathrm{A\overline{B}CD} + \mathrm{\overline{A}BCD} + \mathrm{\overline{A}BC\overline{D}} + \mathrm{\overline{A}B\overline{C}D} + \mathrm{\overline{A}\,\overline{B}CD}$)

Product Term	Index	A	B	C	D	
$\mathrm{\overline{A}\,\overline{B}CD}$	1	0	0	0	1	✓
$\mathrm{\overline{A}BCD}$	5	0	1	0	1	✓
$\mathrm{\overline{A}BC\overline{D}}$	6	0	1	1	0	✓
$\mathrm{AB\overline{C}\,\overline{D}}$	12	1	1	0	0	✓
$\mathrm{\overline{A}BCD}$	7	0	1	1	1	✓
$\mathrm{A\overline{B}CD}$	11	1	0	1	1	✓
$\mathrm{AB\overline{C}D}$	13	1	1	0	1	✓
ABCD	15	1	1	1	1	✓

The new table is organized into groups, as indicated, in the same fashion as the first table. The second table is then processed in the same manner as the first. That is, terms that differ in only one variable are checked and a new term produced for a third table. In this example, the third table that is produced contains only one term: BD.

In general, the process would proceed through successive tables until a table with no matches was produced. In this case, this has involved three tables.

Once the process just described is completed, we have eliminated many of the possible terms of the expression. Those terms that have not been eliminated are used to construct a matrix, as illustrated in Table 11.6. Each row of the matrix corresponds to one of the terms that have not been eliminated (has no check) in any of the tables used so far. Each column corresponds to one of the terms in the original expression. An X is placed at each intersection of a row and a column such that the row element is "compatible" with the column element. That is, the variables present in the row element have the same value as the variables present in the column element. Next, circle each X that is alone in a column. Then place a square around each X in any row in which there is a circled X. If every column now has either a squared or a circled X, then we are done, and those row elements whose Xs have been marked constitute the minimal expression. Thus, in our example, the final expression is

$$AB\overline{C} + ACD + \overline{A}BC + \overline{A}\,\overline{C}D$$

In cases in which some columns have neither a circle nor a square, additional processing is required. Essentially, we keep adding row elements until all columns are covered.

Let us summarize the Quine–McCluskey method to try to justify intuitively why it works. The first phase of the operation is reasonably straightforward. The process eliminates unneeded variables in product terms. Thus, the expression $ABC + AB\overline{C}$ is equivalent to AB, because

$$ABC + AB\overline{C} = AB(C + \overline{C}) = AB$$

After the elimination of variables, we are left with an expression that is clearly equivalent to the original expression. However, there may be redundant terms in this expression, just as we found redundant groupings in Karnaugh maps. The matrix layout assures that each term in the original expression is covered and does so in a way that minimizes the number of terms in the final expression.

Table 11.6 Last Stage of Quine–McCluskey Method
(for F = ABCD + AB$\overline{C}$D + ABC$\overline{D}$ + A$\overline{B}$CD + $\overline{A}$BCD + $\overline{A}$BC$\overline{D}$ + $\overline{A}$B$\overline{C}$D + $\overline{A}\,\overline{B}$CD)

	ABCD	**AB$\overline{C}$D**	**ABC$\overline{D}$**	**A$\overline{B}$CD**	**$\overline{A}$BCD**	**$\overline{A}$BC$\overline{D}$**	**$\overline{A}$B$\overline{C}$D**	**$\overline{A}\,\overline{B}$CD**
BD	X	X			X		X	
$\overline{A}$CD							[X]	⊗
$\overline{A}$BC					[X]	⊗		
AB$\overline{C}$		[X]	⊗					
ACD	[X]			⊗				

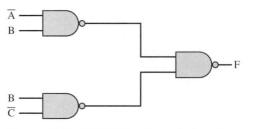

Figure 11.11 NAND Implementation of Table 11.3

NAND AND NOR IMPLEMENTATIONS Another consideration in the implementation of Boolean functions concerns the types of gates used. It is sometimes desirable to implement a Boolean function solely with NAND gates or solely with NOR gates. Although this may not be the minimum-gate implementation, it has the advantage of regularity, which can simplify the manufacturing process. Consider again Equation (11.3):

$$F = B(\overline{A} + \overline{C})$$

Because the complement of the complement of a value is just the original value,

$$F = B(\overline{A} + \overline{C}) = \overline{\overline{(AB + (BC)}}$$

Applying DeMorgan's theorem,

$$F = \overline{(\overline{A}B) \bullet (B\overline{C})}$$

which has three NAND forms, as illustrated in Figure 11.11.

Multiplexers

The **multiplexer** connects multiple inputs to a single output. At any time, one of the inputs is selected to be passed to the output. A general block diagram representation is shown in Figure 11.12. This represents a 4-to-1 multiplexer. There are four input lines, labeled D0, D1, D2, and D3. One of these lines is selected to provide the

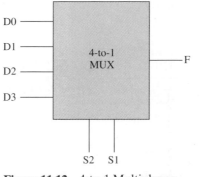

Figure 11.12 4-to-1 Multiplexer Representation

Table 11.7 4-to-1 Multiplexer Truth Table

S2	S1	F
0	C	D0
0	1	D1
1	C	D2
1	1	D3

output signal F. To select one of the four possible inputs, a 2-bit selection code is needed, and this is implemented as two select lines labeled S1 and S2.

An example 4-to-1 multiplexer is defined by the truth table in Table 11.7. This is a simplified form of a truth table. Instead of showing all possible combinations of input variables, it shows the output as data from line D0, D1, D2, or D3. Figure 11.13 shows an implementation using AND, OR, and NOT gates. S1 and S2 are connected to the AND gates in such a way that, for any combination of S1 and S2, three of the AND gates will output 0. The fourth **AND gate** will output the value of the selected line, which is either 0 or 1. Thus, three of the inputs to the OR gate are always 0, and the output of the OR gate will equal the value of the selected input gate. Using this regular organization, it is easy to construct multiplexers of size 8-to-1, 16-to-1, and so on.

Multiplexers are used in digital circuits to control signal and data routing. An example is the loading of the program **counter** (PC). The value to be loaded into the program counter may come from one of several different sources:

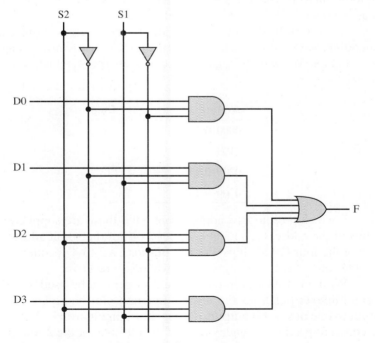

Figure 11.13 Multiplexer Implementation

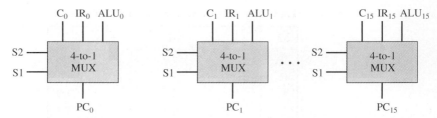

Figure 11.14   Multiplexer Input to Program Counter

- A binary counter, if the PC is to be incremented for the next instruction
- The instruction **register**, if a branch instruction using a direct address has just been executed
- The output of the ALU, if the branch instruction specifies the address using a displacement mode

These various inputs could be connected to the input lines of a multiplexer, with the PC connected to the output line. The select lines determine which value is loaded into the PC. Because the PC contains multiple bits, multiple multiplexers are used, one per bit. Figure 11.14 illustrates this for 16-bit addresses.

Decoders

A **decoder** is a combinational circuit with a number of output lines, only one of which is asserted at any time. Which output line is asserted depends on the pattern of input lines. In general, a decoder has n inputs and 2^n outputs. Figure 11.15 shows a decoder with three inputs and eight outputs.

Decoders find many uses in digital computers. One example is address decoding. Suppose we wish to construct a 1K-byte memory using four 256×8–bit RAM chips. We want a single unified address space, which can be broken down as follows:

Address	Chip
0000–00FF	0
0100–01FF	1
0200–02FF	2
0300–03FF	3

Each chip requires 8 address lines, and these are supplied by the lower-order 8 bits of the address. The higher-order 2 bits of the 10-bit address are used to select one of the four RAM chips. For this purpose, a 2-to-4 decoder is used whose output enables one of the four chips, as shown in Figure 11.16.

With an additional input line, a decoder can be used as a demultiplexer. The demultiplexer performs the inverse function of a multiplexer; it connects a single input to one of several outputs. This is shown in Figure 11.17. As before, n inputs are decoded to produce a single one of 2^n outputs. All of the 2^n output lines are ANDed

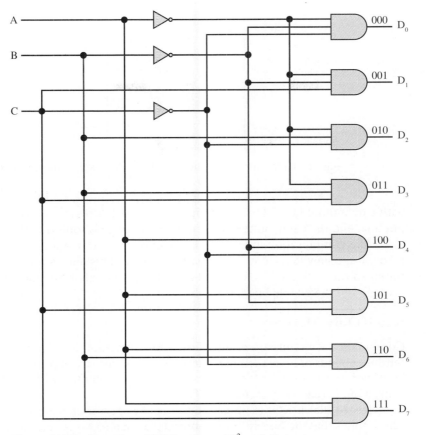

Figure 11.15   Decoder with 3 Inputs and $2^3 = 8$ Outputs

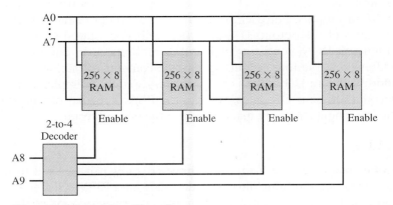

Figure 11.16   Address Decoding

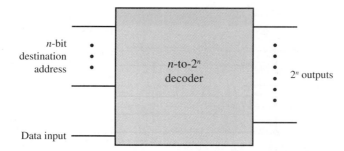

Figure 11.17 Implementation of a Demultiplexer Using a Decoder

with a data input line. Thus, the n inputs act as an address to select a particular output line, and the value on the data input line (0 or 1) is routed to that output line.

The configuration in Figure 11.17 can be viewed in another way. Change the label on the new line from *Data Input* to *Enable*. This allows for the control of the timing of the decoder. The decoded output appears only when the encoded input is present *and* the enable line has a value of 1.

Read-Only Memory

Combinational circuits are often referred to as "memoryless" circuits, because their output depends only on their current input and no history of prior inputs is retained. However, there is one sort of memory that is implemented with combinational circuits, namely **read-only memory (ROM)**.

Recall that a ROM is a memory unit that performs only the read operation. This implies that the binary information stored in a ROM is permanent and was created during the fabrication process. Thus, a given input to the ROM (address lines) always produces the same output (data lines). Because the outputs are a function only of the present inputs, the ROM is in fact a combinational circuit.

A ROM can be implemented with a decoder and a set of OR gates. As an example, consider Table 11.8. This can be viewed as a truth table with four inputs and four outputs. For each of the 16 possible input values, the corresponding set of values of the outputs is shown. It can also be viewed as defining the contents of a 64-bit ROM consisting of 16 words of 4 bits each. The four inputs specify an address, and the four outputs specify the contents of the location specified by the address. Figure 11.18 shows how this memory could be implemented using a 4-to-16 decoder and four OR gates. As with the PLA, a regular organization is used, and the interconnections are made to reflect the desired result.

Adders

So far, we have seen how interconnected gates can be used to implement such functions as the routing of signals, decoding, and ROM. One essential area not yet addressed is that of arithmetic. In this brief overview, we will content ourselves with looking at the addition function.

Binary addition differs from Boolean algebra in that the result includes a carry term. Thus,

Table 11.8 Truth Table for a ROM

Input				Output			
X_1	X_2	X_3	X_4	Z_1	Z_2	Z_3	Z_4
0	0	0	0	0	0	0	0
0	0	0	1	0	0	0	1
0	0	1	0	0	0	1	1
0	0	1	1	0	0	1	0
0	1	0	0	0	1	1	0
0	1	0	1	0	1	1	1
0	1	1	0	0	1	0	1
0	1	1	1	0	1	0	0
1	0	0	0	1	1	0	0
1	0	0	1	1	1	0	1
1	0	1	0	1	1	1	1
1	0	1	1	1	1	1	0
1	1	0	0	1	0	1	0
1	1	0	1	1	0	1	1
1	1	1	0	1	0	0	1
1	1	1	1	1	0	0	0

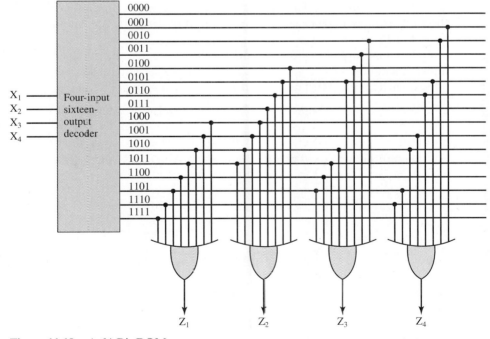

Figure 11.18 A 64-Bit ROM

Table 11.9 Binary Addition Truth Tables

(a) Single-Bit Addition			
A	B	Sum	Carry
0	0	0	0
0	1	1	0
1	0	1	0
1	1	0	1

(b) Addition with Carry Input				
C_{in}	A	B	Sum	C_{out}
0	0	0	0	0
0	0	1	1	0
0	1	0	1	0
0	1	1	0	1
1	0	0	1	0
1	0	1	0	1
1	1	0	0	1
1	1	1	1	1

0	0	1	1
+0	+1	+0	+1
0	1	1	10

However, addition can still be dealt with in Boolean terms. In Table 11.9a, we show the logic for adding two input bits to produce a 1-bit sum and a carry bit. This truth table could easily be implemented in digital logic. However, we are not interested in performing addition on just a single pair of bits. Rather, we wish to add two n-bit numbers. This can be done by putting together a set of adders so that the carry from one **adder** is provided as input to the next. A 4-bit adder is depicted in Figure 11.19.

For a multiple-bit adder to work, each of the single-bit adders must have three inputs, including the carry from the next-lower-order adder. The revised truth table appears in Table 11.9b. The two outputs can be expressed:

$$\text{Sum} = \overline{A}\,\overline{B}C + \overline{A}B\overline{C} + ABC + A\overline{B}\,\overline{C}$$

$$\text{Carry} = AB + AC + BC$$

Figure 11.20 is an implementation using AND, OR, and NOT gates.

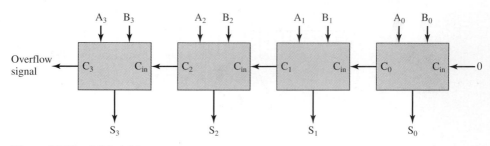

Figure 11.19 4-Bit Adder

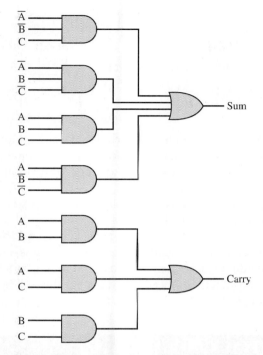

Figure 11.20 Implementation of an Adder

Thus we have the necessary logic to implement a multiple-bit adder such as shown in Figure 11.21. Note that because the output from each adder depends on the carry from the previous adder, there is an increasing delay from the least significant to the most significant bit. Each single-bit adder experiences a certain amount of gate delay, and this gate delay accumulates. For larger adders, the accumulated delay can become unacceptably high.

If the carry values could be determined without having to ripple through all the previous stages, then each single-bit adder could function independently, and delay would not accumulate. This can be achieved with an approach known as *carry lookahead*. Let us look again at the 4-bit adder to explain this approach.

We would like to come up with an expression that specifies the carry input to any stage of the adder without reference to previous carry values. We have

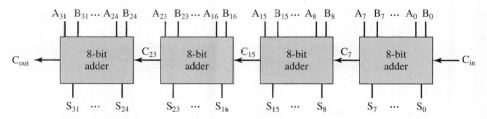

Figure 11.21 Construction of a 32-Bit Adder Using 8-Bit Adders

$$C_0 = A_0 B_0 \qquad\qquad (11.4)$$

$$C_1 = A_1 B_1 + A_1 A_0 B_0 + B_1 A_0 B_0 \qquad\qquad (11.5)$$

Following the same procedure, we get

$$C_2 = A_2 B_2 + A_2 A_1 B_1 + A_2 A_1 A_0 B_0 + A_2 B_1 A_0 B_0 + B_2 A_1 B_1$$
$$+ B_2 A_1 A_0 B_0 + B_2 B_1 A_0 B_0$$

This process can be repeated for arbitrarily long adders. Each carry term can be expressed in SOP form as a function only of the original inputs, with no dependence on the carries. Thus, only two levels of gate delay occur regardless of the length of the adder.

For long numbers, this approach becomes excessively complicated. Evaluating the expression for the most significant bit of an n-bit adder requires an OR gate with $2^n - 1$ inputs and $2^n - 1$ AND gates with from 2 to $n + 1$ inputs. Accordingly, full carry lookahead is typically done only 4 to 8 bits at a time. Figure 11.21 shows how a 32-bit adder can be constructed out of four 8-bit adders. In this case, the carry must ripple through the four 8-bit adders, but this will be substantially quicker than a ripple through thirty-two 1-bit adders.

11.4 SEQUENTIAL CIRCUITS

Combinational circuits implement the essential functions of a digital computer. However, except for the special case of ROM, they provide no memory or state information, elements also essential to the operation of a digital computer. For the latter purposes, a more complex form of digital logic circuit is used: the **sequential circuit**. The current output of a sequential circuit depends not only on the current input, but also on the past history of inputs. Another and generally more useful way to view it is that the current output of a sequential circuit depends on the current input and the current state of that circuit.

In this section, we examine some simple but useful examples of sequential circuits. As will be seen, the sequential circuit makes use of combinational circuits.

Flip-Flops

The simplest form of sequential circuit is the **flip-flop**. There are a variety of flip-flops, all of which share two properties:

- The flip-flop is a bistable device. It exists in one of two states and, in the absence of input, remains in that state. Thus, the flip-flop can function as a 1-bit memory.
- The flip-flop has two outputs, which are always the complements of each other. These are generally labeled Q and $\overline{Q}$.

THE S–R LATCH Figure 11.22 shows a common configuration known as the S–R flip-flop or **S–R latch**. The circuit has two inputs, S (Set) and R (Reset), and two outputs, Q and $\overline{Q}$, and consists of two NOR gates connected in a feedback arrangement.

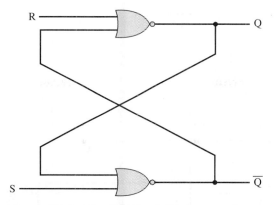

Figure 11.22 The S–R Latch Implemented with NOR Gates

First, let us show that the circuit is bistable. Assume that both S and R are 0 and that Q is 0. The inputs to the lower NOR gate are Q = 0 and S = 0. Thus, the output $\overline{Q}$ = 1 means that the inputs to the upper NOR gate are $\overline{Q}$ = 1 and R = 0, which has the output Q = 0. Thus, the state of the circuit is internally consistent and remains stable as long as S = R = 0. A similar line of reasoning shows that the state Q = 1, $\overline{Q}$ = 0 is also stable for R = S = 0.

Thus, this circuit can function as a 1-bit memory. We can view the output Q as the "value" of the bit. The inputs S and R serve to write the values 1 and 0, respectively, into memory. To see this, consider the state Q = 0, $\overline{Q}$ = 1, S = 0, R = 0. Suppose that S changes to the value 1. Now the inputs to the lower NOR gate are S = 1, Q = 0. After some time delay $\triangle t$, the output of the lower NOR gate will be $\overline{Q}$ = 0 (see Figure 11.23). So, at this point in time, the inputs to the upper NOR gate become R = 0, $\overline{Q}$ = 0. After another gate delay of $\triangle t$ the output Q becomes 1. This is again a stable state. The inputs to the lower gate are now S = 1, Q = 1, which maintain the output $\overline{Q}$ = 0. As long as S = 1 and R = 0, the outputs will remain Q = 1, $\overline{Q}$ = 0. Furthermore, if S returns to 0, the outputs will remain unchanged.

The R output performs the opposite function. When R goes to 1, it forces Q = 0, $\overline{Q}$ = 1 regardless of the previous state of Q and $\overline{Q}$. Again, a time delay of $2\triangle t$ occurs before the final state is established (Figure 11.23).

The S–R latch can be defined with a table similar to a truth table, called a *characteristic table*, which shows the next state or states of a sequential circuit as a function of current states and inputs. In the case of the S–R latch, the state can be defined by the value of Q. Table 11.10a shows the resulting characteristic table. Observe that the inputs S = 1, R = 1 are not allowed, because these would produce an inconsistent output (both Q and $\overline{Q}$ equal 0). The table can be expressed more compactly, as in Table 11.10b. An illustration of the behavior of the S–R latch is shown in Table 11.10c.

CLOCKED S–R FLIP–FLOP The output of the S–R latch changes, after a brief time delay, in response to a change in the input. This is referred to as asynchronous operation. More typically, events in the digital computer are synchronized to a clock pulse, so that changes occur only when a clock pulse occurs. Figure 11.24 shows this

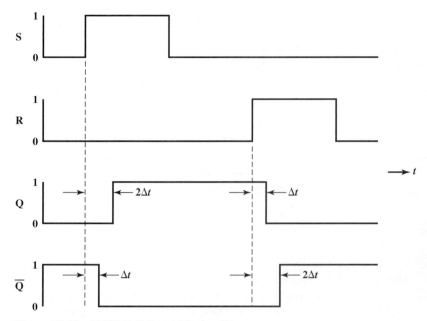

Figure 11.23 NOR S–R Latch Timing Diagram

Table 11.10 The S–R Latch

(a) Characteristic Table				(b) Simplified Characteristic Table		
Current Inputs	**Current State**	**Next State**		**S**	**R**	**Q_{n+1}**
SR	Q_n	Q_{n+1}		0	0	Q_n
00	0	0		0	1	0
00	1	1		1	0	1
01	0	0		1	1	—
01	1	0				
10	0	1				
10	1	1				
11	0	—				
11	1	—				

(c) Response to Series of Inputs										
t	0	1	2	3	4	5	6	7	8	9
S	1	0	0	0	0	0	0	0	1	0
R	0	0	0	1	0	0	1	0	0	0
Q_{n+1}	1	1	1	0	0	0	0	0	1	1

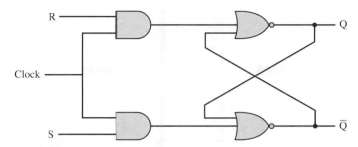

Figure 11.24 Clocked S–R Flip-Flop

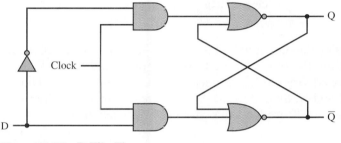

Figure 11.25 D Flip-Flop

arrangement. This device is referred to as a **clocked S–R flip-flop**. Note that the R and S inputs are passed to the NOR gates only during the clock pulse.

D FLIP-FLOP One problem with S–R flip-flop is that the condition $R = 1, S = 1$ must be avoided. One way to do this is to allow just a single input. The **D flip-flop** accomplishes this. Figure 11.25 shows a gate implementation of the D flip-flop. By using an inverter, the nonclock inputs to the two AND gates are guaranteed to be the opposite of each other.

The D flip-flop is sometimes referred to as the data flip-flop because it is, in effect, storage for one bit of data. The output of the D flip-flop is always equal to the most recent value applied to the input. Hence, it remembers and produces the last input. It is also referred to as the delay flip-flop, because it delays a 0 or 1 applied to its input for a single clock pulse. We can capture the logic of the D flip-flop in the following truth table:

D	Q_{n+1}
0	0
1	1

J–K FLIP-FLOP Another useful flip-flop is the **J–K flip-flop**. Like the S–R flip-flop, it has two inputs. However, in this case all possible combinations of input values are valid. Figure 11.26 shows a gate implementation of the J–K flip-flop, and Figure 11.27 shows its characteristic table (along with those for the S–R and D flip-flops). Note that the first three combinations are the same as for the S–R flip-flop. With no input asserted, the output is stable. If only the J input is asserted, the result is a set function,

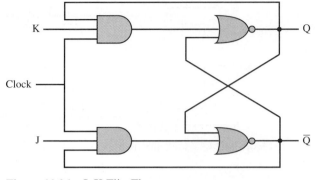

Figure 11.26 J–K Flip-Flop

causing the output to be 1; if only the K input is asserted, the result is a reset function, causing the output to be 0. When both J and K are 1, the function performed is referred to as the toggle function: the output is reversed. Thus, if Q is 1 and 1 is applied to J and K, then Q becomes 0. The reader should verify that the implementation of Figure 11.26 produces this characteristic function.

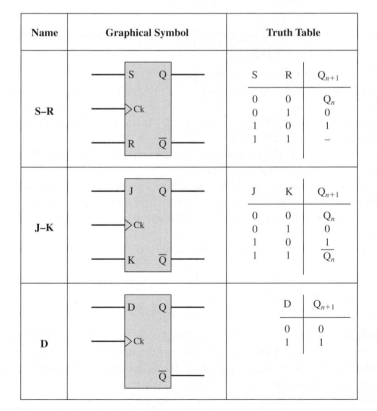

Figure 11.27 Basic Flip-Flops

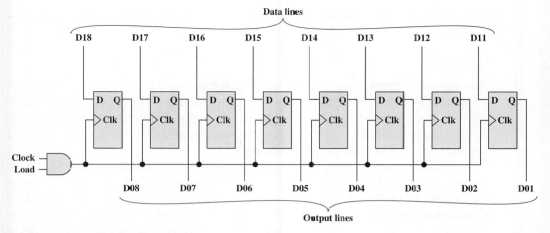

Figure 11.28 8-Bit Parallel Register

Registers

As an example of the use of flip-flops, let us first examine one of the essential elements of the CPU: the register. As we know, a register is a digital circuit used within the CPU to store one or more bits of data. Two basic types of registers are commonly used: parallel registers and shift registers.

PARALLEL REGISTERS A **parallel register** consists of a set of 1-bit memories that can be read or written simultaneously. It is used to store data. The registers that we have discussed throughout this book are parallel registers.

The 8-bit register of Figure 11.28 illustrates the operation of a parallel register using D flip-flops. A control signal, labeled *load*, controls writing into the register from signal lines, D11 through D18. These lines might be the output of multiplexers, so that data from a variety of sources can be loaded into the register.

SHIFT REGISTER A **shift register** accepts and/or transfers information serially. Consider, for example, Figure 11.29, which shows a 5-bit shift register constructed from clocked D flip-flops. Data are input only to the leftmost flip-flop. With each clock pulse, data are shifted to the right one position, and the rightmost bit is transferred out.

Shift registers can be used to interface to serial I/O devices. In addition, they can be used within the ALU to perform logical shift and rotate functions. In this

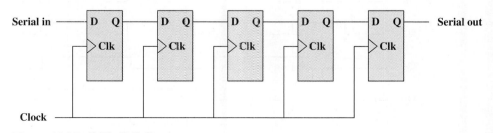

Figure 11.29 5-Bit Shift Register

latter capacity, they need to be equipped with parallel read/write circuitry as well as serial.

Counters

Another useful category of sequential circuit is the counter. A counter is a register whose value is easily incremented by 1 modulo the capacity of the register; that is, after the maximum value is achieved the next increment sets the counter value to 0. Thus, a register made up of n flip-flops can count up to $2^n - 1$. An example of a counter in the CPU is the program counter.

Counters can be designated as asynchronous or synchronous, depending on the way in which they operate. Asynchronous counters are relatively slow because the output of one flip-flop triggers a change in the status of the next flip-flop. In a **synchronous counter**, all of the flip-flops change state at the same time. Because the latter type is much faster, it is the kind used in CPUs. However, it is useful to begin the discussion with a description of an asynchronous counter.

RIPPLE COUNTER An asynchronous counter is also referred to as a **ripple counter**, because the change that occurs to increment the counter starts at one end and "ripples" through to the other end. Figure 11.30 shows an implementation of a 4-bit counter using J–K flip-flops, together with a timing diagram that illustrates its behavior. The timing diagram is idealized in that it does not show the propagation delay that occurs as the signals move down the series of flip-flops. The output of the leftmost flip-flop (Q_0) is the least significant bit. The design could clearly be extended to an arbitrary number of bits by cascading more flip-flops.

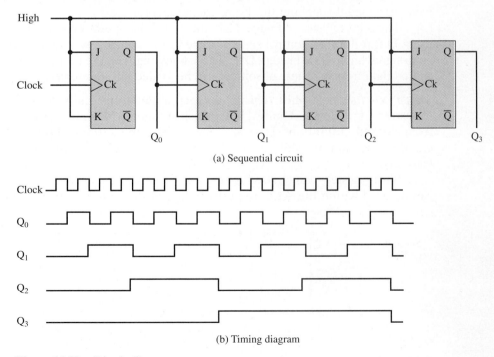

(a) Sequential circuit

(b) Timing diagram

Figure 11.30 Ripple Counter

In the illustrated implementation, the counter is incremented with each clock pulse. The J and K inputs to each flip-flop are held at a constant 1. This means that, when there is a clock pulse, the output at Q will be inverted (1 to 0; 0 to 1). Note that the change in state is shown as occurring with the falling edge of the clock pulse; this is known as an edge-triggered flip-flop. Using flip-flops that respond to the transition in a clock pulse rather than the pulse itself provides better timing control in complex circuits. If one looks at patterns of output for this counter, it can be seen that it cycles through 0000, 0001, ..., 1110. 1111, 0000, and so on.

SYNCHRONOUS COUNTERS The ripple counter has the disadvantage of the delay involved in changing value, which is proportional to the length of the counter. To overcome this disadvantage, CPUs make use of synchronous counters, in which all of the flip-flops of the counter change at the same time. In this subsection, we present a design for a 3-bit synchronous counter. In doing so, we illustrate some basic concepts in the design of a synchronous circuit.

For a 3-bit counter, three flip-flops will be needed. Let us use J–K flip-flops. Label the uncomplemented output of the three flip-flops A, B, and C, respectively, with C representing the least significant bit. The first step is to construct a truth table that relates the J–K inputs and outputs, to allow us to design the overall circuit. Such a truth table is shown in Figure 11.31a. The first three columns show the possible combinations of outputs A, B, and C. They are listed in the order that they will appear as the counter is incremented. Each row lists the current value of A, B, C and the inputs to the three flip-flops that will be required to reach the next value of A, B, C.

To understand the way in which the truth table of Figure 11.31a is constructed, it may be helpful to recast the characteristic table for the J–K flip-flop. Recall that this table was presented as follows:

J	K	Q_{n+1}
0	0	Q_n
0	1	0
1	0	1
1	1	Q_{n+1}

In this form, the table shows the effect that the J and K inputs have on the output. Now consider the following organization of the same information:

Q_n	J	K	Q_{n+1}
0	0	d	0
0	1	d	1
1	d	1	0
1	d	0	1

In this form, the table provides the value of the next output when the inputs and the present output are known. This is exactly the information needed to design the counter or, indeed, any sequential circuit. In this form, the table is referred to as an **excitation table**.

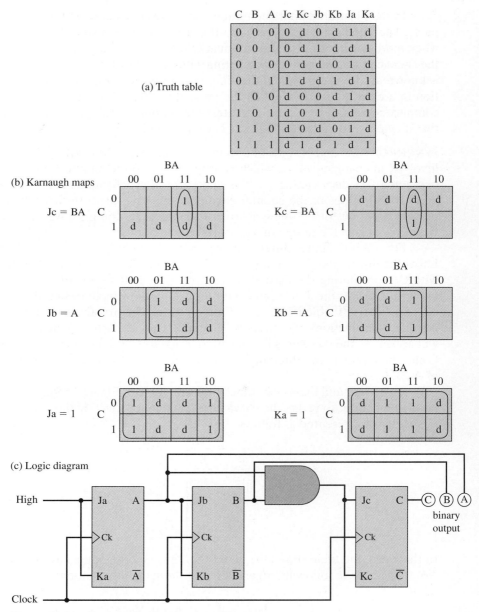

Figure 11.31 Design of a Synchronous Counter

Let us return to Figure 11.31a. Consider the first row. We want the value of A to remain 0, the value of B to remain 0, and the value of C to go from 0 to 1 with the next application of a clock pulse. The excitation table shows that to maintain an output of 0, we must have inputs of $J = 0$ and don't care for K. To effect a transition from 0 to 1, the inputs must be $J = 1$ and $K = d$. These values are shown in the first row of the table. By similar reasoning, the remainder of the table can be filled in.

Having constructed the truth table of Figure 11.31a, we see that the table shows the required values of all of the J and K inputs as functions of the current values of A, B, and C. With the aid of Karnaugh maps, we can develop Boolean expressions for these six functions. This is shown in part b of the figure. For example, the Karnaugh map for the variable Ja (the J input to the flip-flop that produces the A output) yields the expression Ja = BC. When all six expressions are derived, it is a straightforward matter to design the actual circuit, as shown in part c of the figure.

11.5 PROGRAMMABLE LOGIC DEVICES

Thus far, we have treated individual gates as building blocks, from which arbitrary functions can be realized. The designer could pursue a strategy of minimizing the number of gates to be used by manipulating the corresponding Boolean expressions.

As the level of integration provided by integrated circuits increases, other considerations apply. Early integrated circuits, using small-scale integration (SSI), provided from one to ten gates on a chip. Each gate is treated independently, in the building-block approach described so far. To construct a logic function, a number of these chips are laid out on a printed circuit board and the appropriate pin interconnections are made.

Increasing levels of integration made it possible to put more gates on a chip and to make gate interconnections on the chip as well. This yields the advantages of decreased cost, decreased size, and increased speed (because on-chip delays are of shorter duration than off-chip delays). A design problem arises, however. For each particular logic function or set of functions, the layout of gates and interconnections on the chip must be designed. The cost and time involved in such custom chip design is high. Thus, it becomes attractive to develop a general-purpose chip that can be readily adapted to specific purposes. This is the intent of the *programmable logic device* (PLD).

There are a number of different types of PLDs in commercial use. Table 11.11 lists some of the key terms and defines some of the most important types. In this section, we first look at one of the simplest such devices, the programmable logic array (PLA) and then introduce perhaps the most important and widely used type of PLD, the field-programmable gate array (FPGA).

Programmable Logic Array

The PLA is based on the fact that any Boolean function (truth table) can be expressed in a sum-of-products (SOP) form, as we have seen. The PLA consists of a regular arrangement of NOT, AND, and OR gates on a chip. Each chip input is passed through a NOT gate so that each input and its complement are available to each AND gate. The output of each AND gate is available to each OR gate, and the output of each OR gate is a chip output. By making the appropriate connections, arbitrary SOP expressions can be implemented.

Figure 11.32a shows a PLA with three inputs, eight gates, and two outputs. On the left is a programmable AND array. The AND array is programmed by establishing a connection between any PLA input or its negation and any AND gate input by connecting the corresponding lines at their point of intersection. On the

Table 11.11 PLD Terminology

Programmable Logic Device (PLD)

A general term that refers to any type of integrated circuit used for implementing digital hardware, where the chip can be configured by the end user to realize different designs. Programming of such a device often involves placing the chip into a special programming unit, but some chips can also be configured "in-system." Also referred to as a field-programmable device (FPD).

Programmable Logic Array (PLA)

A relatively small PLD that contains two levels of logic, an AND-plane and an OR-plane, where both levels are programmable.

Programmable Array Logic (PAL)

A relatively small PLD that has a programmable AND-plane followed by a fixed OR-plane.

Simple PLD (SPLD)

A PLA or PAL.

Complex PLD (CPLD)

A more complex PLD that consists of an arrangement of multiple SPLD-like blocks on a single chip.

Field-Programmable Gate Array (FPGA)

A PLD featuring a general structure that allows very high logic capacity. Whereas CPLDs feature logic resources with a wide number of inputs (AND planes), FPGAs offer more narrow logic resources. FPGAs also offer a higher ratio of flip-flops to logic resources than do CPLDs.

Logic Block

A relatively small circuit block that is replicated in an array in an FPD. When a circuit is implemented in an FPD, it is first decomposed into smaller subcircuits that can each be mapped into a logic block. The term *logic block* is mostly used in the context of FPGAs, but it could also refer to a block of circuitry in a CPLD.

---

right is a programmable OR array, which involves connecting AND gate outputs to OR gate inputs. Most larger PLAs contain several hundred gates, 15 to 25 inputs, and 5 to 15 outputs. The connections from the inputs to the AND gates, and from the AND gates to the OR gates, are not specified until programming time.

PLAs are manufactured in two different ways to allow easy programming (making of connections). In the first, every possible connection is made through a fuse at every intersection point. The undesired connections can then be later removed by blowing the fuses. This type of PLA is referred to as a *field-programmable logic array*. Alternatively, the proper connections can be made during chip fabrication by using an appropriate mask supplied for a particular interconnection pattern. In either case, the PLA provides a flexible, inexpensive way of implementing digital logic functions.

Figure 11.32b shows a programmed PLA that realizes two Boolean expressions.

Field–Programmable Gate Array

The PLA is an example of a simple PLD (SPLD). The difficulty with increasing capacity of a strict SPLD architecture is that the structure of the programmable logic-planes grows too quickly in size as the number of inputs is increased. The only feasible way to provide large capacity devices based on SPLD architectures is then to integrate multiple SPLDs onto a single chip and provide interconnect to programmably connect the SPLD blocks together. Many commercial PLD products

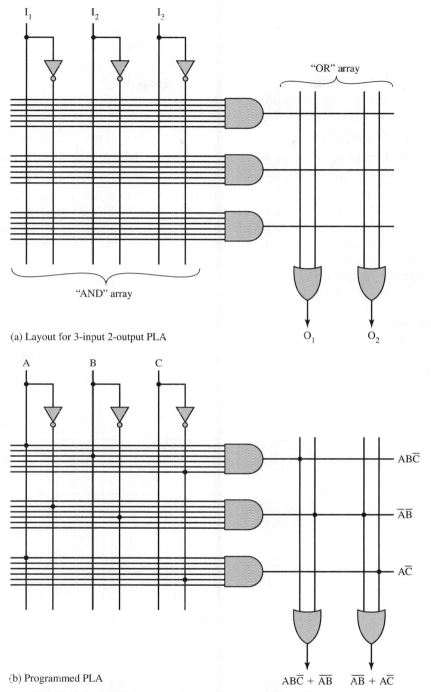

(a) Layout for 3-input 2-output PLA

(b) Programmed PLA

Figure 11.32   An Example of a Programmable Logic Array

exist on the market today with this basic structure, and are collectively referred to as Complex PLDs (CPLDs). The most important type of CPLD is the FPGA.

An FPGA consists of an array of uncommitted circuit elements, called **logic blocks**, and interconnect resources. An illustration of a typical FPGA architecture is shown in Figure 11.33. The key components of an FPGA are;

- **Logic block:** The configurable logic blocks are where the computation of the user's circuit takes place.
- **I/O block:** The I/O blocks connect I/O pins to the circuitry on the chip.
- **Interconnect:** These are signal paths available for establishing connections among I/O blocks and logic blocks.

The logic block can be either a combinational circuit or a sequential circuit. In essence, the programming of a logic block is done by downloading the contents of a truth table for a logic function. Figure 11.34 shows an example of a simple logic block consisting of a D flip-flop, a 2-to-1 multiplexer, and a 16-bit **lookup table**. The lookup table is a memory consisting of 16 1-bit elements, so that 4 input lines are required to select one of the 16 bits. Larger logic blocks have larger lookup tables and multiple interconnected lookup tables. The combinational logic realized by the lookup table can be output directly or stored in the D flip-flop and output synchronously. A separate one-bit memory controls the multiplexer to determine whether the output comes directly from the lookup table or from the flip-flop.

By interconnecting numerous logic blocks, very complex logic functions can be easily implemented.

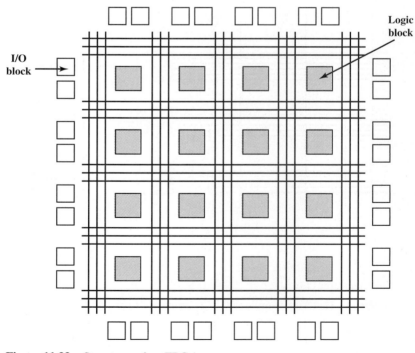

Figure 11.33   Structure of an FPGA

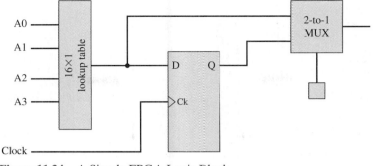

Figure 11.34 A Simple FPGA Logic Block

11.6 RECOMMENDED READING

[GREG98] is an easy-to-read introduction to the concepts of this chapter. [STON96] is an excellent short introduction. A number of textbooks provide more in-depth treatment; these include [MANO08] and [FARH04].

[BROW96] is a worthwhile tutorial on programmable logic devices. [LEON08] looks at recent developments in FPGA devices, platforms, and applications.

BROW96 Brown, S., and Rose, S. "Architecture of FPGAs and CPLDs: A Tutorial." *IEEE Design and Test of Computers*, Vol. 13, No. 2, 1996.

FARH04 Farhat, H. *Digital Design and Computer Organization.* Boca Rato, FL CRC Press, 2004.

GREG98 Gregg, J. *Ones and Zeros: Understanding Boolean Algebra, Digital Circuits, and the Logic of Sets.* New York: Wiley, 1998.

LEON08 Leong, p. "Recent Trends in FPGA Architectures and Applications." *Proceedings, 4th IEEE International symposium on Electronic Design, Test, and Applications*, 2008.

MANO08 Mano, M., and Kime, C. *Logic and Computer Design Fundamentals.* Upper Saddle River, NJ: Prentice Hall, 2008.

STON96 Stonham, T. *Digital Logic Techniques.* London: Chapman & Hall, 1996.

11.7 KEY TERMS AND PROBLEMS

Key Terms

adder	combinational circuit	excitation table
AND gate	complex PLD (CPLD)	field-programmable gate
assert	counter	array (FPGA)
Boolean algebra	decoder	flip-flop
clocked S–R flip-flop	D flip-flop	gates

graphical symbol	product of sums (POS)	ripple counter
J–K flip-flop	programmable array logic	sequential circuit
Karnaugh map	(PAL)	shift register
logic block	programmable logic array	simple PLD (SPLD)
lookup table	(PLA)	sum of products (SOP)
multiplexer	programmable logic device	synchronous counter
NAND gate	(PLD)	S–R Latch
NOR	Quine–McCluskey method	truth table
OR gate	read-only memory (ROM)	XOR gate
parallel register	register	

Problems

11.1 Construct a truth table for the following Boolean expressions:
  a. $ABC + \overline{A}\,\overline{B}\,\overline{C}$
  b. $ABC + A\,\overline{B}\,\overline{C} + \overline{A}\,\overline{B}\,\overline{C}$
  c. $A(B\overline{C} + \overline{B}C)$
  d. $(A + B)(A + C)(\overline{A} + \overline{B})$

11.2 Simplify the following expressions according to the commutative law:
  a. $A \cdot \overline{B} + \overline{B} \cdot A + C \cdot D \cdot E + \overline{C} \cdot D \cdot E + E \cdot \overline{C} \cdot D$
  b. $A \cdot B + A \cdot C + B \cdot A$
  c. $(L \cdot M \cdot N)(A \cdot B)(C \cdot D \cdot E)(M \cdot N \cdot L)$
  d. $F \cdot (K + R) + S \cdot V + W \cdot \overline{X} + V \cdot S + \overline{X} \cdot W + (R + K) \cdot F$

11.3 Apply DeMorgan's theorem to the following equations:
  a. $F = \overline{V} + \overline{A} + \overline{L}$
  b. $F = \overline{A} + \overline{B} + \overline{C} + \overline{D}$

11.4 Simplify the following expressions:
  a. $A = S \cdot T + V \cdot W + R \cdot S \cdot T$
  b. $A = T \cdot U \cdot V + X \cdot Y + Y$
  c. $A = F \cdot (E + F + G)$
  d. $A = (P \cdot Q + R + S \cdot T)T \cdot S$
  e. $A = \overline{\overline{D} \cdot \overline{D}} \cdot E$
  f. $A = Y \cdot (W + X + \overline{Y} + \overline{Z}) \cdot Z$
  g. $A = (B \cdot E + C + F) \cdot C$

11.5 Construct the operation XOR from the basic Boolean operations AND, OR, and NOT.

11.6 Given a NOR gate and NOT gates, draw a logic diagram that will perform the three-input AND function.

11.7 Write the Boolean expression for a four-input **NAND gate**.

11.8 A combinational circuit is used to control a seven-segment display of decimal digits, as shown in Figure 11.35. The circuit has four inputs, which provide the four-bit code used in packed decimal representation ($0_{10} = 0000, \ldots, 9_{10} = 1001$). The seven outputs define which segments will be activated to display a given decimal digit. Note that some combinations of inputs and outputs are not needed.
  a. Develop a truth table for this circuit.
  b. Express the truth table in SOP form.
  c. Express the truth table in POS form.
  d. Provide a simplified expression.

11.9 Design an 8-to-1 multiplexer.

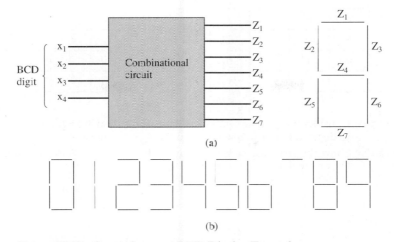

(a)

(b)

Figure 11.35   Seven-Segment LED Display Example

11.10 Add an additional line to Figure 11.15 so that it functions as a demultiplexer.

11.11 The Gray code is a binary code for integers. It differs from the ordinary binary representation in that there is just a single bit change between the representations of any two numbers. This is useful for applications such as counters or analog-to-digital converters where a sequence of numbers is generated. Because only one bit changes at a time, there is never any ambiguity due to slight timing differences. The first eight elements of the code are

Binary Code	Gray Code
000	000
001	001
010	011
011	010
100	110
101	111
110	101
111	100

Design a circuit that converts from binary to Gray code.

11.12 Design a 5×32 decoder using four 3×8 decoders (with enable inputs) and one 2×4 decoder.

11.13 Implement the full adder of Figure 11.20 with just five gates. (*Hint:* Some of the gates are **XOR gates**.)

11.14 Consider Figure 11.20. Assume that each gate produces a delay of 10 ns. Thus, the sum output is valid after 30 ns and the carry output after 0 ns. What is the total add time for a 32-bit adder
  a. Implemented without carry lookahead, as in Figure 11.19?
  b. Implemented with carry lookahead and using 8-bit adders, as in Figure 11.21?

11.15 An alternative form of the S–R latch has the same structure as Figure 11.22 but uses NAND gates instead of NOR gates.
  a. Redo Table 11.10a and 11.10b for S–R latch implemented with NAND gates.
  b. Complete the following table, similar to Table 11.10c

t	0	1	2	3	4	5	6	7	8	9
S	0	1	1	1	1	1	0	1	0	1
R	1	1	0	1	0	1	1	1	0	0

11.16 Consider the graphic symbol for the S–R flip-flop in Figure 11.27. Add additional lines to depict a D flip-flop wired from the S–R flip-flop.

11.17 Show the structure of a PLA with three inputs (C, B, A) and four outputs (O_0, O_1, O_2, O_3) with the outputs defined as follows:

$$O_0 = \overline{A}\,\overline{B}C + A\overline{B} + AB\overline{C}$$
$$O_1 = \overline{A}\,\overline{B}C + AB\overline{C}$$
$$O_2 = C$$
$$O_3 = A\overline{B} + AB\overline{C}$$

11.18 An interesting application of a PLA is conversion from the old, obsolete punched cards character codes to ASCII codes. The standard punched cards that were so popular with computers in the past had 12 rows and 80 columns where holes could be punched. Each column corresponded to one character, so each character had a 12-bit code. However, only 96 characters were actually used. Consider an application that reads punched cards and converts the character codes to ASCII.

    a. Describe a PLA implementation of this application.

    b. Can this problem be solved with a ROM? Explain.

INSTRUCTION SETS: CHARACTERISTICS AND FUNCTIONS

LEARNING OBJECTIVES

After studying this chapter, you should be able to:

◆ Present an overview of essential characteristics of machine instructions.

◆ Describe the types of operands used in typical machine instruction sets.

◆ Present an overview of x86 and ARM data types.

◆ Describe the types of operands supported by typical machine instruction sets.

◆ Present an overview of x86 and ARM operation types.

◆ Understand the differences among big endian, little endian, and bi-endian.

Much of what is discussed in this book is not readily apparent to the user or programmer of a computer. If a programmer is using a high-level language, such as Pascal or Ada, very little of the architecture of the underlying machine is visible.

One boundary where the computer designer and the computer programmer can view the same machine is the machine instruction set. From the designer's point of view, the machine instruction set provides the functional requirements for the processor: implementing the processor is a task that in large part involves implementing the machine instruction set. The user who chooses to program in machine language (actually, in assembly language; see Appendix B) becomes aware of the register and memory structure, the types of data directly supported by the machine, and the functioning of the ALU.

A description of a computer's machine instruction set goes a long way toward explaining the computer's processor. Accordingly, we focus on machine instructions in this chapter and the next.

12.1 MACHINE INSTRUCTION CHARACTERISTICS

The operation of the processor is determined by the instructions it executes, referred to as *machine instructions* or *computer instructions*. The collection of different instructions that the processor can execute is referred to as the processor's *instruction set*.

Elements of a Machine Instruction

Each instruction must contain the information required by the processor for execution. Figure 12.1, which repeats Figure 3.6, shows the steps involved in instruction execution and, by implication, defines the elements of a machine instruction. These elements are as follows:

- **Operation code:** Specifies the operation to be performed (e.g., ADD, I/O). The operation is specified by a binary code, known as the operation code, or **opcode**.

- **Source operand reference:** The operation may involve one or more source operands, that is, operands that are inputs for the operation.

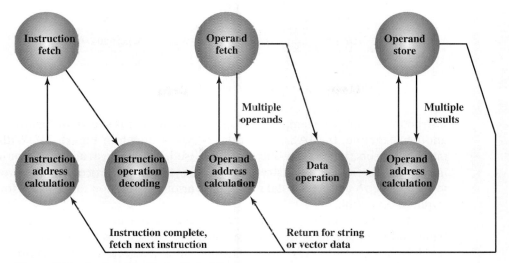

Figure 12.1 Instruction Cycle State Diagram

- **Result operand reference:** The operation may produce a result.
- **Next instruction reference:** This tells the processor where to fetch the next instruction after the execution of this instruction is complete.

The address of the next instruction to be fetched could be either a real address or a virtual address, depending on the architecture. Generally, the distinction is transparent to the instruction set architecture. In most cases, the next instruction to be fetched immediately follows the current instruction. In those cases, there is no explicit reference to the next instruction. When an explicit reference is needed, then the main memory or virtual memory address must be supplied. The form in which that address is supplied is discussed in Chapter 13.

Source and result operands can be in one of four areas:

- **Main or virtual memory:** As with next instruction references, the main or virtual memory address must be supplied.
- **Processor register:** With rare exceptions, a processor contains one or more registers that may be referenced by machine instructions. If only one register exists, reference to it may be implicit. If more than one register exists, then each register is assigned a unique name or number, and the instruction must contain the number of the desired register.
- **Immediate:** The value of the operand is contained in a field in the instruction being executed.
- **I/O device:** The instruction must specify the I/O module and device for the operation. If memory-mapped I/O is used, this is just another main or virtual memory address.

Instruction Representation

Within the computer, each instruction is represented by a sequence of bits. The instruction is divided into fields, corresponding to the constituent elements of the

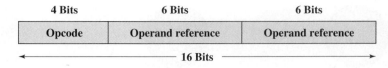

Figure 12.2 A Simple Instruction Format

instruction. A simple example of an instruction format is shown in Figure 12.2. As another example, the IAS instruction format is shown in Figure 2.2. With most instruction sets, more than one format is used. During instruction execution, an instruction is read into an instruction register (IR) in the processor. The processor must be able to extract the data from the various instruction fields to perform the required operation.

It is difficult for both the programmer and the reader of textbooks to deal with binary representations of machine instructions. Thus, it has become common practice to use a *symbolic representation* of machine instructions. An example of this was used for the IAS instruction set, in Table 2.1.

Opcodes are represented by abbreviations, called *mnemonics,* that indicate the operation. Common examples include

ADD	Add
SUB	Subtract
MUL	Multiply
DIV	Divide
LOAD	Load data from memory
STOR	Store data to memory

Operands are also represented symbolically. For example, the instruction

ADD R, Y

may mean add the value contained in data location Y to the contents of register R. In this example, Y refers to the address of a location in memory, and R refers to a particular register. Note that the operation is performed on the contents of a location, not on its address.

Thus, it is possible to write a machine-language program in symbolic form. Each symbolic opcode has a fixed binary representation, and the programmer specifies the location of each symbolic operand. For example, the programmer might begin with a list of definitions:

$$X = 513$$
$$Y = 514$$

and so on. A simple program would accept this symbolic input, convert opcodes and operand references to binary form, and construct binary machine instructions.

Machine-language programmers are rare to the point of nonexistence. Most programs today are written in a high-level language or, failing that, assembly language, which is discussed in Appendix B. However, symbolic machine language remains a useful tool for describing machine instructions, and we will use it for that purpose.

Instruction Types

Consider a high-level language instruction that could be expressed in a language such as BASIC or FORTRAN. For example,

$$X = X - Y$$

This statement instructs the computer to add the value stored in Y to the value stored in X and put the result in X. How might this be accomplished with machine instructions? Let us assume that the variables X and Y correspond to locations 513 and 514. If we assume a simple set of machine instructions, this operation could be accomplished with three instructions:

1. Load a register with the contents of memory location 513.
2. Add the contents of memory location 514 to the register.
3. Store the contents of the register in memory location 513.

As can be seen, the single BASIC instruction may require three machine instructions. This is typical of the relationship between a high-level language and a machine language. A high-level language expresses operations in a concise algebraic form, using variables. A machine language expresses operations in a basic form involving the movement of data to or from registers.

With this simple example to guide us, let us consider the types of instructions that must be included in a practical computer. A computer should have a set of instructions that allows the user to formulate any data processing task. Another way to view it is to consider the capabilities of a high-level programming language. Any program written in a high-level language must be translated into machine language to be executed. Thus, the set of machine instructions must be sufficient to express any of the instructions from a high-level language. With this in mind we can categorize instruction types as follows:

- **Data processing:** Arithmetic and logic instructions
- **Data storage:** Movement of data into or out of register and or memory locations
- **Data movement:** I/O instructions
- **Control:** Test and branch instructions

Arithmetic instructions provide computational capabilities for processing numeric data. *Logic* (Boolean) instructions operate on the bits of a word as bits rather than as numbers; thus, they provide capabilities for processing any other type of data the user may wish to employ. These operations are performed primarily on data in processor registers. Therefore, there must be *memory* instructions for moving data between memory and the registers. *I/O* instructions are needed to transfer programs and data into memory and the results of computations back out to the user. *Test* instructions are used to test the value of a data word or the status of a computation. Branch instructions are then used to branch to a different set of instructions depending on the decision made.

We will examine the various types of instructions in greater detail later in this chapter.

Number of Addresses

One of the traditional ways of describing processor architecture is in terms of the number of addresses contained in each instruction. This dimension has become less significant with the increasing complexity of processor design. Nevertheless, it is useful at this point to draw and analyze this distinction.

What is the maximum number of addresses one might need in an instruction? Evidently, arithmetic and logic instructions will require the most operands. Virtually all arithmetic and logic operations are either unary (one source operand) or binary (two source operands). Thus, we would need a maximum of two addresses to reference source operands. The result of an operation must be stored, suggesting a third address, which defines a destination operand. Finally, after completion of an instruction, the next instruction must be fetched, and its address is needed.

This line of reasoning suggests that an instruction could plausibly be required to contain four address references: two source operands, one destination operand, and the address of the next instruction. In most architectures, most instructions have one, two, or three operand addresses, with the address of the next instruction being implicit (obtained from the program counter). Most architectures also have a few special-purpose instructions with more operands. For example, the load and store multiple instructions of the ARM architecture, described in Chapter 13, designate up to 17 register operands in a single instruction.

Figure 12.3 compares typical one-, two-, and three-address instructions that could be used to compute $Y = (A - B)/[C + (D \times E)]$. With three addresses, each instruction specifies two source operand locations and a destination operand location. Because we choose not to alter the value of any of the operand locations, a temporary location, T, is used to store some intermediate results. Note that there are four instructions and that the original expression had five operands.

Instruction		Comment
SUB	Y, A, B	$Y \leftarrow A - B$
MPY	T, D, E	$T \leftarrow D \times E$
ADD	T, T, C	$T \leftarrow T + C$
DIV	Y, Y, T	$Y \leftarrow Y \div T$

(a) Three-address instructions

Instruction		Comment
MOVE	Y, A	$Y \leftarrow A$
SUB	Y, B	$Y \leftarrow Y - B$
MOVE	T, D	$T \leftarrow D$
MPY	T, E	$T \leftarrow T \times E$
ADD	T, C	$T \leftarrow T + C$
DIV	Y, T	$Y \leftarrow Y \div T$

(b) Two-address instructions

Instruction		Comment
LOAD	D	$AC \leftarrow D$
MPY	E	$AC \leftarrow AC \times E$
ADD	C	$AC \leftarrow AC + C$
STOR	Y	$Y \leftarrow AC$
LOAD	A	$AC \leftarrow A$
SUB	B	$AC \leftarrow AC - B$
DIV	Y	$AC \leftarrow AC \div Y$
STOR	Y	$Y \leftarrow AC$

(c) One-address instructions

Figure 12.3 Programs to Execute $Y = \dfrac{A - B}{C + (D \times E)}$

Three-address instruction formats are not common because they require a relatively long instruction format to hold the three address references. With two-address instructions, and for binary operations, one address must do double duty as both an operand and a result. Thus, the instruction SUB Y, B carries out the calculation Y − B and stores the result in Y. The two-address format reduces the space requirement but also introduces some awkwardness. To avoid altering the value of an operand, a MOVE instruction is used to move one of the values to a result or temporary location before performing the operation. Our sample program expands to six instructions.

Simpler yet is the one-address instruction. For this to work, a second address must be implicit. This was common in earlier machines, with the implied address being a processor register known as the **accumulator** (AC). The accumulator contains one of the operands and is used to store the result. In our example, eight instructions are needed to accomplish the task.

It is, in fact, possible to make do with zero addresses for some instructions. Zero-address instructions are applicable to a special memory organization called a *stack*. A stack is a last-in-first-out set of locations. The stack is in a known location and, often, at least the top two elements are in processor registers. Thus, zero-address instructions would reference the top two stack elements. Stacks are described in Appendix O. Their use is explored further later in this chapter and in Chapter 13.

Table 12.1 summarizes the interpretations to be placed on instructions with zero, one, two, or three addresses. In each case in the table, it is assumed that the address of the next instruction is implicit, and that one operation with two source operands and one result operand is to be performed.

The number of addresses per instruction is a basic design decision. Fewer addresses per instruction result in instructions that are more primitive, requiring a less complex processor. It also results in instructions of shorter length. On the other hand, programs contain more total instructions, which in general results in longer execution times and longer, more complex programs. Also, there is an important threshold between one-address and multiple-address instructions. With one-address instructions, the programmer generally has available only one general-purpose register, the accumulator. With multiple-address instructions, it is common to have multiple general-purpose registers. This allows some operations to be performed

Table 12.1   Utilization of Instruction Addresses (Nonbranching Instructions)

Number of Addresses	Symbolic Representation	Interpretation
3	OP A, B, C	A ← B OP C
2	OP A, B	A ← A OP B
1	OP A	AC ← AC OP A
0	OP	T ← (T − 1) OP T

AC   = accumulator
T   = top of stack
(T − 1) = second element of stack
A, B, C = memory or register locations

solely on registers. Because register references are faster than memory references, this speeds up execution. For reasons of flexibility and ability to use multiple registers, most contemporary machines employ a mixture of two- and three-address instructions.

The design trade-offs involved in choosing the number of addresses per instruction are complicated by other factors. There is the issue of whether an address references a memory location or a register. Because there are fewer registers, fewer bits are needed for a register reference. Also, as we shall see in Chapter 13, a machine may offer a variety of addressing modes, and the specification of mode takes one or more bits. The result is that most processor designs involve a variety of instruction formats.

Instruction Set Design

One of the most interesting, and most analyzed, aspects of computer design is instruction set design. The design of an instruction set is very complex because it affects so many aspects of the computer system. The instruction set defines many of the functions performed by the processor and thus has a significant effect on the implementation of the processor. The instruction set is the programmer's means of controlling the processor. Thus, programmer requirements must be considered in designing the instruction set.

It may surprise you to know that some of the most fundamental issues relating to the design of instruction sets remain in dispute. Indeed, in recent years, the level of disagreement concerning these fundamentals has actually grown. The most important of these fundamental design issues include the following:

- **Operation repertoire:** How many and which operations to provide, and how complex operations should be
- **Data types:** The various types of data upon which operations are performed
- **Instruction format:** Instruction length (in bits), number of addresses, size of various fields, and so on
- **Registers:** Number of processor registers that can be referenced by instructions, and their use
- **Addressing:** The mode or modes by which the address of an operand is specified

These issues are highly interrelated and must be considered together in designing an instruction set. This book, of course, must consider them in some sequence, but an attempt is made to show the interrelationships.

Because of the importance of this topic, much of Part Three is devoted to instruction set design. Following this overview section, this chapter examines data types and operation repertoire. Chapter 13 examines addressing modes (which includes a consideration of registers) and instruction formats. Chapter 15 examines the reduced instruction set computer (RISC). RISC architecture calls into question many of the instruction set design decisions traditionally made in commercial computers.

12.2 TYPES OF OPERANDS

Machine instructions operate on data. The most important general categories of data are

- Addresses
- Numbers
- Characters
- Logical data

We shall see, in discussing addressing modes in Chapter 13, that addresses are, in fact, a form of data. In many cases, some calculation must be performed on the operand reference in an instruction to determine the main or virtual memory address. In this context, addresses can be considered to be unsigned integers.

Other common data types are numbers, characters, and logical data, and each of these is briefly examined in this section. Beyond that, some machines define specialized data types or data structures. For example, there may be machine operations that operate directly on a list or a string of characters.

Numbers

All machine languages include numeric data types. Even in nonnumeric data processing, there is a need for numbers to act as counters, field widths, and so forth. An important distinction between numbers used in ordinary mathematics and numbers stored in a computer is that the latter are limited. This is true in two senses. First, there is a limit to the magnitude of numbers representable on a machine and second, in the case of floating-point numbers, a limit to their precision. Thus, the programmer is faced with understanding the consequences of rounding, overflow, and underflow.

Three types of numerical data are common in computers:

- Binary integer or binary fixed point
- Binary floating point
- Decimal

We examined the first two in some detail in Chapter 10. It remains to say a few words about decimal numbers.

Although all internal computer operations are binary in nature, the human users of the system deal with decimal numbers. Thus, there is a necessity to convert from decimal to binary on input and from binary to decimal on output. For applications in which there is a great deal of I/O and comparatively little, comparatively simple computation, it is preferable to store and operate on the numbers in decimal form. The most common representation for this purpose is **packed decimal**.[1]

---

[1]Textbooks often refer to this as binary coded decimal (BCD). Strictly speaking, BCD refers to the encoding of each decimal digit by a unique 4-bit sequence. Packed decimal refers to the storage of BCD-encoded digits using one byte for each two digits.

With packed decimal, each decimal digit is represented by a 4-bit code, in the obvious way, with two digits stored per byte. Thus, $0 = 000$, $1 = 0001$, ..., $8 = 1000$, and $9 = 1001$. Note that this is a rather inefficient code because only 10 of 16 possible 4-bit values are used. To form numbers, 4-bit codes are strung together, usually in multiples of 8 bits. Thus, the code for 246 is 0000 0010 0100 0110. This code is clearly less compact than a straight binary representation, but it avoids the conversion overhead. Negative numbers can be represented by including a 4-bit sign digit at either the left or right end of a string of packed decimal digits. Standard sign values are 1100 for positive $(+)$ and 1101 for negative $(-)$.

Many machines provide arithmetic instructions for performing operations directly on packed decimal numbers. The algorithms are quite similar to those described in Section 9.3 but must take into account the decimal carry operation.

Characters

A common form of data is text or character strings. While textual data are most convenient for human beings, they cannot, in character form, be easily stored or transmitted by data processing and communications systems. Such systems are designed for binary data. Thus, a number of codes have been devised by which characters are represented by a sequence of bits. Perhaps the earliest common example of this is the Morse code. Today, the most commonly used character code in the International Reference Alphabet (IRA), referred to in the United States as the American Standard Code for Information Interchange (ASCII; see Appendix F). Each character in this code is represented by a unique 7-bit pattern; thus, 128 different characters can be represented. This is a larger number than is necessary to represent printable characters, and some of the patterns represent *control* characters. Some of these control characters have to do with controlling the printing of characters on a page. Others are concerned with communications procedures. IRA-encoded characters are almost always stored and transmitted using 8 bits per character. The eighth bit may be set to 0 or used as a parity bit for error detection. In the latter case, the bit is set such that the total number of binary 1s in each octet is always odd (odd parity) or always even (even parity).

Note in Table F.1 (Appendix F) that for the IRA bit pattern 011XXXX, the digits 0 through 9 are represented by their binary equivalents, 0000 through 1001, in the rightmost 4 bits. This is the same code as packed decimal. This facilitates conversion between 7-bit IRA and 4-bit packed decimal representation.

Another code used to encode characters is the Extended Binary Coded Decimal Interchange Code (EBCDIC). EBCDIC is used on IBM mainframes. It is an 8-bit code. As with IRA, EBCDIC is compatible with packed decimal. In the case of EBCDIC, the codes 11110000 through 11111001 represent the digits 0 through 9.

Logical Data

Normally, each word or other addressable unit (byte, halfword, and so on) is treated as a single unit of data. It is sometimes useful, however, to consider an n-bit unit as consisting of n 1-bit items of data, each item having the value 0 or 1. When data are viewed this way, they are considered to be *logical* data.

There are two advantages to the bit-oriented view. First, we may sometimes wish to store an array of Boolean or binary data items, in which each item can take on only the values 1 (true) and 0 (false). With logical data, memory can be used most efficiently for this storage. Second, there are occasions when we wish to manipulate the bits of a data item. For example, if floating-point operations are implemented in software, we need to be able to shift significant bits in some operations. Another example: To convert from IRA to packed decimal, we need to extract the rightmost 4 bits of each byte.

Note that, in the preceding examples, the same data are treated sometimes as logical and other times as numerical or text. The "type" of a unit of data is determined by the operation being performed on it. While this is not normally the case in high-level languages, it is almost always the case with machine language.

12.3 INTEL x86 AND ARM DATA TYPES

x86 Data Types

The x86 can deal with data types of 8 (byte), 16 (word), 32 (doubleword), 64 (quadword), and 128 (double quadword) bits in length. To allow maximum flexibility in data structures and efficient memory utilization, words need not be aligned at even-numbered addresses; doublewords need not be aligned at addresses evenly divisible by 4; and quadwords need not be aligned at addresses evenly divisible by 8; and so on. However, when data are accessed across a 32-bit bus, data transfers take place in units of doublewords, beginning at addresses divisible by 4. The processor converts the request for misaligned values into a sequence of requests for the bus transfer. As with all of the Intel 80x86 machines, the x86 uses the little-endian style; that is, the least significant byte is stored in the lowest address (see Appendix 12A for a discussion of endianness).

The byte, word, doubleword, quadword, and double quadword are referred to as general data types. In addition, the x86 supports an impressive array of specific data types that are recognized and operated on by particular instructions. Table 12.2 summarizes these types.

Figure 12.4 illustrates the x86 numerical data types. The signed integers are in twos complement representation and may be 16, 32, or 64 bits long. The floating-point type actually refers to a set of types that are used by the floating-point unit and operated on by floating-point instructions. The three floating-point representations conform to the IEEE 754 standard.

The packed SIMD (single-instruction-multiple-data) data types were introduced to the x86 architecture as part of the extensions of the instruction set to optimize performance of multimedia applications. These extensions include MMX (multimedia extensions) and SSE (streaming SIMD extensions). The basic concept is that multiple operands are packed into a single referenced memory item and that these multiple operands are operated on in parallel. The data types are as follows:

- **Packed byte and packed byte integer:** Bytes packed into a 64-bit quadword or 128-bit double quadword, interpreted as a bit field or as an integer
- **Packed word and packed word integer:** 16-bit words packed into a 64-bit quadword or 128-bit double quadword, interpreted as a bit field or as an integer

Table 12.2   x86 Data Types

Data Type	Description
General	Byte, word (16 bits), doubleword (32 bits), quadword (64 bits), and double quadword (128 bits) locations with arbitrary binary contents.
Integer	A signed binary value contained in a byte, word, or doubleword, using twos complement representation.
Ordinal	An unsigned integer contained in a byte, word, or doubleword.
Unpacked binary coded decimal (BCD)	A representation of a BCD digit in the range 0 through 9, with one digit in each byte.
Packed BCD	Packed byte representation of two BCD digits; value in the range 0 to 99.
Near pointer	A 16-bit, 32-bit, or 64-bit effective address that represents the offset within a segment. Used for all pointers in a nonsegmented memory and for references within a segment in a segmented memory.
Far pointer	A logical address consisting of a 16-bit segment selector and an offset of 16, 32, or 64 bits. Far pointers are used for memory references in a segmented memory model where the identity of a segment being accessed must be specified explicitly.
Bit field	A contiguous sequence of bits in which the position of each bit is considered as an independent unit. A bit string can begin at any bit position of any byte and can contain up to 32 bits.
Bit string	A contiguous sequence of bits, containing from zero to $2^{32} - 1$ bits.
Byte string	A contiguous sequence of bytes, words, or doublewords, containing from zero to $2^{32} - 1$ bytes.
Floating point	See Figure 12.4.
Packed SIMD (single instruction, multiple data)	Packed 64-bit and 128-bit data types

- **Packed doubleword and packed doubleword integer:** 32-bit doublewords packed into a 64-bit quadword or 128-bit double quadword, interpreted as a bit field or as an integer

- **Packed quadword and packed qaudword integer:** Two 64-bit quadwords packed into a 128-bit double quadword, interpreted as a bit field or as an integer

- **Packed single-precision floating-point and packed double-precision floating-point:** Four 32-bit floating-point or two 64-bit floating-point values packed into a 128-bit double quadword

ARM Data Types

ARM processors support data types of 8 (byte), 16 (halfword), and 32 (word) bits in length. Normally, halfword access should be halfword aligned and word accesses should be word aligned. For nonaligned access attempts, the architecture supports three alternatives.

- Default case:
  - The address is treated as truncated, with address bits[1:0] treated as zero for word accesses, and address bit[0] treated as zero for halfword accesses.

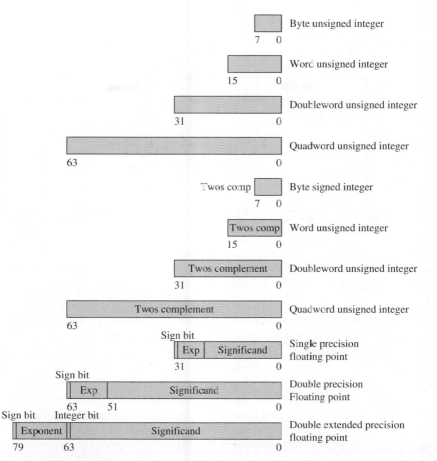

Figure 12.4 x86 Numeric Data Formats

– Load single word ARM instructions are architecturally defined to rotate right the word-aligned data transferred by a non word-aligned address one, two, or three bytes depending on the value of the two least significant address bits.

- **Alignment checking:** When the appropriate control bit is set, a data abort signal indicates an alignment fault for attempting unaligned access.

- **Unaligned access:** When this option is enabled, the processor uses one or more memory accesses to generate the required transfer of adjacent bytes transparently to the programmer.

For all three data types (byte, halfword, and word) an unsigned interpretation is supported, in which the value represents an unsigned, nonnegative integer. All three data types can also be used for twos complement signed integers.

The majority of ARM processor implementations do not provide floating-point hardware, which saves power and area. If floating-point arithmetic is required in such processors, it must be implemented in software. ARM does support an optional floating-point coprocessor that supports the single- and double-precision floating point data types defined in IEEE 754.

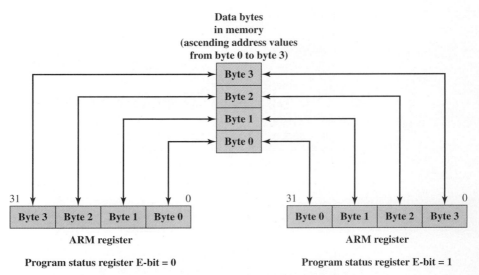

Figure 12.5   ARM Endian Support—Word Load/Store with E-Bit

ENDIAN SUPPORT A state bit (E-bit) in the system control register is set and cleared under program control using the SETEND instruction. The E-bit defines which endian to load and store data. Figure 12.5 illustrates the functionality associated with the E-bit for a word load or store operation. This mechanism enables efficient dynamic data load/store for system designers who know they need to access data structures in the opposite endianness to their OS/environment. Note that the address of each data byte is fixed in memory. However, the byte lane in a register is different.

12.4 TYPES OF OPERATIONS

The number of different opcodes varies widely from machine to machine. However, the same general types of operations are found on all machines. A useful and typical categorization is the following:

- Data transfer
- Arithmetic
- Logical
- Conversion
- I/O
- System control
- Transfer of control

Table 12.3 (based on [HAYE98]) lists common instruction types in each category. This section provides a brief survey of these various types of operations, together with a brief discussion of the actions taken by the processor to execute a particular type of operation (summarized in Table 12.4). The latter topic is examined in more detail in Chapter 14.

Table 12.3   Common Instruction Set Operations

Type	Operation Name	Description
Data transfer	Move (transfer)	Transfer word or block from source to destination
	Store	Transfer word from processor to memory
	Load (fetch)	Transfer word from memory to processor
	Exchange	Swap contents of source and destination
	Clear (reset)	Transfer word of 0s to destination
	Set	Transfer word of 1s to destination
	Push	Transfer word from source to top of stack
	Pop	Transfer word from top of stack to destination
Arithmetic	Add	Compute sum of two operands
	Subtract	Compute difference of two operands
	Multiply	Compute product of two operands
	Divide	Compute quotient of two operands
	Absolute	Replace operand by its absolute value
	Negate	Change sign of operand
	Increment	Add 1 to operand
	Decrement	Subtract 1 from operand
Logical	AND	Perform logical AND
	OR	Perform logical OR
	NOT (complement)	Perform logical NOT
	Exclusive-OR	Perform logical XOR
	Test	Test specified condition; set flag(s) based on outcome
	Compare	Make logical or arithmetic comparison of two or more operands; set flag(s) based on outcome
	Set Control Variables	Class of instructions to set controls for protection purposes, interrupt handling, timer control, etc.
	Shift	Left (right) shift operand, introducing constants at end
	Rotate	Left (right) shift operand, with wraparound end
Transfer of control	Jump (branch)	Unconditional transfer; load PC with specified address
	Jump Conditional	Test specified condition; either load PC with specified address or do nothing, based on condition
	Jump to Subroutine	Place current program control information in known location; jump to specified address
	Return	Replace contents of PC and other register from known location
	Execute	Fetch operand from specified location and execute as instruction; do not modify PC
	Skip	Increment PC to skip next instruction
	Skip Conditional	Test specified condition; either skip or do nothing based on condition
	Halt	Stop program execution
	Wait (hold)	Stop program execution; test specified condition repeatedly; resume execution when condition is satisfied
	No operation	No operation is performed, but program execution is continued

(continued)

Table 12.3 Continued

Type	Operation Name	Description
Input/output	Input (read)	Transfer data from specified I/O port or device to destination (e.g., main memory or processor register)
	Output (write)	Transfer data from specified source to I/O port or device
	Start I/O	Transfer instructions to I/O processor to initiate I/O operation
	Test I/O	Transfer status information from I/O system to specified destination
Conversion	Translate	Translate values in a section of memory based on a table of correspondences
	Convert	Convert the contents of a word from one form to another (e.g., packed decimal to binary)

Table 12.4 Processor Actions for Various Types of Operations

Data transfer	Transfer data from one location to another

	If memory is involved:
	    Determine memory address
	    Perform virtual-to-actual-memory address transformation
	    Check cache
	    Initiate memory read/write

Arithmetic	May involve data transfer, before and/or after
	Perform function in ALU
	Set condition codes and flags
Logical	Same as arithmetic
Conversion	Similar to arithmetic and logical. May involve special logic to perform conversion
Transfer of control	Update program counter. For subroutine call/return, manage parameter passing and linkage
I/O	Issue command to I/O module
	If memory-mapped I/O, determine memory-mapped address

Data Transfer

The most fundamental type of machine instruction is the data transfer instruction. The data transfer instruction must specify several things. First, the location of the source and destination operands must be specified. Each location could be memory, a register, or the top of the stack. Second, the length of data to be transferred must be indicated. Third, as with all instructions with operands, the mode of addressing for each operand must be specified. This latter point is discussed in Chapter 13.

The choice of data transfer instructions to include in an instruction set exemplifies the kinds of trade-offs the designer must make. For example, the general location (memory or register) of an operand can be indicated in either the specification of the opcode or the operand. Table 12.5 shows examples of the most common IBM EAS/390 data transfer instructions. Note that there are variants to indicate

Table 12.5   Examples of IBM EAS/390 Data Transfer Operations

Operation Mnemonic	Name	Number of Bits Transferred	Description
L	Load	32	Transfer from memory to register
LH	Load Halfword	16	Transfer from memory to register
LR	Load	32	Transfer from register to register
LER	Load (short)	32	Transfer from floating-point register to floating-point register
LE	Load (short)	32	Transfer from memory to floating-point register
LDR	Load (long)	64	Transfer from floating-point register to floating-point register
LD	Load (long)	64	Transfer from memory to floating-point register
ST	Store	32	Transfer from register to memory
STH	Store Halfword	16	Transfer from register to memory
STC	Store Character	8	Transfer from register to memory
STE	Store (short)	32	Transfer from floating-point register to memory
STD	Store (long)	64	Transfer from floating-point register to memory

the amount of data to be transferred (8, 16, 32, or 64 bits). Also, there are different instructions for register to register, register to memory, memory to register, and memory to memory transfers. In contrast, the VAX has a move (MOV) instruction with variants for different amounts of data to be moved, but it specifies whether an operand is register or memory as part of the operand. The VAX approach is somewhat easier for the programmer, who has fewer mnemonics to deal with. However, it is also somewhat less compact than the IBM EAS/390 approach because the location (register versus memory) of each operand must be specified separately in the instruction. We will return to this distinction when we discuss instruction formats in Chapter 13.

In terms of processor action, data transfer operations are perhaps the simplest type. If both source and destination are registers, then the processor simply causes data to be transferred from one register to another; this is an operation internal to the processor. If one or both operands are in memory, then the processor must perform some or all of the following actions:

1. Calculate the memory address, based on the address mode (discussed in Chapter 13).

2. If the address refers to virtual memory, translate from virtual to real memory address.

3. Determine whether the addressed item is in cache.

4. If not, issue a command to the memory module.

Arithmetic

Most machines provide the basic arithmetic operations of add, subtract, multiply, and divide. These are invariably provided for signed integer (fixed-point) numbers. Often they are also provided for floating-point and packed decimal numbers.

Other possible operations include a variety of single-operand instructions; for example,

- **Absolute:** Take the absolute value of the operand.
- **Negate:** Negate the operand.
- **Increment:** Add 1 to the operand.
- **Decrement:** Subtract 1 from the operand.

The execution of an arithmetic instruction may involve data transfer operations to position operands for input to the ALU, and to deliver the output of the ALU. Figure 3.5 illustrates the movements involved in both data transfer and arithmetic operations. In addition, of course, the ALU portion of the processor performs the desired operation.

Logical

Most machines also provide a variety of operations for manipulating individual bits of a word or other addressable units, often referred to as "bit twiddling." They are based upon Boolean operations (see Chapter 11).

Some of the basic logical operations that can be performed on Boolean or binary data are shown in Table 12.6. The NOT operation inverts a bit. AND, OR, and Exclusive-OR (XOR) are the most common logical functions with two operands. EQUAL is a useful binary test.

These logical operations can be applied bitwise to n-bit logical data units. Thus, if two registers contain the data

$$(R1) = 10100101$$
$$(R2) = 00001111$$

then

$$(R1) \text{ AND } (R2) = 00000101$$

Table 12.6 Basic Logical Operations

P	Q	NOT P	P AND Q	P OR Q	P XOR Q	P = Q
0	0	1	0	0	0	1
0	1	1	0	1	1	0
1	0	0	0	1	1	0
1	1	0	1	1	0	1

where the notation (X) means the contents of location X. Thus, the AND operation can be used as a *mask* that selects certain bits in a word and zeros out the remaining bits. As another example, if two registers contain

$$(R1) = 10100101$$
$$(R2) = 11111111$$

then

$$(R1) \text{ XOR } (R2) = 01011010$$

With one word set to all 1s, the XOR operation inverts all of the bits in the other word (ones complement).

In addition to bitwise logical operations, most machines provide a variety of shifting and rotating functions. The most basic operations are illustrated in Figure 12.6. With a **logical shift**, the bits of a word are shifted left or right. On one end, the bit shifted out is lost. On the other end, a 0 is shifted in. Logical shifts are useful primarily for isolating fields within a word. The 0s that are shifted into a word displace unwanted information that is shifted off the other end.

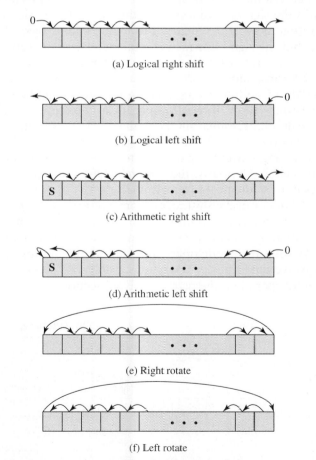

(a) Logical right shift

(b) Logical left shift

(c) Arithmetic right shift

(d) Arithmetic left shift

(e) Right rotate

(f) Left rotate

Figure 12.6 Shift and Rotate Operations

As an example, suppose we wish to transmit characters of data to an I/O device 1 character at a time. If each memory word is 16 bits in length and contains two characters, we must *unpack* the characters before they can be sent. To send the two characters in a word,

1. Load the word into a register.
2. Shift to the right eight times. This shifts the remaining character to the right half of the register.
3. Perform I/O. The I/O module reads the lower-order 8 bits from the data bus.

The preceding steps result in sending the left-hand character. To send the right-hand character,

1. Load the word again into the register.
2. AND with 0000000011111111. This masks out the character on the left.
3. Perform I/O.

The **arithmetic shift** operation treats the data as a signed integer and does not shift the sign bit. On a right arithmetic shift, the sign bit is replicated into the bit position to its right. On a left arithmetic shift, a logical left shift is performed on all bits but the sign bit, which is retained. These operations can speed up certain arithmetic operations. With numbers in twos complement notation, a right arithmetic shift corresponds to a division by 2, with truncation for odd numbers. Both an arithmetic left shift and a logical left shift correspond to a multiplication by 2 when there is no overflow. If overflow occurs, arithmetic and logical left shift operations produce different results, but the arithmetic left shift retains the sign of the number. Because of the potential for overflow, many processors do not include this instruction, including PowerPC and Itanium. Others, such as the IBM EAS/390, do offer the instruction. Curiously, the x86 architecture includes an arithmetic left shift but defines it to be identical to a logical left shift.

Rotate, or cyclic shift, operations preserve all of the bits being operated on. One use of a rotate is to bring each bit successively into the leftmost bit, where it can be identified by testing the sign of the data (treated as a number).

As with arithmetic operations, logical operations involve ALU activity and may involve data transfer operations. Table 12.7 gives examples of all of the shift and rotate operations discussed in this subsection.

Table 12.7   Examples of Shift and Rotate Operations

Input	Operation	Result
10100110	Logical right shift (3 bits)	00010100
10100110	Logical left shift (3 bits)	00110000
10100110	Arithmetic right shift (3 bits)	11110100
10100110	Arithmetic left shift (3 bits)	10110000
10100110	Right rotate (3 bits)	11010100
10100110	Left rotate (3 bits)	00110101

Conversion

Conversion instructions are those that change the format or operate on the format of data. An example is converting from decimal to binary. An example of a more complex editing instruction is the EAS/390 Translate (TR) instruction. This instruction can be used to convert from one 8-bit code to another, and it takes three operands:

$$TR \ R1 \ (L), \ R2$$

The operand R2 contains the address of the start of a table of 8-bit codes. The L bytes starting at the address specified in R1 are translated, each byte being replaced by the contents of a table entry indexed by that byte. For example, to translate from EBCDIC to IRA, we first create a 256-byte table in storage locations, say, 1000-10FF hexadecimal. The table contains the characters of the IRA code in the sequence of the binary representation of the EBCDIC code; that is, the IRA code is placed in the table at the relative location equal to the binary value of the EBCDIC code of the same character. Thus, locations 10F0 through 10F9 will contain the values 30 through 39, because F0 is the EBCDIC code for the digit 0, and 30 is the IRA code for the digit 0, and so on through digit 9. Now suppose we have the EBCDIC for the digits 1984 starting at location 2100 and we wish to translate to IRA. Assume the following:

- Locations 2100–2103 contain F1 F9 F8 F4.
- R1 contains 2100.
- R2 contains 1000.

Then, if we execute

$$TR \ R1 \ (4), \ R2$$

locations 2100–2103 will contain 31 39 38 34.

Input/Output

Input/output instructions were discussed in some detail in Chapter 7. As we saw, there are a variety of approaches taken, including isolated programmed I/O, memory-mapped programmed I/O, DMA, and the use of an I/O processor. Many implementations provide only a few I/O instructions, with the specific actions specified by parameters, codes, or command words.

System Control

System control instructions are those that can be executed only while the processor is in a certain privileged state or is executing a program in a special privileged area of memory. Typically, these instructions are reserved for the use of the operating system.

Some examples of system control operations are as follows. A system control instruction may read or alter a control register; we discuss control registers in Chapter 14. Another example is an instruction to read or modify a storage protection key, such as is used in the EAS/390 memory system. Another example is access to process control blocks in a multiprogramming system.

Transfer of Control

For all of the operation types discussed so far, the next instruction to be performed is the one that immediately follows, in memory, the current instruction. However, a significant fraction of the instructions in any program have as their function changing the sequence of instruction execution. For these instructions, the operation performed by the processor is to update the program counter to contain the address of some instruction in memory.

There are a number of reasons why transfer-of-control operations are required. Among the most important are the following:

1. In the practical use of computers, it is essential to be able to execute each instruction more than once and perhaps many thousands of times. It may require thousands or perhaps millions of instructions to implement an application. This would be unthinkable if each instruction had to be written out separately. If a table or a list of items is to be processed, a program loop is needed. One sequence of instructions is executed repeatedly to process all the data.

2. Virtually all programs involve some decision making. We would like the computer to do one thing if one condition holds, and another thing if another condition holds. For example, a sequence of instructions computes the square root of a number. At the start of the sequence, the sign of the number is tested. If the number is negative, the computation is not performed, but an error condition is reported.

3. To compose correctly a large or even medium-size computer program is an exceedingly difficult task. It helps if there are mechanisms for breaking the task up into smaller pieces that can be worked on one at a time.

We now turn to a discussion of the most common transfer-of-control operations found in instruction sets: branch, skip, and procedure call.

BRANCH INSTRUCTIONS A branch instruction, also called a jump instruction, has as one of its operands the address of the next instruction to be executed. Most often, the instruction is a **conditional branch** instruction. That is, the branch is made (update program counter to equal address specified in operand) only if a certain condition is met. Otherwise, the next instruction in sequence is executed (increment program counter as usual). A branch instruction in which the branch is always taken is an **unconditional branch**.

There are two common ways of generating the condition to be tested in a conditional branch instruction. First, most machines provide a 1-bit or multiple-bit condition code that is set as the result of some operations. This code can be thought of as a short user-visible register. As an example, an arithmetic operation (ADD, SUBTRACT, and so on) could set a 2-bit condition code with one of the following four values: 0, positive, negative, overflow. On such a machine, there could be four different conditional branch instructions:

BRP X   Branch to location X if result is positive.

BRN X   Branch to location X if result is negative.

BRZ X   Branch to location X if result is zero.

BRO X   Branch to location X if overflow occurs.

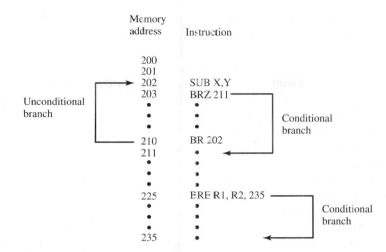

Figure 12.7   Branch Instructions

In all of these cases, the result referred to is the result of the most recent operation that set the condition code.

Another approach that can be used with a three-address instruction format is to perform a comparison and specify a branch in the same instruction. For example,

BRE R1, R2, X   Branch to X if contents of R1 = contents of R2.

Figure 12.7 shows examples of these operations. Note that a branch can be either *forward* (an instruction with a higher address) or *backward* (lower address). The example shows how an unconditional and a conditional branch can be used to create a repeating loop of instructions. The instructions in locations 202 through 210 will be executed repeatedly until the result of subtracting Y from X is 0.

SKIP INSTRUCTIONS Another form of transfer-of-control instruction is the skip instruction. The skip instruction includes an implied address. Typically, the skip implies that one instruction be skipped; thus, the implied address equals the address of the next instruction plus one instruction length.

Because the skip instruction does not require a destination address field, it is free to do other things. A typical example is the increment-and-skip-if-zero (ISZ) instruction. Consider the following program fragment:

```
301
 •
 •
 •
309   ISZ   R1
310   BR    301
311
```

In this fragment, the two transfer-of-control instructions are used to implement an iterative loop. R1 is set with the negative of the number of iterations to be performed. At the end of the loop, R1 is incremented. If it is not 0, the program branches back to the beginning of the loop. Otherwise, the branch is skipped, and the program continues with the next instruction after the end of the loop.

PROCEDURE CALL INSTRUCTIONS Perhaps the most important innovation in the development of programming languages is the *procedure.* A procedure is a self-contained computer program that is incorporated into a larger program. At any point in the program the procedure may be invoked, or *called.* The processor is instructed to go and execute the entire procedure and then return to the point from which the call took place.

The two principal reasons for the use of procedures are economy and modularity. A procedure allows the same piece of code to be used many times. This is important for economy in programming effort and for making the most efficient use of storage space in the system (the program must be stored). Procedures also allow large programming tasks to be subdivided into smaller units. This use of *modularity* greatly eases the programming task.

The procedure mechanism involves two basic instructions: a call instruction that branches from the present location to the procedure, and a return instruction that returns from the procedure to the place from which it was called. Both of these are forms of branching instructions.

Figure 12.8a illustrates the use of procedures to construct a program. In this example, there is a main program starting at location 4000. This program includes a call to procedure PROC1, starting at location 4500. When this call instruction is encountered, the processor suspends execution of the main program and begins execution of PROC1 by fetching the next instruction from location 4500. Within PROC1, there are two calls to PROC2 at location 4800. In each case, the execution of PROC1

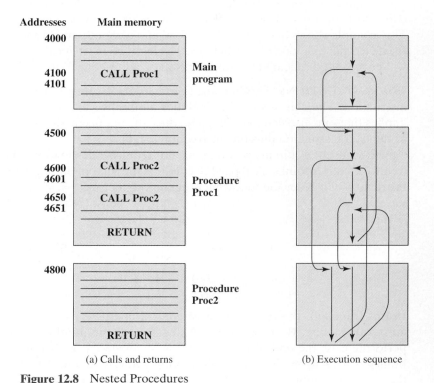

(a) Calls and returns   (b) Execution sequence

Figure 12.8 Nested Procedures

is suspended and PROC2 is executed. The RETURN statement causes the processor to go back to the calling program and continue execution at the instruction after the corresponding CALL instruction. This behavior is illustrated in Figure 12.8b.

Three points are worth noting:

1. A procedure can be called from more than one location.
2. A procedure call can appear in a procedure. This allows the *nesting* of procedures to an arbitrary depth.
3. Each procedure call is matched by a return in the called program.

Because we would like to be able to call a procedure from a variety of points, the processor must somehow save the return address so that the return can take place appropriately. There are three common places for storing the return address:

- Register
- Start of called procedure
- Top of stack

Consider a machine-language instruction CALL X, which stands for *call procedure at location X*. If the register approach is used, CALL X causes the following actions:

$$RN \longleftarrow PC + \Delta$$
$$PC \longleftarrow X$$

where RN is a register that is always used for this purpose, PC is the program counter, and Δ is the instruction length. The called procedure can now save the contents of RN to be used for the later return.

A second possibility is to store the return address at the start of the procedure. In this case, CALL X causes

$$X \longleftarrow PC + \Delta$$
$$PC \longleftarrow X + 1$$

This is quite handy. The return address has been stored safely away.

Both of the preceding approaches work and have been used. The only limitation of these approaches is that they complicate the use of *reentrant* procedures. A reentrant procedure is one in which it is possible to have several calls open to it at the same time. A recursive procedure (one that calls itself) is an example of the use of this feature (see Appendix H). If parameters are passed via registers or memory for a reentrant procedure, some code must be responsible for saving the parameters so that the registers or memory space are available for other procedure calls.

A more general and powerful approach is to use a stack (see Appendix O for a discussion of stacks). When the processor executes a call, it places the return address on the stack. When it executes a return, it uses the address on the stack. Figure 12.9 illustrates the use of the stack.

In addition to providing a return address, it is also often necessary to pass parameters with a procedure call. These can be passed in registers. Another possibility is to store the parameters in memory just after the CALL instruction. In this case, the return must be to the location following the parameters. Again, both of

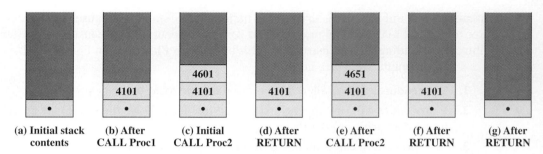

(a) Initial stack contents   (b) After CALL Proc1   (c) Initial CALL Proc2   (d) After RETURN   (e) After CALL Proc2   (f) After RETURN   (g) After RETURN

Figure 12.9   Use of Stack to Implement Nested Subroutines of Figure 12.8

these approaches have drawbacks. If registers are used, the called program and the calling program must be written to assure that the registers are used properly. The storing of parameters in memory makes it difficult to exchange a variable number of parameters. Both approaches prevent the use of reentrant procedures.

A more flexible approach to parameter passing is the stack. When the processor executes a call, it not only stacks the return address, it stacks parameters to be passed to the called procedure. The called procedure can access the parameters from the stack. Upon return, return parameters can also be placed on the stack. The entire set of parameters, including return address, that is stored for a procedure invocation is referred to as a *stack frame.*

An example is provided in Figure 12.10. The example refers to procedure P in which the local variables $x1$ and $x2$ are declared, and procedure Q, which P can call and in which the local variables $y1$ and $y2$ are declared. In this figure, the return

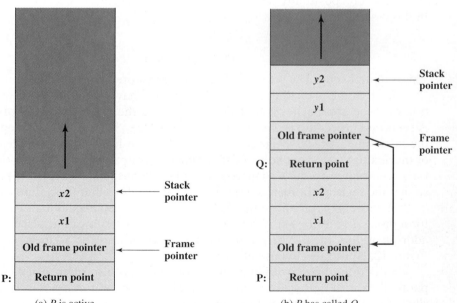

(a) *P* is active   (b) *P* has called *Q*

Figure 12.10   Stack Frame Growth Using Sample Procedures P and Q

point for each procedure is the first item stored in the corresponding stack frame. Next is stored a pointer to the beginning of the previous frame. This is needed if the number or length of parameters to be stacked is variable.

12.5 INTEL x86 AND ARM OPERATION TYPES

x86 Operation Types

The x86 provides a complex array of operation types, including a number of specialized instructions. The intent was to provide tools for the compiler writer to produce optimized machine language translation of high-level language programs. Table 12.8 lists the types and gives examples of each. Most of these are the conventional instructions found in most machine instruction sets, but several types of instructions are tailored to the x86 architecture and are of particular interest. Appendix A of

Table 12.8   x86 Operation Types (with Examples of Typical Operations)

Instruction	Description
Data Movement	
MOV	Move operand, between registers or between register and memory.
PUSH	Push operand onto stack.
PUSHA	Push all registers on stack.
MOVSX	Move byte, word, dword, sign extended. Moves a byte to a word or a word to a doubleword with twos-complement sign extension.
LEA	Load effective address. Loads the offset of the source operand, rather than its value to the destination operand.
XLAT	Table lookup translation. Replaces a byte in AL with a byte from a user-coded translation table. When XLAT is executed, AL should have an unsigned index to the table. XLAT changes the contents of AL from the table index to the table entry.
IN, OUT	Input, output operand from I/O space.
Arithmetic	
ADD	Add operands.
SUB	Subtract operands.
MUL	Unsigned integer multiplication, with byte, word, or double word operands, and word, doubleword, or quadword result.
IDIV	Signed divide.
Logical	
AND	AND operands.
BTS	Bit test and set. Operates on a bit field operand. The instruction copies the current value of a bit to flag CF and sets the original bit to 1.
BSF	Bit scan forward. Scans a word or doubleword for a 1-bit and stores the number of the first 1-bit into a register.
SHL/SHR	Shift logical left or right.
SAL/SAR	Shift arithmetic left or right.

(continued)

Table 12.8 Continued

Instruction	Description
ROL/ROR	Rotate left or right.
SETcc	Sets a byte to zero or one depending on any of the 16 conditions defined by status flags.
Control Transfer	
JMP	Unconditional jump.
CALL	Transfer control to another location. Before transfer, the address of the instruction following the CALL is placed on the stack.
JE/JZ	Jump if equal/zero.
LOOPE/LOOPZ	Loops if equal/zero. This is a conditional jump using a value stored in register ECX. The instruction first decrements ECX before testing ECX for the branch condition.
INT/INTO	Interrupt/Interrupt if overflow. Transfer control to an interrupt service routine.
String Operations	
MOVS	Move byte, word, dword string. The instruction operates on one element of a string, indexed by registers ESI and EDI. After each string operation, the registers are automatically incremented or decremented to point to the next element of the string.
LODS	Load byte, word, dword of string.
High-Level Language Support	
ENTER	Creates a stack frame that can be used to implement the rules of a block-structured high-level language.
LEAVE	Reverses the action of the previous ENTER.
BOUND	Check array bounds. Verifies that the value in operand 1 is within lower and upper limits. The limits are in two adjacent memory locations referenced by operand 2. An interrupt occurs if the value is out of bounds. This instruction is used to check an array index.
Flag Control	
STC	Set Carry flag.
LAHF	Load AH register from flags. Copies SF, ZF, AF, PF, and CF bits into A register.
Segment Register	
LDS	Load pointer into DS and another register.
	System Control
HLT	Halt.
LOCK	Asserts a hold on shared memory so that the Pentium has exclusive use of it during the instruction that immediately follows the LOCK.
ESC	Processor extension escape. An escape code that indicates the succeeding instructions are to be executed by a numeric coprocessor that supports high-precision integer and floating-point calculations.
WAIT	Wait until BUSY# negated. Suspends Pentium program execution until the processor detects that the BUSY pin is inactive, indicating that the numeric coprocessor has finished execution.
Protection	
SGDT	Store global descriptor table.
LSL	Load segment limit. Loads a user-specified register with a segment limit.
VERR/VERW	Verify segment for reading/writing.

Instruction	Description
Cache Management	
INVD	Flushes the internal cache memory.
WBINVD	Flushes the internal cache memory after writing dirty lines to memory.
INVLPG	Invalidates a translation lookaside buffer (TLB) entry.

[CART06] lists the x86 instructions, together with the operands for each and the effect of the instruction on the condition codes. Appendix B of the NASM assembly language manual provides a more detailed description of each x86 instruction. Both documents are available at this book's Web site.

CALL/RETURN INSTRUCTIONS The x86 provides four instructions to support procedure call/return: CALL, ENTER, LEAVE, RETURN. It will be instructive to look at the support provided by these instructions. Recall from Figure 12.10 that a common means of implementing the procedure call/return mechanism is via the use of stack frames. When a new procedure is called, the following must be performed upon entry to the new procedure:

- Push the return point on the stack.
- Push the current frame pointer on the stack.
- Copy the stack pointer as the new value of the frame pointer.
- Adjust the stack pointer to allocate a frame.

The CALL instruction pushes the current instruction pointer value onto the stack and causes a jump to the entry point of the procedure by placing the address of the entry point in the instruction pointer. In the 8088 and 8086 machines, the typical procedure began with the sequence

```
PUSH      EBP
MOV       EBP, ESP
SUB       ESP, space_for_locals
```

where EBP is the frame pointer and ESP is the stack pointer. In the 80286 and later machines, the ENTER instruction performs all the aforementioned operations in a single instruction.

The ENTER instruction was added to the instruction set to provide direct support for the compiler. The instruction also includes a feature for support of what are called nested procedures in languages such as Pascal, COBOL, and Ada (not found in C or FORTRAN). It turns out that there are better ways of handling nested procedure calls for these languages. Furthermore, although the ENTER instruction saves a few bytes of memory compared with the PUSH, MOV, SUB sequence (4 bytes versus 6 bytes), it actually takes longer to execute (10 clock cycles versus 6 clock cycles). Thus, although it may have seemed a good idea to the instruction set designers to add this feature, it complicates the implementation of the processor while providing little or no benefit. We will see that, in contrast, a RISC approach to processor design would avoid complex instructions such as ENTER and might produce a more efficient implementation with a sequence of simpler instructions.

MEMORY MANAGEMENT Another set of specialized instructions deals with memory segmentation. These are privileged instructions that can only be executed from the operating system. They allow local and global segment tables (called descriptor tables) to be loaded and read, and for the privilege level of a segment to be checked and altered.

The special instructions for dealing with the on-chip cache were discussed in Chapter 4.

STATUS FLAGS AND CONDITION CODES Status flags are bits in special registers that may be set by certain operations and used in conditional branch instructions. The term *condition code* refers to the settings of one or more status flags. In the x86 and many other architectures, status flags are set by arithmetic and compare operations. The compare operation in most languages subtracts two operands, as does a subtract operation. The difference is that a compare operation only sets status flags, whereas a subtract operation also stores the result of the subtraction in the destination operand. Some architectures also set status flags for data transfer instructions.

Table 12.9 lists the status flags used on the x86. Each flag, or combinations of these flags, can be tested for a conditional jump. Table 12.10 shows the condition codes (combinations of status flag values) for which conditional jump opcodes have been defined.

Several interesting observations can be made about this list. First, we may wish to test two operands to determine if one number is bigger than another. But this will depend on whether the numbers are signed or unsigned. For example, the 8-bit number 11111111 is bigger than 00000000 if the two numbers are interpreted as unsigned integers ($255 > 0$) but is less if they are considered as 8-bit twos complement numbers ($-1 < 0$). Many assembly languages therefore introduce two sets of terms to distinguish the two cases: If we are comparing two numbers as signed integers, we use the terms *less than* and *greater than;* if we are comparing them as unsigned integers, we use the terms *below* and *above.*

A second observation concerns the complexity of comparing signed integers. A signed result is greater than or equal to zero if (1) the sign bit is zero and there is no overflow ($S = 0$ AND $O = 0$), or (2) the sign bit is one and there is an overflow.

Table 12.9 x86 Status Flags

Status Bit	Name	Description
C	Carry	Indicates carrying or borrowing out of the left-most bit position following an arithmetic operation. Also modified by some of the shift and rotate operations.
P	Parity	Parity of the least-significant byte of the result of an arithmetic or logic operation. 1 indicates even parity; 0 indicates odd parity.
A	Auxiliary Carry	Represents carrying or borrowing between half-bytes of an 8-bit arithmetic or logic operation. Used in binary-coded decimal arithmetic.
Z	Zero	Indicates that the result of an arithmetic or logic operation is 0.
S	Sign	Indicates the sign of the result of an arithmetic or logic operation.
O	Overflow	Indicates an arithmetic overflow after an addition or subtraction for twos complement arithmetic.

Table 12.10   x86 Condition Codes for Conditional Jump and SETcc Instructions

Symbol	Condition Tested	Comment
A, NBE	$C = 0$ AND $Z = 0$	Above: Not below or equal (greater than, unsigned)
AE, NB, NC	$C = 0$	Above or equal; Not below (greater than or equal, unsigned); Not carry
B, NAE, C	$C = 1$	Below; Not above or equal (less than, unsigned); Carry set
BE, NA	$C = 1$ OR $Z = 1$	Below or equal; Not above (less than or equal, unsigned)
E, Z	$Z = 1$	Equal; Zero (signed or unsigned)
G, NLE	$[(S = 1$ AND $O = 1)$ OR $(S = 0$ and $O = 0)]$ AND $[Z = 0]$	Greater than; Not less than or equal (signed)
GE, NL	$(S = 1$ AND $O = 1)$ OR $(S = 0$ AND $O = 0)$	Greater than or equal; Not less than (signed)
L, NGE	$(S = 1$ AND $O = 0)$ OR $(S = 0$ AND $O = 1)$	Less than; Not greater than or equal (signed)
LE, NG	$(S = 1$ AND $O = 0)$ OR $(S = 0$ AND $O = 1)$ OR $(Z = 1)$	Less than or equal; Not greater than (signed)
NE, NZ	$Z = 0$	Not equal; Not zero (signed or unsigned)
NO	$O = 0$	No overflow
NS	$S = 0$	Not sign (not negative)
NP, PO	$P = 0$	Not parity; Parity odd
O	$O = 1$	Overflow
P	$P = 1$	Parity; Parity even
S	$S = 1$	Sign (negative)

A study of Figure 10.4 should convince you that the conditions tested for the various signed operations are appropriate.

x86 SIMD INSTRUCTIONS In 1996, Intel introduced MMX technology into its Pentium product line. MMX is set of highly optimized instructions for multimedia tasks. There are 57 new instructions that treat data in a SIMD (single-instruction, multiple-data) fashion, which makes it possible to perform the same operation, such as addition or multiplication, on multiple data elements at once. Each instruction typically takes a single clock cycle to execute. For the proper application, these fast parallel operations can yield a speedup of two to eight times over comparable algorithms that do not use the MMX instructions [ATKI96]. With the introduction of 64-bit x86 architecture, Intel has expanded this extension to include double quadword (128 bits) operands and floating-point operations. In this subsection, we describe the MMX features.

The focus of MMX is multimedia programming. Video and audio data are typically composed of large arrays of small data types, such as 8 or 16 bits, whereas conventional instructions are tailored to operate on 32- or 64-bit data. Here are some examples: In graphics and video, a single scene consists of an array of pixels,[2] and

---

[2]A pixel, or picture element, is the smallest element of a digital image that can be assigned a gray level. Equivalently, a pixel is an individual dot in a dot-matrix representation of a picture.

there are 8 bits for each pixel or 8 bits for each pixel color component (red, green, blue). Typical audio samples are quantized using 16 bits. For some 3D graphics algorithms, 32 bits are common for basic data types. To provide for parallel operation on these data lengths, three new data types are defined in MMX. Each data type is 64 bits in length and consists of multiple smaller data fields, each of which holds a fixed-point integer. The types are as follows:

- **Packed byte:** Eight bytes packed into one 64-bit quantity
- **Packed word:** Four 16-bit words packed into 64 bits
- **Packed doubleword:** Two 32-bit doublewords packed into 64 bits

Table 12.11 lists the MMX instruction set. Most of the instructions involve parallel operation on bytes, words, or doublewords. For example, the PSLLW instruction performs a left logical shift separately on each of the four words in the packed word operand; the PADDB instruction takes packed byte operands as input and performs parallel additions on each byte position independently to produce a packed byte output.

One unusual feature of the new instruction set is the introduction of **saturation arithmetic** for byte and 16-bit word operands. With ordinary unsigned arithmetic, when an operation overflows (i.e., a carry out of the most significant bit), the extra bit is truncated. This is referred to as wraparound, because the effect of the truncation can be, for example, to produce an addition result that is smaller than the two input operands. Consider the addition of the two words, in hexadecimal, F000h and 3000h. The sum would be expressed as

$$\begin{array}{r} \text{F000h} = 1111\ 0000\ 0000\ 0000 \\ \underline{+3000\text{h} = 0011\ 0000\ 0000\ 0000} \\ 10010\ 0000\ 0000\ 0000 \end{array} = 2000\text{h}$$

If the two numbers represented image intensity, then the result of the addition is to make the combination of two dark shades turn out to be lighter. This is typically not what is intended. With saturation arithmetic, if addition results in overflow or subtraction results in underflow, the result is set to the largest or smallest value representable. For the preceding example, with saturation arithmetic, we have

$$\begin{array}{r} \text{F000h} = 1111\ 0000\ 0000\ 0000 \\ \underline{+3000\text{h} = 0011\ 0000\ 0000\ 0000} \\ 10010\ 0000\ 0000\ 0000 \end{array}$$

$$1111\ 1111\ 1111\ 1111 = \text{FFFFh}$$

To provide a feel for the use of MMX instructions, we look at an example, taken from [PELE97]. A common video application is the fade-out, fade-in effect, in which one scene gradually dissolves into another. Two images are combined with a weighted average:

$$\text{Result\_pixel} = \text{A\_pixel} \times \text{fade} + \text{B\_pixel} \times (1 - \text{fade})$$

Table 12.11 MMX Instruction Set

Category	Instruction	Description
Arithmetic	PADD [B, W, D]	Parallel add of packed eight bytes, four 16-bit words, or two 32-bit doublewords, with wraparound.
	PADDS [B, W]	Add with saturation.
	PADDUS [B, W]	Add unsigned with saturation.
	PSUB [B, W, D]	Subtract with wraparound.
	PSUBS [B, W]	Subtract with saturation.
	PSUBUS [B, W]	Subtract unsigned with saturation.
	PMULHW	Parallel multiply of four signed 16-bit words, with high-order 16 bits of 32-bit result chosen.
	PMULLW	Parallel multiply of four signed 16-bit words, with low-order 16 bits of 32-bit result chosen.
	PMADDWD	Parallel multiply of four signed 16-bit words; add together adjacent pairs of 32-bit results.
Comparison	PCMPEQ [B, W, D]	Parallel compare for equality; result is mask of 1s if true or 0s if false.
	PCMPGT [B, W, D]	Parallel compare for greater than; result is mask of 1s if true or 0s if false.
Conversion	PACKUSWB	Pack words into bytes with unsigned saturation.
	PACKSS [WB, DW]	Pack words into bytes, or doublewords into words, with signed saturation.
	PUNPCKH [BW, WD, DQ]	Parallel unpack (interleaved merge) high-order bytes, words, or doublewords from MMX register.
	PUNPCKL [BW, WD, DQ]	Parallel unpack (interleaved merge) low-order bytes, words, or doublewords from MMX register.
Logical	PAND	64-bit bitwise logical AND
	PNDN	64-bit bitwise logical AND NOT
	POR	64-bit bitwise logical OR
	PXOR	64-bit bitwise logical XOR
Shift	PSLL [W, D, Q]	Parallel logical left shift of packed words, doublewords, or quadword by amount specified in MMX register or immediate value.
	PSRL [W, D, Q]	Parallel logical right shift of packed words, doublewords, or quadword.
	PSRA [W, D]	Parallel arithmetic right shift of packed words, doublewords, or quadword.
Data transfer	MOV [D, Q]	Move doubleword or quadword to/from MMX register.
State mgt	EMMS	Empty MMX state (empty FP registers tag bits).

Note: If an instruction supports multiple data types [byte (B), word (W), doubleword (D), quadword (Q)], the data types are indicated in brackets.

This calculation is performed on each pixel position in A and B. If a series of video frames is produced while gradually changing the fade value from 1 to 0 (scaled appropriately for an 8-bit integer), the result is to fade from image A to image B.

Figure 12.11 shows the sequence of steps required for one set of pixels. The 8-bit pixel components are converted to 16-bit elements to accommodate the MMX 16-bit multiply capability. If these images use 640 × 480 resolution, and the dissolve technique uses all 255 possible values of the fade value, then the total number of instructions executed using MMX is 535 million. The same calculation, performed without the MMX instructions, requires 1.4 billion instruction executions [INTE98].

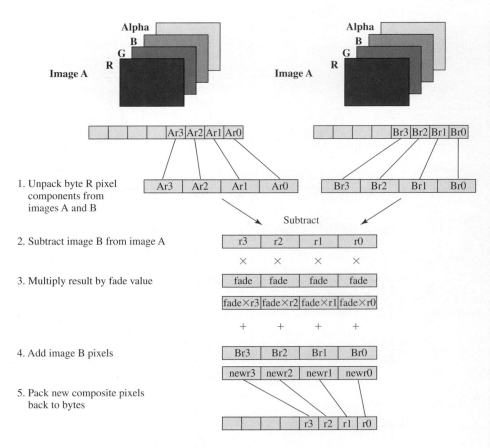

MMX code sequence performing this operation:

```
pxor        mm7, mm7        ;zero out mm7
movq        mm3, fad_val    ;load fade value replicated 4 times
movd        mm0, imageA     ;load 4 red pixel components from image A
movd        mm1, imageB     ;load 4 red pixel components from image B
punpckblw   mm0, mm7        ;unpack 4 pixels to 16 bits
punpckblw   mm1, mm7        ;unpack 4 pixels to 16 bits
psubw       mm0, mm1        ;subtract image B from image A
pmulhw      mm0, mm3        ;multiply the subtract result by fade values
padddw      mm0, mm1        ;add result to image B
packuswb    mm0, mm7        ;pack 16-bit results back to bytes
```

Figure 12.11 Image Compositing on Color Plane Representation

ARM Operation Types

The ARM architecture provides a large collection of operation types. The following are the principal categories:

- **Load and store instructions:** In the ARM architecture, only load and store instructions access memory locations; arithmetic and logical instructions are performed only on registers and immediate values encoded in the instruction. This limitation is characteristic of RISC design and it is explored further in Chapter 15. The ARM architecture supports two broad types of instruction that load or store the value of a single register, or a pair of registers, from or to memory: (1) load or store a 32-bit word or an 8-bit unsigned byte, and (2) load or store a 16-bit unsigned halfword, and load and sign extend a 16-bit halfword or an 8-bit byte.

- **Branch instructions:** ARM supports a branch instruction that allows a conditional branch forwards or backwards up to 32 MB. As the program counter is one of the general-purpose registers (R15), a branch or jump can also be generated by writing a value to R15. A subroutine call can be performed by a variant of the standard branch instruction. As well as allowing a branch forward or backward up to 32 MB, the Branch with Link (BL) instruction preserves the address of the instruction after the branch (the return address) in the LR (R14). Branches are determined by a 4-bit condition field in the instruction.

- **Data-processing instructions:** This category includes logical instructions (AND, OR, XOR), add and subtract instructions, and test and compare instructions.

- **Multiply instructions:** The integer multiply instructions operate on word or halfword operands and can produce normal or long results. For example, there is a multiply instruction that takes two 32-bit operands and produces a 64-bit result.

- **Parallel addition and subtraction instructions:** In addition to the normal data processing and multiply instructions, there are a set of parallel addition and subtraction instructions, in which portions of two operands are operated on in parallel. For example, ADD16 adds the top halfwords of two registers to form the top halfword of the result and adds the bottom halfwords of the same two registers to form the bottom halfword of the result. These instructions are useful in image processing applications, similar to the x86 MMX instructions.

- **Extend instructions:** There are several instructions for unpacking data by sign or zero extending bytes to halfwords or words, and halfwords to words.

- **Status register access instructions:** ARM provides the ability to read and also to write portions of the status register.

CONDITION CODES The ARM architecture defines four condition flags that are stored in the program status register: N, Z, C, and V (Negative, Zero, Carry and oVerflow), with meanings essentially the same as the S, Z, C, and V flags

Table 12.12 ARM Conditions for Conditional Instruction Execution

Code	Symbol	Condition Tested	Comment
0000	EQ	Z = 1	Equal
0001	NE	Z = 0	Not equal
0010	CS/HS	C = 1	Carry set/unsigned higher or same
0011	CC/LO	C = 0	Carry clear/unsigned lower
0100	MI	N = 1	Minus/negative
0101	PL	N = 0	Plus/positive or zero
0110	VS	V = 1	Overflow
0111	VC	V = 0	No overflow
1000	HI	C = 1 AND Z = 0	Unsigned higher
1001	LS	C = 0 OR Z = 1	Unsigned lower or same
1010	GE	N = V [(N = 1 AND V = 1) OR (N = 0 AND V = 0)]	Signed greater than or equal
1011	LT	N ≠ V [(N = 1 AND V = 0) OR (N = 0 AND V = 1)]	Signed less than
1100	GT	(Z = 0) AND (N = V)	Signed greater than
1101	LE	(Z = 1) OR (N ≠ V)	Signed less than or equal
1110	AL	—	Always (unconditional)
1111	—	—	This instruction can only be executed unconditionally

in the x86 architecture. These four flags constitute a condition code in ARM. Table 12.12 shows the combination of conditions for which conditional execution is defined.

There are two unusual aspects to the use of condition codes in ARM:

1. All instructions, not just branch instructions, include a condition code field, which means that virtually all instructions may be conditionally executed. Any combination of flag settings except 1110 or 1111 in an instruction's condition code field signifies that the instruction will be executed only if the condition is met.

2. All data processing instructions (arithmetic, logical) include an S bit that signifies whether the instruction updates the condition flags.

The use of conditional execution and conditional setting of the condition flags helps in the design of shorter programs that use less memory. On the other hand, all instructions include 4 bits for the condition code, so there is a trade-off in that fewer bits in the 32-bit instruction are available for opcode and operands. Because the ARM is a RISC design that relies heavily on register addressing, this seems to be a reasonable trade-off.

2.6 RECOMMENDED READING

The x86 instruction set is well covered by [BREY09]. The ARM instruction set is covered in [SLOS04] and [KNAG04]. [INTE04c] describes software considerations related to microprocessor Endian architecture and discusses guidelines for developing Endian-neutral code (paper available in the premium content section for this book).

BREY09 Brey, B. *The Intel Microprocessors: 8086/8066, 80186/80188, 80286, 80386, 80486, Pentium, Pentium Pro Processor, Pentium II, Pentium III, Pentium 4 and Core2 with 64-bit Extensions.* Upper Saddle River, NJ: Prentice Hall, 2009.

INTE04c Intel Corp. *Endianness White Paper.* November 15, 2004.

KNAG04 Knaggs, P., and Welsh, S. *ARM: Assembly Language Programming.* Bournemouth University, School of Design, Engineering, and Computing, August 31, 2004. www.freetechbooks.com/arm-assembly-language-programming-t729.html

SLOS04 Sloss, A.; Symes, D.; and Wright, C. *ARM System Developer's Guide.* San Francisco: Morgan Kaufmann, 2004.

2.7 KEY TERMS, REVIEW QUESTIONS, AND PROBLEMS

Key Terms

accumulator	jump	procedure call
address	little endian	procedure return
arithmetic shift	logical shift	push
bi-endian	machine instruction	reentrant procedure
big endian	operand	reverse Polish notation
branch	operation	rotate
conditional branch	packed decimal	skip
instruction set	pop	stack

Review Questions

12.1 What are the typical elements of a machine instruction?

12.2 What types of locations can hold source and destination operands?

12.3 If an instruction contains four addresses, what might be the purpose of each address?

12.4 List and briefly explain five important instruction set design issues.

12.5 What types of operands are typical in machine instruction sets?

12.6 What is the relationship between the IRA character code and the packed decimal representation?

12.7 What is the difference between an arithmetic shift and a logical shift?

12.8 Why are transfer of control instructions needed?

12.9 List and briefly explain two common ways of generating the condition to be tested in a conditional branch instruction.

12.10 What is meant by the term *nesting of procedures*?

12.11 List three possible places for storing the return address for a procedure return.

12.12 What is a reentrant procedure?

12.13 What is reverse Polish notation?

12.14 What is the difference between big endian and little endian?

Problems

12.1 Show in hex notation:
  a. The packed decimal format for 23
  b. The ASCII characters 23

12.2 For each of the following packed decimal numbers, show the decimal value:
  a. 0111 0011 0000 1001
  b. 0101 1000 0010
  c. 0100 1010 0110

12.3 A given microprocessor has words of 1 byte. What is the smallest and largest integer that can be represented in the following representations:
  a. Unsigned
  b. Sign-magnitude
  c. Ones complement
  d. Twos complement
  e. Unsigned packed decimal
  f. Signed packed decimal

12.4 Many processors provide logic for performing arithmetic on packed decimal numbers. Although the rules for decimal arithmetic are similar to those for binary operations, the decimal results may require some corrections to the individual digits if binary logic is used.

  Consider the decimal addition of two unsigned numbers. If each number consists of N digits, then there are $4N$ bits in each number. The two numbers are to be added using a binary adder. Suggest a simple rule for correcting the result. Perform addition in this fashion on the numbers 1698 and 1786.

12.5 The tens complement of the decimal number X is defined to be $10^N - X$, where N is the number of decimal digits in the number. Describe the use of ten's complement representation to perform decimal subtraction. Illustrate the procedure by subtracting $(0326)_{10}$ from $(0736)_{10}$.

12.6 Compare zero-, one-, two-, and three-address machines by writing programs to compute

$$X = (A + B \times C)/(D - E \times F)$$

for each of the four machines. The instructions available for use are as follows:

0 Address	1 Address	2 Address	3 Address
PUSH M	LOAD M	MOVE $(X \leftarrow Y)$	MOVE $(X \leftarrow Y)$
POP M	STORE M	ADD $(X \leftarrow X + Y)$	ADD $(X \leftarrow Y + Z)$
ADD	ADD M	SUB $(X \leftarrow X - Y)$	SUB $(X \leftarrow Y - Z)$
SUB	SUB M	MUL $(X \leftarrow X \times Y)$	MUL $(X \leftarrow Y \times Z)$
MUL	MUL M	DIV $(X \leftarrow X/Y)$	DIV $(X \leftarrow Y/Z)$
DIV	DIV M		

12.7 Consider a hypothetical computer with an instruction set of only two n-bit instructions. The first bit specifies the opcode, and the remaining bits specify one of the 2^{n-1} n-bit words of main memory. The two instructions are as follows:

SUBS X   Subtract the contents of location X from the accumulator, and store the result in location X and the accumulator.

JUMP X   Place address X in the program counter.

A word in main memory may contain either an instruction or a binary number in twos complement notation. Demonstrate that this instruction repertoire is reasonably complete by specifying how the following operations can be programmed:
  a. Data transfer: Location X to accumulator, accumulator to location X
  b. Addition: Add contents of location X to accumulator
  c. Conditional branch
  d. Logical OR
  e. I/O Operations

12.8 Many instruction sets contain the instruction NOOP, meaning no operation, which has no effect on the processor state other than incrementing the program counter. Suggest some uses of this instruction.

12.9 In Section 12.4, it was stated that both an arithmetic left shift and a logical left shift correspond to a multiplication by 2 when there is no overflow, and if overflow occurs, arithmetic and logical left shift operations produce different results, but the arithmetic left shift retains the sign of the number. Demonstrate that these statements are true for 5-bit twos complement integers.

12.10 In what way are numbers rounded using arithmetic right shift (e.g., round toward $+\infty$, round toward $-\infty$, toward zero, away from 0)?

12.11 Suppose a stack is to be used by the processor to manage procedure calls and returns. Can the program counter be eliminated by using the top of the stack as a program counter?

12.12 The x86 architecture includes an instruction called Decimal Adjust after Addition (DAA). DAA performs the following sequence of instructions:

```
if  ((AL AND 0FH) >9) OR (AF = 1) then
        AL ← AL + 6;
        AF ← 1;
else
        AF ← 0;
endif;
if  (AL > 9FH) OR (CF = 1) then
        AL ← AL + 60H;
        CF ← 1;
else
        CF ← 0;
endif.
```

"H" indicates hexadecimal. AL is an 8-bit register that holds the result of addition of two unsigned 8-bit integers. AF is a flag set if there is a carry from bit 3 to bit 4 in the result of an addition. CF is a flag set if there is a carry from bit 7 to bit 8. Explain the function performed by the DAA instruction.

12.13 The x86 Compare instruction (CMP) subtracts the source operand from the destination operand; it updates the status flags (C, P, A, Z, S, O) but does not alter either of the operands. The CMP instruction can be used to determine if the destination operand is greater than, equal to, or less than the source operand.

   a. Suppose the two operands are treated as unsigned integers. Show which status flags are relevant to determine the relative size of the two integer and what values of the flags correspond to greater than, equal to, or less than.

   b. Suppose the two operands are treated as twos complement signed integers. Show which status flags are relevant to determine the relative size of the two integer and what values of the flags correspond to greater than, equal to, or less than.

   c. The CMP instruction may be followed by a conditional Jump (Jcc) or Set Condition (SETcc) instruction, where cc refers to one of the 16 conditions listed in Table 12.12. Demonstrate that the conditions tested for a signed number comparison are correct.

12.14 Suppose we wished to apply the x86 CMP instruction to 32-bit operands that contained numbers in a floating-point format. For correct results, what requirements have to be met in the following areas?

   a. The relative position of the significand, sign, and exponent fields.

   b. The representation of the value zero.

   c. The representation of the exponent.

   d. Does the IEEE format meet these requirements? Explain.

12.15 Many microprocessor instruction sets include an instruction that tests a condition and sets a destination operand if the condition is true. Examples include the SETcc on the x86, the Scc on the Motorola MC68000, and the Scond on the National NS32000.

   a. There are a few differences among these instructions:

   - SETcc and Scc operate only on a byte, whereas Scond operates on byte, word, and doubleword operands.

   - SETcc and Scond set the operand to integer one if true and to zero if false. Scc sets the byte to all binary ones if true and all zeros if false.

   What are the relative advantages and disadvantages of these differences?

   b. None of these instructions set any of the condition code flags, and thus an explicit test of the result of the instruction is required to determine its value. Discuss whether condition codes should be set as a result of this instruction.

   c. A simple IF statement such as IF a > b THEN can be implemented using a numerical representation method, that is, making the Boolean value manifest, as opposed to a *flow of control* method, which represents the value of a Boolean expression by a point reached in the program. A compiler might implement IF a > ssb THEN with the following x86 code:

```
             SUB     CX, CX    ;set register CX to 0
             MOV     AX, B     ;move contents of location B to register AX
             CMP     AX, A     ;compare contents of register AX and location A
             JLE     TEST      ;jump if A ≤ B
             INC     CX        ;add 1 to contents of register CX
TEST         JCXZ    OUT       ;jump if contents of CX equal 0
THEN                 OUT
```

   The result of (A > B) is a Boolean value held in a register and available later on, outside the context of the flow of code just shown. It is convenient to use register CX for this, because many of the branch and loop opcodes have a built-in test for CX.

   Show an alternative implementation using the SETcc instruction that saves memory and execution time. (*Hint:* No additional new x86 instructions are needed, other than the SETcc.)

   d. Now consider the high-level language statement:

$$A: = (B > C) OR (D = F)$$

A compiler might generate the following code:

```
        MOV    EAX, B      ;move contents of location B to register EAX
        CMP    EAX, C      ;compare contents of register EAX and location C
        MOV    BL, 0       ;0 represents false
        JLE    N1          ;jump if (B ≤ C)
        MOV    BL, 1       ;1 represents false
N1      MOV    EAX, D
        CMP    EAX, F
        MOV    BH, 0
        JNE    N2
        MOV    BH, 1
N2      OR     BL. BH
```

Show an alternative implementation using the SETcc instruction that saves memory and execution time.

12.16 Suppose that two registers contain the following hexadecimal values: AB0890C2, 4598EE50. What is the result of adding them using MMX instructions:
  a. for packed byte
  b. for packed word

Assume saturation arithmetic is not used.

12.17 Appendix O points out that there are no stack-oriented instructions in an instruction set if the stack is to be used only by the processor for such purposes as procedure handling. How can the processor use a stack for any purpose without stack-oriented instructions?

12.18 Convert the following formulas from reverse Polish to infix:
  a. $AB + C + D \times$
  b. $AB/CD/ +$
  c. $ABCDE +\times\times/$
  d. $ABCDE + F/ + G - H/ \times +$

12.19 Convert the following formulas from infix to reverse Polish:
  a. $A + B + C + D + E$
  b. $(A + B) \times (C + D) + E$
  c. $(A \times B) + (C \times D) + E$
  d. $(A - B) \times (((C - D \times E)/F)/G) \times H$

12.20 Convert the expression $A + B - C$ to postfix notation using Dijkstra's algorithm. Show the steps involved. Is the result equivalent to $(A + B) - C$ or $A + (B - C)$? Does it matter?

12.21 Using the algorithm for converting infix to postfix defined in Appendix O, show the steps involved in converting the expression of Figure O.3 into postfix. Use a presentation similar to Figure O.5.

12.22 Show the calculation of the expression in Figure O.5, using a presentation similar to Figure O.4.

12.23 Redraw the little-endian layout in Figure 12.13 so that the bytes appear as numbered in the big-endian layout. That is, show memory in 64-bit rows, with the bytes listed left to right, top to bottom.

12.24 For the following data structures, draw the big-endian and little-endian layouts, using the format of Figure 12.13, and comment on the results.
```
        a.   struct {
                double i;      //0x1112131415161718
             } s1;
        b.   struct {
                int i;         //0x11121314
                int j;         //0x15161718
             } s2;
```

c. struct {
        short i;   //0x1112
        short j;   //0x1314
        short k; //0x1516
        short l;   //0x1718
  } s3;

12.25 The IBM Power architecture specification does not dictate how a processor should implement little-endian mode. It specifies only the view of memory a processor must have when operating in little-endian mode. When converting a data structure from big endian to little endian, processors are free to implement a true byte-swapping mechanism or to use some sort of an address modification mechanism. Current Power processors are all default big-endian machines and use address modification to treat data as little-endian.

Consider the structure s defined in Figure 12.13. The layout in the lower-right portion of the figure shows the structure s as seen by the processor. In fact, if structure s is compiled in little-endian mode, its layout in memory is shown in Figure 12.12. Explain the mapping that is involved, describe an easy way to implement the mapping, and discuss the effectiveness of this approach.

12.26 Write a small program to determine the endianness of machine and report the results. Run the program on a computer available to you and turn in the output.

12.27 The MIPS processor can be set to operate in either big-endian or little-endian mode. Consider the Load Byte Unsigned (LBU) instruction, which loads a byte from memory into the low-order 8 bits of a register and fills the high-order 24 bits of the register with zeros. The description of LBU is given in the MIPS reference manual using a register-transfer language as

mem ← LoadMemory (...)
byte ← VirtualAddress$_{1..0}$
if CONDITION **then**
       GPR[rt] ← 0^{24}‖mem$_{31 - 8}$ $\times$ byte .. 24 $-$ 8 $\times$ byte
else
       GPR[rt] ← 0^{24}‖mem$_{7 + 8}$ $\times$ byte .. 8 $\times$ byte
endif

where *byte* refers to the two low-order bits of the effective address and *mem* refers to the value loaded from memory. In the manual, instead of the word CONDITION, one of the following two words is used: BigEndian, LittleEndian. Which word is used?

12.28 Most, but not all, processors use big- or little-endian bit ordering within a byte that is consistent with big- or little-endian ordering of bytes within a multibyte scalar. Let us

Little-endian address mapping

Byte address								
					11	**12**	**13**	**14**
00	00	01	02	03	04	05	06	07
	21	**22**	**23**	**24**	**25**	**26**	**27**	**28**
08	08	09	0A	0B	0C	0D	0E	0F
	'D'	**'C'**	**'B'**	**'A'**	**31**	**32**	**33**	**34**
10	10	11	12	13	14	15	16	17
			51	**52**		**'G'**	**'F'**	**'E'**
18	18	19	1A	1B	1C	1D	1E	1F
					61	**62**	**63**	**64**
20	20	21	22	23	24	25	26	27

Figure 12.12 Power Architecture Little-Endian Structure s in Memory

consider the Motorola 68030, which uses big-endian byte ordering. The documentation of the 68030 concerning formats is confusing. The user's manual explains that the bit ordering of bit fields is the opposite of bit ordering of integers. Most bit field operations operate with one endian ordering, but a few bit field operations require the opposite ordering. The following description from the user's manual describes most of the bit field operations:

> A bit operand is specified by a base address that selects one byte in memory (the base byte), and a bit number that selects the one bit in this byte. The most significant bit is bit seven. A bit field operand is specified by: **(1)** a base address that selects one byte in memory; **(2)** a bit field offset that indicates the leftmost (base) bit of the bit field in relation to the most significant bit of the base byte; and **(3)** a bit field width that determines how many bits to the right of the base byte are in the bit field. The most significant bit of the base byte is bit field offset 0, the least significant bit of the base byte is bit field offset 7.

Do these instructions use big-endian or little-endian bit ordering?

APPENDIX 12A   LITTLE-, BIG-, AND BI-ENDIAN

An annoying and curious phenomenon relates to how the bytes within a word and the bits within a byte are both referenced and represented. We look first at the problem of byte ordering and then consider that of bits.

Byte Ordering

The concept of endianness was first discussed in the literature by Cohen [COHE81]. With respect to bytes, endianness has to do with the byte ordering of multibyte scalar values. The issue is best introduced with an example. Suppose we have the 32-bit hexadecimal value 12345678 and that it is stored in a 32-bit word in byte-addressable memory at byte location 184. The value consists of 4 bytes, with the least significant byte containing the value 78 and the most significant byte containing the value 12. There are two obvious ways to store this value:

Address	Value
184	12
185	34
186	56
187	78

Address	Value
184	78
185	56
186	34
187	12

The mapping on the left stores the most significant byte in the lowest numerical byte address; this is known as **big endian** and is equivalent to the left-to-right order of writing in Western culture languages. The mapping on the right stores the least significant byte in the lowest numerical byte address; this is known as **little endian** and is reminiscent of the right-to-left order of arithmetic operations in arithmetic units.[3] For a given multibyte scalar value, big endian and little endian are byte-reversed mappings of each other.

---

[3]The terms *big endian* and *little endian* come from Part I, Chapter 4 of Jonathan Swift's *Gulliver's Travels*. They refer to a religious war between two groups, one that breaks eggs at the big end and the other that breaks eggs at the little end.

The concept of endianness arises when it is necessary to treat a multiple-byte entity as a single data item with a single address, even though it is composed of smaller addressable units. Some machines, such as the Intel 80x86, x86, VAX, and Alpha, are little-endian machines, whereas others, such as the IBM System 370/390, the Motorola 680x0, Sun SPARC, and most RISC machines, are big endian. This presents problems when data are transferred from a machine of one endian type to the other and when a programmer attempts to manipulate individual bytes or bits within a multibyte scalar.

The property of endianness does not extend beyond an individual data unit. In any machine, aggregates such as files, data structures, and arrays are composed of multiple data units, each with endianness. Thus, conversion of a block of memory from one style of endianness to the other requires knowledge of the data structure.

Figure 12.13 illustrates how endianness determines addressing and byte order. The C structure at the top contains a number of data types. The memory layout in the lower left results from compilation of that structure for a big-endian machine, and that in the lower right for a little-endian machine. In each case, memory is depicted as a series of 64-bit rows. For the big-endian case, memory typically is viewed left to right, top to bottom, whereas for the little-endian case, memory typically is viewed as right to left, top to bottom. Note that these layouts are arbitrary. Either scheme could use either left to right or right to left within a row; this is a matter of depiction, not memory assignment. In fact, in looking at programmer manuals for a variety of machines, a bewildering collection of depictions is to be found, even within the same manual.

```
struct{
    int     a;      //0x1112_1314                          word
    int     pad;    //
    double  b;      //0x2122_2324_2526_2728                doubleword
    char*   c;      //0x3132_3334                          word
    char    d[7];   //'A'.'B','C','D','E','F','G'          byte array
    short   e;      //0x5152                               halfword
    int     f;      //0x6162_6364                          word
} s;
```

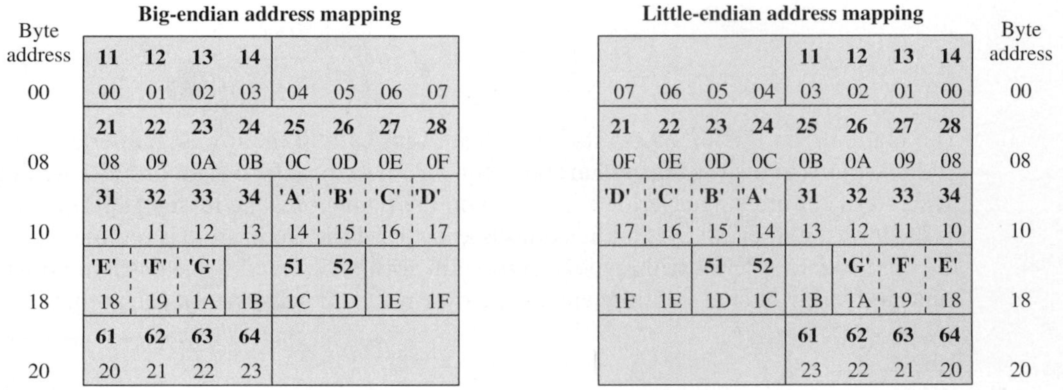

Big-endian address mapping

Byte address								
	11	**12**	**13**	**14**				
00	00	01	02	03	04	05	06	07
	21	**22**	**23**	**24**	**25**	**26**	**27**	**28**
08	08	09	0A	0B	0C	0D	0E	0F
	31	**32**	**33**	**34**	**'A'**	**'B'**	**'C'**	**'D'**
10	10	11	12	13	14	15	16	17
	'E'	**'F'**	**'G'**		**51**	**52**		
18	18	19	1A	1B	1C	1D	1E	1F
	61	**62**	**63**	**64**				
20	20	21	22	23				

Little-endian address mapping

								Byte address
				11	**12**	**13**	**14**	
07	06	05	04	03	02	01	00	00
21	**22**	**23**	**24**	**25**	**26**	**27**	**28**	
0F	0E	0D	0C	0B	0A	09	08	08
'D'	**'C'**	**'B'**	**'A'**	**31**	**32**	**33**	**34**	
17	16	15	14	13	12	11	10	10
		51	**52**		**'G'**	**'F'**	**'E'**	
1F	1E	1D	1C	1B	1A	19	18	18
				61	**62**	**63**	**64**	
				23	22	21	20	20

Figure 12.13   Example C Data Structure and Its Endian Maps

We can make several observations about this data structure:

- Each data item has the same address in both schemes. For example, the address of the doubleword with hexadecimal value 2122232425262728 is 08.

- Within any given multibyte scalar value, the ordering of bytes in the little-endian structure is the reverse of that for the big-endian structure.

- Endianness does not affect the ordering of data items within a structure. Thus, the four-character word c exhibits byte reversal, but the seven-character byte array d does not. Hence, the address of each individual element of d is the same in both structures.

The effect of endianness is perhaps more clearly demonstrated when we view memory as a vertical array of bytes, as shown in Figure 12.14.

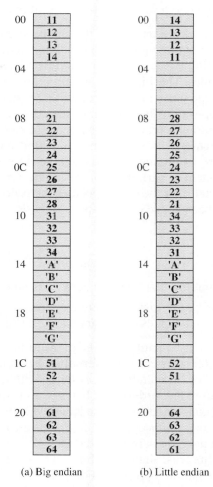

(a) Big endian   (b) Little endian

Figure 12.14   Another View of Figure 12.13

There is no general consensus as to which is the superior style of endianness.[4] The following points favor the big-endian style:

- **Character-string sorting:** A big-endian processor is faster in comparing integer-aligned character strings; the integer ALU can compare multiple bytes in parallel.
- **Decimal/IRA dumps:** All values can be printed left to right without causing confusion.
- **Consistent order:** Big-endian processors store their integers and character strings in the same order (most significant byte comes first).

The following points favor the little-endian style:

- A big-endian processor has to perform addition when it converts a 32-bit integer address to a 16-bit integer address, to use the least significant bytes.
- It is easier to perform higher-precision arithmetic with the little-endian style; you don't have to find the least-significant byte and move backward.

The differences are minor and the choice of endian style is often more a matter of accommodating previous machines than anything else.

The PowerPC is a bi-endian processor that supports both big-endian and little-endian modes. The bi-endian architecture enables software developers to choose either mode when migrating operating systems and applications from other machines. The operating system establishes the endian mode in which processes execute. Once a mode is selected, all subsequent memory loads and stores are determined by the memory-addressing model of that mode. To support this hardware feature, 2 bits are maintained in the machine state register (MSR) maintained by the operating system as part of the process state. One bit specifies the endian mode in which the kernel runs; the other specifies the processor's current operating mode. Thus, mode can be changed on a per-process basis.

Bit Ordering

In ordering the bits within a byte, we are immediately faced with two questions:

1. Do you count the first bit as bit zero or as bit one?
2. Do you assign the lowest bit number to the byte's least significant bit (little endian) or to the bytes most significant bit (big endian)?

These questions are not answered in the same way on all machines. Indeed, on some machines, the answers are different in different circumstances. Furthermore, the choice of big- or little-endian bit ordering within a byte is not always consistent with big- or little-endian ordering of bytes within a multibyte scalar. The programmer needs to be concerned with these issues when manipulating individual bits.

Another area of concern is when data are transmitted over a bit-serial line. When an individual byte is transmitted, does the system transmit the most significant bit first or the least significant bit first? The designer must make certain that incoming bits are handled properly. For a discussion of this issue, see [JAME90].

---

[4]The prophet revered by both groups in the Endian Wars of *Gulliver's Travels* had this to say. "All true Believers shall break their Eggs at the convenient End." Not much help!

CHAPTER 13

INSTRUCTION SETS: ADDRESSING MODES AND FORMATS

LEARNING OBJECTIVES

After studying this chapter, you should be able to:

◆ Describe the various types of addressing modes common in instruction sets.

◆ Present an overview of x86 and ARM addressing modes.

◆ Summarize the issues and trade-offs involved in designing an **instruction format**.

◆ Present an overview of x86 and ARM instruction formats.

◆ Understand the distinction between machine language and assembly language.

In Chapter 12, we focused on *what* an instruction set does. Specifically, we examined the types of operands and operations that may be specified by machine instructions. This chapter turns to the question of *how* to specify the operands and operations of instructions. Two issues arise. First, how is the address of an operand specified, and second, how are the bits of an instruction organized to define the operand addresses and operation of that instruction?

13.1 ADDRESSING MODES

The address field or fields in a typical instruction format are relatively small. We would like to be able to reference a large range of locations in main memory or, for some systems, virtual memory. To achieve this objective, a variety of addressing techniques has been employed. They all involve some trade-off between address range and/or addressing flexibility, on the one hand, and the number of memory references in the instruction and/or the complexity of address calculation, on the other. In this section, we examine the most common addressing techniques, or modes:

- Immediate
- Direct
- Indirect
- Register
- Register indirect
- Displacement
- Stack

These modes are illustrated in Figure 13.1. In this section, we use the following notation:

A = contents of an address field in the instruction

R = contents of an address field in the instruction that refers to a register

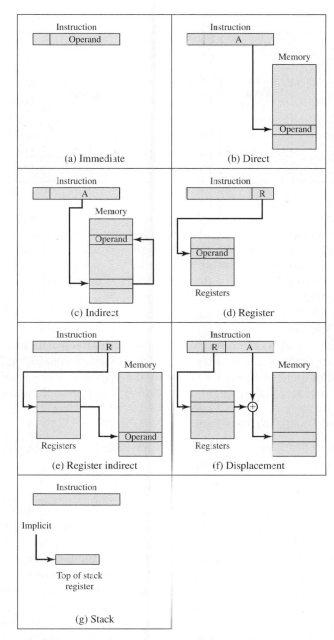

Figure 13.1 Addressing Modes

EA = actual (effective) address of the location containing the referenced operand

(X) = contents of memory location X or register X

Table 13.1 indicates the address calculation performed for each addressing mode.

Table 13.1   Basic Addressing Modes

Mode	Algorithm	Principal Advantage	Principal Disadvantage
Immediate	Operand = A	No memory reference	Limited operand magnitude
Direct	EA = A	Simple	Limited address space
Indirect	EA = (A)	Large address space	Multiple memory references
Register	EA = R	No memory reference	Limited address space
Register indirect	EA = (R)	Large address space	Extra memory reference
Displacement	EA = A + (R)	Flexibility	Complexity
Stack	EA = top of stack	No memory reference	Limited applicability

Before beginning this discussion, two comments need to be made. First, virtually all computer architectures provide more than one of these addressing modes. The question arises as to how the processor can determine which address mode is being used in a particular instruction. Several approaches are taken. Often, different opcodes will use different addressing modes. Also, one or more bits in the instruction format can be used as a *mode field*. The value of the mode field determines which addressing mode is to be used.

The second comment concerns the interpretation of the effective address (EA). In a system without virtual memory, the **effective address** will be either a main memory address or a register. In a virtual memory system, the effective address is a virtual address or a register. The actual mapping to a physical address is a function of the memory management unit (MMU) and is invisible to the programmer.

Immediate Addressing

The simplest form of addressing is **immediate addressing**, in which the operand value is present in the instruction

$$\text{Operand} = A$$

This mode can be used to define and use constants or set initial values of variables. Typically, the number will be stored in twos complement form; the leftmost bit of the operand field is used as a sign bit. When the operand is loaded into a data register, the sign bit is extended to the left to the full data **word** size. In some cases, the immediate binary value is interpreted as an unsigned nonnegative integer.

The advantage of immediate addressing is that no memory reference other than the instruction fetch is required to obtain the operand, thus saving one memory or cache cycle in the instruction cycle. The disadvantage is that the size of the number is restricted to the size of the address field, which, in most instruction sets, is small compared with the word length.

Direct Addressing

A very simple form of addressing is direct addressing, in which the address field contains the effective address of the operand:

$$EA = A$$

The technique was common in earlier generations of computers but is not common on contemporary architectures. It requires only one memory reference and no special calculation. The obvious limitation is that it provides only a limited address space.

Indirect Addressing

With direct addressing, the length of the address field is usually less than the word length, thus limiting the address range. One solution is to have the address field refer to the address of a word in memory, which in turn contains a full-length address of the operand. This is known as **indirect addressing**:

$$EA = (A)$$

As defined earlier, the parentheses are to be interpreted as meaning *contents of.* The obvious advantage of this approach is that for a word length of N, an address space of 2^N is now available. The disadvantage is that instruction execution requires two memory references to fetch the operand: one to get its address and a second to get its value.

Although the number of words that can be addressed is now equal to 2^N, the number of different effective addresses that may be referenced at any one time is limited to 2^K, where K is the length of the address field. Typically, this is not a burdensome restriction, and it can be an asset. In a virtual memory environment, all the effective address locations can be confined to page 0 of any process. Because the address field of an instruction is small, it will naturally produce low-numbered direct addresses, which would appear in page 0. (The only restriction is that the page size must be greater than or equal to 2^K.) When a process is active, there will be repeated references to page 0, causing it to remain in real memory. Thus, an indirect memory reference will involve, at most, one page fault rather than two.

A rarely used variant of indirect addressing is multilevel or cascaded indirect addressing:

$$EA = (\ldots (A) \ldots)$$

In this case, one bit of a full-word address is an indirect flag (I). If the I bit is 0, then the word contains the EA. If the I bit is 1, then another level of indirection is invoked. There does not appear to be any particular advantage to this approach, and its disadvantage is that three or more memory references could be required to fetch an operand.

Register Addressing

Register addressing is similar to direct addressing. The only difference is that the address field refers to a register rather than a main memory address:

$$EA = R$$

To clarify, if the contents of a register address field in an instruction is 5, then register R5 is the intended address, and the operand value is contained in R5. Typically, an address field that references registers will have from 3 to 5 bits, so that a total of from 8 to 32 general-purpose registers can be referenced.

The advantages of register addressing are that (1) only a small address field is needed in the instruction, and (2) no time-consuming memory references are required. As was discussed in Chapter 4, the memory access time for a register internal to the processor is much less than that for a main memory address. The disadvantage of register addressing is that the address space is very limited.

If register addressing is heavily used in an instruction set, this implies that the processor registers will be heavily used. Because of the severely limited number of registers (compared with main memory locations), their use in this fashion makes sense only if they are employed efficiently. If every operand is brought into a register from main memory, operated on once, and then returned to main memory, then a wasteful intermediate step has been added. If, instead, the operand in a register remains in use for multiple operations, then a real savings is achieved. An example is the intermediate result in a calculation. In particular, suppose that the algorithm for twos complement multiplication were to be implemented in software. The location labeled A in the flowchart (Figure 10.12) is referenced many times and should be implemented in a register rather than a main memory location.

It is up to the programmer or compiler to decide which values should remain in registers and which should be stored in main memory. Most modern processors employ multiple general-purpose registers, placing a burden for efficient execution on the assembly-language programmer (e.g., compiler writer).

Register Indirect Addressing

Just as register addressing is analogous to direct addressing, **register indirect addressing** is analogous to indirect addressing. In both cases, the only difference is whether the address field refers to a memory location or a register. Thus, for register indirect address,

$$EA = (R)$$

The advantages and limitations of register indirect addressing are basically the same as for indirect addressing. In both cases, the address space limitation (limited range of addresses) of the address field is overcome by having that field refer to a word-length location containing an address. In addition, register indirect addressing uses one less memory reference than indirect addressing.

Displacement Addressing

A very powerful mode of addressing combines the capabilities of direct addressing and register indirect addressing. It is known by a variety of names depending on the context of its use, but the basic mechanism is the same. We will refer to this as **displacement addressing**:

$$EA = A + (R)$$

Displacement addressing requires that the instruction have two address fields, at least one of which is explicit. The value contained in one address field (value = A) is used directly. The other address field, or an implicit reference based on opcode, refers to a register whose contents are added to A to produce the effective address.

We will describe three of the most common uses of displacement addressing:

- Relative addressing
- Base-register addressing
- Indexing

RELATIVE ADDRESSING For relative addressing, also called PC-relative addressing, the implicitly referenced register is the program counter (PC). That is, the next instruction address is added to the address field to produce the EA. Typically, the address field is treated as a twos complement number for this operation. Thus, the effective address is a displacement relative to the address of the instruction.

Relative addressing exploits the concept of locality that was discussed in Chapters 4 and 8. If most memory references are relatively near to the instruction being executed, then the use of relative addressing saves address bits in the instruction.

BASE–REGISTER ADDRESSING For **base-register addressing**, the interpretation is the following: The referenced register contains a main memory address, and the address field contains a displacement (usually an unsigned integer representation) from that address. The register reference may be explicit or implicit.

Base-register addressing also exploits the locality of memory references. It is a convenient means of implementing segmentation, which was discussed in Chapter 8. In some implementations, a single segment-base register is employed and is used implicitly. In others, the programmer may choose a register to hold the base address of a segment, and the instruction must reference it explicitly. In this latter case, if the length of the address field is K and the number of possible registers is N, then one instruction can reference any one of N areas of 2^K words.

INDEXING For indexing, the interpretation is typically the following: The address field references a main memory address, and the referenced register contains a positive displacement from that address. Note that this usage is just the opposite of the interpretation for base-register addressing. Of course, it is more than just a matter of user interpretation. Because the address field is considered to be a memory address in indexing, it generally contains more bits than an address field in a comparable base-register instruction. Also, we shall see that there are some refinements to indexing that would not be as useful in the base-register context. Nevertheless, the method of calculating the EA is the same for both base-register addressing and indexing, and in both cases the register reference is sometimes explicit and sometimes implicit (for different processor types).

An important use of indexing is to provide an efficient mechanism for performing iterative operations. Consider, for example, a list of numbers stored starting at location A. Suppose that we would like to add 1 to each element on the list. We need to fetch each value, add 1 to it, and store it back. The sequence of effective addresses that we need is A, A + 1, A + 2,..., up to the last location on the list. With indexing, this is easily done. The value A is stored in the instruction's address field, and the chosen register, called an *index register,* is initialized to 0. After each operation, the index register is incremented by 1.

Because index registers are commonly used for such iterative tasks, it is typical that there is a need to increment or decrement the index register after each reference to it. Because this is such a common operation, some systems will automatically do this as part of the same instruction cycle. This is known as **autoindexing**. If certain registers are devoted exclusively to indexing, then autoindexing can be invoked implicitly and automatically. If general-purpose registers are used, the autoindex operation may need to be signaled by a bit in the instruction. Autoindexing using increment can be depicted as follows.

$$EA = A + (R)$$

$$(R) \leftarrow (R) + 1$$

In some machines, both indirect addressing and indexing are provided, and it is possible to employ both in the same instruction. There are two possibilities: the indexing is performed either before or after the indirection.

If indexing is performed after the indirection, it is termed **postindexing**:

$$EA = (A) + (R)$$

First, the contents of the address field are used to access a memory location containing a direct address. This address is then indexed by the register value. This technique is useful for accessing one of a number of blocks of data of a fixed format. For example, it was described in Chapter 8 that the operating system needs to employ a process control block for each process. The operations performed are the same regardless of which block is being manipulated. Thus, the addresses in the instructions that reference the block could point to a location (value = A) containing a variable pointer to the start of a process control block. The index register contains the displacement within the block.

With **preindexing**, the indexing is performed before the indirection:

$$EA = (A + (R))$$

An address is calculated as with simple indexing. In this case, however, the calculated address contains not the operand, but the address of the operand. An example of the use of this technique is to construct a multiway branch table. At a particular point in a program, there may be a branch to one of a number of locations depending on conditions. A table of addresses can be set up starting at location A. By indexing into this table, the required location can be found.

Typically, an instruction set will not include both preindexing and postindexing.

Stack Addressing

The final addressing mode that we consider is stack addressing. As defined in Appendix O, a stack is a linear array of locations. It is sometimes referred to as a *pushdown list* or *last-in-first-out queue*. The stack is a reserved block of locations. Items are appended to the top of the stack so that, at any given time, the block is partially filled. Associated with the stack is a pointer whose value is the address of the top of the stack. Alternatively, the top two elements of the stack may be in processor registers, in which case the stack pointer references the third element of the stack. The stack pointer is maintained in a register. Thus, references to stack locations in memory are in fact register indirect addresses.

The stack mode of addressing is a form of implied addressing. The machine instructions need not include a memory reference but implicitly operate on the top of the stack.

13.2 x86 AND ARM ADDRESSING MODES

x86 Addressing Modes

Recall from Figure 8.21 that the x86 address translation mechanism produces an address, called a virtual or effective address, that is an offset into a segment. The sum of the starting address of the segment and the effective address produces a linear address. If paging is being used, this linear address must pass through a page-translation mechanism to produce a physical address. In what follows, we ignore this last step because it is transparent to the instruction set and to the programmer.

The x86 is equipped with a variety of addressing modes intended to allow the efficient execution of high-level languages. Figure 13.2 indicates the logic involved. The segment register determines the segment that is the subject of the reference. There are six segment registers; the one being used for a particular reference depends on the context of execution and the instruction. Each segment register

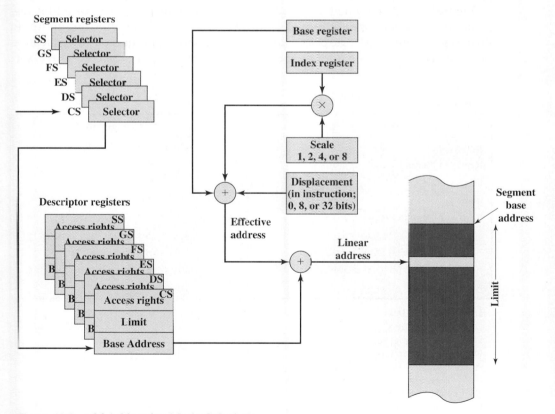

Figure 13.2   x86 Addressing Mode Calculation

holds an index into the segment descriptor table (Figure 8.20), which holds the starting address of the corresponding segments. Associated with each user-visible segment register is a segment descriptor register (not programmer visible), which records the access rights for the segment as well as the starting address and limit (length) of the segment. In addition, there are two registers that may be used in constructing an address: the base register and the index register.

Table 13.2 lists the x86 addressing modes. Let us consider each of these in turn.

For the **immediate mode**, the operand is included in the instruction. The operand can be a byte, word, or doubleword of data.

For **register operand mode**, the operand is located in a register. For general instructions, such as data transfer, arithmetic, and logical instructions, the operand can be one of the 32-bit general registers (EAX, EBX, ECX, EDX, ESI, EDI, ESP, EBP), one of the 16-bit general registers (AX, BX, CX, DX, SI, DI, SP, BP), or one of the 8-bit general registers (AH, BH, CH, DH, AL, BL, CL, DL). There are also some instructions that reference the segment selector registers (CS, DS, ES, SS, FS, GS).

The remaining addressing modes reference locations in memory. The memory location must be specified in terms of the segment containing the location and the offset from the beginning of the segment. In some cases, a segment is specified explicitly; in others, the segment is specified by simple rules that assign a segment by default.

In the **displacement mode**, the operand's offset (the effective address of Figure13.2) is contained as part of the instruction as an 8-, 16-, or 32-bit displacement. With segmentation, all addresses in instructions refer merely to an offset in a segment. The displacement addressing mode is found on few machines because, as mentioned earlier, it leads to long instructions. In the case of the x86,

Table 13.2 x86 Addressing Modes

Mode	Algorithm
Immediate	Operand = A
Register Operand	LA = R
Displacement	LA = (SR) + A
Base	LA = (SR) + (B)
Base with Displacement	LA = (SR) + (B) + A
Scaled Index with Displacement	LA = (SR) + (I) × S + A
Base with Index and Displacement	LA = (SR) + (B) + (I) + A
Base with Scaled Index and Displacement	LA = (SR) + (I) × S + (B) + A
Relative	LA = (PC) + A

LA = linear address
(X) = contents of X
SR = segment register
PC = program counter
A = contents of an address field in the instruction
R = register
B = base register
I = index register
S = scaling factor

the displacement value can be as long as 32 bits, making for a 6-byte instruction. Displacement addressing can be useful for referencing global variables.

The remaining addressing modes are indirect, in the sense that the address portion of the instruction tells the processor where to look to find the address. The **base mode** specifies that one of the 8- 16-, or 32-bit registers contains the effective address. This is equivalent to what we have referred to as register indirect addressing.

In the **base with displacement mode**, the instruction includes a displacement to be added to a base register, which may be any of the general-purpose registers. Examples of uses of this mode are as follows:

- Used by a compiler to point to the start of a local variable area. For example, the base register could point to the beginning of a stack frame, which contains the local variables for the corresponding procedure.

- Used to index into an array when the element size is not 1, 2, 4, or 8 bytes and which therefore cannot be indexed using an index register. In this case, the displacement points to the beginning of the array, and the base register holds the results of a calculation to determine the offset to a specific element within the array.

- Used to access a field of a record. The base register points to the beginning of the record, while the displacement is an offset to the field.

In the **scaled index with displacement mode**, the instruction includes a displacement to be added to a register, in this case called an index register. The index register may be any of the general-purpose registers except the one called ESP, which is generally used for stack processing. In calculating the effective address, the contents of the index register are multiplied by a scaling factor of 1, 2, 4, or 8, and then added to a displacement. This mode is very convenient for indexing arrays. A scaling factor of 2 can be used for an array of 16-bit integers. A scaling factor of 4 can be used for 32-bit integers or floating-point numbers. Finally, a scaling factor of 8 can be used for an array of double-precision floating-point numbers.

The **base with index and displacement mode** sums the contents of the base register, the index register, and a displacement to form the effective address. Again, the base register can be any general-purpose register and the index register can be any general-purpose register except ESP. As an example, this addressing mode could be used for accessing a local array on a stack frame. This mode can also be used to support a two-dimensional array; in this case, the displacement points to the beginning of the array, and each register handles one dimension of the array.

The **based scaled index with displacement mode** sums the contents of the index register multiplied by a scaling factor, the contents of the base register, and the displacement. This is useful if an array is stored in a stack frame; in this case, the array elements would be 2, 4, or 8 bytes each in length. This mode also provides efficient indexing of a two-dimensional array when the array elements are 2, 4, or 8 bytes in length.

Finally, **relative addressing** can be used in transfer-of-control instructions. A displacement is added to the value of the program counter, which points to the next instruction. In this case, the displacement is treated as a signed byte, word, or doubleword value, and that value either increases or decreases the address in the program counter.

ARM Addressing Modes

Typically, a RISC machine, unlike a CISC machine, uses a simple and relatively straightforward set of addressing modes. The ARM architecture departs somewhat from this tradition by providing a relatively rich set of addressing modes. These modes are most conveniently classified with respect to the type of instruction.[1]

LOAD/STORE ADDRESSING Load and store instructions are the only instructions that reference memory. This is always done indirectly through a base register plus offset. There are three alternatives with respect to indexing (Figure 13.3):

- **Offset:** For this addressing method, **indexing** is not used. An offset value is added to or subtracted from the value in the base register to form the memory address. As an example Figure 13.3a illustrates this method with the assembly language instruction STRB r0, [r1, #12]. This is the store byte instruction. In this case the base address is in register r1 and the displacement is an immediate value of decimal 12. The resulting address (base plus offset) is the location where the least significant byte from r0 is to be stored.
- **Preindex:** The memory address is formed in the same way as for offset addressing. The memory address is also written back to the base register. In other words, the base register value is incremented or decremented by the offset value. Figure 13.3b illustrates this method with the assembly language instruction STRB r0, [r1, #12]!. The exclamation point signifies preindexing.
- **Postindex:** The memory address is the base register value. An offset is added to or subtracted from the base register value and the result is written back to the base register. Figure 13.3c illustrates this method with the assembly language instruction STRB r0, [r1], #12.

Note that what ARM refers to as a base register acts as an index register for preindex and postindex addressing. The offset value can either be an immediate value stored in the instruction or it can be in another register. If the offset value is in a register, another useful feature is available: scaled register addressing. The value in the offset register is scaled by one of the shift operators: Logical Shift Left, Logical Shift Right, Arithmetic Shift Right, Rotate Right, or Rotate Right Extended (which includes the carry bit in the rotation). The amount of the shift is specified as an immediate value in the instruction.

DATA PROCESSING INSTRUCTION ADDRESSING Data processing instructions use either register addressing or a mixture of register and immediate addressing. For register addressing, the value in one of the register operands may be scaled using one of the five shift operators defined in the preceding paragraph.

BRANCH INSTRUCTIONS The only form of addressing for branch instructions is immediate addressing. The branch instruction contains a 24-bit value. For address calculation, this value is shifted left 2 bits, so that the address is on a word boundary. Thus the effective address range is ± 32 MB from the program counter.

---

[1]As with our discussion of x86 addressing, we ignore the translation from virtual to physical address in the following discussion.

```
STRB r0, [r1, #12]
```

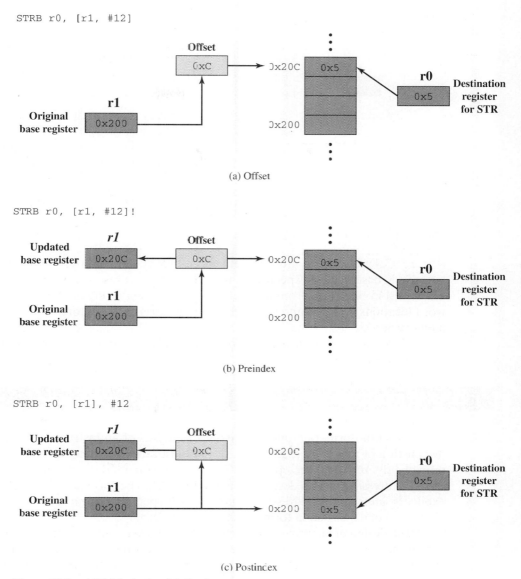

(a) Offset

```
STRB r0, [r1, #12]!
```

(b) Preindex

```
STRB r0, [r1], #12
```

(c) Postindex

Figure 13.3   ARM Indexing Methods

LOAD/STORE MULTIPLE ADDRESSING Load Multiple instructions load a subset (possibly all) of the general-purpose registers from memory. Store Multiple instructions store a subset (possibly all) of the general-purpose registers to memory. The list of registers for the load or store is specified in a 16-bit field in the instruction with each bit corresponding to one of the 16 registers. Load and Store Multiple addressing modes produce a sequential range of memory addresses. The lowest-numbered register is stored at the lowest memory address and the highest-numbered register at the highest memory address. Four addressing modes are used

```
LDMxx r10, {r0, r1, r4}
STMxx r10, {r0, r1, r4}
```

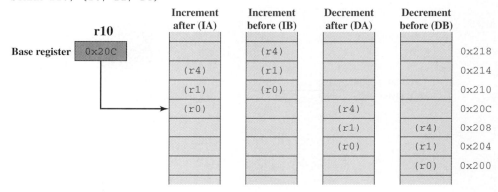

Figure 13.4 ARM Load/Store Multiple Addressing

(Figure 13.4): increment after, increment before, decrement after, and decrement before. A base register specifies a main memory address where register values are stored in or loaded from in ascending (increment) or descending (decrement) word locations. Incrementing or decrementing starts either before or after the first memory access.

These instructions are useful for block loads or stores, stack operations, and procedure exit sequences.

13.3 INSTRUCTION FORMATS

An instruction format defines the layout of the bits of an instruction, in terms of its constituent fields. An instruction format must include an opcode and, implicitly or explicitly, zero or more operands. Each explicit operand is referenced using one of the addressing modes described in Section 13.1. The format must, implicitly or explicitly, indicate the addressing mode for each operand. For most instruction sets, more than one instruction format is used.

The design of an instruction format is a complex art, and an amazing variety of designs have been implemented. We examine the key design issues, looking briefly at some designs to illustrate points, and then we examine the x86 and ARM solutions in detail.

Instruction Length

The most basic design issue to be faced is the instruction format length. This decision affects, and is affected by, memory size, memory organization, bus structure, processor complexity, and processor speed. This decision determines the richness and flexibility of the machine as seen by the assembly-language programmer.

The most obvious trade-off here is between the desire for a powerful instruction repertoire and a need to save space. Programmers want more opcodes, more operands, more addressing modes, and greater address range. More opcodes and more operands make life easier for the programmer, because shorter programs can be written to accomplish given tasks. Similarly, more addressing modes give the programmer greater flexibility in implementing certain functions, such as table manipulations and multiple-way branching. And, of course, with the increase in main memory size and the increasing use of virtual memory, programmers want to be able to address larger memory ranges. All of these things (opcodes, operands, addressing modes, address range) require bits and push in the direction of longer instruction lengths. But longer instruction length may be wasteful. A 64-bit instruction occupies twice the space of a 32-bit instruction but is probably less than twice as useful.

Beyond this basic trade-off, there are other considerations. Either the instruction length should be equal to the memory-transfer length (in a bus system, data-bus length) or one should be a multiple of the other. Otherwise, we will not get an integral number of instructions during a fetch cycle. A related consideration is the memory transfer rate. This rate has not kept up with increases in processor speed. Accordingly, memory can become a bottleneck if the processor can execute instructions faster than it can fetch them. One solution to this problem is to use cache memory (see Section 4.3); another is to use shorter instructions. Thus, 16-bit instructions can be fetched at twice the rate of 32-bit instructions but probably can be executed less than twice as rapidly.

A seemingly mundane but nevertheless important feature is that the instruction length should be a multiple of the character length, which is usually 8 bits, and of the length of fixed-point numbers. To see this, we need to make use of that unfortunately ill-defined word, *word* [FRAI83]. The word length of memory is, in some sense, the "natural" unit of organization. The size of a word usually determines the size of fixed-point numbers (usually the two are equal). Word size is also typically equal to, or at least integrally related to, the memory transfer size. Because a common form of data is character data, we would like a word to store an integral number of characters. Otherwise, there are wasted bits in each word when storing multiple characters, or a character will have to straddle a word boundary. The importance of this point is such that IBM, when it introduced the System/360 and wanted to employ 8-bit characters, made the wrenching decision to move from the 36-bit architecture of the scientific members of the 700/7000 series to a 32-bit architecture.

Allocation of Bits

We've looked at some of the factors that go into deciding the length of the instruction format. An equally difficult issue is how to allocate the bits in that format. The trade-offs here are complex.

For a given instruction length, there is clearly a trade-off between the number of opcodes and the power of the addressing capability. More opcodes obviously mean more bits in the opcode field. For an instruction format of a given length, this reduces the number of bits available for addressing. There is one interesting refinement to this trade-off, and that is the use of variable-length opcodes. In this approach, there is a minimum opcode length but, for some opcodes, additional operations may be specified by using additional bits in the instruction. For a fixed-length instruction, this leaves fewer bits for addressing. Thus, this feature is used for those instructions that require fewer operands and/or less powerful addressing.

The following interrelated factors go into determining the use of the addressing bits.

- **Number of addressing modes:** Sometimes an addressing mode can be indicated implicitly. For example, certain opcodes might always call for indexing. In other cases, the addressing modes must be explicit, and one or more mode bits will be needed.

- **Number of operands:** We have seen that fewer addresses can make for longer, more awkward programs (e.g., Figure 10.3). Typical instruction formats on today's machines include two operands. Each operand address in the instruction might require its own mode indicator, or the use of a mode indicator could be limited to just one of the address fields.

- **Register versus memory:** A machine must have registers so that data can be brought into the processor for processing. With a single user-visible register (usually called the accumulator), one operand address is implicit and consumes no instruction bits. However, single-register programming is awkward and requires many instructions. Even with multiple registers, only a few bits are needed to specify the register. The more that registers can be used for operand references, the fewer bits are needed. A number of studies indicate that a total of 8 to 32 user-visible registers is desirable [LUND77, HUCK83]. Most contemporary architectures have at least 32 registers.

- **Number of register sets:** Most contemporary machines have one set of general-purpose registers, with typically 32 or more registers in the set. These registers can be used to store data and can be used to store addresses for displacement addressing. Some architectures, including that of the x86, have a collection of two or more specialized sets (such as data and displacement). One advantage of this latter approach is that, for a fixed number of registers, a functional split requires fewer bits to be used in the instruction. For example, with two sets of eight registers, only 3 bits are required to identify a register; the opcode or mode register will determine which set of registers is being referenced.

- **Address range:** For addresses that reference memory, the range of addresses that can be referenced is related to the number of address bits. Because this imposes a severe limitation, direct addressing is rarely used. With displacement addressing, the range is opened up to the length of the address register. Even so, it is still convenient to allow rather large displacements from the register address, which requires a relatively large number of address bits in the instruction.

- **Address granularity:** For addresses that reference memory rather than registers, another factor is the granularity of addressing. In a system with 16- or 32-bit words, an address can reference a word or a byte at the designer's choice. Byte addressing is convenient for character manipulation but requires, for a fixed-size memory, more address bits.

Thus, the designer is faced with a host of factors to consider and balance. How critical the various choices are is not clear. As an example, we cite one study [CRAG79] that compared various instruction format approaches, including the use of a stack, general-purpose registers, an accumulator, and only memory-to-register approaches. Using a consistent set of assumptions, no significant difference in code space or execution time was observed.

Let us briefly look at how two historical machine designs balance these various factors.

PDP-8 One of the simplest instruction designs for a general-purpose computer was for the PDP-8 [BELL78b]. The PDP-8 uses 12-bit instructions and operates on 12-bit words. There is a single general-purpose register, the accumulator.

Despite the limitations of this design, the addressing is quite flexible. Each memory reference consists of 7 bits plus two 1-bit modifiers. The memory is divided into fixed-length pages of $2^7 = 128$ words each. Address calculation is based on references to page 0 or the current page (page containing this instruction) as determined by the page bit. The second modifier bit indicates whether direct or indirect addressing is to be used. These two modes can be used in combination, so that an indirect address is a 12-bit address contained in a word of page 0 or the current page. In addition, 8 dedicated words on page 0 are autoindex "registers." When an indirect reference is made to one of these locations, preindexing occurs.

Figure 13.5 shows the PDP-8 instruction format. There are a 3-bit opcode and three types of instructions. For opcodes 0 through 5, the format is a single-address memory reference instruction including a page bit and an indirect bit. Thus, there are only six basic operations. To enlarge the group of operations, opcode 7 defines

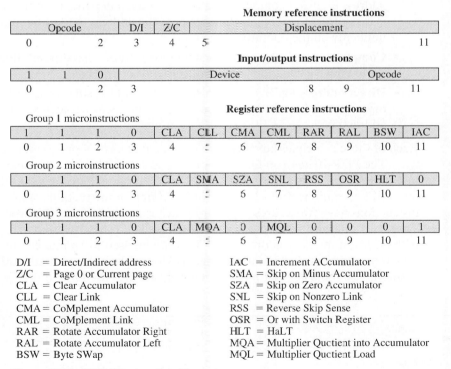

Figure 13.5 PDP-8 Instruction Formats

a register reference or *microinstruction.* In this format, the remaining bits are used to encode additional operations. In general, each bit defines a specific operation (e.g., clear accumulator), and these bits can be combined in a single instruction. The microinstruction strategy was used as far back as the PDP-1 by DEC and is, in a sense, a forerunner of today's microprogrammed machines, to be discussed in Part Four. Opcode 6 is the I/O operation; 6 bits are used to select one of 64 devices, and 3 bits specify a particular I/O command.

The PDP-8 instruction format is remarkably efficient. It supports indirect addressing, displacement addressing, and indexing. With the use of the opcode extension, it supports a total of approximately 35 instructions. Given the constraints of a 12-bit instruction length, the designers could hardly have done better.

PDP-10 A sharp contrast to the instruction set of the PDP-8 is that of the PDP-10. The PDP-10 was designed to be a large-scale time-shared system, with an emphasis on making the system easy to program, even if additional hardware expense was involved.

Among the design principles employed in designing the instruction set were the following [BELL78c]:

- **Orthogonality:** Orthogonality is a principle by which two variables are independent of each other. In the context of an instruction set, the term indicates that other elements of an instruction are independent of (not determined by) the opcode. The PDP-10 designers use the term to describe the fact that an address is always computed in the same way, independent of the opcode. This is in contrast to many machines, where the address mode sometimes depends implicitly on the operator being used.

- **Completeness:** Each arithmetic data type (integer, fixed-point, floating-point) should have a complete and identical set of operations.

- **Direct addressing:** Base plus displacement addressing, which places a memory organization burden on the programmer, was avoided in favor of direct addressing.

Each of these principles advances the main goal of ease of programming.

The PDP-10 has a 36-bit word length and a 36-bit instruction length. The fixed instruction format is shown in Figure 13.6. The opcode occupies 9 bits, allowing up to 512 operations. In fact, a total of 365 different instructions are defined. Most instructions have two addresses, one of which is one of 16 general-purpose registers. Thus, this operand reference occupies 4 bits. The other operand reference starts with an 18-bit memory address field. This can be used as an immediate operand or a memory address. In the latter usage, both indexing and indirect addressing are allowed. The same general-purpose registers are also used as index registers.

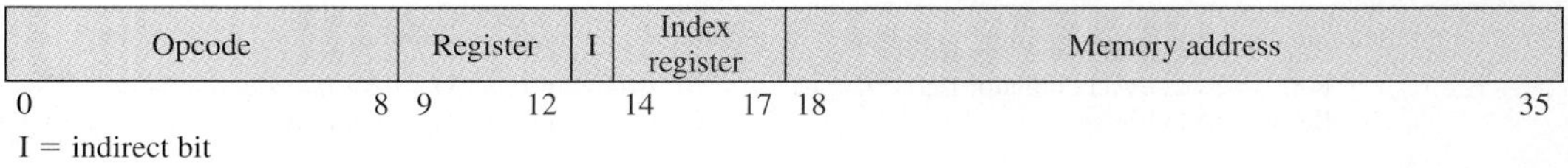

Opcode	Register	I	Index register	Memory address
0 8	9 12	14	17 18	35

I = indirect bit

Figure 13.6 PDP-10 Instruction Format

A 36-bit instruction length is true luxury. There is no need to do clever things to get more opcodes; a 9-bit opcode field is more than adequate. Addressing is also straightforward. An 18-bit address field makes direct addressing desirable. For memory sizes greater than 2^{18}, indirection is provided. For the ease of the programmer, indexing is provided for table manipulation and iterative programs. Also, with an 18-bit operand field, immediate addressing becomes attractive.

The PDP-10 instruction set design does accomplish the objectives listed earlier [LUND77]. It eases the task of the programmer or compiler at the expense of an inefficient utilization of space. This was a conscious choice made by the designers and therefore cannot be faulted as poor design.

Variable-Length Instructions

The examples we have looked at so far have used a single fixed instruction length, and we have implicitly discussed trade-offs in that context. But the designer may choose instead to provide a variety of instruction formats of different lengths. This tactic makes it easy to provide a large repertoire of opcodes, with different opcode lengths. Addressing can be more flexible, with various combinations of register and memory references plus addressing modes. With variable-length instructions, these many variations can be provided efficiently and compactly.

The principal price to pay for variable-length instructions is an increase in the complexity of the processor. Falling hardware prices, the use of microprogramming (discussed in Part Four), and a general increase in understanding the principles of processor design have all contributed to making this a small price to pay. However, we will see that RISC and superscalar machines can exploit the use of fixed-length instructions to provide improved performance.

The use of variable-length instructions does not remove the desirability of making all of the instruction lengths integrally related to the word length. Because the processor does not know the length of the next instruction to be fetched, a typical strategy is to fetch a number of bytes or words equal to at least the longest possible instruction. This means that sometimes multiple instructions are fetched. However, as we shall see in Chapter 14, this is a good strategy to follow in any case.

PDP-11 The PDP-11 was designed to provide a powerful and flexible instruction set within the constraints of a 16-bit minicomputer [BELL70].

The PDP-11 employs a set of eight 16-bit general-purpose registers. Two of these registers have additional significance: one is used as a stack pointer for special-purpose stack operations, and one is used as the program counter, which contains the address of the next instruction.

Figure 13.7 shows the PDP-11 instruction formats. Thirteen different formats are used, encompassing zero-, one-, and two-address instruction types. The opcode can vary from 4 to 16 bits in length. Register references are 6 bits in length. Three bits identify the register, and the remaining 3 bits identify the addressing mode. The PDP-11 is endowed with a rich set of addressing modes. One advantage of linking the addressing mode to the operand rather than the opcode, as is sometimes done, is that any addressing mode can be used with any opcode. As was mentioned, this independence is referred to as *orthogonality*.

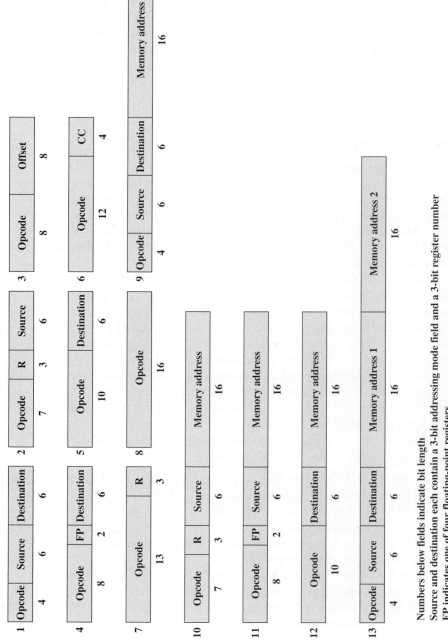

Figure 13.7 Instruction Formats for the PDP-11

Numbers below fields indicate bit length
Source and destination each contain a 3-bit addressing mode field and a 3-bit register number
FP indicates one of four floating-point registers
R indicates one of the general-purpose registers
CC is the condition code field

PDP-11 instructions are usually one word (16 bits) long. For some instructions, one or two memory addresses are appended, so that 32-bit and 48-bit instructions are part of the repertoire. This provides for further flexibility in addressing.

The PDP-11 instruction set and addressing capability are complex. This increases both hardware cost and programming complexity. The advantage is that more efficient or compact programs can be developed.

VAX Most architectures provide a relatively small number of fixed instruction formats. This can cause two problems for the programmer. First, addressing mode and opcode are not orthogonal. For example, for a given operation, one operand must come from a register and another from memory, or both from registers, and so on. Second, only a limited number of operands can be accommodated: typically up to two or three. Because some operations inherently require more operands, various strategies must be used to achieve the desired result using two or more instructions.

To avoid these problems, two criteria were used in designing the VAX instruction format [STRE78]:

1. All instructions should have the "natural" number of operands.
2. All operands should have the same generality in specification.

The result is a highly variable instruction format. An instruction consists of a 1- or 2-byte opcode followed by from zero to six operand specifiers, depending on the opcode. The minimal instruction length is 1 byte, and instructions up to 37 bytes can be constructed. Figure 13.8 gives a few examples.

The VAX instruction begins with a 1-byte opcode. This suffices to handle most VAX instructions. However, as there are over 300 different instructions, 8 bits are not enough. The hexadecimal codes FD and FF indicate an extended opcode, with the actual opcode being specified in the second byte.

The remainder of the instruction consists of up to six operand specifiers. An operand specifier is, at minimum, a 1-byte format in which the leftmost 4 bits are the address mode specifier. The only exception to this rule is the literal mode, which is signaled by the pattern 00 in the leftmost 2 bits, leaving space for a 6-bit literal. Because of this exception, a total of 12 different addressing modes can be specified.

An operand specifier often consists of just one byte, with the rightmost 4 bits specifying one of 16 general-purpose registers. The length of the operand specifier can be extended in one of two ways. First, a constant value of one or more bytes may immediately follow the first byte of the operand specifier. An example of this is the displacement mode, in which an 8-, 16-, or 32-bit displacement is used. Second, an index mode of addressing may be used. In this case, the first byte of the operand specifier consists of the 4-bit addressing mode code of 0100 and a 4-bit index register identifier. The remainder of the operand specifier consists of the base address specifier, which may itself be one or more bytes in length.

The reader may be wondering, as the author did, what kind of instruction requires six operands. Surprisingly, the VAX has a number of such instructions. Consider

ADDP6 OP1, OP2, OP3, OP4, OP5, OP6

Hexadecimal Format	Explanation	Assembler Notation and Description
8 bits ← → 0 5	Opcode for RSB	RSB Return from subroutine
D 4 5 9	Opcode for CLRL Register R9	CLRL R9 Clear register R9
B 0 C 4 6 4 0 1 A B 1 9	Opcode for MOVW Word displacement mode, Register R4 356 in hexadecimal Byte displacement mode, Register R11 25 in hexadecimal	MOVW 356(R4), 25(R11) Move a word from address that is 356 plus contents of R4 to address that is 25 plus contents of R11
C 1 0 5 5 0 4 2 D F	Opcode for ADDL3 Short literal 5 Register mode R0 Index prefix R2 Indirect word relative (displacement from PC) Amount of displacement from PC relative to location A	ADDL3 #5, R0, @A[R2] Add 5 to a 32-bit integer in R0 and store the result in location whose address is sum of A and 4 times the contents of R2

Figure 13.8 Example of VAX Instructions

This instruction adds two packed decimal numbers. OP1 and OP2 specify the length and starting address of one decimal string; OP3 and OP4 specify a second string. These two strings are added and the result is stored in the decimal string whose length and starting location are specified by OP5 and OP6.

The VAX instruction set provides for a wide variety of operations and addressing modes. This gives a programmer, such as a compiler writer, a very powerful and flexible tool for developing programs. In theory, this should lead to efficient machine-language compilations of high-level language programs and, in general, to effective and efficient use of processor resources. The penalty to be paid for these benefits is the increased complexity of the processor compared with a processor with a simpler instruction set and format.

We return to these matters in Chapter 15, where we examine the case for very simple instruction sets.

13.4 x86 AND ARM INSTRUCTION FORMATS

x86 Instruction Formats

The x86 is equipped with a variety of instruction formats. Of the elements described in this subsection, only the opcode field is always present. Figure 13.9 illustrates the general instruction format. Instructions are made up of from zero to four optional instruction prefixes, a 1- or 2-byte opcode, an optional address specifier (which consists of the ModR/M byte and the Scale Index Base byte) an optional displacement, and an optional immediate field.

Let us first consider the prefix bytes:

- **Instruction prefixes:** The instruction prefix, if present, consists of the LOCK prefix or one of the repeat prefixes. The LOCK prefix is used to ensure exclusive use of shared memory in multiprocessor environments. The repeat prefixes specify repeated operation of a string, which enables the x86 to process strings much faster than with a regular software loop. There are five different repeat prefixes: REP, REPE, REPZ, REPNE, and REPNZ. When the absolute REP prefix is present, the operation specified in the instruction is executed repeatedly on successive elements of the string; the number of repetitions is specified in register CX. The conditional REP prefix causes the instruction to repeat until the count in CX goes to zero or until the condition is met.

- **Segment override:** Explicitly specifies which segment register an instruction should use, overriding the default segment-register selection generated by the x86 for that instruction.

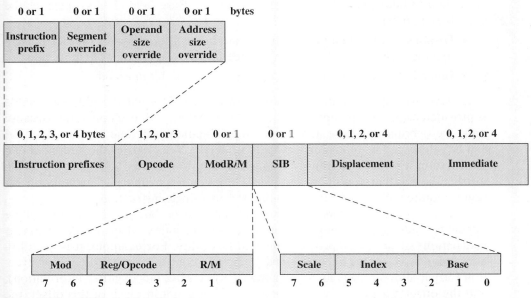

Figure 13.9 x86 Instruction Format

- **Operand size:** An instruction has a default operand size of 16 or 32 bits, and the operand prefix switches between 32-bit and 16-bit operands.
- **Address size:** The processor can address memory using either 16- or 32-bit addresses. The address size determines the displacement size in instructions and the size of address offsets generated during effective address calculation. One of these sizes is designated as default, and the address size prefix switches between 32-bit and 16-bit address generation.

The instruction itself includes the following fields:

- **Opcode:** The opcode field is 1, 2, or 3 bytes in length. The opcode may also include bits that specify if data is byte- or full-size (16 or 32 bits depending on context), direction of data operation (to or from memory), and whether an immediate data field must be sign extended.
- **ModR/M:** This byte, and the next, provide addressing information. The ModR/M byte specifies whether an operand is in a register or in memory; if it is in memory, then fields within the byte specify the addressing mode to be used. The ModR/M byte consists of three fields: The Mod field (2 bits) combines with the R/M field to form 32 possible values: 8 registers and 24 indexing modes; the Reg/Opcode field (3 bits) specifies either a register number or three more bits of opcode information; the r/m field (3 bits) can specify a register as the location of an operand, or it can form part of the addressing-mode encoding in combination with the Mod field.
- **SIB:** Certain encoding of the ModR/M byte specifies the inclusion of the SIB byte to specify fully the addressing mode. The SIB byte consists of three fields: The Scale field (2 bits) specifies the scale factor for scaled indexing; the Index field (3 bits) specifies the index register; the Base field (3 bits) specifies the base register.
- **Displacement:** When the addressing-mode specifier indicates that a displacement is used, an 8-, 16-, or 32-bit signed integer displacement field is added.
- **Immediate:** Provides the value of an 8-, 16-, or 32-bit operand.

Several comparisons may be useful here. In the x86 format, the addressing mode is provided as part of the opcode sequence rather than with each operand. Because only one operand can have address-mode information, only one memory operand can be referenced in an instruction. In contrast, the VAX carries the address-mode information with each operand, allowing memory-to-memory operations. The x86 instructions are therefore more compact. However, if a memory-to-memory operation is required, the VAX can accomplish this in a single instruction.

The x86 format allows the use of not only 1-byte, but also 2-byte and 4-byte offsets for indexing. Although the use of the larger index offsets results in longer instructions, this feature provides needed flexibility. For example, it is useful in addressing large arrays or large stack frames. In contrast, the IBM S/370 instruction format allows offsets no greater than 4 Kbytes (12 bits of offset information), and the offset must be positive. When a location is not in reach of this offset, the compiler must generate extra code to generate the needed address. This problem is especially apparent in dealing with stack frames that have local variables occupying in excess of 4 Kbytes. As [DEWA90] puts it, "generating code for the 370 is so painful as a result of that restriction that there have even been compilers for the 370 that simply chose to limit the size of the stack frame to 4 Kbytes."

As can be seen, the encoding of the x86 instruction set is very complex. This has to do partly with the need to be backward compatible with the 8086 machine and partly with a desire on the part of the designers to provide every possible assistance to the compiler writer in producing efficient code. It is a matter of some debate whether an instruction set as complex as this is preferable to the opposite extreme of the RISC instruction sets.

ARM Instruction Formats

All instructions in the ARM architecture are 32 bits long and follow a regular format (Figure 13.10). The first four bits of an instruction are the condition code. As discussed in Chapter 12, virtually all ARM instructions can be conditionally executed. The next three bits specify the general type of instruction. For most instructions other than branch instructions, the next five bits constitute an opcode and/or modifier bits for the operation. The remaining 20 bits are for operand addressing. The regular structure of the instruction formats eases the job of the instruction decode units.

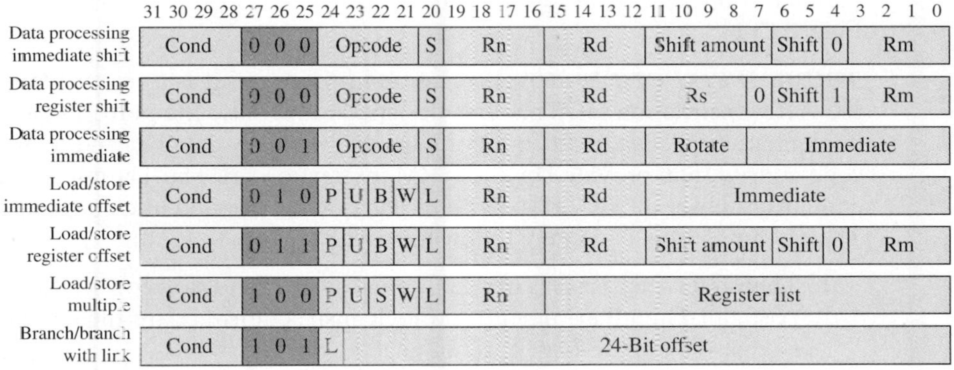

	31 30 29 28	27 26 25	24 23 22 21 20	19 18 17 16	15 14 13 12	11 10 9 8	7 6 5	4	3 2 1 0
Data processing immediate shift	Cond	0 0 0	Opcode S	Rn	Rd	Shift amount	Shift	0	Rm
Data processing register shift	Cond	0 0 0	Opcode S	Rn	Rd	Rs	0 Shift	1	Rm
Data processing immediate	Cond	0 0 1	Opcode S	Rn	Rd	Rotate	Immediate		
Load/store immediate offset	Cond	0 1 0	P U B W L	Rn	Rd	Immediate			
Load/store register offset	Cond	0 1 1	P U B W L	Rn	Rd	Shift amount	Shift	0	Rm
Load/store multiple	Cond	1 0 0	P U S W L	Rn	Register list				
Branch/branch with link	Cond	1 0 1	L	24-Bit offset					

S = For data processing instructions, signifies that the instruction updates the condition codes
S = For load/store multiple instructions, signifies whether instruction execution is restricted to supervisor mode
P, U, W = Bits that distinguish among different types of addressing_mode
B = Distinguishes between an unsigned byte (B==1) and a word (B==0) access
L = For load/store instructions, distinguishes between a Load (L==1) and a Store (L==0)
L = For branch instructions, determines whether a return address is stored in the link register

Figure 13.10 ARM Instruction Formats

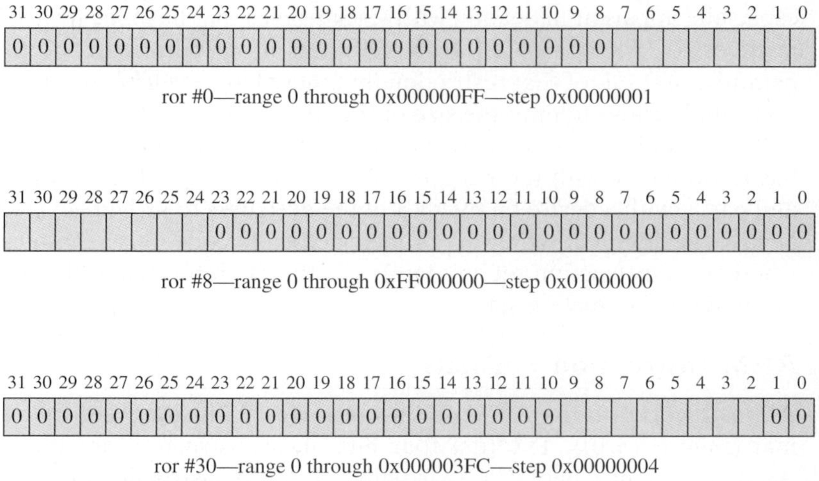

31 30 29 28 27 26 25 24 23 22 21 20 19 18 17 16 15 14 13 12 11 10 9 8 7 6 5 4 3 2 1 0

| 0 | 0 | 0 | 0 | 0 | 0 | 0 | 0 | 0 | 0 | 0 | 0 | 0 | 0 | 0 | 0 | 0 | 0 | 0 | 0 | 0 | 0 | 0 | 0 | | | | | | | | |

ror #0—range 0 through 0x000000FF—step 0x00000001

31 30 29 28 27 26 25 24 23 22 21 20 19 18 17 16 15 14 13 12 11 10 9 8 7 6 5 4 3 2 1 0

| | | | | | | | | 0 | 0 | 0 | 0 | 0 | 0 | 0 | 0 | 0 | 0 | 0 | 0 | 0 | 0 | 0 | 0 | 0 | 0 | 0 | 0 | 0 | 0 | 0 | 0 |

ror #8—range 0 through 0xFF000000—step 0x01000000

31 30 29 28 27 26 25 24 23 22 21 20 19 18 17 16 15 14 13 12 11 10 9 8 7 6 5 4 3 2 1 0

| 0 | 0 | 0 | 0 | 0 | 0 | 0 | 0 | 0 | 0 | 0 | 0 | 0 | 0 | 0 | 0 | 0 | 0 | 0 | 0 | 0 | 0 | 0 | 0 | | | | | | | 0 | 0 |

ror #30—range 0 through 0x000003FC—step 0x00000004

Figure 13.11   Examples of Use of ARM Immediate Constants

IMMEDIATE CONSTANTS To achieve a greater range of immediate values, the data processing immediate format specifies both an immediate value and a rotate value. The 8-bit immediate value is expanded to 32 bits and then rotated right by a number of bits equal to twice the 4-bit rotate value. Several examples are shown in Figure 13.11.

THUMB INSTRUCTION SET The Thumb instruction set is a re-encoded subset of the ARM instruction set. Thumb is designed to increase the performance of ARM implementations that use a 16-bit or narrower memory data bus and to allow better code density than provided by the ARM instruction set. The Thumb instruction set contains a subset of the ARM 32-bit instruction set recoded into 16-bit instructions. The savings is achieved in the following way:

1. Thumb instructions are unconditional, so the condition code field is not used. Also, all Thumb arithmetic and logic instructions update the condition flags, so that the update-flag bit is not needed. Savings: 5 bits.

2. Thumb has only a subset of the operations in the full instruction set and uses only a 2-bit opcode field, plus a 3-bit type field. Savings: 2 bits.

3. The remaining savings of 9 bits comes from reductions in the operand specifications. For example, Thumb instructions reference only registers r0 through r7, so only 3 bits are required for register references, rather than 4 bits. Immediate values do not include a 4-bit rotate field.

The ARM processor can execute a program consisting of a mixture of Thumb instructions and 32-bit ARM instructions. A bit in the processor control register determines which type of instruction is currently being executed. Figure 13.12 shows an example. The figure shows both the general format and a specific instance of an instruction in both 16-bit and 32-bit formats.

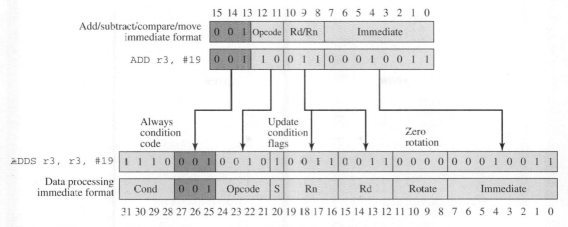

Figure 13.12 Expanding a Thumb ADD Instruction into its ARM Equivalent

13.5 ASSEMBLY LANGUAGE

A processor can understand and execute machine instructions. Such instructions are simply binary numbers stored in the computer. If a programmer wished to program directly in machine language, then it would be necessary to enter the program as binary data.

Consider the simple BASIC statement

$$N = I + J + K$$

Suppose we wished to program this statement in machine language and to initialize I, J, and K to 2, 3, and 4, respectively. This is shown in Figure 13.13a. The program starts in location 101 (hexadecimal). Memory is reserved for the four variables starting at location 201. The program consists of four instructions:

1. Load the contents of location 201 into the AC.
2. Add the contents of location 202 to the AC.
3. Add the contents of location 203 to the AC.
4. Store the contents of the AC in location 204.

This is clearly a tedious and very error-prone process.

A slight improvement is to write the program in hexadecimal rather than binary notation (Figure 10.11b). We could write the program as a series of lines. Each line contains the address of a memory location and the hexadecimal code of the binary value to be stored in that location. Then we need a program that will accept this input, translate each line into a binary number, and store it in the specified location.

For more improvement, we can make use of the symbolic name or mnemonic of each instruction. This results in the *symbolic program* shown in Figure 10.11c. Each line of input still represents one memory location. Each line consists of three

Address	Contents			
101	0010	0010	101	2201
102	0001	0010	102	1202
103	0001	0010	103	1203
104	0011	0010	104	3204
201	0000	0000	201	0002
202	0000	0000	202	0003
203	0000	0000	203	0004
204	0000	0000	204	0000

(a) Binary program

Address	Contents
101	2201
102	1202
103	1203
104	3204
201	0002
202	0003
203	0004
204	0000

(b) Hexadecimal program

Address	Instruction	
101	LDA	201
102	ADD	202
103	ADD	203
104	STA	204
201	DAT	2
202	DAT	3
203	DAT	4
204	DAT	0

(c) Symbolic program

Label	Operation	Operand
FORMUL	LDA	I
	ADD	J
	ADD	K
	STA	N
I	DATA	2
J	DATA	3
K	DATA	4
N	DATA	0

(d) Assembly program

Figure 13.13   Computation of the Formula $N = I + J + K$

fields, separated by spaces. The first field contains the address of a location. For an instruction, the second field contains the three-letter symbol for the opcode. If it is a memory-referencing instruction, then a third field contains the address. To store arbitrary data in a location, we invent a *pseudoinstruction* with the symbol DAT. This is merely an indication that the third field on the line contains a hexadecimal number to be stored in the location specified in the first field.

For this type of input we need a slightly more complex program. The program accepts each line of input, generates a binary number based on the second and third (if present) fields, and stores it in the location specified by the first field.

The use of a symbolic program makes life much easier but is still awkward. In particular, we must give an absolute address for each word. This means that the program and data can be loaded into only one place in memory, and we must know that place ahead of time. Worse, suppose we wish to change the program some day by adding or deleting a line. This will change the addresses of all subsequent words.

A much better system, and one commonly used, is to use symbolic addresses. This is illustrated in Figure 10.11d. Each line still consists of three fields. The first field is still for the address, but a symbol is used instead of an absolute numerical address. Some lines have no address, implying that the address of that line is one more than the address of the previous line. For memory-reference instructions, the third field also contains a symbolic address.

With this last refinement, we have an *assembly language*. Programs written in assembly language (assembly programs) are translated into machine language by an *assembler*. This program must not only do the symbolic translation discussed earlier but also assign some form of memory addresses to symbolic addresses.

The development of assembly language was a major milestone in the evolution of computer technology. It was the first step to the high-level languages in use today. Although few programmers use assembly language, virtually all machines provide one. They are used, if at all, for systems programs such as compilers and I/O routines.

Appendix B provides a more detailed examination of assembly language.

13.6 RECOMMENDED READING

The references cited in Chapter 12 are equally applicable to the material of this chapter. [BLAA97] contains a detailed discussion of instruction formats and addressing modes. In addition, the reader may wish to consult [FLYN85] for a discussion and analysis of instruction set design issues, particularly those relating to formats.

BLAA97 Blaauw, G., and Brooks, F. *Computer Architecture: Concepts and Evolution.* Reading, MA: Addison-Wesley, 1997.

FLYN85 Flynn, M.; Johnson, J.; and Wakefield, S. "On Instruction Sets and Their Formats." *IEEE Transactions on Computers,* March 1985.

13.7 KEY TERMS, REVIEW QUESTIONS, AND PROBLEMS

Key Terms

autoindexing	immediate addressing	preindexing
base-register addressing	indexing	register addressing
direct addressing	indirect addressing	register indirect addressing
displacement addressing	instruction format	relative addressing
effective address	postindexing	word

Review Questions

13.1 Briefly define immediate addressing.

13.2 Briefly define **direct addressing**.

13.3 Briefly define indirect addressing.

13.4 Briefly define register addressing.

13.5 Briefly define register indirect addressing.

13.6 Briefly define displacement addressing.

13.7 Briefly define relative addressing.

13.8 What is the advantage of autoindexing?

13.9 What is the difference between postindexing and preindexing?

13.10 What facts go into determining the use of the addressing bits of an instruction?

13.11 What are the advantages and disadvantages of using a variable-length instruction format?

Problems

13.1 Given the following memory values and a one-address machine with an accumulator, what values do the following instructions load into the accumulator?

- Word 20 contains 40.
- Word 30 contains 50.
- Word 40 contains 60.
- Word 50 contains 70.

    a. LOAD IMMEDIATE 20
    b. LOAD DIRECT 20
    c. LOAD INDIRECT 20
    d. LOAD IMMEDIATE 30
    e. LOAD DIRECT 30
    f. LOAD INDIRECT 30

13.2 Let the address stored in the program counter be designated by the symbol X1. The instruction stored in X1 has an address part (operand reference) X2. The operand needed to execute the instruction is stored in the memory word with address X3. An index register contains the value X4. What is the relationship between these various quantities if the addressing mode of the instruction is (a) direct; (b) indirect; (c) PC relative; (d) indexed?

13.3 An address field in an instruction contains decimal value 14. Where is the corresponding operand located for
    a. immediate addressing?
    b. direct addressing?
    c. indirect addressing?
    d. register addressing?
    e. register indirect addressing?

13.4 Consider a 16-bit processor in which the following appears in main memory, starting at location 200:

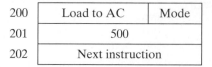

200	Load to AC	Mode
201	500	
202	Next instruction	

The first part of the first word indicates that this instruction loads a value into an accumulator. The Mode field specifies an addressing mode and, if appropriate, indicates a source register; assume that when used, the source register is R1, which has a value of 400. There is also a base register that contains the value 100. The value of 500 in location 201 may be part of the address calculation. Assume that location 399 contains the value 999, location 400 contains the value 1000, and so on. Determine the effective address and the operand to be loaded for the following address modes:

a. Direct	**d.** PC relative	**g.** Register indirect
b. Immediate	**e.** Displacement	**h.** Autoindexing with increment, using R1
c. Indirect	**f.** Register	

13.5 A PC-relative mode branch instruction is 3 bytes long. The address of the instruction, in decimal, is 256028. Determine the branch target address if the signed displacement in the instruction is -31.

13.6 A PC-relative mode branch instruction is stored in memory at address 620_{10}. The branch is made to location 530_{10}. The address field in the instruction is 10 bits long. What is the binary value in the instruction?

13.7   How many times does the processor need to refer to memory when it fetches and executes an indirect-address-mode instruction if the instruction is (a) a computation requiring a single operand; (b) a branch?

13.8   The IBM 370 does not provide indirect addressing. Assume that the address of an operand is in main memory. How would you access the operand?

13.9   In [COOK82], the author proposes that the PC-relative addressing modes be eliminated in favor of other modes, such as the use of a stack. What is the disadvantage of this proposal?

13.10   The x86 includes the following instruction:

IMUL op1, op2, immediate

This instruction multiplies op2, which may be either register or memory, by the immediate operand value, and places the result in op1, which must be a register. There is no other three-operand instruction of this sort in the instruction set. What is the possible use of such an instruction? (*Hint*: Consider indexing.)

13.11   Consider a processor that includes a base with indexing addressing mode. Suppose an instruction is encountered that employs this addressing mode and specifies a displacement of 1970, in decimal. Currently the base and index register contain the decimal numbers 48,022 and 8, respectively. What is the address of the operand?

13.12   Define: EA = (X)+ is the effective address equal to the contents of location X, with X incremented by one word length after the effective address is calculated; EA = −(X) is the effective address equal to the contents of location X, with X decremented by one word length before the effective address is calculated; EA = (X)− is the effective address equal to the contents of location X, with X decremented by one word length after the effective address is calculated. Consider the following instructions, each in the format (Operation Source Operand, Destination Operand), with the result of the operation placed in the destination operand.
  a.   OP X, (X)
  b.   OP (X), (X)+
  c.   OP (X)+, (X)
  d.   OP − (X), (X)
  e.   OP − (X), (X)+
  f.   OP (X)+, (X)+
  g.   OP (X)−, (X)
Using X as the stack pointer, which of these instructions can pop the top two elements from the stack, perform the designated operation (e.g., ADD source to destination and store in destination), and push the result back on the stack? For each such instruction, does the stack grow toward memory location 0 or in the opposite direction?

13.13   Assume a stack-oriented processor that includes the stack operations PUSH and POP. Arithmetic operations automatically involve the top one or two stack elements. Begin with an empty stack. What stack elements remain after the following instructions are executed?
PUSH   4
PUSH   7
PUSH   8
ADD
PUSH   10
SUB
MUL

13.14   Justify the assertion that a 32-bit instruction is probably much less than twice as useful as a 16-bit instruction.

13.15   Why was IBM's decision to move from 36 bits to 32 bits per word wrenching, and to whom?

13.16   Assume an instruction set that uses a fixed 16-bit instruction length. Operand specifiers are 6 bits in length. There are K two-operand instructions and L zero-operand instructions. What is the maximum number of one-operand instructions that can be supported?

13.17   Design a variable-length opcode to allow all of the following to be encoded in a 36-bit instruction:

- instructions with two 15-bit addresses and one 3-bit register number
- instructions with one 15-bit address and one 3-bit register number
- instructions with no addresses or registers

13.18   Consider the results of Problem 10.6. Assume that M is a 16-bit memory address and that X, Y, and Z are either 16-bit addresses or 4-bit register numbers. The one-address machine uses an accumulator, and the two- and three-address machines have 16 registers and instructions operating on all combinations of memory locations and registers. Assuming 8-bit opcodes and instruction lengths that are multiples of 4 bits, how many bits does each machine need to compute X?

13.19   Is there any possible justification for an instruction with two opcodes?

13.20   The 16-bit Zilog Z8001 has the following general instruction format:

15	14	13	12	11	10	9	8	7	6	5	4	3	2	1	0

Mode		Opcode					w/b		Operand 2			Operand 1			

The *mode* field specifies how to locate the operands from the *operand* fields. The *w/b* field is used in certain instructions to specify whether the operands are bytes or 16-bit words. The *operand 1* field may (depending on the *mode field* contents) specify one of 16 general-purpose registers. The *operand 2* field may specify any general-purpose registers except register 0. When the *operand 2* field is all zeros, each of the original opcodes takes on a new meaning.

a.   How many opcodes are provided on the Z8001?

b.   Suggest an efficient way to provide more opcodes and indicate the trade-off involved.

PROCESSOR STRUCTURE AND FUNCTION

LEARNING OBJECTIVES

After studying this chapter, you should be able to:

◆ Distinguish between user-visible and control/status registers, and discuss the purposes of registers in each category.

◆ Summarize the instruction cycle.

◆ Discuss the principle behind instruction pipelining and how it works in practice.

◆ Compare and contrast the various forms of pipeline hazards.

◆ Present an overview of the x86 processor structure.

◆ Present an overview of the ARM processor structure.

This chapter discusses aspects of the processor not yet covered in Part Three and sets the stage for the discussion of RISC and superscalar architecture in Chapters 15 and 16.

We begin with a summary of processor organization. Registers, which form the internal memory of the processor, are then analyzed. We are then in a position to return to the discussion (begun in Section 3.2) of the instruction cycle. A description of the instruction cycle and a common technique known as instruction pipelining complete our description. The chapter concludes with an examination of some aspects of the x86 and ARM organizations.

14.1 PROCESSOR ORGANIZATION

To understand the organization of the processor, let us consider the requirements placed on the processor, the things that it must do:

- **Fetch instruction:** The processor reads an instruction from memory (register, cache, main memory).

- **Interpret instruction:** The instruction is decoded to determine what action is required.

- **Fetch data:** The execution of an instruction may require reading data from memory or an I/O module.

- **Process data:** The execution of an instruction may require performing some arithmetic or logical operation on data.

- **Write data:** The results of an execution may require writing data to memory or an I/O module.

To do these things, it should be clear that the processor needs to store some data temporarily. It must remember the location of the last instruction so that it can know where to get the next instruction. It needs to store instructions and data temporarily while an instruction is being executed. In other words, the processor needs a small internal memory.

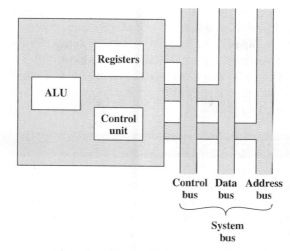

Figure 14.1   The CPU with the System Bus

Figure 14.1 is a simplified view of a processor, indicating its connection to the rest of the system via the system bus. A similar interface would be needed for any of the interconnection structures described in Chapter 3. The reader will recall that the major components of the processor are an *arithmetic and logic unit* (ALU) and a *control unit* (CU). The ALU does the actual computation or processing of data. The control unit controls the movement of data and instructions into and out of the processor and controls the operation of the ALU. In addition, the figure shows a minimal internal memory, consisting of a set of storage locations, called *registers.*

Figure 14.2 is a slightly more detailed view of the processor. The data transfer and logic control paths are indicated, including an element labeled *internal*

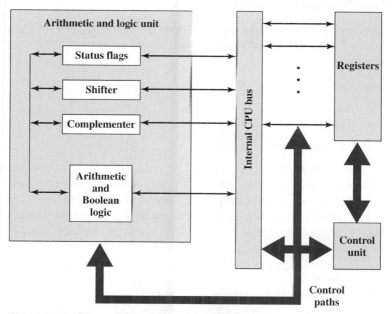

Figure 14.2   Internal Structure of the CPU

processor bus. This element is needed to transfer data between the various registers and the ALU because the ALU in fact operates only on data in the internal processor memory. The figure also shows typical basic elements of the ALU. Note the similarity between the internal structure of the computer as a whole and the internal structure of the processor. In both cases, there is a small collection of major elements (computer: processor, I/O, memory; processor: control unit, ALU, registers) connected by data paths.

14.2 REGISTER ORGANIZATION

As we discussed in Chapter 4, a computer system employs a memory hierarchy. At higher levels of the hierarchy, memory is faster, smaller, and more expensive (per bit). Within the processor, there is a set of registers that function as a level of memory above main memory and cache in the hierarchy. The registers in the processor perform two roles:

- **User-visible registers:** Enable the machine- or assembly language programmer to minimize main memory references by optimizing use of registers.
- **Control and status registers:** Used by the control unit to control the operation of the processor and by privileged, operating system programs to control the execution of programs.

There is not a clean separation of registers into these two categories. For example, on some machines the program counter is user visible (e.g., x86), but on many it is not. For purposes of the following discussion, however, we will use these categories.

User–Visible Registers

A user-visible register is one that may be referenced by means of the machine language that the processor executes. We can characterize these in the following categories:

- General purpose
- Data
- Address
- Condition codes

General-purpose registers can be assigned to a variety of functions by the programmer. Sometimes their use within the instruction set is orthogonal to the operation. That is, any general-purpose register can contain the operand for any opcode. This provides true general-purpose register use. Often, however, there are restrictions. For example, there may be dedicated registers for floating-point and stack operations.

In some cases, general-purpose registers can be used for addressing functions (e.g., register indirect, displacement). In other cases, there is a partial or clean separation between data registers and address registers. **Data registers** may be used only to hold data and cannot be employed in the calculation of an operand address.

Address registers may themselves be somewhat general purpose, or they may be devoted to a particular addressing mode. Examples include the following:

- **Segment pointers:** In a machine with segmented addressing (see Section 8.3), a segment register holds the address of the base of the segment. There may be multiple registers: for example, one for the operating system and one for the current process.

- **Index registers:** These are used for indexed addressing and may be autoindexed.

- **Stack pointer:** If there is user-visible stack addressing, then typically there is a dedicated register that points to the top of the stack. This allows implicit addressing; that is, push, pop, and other stack instructions need not contain an explicit stack operand.

There are several design issues to be addressed here. An important issue is whether to use completely general-purpose registers or to specialize their use. We have already touched on this issue in the preceding chapter because it affects instruction set design. With the use of specialized registers, it can generally be implicit in the opcode which type of register a certain operand specifier refers to. The operand specifier must only identify one of a set of specialized registers rather than one out of all the registers, thus saving bits. On the other hand, this specialization limits the programmer's flexibility.

Another design issue is the number of registers, either general purpose or data plus address, to be provided. Again, this affects instruction set design because more registers require more operand specifier bits. As we previously discussed, somewhere between 8 and 32 registers appears optimum [LUND77]. Fewer registers result in more memory references; more registers do not noticeably reduce memory references (e.g., see [WILL90]). However, a new approach, which finds advantage in the use of hundreds of registers, is exhibited in some RISC systems and is discussed in Chapter 15.

Finally, there is the issue of register length. Registers that must hold addresses obviously must be at least long enough to hold the largest address. Data registers should be able to hold values of most data types. Some machines allow two contiguous registers to be used as one for holding double-length values.

A final category of registers, which is at least partially visible to the user, holds **condition codes** (also referred to as *flags*). Condition codes are bits set by the processor hardware as the result of operations. For example, an arithmetic operation may produce a positive, negative, zero, or overflow result. In addition to the result itself being stored in a register or memory, a condition code is also set. The code may subsequently be tested as part of a conditional branch operation.

Condition code bits are collected into one or more registers. Usually, they form part of a control register. Generally, machine instructions allow these bits to be read by implicit reference, but the programmer cannot alter them.

Many processors, including those based on the IA-64 architecture and the MIPS processors, do not use condition codes at all. Rather, conditional branch instructions specify a comparison to be made and act on the result of the comparison, without storing a condition code. Table 14.1, based on [DERO87], lists key advantages and disadvantages of condition codes.

Table 14.1   Condition Codes

Advantages	Disadvantages
1. Because condition codes are set by normal arithmetic and data movement instructions, they should reduce the number of COMPARE and TEST instructions needed. 2. Conditional instructions, such as BRANCH are simplified relative to composite instructions, such as TEST AND BRANCH. 3. Condition codes facilitate multiway branches. For example, a TEST instruction can be followed by two branches, one on less than or equal to zero and one on greater than zero. 4. Condition codes can be saved on the stack during subroutine calls along with other register information.	1. Condition codes add complexity, both to the hardware and software. Condition code bits are often modified in different ways by different instructions, making life more difficult for both the microprogrammer and compiler writer. 2. Condition codes are irregular; they are typically not part of the main data path, so they require extra hardware connections. 3. Often condition code machines must add special non-condition-code instructions for special situations anyway, such as bit checking, loop control, and atomic semaphore operations. 4. In a pipelined implementation, condition codes require special synchronization to avoid conflicts.

In some machines, a subroutine call will result in the automatic saving of all user-visible registers, to be restored on return. The processor performs the saving and restoring as part of the execution of call and return instructions. This allows each subroutine to use the user-visible registers independently. On other machines, it is the responsibility of the programmer to save the contents of the relevant user-visible registers prior to a subroutine call, by including instructions for this purpose in the program.

Control and Status Registers

There are a variety of processor registers that are employed to control the operation of the processor. Most of these, on most machines, are not visible to the user. Some of them may be visible to machine instructions executed in a control or operating system mode.

Of course, different machines will have different register organizations and use different terminology. We list here a reasonably complete list of register types, with a brief description.

Four registers are essential to instruction execution:

- **Program counter (PC):** Contains the address of an instruction to be fetched.
- **Instruction register (IR):** Contains the instruction most recently fetched.
- **Memory address register (MAR):** Contains the address of a location in memory.
- **Memory buffer register (MBR):** Contains a word of data to be written to memory or the word most recently read.

Not all processors have internal registers designated as MAR and MBR, but some equivalent buffering mechanism is needed whereby the bits to be transferred to the system bus are staged and the bits to be read from the data bus are temporarily stored.

Typically, the processor updates the PC after each instruction fetch so that the PC always points to the next instruction to be executed. A branch or skip instruction will also modify the contents of the PC. The fetched instruction is loaded into an IR, where the opcode and operand specifiers are analyzed. Data are exchanged with memory using the MAR and MBR. In a bus-organized system, the MAR connects directly to the address bus, and the MBR connects directly to the data bus. User-visible registers, in turn, exchange data with the MBR.

The four registers just mentioned are used for the movement of data between the processor and memory. Within the processor, data must be presented to the ALU for processing. The ALU may have direct access to the MBR and user-visible registers. Alternatively, there may be additional buffering registers at the boundary to the ALU; these registers serve as input and output registers for the ALU and exchange data with the MBR and user-visible registers.

Many processor designs include a register or set of registers, often known as the *program status word* (PSW), that contain status information. The PSW typically contains condition codes plus other status information. Common fields or flags include the following:

- **Sign:** Contains the sign bit of the result of the last arithmetic operation.
- **Zero:** Set when the result is 0.
- **Carry:** Set if an operation resulted in a carry (addition) into or borrow (subtraction) out of a high-order bit. Used for multiword arithmetic operations.
- **Equal:** Set if a logical compare result is equality.
- **Overflow:** Used to indicate arithmetic overflow.
- **Interrupt Enable/Disable:** Used to enable or disable interrupts.
- **Supervisor:** Indicates whether the processor is executing in supervisor or user mode. Certain privileged instructions can be executed only in supervisor mode, and certain areas of memory can be accessed only in supervisor mode.

A number of other registers related to status and control might be found in a particular processor design. There may be a pointer to a block of memory containing additional status information (e.g., process control blocks). In machines using vectored interrupts, an interrupt vector register may be provided. If a stack is used to implement certain functions (e.g., subroutine call), then a system stack pointer is needed. A page table pointer is used with a virtual memory system. Finally, registers may be used in the control of I/O operations.

A number of factors go into the design of the control and status register organization. One key issue is operating system support. Certain types of control information are of specific utility to the operating system. If the processor designer has a functional understanding of the operating system to be used, then the register organization can to some extent be tailored to the operating system.

Another key design decision is the allocation of control information between registers and memory. It is common to dedicate the first (lowest) few hundred or

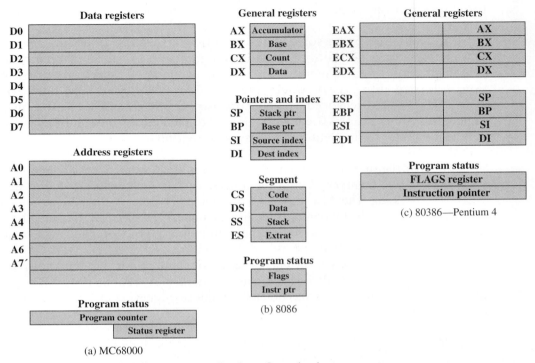

Figure 14.3 Example Microprocessor Register Organizations

thousand words of memory for control purposes. The designer must decide how much control information should be in registers and how much in memory. The usual trade-off of cost versus speed arises.

Example Microprocessor Register Organizations

It is instructive to examine and compare the register organization of comparable systems. In this section, we look at two 16-bit microprocessors that were designed at about the same time: the Motorola MC68000 [STRI79] and the Intel 8086 [MORS78]. Figures 14.3a and b depict the register organization of each; purely internal registers, such as a memory address register, are not shown.

The MC68000 partitions its 32-bit registers into eight data registers and nine address registers. The eight data registers are used primarily for data manipulation and are also used in addressing as index registers. The width of the registers allows 8-, 16-, and 32-bit data operations, determined by opcode. The address registers contain 32-bit (no segmentation) addresses; two of these registers are also used as stack pointers, one for users and one for the operating system, depending on the current execution mode. Both registers are numbered 7, because only one can be used at a time. The MC68000 also includes a 32-bit program counter and a 16-bit status register.

The Motorola team wanted a very regular instruction set, with no special-purpose registers. A concern for code efficiency led them to divide the registers into two functional components, saving one bit on each register specifier. This seems a reasonable compromise between complete generality and code compaction.

The Intel 8086 takes a different approach to register organization. Every register is special purpose, although some registers are also usable as general purpose. The 8086 contains four 16-bit data registers that are addressable on a byte or 16-bit basis, and four 16-bit pointer and index registers. The data registers can be used as general purpose in some instructions. In others, the registers are used implicitly. For example, a multiply instruction always uses the accumulator. The four pointer registers are also used implicitly in a number of operations; each contains a segment offset. There are also four 16-bit segment registers. Three of the four segment registers are used in a dedicated, implicit fashion, to point to the segment of the current instruction (useful for branch instructions), a segment containing data, and a segment containing a stack, respectively. These dedicated and implicit uses provide for compact encoding at the cost of reduced flexibility. The 8086 also includes an instruction pointer and a set of 1-bit status and control flags.

The point of this comparison should be clear. There is no universally accepted philosophy concerning the best way to organize processor registers [TOON81]. As with overall instruction set design and so many other processor design issues, it is still a matter of judgment and taste.

A second instructive point concerning register organization design is illustrated in Figure 14.3c. This figure shows the user-visible register organization for the Intel 80386 [ELAY85], which is a 32-bit microprocessor designed as an extension of the 8086.[1] The 80386 uses 32-bit registers. However, to provide upward compatibility for programs written on the earlier machine, the 80386 retains the original register organization embedded in the new organization. Given this design constraint, the architects of the 32-bit processors had limited flexibility in designing the register organization.

14.3 INSTRUCTION CYCLE

In Section 3.2, we described the processor's instruction cycle (Figure 3.9). To recall, an instruction cycle includes the following stages:

- **Fetch:** Read the next instruction from memory into the processor.
- **Execute:** Interpret the opcode and perform the indicated operation.
- **Interrupt:** If interrupts are enabled and an interrupt has occurred, save the current process state and service the interrupt.

We are now in a position to elaborate somewhat on the instruction cycle. First, we must introduce one additional stage, known as the indirect cycle.

---

[1]Because the MC68000 already uses 32-bit registers, the MC68020 [MACD84], which is a full 32-bit architecture, uses the same register organization.

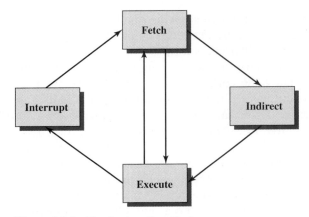

Figure 14.4   The Instruction Cycle

The Indirect Cycle

We have seen, in Chapter 13, that the execution of an instruction may involve one or more operands in memory, each of which requires a memory access. Further, if indirect addressing is used, then additional memory accesses are required.

We can think of the fetching of indirect addresses as one more instruction stages. The result is shown in Figure 14.4. The main line of activity consists of alternating instruction fetch and instruction execution activities. After an instruction is fetched, it is examined to determine if any indirect addressing is involved. If so, the required operands are fetched using indirect addressing. Following execution, an interrupt may be processed before the next instruction fetch.

Another way to view this process is shown in Figure 14.5, which is a revised version of Figure 3.12. This illustrates more correctly the nature of the instruction cycle. Once an instruction is fetched, its operand specifiers must be identified. Each input operand in memory is then fetched, and this process may require indirect addressing. Register-based operands need not be fetched. Once the opcode is executed, a similar process may be needed to store the result in main memory.

Data Flow

The exact sequence of events during an instruction cycle depends on the design of the processor. We can, however, indicate in general terms what must happen. Let us assume that a processor that employs a memory address register (MAR), a memory buffer register (MBR), a program counter (PC), and an instruction register (IR).

During the *fetch cycle,* an instruction is read from memory. Figure 14.6 shows the flow of data during this cycle. The PC contains the address of the next instruction to be fetched. This address is moved to the MAR and placed on the address bus. The control unit requests a memory read, and the result is placed on the data bus and copied into the MBR and then moved to the IR. Meanwhile, the PC is incremented by 1, preparatory for the next fetch.

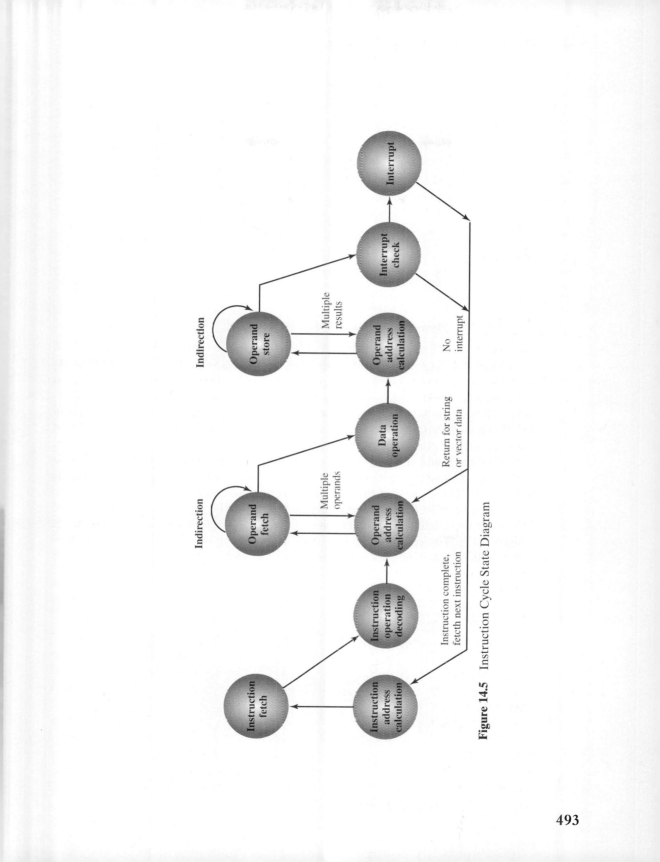

Figure 14.5 Instruction Cycle State Diagram

493

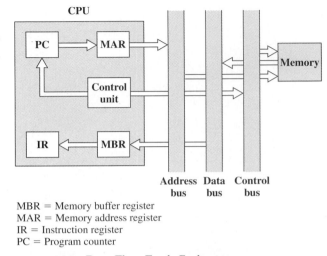

MBR = Memory buffer register
MAR = Memory address register
IR = Instruction register
PC = Program counter

Figure 14.6 Data Flow, Fetch Cycle

Once the fetch cycle is over, the control unit examines the contents of the IR to determine if it contains an operand specifier using indirect addressing. If so, an *indirect cycle* is performed. As shown in Figure 14.7, this is a simple cycle. The rightmost *N* bits of the MBR, which contain the address reference, are transferred to the MAR. Then the control unit requests a memory read, to get the desired address of the operand into the MBR.

The fetch and indirect cycles are simple and predictable. The *execute cycle* takes many forms; the form depends on which of the various machine instructions is in the IR. This cycle may involve transferring data among registers, read or write from memory or I/O, and/or the invocation of the ALU.

Like the fetch and indirect cycles, the *interrupt cycle* is simple and predictable (Figure 14.8). The current contents of the PC must be saved so that the processor can resume normal activity after the interrupt. Thus, the contents of the PC are

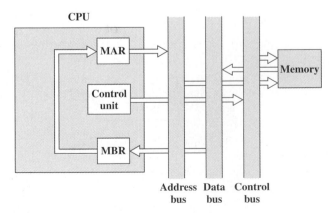

Figure 14.7 Data Flow, Indirect Cycle

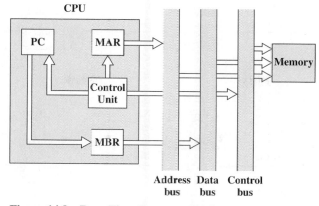

Figure 14.8 Data Flow, Interrupt Cycle

transferred to the MBR to be written into memory. The special memory location reserved for this purpose is loaded into the MAR from the control unit. It might, for example, be a stack pointer. The PC is loaded with the address of the interrupt routine. As a result, the next instruction cycle will begin by fetching the appropriate instruction.

14.4 INSTRUCTION PIPELINING

As computer systems evolve, greater performance can be achieved by taking advantage of improvements in technology, such as faster circuitry. In addition, organizational enhancements to the processor can improve performance. We have already seen some examples of this, such as the use of multiple registers rather than a single accumulator, and the use of a cache memory. Another organizational approach, which is quite common, is instruction pipelining.

Pipelining Strategy

Instruction pipelining is similar to the use of an assembly line in a manufacturing plant. An assembly line takes advantage of the fact that a product goes through various stages of production. By laying the production process out in an assembly line, products at various stages can be worked on simultaneously. This process is also referred to as *pipelining,* because, as in a pipeline, new inputs are accepted at one end before previously accepted inputs appear as outputs at the other end.

To apply this concept to instruction execution, we must recognize that, in fact, an instruction has a number of stages. Figures 14.5, for example, breaks the instruction cycle up into 10 tasks, which occur in sequence. Clearly, there should be some opportunity for pipelining.

As a simple approach, consider subdividing instruction processing into two stages: fetch instruction and execute instruction. There are times during the execution of an instruction when main memory is not being accessed. This time could be used to fetch the next instruction in parallel with the execution of the current

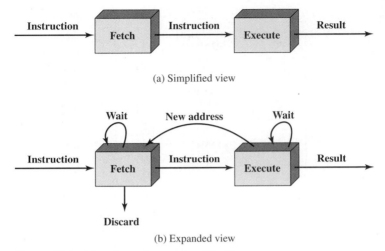

(a) Simplified view

(b) Expanded view

Figure 14.9 Two-Stage Instruction Pipeline

one. Figure 14.9a depicts this approach. The pipeline has two independent stages. The first stage fetches an instruction and buffers it. When the second stage is free, the first stage passes it the buffered instruction. While the second stage is executing the instruction, the first stage takes advantage of any unused memory cycles to fetch and buffer the next instruction. This is called instruction prefetch or *fetch overlap*. Note that this approach, which involves instruction buffering, requires more registers. In general, pipelining requires registers to store data between stages.

It should be clear that this process will speed up instruction execution. If the fetch and execute stages were of equal duration, the instruction cycle time would be halved. However, if we look more closely at this pipeline (Figure 14.9b), we will see that this doubling of execution rate is unlikely for two reasons:

1. The execution time will generally be longer than the fetch time. Execution will involve reading and storing operands and the performance of some operation. Thus, the fetch stage may have to wait for some time before it can empty its buffer.

2. A conditional branch instruction makes the address of the next instruction to be fetched unknown. Thus, the fetch stage must wait until it receives the next instruction address from the execute stage. The execute stage may then have to wait while the next instruction is fetched.

Guessing can reduce the time loss from the second reason. A simple rule is the following: When a conditional branch instruction is passed on from the fetch to the execute stage, the fetch stage fetches the next instruction in memory after the branch instruction. Then, if the branch is not taken, no time is lost. If the branch is taken, the fetched instruction must be discarded and a new instruction fetched.

While these factors reduce the potential effectiveness of the two-stage pipeline, some speedup occurs. To gain further speedup, the pipeline must have more stages. Let us consider the following decomposition of the instruction processing.

- **Fetch instruction (FI):** Read the next expected instruction into a buffer.
- **Decode instruction (DI):** Determine the opcode and the operand specifiers.
- **Calculate operands (CO):** Calculate the effective address of each source operand. This may involve displacement, register indirect, indirect, or other forms of address calculation.
- **Fetch operands (FO):** Fetch each operand from memory. Operands in registers need not be fetched.
- **Execute instruction (EI):** Perform the indicated operation and store the result, if any, in the specified destination operand location.
- **Write operand (WO):** Store the result in memory.

With this decomposition, the various stages will be of more nearly equal duration. For the sake of illustration, let us assume equal duration. Using this assumption, Figure 14.10 shows that a six-stage pipeline can reduce the execution time for 9 instructions from 54 time units to 14 time units.

Several comments are in order: The diagram assumes that each instruction goes through all six stages of the pipeline. This will not always be the case. For example, a load instruction does not need the WO stage. However, to simplify the pipeline hardware, the timing is set up assuming that each instruction requires all six stages. Also, the diagram assumes that all of the stages can be performed in parallel. In particular, it is assumed that there are no memory conflicts. For example, the FI, FO, and WO stages involve a memory access. The diagram implies that all these accesses can occur simultaneously. Most memory systems will not permit that. However, the desired value may be in cache, or the FO or WO stage may be null. Thus, much of the time, memory conflicts will not slow down the pipeline.

Time

	1	2	3	4	5	6	7	8	9	10	11	12	13	14
Instruction 1	FI	DI	CO	FO	EI	WO								
Instruction 2		FI	DI	CO	FO	EI	WO							
Instruction 3			FI	DI	CO	FO	EI	WO						
Instruction 4				FI	DI	CO	FO	EI	WO					
Instruction 5					FI	DI	CO	FO	EI	WO				
Instruction 6						FI	DI	CO	FO	EI	WO			
Instruction 7							FI	DI	CO	FO	EI	WO		
Instruction 8								FI	DI	CO	FO	EI	WO	
Instruction 9									FI	DI	CO	FO	EI	WO

Figure 14.10   Timing Diagram for Instruction Pipeline Operation

	Time →								Branch penalty ↔					
	1	2	3	4	5	6	7	8	9	10	11	12	13	14
Instruction 1	FI	DI	CO	FO	EI	WO								
Instruction 2		FI	DI	CO	FO	EI	WO							
Instruction 3			FI	DI	CO	FO	EI	WO						
Instruction 4				FI	DI	CO	FO							
Instruction 5					FI	DI	CO							
Instruction 6						FI	DI							
Instruction 7							FI							
Instruction 15									FI	DI	CO	FO	EI	WO
Instruction 16										FI	DI	CO	FO	EI	WO

Figure 14.11   The Effect of a Conditional Branch on Instruction Pipeline Operation

Several other factors serve to limit the performance enhancement. If the six stages are not of equal duration, there will be some waiting involved at various pipeline stages, as discussed before for the two-stage pipeline. Another difficulty is the conditional branch instruction, which can invalidate several instruction fetches. A similar unpredictable event is an interrupt. Figure 14.11 illustrates the effects of the conditional branch, using the same program as Figure 14.10. Assume that instruction 3 is a conditional branch to instruction 15. Until the instruction is executed, there is no way of knowing which instruction will come next. The pipeline, in this example, simply loads the next instruction in sequence (instruction 4) and proceeds. In Figure 14.10, the branch is not taken, and we get the full performance benefit of the enhancement. In Figure 14.11, the branch is taken. This is not determined until the end of time unit 7. At this point, the pipeline must be cleared of instructions that are not useful. During time unit 8, instruction 15 enters the pipeline. No instructions complete during time units 9 through 12; this is the performance penalty incurred because we could not anticipate the branch. Figure 14.12 indicates the logic needed for pipelining to account for branches and interrupts.

Other problems arise that did not appear in our simple two-stage organization. The CO stage may depend on the contents of a register that could be altered by a previous instruction that is still in the pipeline. Other such register and memory conflicts could occur. The system must contain logic to account for this type of conflict.

To clarify pipeline operation, it might be useful to look at an alternative depiction. Figures 14.10 and 14.11 show the progression of time horizontally across the figures, with each row showing the progress of an individual instruction. Figure 14.13 shows same sequence of events, with time progressing vertically down the figure,

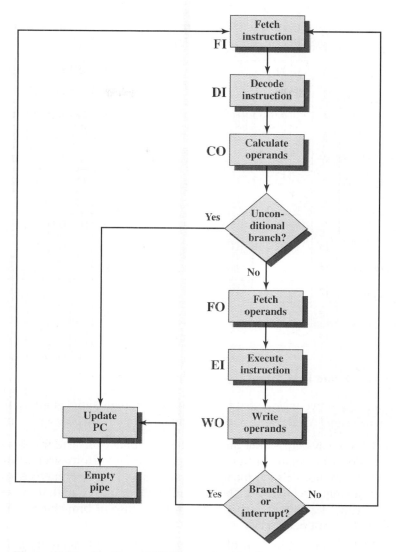

Figure 14.12 Six-Stage CPU Instruction Pipeline

and each row showing the state of the pipeline at a given point in time. In Figure 14.13a (which corresponds to Figure 14.10), the pipeline is full at time 6, with 6 different instructions in various stages of execution, and remains full through time 9; we assume that instruction I9 is the last instruction to be executed. In Figure 14.13b, (which corresponds to Figure 14.11), the pipeline is full at times 6 and 7. At time 7, instruction 3 is in the execute stage and executes a branch to instruction 15. At this point, instructions I4 through I7 are flushed from the pipeline, so that at time 8, only two instructions are in the pipeline, I3 and I15.

From the preceding discussion, it might appear that the greater the number of stages in the pipeline, the faster the execution rate. Some of the IBM S/360 designers

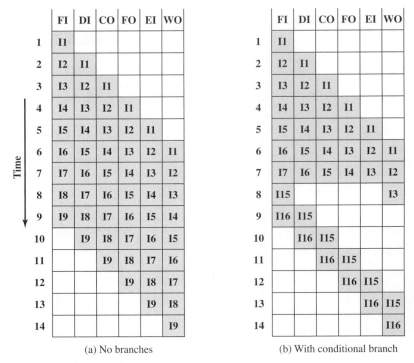

Figure 14.13 An Alternative Pipeline Depiction

pointed out two factors that frustrate this seemingly simple pattern for high-perform-ance design [ANDE67a], and they remain elements that designer must still consider:

1. At each stage of the pipeline, there is some overhead involved in moving data from buffer to buffer and in performing various preparation and delivery functions. This overhead can appreciably lengthen the total execution time of a single instruction. This is significant when sequential instructions are logi-cally dependent, either through heavy use of branching or through memory access dependencies.

2. The amount of control logic required to handle memory and register depen-dencies and to optimize the use of the pipeline increases enormously with the number of stages. This can lead to a situation where the logic controlling the gating between stages is more complex than the stages being controlled.

Another consideration is latching delay: It takes time for pipeline buffers to operate and this adds to instruction cycle time.

Instruction pipelining is a powerful technique for enhancing performance but requires careful design to achieve optimum results with reasonable complexity.

Pipeline Performance

In this subsection, we develop some simple measures of pipeline performance and relative speedup (based on a discussion in [HWAN93]). The cycle time τ of an **instruction pipeline** is the time needed to advance a set of instructions one stage through the pipeline; each column in Figures 14.10 and 14.11 represents one cycle time. The cycle time can be determined as

$$\tau = \max_i[\tau_i] + d = \tau_m + d \quad 1 \le i \le k$$

where

τ_i = time delay of the circuitry in the ith stage of the pipeline

τ_m = maximum stage delay (delay through stage which experiences the largest delay)

k = number of stages in the instruction pipeline

d = time delay of a latch, needed to advance signals and data from one stage to the next

In general, the time delay d is equivalent to a clock pulse and $\tau_m \gg d$. Now suppose that n instructions are processed, with no branches. Let $T_{k,n}$ be the total time required for a pipeline with k stages to execute n instructions. Then

$$T_{k,n} = [k + (n - 1)]\tau \tag{14.1}$$

A total of k cycles are required to complete the execution of the first instruction, and the remaining $n - 1$ instructions require $n - 1$ cycles.[2] This equation is easily verified from Figures 14.10. The ninth instruction completes at time cycle 14:

$$14 = [6 + (9 - 1)]$$

Now consider a processor with equivalent functions but no pipeline, and assume that the instruction cycle time is $k\tau$. The speedup factor for the instruction pipeline compared to execution without the pipeline is defined as

$$S_k = \frac{T_{1,n}}{T_{k,n}} = \frac{nk\tau}{[k + (n - 1)]\tau} = \frac{nk}{k + (n - 1)} \tag{14.2}$$

Figure 14.14a plots the speedup factor as a function of the number of instructions that are executed without a branch. As might be expected, at the limit ($n \to \infty$), we have a k-fold speedup. Figure 14.14b shows the speedup factor as a function of the number of stages in the instruction pipeline.[3] In this case, the speedup factor approaches the number of instructions that can be fed into the pipeline without branches. Thus, the larger the number of pipeline stages, the greater the potential for speedup. However, as a practical matter, the potential gains of additional pipeline stages are countered by increases in cost, delays between stages, and the fact that branches will be encountered requiring the flushing of the pipeline.

Pipeline Hazards

In the previous subsection, we mentioned some of the situations that can result in less than optimal pipeline performance. In this subsection, we examine this issue in

---

[2]We are being a bit sloppy here. The cycle time will only equal the maximum value of τ when all the stages are full. At the beginning, the cycle time may be less for the first one or few cycles.

[3]Note that the x-axis is logarithmic in Figure 14.14a and linear in Figure 14.14b.

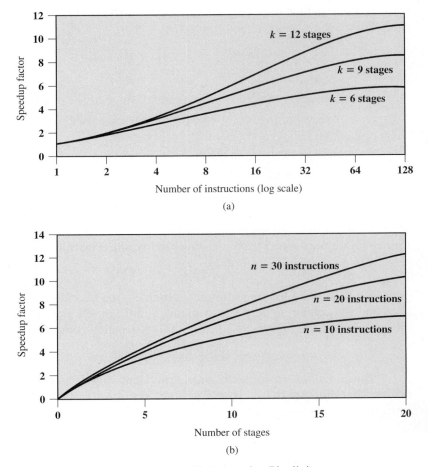

Figure 14.14 Speedup Factors with Instruction Pipelining

a more systematic way. Chapter 16 revisits this issue, in more detail, after we have introduced the complexities found in superscalar pipeline organizations.

A **pipeline hazard** occurs when the pipeline, or some portion of the pipeline, must stall because conditions do not permit continued execution. Such a pipeline stall is also referred to as a *pipeline bubble*. There are three types of hazards: resource, data, and control.

RESOURCE HAZARDS A resource hazard occurs when two (or more) instructions that are already in the pipeline need the same resource. The result is that the instructions must be executed in serial rather than parallel for a portion of the pipeline. A resource hazard is sometime referred to as a *structural hazard*.

Let us consider a simple example of a resource hazard. Assume a simplified five-stage pipeline, in which each stage takes one clock cycle. Figure 14.15a shows the ideal case, in which a new instruction enters the pipeline each clock cycle. Now assume that main memory has a single port and that all instruction fetches and data reads and writes must be performed one at a time. Further, ignore the cache. In this

Clock cycle

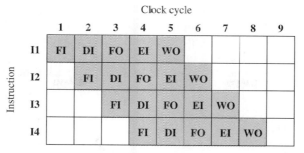

(a) Five-stage pipeline, ideal case

Clock cycle

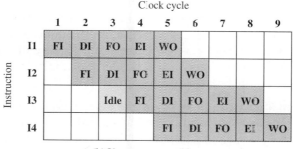

(b) I1 source operand in memory

Figure 14.15 Example of Resource Hazard

case, an operand read to or write from memory cannot be performed in parallel with an instruction fetch. This is illustrated in Figure 14.15b, which assumes that the source operand for instruction I1 is in memory, rather than a register. Therefore, the fetch instruction stage of the pipeline must idle for one cycle before beginning the instruction fetch for instruction I3. The figure assumes that all other operands are in registers.

Another example of a resource conflict is a situation in which multiple instructions are ready to enter the execute instruction phase and there is a single ALU. One solutions to such resource hazards is to increase available resources, such as having multiple ports into main memory and multiple ALU units.

Reservation Table Analyzer

One approach to analyzing resource conflicts and aiding in the design of pipelines is the reservation table. We examine reservation tables in Appendix I.

DATA HAZARDS A data hazard occurs when there is a conflict in the access of an operand location. In general terms, we can state the hazard in this form: Two instructions in a program are to be executed in sequence and both access a particular memory or register operand. If the two instructions are executed in strict sequence, no problem occurs. However, if the instructions are executed in a pipeline, then it is possible for the operand value to be updated in such a way as to produce a different result than would occur with strict sequential execution. In other words, the program produces an incorrect result because of the use of pipelining.

As an example, consider the following x86 machine instruction sequence:

```
ADD EAX,    EBX /* EAX = EAX + EBX
SUB ECX,    EAX /* ECX = ECX - EAX
```

The first instruction adds the contents of the 32-bit registers EAX and EBX and stores the result in EAX. The second instruction subtracts the contents of EAX from ECX and stores the result in ECX. Figure 14.16 shows the pipeline behavior. The ADD instruction does not update register EAX until the end of stage 5, which occurs at clock cycle 5. But the SUB instruction needs that value at the beginning of its stage 2, which occurs at clock cycle 4. To maintain correct operation, the pipeline must stall for two clocks cycles. Thus, in the absence of special hardware and specific avoidance algorithms, such a data hazard results in inefficient pipeline usage.

There are three types of data hazards;

- **Read after write (RAW), or true dependency:** An instruction modifies a register or memory location and a succeeding instruction reads the data in that memory or register location. A hazard occurs if the read takes place before the write operation is complete.

- **Write after read (WAR), or antidependency:** An instruction reads a register or memory location and a succeeding instruction writes to the location. A hazard occurs if the write operation completes before the read operation takes place.

- **Write after write (WAW), or output dependency:** Two instructions both write to the same location. A hazard occurs if the write operations take place in the reverse order of the intended sequence.

The example of Figure 14.16 is a RAW hazard. The other two hazards are best discussed in the context of superscalar organization, discussed in Chapter 16.

CONTROL HAZARDS A control hazard, also known as a *branch hazard,* occurs when the pipeline makes the wrong decision on a branch prediction and therefore brings instructions into the pipeline that must subsequently be discarded. We discuss approaches to dealing with control hazards next.

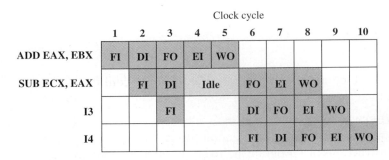

Figure 14.16 Example of Data Hazard

Dealing with Branches

One of the major problems in designing an instruction pipeline is assuring a steady flow of instructions to the initial stages of the pipeline. The primary impediment, as we have seen, is the conditional branch instruction. Until the instruction is actually executed, it is impossible to determine whether the branch will be taken or not.

A variety of approaches have been taken for dealing with conditional branches:

- Multiple streams
- Prefetch branch target
- Loop buffer
- Branch prediction
- Delayed branch

MULTIPLE STREAMS A simple pipeline suffers a penalty for a branch instruction because it must choose one of two instructions to fetch next and may make the wrong choice. A brute-force approach is to replicate the initial portions of the pipeline and allow the pipeline to fetch both instructions, making use of two streams. There are two problems with this approach:

- With multiple pipelines there are contention delays for access to the registers and to memory.
- Additional branch instructions may enter the pipeline (either stream) before the original branch decision is resolved. Each such instruction needs an additional stream.

Despite these drawbacks, this strategy can improve performance. Examples of machines with two or more pipeline streams are the IBM 370/168 and the IBM 3033.

PREFETCH BRANCH TARGET When a conditional branch is recognized, the target of the branch is prefetched, in addition to the instruction following the branch. This target is then saved until the branch instruction is executed. If the branch is taken, the target has already been prefetched.

The IBM 360/91 uses this approach.

LOOP BUFFER A loop buffer is a small, very-high-speed memory maintained by the instruction fetch stage of the pipeline and containing the n most recently fetched instructions, in sequence. If a branch is to be taken, the hardware first checks whether the branch target is within the buffer. If so, the next instruction is fetched from the buffer. The loop buffer has three benefits:

1. With the use of prefetching, the loop buffer will contain some instruction sequentially ahead of the current instruction fetch address. Thus, instructions fetched in sequence will be available without the usual memory access time.
2. If a branch occurs to a target just a few locations ahead of the address of the branch instruction, the target will already be in the buffer. This is useful for the rather common occurrence of IF–THEN and IF–THEN–ELSE sequences.

Branch address

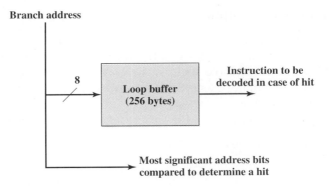

Figure 14.17   Loop Buffer

3. This strategy is particularly well suited to dealing with loops, or iterations; hence the name *loop buffer*. If the loop buffer is large enough to contain all the instructions in a loop, then those instructions need to be fetched from memory only once, for the first iteration. For subsequent iterations, all the needed instructions are already in the buffer.

The loop buffer is similar in principle to a cache dedicated to instructions. The differences are that the loop buffer only retains instructions in sequence and is much smaller in size and hence lower in cost.

Figure 14.17 gives an example of a loop buffer. If the buffer contains 256 bytes, and byte addressing is used, then the least significant 8 bits are used to index the buffer. The remaining most significant bits are checked to determine if the branch target lies within the environment captured by the buffer.

Among the machines using a loop buffer are some of the CDC machines (Star-100, 6600, 7600) and the CRAY-1. A specialized form of loop buffer is available on the Motorola 68010, for executing a three-instruction loop involving the DBcc (decrement and branch on condition) instruction (see Problem 14.14). A three-word buffer is maintained, and the processor executes these instructions repeatedly until the loop condition is satisfied.

Branch Prediction Simulator
Branch Target Buffer

BRANCH PREDICTION Various techniques can be used to predict whether a branch will be taken. Among the more common are the following:

- Predict never taken
- Predict always taken
- Predict by opcode
- Taken/not taken switch
- Branch history table

The first three approaches are static: they do not depend on the execution history up to the time of the conditional branch instruction. The latter two approaches are dynamic: They depend on the execution history.

The first two approaches are the simplest. These either always assume that the branch will not be taken and continue to fetch instructions in sequence, or they always assume that the branch will be taken and always fetch from the branch target. The predict-never-taken approach is the most popular of all the branch prediction methods.

Studies analyzing program behavior have shown that conditional branches are taken more than 50% of the time [LILJ88], and so if the cost of prefetching from either path is the same, then always prefetching from the branch target address should give better performance than always prefetching from the sequential path. However, in a paged machine, prefetching the branch target is more likely to cause a page fault than prefetching the next instruction in sequence, and so this performance penalty should be taken into account. An avoidance mechanism may be employed to reduce this penalty.

The final static approach makes the decision based on the opcode of the branch instruction. The processor assumes that the branch will be taken for certain branch opcodes and not for others. [LILJ88] reports success rates of greater than 75% with this strategy.

Dynamic branch strategies attempt to improve the accuracy of prediction by recording the history of conditional branch instructions in a program. For example, one or more bits can be associated with each conditional branch instruction that reflect the recent history of the instruction. These bits are referred to as a taken/ not taken switch that directs the processor to make a particular decision the next time the instruction is encountered. Typically, these history bits are not associated with the instruction in main memory. Rather, they are kept in temporary high-speed storage. One possibility is to associate these bits with any conditional branch instruction that is in a cache. When the instruction is replaced in the cache, its history is lost. Another possibility is to maintain a small table for recently executed branch instructions with one or more history bits in each entry. The processor could access the table associatively, like a cache, or by using the low-order bits of the branch instruction's address.

With a single bit, all that can be recorded is whether the last execution of this instruction resulted in a branch or not. A shortcoming of using a single bit appears in the case of a conditional branch instruction that is almost always taken, such as a loop instruction. With only one bit of history, an error in prediction will occur twice for each use of the loop: once on entering the loop, and once on exiting.

If two bits are used, they can be used to record the result of the last two instances of the execution of the associated instruction, or to record a state in some other fashion. Figure 14.18 shows a typical approach (see Problem 14.13 for other possibilities). Assume that the algorithm starts at the upper-left-hand corner of the flowchart. As long as each succeeding conditional branch instruction that is encountered is taken, the decision process predicts that the next branch will be taken. If a single prediction is wrong, the algorithm continues to predict that the next branch is taken. Only if two successive branches are not taken does the algorithm shift to the right-hand side of the flowchart. Subsequently, the algorithm

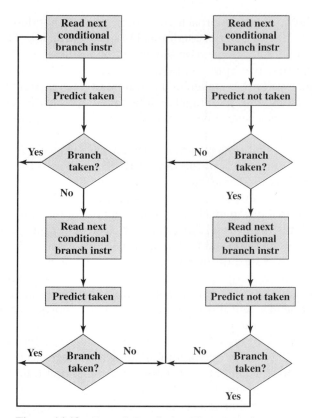

Figure 14.18 Branch Prediction Flowchart

will predict that branches are not taken until two branches in a row are taken. Thus, the algorithm requires two consecutive wrong predictions to change the prediction decision.

The decision process can be represented more compactly by a finite-state machine, shown in Figure 14.19. The finite-state machine representation is commonly used in the literature.

The use of history bits, as just described, has one drawback: If the decision is made to take the branch, the target instruction cannot be fetched until the target address, which is an operand in the conditional branch instruction, is decoded. Greater efficiency could be achieved if the instruction fetch could be initiated as soon as the branch decision is made. For this purpose, more information must be saved, in what is known as a branch target buffer, or a branch history table.

The branch history table is a small cache memory associated with the instruction fetch stage of the pipeline. Each entry in the table consists of three elements: the address of a branch instruction, some number of history bits that record the state of use of that instruction, and information about the target instruction. In most proposals and implementations, this third field contains the address of the target instruction. Another possibility is for the third field to actually contain the target instruction. The trade-off is clear: Storing the target address yields a smaller

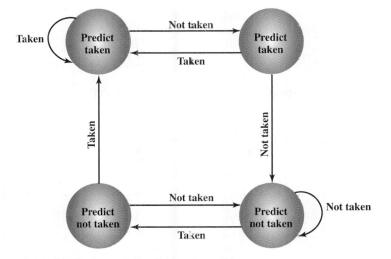

Figure 14.19 Branch Prediction State Diagram

table but a greater instruction fetch time compared with storing the target instruction [RECH98].

Figure 14.20 contrasts this scheme with a predict-never-taken strategy. With the former strategy, the instruction fetch stage always fetches the next sequential address. If a branch is taken, some logic in the processor detects this and instructs that the next instruction be fetched from the target address (in addition to flushing the pipeline). The branch history table is treated as a cache. Each prefetch triggers a lookup in the branch history table. If no match is found, the next sequential address is used for the fetch. If a match is found, a prediction is made based on the state of the instruction: Either the next sequential address or the branch target address is fed to the select logic.

When the branch instruction is executed, the execute stage signals the branch history table logic with the result. The state of the instruction is updated to reflect a correct or incorrect prediction. If the prediction is incorrect, the select logic is redirected to the correct address for the next fetch. When a conditional branch instruction is encountered that is not in the table, it is added to the table and one of the existing entries is discarded, using one of the cache replacement algorithms discussed in Chapter 4.

A refinement of the branch history approach is referred to as two-level or correlation-based branch history [YEH91]. This approach is based on the assumption that whereas in loop-closing branches, the past history of a particular branch instruction is a good predictor of future behavior, with more complex control-flow structures, the direction of a branch is frequently correlated with the direction of related branches. An example is an if-then-else or case structure. There are a number of strategies possible. Typically, recent global branch history (i.e., the history of the most recent branches not just of this branch instruction) is used in addition to the history of the current branch instruction. The general structure is defined as an (m, n) correlator, which uses the behavior of the last m branches to choose from 2^m n-bit branch predictors for the current branch instruction. In other words, an

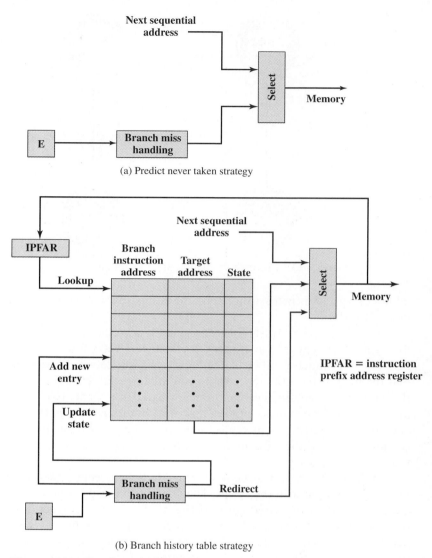

Figure 14.20 Dealing with Branches

n-bit history is kept for a give branch for each possible combination of branches taken by the most recent m branches.

DELAYED BRANCH It is possible to improve pipeline performance by automatically rearranging instructions within a program, so that branch instructions occur later than actually desired. This intriguing approach is examined in Chapter 15.

Intel 80486 Pipelining

An instructive example of an instruction pipeline is that of the Intel 80486. The 80486 implements a five-stage pipeline:

- **Fetch:** Instructions are fetched from the cache or from external memory and placed into one of the two 16-byte prefetch buffers. The objective of the fetch stage is to fill the prefetch buffers with new data as soon as the old data have been consumed by the instruction decoder. Because instructions are of variable length (from 1 to 11 bytes not counting prefixes), the status of the prefetcher relative to the other pipeline stages varies from instruction to instruction. On average, about five instructions are fetched with each 16-byte load [CRAW90]. The fetch stage operates independently of the other stages to keep the prefetch buffers full.

- **Decode stage 1:** All opcode and addressing-mode information is decoded in the D1 stage. The required information, as well as instruction-length information, is included in at most the first 3 bytes of the instruction. Hence, 3 bytes are passed to the D1 stage from the prefetch buffers. The D1 decoder can then direct the D2 stage to capture the rest of the instruction (displacement and immediate data), which is not involved in the D1 decoding.

- **Decode stage 2:** The D2 stage expands each opcode into control signals for the ALU. It also controls the computation of the more complex addressing modes.

- **Execute:** This stage includes ALU operations, cache access, and register update.

- **Write back:** This stage, if needed, updates registers and status flags modified during the preceding execute stage. If the current instruction updates memory, the computed value is sent to the cache and to the bus-interface write buffers at the same time.

With the use of two decode stages, the pipeline can sustain a throughput of close to one instruction per clock cycle. Complex instructions and conditional branches can slow down this rate.

Figure 14.21 shows examples of the operation of the pipeline. Figure 14.21a shows that there is no delay introduced into the pipeline when a memory access is required. However, as Figure 14.21b shows, there can be a delay for values used to compute memory addresses. That is, if a value is loaded from memory into a register and that register is then used as a base register in the next instruction, the processor will stall for one cycle. In this example, the processor accesses the cache in the EX stage of the first instruction and stores the value retrieved in the register during the WB stage. However, the next instruction needs this register in its D2 stage. When the D2 stage lines up with the WB stage of the previous instruction, bypass signal paths allow the D2 stage to have access to the same data being used by the WB stage for writing, saving one pipeline stage.

Figure 14.21c illustrates the timing of a branch instruction, assuming that the branch is taken. The compare instruction updates condition codes in the WB stage, and bypass paths make this available to the EX stage of the jump instruction at the same time. In parallel, the processor runs a speculative fetch cycle to the target of the jump during the EX stage of the jump instruction. If the processor determines a false branch condition, it discards this prefetch and continues execution with the next sequential instruction (already fetched and decoded).

Fetch	D1	D2	EX	WB				MOV Reg1, Mem1
	Fetch	D1	D2	EX	WB			MOV Reg1, Reg2
		Fetch	D1	D2	EX	WB		MOV Mem2, Reg1

(a) No data load delay in the pipeline

| Fetch | D1 | D2 | EX | WB | | | MOV Reg1, Mem1 |
| | Fetch | D1 | | D2 | EX | | MOV Reg2, (Reg1) |

(b) Pointer load delay

Fetch	D1	D2	EX	WB				CMP Reg1, Imm
	Fetch	D1	D2	EX				Jcc Target
			Fetch	D1	D2	EX		Target

(c) Branch instruction timing

Figure 14.21   80486 Instruction Pipeline Examples

14.5 THE x86 PROCESSOR FAMILY

The x86 organization has evolved dramatically over the years. In this section we examine some of the details of the most recent processor organizations, concentrating on common elements in single processors. Chapter 16 looks at superscalar aspects of the x86, and Chapter 18 examines the multicore organization. An overview of the Pentium 4 processor organization is depicted in Figure 4.18.

Register Organization

The register organization includes the following types of registers (Table 14.2):

- **General:** There are eight 32-bit general-purpose registers (see Figure 14.3c). These may be used for all types of x86 instructions; they can also hold operands for address calculations. In addition, some of these registers also serve special purposes. For example, string instructions use the contents of the ECX, ESI, and EDI registers as operands without having to reference these registers explicitly in the instruction. As a result, a number of instructions can be encoded more compactly. In 64-bit mode, there are 16 64-bit general-purpose registers.

- **Segment:** The six 16-bit segment registers contain segment selectors, which index into segment tables, as discussed in Chapter 8. The code segment (CS) register references the segment containing the instruction being executed. The stack segment (SS) register references the segment containing a user-visible stack. The remaining segment registers (DS, ES, FS, GS) enable the user to reference up to four separate data segments at a time.

- **Flags:** The 32-bit EFLAGS register contains condition codes and various mode bits. In 64-bit mode, this register is extended to 64 bits and referred

Table 14.2 x86 Processor Registers

(a) Integer Unit in 32-bit Mode

Type	Number	Length (bits)	Purpose
General	8	32	General-purpose user registers
Segment	6	16	Contain segment selectors
EFLAGS	1	32	Status and control bits
Instruction Pointer	1	32	Instruction pointer

(b) Integer Unit in 64-bit Mode

Type	Number	Length (bits)	Purpose
General	16	32	General-purpose user registers
Segment	6	16	Contain segment selectors
RFLAGS	1	64	Status and control bits
Instruction Pointer	1	64	Instruction pointer

(c) Floating-Point Unit

Type	Number	Length (bits)	Purpose
Numeric	8	80	Hold floating-point numbers
Control	1	16	Control bits
Status	1	16	Status bits
Tag Word	1	16	Specifies contents of numeric registers
Instruction Pointer	1	48	Points to instruction interrupted by exception
Data Pointer	1	48	Points to operand interrupted by exception

to as RFLAGS. In the current architecture definition, the upper 32 bits of RFLAGS are unused.

- **Instruction pointer:** Contains the address of the current instruction.

There are also registers specifically devoted to the floating-point unit:

- **Numeric:** Each register holds an extended-precision 80-bit floating-point number. There are eight registers that function as a stack, with push and pop operations available in the instruction set.
- **Control:** The 16-bit control register contains bits that control the operation of the floating-point unit, including the type of rounding control; single, double, or extended precision; and bits to enable or disable various exception conditions.
- **Status:** The 16-bit status register contains bits that reflect the current state of the floating-point unit, including a 3-bit pointer to the top of the stack; condition codes reporting the outcome of the last operation; and exception flags.
- **Tag word:** This 16-bit register contains a 2-bit tag for each floating-point numeric register, which indicates the nature of the contents of the corresponding register.

The four possible values are valid, zero, special (NaN, infinity, denormalized), and empty. These tags enable programs to check the contents of a numeric register without performing complex decoding of the actual data in the register. For example, when a context switch is made, the processor need not save any floating-point registers that are empty.

The use of most of the aforementioned registers is easily understood. Let us elaborate briefly on several of the registers.

EFLAGS REGISTER The EFLAGS register (Figure 14.22) indicates the condition of the processor and helps to control its operation. It includes the six condition codes defined in Table 12.9 (carry, parity, auxiliary, zero, sign, overflow), which report the results of an integer operation. In addition, there are bits in the register that may be referred to as control bits:

- **Trap flag (TF):** When set, causes an interrupt after the execution of each instruction. This is used for debugging.
- **Interrupt enable flag (IF):** When set, the processor will recognize external interrupts.
- **Direction flag (DF):** Determines whether string processing instructions increment or decrement the 16-bit half-registers SI and DI (for 16-bit operations) or the 32-bit registers ESI and EDI (for 32-bit operations).
- **I/O privilege flag (IOPL):** When set, causes the processor to generate an exception on all accesses to I/O devices during protected-mode operation.
- **Resume flag (RF):** Allows the programmer to disable debug exceptions so that the instruction can be restarted after a debug exception without immediately causing another debug exception.
- **Alignment check (AC):** Activates if a word or doubleword is addressed on a nonword or nondoubleword boundary.
- **Identification flag (ID):** If this bit can be set and cleared, then this processor supports the processorID instruction. This instruction provides information about the vendor, family, and model.

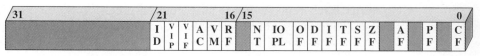

ID	= Identification flag	DF	= Direction flag
VIP	= Virtual interrupt pending	IF	= Interrupt enable flag
VIF	= Virtual interrupt flag	TF	= Trap flag
AC	= Alignment check	SF	= Sign flag
VM	= Virtual 8086 mode	ZF	= Zero flag
RF	= Resume flag	AF	= Auxiliary carry flag
NT	= Nested task flag	PF	= Parity flag
IOPL	= I/O privilege level	CF	= Carry flag
OF	= Overflow flag		

Figure 14.22 Pentium II EFLAGS Register

In addition, there are 4 bits that relate to operating mode. The Nested Task (NT) flag indicates that the current task is nested within another task in protected-mode operation. The Virtual Mode (VM) bit allows the programmer to enable or disable virtual 8086 mode, which determines whether the processor runs as an 8086 machine. The Virtual Interrupt Flag (VIF) and Virtual Interrupt Pending (VIP) flag are used in a multitasking environment.

CONTROL REGISTERS The x86 employs four control registers (register CR1 is unused) to control various aspects of processor operation (Figure 14.23). All of the registers except CR0 are either 32 bits or 64 bits long, depending on whether the implementation supports the x86 64-bit architecture. The CR0 register contains system control flags,

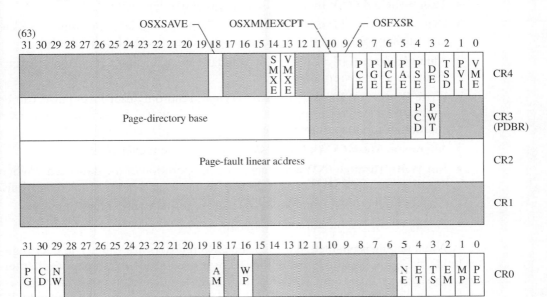

Shaded area indicates reserved bits.

OSXSAVE	=	XSAVE enable bit
SMXE	=	Enable safer mode extensions
VMXE	=	Enable virtual machine extensions
OSXMMEXCPT	=	Support unmasked SIMD FP exceptions
OSFXSR	=	Support FXSAVE, FXSTOR
PCE	=	Performance counter enable
PGE	=	Page global enable
MCE	=	Machine check enable
PAE	=	Physical address extension
PSE	=	Page size extensions
DE	=	Debug extensions
TSD	=	Time stamp disable
PVI	=	Protected mode virtual interrupt
VME	=	Virtual 8086 mode extensions

PCD	=	Page-level cache disable
PWT	=	Page-level writes transparent
PG	=	Paging
CD	=	Cache disable
NW	=	Not write through
AM	=	Alignment mask
WP	=	Write protect
NE	=	Numeric error
ET	=	Extension type
TS	=	Task switched
EM	=	Emulation
MP	=	Monitor coprocessor
PE	=	Protection enable

Figure 14.23   x86 Control Registers

which control modes or indicate states that apply generally to the processor rather than to the execution of an individual task. The flags are as follows:

- **Protection Enable (PE):** Enable/disable protected mode of operation.
- **Monitor Coprocessor (MP):** Only of interest when running programs from earlier machines on the x86; it relates to the presence of an arithmetic coprocessor.
- **Emulation (EM):** Set when the processor does not have a floating-point unit, and causes an interrupt when an attempt is made to execute floating-point instructions.
- **Task Switched (TS):** Indicates that the processor has switched tasks.
- **Extension Type (ET):** Not used on the Pentium and later machines; used to indicate support of math coprocessor instructions on earlier machines.
- **Numeric Error (NE):** Enables the standard mechanism for reporting floating-point errors on external bus lines.
- **Write Protect (WP):** When this bit is clear, read-only user-level pages can be written by a supervisor process. This feature is useful for supporting process creation in some operating systems.
- **Alignment Mask (AM):** Enables/disables alignment checking.
- **Not Write Through (NW):** Selects mode of operation of the data cache. When this bit is set, the data cache is inhibited from cache write-through operations.
- **Cache Disable (CD):** Enables/disables the internal cache fill mechanism.
- **Paging (PG):** Enables/disables paging.

When paging is enabled, the CR2 and CR3 registers are valid. The CR2 register holds the 32-bit linear address of the last page accessed before a page fault interrupt. The leftmost 20 bits of CR3 hold the 20 most significant bits of the base address of the page directory; the remainder of the address contains zeros. Two bits of CR3 are used to drive pins that control the operation of an external cache. The page-level cache disable (PCD) enables or disables the external cache, and the page-level writes transparent (PWT) bit controls write through in the external cache.

Nine additional control bits are defined in CR4:

- **Virtual-8086 Mode Extension (VME):** Enables support for the virtual interrupt flag in virtual-8086 mode.
- **Protected-mode Virtual Interrupts (PVI):** Enables support for the virtual interrupt flag in protected mode.
- **Time Stamp Disable (TSD):** Disables the read from time stamp counter (RDTSC) instruction, which is used for debugging purposes.
- **Debugging Extensions (DE):** Enables I/O breakpoints; this allows the processor to interrupt on I/O reads and writes.
- **Page Size Extensions (PSE):** Enables large page sizes (2 or 4-MByte pages) when set; restricts pages to 4 KBytes when clear.
- **Physical Address Extension (PAE):** Enables address lines A35 through A32 whenever a special new addressing mode, controlled by the PSE, is enabled.

- **Machine Check Enable (MCE):** Enables the machine check interrupt, which occurs when a data parity error occurs during a read bus cycle or when a bus cycle is not successfully completed.

- **Page Global Enable (PGE):** Enables the use of global pages. When PGE = 1 and a task switch is performed, all of the TLB entries are flushed with the exception of those marked global.

- **Performance Counter Enable (PCE):** Enables the execution of the RDPMC (read performance counter) instruction at any privilege level. Two performance counters are used to measure the duration of a specific event type and the number of occurrences of a specific event type.

MMX REGISTERS Recall from Section 10.3 that the x86 MMX capability makes use of several 64-bit data types. The MMX instructions make use of 3-bit register address fields, so that eight MMX registers are supported. In fact, the processor does not include specific MMX registers. Rather, the processor uses an aliasing technique (Figure 14.24). The existing floating-point registers are used to store MMX values. Specifically, the low-order 64 bits (mantissa) of each floating-point register are used to form the eight MMX registers. Thus, the older 32-bit x86 architecture is easily extended to support the MMX capability. Some key characteristics of the MMX use of these registers are as follows:

- Recall that the floating-point registers are treated as a stack for floating-point operations. For MMX operations, these same registers are accessed directly.

- The first time that an MMX instruction is executed after any floating-point operations, the FP tag word is marked valid. This reflects the change from stack operation to direct register addressing.

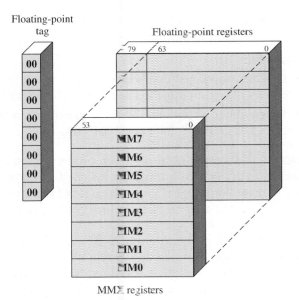

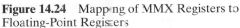

Figure 14.24 Mapping of MMX Registers to Floating-Point Registers

- The EMMS (Empty MMX State) instruction sets bits of the FP tag word to indicate that all registers are empty. It is important that the programmer insert this instruction at the end of an MMX code block so that subsequent floating-point operations function properly.
- When a value is written to an MMX register, bits [79:64] of the corresponding FP register (sign and exponent bits) are set to all ones. This sets the value in the FP register to NaN (not a number) or infinity when viewed as a floating-point value. This ensures that an MMX data value will not look like a valid floating-point value.

Interrupt Processing

Interrupt processing within a processor is a facility provided to support the operating system. It allows an application program to be suspended, in order that a variety of interrupt conditions can be serviced and later resumed.

INTERRUPTS AND EXCEPTIONS Two classes of events cause the x86 to suspend execution of the current instruction stream and respond to the event: interrupts and exceptions. In both cases, the processor saves the context of the current process and transfers to a predefined routine to service the condition. An *interrupt* is generated by a signal from hardware, and it may occur at random times during the execution of a program. An *exception* is generated from software, and it is provoked by the execution of an instruction. There are two sources of interrupts and two sources of exceptions:

1. Interrupts
   - **Maskable interrupts:** Received on the processor's INTR pin. The processor does not recognize a maskable interrupt unless the interrupt enable flag (IF) is set.
   - **Nonmaskable interrupts:** Received on the processor's NMI pin. Recognition of such interrupts cannot be prevented.

2. Exceptions
   - **Processor-detected exceptions:** Results when the processor encounters an error while attempting to execute an instruction.
   - **Programmed exceptions:** These are instructions that generate an exception (e.g., INTO, INT3, INT, and BOUND).

INTERRUPT VECTOR TABLE Interrupt processing on the x86 uses the interrupt vector table. Every type of interrupt is assigned a number, and this number is used to index into the interrupt vector table. This table contains 256 32-bit interrupt vectors, which is the address (segment and offset) of the interrupt service routine for that interrupt number.

Table 14.3 shows the assignment of numbers in the interrupt vector table; shaded entries represent interrupts, while nonshaded entries are exceptions. The NMI hardware interrupt is type 2. INTR hardware interrupts are assigned numbers in the range of 32 to 255; when an INTR interrupt is generated, it must be accompanied on the bus with the interrupt vector number for this interrupt. The remaining vector numbers are used for exceptions.

Table 14.3   x86 Exception and Interrupt Vector Table

Vector Number	Description
0	Divide error; division overflow or division by zero
1	Debug exception; includes various faults and traps related to debugging
2	NMI pin interrupt; signal on NMI pin
3	Breakpoint; caused by INT 3 instruction, which is a 1-byte instruction useful for debugging
4	INTO-detected overflow; occurs when the processor executes INTO with the OF flag set
5	BOUND range exceeded; the BOUND instruction compares a register with boundaries stored in memory and generates an interrupt if the contents of the register is out of bounds.
6	Undefined opcode
7	Device not available; attempt to use ESC or WAIT instruction fails due to lack of external device
8	Double fault; two interrupts occur during the same instruction and cannot be handled serially
9	Reserved
10	Invalid task state segment; segment describing a requested task is not initialized or not valid
11	Segment not present; required segment not present
12	Stack fault; limit of stack segment exceeded or stack segment not present
13	General protection; protection violation that does not cause another exception (e.g., writing to a read-only segment)
14	Page fault
15	Reserved
16	Floating-point error; generated by a floating-point arithmetic instruction
17	Alignment check; access to a word stored at an odd byte address or a doubleword stored at an address not a multiple of 4
18	Machine check; model specific
19–31	Reserved
32–255	User interrupt vectors; provided when INTR signal is activated

Unshaded: exceptions
Shaded: interrupts

If more than one exception or interrupt is pending, the processor services them in a predictable order. The location of vector numbers within the table does not reflect priority. Instead, priority among exceptions and interrupts is organized into five classes. In descending order of priority, these are

- **Class 1:** Traps on the previous instruction (vector number 1)
- **Class 2:** External interrupts (2, 32–255)
- **Class 3:** Faults from fetching next instruction (3, 14)
- **Class 4:** Faults from decoding the next instruction (6, 7)
- **Class 5:** Faults on executing an instruction (0, 4, 5, 8, 10–14, 16, 17)

INTERRUPT HANDLING Just as with a transfer of execution using a CALL instruction, a transfer to an interrupt-handling routine uses the system stack to store the processor state. When an interrupt occurs and is recognized by the processor, a sequence of events takes place:

1. If the transfer involves a change of privilege level, then the current stack segment register and the current extended stack pointer (ESP) register are pushed onto the stack.

2. The current value of the EFLAGS register is pushed onto the stack.

3. Both the interrupt (IF) and trap (TF) flags are cleared. This disables INTR interrupts and the trap or single-step feature.

4. The current code segment (CS) pointer and the current instruction pointer (IP or EIP) are pushed onto the stack.

5. If the interrupt is accompanied by an error code, then the error code is pushed onto the stack.

6. The interrupt vector contents are fetched and loaded into the CS and IP or EIP registers. Execution continues from the interrupt service routine.

To return from an interrupt, the interrupt service routine executes an IRET instruction. This causes all of the values saved on the stack to be restored; execution resumes from the point of the interrupt.

14.6 THE ARM PROCESSOR

In this section, we look at some of the key elements of the ARM architecture and organization. We defer a discussion of more complex aspects of organization and pipelining until Chapter 16. For the discussion in this section and in Chapter 16, it is useful to keep in mind key characteristics of the ARM architecture. ARM is primarily a RISC system with the following notable attributes:

- A moderate array of uniform registers, more than are found on some CISC systems but fewer than are found on many RISC systems.

- A load/store model of data processing, in which operations only perform on operands in registers and not directly in memory. All data must be loaded into registers before an operation can be performed; the result can then be used for further processing or stored into memory.

- A uniform fixed-length instruction of 32 bits for the standard set and 16 bits for the Thumb instruction set.

- To make each data processing instruction more flexible, either a shift or rotation can preprocess one of the source registers. To efficiently support this feature, there are separate arithmetic logic unit (ALU) and shifter units.

- A small number of addressing modes with all load/store addressees determined from registers and instruction fields. Indirect or indexed addressing involving values in memory are not used.

- Auto-increment and auto-decrement addressing modes are used to improve the operation of program loops.

- Conditional execution of instructions minimizes the need for conditional branch instructions, thereby improving pipeline efficiency, because pipeline flushing is reduced.

Processor Organization

The ARM processor organization varies substantially from one implementation to the next, particularly when based on different versions of the ARM architecture. However, it is useful for the discussion in this section to present a simplified, generic ARM organization, which is illustrated in Figure 14.25. In this figure, the arrows indicate the flow of data. Each box represents a functional hardware unit or a storage unit.

Data are exchanged with the processor from external memory through a data bus. The value transferred is either a data item, as a result of a load or store instruction, or an instruction fetch. Fetched instructions pass through an instruction decoder before execution, under control of a control unit. The latter includes

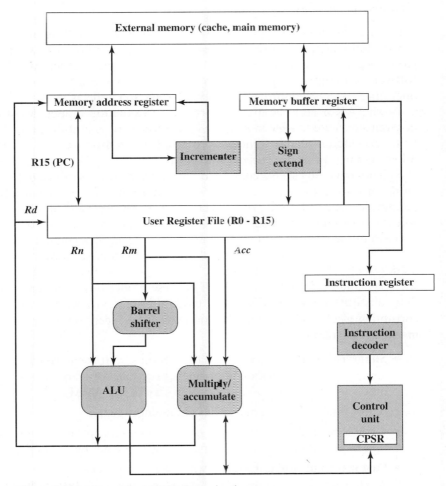

Figure 14.25   Simplified ARM Organization

pipeline logic and provides control signals (not shown) to all the hardware elements of the processor. Data items are placed in the register file, consisting of a set of 32-bit registers. Byte or halfword items treated as twos-complement numbers are sign-extended to 32 bits.

ARM data processing instructions typically have two source registers, *Rn* and *Rm*, and a single result or destination register, *Rd*. The source register values feed into the ALU or a separate multiply unit that makes use of an additional register to accumulate partial results. The ARM processor also includes a hardware unit that can shift or rotate the *Rm* value before it enters the ALU. This shift or rotate occurs within the cycle time of the instruction and increases the power and flexibility of many data processing operations.

The results of an operation are fed back to the destination register. Load/store instructions may also use the output of the arithmetic units to generate the memory address for a load or store.

Processor Modes

It is quite common for a processor to support only a small number of processor modes. For example, many operating systems make use of just two modes: a user mode and a kernel mode, with the latter mode used to execute privileged system software. In contrast, the ARM architecture provides a flexible foundation for operating systems to enforce a variety of protection policies.

The ARM architecture supports seven execution modes. Most application programs execute in **user mode**. While the processor is in user mode, the program being executed is unable to access protected system resources or to change mode, other than by causing an exception to occur.

The remaining six execution modes are referred to as privileged modes. These modes are used to run system software. There are two principal advantages to defining so many different privileged modes: (1) The OS can tailor the use of system software to a variety of circumstances, and (2) certain registers are dedicated for use for each of the privileged modes, allows swifter changes in context.

The exception modes have full access to system resources and can change modes freely. Five of these modes are known as exception modes. These are entered when specific exceptions occur. Each of these modes has some dedicated registers that substitute for some of the user mode registers, and which are used to avoid corrupting User mode state information when the exception occurs. The exception modes are as follows:

- **Supervisor mode:** Usually what the OS runs in. It is entered when the processor encounters a software interrupt instruction. Software interrupts are a standard way to invoke operating system services on ARM.
- **Abort mode:** Entered in response to memory faults.
- **Undefined mode:** Entered when the processor attempts to execute an instruction that is supported neither by the main integer core nor by one of the coprocessors.
- **Fast interrupt mode:** Entered whenever the processor receives an interrupt signal from the designated fast interrupt source. A fast interrupt cannot be interrupted, but a fast interrupt may interrupt a normal interrupt.

- **Interrupt mode:** Entered whenever the processor receives an interrupt signal from any other interrupt source (other than fast interrupt). An interrupt may only be interrupted by a fast interrupt.

The remaining privileged mode is the **System mode**. This mode is not entered by any exception and uses the same registers available in User mode. The System mode is used for running certain privileged operating system tasks. System mode tasks may be interrupted by any of the five exception categories.

Register Organization

Figure 14.26 depicts the user-visible registers for the ARM. The ARM processor has a total of 37 32-bit registers, classified as follows:

- Thirty-one registers referred to in the ARM manual as general-purpose registers. In fact, some of these, such as the program counters, have special purposes.
- Six program status registers.

Registers are arranged in partially overlapping banks, with the current processor mode determining which bank s available. At any time, sixteen numbered registers and one or two program status registers are visible, for a total of 17 or 18 software-visible registers. Figure 14.26 is interpreted as follows:

- Registers R0 through R7, register R15 (the program counter) and the current program status register (CPSR) are visible in and shared by all modes.
- Registers R8 through R12 are shared by all modes except fast interrupt, which has its own dedicated registers R8_fiq through R12_fiq.
- All the exception modes have their own versions of registers R13 and R14.
- All the exception modes have a dedicated saved program status register (SPSR)

GENERAL-PURPOSE REGISTERS Register R13 is normally used as a stack pointer and is also known as the SP. Because each exception mode has a separate R13, each exception mode can have its own dedicated program stack. R14 is known as the link register (LR) and is used to hold subroutine return addresses and exception mode returns. Register R15 is the program counter (PC).

PROGRAM STATUS REGISTERS The CPSR is accessible in all processor modes. Each exception mode also has a dedicated SPSR that is used to preserve the value of the CPSR when the associated exception occurs.

The 16 most significant bits of the CPSR contain user flags visible in User mode, and which can be used to affect the operation of a program (Figure 14.27). These are as follows:

- **Condition code flags:** The N, Z, C, and V flags, which are discussed in Chapter 12.
- **Q flag:** used to indicate whether overflow and/or saturation has occurred in some SIMD-oriented instructions.
- **J bit:** indicates the use of special 8-bit instructions, known as Jazelle instructions, which are beyond the scope of our discussion.
- **GE[3:0] bits:** SIMD instructions use bits [19:16] as Greater than or Equal (GE) flags for individual bytes or halfwords of the result.

Modes						
		Privileged modes				
			Exception modes			
User	**System**	**Supervisor**	**Abort**	**Undefined**	**Interrupt**	**Fast interrupt**
R0	R0	R0	R0	R0	R0	R0
R1	R1	R1	R1	R1	R1	R1
R2	R2	R2	R2	R2	R2	R2
R3	R3	R3	R3	R3	R3	R3
R4	R4	R4	R4	R4	R4	R4
R5	R5	R5	R5	R5	R5	R5
R6	R6	R6	R6	R6	R6	R6
R7	R7	R7	R7	R7	R7	R7
R8	R8	R8	R8	R8	R8	R8_fiq
R9	R9	R9	R9	R9	R9	R9_fiq
R10	R10	R10	R10	R10	R10	R10_fiq
R11	R11	R11	R11	R11	R11	R11_fiq
R12	R12	R12	R12	R12	R12	R12_fiq
R13(SP)	R13(SP)	R13_svc	R13_abt	R13_und	R13_irq	R13_fiq
R14(LR)	R14(LR)	R14_svc	R14_abt	R14_und	R14_irq	R14_fiq
R15(PC)	R15(PC)	R15(PC)	R15(PC)	R15(PC)	R15(PC)	R15(PC)

CPSR	CPSR	CPSR	CPSR	CPSR	CPSR	CPSR
		SPSR_svc	SPSR_abt	SPSR_und	SPSR_irq	SPSR_fiq

Shading indicates that the normal register used by User or System mode has been replaced by an alternative register specific to the exception mode.

SP = stack pointer   CPSR = current program status register
LR = link register   SPSR = saved program status register
PC = program counter

Figure 14.26 ARM Register Organization

The 16 least significant bits of the CPSR contain system control flags that can only be altered when the processor is in a privileged mode. The fields are as follows:

- **E bit:** Controls load and store endianness for data; ignored for instruction fetches.
- **Interrupt disable bits:** The A bit disables imprecise data aborts when set; the I bit disables IRQ interrupts when set; and the F bit disables FIQ interrupts when set.
- **T bit:** Indicates whether instructions should be interpreted as normal ARM instructions or Thumb instructions.
- **Mode bits:** Indicates the processor mode.

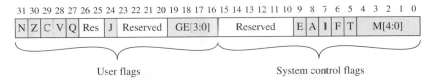

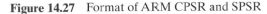

Figure 14.27   Format of ARM CPSR and SPSR

Interrupt Processing

As with any processor, the ARM includes a facility that enables the processor to interrupt the currently executing program to deal with exception conditions. Exceptions are generated by internal and external sources to cause the processor to handle an event. The processor state just before handling the exception is normally preserved so that the original program can be resumed when the exception routine has completed. More than one exception can arise at the same time. The ARM architecture supports seven types of exception. Table 14.4 lists the types of exception and the processor mode that is used to process each type. When an exception occurs, execution is forced

Table 14.4   ARM Interrupt Vector

Exception type	Mode	Normal entry address	Description
Reset	Supervisor	0x00000000	Occurs when the system is initialized.
Data abort	Abort	0x00000010	Occurs when an invalid memory address has been accessed, such as if there is no physical memory for an address or the correct access permission is lacking.
FIQ (fast interrupt)	FIQ	0x0000001C	Occurs when an external device asserts the FIQ pin on the processor. An interrupt cannot be interrupted except by an FIQ. FIQ is designed to support a data transfer or channel process, and has sufficient private registers to remove the need for register saving in such applications, therefore minimizing the overhead of context switching. A fast interrupt cannot be interrupted.
IRQ (interrupt)	IRQ	0x00000018	Occurs when an external device asserts the IRQ pin on the processor. An interrupt cannot be interrupted except by an FIQ.
Prefetch abort	Abort	0x0000000C	Occurs when an attempt to fetch an instruction results in a memory fault. The exception is raised when the instruction enters the execute stage of the pipeline.
Undefined instructions	Undefined	0x00000004	Occurs when an instruction not in the instruction set reaches the execute stage of the pipeline.
Software interrupt	Supervisor	0x00000008	Generally used to allow user mode programs to call the OS. The user program executes a SWI instruction with an argument that identifies the function the user wishes to perform.

from a fixed memory address corresponding to the type of exception. These fixed addresses are called the exception vectors.

If more than one interrupt is outstanding, they are handled in priority order. Table 14.4 lists the exceptions in priority order, highest to lowest.

When an exception occurs, the processor halts execution after the current instruction. The state of the processor is preserved in the SPSR that corresponds to the type of exception, so that the original program can be resumed when the exception routine has completed. The address of the instruction the processor was just about to execute is placed in the link register of the appropriate processor mode. To return after handling the exception, the SPSR is moved into the CPSR and R14 is moved into the PC.

14.7 RECOMMENDED READING

[PATT01] and [MOSH01] provide excellent coverage of the pipelining issues discussed in this chapter. [HENN91] contains a detailed discussions of pipelining. [SOHI90] provides an excellent, detailed discussion of the hardware design issues involved in an instruction pipeline. [RAMA77] is a classic paper on the subject still well worth reading.

[EVER01] examines the evolution of branch prediction strategies. [CRAG92] is a detailed study of branch prediction in instruction pipelines. [DUBE91] and [LILJ88] examine various branch prediction strategies that can be used to enhance the performance of instruction pipelining. [KAEL91] examines the difficulty introduced into branch prediction by instructions whose target address is variable.

[BREY09] provides good coverage of interrupt processing on the x86. [FOG08b] provides a detailed discussion of pipeline architecture for the x86 family.

BREY09 Brey, B. *The Intel Microprocessors: 8086/8066, 80186/80188, 80286, 80386, 80486, Pentium, Pentium Pro Processor, Pentium II, Pentium III, Pentium 4 and Core2 with 64-bit Extensions.* Upper Saddle River, NJ: Prentice Hall, 2009.

CRAG92 Cragon, H. *Branch Strategy Taxonomy and Performance Models.* Los Alamitos, CA: IEEE Computer Society Press, 1992.

DUBE91 Dubey, P., and Flynn, M. "Branch Strategies: Modeling and Optimization." *IEEE Transactions on Computers*, October 1991.

EVER01 Evers, M., and Yeh, T. "Understanding Branches and Designing Branch Predictors for High-Performance Microprocessors." *Proceedings of the IEEE*, November 2001.

FOG08b Fog, A. *The Microarchitecture of Intel and AMD CPUs.* Copenhagen University College of Engineering, 2008. www.agner.org/optimize/

HENN91 Hennessy, J., and Jouppi, N. "Computer Technology and Architecture: An Evolving Interaction." *Computer*, September 1991.

KAEL91 Kaeli, D., and Emma, P. "Branch History Table Prediction of Moving Target Branches Due to Subroutine Returns." *Proceedings, 18th Annual International Symposium on Computer Architecture*, May 1991.

LILJ88 Lilja, D. "Reducing the Branch Penalty in Pipelined Processors." *Computer*, July 1988.

MOSH01 Moshovos, A., and Sohi, G. "Microarchitectural Innovations: Boosting Microprocessor Performance Beyond Semiconductor Technology Scaling." *Proceedings of the IEEE*, November 2001.

PATT01 Patt, Y. "Requirements, Bottlenecks, and Good Fortune: Agents for Micro-processor Evolution." *Proceedings of the IEEE*, November 2001.

RAMA77 Ramamoorthy, C. "Pipeline Architecture." *Computing Surveys*, March 1977.

SOHI90 Sohi, G. "Instruction Issue Logic for High-Performance Interruptable, Multiple Functional Unit, Pipelined Computers." *IEEE Transactions on Computers*, March 1990.

14.8 KEY TERMS, REVIEW QUESTIONS, AND PROBLEMS

Key Terms

branch prediction condition code delayed branch	flag instruction cycle instruction pipeline	instruction prefetch program status word (PSW)

Review Questions

14.1 What general roles are performed by processor registers?

14.2 What categories of data are commonly supported by user-visible registers?

14.3 What is the function of condition codes?

14.4 What is a program status word?

14.5 Why is a two-stage instruction pipeline unlikely to cut the instruction cycle time in half, compared with the use of no pipeline?

14.6 List and briefly explain various ways in which an instruction pipeline can deal with conditional branch instructions.

14.7 How are history bits used for branch prediction?

Problems

14.1 **a.** If the last operation performed on a computer with an 8-bit word was an addition in which the two operands were 00000010 and 00000011, what would be the value of the following flags?
- Carry
- Zero
- Overflow
- Sign
- Even Parity
- Half-Carry

b. Repeat for the addition of −1 (twos complement) and +1.

14.2 Repeat Problem 14.1 for the operation A − B, where A contains 11110000 and B contains 0010100.

14.3 A microprocessor is clocked at a rate of 5 GHz.
a. How long is a clock cycle?
b. What is the duration of a particular type of machine instruction consisting of three clock cycles?

14.4 A microprocessor provides an instruction capable of moving a string of bytes from one area of memory to another. The fetching and initial decoding of the instruction takes 10 clock cycles. Thereafter, it takes 15 clock cycles to transfer each byte. The microprocessor is clocked at a rate of 10 GHz.

    a. Determine the length of the instruction cycle for the case of a string of 64 bytes.

    b. What is the worst-case delay for acknowledging an interrupt if the instruction is noninterruptible?

    c. Repeat part (b) assuming the instruction can be interrupted at the beginning of each byte transfer.

14.5 The Intel 8088 consists of a bus interface unit (BIU) and an execution unit (EU), which form a 2-stage pipeline. The BIU fetches instructions into a 4-byte instruction queue. The BIU also participates in address calculations, fetches operands, and writes results in memory as requested by the EU. If no such requests are outstanding and the bus is free, the BIU fills any vacancies in the instruction queue. When the EU completes execution of an instruction, it passes any results to the BIU (destined for memory or I/O) and proceeds to the next instruction.

    a. Suppose the tasks performed by the BIU and EU take about equal time. By what factor does pipelining improve the performance of the 8088? Ignore the effect of branch instructions.

    b. Repeat the calculation assuming that the EU takes twice as long as the BIU.

14.6 Assume an 8088 is executing a program in which the probability of a program jump is 0.1. For simplicity, assume that all instructions are 2 bytes long.

    a. What fraction of instruction fetch bus cycles is wasted?

    b. Repeat if the instruction queue is 8 bytes long.

14.7 Consider the timing diagram of Figures 14.10. Assume that there is only a two-stage pipeline (fetch, execute). Redraw the diagram to show how many time units are now needed for four instructions.

14.8 Assume a pipeline with four stages: fetch instruction (FI), decode instruction and calculate addresses (DA), fetch operand (FO), and execute (EX). Draw a diagram similar to Figure 14.10 for a sequence of 7 instructions, in which the third instruction is a branch that is taken and in which there are no data dependencies.

14.9 A pipelined processor has a clock rate of 2.5 GHz and executes a program with 1.5 million instructions. The pipeline has five stages, and instructions are issued at a rate of one per clock cycle. Ignore penalties due to branch instructions and out-of-sequence executions.

    a. What is the speedup of this processor for this program compared to a nonpipelined processor, making the same assumptions used in Section 14.4?

    b. What is throughput (in MIPS) of the pipelined processor?

14.10 A nonpipelined processor has a clock rate of 2.5 GHz and an average CPI (cycles per instruction) of 4. An upgrade to the processor introduces a five-stage pipeline. However, due to internal pipeline delays, such as latch delay, the clock rate of the new processor has to be reduced to 2 GHz.

    a. What is the speedup achieved for a typical program?

    b. What is the MIPS rate for each processor?

14.11 Consider an instruction sequence of length n that is streaming through the instruction pipeline. Let p be the probability of encountering a conditional or unconditional branch instruction, and let q be the probability that execution of a branch instruction I causes a jump to a nonconsecutive address. Assume that each such jump requires the pipeline to be cleared, destroying all ongoing instruction processing, when I emerges from the last stage. Revise Equations (14.1) and (14.2) to take these probabilities into account.

14.12 One limitation of the multiple-stream approach to dealing with branches in a pipeline is that additional branches will be encountered before the first branch is resolved. Suggest two additional limitations or drawbacks.

14.13 Consider the state diagrams of Figure 14.28.

    a. Describe the behavior of each.

    b. Compare these with the branch prediction state diagram in Section 14.4. Discuss the relative merits of each of the three approaches to branch prediction.

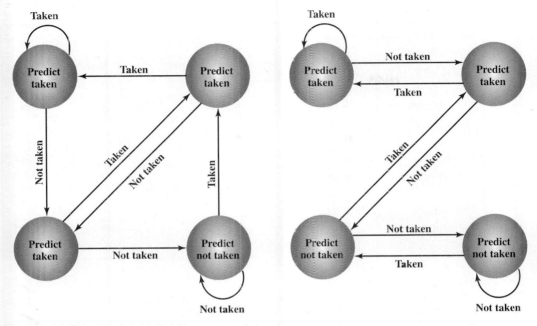

Figure 14.28 Two Branch Prediction State Diagrams

14.14 The Motorola 680x0 machines include the instruction Decrement and Branch According to Condition, which has the following form:

DBcc Dn, displacement

where cc is one of the testable conditions, Dn is a general-purpose register, and displacement specifies the target address relative to the current address. The instruction can be defined as follows:

if (cc = False)
then begin
    Dn := (Dn) − 1;
    if Dn ≠ −1 **then** PC := (PC) + displacement **end**
else PC := (PC) + 2;

When the instruction is executed, the condition is first tested to determine whether the termination condition for the loop is satisfied. If so, no operation is performed and execution continues at the next instruction in sequence. If the condition is false, the specified data register is decremented and checked to see if it is less than zero. If it is less than zero, the loop is terminated and execution continues at the next instruction in sequence. Otherwise, the program branches to the specified location. Now consider the following assembly-language program fragment:

AGAIN   CMPM.L   (A0)+,(A1)+
            DBNE   D1,AGAIN
            NOP

Two strings addressed by A0 and A1 are compared for equality; the string pointers are incremented with each reference. D1 initially contains the number of longwords (4 bytes) to be compared.
a. The initial contents of the registers are A0 = $00004000, A1 = $00005000 and D1 = $000000FF (the $ indicates hexadecimal notation). Memory between $4000 and $6000 is loaded with words $AAAA. If the foregoing program is run, specify

Table 14.5 Branch Behavior in Sample Applications

Occurrence of branch classes:			
Type 1: Branch	72.5%		
Type 2: Loop control	9.8%		
Type 3: Procedure call, return	17.7%		
Type 1 branch: where it goes	**Scientific**	**Commercial**	**Systems**
Unconditional—100% go to target	20%	40%	35%
Conditional—went to target	43.2%	24.3%	32.5%
Conditional—did not go to target (inline)	36.8%	35.7%	32.5%
Type 2 branch (all environments)			
That go to target	91%		
That go inline	9%		
Type 3 branch			
100% go to target			

the number of times the DBNE loop is executed and the contents of the three registers when the NOP instruction is reached.

b. Repeat (a), but now assume that memory between $4000 and $4FEE is loaded with $0000 and between $5000 and $6000 is loaded with $AAA.

14.15 Redraw Figures 14.19c, assuming that the conditional branch is not taken.

14.16 Table 14.5 summarizes statistics from [MACD84] concerning branch behavior for various classes of applications. With the exception of type 1 branch behavior, there is no noticeable difference among the application classes. Determine the fraction of all branches that go to the branch target address for the scientific environment. Repeat for commercial and systems environments.

14.17 Pipelining can be applied within the ALU to speed up floating-point operations. Consider the case of floating-point addition and subtraction. In simplified terms, the pipeline could have four stages: (1) Compare the exponents; (2) Choose the exponent and align the significands; (3) Add or subtract significands; (4) Normalize the results. The pipeline can be considered to have two parallel threads, one handling exponents and one handling significands, and could start out like this:

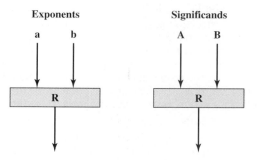

In this figure, the boxes labeled R refer to a set of registers used to hold temporary results. Complete the block diagram that shows at a top level the structure of the pipeline.

REDUCED INSTRUCTION SET COMPUTERS

LEARNING OBJECTIVES

After studying this chapter, you should be able to:

◆ Provide an overview research results on instruction execution characteristics that motivated the development of the RISC approach.

◆ Summarize the key characteristics of RISC machines.

◆ Understand the design and performance implications of using a large register file.

◆ Understand the use of compiler-based register optimization to improve performance.

◆ Discuss the implication of a RISC architecture for pipeline design and performance.

◆ List and explain key approaches to pipeline optimization on a RISC machine.

Since the development of the stored-program computer around 1950, there have been remarkably few true innovations in the areas of computer organization and architecture. The following are some of the major advances since the birth of the computer:

- **The family concept:** Introduced by IBM with its System/360 in 1964, followed shortly thereafter by DEC, with its PDP-8. The family concept decouples the architecture of a machine from its implementation. A set of computers is offered, with different price/performance characteristics, that presents the same architecture to the user. The differences in price and performance are due to different implementations of the same architecture.

- **Microprogrammed control unit:** Suggested by Wilkes in 1951 and introduced by IBM on the S/360 line in 1964. Microprogramming eases the task of designing and implementing the control unit and provides support for the family concept.

- **Cache memory:** First introduced commercially on IBM S/360 Model 85 in 1968. The insertion of this element into the memory hierarchy dramatically improves performance.

- **Pipelining:** A means of introducing parallelism into the essentially sequential nature of a machine-instruction program. Examples are instruction pipelining and vector processing.

- **Multiple processors:** This category covers a number of different organizations and objectives.

- **Reduced instruction set computer (RISC) architecture:** This is the focus of this chapter.

When it appeared, RISC architecture was a dramatic departure from the historical trend in processor architecture. An analysis of the RISC architecture brings into focus many of the important issues in computer organization and architecture.

Although RISC architectures have been defined and designed in a variety of ways by different groups, the key elements shared by most designs are these:

- A large number of general-purpose registers, and/or the use of compiler technology to optimize register usage
- A limited and simple instruction set
- An emphasis on optimizing the instruction pipeline

Table 15.1 compares several RISC and non-RISC systems.

We begin this chapter with a brief survey of some results on instruction sets, and then examine each of the three topics just listed. This is followed by a description of two of the best-documented RISC designs.

15.1 INSTRUCTION EXECUTION CHARACTERISTICS

One of the most visible forms of evolution associated with computers is that of programming languages. As the cost of hardware has dropped, the relative cost of software has risen. Along with that, a chronic shortage of programmers has driven up software costs in absolute terms. Thus, the major cost in the life cycle of a system is software, not hardware. Adding to the cost, and to the inconvenience, is the element of unreliability: it is common for programs, both system and application, to continue to exhibit new bugs after years of operation.

The response from researchers and industry has been to develop ever more powerful and complex high-level programming languages. These **high-level languages (HLLs)**: (1) allow the programmer to express algorithms more concisely, (2) allow the compiler to take care of details that are not important in the programmer's expression of algorithms, and (3) often support naturally the use of structured programming and/or object-oriented design.

Alas, this solution gave rise to a perceived problem, known as the *semantic gap,* the difference between the operations provided in HLLs and those provided in computer architecture. Symptoms of this gap are alleged to include execution inefficiency, excessive machine program size, and compiler complexity. Designers responded with architectures intended to close this gap. Key features include large instruction sets, dozens of addressing modes, and various HLL statements implemented in hardware. An example of the latter is the CASE machine instruction on the VAX. Such complex instruction sets are intended to

- Ease the task of the compiler writer.
- Improve execution efficiency, because complex sequences of operations can be implemented in microcode.
- Provide support for even more complex and sophisticated HLLs.

Meanwhile, a number of studies have been done over the years to determine the characteristics and patterns of execution of machine instructions generated from HLL programs. The results of these studies inspired some researchers to look for a different approach: namely, to make the architecture that supports the HLL simpler, rather than more complex.

Table 15.1 Characteristics of Some CISCs, RISCs, and Superscalar Processors

Characteristic	Complex Instruction Set (CISC) Computer			Reduced Instruction Set (RISC) Computer		Superscalar		
	IBM 370/168	VAX 11/780	Intel 80486	SPARC	MIPS R4000	PowerPC	Ultra SPARC	MIPS R10000
Year developed	1973	1978	1989	1987	1991	1993	1996	1996
Number of instructions	208	303	235	69	94	225	—	—
Instruction size (bytes)	2–6	2–57	1–11	4	4	4	4	4
Addressing modes	4	22	11	1	1	2	1	1
Number of general-purpose registers	16	16	8	40–520	32	32	40–520	32
Control memory size (Kbits)	420	480	246	—	—	—	—	—
Cache size (Kbytes)	64	64	8	32	128	16-32	32	64

To understand the line of reasoning of the RISC advocates, we begin with a brief review of instruction execution characteristics. The aspects of computation of interest are as follows:

- **Operations performed:** These determine the functions to be performed by the processor and its interaction with memory.
- **Operands used:** The types of operands and the frequency of their use determine the memory organization for storing them and the addressing modes for accessing them.
- **Execution sequencing:** This determines the control and pipeline organization.

In the remainder of this section, we summarize the results of a number of studies of high-level-language programs. All of the results are based on dynamic measurements. That is, measurements are collected by executing the program and counting the number of times some feature has appeared or a particular property has held true. In contrast, static measurements merely perform these counts on the source text of a program. They give no useful information on performance, because they are not weighted relative to the number of times each statement is executed.

Operations

A variety of studies have been made to analyze the behavior of HLL programs. Table 4.8, discussed in Chapter 4, includes key results from a number of studies. There is quite good agreement in the results of this mixture of languages and applications. Assignment statements predominate, suggesting that the simple movement of data is of high importance. There is also a preponderance of conditional statements (IF, LOOP). These statements are implemented in machine language with some sort of compare and branch instruction. This suggests that the sequence control mechanism of the instruction set is important.

These results are instructive to the machine instruction set designer, indicating which types of statements occur most often and therefore should be supported in an "optimal" fashion. However, these results do not reveal which statements use the most time in the execution of a typical program. That is, we want to answer the question: Given a compiled machine-language program, which statements in the source language cause the execution of the most machine-language instructions and what is the execution time of these instructions?

To get at this underlying phenomenon, the Patterson programs [PATT82a], described in Appendix 4A, were compiled on the VAX, PDP-11, and Motorola 68000 to determine the average number of machine instructions and memory references per statement type. The second and third columns in Table 15.2 show the relative frequency of occurrence of various HLL statements in a variety of programs; the data were obtained by observing the occurrences in running programs rather than just the number of times that statements occur in the source code. Hence these metrics capture dynamic behavior. To obtain the data in columns four and five (machine-instruction weighted), each value in the second and third columns is multiplied by the number of machine instructions produced by the compiler. These results are then normalized so that columns four and five show the relative frequency of occurrence, weighted by the number of machine instructions per HLL

Table 15.2   Weighted Relative Dynamic Frequency of HLL Operations [PATT82a]

	Dynamic Occurrence		Machine-Instruction Weighted		Memory-Reference Weighted	
	Pascal	C	Pascal	C	Pascal	C
ASSIGN	45%	38%	13%	13%	14%	15%
LOOP	5%	3%	42%	32%	33%	26%
CALL	15%	12%	31%	33%	44%	45%
IF	29%	43%	11%	21%	7%	13%
GOTO	—	3%	—	—	—	—
OTHER	6%	1%	3%	1%	2%	1%

statement. Similarly, the sixth and seventh columns are obtained by multiplying the frequency of occurrence of each statement type by the relative number of memory references caused by each statement. The data in columns four through seven provide surrogate measures of the actual time spent executing the various statement types. The results suggest that the procedure call/return is the most time-consuming operation in typical HLL programs.

The reader should be clear on the significance of Table 15.2. This table indicates the relative performance impact of various statement types in an HLL, when that HLL is compiled for a typical contemporary instruction set architecture. Some other architecture could conceivably produce different results. However, this study produces results that are representative for contemporary **complex instruction set computer (CISC)** architectures. Thus, they can provide guidance to those looking for more efficient ways to support HLLs.

Operands

Much less work has been done on the occurrence of types of operands, despite the importance of this topic. There are several aspects that are significant.

The Patterson study already referenced [PATT82a] also looked at the dynamic frequency of occurrence of classes of variables (Table 15.3). The results, consistent between Pascal and C programs, show that most references are to simple scalar variables. Further, more than 80% of the scalars were local (to the procedure) variables. In addition, each reference to an array or a structure requires a reference to an index or pointer, which again is usually a local scalar. Thus, there is a preponderance of references to scalars, and these are highly localized.

The Patterson study examined the dynamic behavior of HLL programs, independent of the underlying architecture. As discussed before, it is necessary

Table 15.3   Dynamic Percentage of Operands

	Pascal	C	Average
Integer Constant	16%	23%	20%
Scalar Variable	58%	53%	55%
Array/Structure	26%	24%	25%

to deal with actual architectures to examine program behavior more deeply. One study, [LUND77], examined DEC-10 instructions dynamically and found that each instruction on the average references 0.5 operand in memory and 1.4 registers. Similar results are reported in [HUCK83] for C, Pascal, and FORTRAN programs on S/370, PDP-11, and VAX. Of course, these figures depend highly on both the architecture and the compiler, but they do illustrate the frequency of operand accessing.

These latter studies suggest the importance of an architecture that lends itself to fast operand accessing, because this operation is performed so frequently. The Patterson study suggests that a prime candidate for optimization is the mechanism for storing and accessing local scalar variables.

Procedure Calls

We have seen that procedure calls and returns are an important aspect of HLL programs. The evidence (Table 15.2) suggests that these are the most time-consuming operations in compiled HLL programs. Thus, it will be profitable to consider ways of implementing these operations efficiently. Two aspects are significant: the number of parameters and variables that a procedure deals with, and the depth of nesting.

Tanenbaum's study [TANE78] found that 98% of dynamically called procedures were passed fewer than six arguments and that 92% of them used fewer than six local scalar variables. Similar results were reported by the Berkeley RISC team [KATE83], as shown in Table 15.4. These results show that the number of words required per procedure activation is not large. The studies reported earlier indicated that a high proportion of operand references is to local scalar variables. These studies show that those references are in fact confined to relatively few variables.

The same Berkeley group also looked at the pattern of procedure calls and returns in HLL programs. They found that it is rare to have a long uninterrupted sequence of procedure calls followed by the corresponding sequence of returns. Rather, they found that a program remains confined to a rather narrow window of procedure-invocation depth. This is illustrated in Figure 4.21, which was discussed in Chapter 4. These results reinforce the conclusion that operand references are highly localized.

Implications

A number of groups have looked at results such as those just reported and have concluded that the attempt to make the instruction set architecture close to HLLs

Table 15.4 Procedure Arguments and Local Scalar Variables

Percentage of Executed Procedure Calls With	Compiler, Interpreter, and Typesetter	Small Nonnumeric Programs
>3 arguments	0–7%	0–5%
>5 arguments	0–3%	0%
>8 words of arguments and local scalars	1–20%	0–6%
>12 words of arguments and local scalars	1–6%	0–3%

is not the most effective design strategy. Rather, the HLLs can best be supported by optimizing performance of the most time-consuming features of typical HLL programs.

Generalizing from the work of a number of researchers, three elements emerge that, by and large, characterize RISC architectures. First, use a large number of registers or use a compiler to optimize register usage. This is intended to optimize operand referencing. The studies just discussed show that there are several references per HLL statement and that there is a high proportion of move (assignment) statements. This, coupled with the locality and predominance of scalar references, suggests that performance can be improved by reducing memory references at the expense of more register references. Because of the locality of these references, an expanded register set seems practical.

Second, careful attention needs to be paid to the design of instruction pipelines. Because of the high proportion of conditional branch and procedure call instructions, a straightforward instruction pipeline will be inefficient. This manifests itself as a high proportion of instructions that are prefetched but never executed.

Finally, an instruction set consisting of high-performance primitives is indicated. Instructions should have predictable costs (measured in execution time and code size, and increasingly, in energy dissipation) and be consistent with a high-performance implementation (which harmonizes with predictable execution-time cost).

15.2 THE USE OF A LARGE REGISTER FILE

The results summarized in Section 15.1 point out the desirability of quick access to operands. We have seen that there is a large proportion of assignment statements in HLL programs, and many of these are of the simple form A ← B. Also, there is a significant number of operand accesses per HLL statement. If we couple these results with the fact that most accesses are to local scalars, heavy reliance on register storage is suggested.

The reason that register storage is indicated is that it is the fastest available storage device, faster than both main memory and cache. The register file is physically small, on the same chip as the ALU and control unit, and employs much shorter addresses than addresses for cache and memory. Thus, a strategy is needed that will allow the most frequently accessed operands to be kept in registers and to minimize register-memory operations.

Two basic approaches are possible, one based on software and the other on hardware. The software approach is to rely on the compiler to maximize register usage. The compiler will attempt to assign registers to those variables that will be used the most in a given time period. This approach requires the use of sophisticated program-analysis algorithms. The hardware approach is simply to use more registers so that more variables can be held in registers for longer periods of time.

In this section, we will discuss the hardware approach. This approach has been pioneered by the Berkeley RISC group [PATT82a]; was used in the first commercial RISC product, the Pyramid [RAGA83]; and is currently used in the popular **SPARC** architecture.

Register Windows

On the face of it, the use of a large set of registers should decrease the need to access memory. The design task is to organize the registers in such a fashion that this goal is realized.

Because most operand references are to local scalars, the obvious approach is to store these in registers, with perhaps a few registers reserved for global variables. The problem is that the definition of *local* changes with each procedure call and return, operations that occur frequently. On every call, local variables must be saved from the registers into memory, so that the registers can be reused by the called procedure. Furthermore, parameters must be passed. On return, the variables of the calling procedure must be restored (loaded back into registers) and results must be passed back to the calling procedure.

The solution is based on two other results reported in Section 15.1. First, a typical procedure employs only a few passed parameters and local variables (Table 15.4). Second, the depth of procedure activation fluctuates within a relatively narrow range (Figure 4.21). To exploit these properties, multiple small sets of registers are used, each assigned to a different procedure. A procedure call automatically switches the processor to use a different fixed-size window of registers, rather than saving registers in memory. Windows for adjacent procedures are overlapped to allow parameter passing.

The concept is illustrated in Figure 15.1. At any time, only one window of registers is visible and is addressable as if it were the only set of registers (e.g., addresses 0 through $N - 1$). The window is divided into three fixed-size areas. Parameter registers hold parameters passed down from the procedure that called the current procedure and hold results to be passed back up. Local registers are used for local variables, as assigned by the compiler. Temporary registers are used to exchange parameters and results with the next lower level (procedure called by current procedure). The temporary registers at one level are physically the same as the parameter registers at the next lower level. This overlap permits parameters to be passed without the actual movement of data. Keep in mind that, except for the overlap, the registers at two different levels are physically distinct. That is, the parameter and local registers at level J are disjoint from the local and temporary registers at level $J + 1$.

To handle any possible pattern of calls and returns, the number of **register windows** would have to be unbounded. Instead, the register windows can be used to hold the few most recent procedure activations. Older activations must be saved

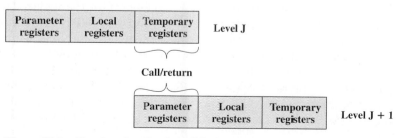

Figure 15.1 Overlapping Register Windows

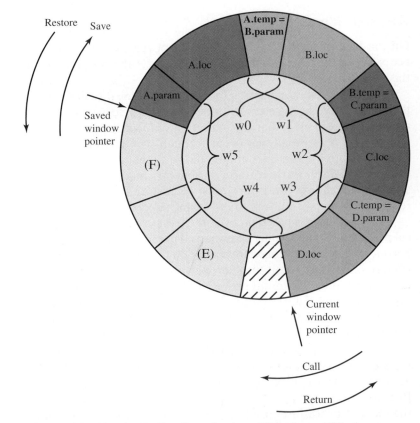

Figure 15.2 Circular-Buffer Organization of Overlapped Windows

in memory and later restored when the nesting depth decreases. Thus, the actual organization of the register file is as a circular buffer of overlapping windows. Two notable examples of this approach are Sun's SPARC architecture, described in Section 15.7, and the IA-64 architecture used in Intel's Itanium processor.

The circular organization is shown in Figure 15.2, which depicts a circular buffer of six windows. The buffer is filled to a depth of 4 (A called B; B called C; C called D) with procedure D active. The current-window pointer (CWP) points to the window of the currently active procedure. Register references by a machine instruction are offset by this pointer to determine the actual physical register. The saved-window pointer (SWP) identifies the window most recently saved in memory. If procedure D now calls procedure E, arguments for E are placed in D's temporary registers (the overlap between w3 and w4) and the CWP is advanced by one window.

If procedure E then makes a call to procedure F, the call cannot be made with the current status of the buffer. This is because F's window overlaps A's window. If F begins to load its temporary registers, preparatory to a call, it will overwrite the parameter registers of A (A.in). Thus, when CWP is incremented (modulo 6) so that it becomes equal to SWP, an interrupt occurs, and A's window is saved. Only the first two portions (A.in and A.loc) need be saved. Then, the SWP is incremented and the call to F proceeds. A similar interrupt can occur on returns. For example, subsequent to the activation of F, when B returns to A, CWP is decremented and becomes equal to SWP. This causes an interrupt that results in the restoration of A's window.

From the preceding, it can be seen that an N-window register file can hold only $N - 1$ procedure activations. The value of N need not be large. As was mentioned in Appendix 4A, one study [TAMI83] found that, with 8 windows, a save or restore is needed on only 1% of the calls or returns. The Berkeley RISC computers use 8 windows of 16 registers each. The Pyramid computer employs 16 windows of 32 registers each.

Global Variables

The window scheme just described provides an efficient organization for storing local scalar variables in registers. However, this scheme does not address the need to store global variables, those accessed by more than one procedure. Two options suggest themselves. First, variables declared as global in an HLL can be assigned memory locations by the compiler, and all machine instructions that reference these variables will use memory-reference operands. This is straightforward, from both the hardware and software (compiler) points of view. However, for frequently accessed global variables, this scheme is inefficient.

An alternative is to incorporate a set of global registers in the processor. These registers would be fixed in number and available to all procedures. A unified numbering scheme can be used to simplify the instruction format. For example, references to registers 0 through 7 could refer to unique global registers, and references to registers 8 through 31 could be offset to refer to physical registers in the current window. There is an increased hardware burden to accommodate the split in register addressing. In addition, the linker must decide which global variables should be assigned to registers.

Large Register File versus Cache

The register file, organized into windows, acts as a small, fast buffer for holding a subset of all variables that are likely to be used the most heavily. From this point of view, the register file acts much like a cache memory, although a much faster memory. The question therefore arises as to whether it would be simpler and better to use a cache and a small traditional register file.

Table 15.5 compares characteristics of the two approaches. The window-based register file holds all the local scalar variables (except in the rare case of window overflow) of the most recent $N - 1$ procedure activations. The cache holds a selection of recently used scalar variables. The register file should save time, because all local scalar variables are retained. On the other hand, the cache may make more efficient use of space, because it is reacting to the situation dynamically. Furthermore, caches generally treat all memory references alike, including instructions and other types of data. Thus, savings in these other areas are possible with a cache and not a register file.

Table 15.5 Characteristics of Large-Register-File and Cache Organizations

Large Register File	Cache
All local scalars	Recently-used local scalars
Individual variables	Blocks of memory
Compiler-assigned global variables	Recently-used global variables
Save/Restore based on procedure nesting depth	Save/Restore based on cache replacement algorithm
Register addressing	Memory addressing
Multiple operands addressed and accessed in one cycle	One operand addressed and accessed per cycle

A register file may make inefficient use of space, because not all procedures will need the full window space allotted to them. On the other hand, the cache suffers from another sort of inefficiency: Data are read into the cache in blocks. Whereas the register file contains only those variables in use, the cache reads in a block of data, some or much of which will not be used.

The cache is capable of handling global as well as local variables. There are usually many global scalars, but only a few of them are heavily used [KATE83]. A cache will dynamically discover these variables and hold them. If the window-based register file is supplemented with global registers, it too can hold some global scalars. However, when program modules are separately compiled, it is impossible for the compiler to assign global values to registers; the linker must perform this task.

With the register file, the movement of data between registers and memory is determined by the procedure nesting depth. Because this depth usually fluctuates within a narrow range, the use of memory is relatively infrequent. Most cache memories are set associative with a small set size. Thus, there is the danger that other data or instructions will compete for cache residency.

Based on the discussion so far, the choice between a large window-based register file and a cache is not clear-cut. There is one characteristic, however, in which the register approach is clearly superior and which suggests that a cache-based system will be noticeably slower. This distinction shows up in the amount of addressing overhead experienced by the two approaches.

Figure 15.3 illustrates the difference. To reference a local scalar in a window-based register file, a "virtual" register number and a window number are used. These can pass through a relatively simple decoder to select one of the physical registers. To reference a memory location in cache, a full-width memory address must be generated. The complexity of this operation depends on the addressing mode. In a set associative cache, a portion of the address is used to read a number of words and tags equal to the set size. Another portion of the address is compared with the tags, and one of the words that were read is selected. It should be clear that even if the cache is as fast as the register file, the access time will be considerably longer. Thus, from the point of view of performance, the window-based register file is superior for local scalars. Further performance improvement could be achieved by the addition of a cache for instructions only.

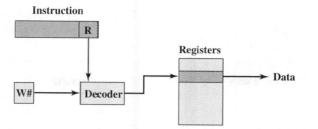

(a) Windows-based register file

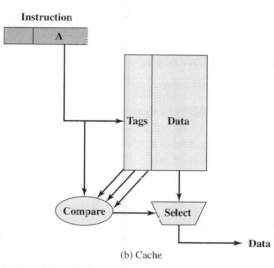

(b) Cache

Figure 15.3 Referencing a Scalar

15.3 COMPILER-BASED REGISTER OPTIMIZATION

Let us assume now that only a small number (e.g., 16–32) of registers is available on the target RISC machine. In this case, optimized register usage is the responsibility of the compiler. A program written in a high-level language has, of course, no explicit references to registers (the C-language keyword register notwithstanding). Rather, program quantities are referred to symbolically. The objective of the compiler is to keep the operands for as many computations as possible in registers rather than main memory, and to minimize load-and-store operations.

In general, the approach taken is as follows. Each program quantity that is a candidate for residing in a register is assigned to a symbolic or virtual register. The compiler then maps the unlimited number of symbolic registers into a fixed number of real registers. Symbolic registers whose usage does not overlap can share the same real register. If, in a particular portion of the program, there are more quantities to deal with than real registers, then some of the quantities are assigned to memory locations. Load-and-store instructions are used to position quantities in registers temporarily for computational operations.

The essence of the optimization task is to decide which quantities are to be assigned to registers at any given point in the program. The technique most commonly used in RISC compilers is known as graph coloring, which is a technique borrowed from the discipline of topology [CHAI82, CHOW86, COUT86, CHOW90].

The graph coloring problem is this. Given a graph consisting of nodes and edges, assign colors to nodes such that adjacent nodes have different colors, and do this in such a way as to minimize the number of different colors. This problem is adapted to the compiler problem in the following way. First, the program is analyzed to build a register interference graph. The nodes of the graph are the symbolic registers. If two symbolic registers are "live" during the same program fragment, then they are joined by an edge to depict interference. An attempt is then made to color the graph with n colors, where n is the number of registers. Nodes that share the same color can be assigned to the same register. If this process does not fully succeed, then those nodes that cannot be colored must be placed in memory, and loads and stores must be used to make space for the affected quantities when they are needed.

Figure 15.4 is a simple example of the process. Assume a program with six symbolic registers to be compiled into three actual registers. Figure 15.4a shows the time sequence of active use of each symbolic register. The dashed horizontal lines indicate successive instruction executions. Figure 15.4b shows the register interference graph (shading and cross-hatching are used instead of colors). A possible coloring with three colors is indicated. Because symbolic registers A and D do not interfere, the compile can assign both of these to physical register R1. Similarly, symbolic registers C and E can be assigned to register R3. One symbolic register, F, is left uncolored and must be dealt with using loads and stores.

In general, there is a trade-off between the use of a large set of registers and compiler-based register optimization. For example, [BRAD91a] reports on a study

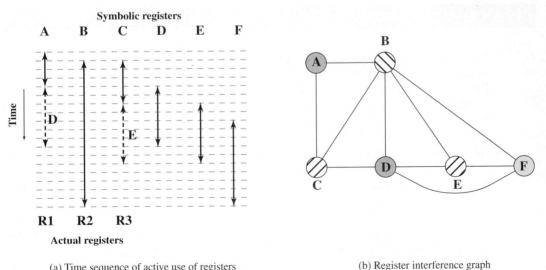

(a) Time sequence of active use of registers

(b) Register interference graph

Figure 15.4 Graph Coloring Approach

that modeled a RISC architecture with features similar to the Motorola 88000 and the MIPS R2000. The researchers varied the number of registers from 16 to 128, and they considered both the use of all general-purpose registers and registers split between integer and floating-point use. Their study showed that with even simple register optimization, there is little benefit to the use of more than 64 registers. With reasonably sophisticated register optimization techniques, there is only marginal performance improvement with more than 32 registers. Finally, they noted that with a small number of registers (e.g., 16), a machine with a shared register organization executes faster than one with a split organization. Similar conclusions can be drawn from [HUGU91], which reports on a study that is primarily concerned with optimizing the use of a small number of registers rather than comparing the use of large register sets with optimization efforts.

15.4 REDUCED INSTRUCTION SET ARCHITECTURE

In this section, we look at some of the general characteristics of and the motivation for a reduced instruction set architecture. Specific examples will be seen later in this chapter. We begin with a discussion of motivations for contemporary complex instruction set architectures.

Why CISC

We have noted the trend to richer instruction sets, which include a larger number of instructions and more complex instructions. Two principal reasons have motivated this trend: a desire to simplify compilers and a desire to improve performance. Underlying both of these reasons was the shift to HLLs on the part of programmers; architects attempted to design machines that provided better support for HLLs.

It is not the intent of this chapter to say that the CISC designers took the wrong direction. Indeed, because technology continues to evolve and because architectures exist along a spectrum rather than in two neat categories, a black-and-white assessment is unlikely ever to emerge. Thus, the comments that follow are simply meant to point out some of the potential pitfalls in the CISC approach and to provide some understanding of the motivation of the RISC adherents.

The first of the reasons cited, compiler simplification, seems obvious, but it is not. The task of the compiler writer is to build a compiler that generates good (fast, small, fast and small) sequences of machine instructions for HLL programs (i.e., the compiler views individual HLL statements in the context of surrounding HLL statements). If there are machine instructions that resemble HLL statements, this task is simplified. This reasoning has been disputed by the RISC researchers ([HENN82], [RADI83], [PATT82b]). They have found that complex machine instructions are often hard to exploit because the compiler must find those cases that exactly fit the construct. The task of optimizing the generated code to minimize code size, reduce instruction execution count, and enhance pipelining is much more difficult with a complex instruction set. As evidence of this, studies cited earlier in this chapter indicate that most of the instructions in a compiled program are the relatively simple ones.

The other major reason cited is the expectation that a CISC will yield smaller, faster programs. Let us examine both aspects of this assertion: that programs will be smaller and that they will execute faster.

There are two advantages to smaller programs. First, because the program takes up less memory, there is a savings in that resource. With memory today being so inexpensive, this potential advantage is no longer compelling. More important, smaller programs should improve performance, and this will happen in three ways. First, fewer instructions means fewer instruction bytes to be fetched. Second, in a paging environment, smaller programs occupy fewer pages, reducing page faults. Third, more instructions fit in cache(s).

The problem with this line of reasoning is that it is far from certain that a CISC program will be smaller than a corresponding RISC program. In many cases, the CISC program, expressed in symbolic machine language, may be *shorter* (i.e., fewer instructions), but the number of bits of memory occupied may not be noticeably *smaller*. Table 15.6 shows results from three studies that compared the size of compiled C programs on a variety of machines, including RISC I, which has a reduced instruction set architecture. Note that there is little or no savings using a CISC over a RISC. It is also interesting to note that the VAX, which has a much more complex instruction set than the PDP-11, achieves very little savings over the latter. These results were confirmed by IBM researchers [RADI83], who found that the IBM 801 (a RISC) produced code that was 0.9 times the size of code on an IBM S/370. The study used a set of PL/I programs.

There are several reasons for these rather surprising results. We have already noted that compilers on CISCs tend to favor simpler instructions, so that the conciseness of the complex instructions seldom comes into play. Also, because there are more instructions on a CISC, longer opcodes are required, producing longer instructions. Finally, RISCs tend to emphasize register rather than memory references, and the former require fewer bits. An example of this last effect is discussed presently.

So the expectation that a CISC will produce smaller programs, with the attendant advantages, may not be realized. The second motivating factor for increasingly complex instruction sets was that instruction execution would be faster. It seems to make sense that a complex HLL operation will execute more quickly as a single machine instruction rather than as a series of more primitive instructions. However, because of the bias toward the use of those simpler instructions, this may not be so.

Table 15.6   Code Size Relative to RISC I

	[PATT82a] 11 C Programs	[KATE83] 12 C Programs	[HEAT84] 5 C Programs
RISC I	1.0	1.0	1.0
VAX-11/780	0.8	0.67	
M68000	0.9		0.9
Z8002	1.2		1.12
PDP-11/70	0.9	0.71	

The entire control unit must be made more complex, and/or the microprogram control store must be made larger, to accommodate a richer instruction set. Either factor increases the execution time of the simple instructions.

In fact, some researchers have found that the speedup in the execution of complex functions is due not so much to the power of the complex machine instructions as to their residence in high-speed control store [RADI83]. In effect, the control store acts as an instruction cache. Thus, the hardware architect is in the position of trying to determine which subroutines or functions will be used most frequently and assigning those to the control store by implementing them in microcode. The results have been less than encouraging. On S/390 systems, instructions such as Translate and Extended-Precision-Floating-Point-Divide reside in high-speed storage, while the sequence involved in setting up procedure calls or initiating an interrupt handler are in slower main memory.

Thus, it is far from clear that a trend to increasingly complex instruction sets is appropriate. This has led a number of groups to pursue the opposite path.

Characteristics of Reduced Instruction Set Architectures

Although a variety of different approaches to reduced instruction set architecture have been taken, certain characteristics are common to all of them:

- One instruction per cycle
- Register-to-register operations
- Simple addressing modes
- Simple instruction formats

Here, we provide a brief discussion of these characteristics. Specific examples are explored later in this chapter.

The first characteristic listed is that there is **one machine instruction per machine cycle**. A *machine cycle* is defined to be the time it takes to fetch two operands from registers, perform an ALU operation, and store the result in a register. Thus, RISC machine instructions should be no more complicated than, and execute about as fast as, microinstructions on CISC machines (discussed in Part Four). With simple, one-cycle instructions, there is little or no need for microcode; the machine instructions can be hardwired. Such instructions should execute faster than comparable machine instructions on other machines, because it is not necessary to access a microprogram control store during instruction execution.

A second characteristic is that most operations should be **register to register**, with only simple LOAD and STORE operations accessing memory. This design feature simplifies the instruction set and therefore the control unit. For example, a RISC instruction set may include only one or two ADD instructions (e.g., integer add, add with carry); the VAX has 25 different ADD instructions. Another benefit is that such an architecture encourages the optimization of register use, so that frequently accessed operands remain in high-speed storage.

This emphasis on register-to-register operations is notable for RISC designs. Contemporary CISC machines provide such instructions but also include memory-to-memory and mixed register/memory operations. Attempts to compare these approaches were made in the 1970s, before the appearance of RISCs. Figure 15.5a illustrates the approach taken. Hypothetical architectures were evaluated on program size and the number of bits of memory traffic. Results such as this one led one researcher to suggest that future architectures should contain no registers at all [MYER78]. One wonders what he would have thought, at the time, of the RISC machine once produced by Pyramid, which contained no less than 528 registers!

What was missing from those studies was a recognition of the frequent access to a small number of local scalars and that, with a large bank of registers or an optimizing compiler, most operands could be kept in registers for long periods of time. Thus, Figure 15.5b may be a fairer comparison.

A third characteristic is the use of **simple addressing modes**. Almost all RISC instructions use simple register addressing. Several additional modes, such as displacement and PC-relative, may be included. Other, more complex modes can be synthesized in software from the simple ones. Again, this design feature simplifies the instruction set and the control unit.

A final common characteristic is the use of **simple instruction formats**. Generally, only one or a few formats are used. Instruction length is fixed and aligned on word boundaries. Field locations, especially the opcode, are fixed. This design feature has a number of benefits. With fixed fields, opcode decoding and register operand accessing can occur simultaneously. Simplified formats simplify the control unit. Instruction fetching is optimized because word-length units are fetched. Alignment on a word boundary also means that a single instruction does not cross page boundaries.

Taken together, these characteristics can be assessed to determine the potential performance benefits of the RISC approach. A certain amount of "circumstantial

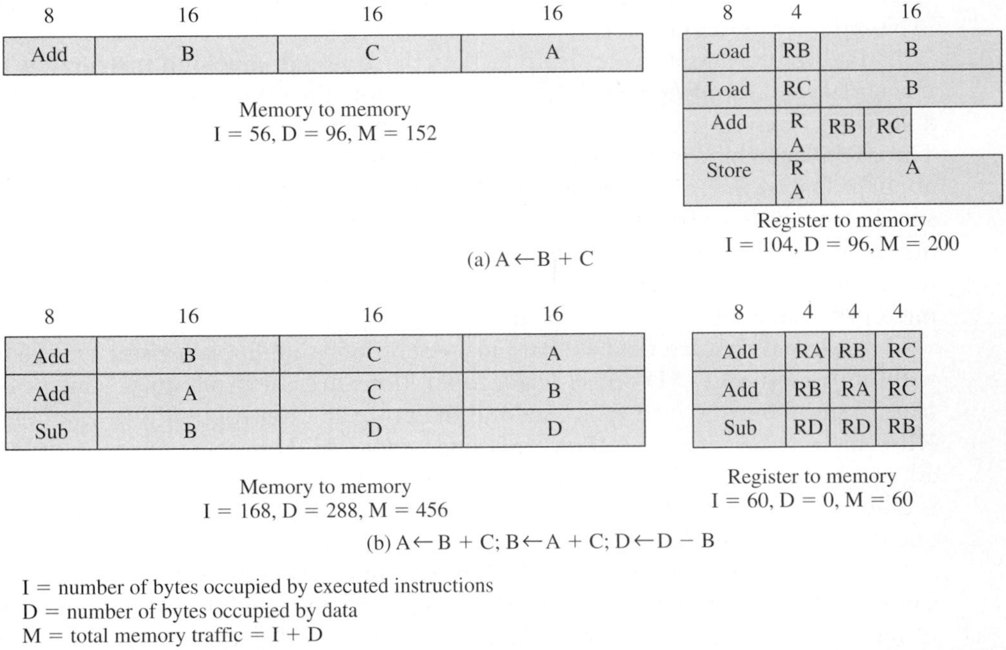

(a) A ← B + C

(b) A ← B + C; B ← A + C; D ← D − B

I = number of bytes occupied by executed instructions
D = number of bytes occupied by data
M = total memory traffic = I + D

Figure 15.5 Two Comparisons of Register-to-Register and Memory-to-Memory Approaches

evidence" can be presented. First, more effective optimizing compilers can be developed. With more-primitive instructions, there are more opportunities for moving functions out of loops, reorganizing code for efficiency, maximizing register utilization, and so forth. It is even possible to compute parts of complex instructions at compile time. For example, the S/390 Move Characters (MVC) instruction moves a string of characters from one location to another. Each time it is executed, the move will depend on the length of the string, whether and in which direction the locations overlap, and what the alignment characteristics are. In most cases, these will all be known at compile time. Thus, the compiler could produce an optimized sequence of primitive instructions for this function.

A second point, already noted, is that most instructions generated by a compiler are relatively simple anyway. It would seem reasonable that a control unit built specifically for those instructions and using little or no microcode could execute them faster than a comparable CISC.

A third point relates to the use of instruction pipelining. RISC researchers feel that the instruction pipelining technique can be applied much more effectively with a reduced instruction set. We examine this point in some detail presently.

A final, and somewhat less significant, point is that RISC processors are more responsive to interrupts because interrupts are checked between rather elementary operations. Architectures with complex instructions either restrict interrupts to instruction boundaries or must define specific interruptible points and implement mechanisms for restarting an instruction.

The case for improved performance for a reduced instruction set architecture is strong, but one could perhaps still make an argument for CISC. A number of studies have been done but not on machines of comparable technology and power. Further, most studies have not attempted to separate the effects of a reduced instruction set and the effects of a large register file. The "circumstantial evidence," however, is suggestive.

CISC versus RISC Characteristics

After the initial enthusiasm for RISC machines, there has been a growing realization that (1) RISC designs may benefit from the inclusion of some CISC features and that (2) CISC designs may benefit from the inclusion of some RISC features. The result is that the more recent RISC designs, notably the PowerPC, are no longer "pure" RISC and the more recent CISC designs, notably the Pentium II and later Pentium models, do incorporate some RISC characteristics.

An interesting comparison in [MASH95] provides some insight into this issue. Table 15.7 lists a number of processors and compares them across a number of characteristics. For purposes of this comparison, the following are considered typical of a classic RISC:

1. A single instruction size.
2. That size is typically 4 bytes.
3. A small number of data addressing modes, typically less than five. This parameter is difficult to pin down. In the table, register and literal modes are not counted and different formats with different offset sizes are counted separately.

Table 15.7 Characteristics of Some Processors

Processor	Number of instruction sizes	Max instruction size in bytes	Number of addressing modes	Indirect addressing	Load/store combined with arithmetic	Max number of memory operands	Unaligned addressing allowed	Max number of MMU uses	Number of bits for integer register specifier	Number of bits for FP register specifier
AMD29000	1	4	1	no	no	1	no	1	8	3^a
MIPS R2000	1	4	1	no	no	1	no	1	5	4
SPARC	1	4	2	no	no	1	no	1	5	4
MC88000	1	4	3	no	no	1	no	1	5	4
HP PA	1	4	10^a	no	no	1	no	1	5	4
IBM RT/PC	2^a	4	1	no	no	1	no	1	4^a	3^a
IBM RS/6000	1	4	4	no	no	1	yes	1	5	5
Intel i860	1	4	4	no	no	1	no	1	5	4
IBM 3090	4	8	2^b	no^b	yes	2	yes	4	4	2
Intel 80486	12	12	15	no^b	yes	2	yes	4	3	3
NSC 32016	21	21	23	yes	yes	2	yes	4	3	3
MC68040	11	22	44	yes	yes	2	yes	8	4	3
VAX	56	56	22	yes	yes	6	yes	24	4	0
Clipper	4^a	8^a	9^a	no	no	1	0	2	4^a	3^a
Intel 80960	2^a	8^a	9^a	no	no	1	yes^a	–	5	3^a

Notes: [a] RISC that does not conform to this characteristic.
[b] CISC that does not conform to this characteristic.

4. No indirect addressing that requires you to make one memory access to get the address of another operand in memory.

5. No operations that combine load/store with arithmetic (e.g., add from memory, add to memory).

6. No more than one memory-addressed operand per instruction.

7. Does not support arbitrary alignment of data for load/store operations.

8. Maximum number of uses of the memory management unit (MMU) for a data address in an instruction.

9. Number of bits for integer register specifier equal to five or more. This means that at least 32 integer registers can be explicitly referenced at a time.

10. Number of bits for floating-point register specifier equal to four or more. This means that at least 16 floating-point registers can be explicitly referenced at a time.

Items 1 through 3 are an indication of instruction decode complexity. Items 4 through 8 suggest the ease or difficulty of pipelining, especially in the presence of virtual memory requirements. Items 9 and 10 are related to the ability to take good advantage of compilers.

In the table, the first eight processors are clearly RISC architectures, the next five are clearly CISC, and the last two are processors often thought of as RISC that in fact have many CISC characteristics.

15.5 RISC PIPELINING

Pipelining with Regular Instructions

As we discussed in Section 12.4, instruction pipelining is often used to enhance performance. Let us reconsider this in the context of a RISC architecture. Most instructions are register to register, and an instruction cycle has the following two stages:

- I: Instruction fetch.
- E: Execute. Performs an ALU operation with register input and output.

For load and store operations, three stages are required:

- I: Instruction fetch.
- E: Execute. Calculates memory address.
- D: Memory. Register-to-memory or memory-to-register operation.

Figure 15.6a depicts the timing of a sequence of instructions using no pipelining. Clearly, this is a wasteful process. Even very simple pipelining can substantially improve performance. Figure 15.6b shows a two-stage pipelining scheme, in which the I and E stages of two different instructions are performed simultaneously. The two stages of the pipeline are an instruction fetch stage, and an execute/memory stage that executes the instruction, including register-to-memory and memory-to-register operations. Thus we see that the instruction fetch stage of the

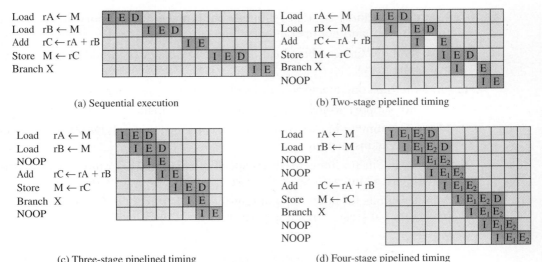

(a) Sequential execution

(b) Two-stage pipelined timing

(c) Three-stage pipelined timing

(d) Four-stage pipelined timing

Figure 15.6 The Effects of Pipelining

second instruction can be performed in parallel with the first part of the execute/ memory stage. However, the execute/memory stage of the second instruction must be delayed until the first instruction clears the second stage of the pipeline. This scheme can yield up to twice the execution rate of a serial scheme. Two problems prevent the maximum speedup from being achieved. First, we assume that a single-port memory is used and that only one memory access is possible per stage. This requires the insertion of a wait state in some instructions. Second, a branch instruction interrupts the sequential flow of execution. To accommodate this with minimum circuitry, a NOOP instruction can be inserted into the instruction stream by the compiler or assembler.

Pipelining can be improved further by permitting two memory accesses per stage. This yields the sequence shown in Figure 15.6c. Now, up to three instructions can be overlapped, and the improvement is as much as a factor of 3. Again, branch instructions cause the speedup to fall short of the maximum possible. Also, note that data dependencies have an effect. If an instruction needs an operand that is altered by the preceding instruction, a delay is required. Again, this can be accomplished by a NOOP.

The pipelining discussed so far works best if the three stages are of approximately equal duration. Because the E stage usually involves an ALU operation, it may be longer. In this case, we can divide into two substages:

- E_1: Register file read
- E_2: ALU operation and register write

Because of the simplicity and regularity of a RISC instruction set, the design of the phasing into three or four stages is easily accomplished. Figure 15.6d shows the result with a four-stage pipeline. Up to four instructions at a time can be under way, and the maximum potential speedup is a factor of 4. Note again the use of NOOPs to account for data and branch delays.

Optimization of Pipelining

Because of the simple and regular nature of RISC instructions, it is easier for a hardware designer to implement a simple, fast pipeline. There are few variations in instruction execution duration, and the pipeline can be tailored to reflect this. However, we have seen that data and branch dependencies reduce the overall execution rate.

DELAYED BRANCH To compensate for these dependencies, code reorganization techniques have been developed. First, let us consider branching instructions. **Delayed branch**, a way of increasing the efficiency of the pipeline, makes use of a branch that does not take effect until after execution of the following instruction (hence the term *delayed*). The instruction location immediately following the branch is referred to as the *delay slot*. This strange procedure is illustrated in Table 15.8. In the column labeled "normal branch," we see a normal symbolic instruction machine-language program. After 102 is executed, the next instruction to be executed is 105. To regularize the pipeline, a NOOP is inserted after this branch. However, increased performance is achieved if the instructions at 101 and 102 are interchanged.

Figure 15.7 shows the result. Figure 15.7a shows the traditional approach to pipelining, of the type discussed in Chapter 14 (e.g., see Figures 14.11 and 14.12). The JUMP instruction is fetched at time 3. At time 4, the JUMP instruction is executed at the same time that instruction 103 (ADD instruction) is fetched. Because a JUMP occurs, which updates the program counter, the pipeline must be cleared of instruction 103; at time 5, instruction 105, which is the target of the JUMP, is loaded. Figure 15.7b shows the same pipeline handled by a typical RISC organization. The timing is the same. However, because of the insertion of the NOOP instruction, we do not need special circuitry to clear the pipeline; the NOOP simply executes with no effect. Figure 15.7c shows the use of the delayed branch. The JUMP instruction is fetched at time 2, before the ADD instruction, which is fetched at time 3. Note, however, that the ADD instruction is fetched before the execution of the JUMP instruction has a chance to alter the program counter. Therefore, during time 4, the ADD instruction is executed at the same time that instruction 105 is fetched.

Table 15.8 Normal and Delayed Branch

Address	Normal Branch		Delayed Branch		Optimized Delayed Branch	
100	LOAD	X, rA	LOAD	X, rA	LOAD	X, rA
101	ADD	1, rA	ADD	1, rA	JUMP	105
102	JUMP	105	JUMP	106	ADD	1, rA
103	ADD	rA, rB	NOOP		ADD	rA, rB
104	SUB	rC, rB	ADD	rA, rB	SUB	rC, rB
105	STORE	rA, Z	SUB	rC, rB	STORE	rA, Z
106			STORE	rA, Z		

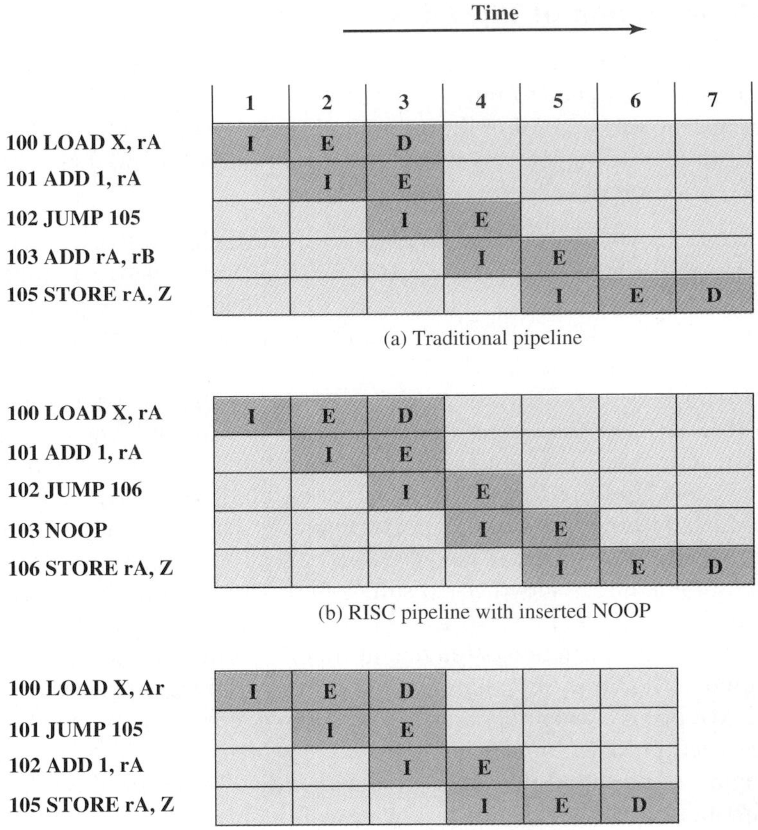

Time

	1	2	3	4	5	6	7
100 LOAD X, rA	I	E	D				
101 ADD 1, rA		I	E				
102 JUMP 105			I	E			
103 ADD rA, rB				I	E		
105 STORE rA, Z					I	E	D

(a) Traditional pipeline

100 LOAD X, rA	I	E	D				
101 ADD 1, rA		I	E				
102 JUMP 106			I	E			
103 NOOP				I	E		
106 STORE rA, Z					I	E	D

(b) RISC pipeline with inserted NOOP

100 LOAD X, Ar	I	E	D				
101 JUMP 105		I	E				
102 ADD 1, rA			I	E			
105 STORE rA, Z				I	E	D	

(c) Reversed instructions

Figure 15.7 Use of the Delayed Branch

Thus, the original semantics of the program are retained but one less clock cycle is required for execution.

This interchange of instructions will work successfully for unconditional branches, calls, and returns. For conditional branches, this procedure cannot be blindly applied. If the condition that is tested for the branch can be altered by the immediately preceding instruction, then the compiler must refrain from doing the interchange and instead insert a NOOP. Otherwise, the compiler can seek to insert a useful instruction after the branch. The experience with both the Berkeley RISC and IBM 801 systems is that the majority of conditional branch instructions can be optimized in this fashion ([PATT82a], [RADI83]).

DELAYED LOAD A similar sort of tactic, called the **delayed load**, can be used on LOAD instructions. On LOAD instructions, the register that is to be the target of the load is locked by the processor. The processor then continues execution of the instruction stream until it reaches an instruction requiring that register, at which point it idles until the load is complete. If the compiler can rearrange instructions so that useful work can be done while the load is in the pipeline, efficiency is increased.

Loop Unrolling Simulator

LOOP UNROLLING Another compiler technique to improve instruction parallelism is loop unrolling [BACO94]. Unrolling replicates the body of a loop some number of times called the unrolling factor (u) and iterates by step u instead of step 1.

Unrolling can improve the performance by

- reducing loop overhead
- increasing instruction parallelism by improving pipeline performance
- improving register, data cache, or TLB locality

Figure 15.8 illustrates all three of these improvements in an example. Loop overhead is cut in half because two iterations are performed before the test and branch at the end of the loop. Instruction parallelism is increased because the second assignment can be performed while the results of the first are being stored and the loop variables are being updated. If array elements are assigned to registers, register locality will improve because a[i] and a[i + 1] are used twice in the loop body, reducing the number of loads per iteration from three to two.

```
do i=2, n-1
        a[i] = a[i] + a[i-1] * a[i+1]
end do
```

(a) Original loop

```
do i=2, n-2, 2
        a[i] = a[i] + a[i-1] * a[i+1]
        a[i+1] = a[i+1] + a[i] * a[i+2]
end do

if (mod(n-2, 2) = 1) then
    a[n-1] = a[n-1] + a[n-2] * a[n]
end if
```

(b) Loop unrolled twice

Figure 15.8 Loop Unrolling

As a final note, we should point out that the design of the instruction pipeline should not be carried out in isolation from other optimization techniques applied to the system. For example, [BRAD91b] shows that the scheduling of instructions for the pipeline and the dynamic allocation of registers should be considered together to achieve the greatest efficiency.

15.6 MIPS R4000

One of the first commercially available RISC chip sets was developed by MIPS Technology Inc. The system was inspired by an experimental system, also using the name MIPS, developed at Stanford [HENN84]. In this section we look at the MIPS R4000. It has substantially the same architecture and instruction set of the earlier MIPS designs: the R2000 and R3000. The most significant difference is that the R4000 uses 64 rather than 32 bits for all internal and external data paths and for addresses, registers, and the ALU.

The use of 64 bits has a number of advantages over a 32-bit architecture. It allows a bigger address space—large enough for an operating system to map more than a terabyte of files directly into virtual memory for easy access. With 1-terabyte and larger disk drives now common, the 4-gigabyte address space of a 32-bit machine becomes limiting. Also, the 64-bit capacity allows the R4000 to process data such as IEEE double-precision floating-point numbers and character strings, up to eight characters in a single action.

The R4000 processor chip is partitioned into two sections, one containing the CPU and the other containing a coprocessor for memory management. The processor has a very simple architecture. The intent was to design a system in which the instruction execution logic was as simple as possible, leaving space available for logic to enhance performance (e.g., the entire memory-management unit).

The processor supports thirty-two 64-bit registers. It also provides for up to 128 Kbytes of high-speed cache, half each for instructions and data. The relatively large cache (the IBM 3090 provides 128 to 256 Kbytes of cache) enables the system to keep large sets of program code and data local to the processor, off-loading the main memory bus and avoiding the need for a large register file with the accompanying windowing logic.

Instruction Set

Table 15.9 lists the basic instruction set for all MIPS R series processors. All processor instructions are encoded in a single 32-bit word format. All data operations are register to register; the only memory references are pure load/store operations.

The R4000 makes no use of condition codes. If an instruction generates a condition, the corresponding flags are stored in a general-purpose register. This avoids the need for special logic to deal with condition codes as they affect the pipelining mechanism and the reordering of instructions by the compiler. Instead, the mechanisms already implemented to deal with register-value dependencies are employed. Further, conditions mapped onto the register files are subject

Table 15.9   MIPS R-Series Instruction Set

OP	Description	OP	Description
	Load/Store Instructions	SRLV	Shift Right Logical Variable
LB	Load Byte	SRAV	Shift Right Arithmetic Variable
LBU	Load Byte Unsigned		**Multiply/Divide Instructions**
LH	Load Halfword	MULT	Multiply
LHU	Load Halfword Unsigned	MULTU	Multiply Unsigned
LW	Load Word	DIV	Divide
LWL	Load Word Left	DIVU	Divide Unsigned
LWR	Load Word Right	MFHI	Move From HI
SB	Store Byte	MTHI	Move To HI
SH	Store Halfword	MFLO	Move From LO
SW	Store Word	MTLO	Move To LO
SWL	Store Word Left		**Jump and Branch Instructions**
SWR	Store Word Right	J	Jump
	Arithmetic Instructions (ALU Immediate)	JAL	Jump and Link
		JR	Jump to Register
ADDI	Add Immediate	JALR	Jump and Link Register
ADDIU	Add Immediate Unsigned	BEQ	Branch on Equal
SLTI	Set on Less Than Immediate	BNE	Branch on Not Equal
SLTIU	Set on Less Than Immediate Unsigned	BLEZ	Branch on Less Than or Equal to Zero
ANDI	AND Immediate	BGTZ	Branch on Greater Than Zero
ORI	OR Immediate	BLTZ	Branch on Less Than Zero
XORI	Exclusive-OR Immediate	BGEZ	Branch on Greater Than or Equal to Zero
LUI	Load Upper Immediate		
	Arithmetic Instructions (3-operand, R-type)	BLTZAL	Branch on Less Than Zero And Link
ADD	Add	BGEZAL	Branch on Greater Than or Equal to Zero And Link
ADDU	Add Unsigned		
SUB	Subtract		**Coprocessor Instructions**
SUBU	Subtract Unsigned	LWCz	Load Word to Coprocessor
SLT	Set on Less Than	SWCz	Store Word to Coprocessor
SLTU	Set on Less Than Unsigned	MTCz	Move To Coprocessor
AND	AND	MFCz	Move From Coprocessor
OR	OR	CTCz	Move Control To Coprocessor
XOR	Exclusive-OR	CFCz	Move Control From Coprocessor
NOR	NOR	COPz	Coprocessor Operation
	Shift Instructions	BCzT	Branch on Coprocessor z True
SLL	Shift Left Logical	BCzF	Branch on Coprocessor z False
SRL	Shift Right Logical		**Special Instructions**
SRA	Shift Right Arithmetic	SYSCALL	System Call
SLLV	Shift Left Logical Variable	BREAK	Break

to the same compile-time optimizations in allocation and reuse as other values stored in registers.

As with most RISC-based machines, the MIPS uses a single 32-bit instruction length. This single instruction length simplifies instruction fetch and decode, and it also simplifies the interaction of instruction fetch with the virtual memory management unit (i.e., instructions do not cross word or page boundaries). The three instruction formats (Figure 15.9) share common formatting of opcodes and register references, simplifying instruction decode. The effect of more complex instructions can be synthesized at compile time.

Only the simplest and most frequently used memory-addressing mode is implemented in hardware. All memory references consist of a 16-bit offset from a 32-bit register. For example, the "load word" instruction is of the form

```
lw r2, 128(r3)    /* load word at address 128 offset from
                     register 3 into register 2
```

Each of the 32 general-purpose registers can be used as the base register. One register, r0, always contains 0.

The compiler makes use of multiple machine instructions to synthesize typical addressing modes in conventional machines. Here is an example from [CHOW87], which uses the instruction lui (load upper immediate). This instruction loads the upper half of a register with a 16-bit immediate value, setting the lower half to zero. Consider an assembly-language instruction that uses a 32-bit immediate argument

```
lw r2, #imm(r4)   /* load word at address using a 32-bit
                     immediate offset #imm
                  /* offset from register 4 into register 2
```

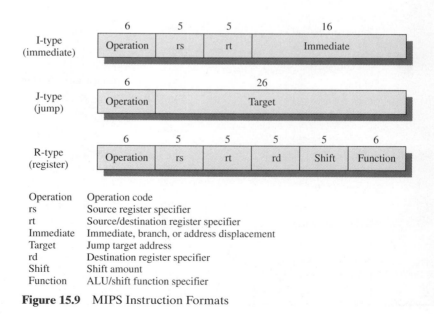

Figure 15.9   MIPS Instruction Formats

This instruction can be compiled into the following MIPS instructions

```
lui  r1, #imm-hi        /* where #imm-hi is the high-order
                           16 bits of #imm
addu r1, r1, r4         /* add unsigned #imm-hi to r4 and
                           put in r1
lw r2, #imm-lo(r1)      /* where #imm-lo is the low-order
                           16 bits of #imm
```

Instruction Pipeline

With its simplified instruction architecture, the MIPS can achieve very efficient pipelining. It is instructive to look at the evolution of the MIPS pipeline, as it illustrates the evolution of RISC pipelining in general.

The initial experimental RISC systems and the first generation of commercial RISC processors achieve execution speeds that approach one instruction per system clock cycle. To improve on this performance, two classes of processors have evolved to offer execution of multiple instructions per clock cycle: superscalar and superpipelined architectures. In essence, a superscalar architecture replicates each of the pipeline stages so that two or more instructions at the same stage of the pipeline can be processed simultaneously. A superpipelined architecture is one that makes use of more, and more fine-grained, pipeline stages. With more stages, more instructions can be in the pipeline at the same time, increasing parallelism.

Both approaches have limitations. With superscalar pipelining, dependencies between instructions in different pipelines can slow down the system. Also, overhead logic is required to coordinate these dependencies. With superpipelining, there is overhead associated with transferring instructions from one stage to the next.

Chapter 16 is devoted to a study of superscalar architecture. The MIPS R4000 is a good example of a RISC-based superpipeline architecture.

MIPS R3000 Five-Stage Pipeline Simulator

Figure 15.10a shows the instruction pipeline of the R3000. In the R3000, the pipeline advances once per clock cycle. The MIPS compiler is able to reorder instructions to fill delay slots with code 70 to 90% of the time. All instructions follow the same sequence of five pipeline stages:

- Instruction fetch
- Source operand fetch from register file
- ALU operation or data operand address generation
- Data memory reference
- Write back into register file

As illustrated in Figure 15.10a, there is not only parallelism due to pipelining but also parallelism within the execution of a single instruction. The 60-ns clock cycle

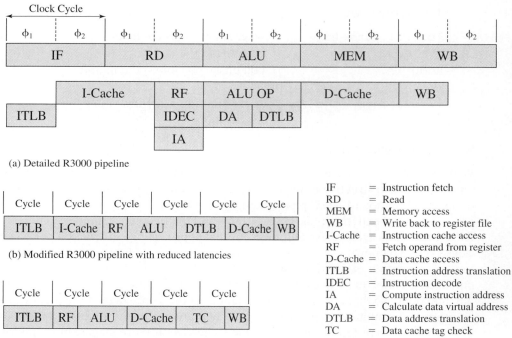

(a) Detailed R3000 pipeline

(b) Modified R3000 pipeline with reduced latencies

(c) Optimized R3000 pipeline with parallel TLB and cache accesses

IF   = Instruction fetch
RD   = Read
MEM   = Memory access
WB   = Write back to register file
I-Cache = Instruction cache access
RF   = Fetch operand from register
D-Cache = Data cache access
ITLB   = Instruction address translation
IDEC   = Instruction decode
IA   = Compute instruction address
DA   = Calculate data virtual address
DTLB   = Data address translation
TC   = Data cache tag check

Figure 15.10   Enhancing the R3000 Pipeline

is divided into two 30-ns stages. The external instruction and data access operations to the cache each require 60 ns, as do the major internal operations (OP, DA, IA). Instruction decode is a simpler operation, requiring only a single 30-ns stage, overlapped with register fetch in the same instruction. Calculation of an address for a branch instruction also overlaps instruction decode and register fetch, so that a branch at instruction i can address the ICACHE access of instruction $i + 2$. Similarly, a load at instruction i fetches data that are immediately used by the OP of instruction $i + 1$, while an ALU/shift result gets passed directly into instruction $i + 1$ with no delay. This tight coupling between instructions makes for a highly efficient pipeline.

In detail, then, each clock cycle is divided into separate stages, denoted as $\phi 1$ and $\phi 2$. The functions performed in each stage are summarized in Table 15.10.

The R4000 incorporates a number of technical advances over the R3000. The use of more advanced technology allows the clock cycle time to be cut in half, to 30 ns, and for the access time to the register file to be cut in half. In addition, there is greater density on the chip, which enables the instruction and data caches to be incorporated on the chip. Before looking at the final R4000 pipeline, let us consider how the R3000 pipeline can be modified to improve performance using R4000 technology.

Figure 15.10b shows a first step. Remember that the cycles in this figure are half as long as those in Figure 15.10a. Because they are on the same chip, the instruction and data cache stages take only half as long; so they still occupy only one clock cycle. Again, because of the speedup of the register file access, register read and write still occupy only half of a clock cycle.

Table 15.10 R3000 Pipeline Stages

Pipeline Stage	Phase	Function
IF	$\phi1$	Using the TLB, translate an instruction virtual address to a physical address (after a branching decision).
IF	$\phi2$	Send the physical address to the instruction address.
RD	$\phi1$	Return instruction from instruction cache.
		Compare tags and validity of fetched instruction.
RD	$\phi2$	Decode instruction.
		Read register file.
		If branch, calculate branch target address.
ALU	$\phi1 + \phi2$	If register-to-register operation, the arithmetic or logical operation is performed.
ALU	$\phi1$	If a branch, decide whether the branch is to be taken or not.
		If a memory reference (load or store), calculate data virtual address.
ALU	$\phi2$	If a memory reference, translate data virtual address to physical using TLB.
MEM	$\phi1$	If a memory reference, send physical address to data cache.
MEM	$\phi2$	If a memory reference, return data from data cache, and check tags.
WB	$\phi1$	Write to register file.

Because the R4000 caches are on-chip, the virtual-to-physical address translation can delay the cache access. This delay is reduced by implementing virtually indexed caches and going to a parallel cache access and address translation. Figure 15.10c shows the optimized R3000 pipeline with this improvement. Because of the compression of events, the data cache tag check is performed separately on the next cycle after cache access. This check determines whether the data item is in the cache.

In a superpipelined system, existing hardware is used several times per cycle by inserting pipeline registers to split up each pipe stage. Essentially, each superpipeline stage operates at a multiple of the base clock frequency, the multiple depending on the degree of superpipelining. The R4000 technology has the speed and density to permit superpipelining of degree 2. Figure 15.11a shows the optimized R3000 pipeline using this superpipelining. Note that this is essentially the same dynamic structure as Figure 15.10c.

Further improvements can be made. For the R4000, a much larger and specialized adder was designed. This makes it possible to execute ALU operations at twice the rate. Other improvements allow the execution of loads and stores at twice the rate. The resulting pipeline is shown in Figure 15.11b.

The R4000 has eight pipeline stages, meaning that as many as eight instructions can be in the pipeline at the same time. The pipeline advances at the rate of two stages per clock cycle. The eight pipeline stages are as follows:

- **Instruction fetch first half:** Virtual address is presented to the instruction cache and the translation lookaside buffer.
- **Instruction fetch second half:** Instruction cache outputs the instruction and the TLB generates the physical address.

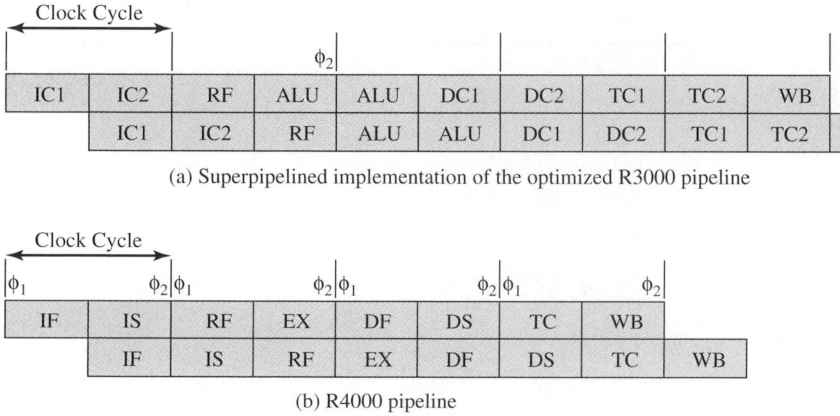

Clock Cycle

IC1	IC2	RF	ALU	ALU	DC1	DC2	TC1	TC2	WB	
	IC1	IC2	RF	ALU	ALU	DC1	DC2	TC1	TC2	WB

(a) Superpipelined implementation of the optimized R3000 pipeline

Clock Cycle

IF	IS	RF	EX	DF	DS	TC	WB	
	IF	IS	RF	EX	DF	DS	TC	WB

(b) R4000 pipeline

IF	=	Instruction fetch first half	DC	= Data cache
IS	=	Instruction fetch second half	DF	= Data cache first half
RF	=	Fetch operands from register	DS	= Data cache second half
EX	=	Instruction execute	TC	= Tag check
IC	=	Instruction cache	WB	= Write back to register file

Figure 15.11 Theoretical R3000 and Actual R4000 Superpipelines

- **Register file**: Three activities occur in parallel:
  - Instruction is decoded and check made for interlock conditions (i.e., this instruction depends on the result of a preceding instruction).
  - Instruction cache tag check is made.
  - Operands are fetched from the register file.
- **Instruction execute:** One of three activities can occur:
  - If the instruction is a register-to-register operation, the ALU performs the arithmetic or logical operation.
  - If the instruction is a load or store, the data virtual address is calculated.
  - If the instruction is a branch, the branch target virtual address is calculated and branch conditions are checked.
- **Data cache first:** Virtual address is presented to the data cache and TLB.
- **Data cache second:** The TLB generates the physical address, and the data cache outputs the data.
- **Tag check:** Cache tag checks are performed for loads and stores.
- **Write back:** Instruction result is written back to register file.

15.7 SPARC

SPARC (Scalable Processor Architecture) refers to an architecture defined by Sun Microsystems. Sun developed its own SPARC implementation but also licenses the architecture to other vendors to produce SPARC-compatible machines. The SPARC architecture is inspired by the Berkeley RISC I machine, and its instruction set and register organization is based closely on the Berkeley RISC model.

SPARC Register Set

As with the Berkeley RISC, the SPARC makes use of register windows. Each window gives addressability to 24 registers, and the total number of windows is implementation dependent and ranges from 2 to 32 windows. Figure 15.12 illustrates an implementation that supports 8 windows, using a total of 136 physical registers; as the discussion in Section 15.2 indicates, this seems a reasonable number of windows. Physical registers 0 through 7 are global registers shared by all procedures. Each procedure sees logical registers 0 through 31. Logical registers 24 through 31, referred to as *ins*, are shared with the calling (parent) procedure; and logical registers 8 through 15, referred to as *outs*, are shared with any called (child) procedure. These two portions overlap with other windows. Logical registers 16 through 23,

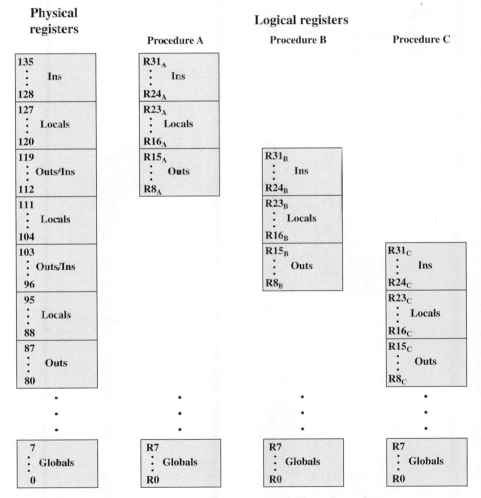

Figure 15.12 SPARC Register Window Layout with Three Procedures

referred to as *locals,* are not shared and do not overlap with other windows. Again, as the discussion of Section 12.1 indicates, the availability of 8 registers for parameter passing should be adequate in most cases (e.g., see Table 15.4).

Figure 15.13 is another view of the register overlap. The calling procedure places any parameters to be passed in its *outs* registers; the called procedure treats these same physical registers as it *ins* registers. The processor maintains a current window pointer (CWP), located in the processor status register (PSR), that points to the window of the currently executing procedure. The window invalid mask (WIM), also in the PSR, indicates which windows are invalid.

With the SPARC register architecture, it is usually not necessary to save and restore registers for a procedure call. The compiler is simplified because the compiler need be concerned only with allocating the local registers for a procedure in an efficient manner and need not be concerned with register allocation between procedures.

Instruction Set

Table 15.11 lists the instructions for the SPARC architecture. Most of the instructions reference only register operands. Register-to-register instructions have three operands and can be expressed in the form

$$R_d \rightarrow R_{S1} \text{ op } S2$$

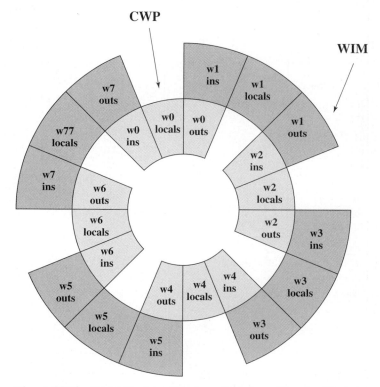

Figure 15.13 Eight Register Windows Forming a Circular Stack in SPARC

Table 15.11   SPARC Instruction Set

OP	Description	OP	Description
Load/Store Instructions		**Arithmetic Instructions**	
LDSB	Load signed byte	ADD	Add
LDSH	Load signed halfword	ADDCC	Add, set icc
LDUB	Load unsigned byte	ADDX	Add with carry
LDUH	Load unsigned halfword	ADDXCC	Add with carry, set icc
LD	Load word	SUB	Subtract
LDD	Load doubleword	SUBCC	Subtract, set icc
STB	Store byte	SUBX	Subtract with carry
STH	Store halfword	SUBXCC	Subtract with carry, set icc
STD	Store word	MULSCC	Multiply step, set icc
STDD	Store doubleword	**Jump/Branch Instructions**	
Shift Instructions		BCC	Branch on condition
SLL	Shift left logical	FBCC	Branch on floating-point condition
SRL	Shift right logical	CBCC	Branch on coprocessor condition
SRA	Shift right arithmetic	CALL	Call procedure
Boolean Instructions		JMPL	Jump and link
AND	AND	TCC	Trap on condition
ANDCC	AND, set icc	SAVE	Advance register window
ANDN	NAND	RESTORE	Move windows backward
ANDNCC	NAND, set icc	RETT	Return from trap
OR	OR	**Miscellaneous Instructions**	
ORCC	OR, set icc	SETHI	Set high 22 bits
ORN	NOR	UNIMP	Unimplemented instruction (trap)
ORNCC	NOR, set icc	RD	Read a special register
XOR	XOR	WR	Write a special register
XORCC	XOR, set icc	IFLUSH	Instruction cache flush
XNOR	Exclusive NOR		
XNORCC	Exclusive NOR, set icc		

where R_d and R_{S1} are register references; S2 can refer either to a register or to a 13-bit immediate operand. Register zero (R_0) is hardwired with the value 0. This form is well suited to typical programs, which have a high proportion of local scalars and constants.

The available ALU operations can be grouped as follows:

- Integer addition (with or without carry)
- Integer subtraction (with or without carry)
- Bitwise Boolean AND, OR, XOR and their negations
- Shift left logical, right logical, or right arithmetic

All of these instructions, except the shifts, can optionally set the four condition codes (ZERO, NEGATIVE, OVERFLOW, CARRY). Signed integers are represented in 32-bit twos complement form.

Only simple load and store instructions reference memory. There are separate load and store instructions for word (32 bits), doubleword, halfword, and byte. For the latter two cases, there are instructions for loading these quantities as signed or unsigned numbers. Signed numbers are sign extended to fill out the 32-bit destination register. Unsigned numbers are padded with zeros.

The only available addressing mode, other than register, is a displacement mode. That is, the effective address (EA) of an operand consists of a displacement from an address contained in a register:

$$EA = (R_{S1}) + S2$$
$$\text{or } EA = (R_{S1}) + (R_{S2})$$

depending on whether the second operand is immediate or a register reference. To perform a load or store, an extra stage is added to the instruction cycle. During the second stage, the memory address is calculated using the ALU; the load or store occurs in a third stage. This single addressing mode is quite versatile and can be used to synthesize other addressing modes, as indicated in Table 15.12.

It is instructive to compare the SPARC addressing capability with that of the MIPS. The MIPS makes use of a 16-bit offset, compared with a 13-bit offset on the SPARC. On the other hand, the MIPS does not permit an address to be constructed from the contents of two registers.

Instruction Format

As with the MIPS R4000, SPARC uses a simple set of 32-bit instruction formats (Figure 15.14). All instructions begin with a 2-bit opcode. For most instructions, this is extended with additional opcode bits elsewhere in the format. For the Call instruction, a 30-bit immediate operand is extended with two zero bits to the right to form a 32-bit PC-relative address in twos complement form. Instructions are aligned on a 32-bit boundary so that this form of addressing suffices.

The Branch instruction includes a 4-bit condition field that corresponds to the four standard condition code bits, so that any combination of conditions can be tested. The 22-bit PC-relative address is extended with two zero bits on the right to form a 24-bit twos complement relative address. An unusual feature of the Branch instruction is the annul bit. When the annul bit is not set, the instruction after the

Table 15.12 Synthesizing Other Addressing Modes with SPARC Addressing Modes

Instruction Type	Addressing Mode	Algorithm	SPARC Equivalent
Register-to-register	Immediate	operand = A	S2
Load, store	Direct	EA = A	$R_0 + S_2$
Register-to-register	Register	EA = R	R_{S1}, R_{S2}
Load, store	Register Indirect	EA = (R)	$R_{S1} + 0$
Load, store	Displacement	EA = (R) + A	$R_{S1} + S2$

Note: S2 = either a register operand or a 13-bit immediate operand.

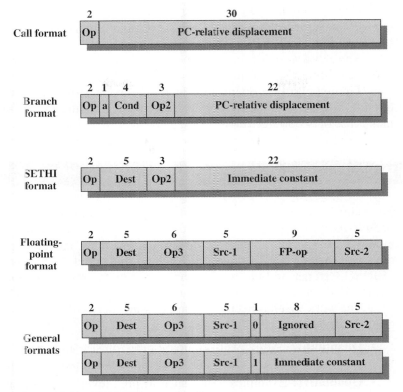

Figure 15.14 SPARC Instruction Formats

branch is always executed, regardless of whether the branch is taken. This is the typical delayed branch operation found on many RISC machines and described in Section 15.5 (see Figure 15.7). However, when the annul bit is set, the instruction following the branch is executed only if the branch is taken. The processor suppresses the effect of that instruction even though it is already in the pipeline. This annul bit is useful because it makes it easier for the compiler to fill the delay slot following a conditional branch. The instruction that is the target of the branch can always be put in the delay slot, because if the branch is not taken, the instruction can be annulled. The reason this technique is desirable is that conditional branches are generally taken more than half the time.

The SETHI instruction is a special instruction used to form a 32-bit constant. This feature is needed to form large data constants; for example, it can be used to form a large offset for a load or store instruction. The SETHI instruction sets the 22 high-order bits of a register with its 22-bit immediate operand, and zeros out the low-order 10 bits. An immediate constant of up to 13 bits can be specified in one of the general formats, and such an instruction could be used to fill in the remaining 10 bits of the register. A load or store instruction can also be used to achieve a direct addressing mode. To load a value from location K in memory, we could use the following SPARC instructions:

```
sethi   %hi(K), %r8          ;load high-order 22 bits of address of location
                             ;K into register r8
ld      [%r8 + %lo(K)], %r8  ;load contents of location K into r8
```

The macros %hi and %lo are used to define immediate operands consisting of the appropriate address bits of a location. This use of SETHI is similar to the use of the lui instruction on the MIPS.

The floating-point format is used for floating-point operations. Two source and one destination registers are designated.

Finally, all other operations, including loads, stores, arithmetic, and logical operations use one of the last two formats shown in Figure 15.14. One of the formats makes use of two source registers and a destination register, while the other uses one source register, one 13-bit immediate operand, and one destination register.

15.8 RISC VERSUS CISC CONTROVERSY

For many years, the general trend in computer architecture and organization has been toward increasing processor complexity: more instructions, more addressing modes, more specialized registers, and so on. The RISC movement represents a fundamental break with the philosophy behind that trend. Naturally, the appearance of RISC systems, and the publication of papers by its proponents extolling RISC virtues, led to a reaction from those involved in the design of CISC architectures.

The work that has been done on assessing merits of the RISC approach can be grouped into two categories:

- **Quantitative:** Attempts to compare program size and execution speed of programs on RISC and CISC machines that use comparable technology
- **Qualitative:** Examines issues such as high-level language support and optimum use of VLSI real estate

Most of the work on quantitative assessment has been done by those working on RISC systems [PATT82b, HEAT84, PATT84], and it has been, by and large, favorable to the RISC approach. Others have examined the issue and come away unconvinced [COLW85a, FLYN87, DAVI87]. There are several problems with attempting such comparisons [SERL86]:

- There is no pair of RISC and CISC machines that are comparable in life-cycle cost, level of technology, gate complexity, sophistication of compiler, operating system support, and so on.
- No definitive test set of programs exists. Performance varies with the program.
- It is difficult to sort out hardware effects from effects due to skill in compiler writing.
- Most of the comparative analysis on RISC has been done on "toy" machines rather than commercial products. Furthermore, most commercially available machines advertised as RISC possess a mixture of RISC and CISC characteristics. Thus, a fair comparison with a commercial, "pure-play" CISC machine (e.g., VAX, Pentium) is difficult.

The qualitative assessment is, almost by definition, subjective. Several researchers have turned their attention to such an assessment [COLW85a, WALL85], but the results are, at best, ambiguous, and certainly subject to rebuttal [PATT85b] and, of course, counterrebuttal [COLW85b].

In more recent years, the RISC versus CISC controversy has died down to a great extent. This is because there has been a gradual convergence of the technologies. As chip densities and raw hardware speeds increase, RISC systems have become more complex. At the same time, in an effort to squeeze out maximum performance, CISC designs have focused on issues traditionally associated with RISC, such as an increased number of general-purpose registers and increased emphasis on instruction pipeline design.

15.9 RECOMMENDED READING

Two classic overview papers on RISC are [PATT85a] and [HENN84]. Another survey article is [STAL88]. Accounts of two pioneering RISC efforts are provided by [RADI83] and [PATT82a].

[KANE92] covers the commercial MIPS machine in detail. [MIRA92] provides a good overview of the MIPS R4000. [BASH91] discusses the evolution from the R3000 pipeline to the R4000 superpipeline. The SPARC is covered in some detail in [DEWA90].

BASH91   Bashteen, A.; Lui, I.; and Mullan, J. "A Superpipeline Approach to the MIPS Architecture." *Proceedings, COMPCON Spring '91,* February 1991.

DEWA90   Dewar, R., and Smosna, M. *Microprocessors: A Programmer's View.* New York: McGraw-Hill, 1990.

HENN84   Hennessy, J. "VLSI Processor Architecture." *IEEE Transactions on Computers,* December 1984.

KANE92   Kane, G., and Heinrich, J. *MIPS RISC Architecture.* Englewood Cliffs, NJ: Prentice Hall, 1992.

MIRA92   Mirapuri, S.; Woodacre, M.; and Vasseghi, N. "The MIPS R4000 Processor." *IEEE Micro,* April 1992.

PATT82a   Patterson, D., and Sequin, C. "A VLSI RISC." *Computer,* September 1982.

PATT85a   Patterson, D. "Reduced Instruction Set Computers." *Communications of the ACM,* January 1985.

RADI83   Radin, G. "The 801 Minicomputer." *IBM Journal of Research and Development,* May 1983.

STAL88   Stallings, W. "Reduced Instruction Set Computer Architecture." *Proceedings of the IEEE,* January 1988.

15.10 KEY TERMS, REVIEW QUESTIONS, AND PROBLEMS

Key Terms

complex instruction set computer (CISC)	high-level language (HLL)	register window
delayed branch	reduced instruction set computer (RISC)	SPARC
delayed load	register file	

Review Questions

15.1 What are some typical distinguishing characteristics of RISC organization?

15.2 Briefly explain the two basic approaches used to minimize register-memory operations on RISC machines.

15.3 If a circular register buffer is used to handle local variables for nested procedures, describe two approaches for handling global variables.

15.4 What are some typical characteristics of a RISC instruction set architecture?

15.5 What is a delayed branch?

Problems

15.1 Considering the call-return pattern in Figure 4.21, how many overflows and underflows (each of which causes a register save/restore) will occur with a window size of
   a. 5?
   b. 8?
   c. 16?

15.2 In the discussion of Figure 15.2, it was stated that only the first two portions of a window are saved or restored. Why is it not necessary to save the temporary registers?

15.3 We wish to determine the execution time for a given program using the various pipelining schemes discussed in Section 15.5. Let

$$N = \text{number of executed instructions}$$
$$D = \text{number of memory accesses}$$
$$J = \text{number of jump instructions}$$

For the simple sequential scheme (Figure 15.6a), the execution time is $2N + D$ stages. Derive formulas for two-stage, three-stage, and four-stage pipelining.

15.4 Reorganize the code sequence in Figure 15.6d to reduce the number of NOOPs.

15.5 Consider the following code fragment in a high-level language:

    for I **in** 1...100 **loop**
       $S \leftarrow S + Q(I). VAL$
    end loop;

Assume that Q is an array of 32-byte records and the VAL field is in the first 4 bytes of each record. Using x86 code, we can compile this program fragment as follows:

```
        MOV     ECX, 1          ;use register ECX to hold I
LP:     IMUL    EAX, ECX, 32    ;get offset in EAX
        MOV     EBX, Q[EAX]     ;load VAL field
        ADD     S, EBX          ;add to S
        INC     ECX             ;increment I
        CMP     ECX, 101        :compare to 101
        JNE     LP              ;loop until I = 100
```

This program makes use of the IMUL instruction, which multiplies the second operand by the immediate value in the third operand and places the result in the first operand (see Problem 10.13). A RISC advocate would like to demonstrate that a clever compiler can eliminate unnecessarily complex instructions such as IMUL. Provide the demonstration by rewriting the above x86 program without using the IMUL instruction.

15.6 Consider the following loop:

    S := 0;
    for K := 1 **to** 100 **do**
       S := S − K;

A straightforward translation of this into a generic assembly language would look something like this:

```
        LD      R1,0            ;keep value of S in R1
        LD      R2,1            ;keep value of K in R2
LP      SUB     R1,R1,R2        ;S := S − K
        BEQ     R2,100,EXIT     ;done if K = 100
        ADD     R2,R2,1         ;else increment K
        JMP     LP              ;back to start of loop
```

A compiler for a RISC machine will introduce delay slots into this code so that the processor can employ the delayed branch mechanism. The JMP instruction is easy to deal with, because this instruction is always followed by the SUB instruction; therefore, we can simply place a copy of the SUB instruction in the delay slot after the JMP. The BEQ presents a difficulty. We can't leave the code as is, because the ADD instruction would then be executed one too many times. Therefore, a NOP instruction is needed. Show the resulting code.

15.7 A RISC machine's compiler may do both a mapping of symbolic registers to actual registers and a rearrangement of instructions for pipeline efficiency. An interesting question arises as to the order in which these two operations should be done. Consider the following program fragment:

```
        LD      SR1,A           ;load A into symbolic register 1
        LD      SR2,B           ;load B into symbolic register 2
        ADD     SR3,SR1,SR2     ;add contents of SR1 and SR2 and store in SR3
        LD      SR4,C
        LD      SR5,D
        ADD     SR6,SR4,SR5
```

  a. First do the register mapping and then any possible instruction reordering. How many machine registers are used? Has there been any pipeline improvement?
  b. Starting with the original program, now do instruction reordering and then any possible mapping. How many machine registers are used? Has there been any pipeline improvement?

15.8 Add entries for the following processors to Table 15.7:
  a. Pentium II
  b. ARM

15.9 In many cases, common machine instructions that are not listed as part of the MIPS instruction set can be synthesized with a single MIPS instruction. Show this for the following:
  a. Register-to-register move
  b. Increment, decrement
  c. Complement
  d. Negate
  e. Clear

15.10 A SPARC implementation has K register windows. What is the number N of physical registers?

15.11 SPARC is lacking a number of instructions commonly found on CISC machines. Some of these are easily simulated using either register R0, which is always set to 0, or a constant operand. These simulated instructions are called pseudoinstructions and are recognized by the SPARC assembler. Show how to simulate the following pseudoinstructions, each with a single SPARC instruction. In all of these, src and dst refer to registers. (*Hint:* A store to R0 has no effect.)
  a. MOV src, dst   **d.** NOT dst   **g.** DEC dst
  b. COMPARE src1, src2   **e.** NEG dst   **h.** CLR dst
  c. TEST src1   **f.** INC dst   **i.** NOP

15.12 Consider the following code fragment:

> **if** K > 10
>> L := K + 1
>
> **else**
>> L := K − 1;

A straightforward translation of this statement into SPARC assembler could take the following form:

```
         sethi   %hi(K), %r8              ;load high-order 22 bits of address of location
                                          ;K into register r8
         ld      [%r8 + %lo(K)], %r8      ;load contents of location K into r8
         cmp     %r8, 10                  ;compare contents of r8 with 10
         ble     L1                       ;branch if (r8) ≤ 10
         nop
         sethi   %hi(K), %r9
         ld      [%r9 + %lo(K)], %r9      ;load contents of location K into r9
         inc     %r9                      ;add 1 to (r9)
         sethi   %hi(L), %r10
         st      %r9, [%r10 + %lo(L)]     ;store (r9) into location L
         b       L2
         nop
L1:      sethi   %hi(K), %r11
         ld      [%r11 + %lo(K)], %r12    ;load contents of location K into r12
         dec     %r12                     ;subtract 1 from (r12)
         sethi   %hi(L), %r13
         st      %r12, [%r13 + %lo(L)]    ;store (r12) into location L
L2:
```

The code contains a nop after each branch instruction to permit delayed branch operation.

a. Standard compiler optimizations that have nothing to do with RISC machines are generally effective in being able to perform two transformations on the foregoing code. Notice that two of the loads are unnecessary and that the two stores can be merged if the store is moved to a different place in the code. Show the program after making these two changes.

b. It is now possible to perform some optimizations peculiar to SPARC. The nop after the ble can be replaced by moving another instruction into that delay slot and setting the annul bit on the ble instruction (expressed as ble,a L1). Show the program after this change.

c. There are now two unnecessary instructions. Remove these and show the resulting program.

INSTRUCTION-LEVEL PARALLELISM AND SUPERSCALAR PROCESSORS

LEARNING OBJECTIVES

After studying this chapter, you should be able to:

◆ Explain the difference between superscalar and superpipelined approaches.
◆ Define instruction-level parallelism.
◆ Discuss dependencies and resource conflicts as limitations to instruction-level parallelism
◆ Present an overview of the design issues involved in instruction-level parallelism.
◆ Compare and contrast techniques of improving pipeline performance in RISC machines and superscalar machines.

A superscalar implementation of a processor architecture is one in which common instructions—integer and floating-point arithmetic, loads, stores, and conditional branches—can be initiated simultaneously and executed independently. Such implementations raise a number of complex design issues related to the instruction pipeline.

Superscalar design arrived on the scene hard on the heels of RISC architecture. Although the simplified instruction set architecture of a RISC machine lends itself readily to superscalar techniques, the superscalar approach can be used on either a RISC or CISC architecture.

Whereas the gestation period for the arrival of commercial RISC machines from the beginning of true RISC research with the IBM 801 and the Berkeley RISC I was seven or eight years, the first superscalar machines became commercially available within just a year or two of the coining of the term **superscalar**. The superscalar approach has now become the standard method for implementing high-performance microprocessors.

In this chapter, we begin with an overview of the superscalar approach, contrasting it with superpipelining. Next, we present the key design issues associated with superscalar implementation. Then we look at several important examples of superscalar architecture.

16.1 OVERVIEW

The term *superscalar,* first coined in 1987 [AGER87], refers to a machine that is designed to improve the performance of the execution of scalar instructions. In most applications, the bulk of the operations are on scalar quantities. Accordingly, the superscalar approach represents the next step in the evolution of high-performance general-purpose processors.

The essence of the superscalar approach is the ability to execute instructions independently and concurrently in different pipelines. The concept can be further exploited by allowing instructions to be executed in an order different from the program order. Figure 16.1 compares, in general terms, the scalar and superscalar approaches. In a traditional scalar organization, there is a single pipelined functional unit for integer operations and one for floating-point operations. Parallelism is achieved by enabling multiple instructions to be at different stages of the pipeline at

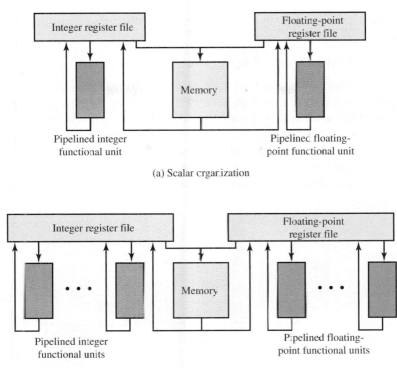

(a) Scalar organization

(b) Superscalar organization

Figure 16.1   Superscalar Organization Compared to Ordinary Scalar Organization

one time. In the superscalar organization, there are multiple functional units, each of which is implemented as a pipeline. Each individual functional unit provides a degree of parallelism by virtue of its pipelined structure. The use of multiple functional units enables the processor to execute streams of instructions in parallel, one stream for each pipeline. It is the responsibility of the hardware, in conjunction with the compiler, to assure that the parallel execution does not violate the intent of the program.

Many researchers have investigated superscalar-like processors, and their research indicates that some degree of performance improvement is possible. Table 16.1 presents the reported performance advantages. The differences in the

Table 16.1   Reported Speedups
of Superscalar-Like Machines

Reference	Speedup
[TJAD70]	1.8
[KUCK77]	8
[WEIS84]	1.58
[ACOS86]	2.7
[SOHI90]	1.8
[SMIT89]	2.3
[JOUP89b]	2.2
[LEE91]	7

results arise from differences both in the hardware of the simulated machine and in the applications being simulated.

Superscalar versus Superpipelined

An alternative approach to achieving greater performance is referred to as super-pipelining, a term first coined in 1988 [JOUP88]. Superpipelining exploits the fact that many pipeline stages perform tasks that require less than half a clock cycle. Thus, a doubled internal clock speed allows the performance of two tasks in one external clock cycle. We have seen one example of this approach with the MIPS R4000.

Figure 16.2 compares the two approaches. The upper part of the diagram illustrates an ordinary pipeline, used as a base for comparison. The base pipeline issues

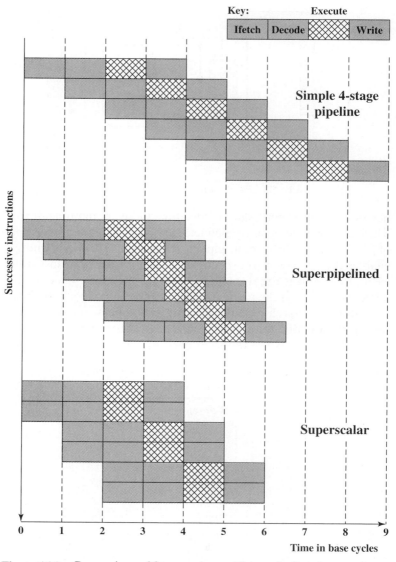

Figure 16.2   Comparison of Superscalar and Superpipeline Approaches

one instruction per clock cycle and can perform one pipeline stage per clock cycle. The pipeline has four stages: instruction fetch, operation decode, operation execution, and result write back. The execution stage is crosshatched for clarity. Note that although several instructions are executing concurrently, only one instruction is in its execution stage at any one time.

The next part of the diagram shows a **superpipelined** implementation that is capable of performing two pipeline stages per clock cycle. An alternative way of looking at this is that the functions performed in each stage can be split into two nonoverlapping parts and each can execute in half a clock cycle. A superpipeline implementation that behaves in this fashion is said to be of degree 2. Finally, the lowest part of the diagram shows a superscalar implementation capable of executing two instances of each stage in parallel. Higher-degree superpipeline and superscalar implementations are of course possible.

Both the superpipeline and the superscalar implementations depicted in Figure 16.2 have the same number of instructions executing at the same time in the steady state. The superpipelined processor falls behind the superscalar processor at the start of the program and at each branch target.

Constraints

The superscalar approach depends on the ability to execute multiple instructions in parallel. The term **instruction-level parallelism** refers to the degree to which, on average, the instructions of a program can be executed in parallel. A combination of compiler-based optimization and hardware techniques can be used to maximize instruction-level parallelism. Before examining the design techniques used in superscalar machines to increase instruction-level parallelism, we need to look at the fundamental limitations to parallelism with which the system must cope. [JOHN91] lists five limitations:

- True data dependency
- Procedural dependency
- Resource conflicts
- Output dependency
- Antidependency

We examine the first three of these limitations in the remainder of this section. A discussion of the last two must await some of the developments in the next section.

TRUE DATA DEPENDENCY Consider the following sequence:[1]

```
ADD EAX, ECX ;load register EAX with the con-
             ;tents of ECX plus the contents
             ;of EAX
MOV EBX, EAX ;load EBX with the contents of EAX
```

The second instruction can be fetched and decoded but cannot execute until the first instruction executes. The reason is that the second instruction needs data

---

[1]For the Intel x86 assembly language, a semicolon starts a comment field.

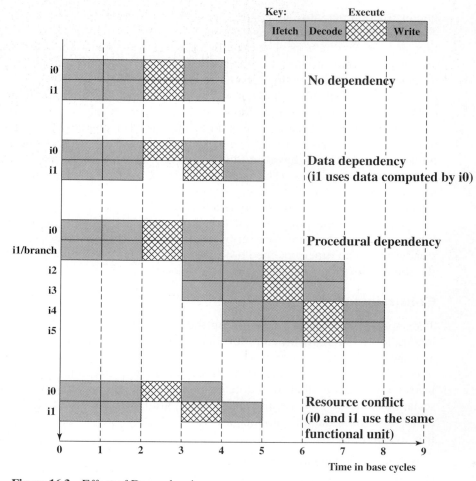

Figure 16.3 Effect of Dependencies

produced by the first instruction. This situation is referred to as a **true data dependency** (also called **flow dependency** or **read after write [RAW] dependency**).

Figure 16.3 illustrates this **dependency** in a superscalar machine of degree 2. With no dependency, two instructions can be fetched and executed in parallel. If there is a data dependency between the first and second instructions, then the second instruction is delayed as many clock cycles as required to remove the dependency. In general, any instruction must be delayed until all of its input values have been produced.

In a simple pipeline, such as illustrated in the upper part of Figure 16.2, the aforementioned sequence of instructions would cause no delay. However, consider the following, in which one of the loads is from memory rather than from a register:

```
MOV EAX, eff ;load register EAX with the con-
                tents of effective memory add-
                ress eff
MOV EBX, EAX ;load EBX with the contents of EAX
```

A typical RISC processor takes two or more cycles to perform a load from memory when the load is a cache hit. It can take tens or even hundreds of cycles for a cache miss on all cache levels, because of the delay of an off-chip memory access. One way to compensate for this delay is for the compiler to reorder instructions so that one or more subsequent instructions that do not depend on the memory load can begin flowing through the pipeline. This scheme is less effective in the case of a superscalar pipeline: The independent instructions executed during the load are likely to be executed on the first cycle of the load, leaving the processor with nothing to do until the load completes.

PROCEDURAL DEPENDENCIES As was discussed in Chapter 14, the presence of branches in an instruction sequence complicates the pipeline operation. The instructions following a branch (taken or not taken) have a **procedural dependency** on the branch and cannot be executed until the branch is executed. Figure 16.3 illustrates the effect of a branch on a superscalar pipeline of degree 2.

As we have seen, this type of procedural dependency also affects a scalar pipeline. The consequence for a superscalar pipeline is more severe, because a greater magnitude of opportunity is lost with each delay.

If variable-length instructions are used, then another sort of procedural dependency arises. Because the length of any particular instruction is not known, it must be at least partially decoded before the following instruction can be fetched. This prevents the simultaneous fetching required in a superscalar pipeline. This is one of the reasons that superscalar techniques are more readily applicable to a RISC or RISC-like architecture, with its fixed instruction length.

RESOURCE CONFLICT A **resource conflict** is a competition of two or more instructions for the same resource at the same time. Examples of resources include memories, caches, buses, register-file ports, and functional units (e.g., ALU adder).

In terms of the pipeline, a resource conflict exhibits similar behavior to a data dependency (Figure 16.3). There are some differences, however. For one thing, resource conflicts can be overcome by duplication of resources, whereas a true data dependency cannot be eliminated. Also, when an operation takes a long time to complete, resource conflicts can be minimized by pipelining the appropriate functional unit.

16.2 DESIGN ISSUES

Instruction-Level Parallelism and Machine Parallelism

[JOUP89a] makes an important distinction between the two related concepts of instruction-level parallelism and machine parallelism. **Instruction-level parallelism** exists when instructions in a sequence are independent and thus can be executed in parallel by overlapping.

As an example of the concept of instruction-level parallelism, consider the following two code fragments [JOUP89b]:

```
Load R1  ←  R2        Add R3   ←  R3, "1"
Add R3   ←  R3, "1"   Add R4   ←  R3, R2
Add R4   ←  R4, R2    Store [R4]  ←  R0
```

The three instructions on the left are independent, and in theory all three could be executed in parallel. In contrast, the three instructions on the right cannot be executed in parallel because the second instruction uses the result of the first, and the third instruction uses the result of the second.

The degree of instruction-level parallelism is determined by the frequency of true data dependencies and procedural dependencies in the code. These factors, in turn, are dependent on the instruction set architecture and on the application. Instruction-level parallelism is also determined by what [JOUP89a] refers to as operation latency: the time until the result of an instruction is available for use as an operand in a subsequent instruction. The latency determines how much of a delay a data or procedural dependency will cause.

Machine parallelism is a measure of the ability of the processor to take advantage of instruction-level parallelism. Machine parallelism is determined by the number of instructions that can be fetched and executed at the same time (the number of parallel pipelines) and by the speed and sophistication of the mechanisms that the processor uses to find independent instructions.

Both instruction-level and machine parallelism are important factors in enhancing performance. A program may not have enough instruction-level parallelism to take full advantage of machine parallelism. The use of a fixed-length instruction set architecture, as in a RISC, enhances instruction-level parallelism. On the other hand, limited machine parallelism will limit performance no matter what the nature of the program.

Instruction Issue Policy

As was mentioned, machine parallelism is not simply a matter of having multiple instances of each pipeline stage. The processor must also be able to identify instruction-level parallelism and orchestrate the fetching, decoding, and execution of instructions in parallel. [JOHN91] uses the term **instruction issue** to refer to the process of initiating instruction execution in the processor's functional units and the term **instruction issue policy** to refer to the protocol used to issue instructions. In general, we can say that instruction issue occurs when instruction moves from the decode stage of the pipeline to the first execute stage of the pipeline.

In essence, the processor is trying to look ahead of the current point of execution to locate instructions that can be brought into the pipeline and executed. Three types of orderings are important in this regard:

- The order in which instructions are fetched
- The order in which instructions are executed
- The order in which instructions update the contents of register and memory locations

The more sophisticated the processor, the less it is bound by a strict relationship between these orderings. To optimize utilization of the various pipeline elements, the processor will need to alter one or more of these orderings with respect to the ordering to be found in a strict sequential execution. The one constraint on the processor is that the result must be correct. Thus, the processor must accommodate the various dependencies and conflicts discussed earlier.

In general terms, we can group superscalar instruction issue policies into the following categories:

- In-order issue with in-order completion
- In-order issue with **out-of-order** completion
- Out-of-order issue with out-of-order completion

IN-ORDER ISSUE WITH IN-ORDER COMPLETION The simplest instruction issue policy is to issue instructions in the exact order that would be achieved by sequential execution (**in-order issue**) and to write results in that same order (**in-order completion**). Not even scalar pipelines follow such a simple-minded policy. However, it is useful to consider this policy as a baseline for comparing more sophisticated approaches.

Figure 16.4a gives an example of this policy. We assume a superscalar pipeline capable of fetching and decoding two instructions at a time, having three separate functional units (e.g., two integer arithmetic and one floating-point arithmetic), and having two instances of the write-back pipeline stage. The example assumes the following constraints on a six-instruction code fragment:

- I1 requires two cycles to execute.
- I3 and I4 conflict for the same functional unit.
- I5 depends on the value produced by I4.
- I5 and I6 conflict for a functional unit.

Instructions are fetched two at a time and passed to the decode unit. Because instructions are fetched in pairs, the next two instructions must wait until the pair of decode pipeline stages has cleared. To guarantee in-order **completion**, when there is a conflict for a functional unit or when a functional unit requires more than one cycle to generate a result, the issuing of instructions temporarily stalls.

In this example, the elapsed time from decoding the first instruction to writing the last results is eight cycles.

IN-ORDER ISSUE WITH OUT-OF-ORDER COMPLETION Out-of-order completion is used in scalar RISC processors to improve the performance of instructions that require multiple cycles. Figure 16.4b illustrates its use on a superscalar processor. Instruction I2 is allowed to run to completion prior to I1. This allows I3 to be completed earlier, with the net result of a savings of one cycle.

With out-of-order completion, any number of instructions may be in the execution stage at any one time, up to the maximum degree of machine parallelism across all functional units. Instruction issuing is stalled by a resource conflict, a data dependency, or a procedural dependency.

In addition to the aforementioned limitations, a new dependency, which we referred to earlier as an **output dependency** (also called **write after write [WAW] dependency**), arises. The following code fragment illustrates this dependency (*op* represents any operation):

```
I1: R3  ←  R3 op R5
I2: R4  ←  R3 + 1
I3: R3  ←  R5 + 1
I4: R7  ←  R3 op R4
```

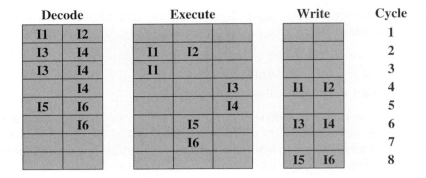

(a) In-order issue and in-order completion

(b) In-order issue and out-of-order completion

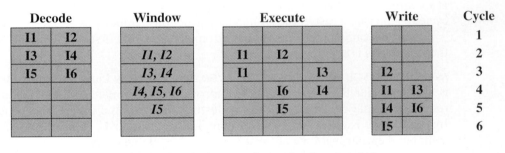

(c) Out-of-order issue and out-of-order completion

Figure 16.4 Superscalar Instruction Issue and Completion Policies

Instruction I2 cannot execute before instruction I1, because it needs the result in register R3 produced in I1; this is an example of a true data dependency, as described in Section 16.1. Similarly, I4 must wait for I3, because it uses a result produced by I3. What about the relationship between I1 and I3? There is no data dependency here, as we have defined it. However, if I3 executes to completion prior to I1, then the wrong value of the contents of R3 will be fetched for the execution of I4. Consequently, I3 must complete after I1 to produce the correct output values. To ensure this, the issuing of the third instruction must be stalled if its result might later be overwritten by an older instruction that takes longer to complete.

Out-of-order completion requires more complex instruction issue logic than in-order completion. In addition, it is more difficult to deal with instruction interrupts and exceptions. When an interrupt occurs, instruction execution at the current point is suspended, to be resumed later. The processor must assure that the resumption takes into account that, at the time of interruption, instructions ahead of the instruction that caused the interrupt may already have completed.

OUT–OF–ORDER ISSUE WITH OUT–OF–ORDER COMPLETION With in-order issue, the processor will only decode instructions up to the point of a dependency or conflict. No additional instructions are decoded until the conflict is resolved. As a result, the processor cannot look ahead of the point of conflict to subsequent instructions that may be independent of those already in the pipeline and that may be usefully introduced into the pipeline.

To allow **out-of-order issue**, it is necessary to decouple the decode and execute stages of the pipeline. This is done with a buffer referred to as an **instruction window**. With this organization, after a processor has finished decoding an instruction, it is placed in the instruction window. As long as this buffer is not full, the processor can continue to fetch and decode new instructions. When a functional unit becomes available in the execute stage, an instruction from the instruction window may be issued to the execute stage. Any instruction may be issued, provided that (1) it needs the particular functional unit that is available, and (2) no conflicts or dependencies block this instruction. Figure 16.5 suggests this organization.

The result of this organization is that the processor has a lookahead capability, allowing it to identify independent instructions that can be brought into the execute stage. Instructions are issued from the instruction window with little regard for their original program order. As before, the only constraint is that the program execution behaves correctly.

Figures 16.4c illustrates this policy. During each of the first three cycles, two instructions are fetched into the decode stage. During each cycle, subject to the constraint of the buffer size, two instructions move from the decode stage to the instruction window. In this example, it is possible to issue instruction I6 ahead of I5 (recall that I5 depends on I4, but I6 does not). Thus, one cycle is saved in both the execute and write-back stages, and the end-to-end savings, compared with Figure 16.4b, is one cycle.

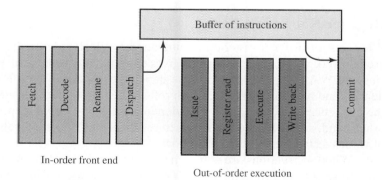

Figure 16.5   Organization for Out-of-Order Issue with Out-of-Order Completion

The instruction window is depicted in Figure 16.4c to illustrate its role. However, this window is not an additional pipeline stage. An instruction being in the window simply implies that the processor has sufficient information about that instruction to decide when it can be issued.

The out-of-order issue, out-of-order completion policy is subject to the same constraints described earlier. An instruction cannot be issued if it violates a dependency or conflict. The difference is that more instructions are available for issuing, reducing the probability that a pipeline stage will have to stall. In addition, a new dependency, which we referred to earlier as an **antidependency** (also called **write after read [WAR] dependency**), arises. The code fragment considered earlier illustrates this dependency:

```
I1:  R3  ←  R3 op R5
I2:  R4  ←  R3 + 1
I3:  R3  ←  R5 + 1
I4:  R7  ←  R3 op R4
```

Instruction I3 cannot complete execution before instruction I2 begins execution and has fetched its operands. This is so because I3 updates register R3, which is a source operand for I2. The term *antidependency* is used because the constraint is similar to that of a true data dependency, but reversed: Instead of the first instruction producing a value that the second instruction uses, the second instruction destroys a value that the first instruction uses.

Reorder Buffer Simulator
Tomasulo's Algorithm Simulator
Alternative Simulation of Tomasulo's Algorithm

One common technique that is used to support out-of-order completion is the reorder buffer. The reorder buffer is temporary storage for results completed out of order that are then committed to the register file in program order. A related concept is Tomasulo's algorithm. Appendix I examines these concepts.

Register Renaming

When out-of-order instruction issuing and/or out-of-order instruction completion are allowed, we have seen that this gives rise to the possibility of WAW dependencies and WAR dependencies. These dependencies differ from RAW data dependencies and resource conflicts, which reflect the flow of data through a program and the sequence of execution. WAW dependencies and WAR dependencies, on the other hand, arise because the values in registers may no longer reflect the sequence of values dictated by the program flow.

When instructions are issued in sequence and complete in sequence, it is possible to specify the contents of each register at each point in the execution. When out-of-order techniques are used, the values in registers cannot be fully known at each point in time just from a consideration of the sequence of instructions dictated by the program. In effect, values are in conflict for the use of registers, and the processor must resolve those conflicts by occasionally stalling a pipeline stage.

Antidependencies and output dependencies are both examples of storage conflicts. Multiple instructions are competing for the use of the same register locations, generating pipeline constraints that retard performance. The problem is made more acute when register optimization techniques are used (as discussed in Chapter 15), because these compiler techniques attempt to maximize the use of registers, hence maximizing the number of storage conflicts.

One method for coping with these types of storage conflicts is based on a traditional resource-conflict solution: duplication of resources. In this context, the technique is referred to as **register renaming**. In essence, registers are allocated dynamically by the processor hardware, and they are associated with the values needed by instructions at various points in time. When a new register value is created (i.e., when an instruction executes that has a register as a destination operand), a new register is allocated for that value. Subsequent instructions that access that value as a source operand in that register must go through a renaming process: the register references in those instructions must be revised to refer to the register containing the needed value. Thus, the same original register reference in several different instructions may refer to different actual registers, if different values are intended.

Let us consider how register renaming could be used on the code fragment we have been examining:

$$
\begin{aligned}
\text{I1:} \quad & R3_b \leftarrow R3_a \text{ op } R5_a \\
\text{I2:} \quad & R4_b \leftarrow R3_b + 1 \\
\text{I3:} \quad & R3_c \leftarrow R5_a + 1 \\
\text{I4:} \quad & R7_b \leftarrow R3_c \text{ op } R4_b
\end{aligned}
$$

The register reference without the subscript refers to the logical register reference found in the instruction. The register reference with the subscript refers to a hardware register allocated to hold a new value. When a new allocation is made for a particular logical register, subsequent instruction references to that logical register as a source operand are made to refer to the most recently allocated hardware register (recent in terms of the program sequence of instructions).

In this example, the creation of register $R3_c$ in instruction I3 avoids the WAR dependency on the second instruction and the WAW on the first instruction, and it does not interfere with the correct value being accessed by I4. The result is that I3 can be issued immediately; without renaming, I3 cannot be issued until the first instruction is complete and the second instruction is issued.

Scoreboarding Simulator

An alternative to register renaming is a scoreboarding. In essence, scoreboarding is a bookkeeping technique that allows instructions to execute whenever they are not dependent on previous instructions and no structural hazards are present. See Appendix I for a discussion.

Machine Parallelism

In the preceding discussion, we have looked at three hardware techniques that can be used in a superscalar processor to enhance performance: duplication of resources, out-of-order issue, and renaming. One study that illuminates the relationship among these techniques was reported in [SMIT89]. The study made use of a simulation that modeled a machine with the characteristics of the MIPS R2000, augmented with various superscalar features. A number of different program sequences were simulated.

Figure 16.6 shows the results. In each of the graphs, the vertical axis corresponds to the mean speedup of the superscalar machine over the scalar machine. The horizontal axis shows the results for four alternative processor organizations. The base machine does not duplicate any of the functional units, but it can issue instructions out of order. The second configuration duplicates the load/store functional unit that accesses a data cache. The third configuration duplicates the ALU, and the fourth configuration duplicates both load/store and ALU. In each graph, results are shown for instruction window sizes of 8, 16, and 32 instructions, which dictates the amount of lookahead the processor can do. The difference between the two graphs is that, in the second, register renaming is allowed. This is equivalent to saying that the first graph reflects a machine that is limited by all dependencies, whereas the second graph corresponds to a machine that is limited only by true dependencies.

The two graphs, combined, yield some important conclusions. The first is that it is probably not worthwhile to add functional units without register renaming.

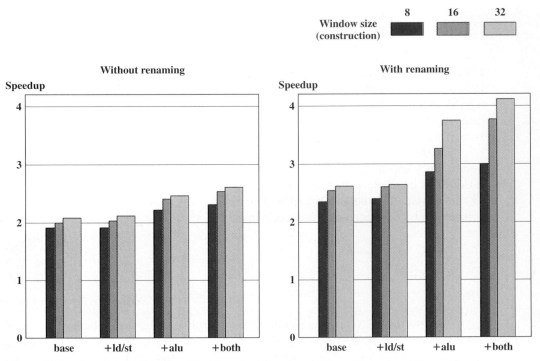

Figure 16.6   Speedups of Various Machine Organizations without Procedural Dependencies

There is some slight improvement in performance, but at the cost of increased hardware complexity. With register renaming, which eliminates antidependencies and output dependencies, noticeable gains are achieved by adding more functional units. Note, however, that there is a significant difference in the amount of gain achievable between using an instruction window of 8 versus a larger instruction window. This indicates that if the instruction window is too small, data dependencies will prevent effective utilization of the extra functional units; the processor must be able to look quite far ahead to find independent instructions to utilize the hardware more fully.

Pipeline with Static vs. Dynamic Scheduling—Simulator

Branch Prediction

Any high-performance pipelined machine must address the issue of dealing with branches. For example, the Intel 80486 addressed the problem by fetching both the next sequential instruction after a branch and speculatively fetching the branch target instruction. However, because there are two pipeline stages between prefetch and execution, this strategy incurs a two-cycle delay when the branch gets taken.

With the advent of RISC machines, the delayed branch strategy was explored. This allows the processor to calculate the result of conditional branch instructions before any unusable instructions have been prefetched. With this method, the processor always executes the single instruction that immediately follows the branch. This keeps the pipeline full while the processor fetches a new instruction stream.

With the development of superscalar machines, the delayed branch strategy has less appeal. The reason is that multiple instructions need to execute in the delay slot, raising several problems relating to instruction dependencies. Thus, superscalar machines have returned to pre-RISC techniques of **branch prediction**. Some, like the PowerPC 601, use a simple static branch prediction technique. More sophisticated processors, such as the PowerPC 620 and the Pentium 4, use dynamic branch prediction based on branch history analysis.

Superscalar Execution

We are now in a position to provide an overview of superscalar execution of programs; this is illustrated in Figure 16.7. The program to be executed consists of a linear sequence of instructions. This is the static program as written by the programmer or generated by the compiler. The instruction fetch stage, which includes branch prediction, is used to form a dynamic stream of instructions. This stream is examined for dependencies, and the processor may remove artificial dependencies. The processor then dispatches the instructions into a window of execution. In this window, instructions no longer form a sequential stream but are structured according to their true data dependencies. The processor executes each instruction in an order determined by the true data dependencies and hardware resource availability. Finally, instructions are conceptually put back into sequential order and their results are recorded.

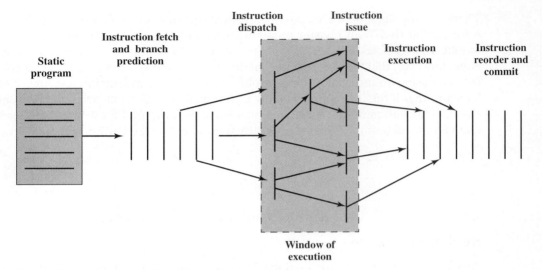

Figure 16.7   Conceptual Depiction of Superscalar Processing

The final step mentioned in the preceding paragraph is referred to as **committing**, or **retiring**, the instruction. This step is needed for the following reason. Because of the use of parallel, multiple pipelines, instructions may complete in an order different from that shown in the static program. Further, the use of branch prediction and speculative execution means that some instructions may complete execution and then must be abandoned because the branch they represent is not taken. Therefore, permanent storage and program-visible registers cannot be updated immediately when instructions complete execution. Results must be held in some sort of temporary storage that is usable by dependent instructions and then made permanent when it is determined that the sequential model would have executed the instruction.

Superscalar Implementation

Based on our discussion so far, we can make some general comments about the processor hardware required for the superscalar approach. [SMIT95] lists the following key elements:

- Instruction fetch strategies that simultaneously fetch multiple instructions, often by predicting the outcomes of, and fetching beyond, conditional branch instructions. These functions require the use of multiple pipeline fetch and decode stages, and branch prediction logic.
- Logic for determining true dependencies involving register values, and mechanisms for communicating these values to where they are needed during execution.
- Mechanisms for initiating, or issuing, multiple instructions in parallel.
- Resources for parallel execution of multiple instructions, including multiple pipelined functional units and memory hierarchies capable of simultaneously servicing multiple memory references.
- Mechanisms for committing the process state in correct order.

16.3 PENTIUM 4

Although the concept of superscalar design is generally associated with the RISC architecture, the same superscalar principles can be applied to a CISC machine. Perhaps the most notable example of this is the Pentium. The evolution of superscalar concepts in the Intel line is interesting to note. The 386 is a traditional CISC non-pipelined machine. The 486 introduced the first pipelined x86 processor, reducing the average latency of integer operations from between two and four cycles to one cycle, but still limited to executing a single instruction each cycle, with no superscalar elements. The original Pentium had a modest superscalar component, consisting of the use of two separate integer execution units. The Pentium Pro introduced a full-blown superscalar design with out-of-order execution. Subsequent x86 models have refined and enhanced the superscalar design.

A general block diagram of the Pentium 4 was shown in Figure 4.18. Figure 16.8 depicts the same structure in a way more suitable for the pipeline discussion in this section. The operation of the Pentium 4 can be summarized as follows:

1. The processor fetches instructions from memory in the order of the static program.

2. Each instruction is translated into one or more fixed-length RISC instructions, known as **micro-operations**, or **micro-ops**.

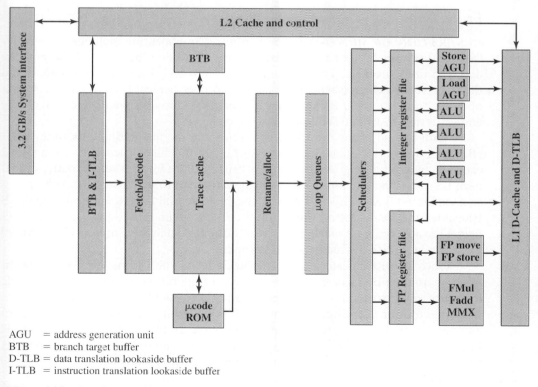

AGU   = address generation unit
BTB   = branch target buffer
D-TLB   = data translation lookaside buffer
I-TLB   = instruction translation lookaside buffer

Figure 16.8   Pentium 4 Block Diagram

1	2	3	4	5	6	7	8	9	10	11	12	13	14	15	16	17	18	19	20
TC Nxt IP		TC Fetch		Drive	Alloc	Rename		Que	Sch	Sch	Sch	Disp	Disp	RF	RF	Ex	Flgs	Br Ck	Drive

TC Next IP = trace cache next instruction pointer   Rename = register renaming   RF = register file
TC Fetch = trace cache fetch   Que = micro-op queuing   Ex = execute
Alloc = allocate   Sch = micro-op scheduling   Flgs = flags
    Disp = Dispatch   Br Ck = branch check

Figure 16.9   Pentium 4 Pipeline

3. The processor executes the micro-ops on a superscalar pipeline organization, so that the micro-ops may be executed out of order.

4. The processor commits the results of each micro-op execution to the processor's register set in the order of the original program flow.

In effect, the Pentium 4 architecture implements a CISC instruction set architecture on a RISC microarchitecture. The inner RISC micro-ops pass through a pipeline with at least 20 stages (Figure 16.9); in some cases, the micro-op requires multiple execution stages, resulting in an even longer pipeline. This contrasts with the five-stage pipeline (Figure 14.21) used on the earlier Intel x86 processors and on the Pentium.

We now trace the operation of the Pentium 4 pipeline, using Figure 16.10 to illustrate its operation.

Front End

GENERATION OF MICRO-OPS The Pentium 4 organization includes an in-order front end (Figure 16.10a) that can be considered outside the scope of the pipeline depicted in Figure 16.9. This front end feeds into an L1 instruction cache, called the trace cache, which is where the pipeline proper begins. Usually, the processor operates from the trace cache; when a trace cache miss occurs, the in-order front end feeds new instructions into the trace cache.

With the aid of the branch target buffer and the instruction lookaside buffer (BTB & I-TLB), the fetch/decode unit fetches x86 machine instructions from the L2 cache 64 bytes at a time. As a default, instructions are fetched sequentially, so that each L2 cache line fetch includes the next instruction to be fetched. Branch prediction via the BTB & I-TLB unit may alter this sequential fetch operation. The ITLB translates the linear instruction pointer address given it into physical addresses needed to access the L2 cache. Static branch prediction in the front-end BTB is used to determine which instructions to fetch next.

Once instructions are fetched, the fetch/decode unit scans the bytes to determine instruction boundaries; this is a necessary operation because of the variable length of x86 instructions. The decoder translates each machine instruction into from one to four micro-ops, each of which is a 118-bit RISC instruction. Note for comparison that most pure RISC machines have an instruction length of just 32 bits. The longer micro-op length is required to accommodate the more complex x86 instructions. Nevertheless, the micro-ops are easier to manage than the original instructions from which they derive.

The generated micro-ops are stored in the trace cache.

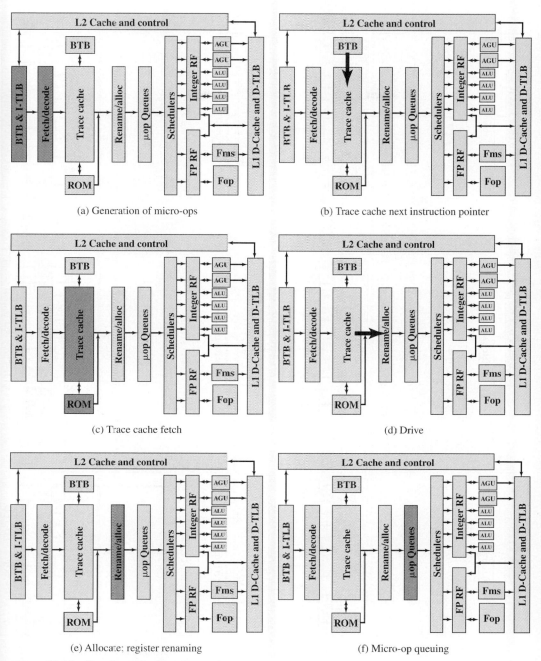

(a) Generation of micro-ops

(b) Trace cache next instruction pointer

(c) Trace cache fetch

(d) Drive

(e) Allocate; register renaming

(f) Micro-op queuing

Figure 16.10 Pentium Pipeline Operation

TRACE CACHE NEXT INSTRUCTION POINTER The first two pipeline stages (Figure 16.10b) deal with the selection of instructions in the trace cache and involve a separate branch prediction mechanism from that described in the previous section. The Pentium 4 uses a dynamic branch prediction strategy based on the

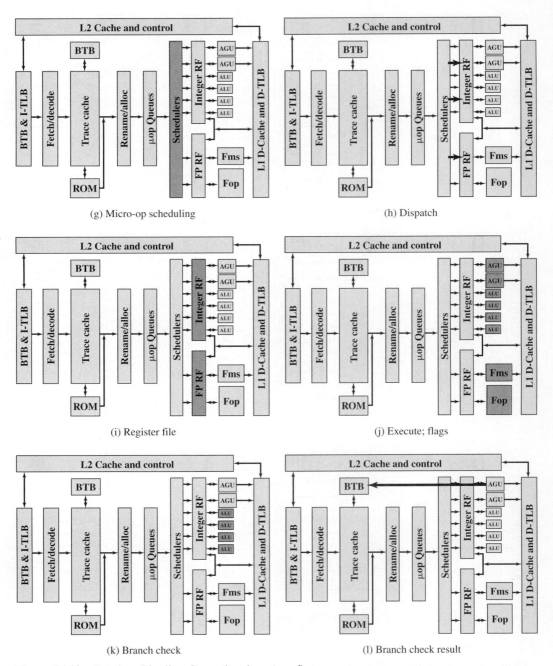

(g) Micro-op scheduling

(h) Dispatch

(i) Register file

(j) Execute; flags

(k) Branch check

(l) Branch check result

Figure 16.10 Pentium Pipeline Operation (*continued*)

history of recent executions of branch instructions. A branch target buffer (BTB) is maintained that caches information about recently encountered branch instructions. Whenever a branch instruction is encountered in the instruction stream, the BTB is checked. If an entry already exists in the BTB, then the instruction unit is guided by the history information for that entry in determining whether to predict that the branch is taken. If a branch is predicted, then the branch destination address associated with this entry is used for prefetching the branch target instruction.

Once the instruction is executed, the history portion of the appropriate entry is updated to reflect the result of the branch instruction. If this instruction is not represented in the BTB, then the address of this instruction is loaded into an entry in the BTB; if necessary, an older entry is deleted.

The description of the preceding two paragraphs fits, in general terms, the branch prediction strategy used on the original Pentium model, as well as the later Pentium models, including Pentium 4. However, in the case of the Pentium, a relatively simple 2-bit history scheme is used. The later Pentium models have much longer pipelines (20 stages for the Pentium 4 compared with 5 stages for the Pentium) and therefore the penalty for misprediction is greater. Accordingly, the later Pentium models use a more elaborate branch prediction scheme with more history bits to reduce the misprediction rate.

The Pentium 4 BTB is organized as a four-way set-associative cache with 512 lines. Each entry uses the address of the branch as a tag. The entry also includes the branch destination address for the last time this branch was taken and a 4-bit history field. Thus use of four history bits contrasts with the 2 bits used in the original Pentium and used in most superscalar processors. With 4 bits, the Pentium 4 mechanism can take into account a longer history in predicting branches. The algorithm that is used is referred to as Yeh's algorithm [YEH91]. The developers of this algorithm have demonstrated that it provides a significant reduction in misprediction compared to algorithms that use only 2 bits of history [EVER98].

Conditional branches that do not have a history in the BTB are predicted using a static prediction algorithm, according to the following rules:

- For branch addresses that are not IP relative, predict taken if the branch is a return and not taken otherwise.
- For IP-relative backward conditional branches, predict taken. This rule reflects the typical behavior of loops.
- For IP-relative forward conditional branches, predict not taken.

TRACE CACHE FETCH The trace cache (Figure 16.10c) takes the already-decoded micro-ops from the instruction decoder and assembles them in to program-ordered sequences of micro-ops called traces. Micro-ops are fetched sequentially from the trace cache, subject to the branch prediction logic.

A few instructions require more than four micro-ops. These instructions are transferred to microcode ROM, which contains the series of micro-ops (five or more) associated with a complex machine instruction. For example, a string instruction may translate into a very large (even hundreds), repetitive sequence of micro-ops. Thus, the microcode ROM is a microprogrammed control unit in the sense discussed in Part Four. After the microcode ROM finishes sequencing micro-ops for the current Pentium instruction, fetching resumes from the trace cache.

DRIVE The fifth stage (Figure 16.10d) of the Pentium 4 pipeline delivers decoded instructions from the trace cache to the rename/allocator module.

Out-of-Order Execution Logic

This part of the processor reorders micro-ops to allow them to execute as quickly as their input operands are ready.

ALLOCATE The allocate stage (Figure 16.10e) allocates resources required for execution. It performs the following functions:

- If a needed resource, such as a register, is unavailable for one of the three micro-ops arriving at the allocator during a clock cycle, the allocator stalls the pipeline.
- The allocator allocates a reorder buffer (ROB) entry, which tracks the completion status of one of the 126 micro-ops that could be in process at any time.[2]
- The allocator allocates one of the 128 integer or floating-point register entries for the result data value of the micro-op, and possibly a load or store buffer used to track one of the 48 loads or 24 stores in the machine pipeline.
- The allocator allocates an entry in one of the two micro-op queues in front of the instruction schedulers.

The ROB is a circular buffer that can hold up to 126 micro-ops and also contains the 128 hardware registers. Each buffer entry consists of the following fields:

- **State:** Indicates whether this micro-op is scheduled for execution, has been dispatched for execution, or has completed execution and is ready for retirement.
- **Memory Address:** The address of the Pentium instruction that generated the micro-op.
- **Micro-op:** The actual operation.
- **Alias Register:** If the micro-op references one of the 16 architectural registers, this entry redirects that reference to one of the 128 hardware registers.

Micro-ops enter the ROB in order. Micro-ops are then dispatched from the ROB to the Dispatch/Execute unit out of order. The criterion for dispatch is that the appropriate execution unit and all necessary data items required for this micro-op are available. Finally, micro-ops are retired from the ROB in order. To accomplish in-order retirement, micro-ops are retired oldest first after each micro-op has been designated as ready for retirement.

REGISTER RENAMING The rename stage (Figure 16.10e) remaps references to the 16 architectural registers (8 floating-point registers, plus EAX, EBX, ECX, EDX, ESI, EDI, EBP, and ESP) into a set of 128 physical registers. The stage removes false dependencies caused by a limited number of architectural registers while preserving the true data dependencies (reads after writes).

MICRO–OP QUEUING After resource allocation and register renaming, micro-ops are placed in one of two micro-op queues (Figure 16.10f), where they are held until there is room in the schedulers. One of the two queues is for memory operations

---

[2]See Appendix I for a discussion of reorder buffers.

(loads and stores) and the other for micro-ops that do not involve memory references. Each queue obeys a FIFO (first-in-first-out) discipline, but no order is maintained between queues. That is, a micro-op may be read out of one queue out of order with respect to micro-ops in the other queue. This provides greater flexibility to the schedulers.

MICRO–OP SCHEDULING AND DISPATCHING The schedulers (Figure 16.10g) are responsible for retrieving micro-ops from the micro-op queues and dispatching these for execution. Each scheduler looks for micro-ops in whose status indicates that the micro-op has all of its operands. If the execution unit needed by that micro-op is available, then the scheduler fetches the micro-op and dispatches it to the appropriate execution unit (Figure 16.10h). Up to six micro-ops can be dispatched in one cycle. If more than one micro-op is available for a given execution unit, then the scheduler dispatches them in sequence from the queue. This is a sort of FIFO discipline that favors in-order execution, but by this time the instruction stream has been so rearranged by dependencies and branches that it is substantially out of order.

Four ports attach the schedulers to the execution units. Port 0 is used for both integer and floating-point instructions, with the exception of simple integer operations and the handling of branch mispredictions, which are allocated to Port 1. In addition, MMX execution units are allocated between these two ports. The remaining ports are for memory loads and stores.

Integer and Floating–Point Execution Units

The integer and floating-point register files are the source for pending operations by the execution units (Figure 16.10i). The execution units retrieve values from the register files as well as from the L1 data cache (Figure 16.10j). A separate pipeline stage is used to compute flags (e.g., zero, negative); these are typically the input to a branch instruction.

A subsequent pipeline stage performs branch checking (Figure 16.10k). This function compares the actual branch result with the prediction. If a branch prediction turns out to have been wrong, then there are micro-operations in various stages of processing that must be removed from the pipeline. The proper branch destination is then provided to the Branch Predictor during a drive stage (Figure 16.10l), which restarts the whole pipeline from the new target address.

16.4 ARM CORTEX-A8

Recent implementations of the ARM architecture have seen the introduction of superscalar techniques in the instruction pipeline. In this section, we focus on the ARM Cortex-A8, which provides a good example of a RISC-based superscalar design.

The Cortex-A8 is in the ARM family of processors that ARM refers to as application processors. An ARM application processor is an embedded processor running complex operating systems for wireless, consumer and imaging applications.

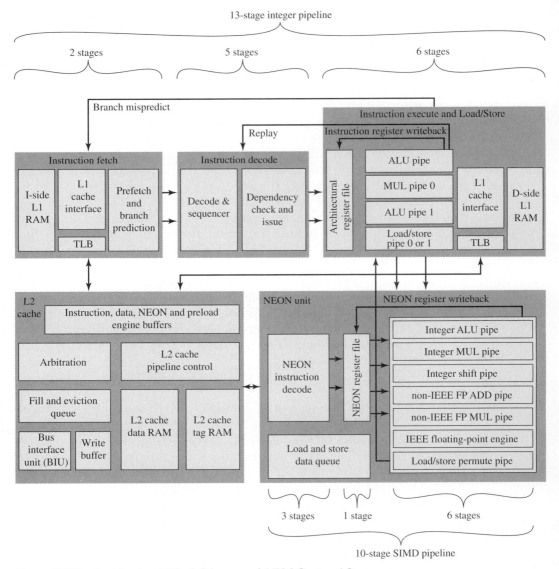

Figure 16.11 Architectural Block Diagram of ARM Cortex-A8

The Cortex-A8 targets a wide variety of mobile and consumer applications including mobile phones, set-top boxes, gaming consoles and automotive navigation/entertainment systems.

Figure 16.11 shows a logical view of the Cortex-A8 architecture, emphasizing the flow of instructions among functional units. The main instruction flow is through three functional units that implement a dual, in-order-issue, 13-stage pipeline. The Cortex designers decided to stay with in-order issue to keep additional power required to a minimum. Out-of-order issue and **retire** can require extensive amounts of logic consuming extra power.

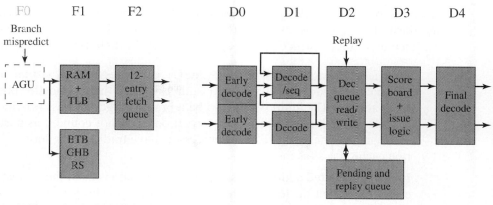

(a) Instruction fetch pipeline

(b) Instruction decode pipeline

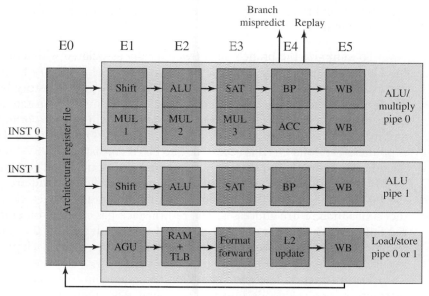

(c) Instruction execute and load/store pipeline

Figure 16.12   ARM Cortex-A8 Integer Pipeline

Figure 16.12 shows the details of the main Cortex-A8 pipeline. There is a separate unit for SIMD (single-instruction-multiple-data) unit that implements a 10-stage pipeline.

Instruction Fetch Unit

The instruction fetch unit predicts the instruction stream, fetches instructions from the L1 instruction cache, and places the fetched instructions into a buffer for consumption by the decode pipeline. The instruction fetch unit also includes the L1 instruction cache. Because there can be several unresolved branches in the pipeline, instruction fetches are speculative, meaning there is no guarantee that they are executed. A branch or exceptional instruction in the code stream can cause a pipeline flush, discarding the currently fetched instructions. The instruction fetch unit can fetch up to four instructions per cycle, and goes through the following stages:

F0 The address generation unit (AGU) generates a new virtual address. Normally, this address is the next address sequentially from the preceding fetch address. The address can also be a branch target address provided by a branch prediction for a previous instruction. F0 is not counted as part of the 13-stage pipeline, because ARM processors have traditionally defined instruction cache access as the first stage.

F1 The calculated address is used to fetch instructions from the L1 instruction cache. In parallel, the fetch address is used to access the branch prediction arrays to determine if the next fetch address should be based on a branch prediction.

F3 Instruction data are placed into the instruction queue. If an instruction results in branch prediction, the new target address is sent to the address generation unit.

To minimize the branch penalties typically associated with a deeper pipeline, the Cortex-A8 processor implements a two-level global history branch predictor, consisting of the branch target buffer (BTB) and the global history buffer (GHB). These data structures are accessed in parallel with instruction fetches. The BTB indicates whether or not the current fetch address will return a branch instruction and its branch target address. It contains 512 entries. On a hit in the BTB a branch is predicted and the GHB is accessed. The GHB consists of 4096 2-bit counters that encode the strength and direction information of branches. The GHB is indexed by 10-bit history of the direction of the last ten branches encountered and 4 bits of the PC. In addition to the dynamic branch predictor, a return stack is used to predict subroutine return addresses. The return stack has eight 32-bit entries that store the link register value in r14 and the ARM or Thumb state of the calling function. When a return-type instruction is predicted taken, the return stack provides the last pushed address and state.

The instruction fetch unit can fetch and queue up to 12 instructions. It issues instructions to the decode unit two at a time. The queue enables the instruction fetch unit to prefetch ahead of the rest of the integer pipeline and build up a backlog of instructions ready for decoding.

Instruction Decode Unit

The instruction decode unit decodes and sequences all ARM and Thumb instructions. It has a dual pipeline structure, called *pipe0* and *pipe1*, so that two instructions can progress through the unit at a time. When two instructions are issued from the instruction decode pipeline, pipe0 will always contain the older instruction in program order. This means that if the instruction in pipe0 cannot issue, then the instruction in pipe1 will not issue. All issued instructions progress in order down the execution pipeline with results written back into the register file at the end of the execution pipeline. This in-order instruction issue and retire prevents WAR hazards and keeps tracking of WAW hazards and recovery from flush conditions straightforward. Thus, the main concern of the instruction decode pipeline is the prevention of RAW hazards.

Each instruction goes through five stages of processing.

D0 Thumb instructions are decompressed into 32-bit ARM instructions. A preliminary decode function is performed.

D1 The instruction decode function is completed.

D2 This stage writes instructions into and read instructions from the pending/replay queue structure.

D3 This stage contains the instruction scheduling logic. A scoreboard predicts register availability using static scheduling techniques.[3] Hazard checking is also done at this stage.

D4 Performs the final decode for all the control signals required by the integer execute and load/store units.

In the first two stages, the instruction type, the source and destination operands, and resource requirements for the instruction are determined. A few less commonly used instructions are referred to as multicycle instructions. The D1 stage breaks these instructions down into multiple instruction opcodes that are sequenced individually through the execution pipeline.

The pending queue serves two purposes. First, it prevents a stall signal from D3 from rippling any further up the pipeline. Second, by buffering instructions, there should always be two instructions available for the dual pipeline. In the case where only one instruction is issued, the pending queue enables two instructions to proceed down the pipeline together, even if they were originally sent from the fetch unit in different cycles.

The replay operation is designed to deal with the effects of the memory system on instruction timing. Instructions are statically scheduled in the D3 stage based on a prediction of when the source operand will be available. Any stall from the memory system can result in the minimum of an 8-cycle delay. This 8-cycle delay minimum is balanced with the minimum number of possible cycles to receive data from the L2 cache in the case of an L1 load miss. Table 16.2 gives the most common cases that can result in an instruction replay because of a memory system stall.

To deal with these stalls, a recovery mechanism is used to flush all subsequent instructions in the execution pipeline and reissue (replay) them. To support replay, instructions are copied into the replay queue before they are issued and removed as they write back their results and retire. If a replay signal is issued instructions are retrieved from the replay queue and reenter the pipeline.

The decode unit issues two instructions in parallel to the execution unit, unless it encounters an issue restriction. Table 16.3 shows the most common restriction cases.

Integer Execute Unit

The instruction execute unit consists of two symmetric arithmetic logic unit (ALU) pipelines, an address generator for load and store instructions, and the multiply

---

[3]See Appendix I for a discussion of scoreboarding.

Table 16.2 Cortex-A8 Memory System Effects on Instruction Timings

Replay Event	Delay	Description
Load data miss	8 cycles	1. A load instruction misses in the L1 data cache. 2. A request is then made to the L2 data cache. 3. If a miss also occurs in the L2 data cache, then a second replay occurs. The number of stall cycles depends on the external system memory timing. The minimum time required to receive the critical word for an L2 cache miss is approximately 25 cycles, but can be much longer because of L3 memory latencies.
Data TLB miss	24 cycles	1. A table walk because of a miss in the L1 TLB causes a 24-cycle delay, assuming the translation table entries are found in the L2 cache. 2. If the translation table entries are not present in the L2 cache, the number of stall cycles depends on the external system memory timing.
Store buffer full	8 cycles plus latency to drain fill buffer	1. A store instruction miss does not result in any stalls unless the store buffer is full. 2. In the case of a full store buffer, the delay is at least eight cycles. The delay can be more if it takes longer to drain some entries from the store buffer.
Unaligned load or store request	8 cycles	1. If a load instruction address is unaligned and the full access is not contained within a 128-bit boundary, there is a 8-cycle penalty. 2. If a store instruction address is unaligned and the full access is not contained within a 64-bit boundary, there is a 8-cycle penalty.

pipeline. The execute pipelines also perform register write back. The instruction execute unit:

- Executes all integer ALU and multiply operations, including flag generation
- Generates the virtual addresses for loads and stores and the base write-back value, when required
- Supplies formatted data for stores and forwards data and flags
- Processes branches and other changes of instruction stream and evaluates instruction condition codes

For ALU instructions, either pipeline can be used, consisting of the following stages:

E0 Access register file. Up to six registers can be read from the register file for two instructions.

E1 The barrel shifter (see Figure 14.25) performs its function, if needed.

E2 The ALU unit (see Figure 14.25) performs its function.

E3 If needed, this stage completes saturation arithmetic used by some ARM data processing instructions.

Table 16.3   Cortex-A8 Dual-Issue Restrictions

Restriction Type	Description	Example	Cycle	Restriction

Load/store resource hazard	There is only one LS pipeline. Only one LS instruction can be issued per cycle. It can be in pipeline 0 or pipeline 1	LDR r5, [r6]
		STR r7, [r8]
		MOV r9, r10
			1
			2
			2
				Wait for LS unit
				Dual issue possible

Multiply resource hazard	There is only one multiply pipeline, and it is only available in pipeline 0.	ADD r1, r2, r3
		MUL r4, r5, r6
		MUL r7, r8, r9
			1
			2
			3
				Wait for pipeline 0
				Wait for multiply unit

Branch resource hazard	There can be only one branch per cycle. It can be in pipeline 0 or pipeline 1. A branch is any instruction that changes the PC.	BX r1 BEQ 0x1000 ADD r1, r2, r3	1 2 2	Wait for branch Dual issue possible

Data output hazard	Instructions with the same destination cannot be issued in the same cycle. This can happen with conditional code.	MOVEQ r1, r2
		MOVNE r1, r3
		LDR r5, [r6]
			1
			2
			2
				Wait because of output dependency
				Dual issue possible

Data source hazard	Instructions cannot be issued if their data is not available. See the scheduling tables for source requirements and stages results.	ADD r1, r2, r3
		ADD r4, r1, r6
		LDR r7, [r4]
			1
			2
			4
				Wait for r1
				Wait two cycles for r4

Multi-cycle instructions	Multi-cycle instructions must issue in pipeline 0 and can only dual issue in their last iteration.	MOV r1, r2
		LDM r3, {r4-r7}
		LDM (cycle 2)
		LDM (cycle 3)
		
		ADD r8, r9, r10
			1
			2
			3
			4
			
			4
				Wait for pipeline 0, transfer r4
				Transfer r5, r6
				Transfer r7
				Dual issue possible on last transfer

E4 Any change in control flow, including branch misprediction, exceptions, and memory system replays are prioritized and processed.

E5 Results of ARM instructions are written back into the register file.

Instructions that invoke the multiply unit (see Figure 14.25) are routed to pipe0; the multiply operation is performed in stages E1 through E3, and the multiply accumulate operation in stage E4.

The load/store pipeline runs parallel to the integer pipeline. The stages are as follows:

E1 The memory address is generated from the base and index register.

E2 The address is applied to the cache arrays.

E3 In the case of a load, data are returned and formatted for forwarding to the ALU or MUL unit. In the case of a store, the data are formatted and ready to be written into the cache.

E4 Performs updates to the L2 cache, if required.

E5 Results of ARM instructions are written back into the register file.

Table 16.4 Cortex-A8 Example Dual Issue Instruction Sequence for Integer Pipeline

Cycle	Program Counter	Instruction	Timing Description
1	0x00000ed0	BX r14	Dual issue pipeline 0
1	0x00000ee4	CMP r0,#0	Dual issue in pipeline 1
2	0x00000ee8	MOV r3,#3	Dual issue pipeline 0
2	0x00000eec	MOV r0,#0	Dual issue in pipeline 1
3	0x00000ef0	STREQ r3,[r1,#0]	Dual issue in pipeline 0, r3 not needed until E3
3	0x00000ef4	CMP r2,#4	Dual issue in pipeline 1
4	0x00000ef8	LDRLS pc,[pc,r2,LSL #2]	Single issue pipeline 0, +1 cycle for load to pc, no extra cycle for shift since LSL #2
5	0x00000f2c	MOV r0,#1	Dual issue with 2nd iteration of load in pipeline 1
6	0x00000f30	B {pc} + 8	#0xf38 dual issue pipeline 0
6	0x00000f38	STR r0,[r1,#0]	Dual issue pipeline 1
7	0x00000f3c:	LDR pc,[r13],#4	Single issue pipeline 0, +1 cycle for load to pc
8	0x0000017c	ADD r2,r4,#0xc	Dual issue with 2nd iteration of load in pipeline 1
9	0x00000180	LDR r0,[r6,#4]	Dual issue pipeline 0
9	0x00000184	MOV r1,#0xa	Dual issue pipeline 1
12	0x00000188	LDR r0,[r0,#0]	Single issue pipeline 0: r0 produced in E3, required in E1, so +2 cycle stall
13	0x0000018c	STR r0,[r4,#0]	Single issue pipeline 0 due to LS resource hazard, no extra delay for r0 since produced in E3 and consumed in E3
14	0x00000190	LDR r0,[r4,#0xc]	Single issue pipeline 0 due to LS resource hazard
15	0x00000194	LDMFD r13!,{r4-r6,r14}	Load multiple: loads r4 in 1st cycle, r5 and r6 in 2nd cycle, r14 in 3rd cycle, 3 cycles total
17	0x00000198	B {pc}+0xda8	#0xf40 dual issue in pipeline 1 with 3rd cycle of LDM
18	0x00000f40	ADD r0,r0,#2 ARM	Single issue in pipeline 0
19	0x00000f44	ADD r0,r1,r0 ARM	Single issue in pipeline 0, no dual issue due to hazard on r0 produced in E2 and required in E2

Table 16.4 shows a sample code segment and indicates how the processor might schedule it.

SIMD and Floating-Point Pipeline

All SIMD and floating-point instructions pass through the integer pipeline and are processed in a separate 10-stage pipeline (Figure 16.13). This unit, referred to as the

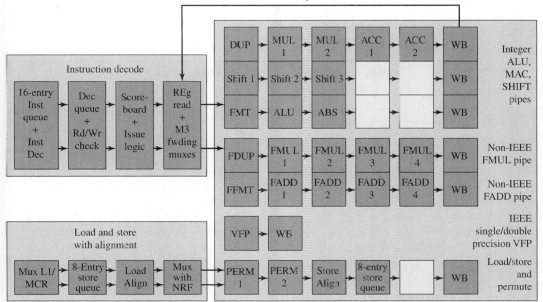

Figure 16.13 ARM Cortex-A8 NEON and Floating-Point Pipeline

NEON unit, handles packed SIMD instructions, and provides two types of floating-point support. If implemented, a vector floating-point (VFP) coprocessor performs floating-point operations in compliance with IEEE 754. If the coprocessor is not present, then separate multiply and add pipelines implement the floating-point operations

16.5 RECOMMENDED READING

Two good book-length treatments of superscalar design are [SHEN05] and [OMON99]. Worthwhile survey articles on the subject are [SMIT95] and [SIMA97]. [JOUP89a] examines instruction-level parallelism, looks at various techniques for maximizing parallelism, and compares superscalar and superpipelined approaches using simulation. Recent papers that provide good coverage of superscalar design issues include [SIMA04], [PATT01], and [MOSH01].

[POPE91] provides a detailed look at a proposed superscalar machine. It also provides an excellent tutorial on the design issues related to out-of-order instruction policies. Another look at a proposed system is found in [KUGA91]; this article raises and considers most of the important design issues for superscalar implementation. [LEE91] examines software techniques that can be used to enhance superscalar performance. [WALL91] is an interesting study of the extent to which instruction-level parallelism can be exploited in a superscalar processor.

Volume I of [INTE04a] provides general description of the Pentium 4 pipeline; more detail is provided in [INTE01a] and [INTE01b]. Another detailed treatment is [FOG08b].

[JOHN08] and [ARM08a] provide thorough coverage of the ARM Cortex-A8 pipeline. [RICH07] is a good overview.

ARM08a   ARM Limited. *Cortex-A8 Technical Reference Manual.* ARM DDI 0344E, 2008. www.arm.com

FOG08b   Fog, A. *The Microarchitecture of Intel and AMD CPUs.* Copenhagen University College of Engineering, 2008. http://www.agner.org/optimize/

HINT01   Hinton, G., et al. "The Microarchitecture of the Pentium 4 Processor." *Intel Technology Journal,* Q1 2001. http://developer.intel.com/technology/itj/

INTE01a   Intel Corp. *Intel Pentium 4 Processor Optimization Reference Manual.* Document 248966-04 2001. http://developer.intel.com/design/Pentium4/documentation.htm

INTE01b   Intel Corp. *Desktop Performance and Optimization for Intel Pentium 4 Processor.* Document 248966-04 2001. http://developer.intel.com/design/Pentium4/documentation.htm

INTE04a   Intel Corp. *IA-32 Intel Architecture Software Developer's Manual (4 volumes).* Document 253665 through 253668. 2004. http://developer.intel.com/design/Pentium4/documentation.htm

JOHN08   John, E., and Rubio, J. *Unique Chips and Systems.* Boca Raton, FL: CRC Press, 2008.

JOUP89a   Jouppi, N., and Wall, D. "Available Instruction-Level Parallelism for Superscalar and Superpipelined Machines." *Proceedings, Third International Conference on Architectural Support for Programming Languages and Operating Systems,* April 1989.

KUGA91   Kuga, M.; Murakami, K.; and Tomita, S. "DSNS (Dynamically-hazard resolved, Statically-code-scheduled, Nonuniform Superscalar): Yet Another Superscalar Processor Architecture." *Computer Architecture News,* June 1991.

LEE91   Lee, R.; Kwok, A.; and Briggs, F. "The Floating Point Performance of a Superscalar SPARC Processor." *Proceedings, Fourth International Conference on Architectural Support for Programming Languages and Operating Systems,* April 1991.

MOSH01   Moshovos, A., and Sohi, G. "Microarchitectural Innovations: Boosting Microprocessor Performance Beyond Semiconductor Technology Scaling." *Proceedings of the IEEE,* November 2001.

OMON99   Omondi, A. *The Microarchitecture of Pipelined and Superscalar Computers.* Boston: Kluwer, 1999.

PATT01   Patt, Y. "Requirements, Bottlenecks, and Good Fortune: Agents for Microprocessor Evolution." *Proceedings of the IEEE,* November 2001.

POPE91   Popescu, V., et al. "The Metaflow Architecture." *IEEE Micro,* June 1991.

RICH07   Riches, S., et al. "A Fully Automated High Performance Implementation of ARM Cortex-A8." *IQ Online,* Vol. 6, No. 3, 2007. www.arm.com/iqonline

SHEN05   Shen, J., and Lipasti, M. *Modern Processor Design: Fundamentals of Superscalar Processors.* New York: McGraw-Hill, 2005.

SIMA97   Sima, D. "Superscalar Instruction Issue." *IEEE Micro,* September/October 1997.

SIMA04   Sima, D. "Decisive Aspects in the Evolution of Microprocessors." *Proceedings of the IEEE,* December 2004.

SMIT95 Smith, J., and Sohi, G. "The Microarchitecture of Superscalar Processors." *Proceedings of the IEEE*, December 1995.

WALL91 Wall, D. "Limits of Instruction-Level Parallelism." *Proceedings, Fourth International Conference on Architectural Support for Programming Languages and Operating Systems*, April 1991.

16.6 KEY TERMS, REVIEW QUESTIONS, AND PROBLEMS

Key Terms

antidependency	machine parallelism	register renaming
branch prediction	micro-operations	resource conflict
commit	micro-ops	retire
flow dependency	out-of-order	superpipelined
in-order completion	completion	superscalar
in-order issue	out-of-order issue	true data dependency
instruction issue	output dependency	write-read dependency
instruction-level parallelism	procedural dependency	write-write
instruction window	read-write dependency	dependency

Review Questions

16.1 What is the essential characteristic of the superscalar approach to processor design?

16.2 What is the difference between the superscalar and superpipelined approaches?

16.3 What is instruction-level parallelism?

16.4 Briefly define the following terms:
- True data dependency
- Procedural dependency
- Resource conflicts
- Output dependency
- Antidependency

16.5 What is the distinction between instruction-level parallelism and machine parallelism?

16.6 List and briefly define three types of superscalar instruction issue policies.

16.7 What is the purpose of an instruction window?

16.8 What is register renaming and what is its purpose?

16.9 What are the key elements of a superscalar processor organization?

Problems

16.1 When out-of-order completion is used in a superscalar processor, resumption of execution after interrupt processing is complicated, because the exceptional condition may have been detected as an instruction that produced its result out of order. The program cannot be restarted at the instruction following the exceptional instruction, because subsequent instructions have already completed, and doing so would cause these instructions to be executed twice. Suggest a mechanism or mechanisms for dealing with this situation.

16.2 Consider the following sequence of instructions, where the syntax consists of an opcode followed by the destination register followed by one or two source registers:

```
 0    ADD     R3, R1, R2
 1    LOAD    R6, [R3]
 2    AND     R7, R5, 3
 3    ADD     R1, R6, R7
 4    SRL     R7, R0, 8
 5    OR      R2, R4, R7
 6    SUB     R5, R3, R4
 7    ADD     R0, R1, 10
 8    LOAD    R6, [R5]
 9    SUB     R2, R1, R6
10    AND     R3, R7, 15
```

Assume the use of a four-stage pipeline: fetch, decode/issue, execute, write back. Assume that all pipeline stages take one clock cycle except for the execute stage. For simple integer arithmetic and logical instructions, the execute stage takes one cycle, but for a LOAD from memory, five cycles are consumed in the execute stage.

If we have a simple scalar pipeline but allow out-of-order execution, we can construct the following table for the execution of the first seven instructions:

Instruction	Fetch	Decode	Execute	Write Back
0	0	1	2	3
1	1	2	4	9
2	2	3	5	6
3	3	4	10	11
4	4	5	6	7
5	5	6	8	10
6	6	7	9	12

The entries under the four pipeline stages indicate the clock cycle at which each instruction begins each phase. In this program, the second ADD instruction (instruction 3) depends on the LOAD instruction (instruction 1) for one of its operands, r6. Because the LOAD instruction takes five clock cycles, and the issue logic encounters the dependent ADD instruction after two clocks, the issue logic must delay the ADD instruction for three clock cycles. With an out-of-order capability, the processor can stall instruction 3 at clock cycle 4, and then move on to issue the following three independent instructions, which enter execution at clocks 6, 8, and 9. The LOAD finishes execution at clock 9, and so the dependent ADD can be launched into execution on clock 10.

a. Complete the preceding table.
b. Redo the table assuming no out-of-order capability. What is the savings using the capability?
c. Redo the table assuming a superscalar implementation that can handle two instructions at a time at each stage.

16.3 Consider the following assembly language program:

```
I1: Move R3, R7        /R3  ←  (R7)/
I2: Load R8, (R3)      /R8  ←  Memory (R3)/
I3: Add R3, R3, 4      /R3  ←  (R3) + 4/
I4: Load R9, (R3)      /R9  ←  Memory (R3)/
I5: BLE R8, R9, L3     /Branch if (R9) > (R8)/
```

This program includes WAW, RAW, and WAR dependencies. Show these.

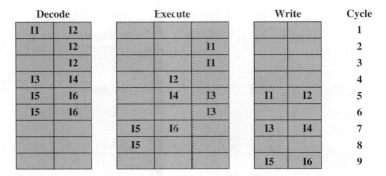

Figure 16.14 An In-Order Issue, In-Order-Completion Execution Sequence

16.4 **a.** Identify the RAW, WAR, and WAW dependencies in the following instruction sequence:

```
I1: R1 = 100
I2: R1 = R2 + R4
I3: R2 = r4 - 25
I4: R4 = R1 + R3
I5: R1 = R1 + 30
```

b. Rename the registers from part (a) to prevent dependency problems. Identify references to initial register values using the subscript "a" to the register reference.

16.5 Consider the "in-order-issue/in-order-completion" execution sequence shown in Figure 16.14.

a. Identify the most likely reason why I2 could not enter the execute stage until the fourth cycle. Will "in-order issue/out-of-order completion" or "out-of-order issue/out-of-order completion" fix this? If so, which?

b. Identify the reason why I6 could not enter the write stage until the nineth cycle. Will "in-order issue/out-of-order completion" or "out-of-order issue/out-of-order completion" fix this? If so, which?

16.6 Figure 16.15 shows an example of a superscalar processor organization. The processor can issue two instructions per cycle if there is no resource conflict and no data dependence problem. There are essentially two pipelines, with four processing stages (fetch, decode, execute, and store). Each pipeline has its own fetch decode and store unit. Four functional units (multiplier, adder, logic unit, and load unit) are available for use in the execute stage and are shared by the two pipelines on a dynamic basis. The two store units can be dynamically used by the two pipelines, depending on availability at a particular cycle. There is a lookahead window with its own fetch and decoding logic. This window is used for instruction lookahead for out-of-order instruction issue.

Consider the following program to be executed on this processor:

```
I1: Load R1, A    /R1 ← Memory (A)/
I2: Add R2, R1    /R2 ← (R2) + R(1)/
I3: Add R3, R4    /R3 ← (R3) + R(4)/
I4: Mul R4, R5    /R4 ← (R4) + R(5)/
I5: Comp R6       /R6 ← (R6)/
I6: Mul R6, R7    /R6 ← (R6) × R(7)/
```

a. What dependencies exist in the program?

b. Show the pipeline activity for this program on the processor of Figure 16.15 using in-order issue with in-order completion policies and using a presentation similar to Figure 16.2.

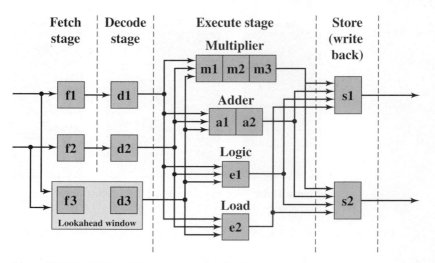

Figure 16.15 A Dual-Pipeline Superscalar Processor

   c. Repeat for in-order issue with out-of-order completion.
   d. Repeat for out-of-order issue with out-of-order completion.

16.7 Figure 16.16 is from a paper on superscalar design. Explain the three parts of the figure, and define w, x, y, and z.

16.8 Yeh's dynamic branch prediction algorithm, used on the Pentium 4, is a two-level branch prediction algorithm. The first level is the history of the last n branches. The second level is the branch behavior of the last s occurrences of that unique pattern of the last n branches. For each conditional branch instruction in a program, there is an entry in a Branch History Table (BHT). Each entry consists of n bits corresponding to the last n executions of the branch instruction, with a 1 if the branch was taken

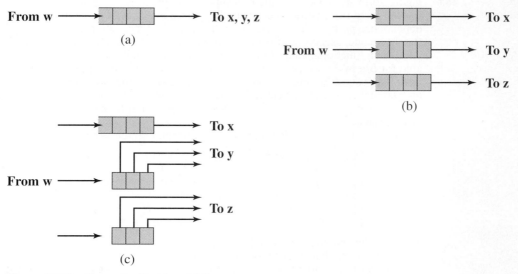

Figure 16.16 Figure for Problem 16.7

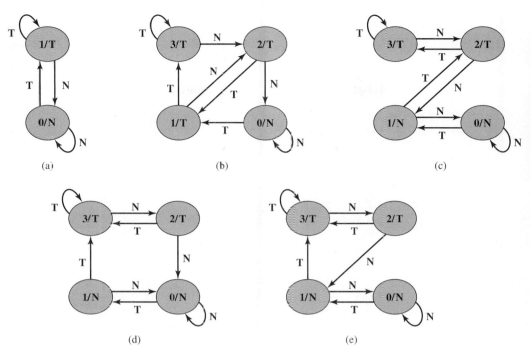

(a)   (b)   (c)

(d)   (e)

Figure 16.17 Figure for Problem 16.8

and a 0 if the branch was not. Each BHT entry indexes into a Pattern Table (PT) that has $2n$ entries, one for each possible pattern of n bits. Each PT entry consists of s bits that are used in branch prediction, as was described in Chapter 14 (e.g., Figure 14.19). When a conditional branch is encountered during instruction fetch and decode, the address of the instruction is used to retrieve the appropriate BHT entry, which shows the recent history of the instruction. Then, the BHT entry is used to retrieve the appropriate PT entry for branch prediction. After the branch is executed, the BHT entry is updated, and then the appropriate PT entry is updated.

a. In testing the performance of this scheme, Yeh tried five different prediction schemes, illustrated in Figure 16.17. Identify which three of these schemes correspond to those shown in Figures 14.19 and 14.28. Describe the remaining two schemes.

b. With this algorithm, the prediction is not based on just the recent history of this particular branch instruction. Rather, it is based on the recent history of all patterns of branches that match the n-bit pattern in the BHT entry for this instruction. Suggest a rationale for such a strategy.

PARALLEL PROCESSING

LEARNING OBJECTIVES

After studying this chapter, you should be able to:

◆ Summarize the types of parallel processor organizations.

◆ Present an overview of design features of symmetric multiprocessors.

◆ Understand the issue of cache coherence in a multiple processor system.

◆ Explain the key features of the MESI protocol.

◆ Explain the difference between implicit and explicit multithreading.

◆ Summarize key design issues for clusters.

◆ Explain the concept of nonuniform memory access.

◆ Present an overview of vector computation.

Traditionally, the computer has been viewed as a sequential machine. Most computer programming languages require the programmer to specify algorithms as sequences of instructions. Processors execute programs by executing machine instructions in a sequence and one at a time. Each instruction is executed in a sequence of operations (fetch instruction, fetch operands, perform operation, store results).

This view of the computer has never been entirely true. At the micro-operation level, multiple control signals are generated at the same time. Instruction pipelining, at least to the extent of overlapping fetch and execute operations, has been around for a long time. Both of these are examples of performing functions in parallel. This approach is taken further with superscalar organization, which exploits instruction-level parallelism. With a superscalar machine, there are multiple execution units within a single processor, and these may execute multiple instructions from the same program in parallel.

As computer technology has evolved, and as the cost of computer hardware has dropped, computer designers have sought more and more opportunities for parallelism, usually to enhance performance and, in some cases, to increase availability. After an overview, this chapter looks at some of the most prominent approaches to parallel organization. First, we examine symmetric multiprocessors (SMPs), one of the earliest and still the most common example of parallel organization. In an SMP organization, multiple processors share a common memory. This organization raises the issue of cache coherence, to which a separate section is devoted. Next, the chapter examines multithreaded processors and chip multiprocessors. Then we describe clusters, which consist of multiple independent computers organized in a cooperative fashion. Clusters have become increasingly common to support workloads that are beyond the capacity of a single SMP. Another approach to the use of multiple processors that we examine is that of nonuniform memory access (NUMA) machines. The NUMA approach is relatively new and not yet proven in the marketplace, but is often considered as an alternative to the SMP or cluster approach. Finally, this chapter looks at hardware organizational approaches to vector computation. These approaches optimize the ALU for processing vectors or arrays of floating-point numbers. They are common on the class of systems known as *supercomputers*.

17.1 MULTIPLE PROCESSOR ORGANIZATIONS

Types of Parallel Processor Systems

A taxonomy first introduced by Flynn [FLYN72] is still the most common way of categorizing systems with parallel processing capability. Flynn proposed the following categories of computer systems:

- **Single instruction, single data (SISD) stream:** A single processor executes a single instruction stream to operate on data stored in a single memory. Uniprocessors fall into this category.
- **Single instruction, multiple data (SIMD) stream:** A single machine instruction controls the simultaneous execution of a number of processing elements on a lockstep basis. Each processing element has an associated data memory, so that instructions are executed on different sets of data by different processors. Vector and array processors fall into this category, and are discussed in Section 18.7.
- **Multiple instruction, single data (MISD) stream:** A sequence of data is transmitted to a set of processors, each of which executes a different instruction sequence. This structure is not commercially implemented.
- **Multiple instruction, multiple data (MIMD) stream:** A set of processors simultaneously execute different instruction sequences on different data sets. SMPs, clusters, and NUMA systems fit into this category.

With the MIMD organization, the processors are general purpose; each is able to process all of the instructions necessary to perform the appropriate data transformation. MIMDs can be further subdivided by the means in which the processors communicate (Figure 17.1). If the processors share a common memory, then each processor accesses programs and data stored in the shared memory, and processors communicate with each other via that memory. The most common form of such system is known as a **symmetric multiprocessor (SMP)**, which we examine in Section 17.2. In an SMP, multiple processors share a single memory or pool of memory by means of a shared bus or other interconnection mechanism; a distinguishing feature is that the memory access time to any region of memory is approximately the same for each processor. A more recent development is the **nonuniform memory access (NUMA)** organization, which is described in Section 17.5. As the name suggests, the memory access time to different regions of memory may differ for a NUMA processor.

A collection of independent uniprocessors or SMPs may be interconnected to form a **cluster**. Communication among the computers is either via fixed paths or via some network facility.

Parallel Organizations

Figure 17.2 illustrates the general organization of the taxonomy of Figure 17.1. Figure 17.2a shows the structure of an SISD. There is some sort of control unit (CU) that provides an instruction stream (IS) to a processing unit (PU). The processing unit operates on a single data stream (DS) from a memory unit (MU). With an

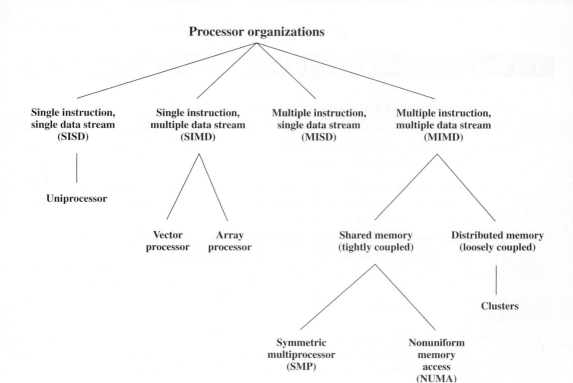

Figure 17.1 A Taxonomy of Parallel Processor Architectures

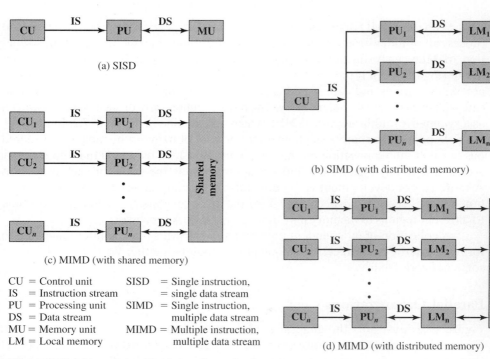

(a) SISD

(b) SIMD (with distributed memory)

(c) MIMD (with shared memory)

(d) MIMD (with distributed memory)

CU = Control unit   SISD = Single instruction,
IS   = Instruction stream   = single data stream
PU = Processing unit   SIMD = Single instruction,
DS = Data stream   multiple data stream
MU = Memory unit   MIMD = Multiple instruction,
LM = Local memory   multiple data stream

Figure 17.2 Alternative Computer Organizations

SIMD, there is still a single control unit, now feeding a single instruction stream to multiple PUs. Each PU may have its own dedicated memory (illustrated in Figure 17.2b), or there may be a shared memory. Finally, with the MIMD, there are multiple control units, each feeding a separate instruction stream to its own PU. The MIMD may be a shared-memory multiprocessor (Figure 17.2c) or a distributed-memory multicomputer (Figure 17.2d).

The design issues relating to SMPs, clusters, and NUMAs are complex, involving issues relating to physical organization, interconnection structures, interprocessor communication, operating system design, and application software techniques. Our concern here is primarily with organization, although we touch briefly on operating system design issues.

17.2 SYMMETRIC MULTIPROCESSORS

Until fairly recently, virtually all single-user personal computers and most workstations contained a single general-purpose microprocessor. As demands for performance increase and as the cost of microprocessors continues to drop, vendors have introduced systems with an SMP organization. The term *SMP* refers to a computer hardware architecture and also to the operating system behavior that reflects that architecture. An SMP can be defined as a standalone computer system with the following characteristics:

1. There are two or more similar processors of comparable capability.
2. These processors share the same main memory and I/O facilities and are interconnected by a bus or other internal connection scheme, such that memory access time is approximately the same for each processor.
3. All processors share access to I/O devices, either through the same channels or through different channels that provide paths to the same device.
4. All processors can perform the same functions (hence the term *symmetric*).
5. The system is controlled by an integrated operating system that provides interaction between processors and their programs at the job, task, file, and data element levels.

Points 1 to 4 should be self-explanatory. Point 5 illustrates one of the contrasts with a loosely coupled multiprocessing system, such as a cluster. In the latter, the physical unit of interaction is usually a message or complete file. In an SMP, individual data elements can constitute the level of interaction, and there can be a high degree of cooperation between processes.

The operating system of an SMP schedules processes or threads across all of the processors. An SMP organization has a number of potential advantages over a uniprocessor organization, including the following:

- **Performance:** If the work to be done by a computer can be organized so that some portions of the work can be done in parallel, then a system with multiple processors will yield greater performance than one with a single processor of the same type (Figure 17.3).

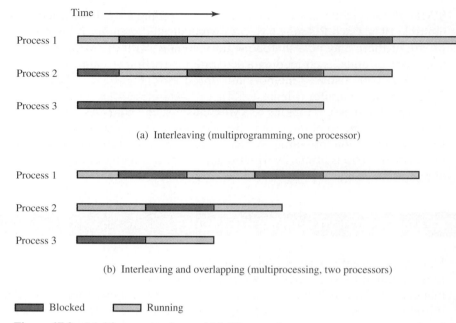

(a) Interleaving (multiprogramming, one processor)

(b) Interleaving and overlapping (multiprocessing, two processors)

Blocked   Running

Figure 17.3 Multiprogramming and Multiprocessing

- **Availability:** In a symmetric multiprocessor, because all processors can perform the same functions, the failure of a single processor does not halt the machine. Instead, the system can continue to function at reduced performance.
- **Incremental growth:** A user can enhance the performance of a system by adding an additional processor.
- **Scaling:** Vendors can offer a range of products with different price and performance characteristics based on the number of processors configured in the system.

It is important to note that these are potential, rather than guaranteed, benefits. The operating system must provide tools and functions to exploit the parallelism in an SMP system.

An attractive feature of an SMP is that the existence of multiple processors is transparent to the user. The operating system takes care of scheduling of threads or processes on individual processors and of synchronization among processors.

Organization

Figure 17.4 depicts in general terms the organization of a multiprocessor system. There are two or more processors. Each processor is self-contained, including a control unit, ALU, registers, and, typically, one or more levels of cache. Each processor has access to a shared main memory and the I/O devices through some form of interconnection mechanism. The processors can communicate with each other through memory (messages and status information left in common data areas). It may also be possible for processors to exchange signals directly. The memory is

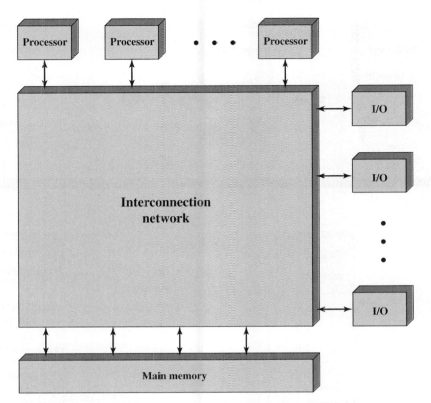

Figure 17.4   Generic Block Diagram of a Tightly Coupled Multiprocessor

often organized so that multiple simultaneous accesses to separate blocks of memory are possible. In some configurations, each processor may also have its own private main memory and I/O channels in addition to the shared resources.

The most common organization for personal computers, workstations, and servers is the time-shared bus. The time-shared bus is the simplest mechanism for constructing a multiprocessor system (Figure 17.5). The structure and interfaces are basically the same as for a single-processor system that uses a bus interconnection. The bus consists of control, address, and data lines. To facilitate DMA transfers from I/O subsystems to processors, the following features are provided:

- **Addressing:** It must be possible to distinguish modules on the bus to determine the source and destination of data.
- **Arbitration:** Any I/O module can temporarily function as "master." A mechanism is provided to arbitrate competing requests for bus control, using some sort of priority scheme.
- **Time-sharing:** When one module is controlling the bus, other modules are locked out and must, if necessary, suspend operation until bus access is achieved.

These uniprocessor features are directly usable in an SMP organization. In this latter case, there are now multiple processors as well as multiple I/O processors all attempting to gain access to one or more memory modules via the bus.

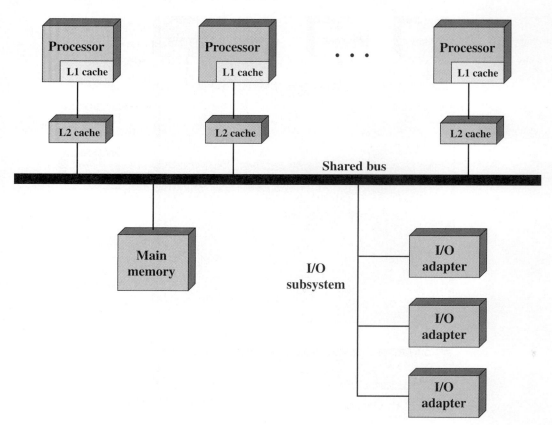

Figure 17.5 Symmetric Multiprocessor Organization

The bus organization has several attractive features:

- **Simplicity:** This is the simplest approach to multiprocessor organization. The physical interface and the addressing, arbitration, and time-sharing logic of each processor remain the same as in a single-processor system.
- **Flexibility:** It is generally easy to expand the system by attaching more processors to the bus.
- **Reliability:** The bus is essentially a passive medium, and the failure of any attached device should not cause failure of the whole system.

The main drawback to the bus organization is performance. All memory references pass through the common bus. Thus, the bus cycle time limits the speed of the system. To improve performance, it is desirable to equip each processor with a cache memory. This should reduce the number of bus accesses dramatically. Typically, workstation and PC SMPs have two levels of cache, with the L1 cache internal (same chip as the processor) and the L2 cache either internal or external. Some processors now employ a L3 cache as well.

The use of caches introduces some new design considerations. Because each local cache contains an image of a portion of memory, if a word is altered in one cache, it could conceivably invalidate a word in another cache. To prevent this, the other processors must be alerted that an update has taken place. This problem is known as the *cache coherence* problem and is typically addressed in hardware rather than by the operating system. We address this issue in Section 17.4.

Multiprocessor Operating System Design Considerations

An SMP operating system manages processor and other computer resources so that the user perceives a single operating system controlling system resources. In fact, such a configuration should appear as a single-processor multiprogramming system. In both the SMP and uniprocessor cases, multiple jobs or processes may be active at one time, and it is the responsibility of the operating system to schedule their execution and to allocate resources. A user may construct applications that use multiple processes or multiple threads within processes without regard to whether a single processor or multiple processors will be available. Thus, a multiprocessor operating system must provide all the functionality of a multiprogramming system plus additional features to accommodate multiple processors. Among the key design issues:

- **Simultaneous concurrent processes:** OS routines need to be reentrant to allow several processors to execute the same IS code simultaneously. With multiple processors executing the same or different parts of the OS, OS tables and management structures must be managed properly to avoid deadlock or invalid operations.
- **Scheduling:** Any processor may perform scheduling, so conflicts must be avoided. The scheduler must assign ready processes to available processors.
- **Synchronization:** With multiple active processes having potential access to shared address spaces or shared I/O resources, care must be taken to provide effective synchronization. Synchronization is a facility that enforces mutual exclusion and event ordering.
- **Memory management:** Memory management on a multiprocessor must deal with all of the issues found on uniprocessor machines, as is discussed in Chapter 8. In addition, the operating system needs to exploit the available hardware parallelism, such as multiported memories, to achieve the best performance. The paging mechanisms on different processors must be coordinated to enforce consistency when several processors share a page or segment and to decide on page replacement.
- **Reliability and fault tolerance:** The operating system should provide graceful degradation in the face of processor failure. The scheduler and other portions of the operating system must recognize the loss of a processor and restructure management tables accordingly.

17.3 CACHE COHERENCE AND THE MESI PROTOCOL

In contemporary multiprocessor systems, it is customary to have one or two levels of cache associated with each processor. This organization is essential to achieve reasonable performance. It does, however, create a problem known as the *cache coherence* problem. The essence of the problem is this: Multiple copies of the same data can exist in different caches simultaneously, and if processors are allowed to update their own copies freely, an inconsistent view of memory can result. In Chapter 4 we defined two common write policies:

- **Write back:** Write operations are usually made only to the cache. Main memory is only updated when the corresponding cache line is flushed from the cache.

- **Write through:** All write operations are made to main memory as well as to the cache, ensuring that main memory is always valid.

It is clear that a write-back policy can result in inconsistency. If two caches contain the same line, and the line is updated in one cache, the other cache will unknowingly have an invalid value. Subsequent reads to that invalid line produce invalid results. Even with the write-through policy, inconsistency can occur unless other caches monitor the memory traffic or receive some direct notification of the update.

In this section, we will briefly survey various approaches to the cache coherence problem and then focus on the approach that is most widely used: the MESI (modified/exclusive/shared/invalid) protocol. A version of this protocol is used on both the Pentium 4 and PowerPC implementations.

For any cache coherence protocol, the objective is to let recently used local variables get into the appropriate cache and stay there through numerous reads and write, while using the protocol to maintain consistency of shared variables that might be in multiple caches at the same time. Cache coherence approaches have generally been divided into software and hardware approaches. Some implementations adopt a strategy that involves both software and hardware elements. Nevertheless, the classification into software and hardware approaches is still instructive and is commonly used in surveying cache coherence strategies.

Software Solutions

Software cache coherence schemes attempt to avoid the need for additional hardware circuitry and logic by relying on the compiler and operating system to deal with the problem. Software approaches are attractive because the overhead of detecting potential problems is transferred from run time to compile time, and the design complexity is transferred from hardware to software. On the other hand, compile-time software approaches generally must make conservative decisions, leading to inefficient cache utilization.

Compiler-based coherence mechanisms perform an analysis on the code to determine which data items may become unsafe for caching, and they mark those items accordingly. The operating system or hardware then prevents noncacheable items from being cached.

The simplest approach is to prevent any shared data variables from being cached. This is too conservative, because a shared data structure may be exclusively used during some periods and may be effectively read-only during other periods. It is only during periods when at least one process may update the variable and at least one other process may access the variable that cache coherence is an issue.

More efficient approaches analyze the code to determine safe periods for shared variables. The compiler then inserts instructions into the generated code to enforce cache coherence during the critical periods. A number of techniques have been developed for performing the analysis and for enforcing the results; see [LILJ93] and [STEN90] for surveys.

Hardware Solutions

Hardware-based solutions are generally referred to as cache coherence protocols. These solutions provide dynamic recognition at run time of potential inconsistency conditions. Because the problem is only dealt with when it actually arises, there is more effective use of caches, leading to improved performance over a software approach. In addition, these approaches are transparent to the programmer and the compiler, reducing the software development burden.

Hardware schemes differ in a number of particulars, including where the state information about data lines is held, how that information is organized, where coherence is enforced, and the enforcement mechanisms. In general, hardware schemes can be divided into two categories: directory protocols and snoopy protocols.

DIRECTORY PROTOCOLS Directory protocols collect and maintain information about where copies of lines reside. Typically, there is a centralized controller that is part of the main memory controller, and a directory that is stored in main memory. The directory contains global state information about the contents of the various local caches. When an individual cache controller makes a request, the centralized controller checks and issues necessary commands for data transfer between memory and caches or between caches. It is also responsible for keeping the state information up to date; therefore, every local action that can affect the global state of a line must be reported to the central controller.

Typically, the controller maintains information about which processors have a copy of which lines. Before a processor can write to a local copy of a line, it must request exclusive access to the line from the controller. Before granting this exclusive access, the controller sends a message to all processors with a cached copy of this line, forcing each processor to invalidate its copy. After receiving acknowledgments back from each such processor, the controller grants exclusive access to the requesting processor. When another processor tries to read a line that is exclusively granted to another processor, it will send a miss notification to the controller. The controller then issues a command to the processor holding that line that requires the processor to do a write back to main memory. The line may now be shared for reading by the original processor and the requesting processor.

Directory schemes suffer from the drawbacks of a central bottleneck and the overhead of communication between the various cache controllers and the central controller. However, they are effective in large-scale systems that involve multiple buses or some other complex interconnection scheme.

SNOOPY PROTOCOLS Snoopy protocols distribute the responsibility for maintaining cache coherence among all of the cache controllers in a multiprocessor. A cache must recognize when a line that it holds is shared with other caches.

When an update action is performed on a shared cache line, it must be announced to all other caches by a broadcast mechanism. Each cache controller is able to "snoop" on the network to observe these broadcasted notifications, and react accordingly.

Snoopy protocols are ideally suited to a bus-based multiprocessor, because the shared bus provides a simple means for broadcasting and snooping. However, because one of the objectives of the use of local caches is to avoid bus accesses, care must be taken that the increased bus traffic required for broadcasting and snooping does not cancel out the gains from the use of local caches.

Two basic approaches to the snoopy protocol have been explored: write invalidate and write update (or write broadcast). With a write-invalidate protocol, there can be multiple readers but only one writer at a time. Initially, a line may be shared among several caches for reading purposes. When one of the caches wants to perform a write to the line, it first issues a notice that invalidates that line in the other caches, making the line exclusive to the writing cache. Once the line is exclusive, the owning processor can make cheap local writes until some other processor requires the same line.

With a write-update protocol, there can be multiple writers as well as multiple readers. When a processor wishes to update a shared line, the word to be updated is distributed to all others, and caches containing that line can update it.

Neither of these two approaches is superior to the other under all circumstances. Performance depends on the number of local caches and the pattern of memory reads and writes. Some systems implement adaptive protocols that employ both write-invalidate and write-update mechanisms.

The write-invalidate approach is the most widely used in commercial multiprocessor systems, such as the Pentium 4 and PowerPC. It marks the state of every cache line (using two extra bits in the cache tag) as modified, exclusive, shared, or invalid. For this reason, the write-invalidate protocol is called MESI. In the remainder of this section, we will look at its use among local caches across a multiprocessor. For simplicity in the presentation, we do not examine the mechanisms involved in coordinating among both level 1 and level 2 locally as well as at the same time coordinating across the distributed multiprocessor. This would not add any new principles but would greatly complicate the discussion.

The MESI Protocol

To provide cache consistency on an SMP, the data cache often supports a protocol known as MESI. For MESI, the data cache includes two status bits per tag, so that each line can be in one of four states:

- **Modified:** The line in the cache has been modified (different from main memory) and is available only in this cache.
- **Exclusive:** The line in the cache is the same as that in main memory and is not present in any other cache.
- **Shared:** The line in the cache is the same as that in main memory and may be present in another cache.
- **Invalid:** The line in the cache does not contain valid data.

Table 17.1 MESI Cache Line States

	M **Modified**	**E** **Exclusive**	**S** **Shared**	**I** **Invalid**
This cache line valid?	Yes	Yes	Yes	No
The memory copy is …	out of date	valid	valid	—
Copies exist in other caches?	No	No	Maybe	Maybe
A write to this line …	does not go to bus	does not go to bus	goes to bus and updates cache	goes directly to bus

Table 17.1 summarizes the meaning of the four states. Figure 17.6 displays a state diagram for the MESI protocol. Keep in mind that each line of the cache has its own state bits and therefore its own realization of the state diagram. Figure 17.6a shows the transitions that occur due to actions initiated by the processor attached to this cache. Figure 17.6b shows the transitions that occur due to events that are snooped on the common bus. This presentation of separate state diagrams for processor-initiated and bus-initiated actions helps to clarify the logic of the MESI protocol.

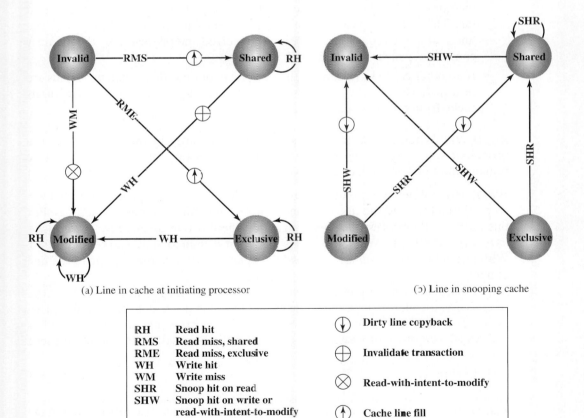

(a) Line in cache at initiating processor (b) Line in snooping cache

RH	Read hit
RMS	Read miss, shared
RME	Read miss, exclusive
WH	Write hit
WM	Write miss
SHR	Snoop hit on read
SHW	Snoop hit on write or read-with-intent-to-modify

- ⬇ Dirty line copyback
- ⊕ Invalidate transaction
- ⊗ Read-with-intent-to-modify
- ⬆ Cache line fill

Figure 17.6 MESI State Transition Diagram

At any time a cache line is in a single state. If the next event is from the attached processor, then the transition is dictated by Figure 17.6a and if the next event is from the bus, the transition is dictated by Figure 17.6b. Let us look at these transitions in more detail.

READ MISS When a read miss occurs in the local cache, the processor initiates a memory read to read the line of main memory containing the missing address. The processor inserts a signal on the bus that alerts all other processor/cache units to snoop the transaction. There are a number of possible outcomes:

- If one other cache has a clean (unmodified since read from memory) copy of the line in the exclusive state, it returns a signal indicating that it shares this line. The responding processor then transitions the state of its copy from exclusive to shared, and the initiating processor reads the line from main memory and transitions the line in its cache from invalid to shared.
- If one or more caches have a clean copy of the line in the shared state, each of them signals that it shares the line. The initiating processor reads the line and transitions the line in its cache from invalid to shared.
- If one other cache has a modified copy of the line, then that cache blocks the memory read and provides the line to the requesting cache over the shared bus. The responding cache then changes its line from modified to shared.[1] The line sent to the requesting cache is also received and processed by the memory controller, which stores the block in memory.
- If no other cache has a copy of the line (clean or modified), then no signals are returned. The initiating processor reads the line and transitions the line in its cache from invalid to exclusive.

READ HIT When a read hit occurs on a line currently in the local cache, the processor simply reads the required item. There is no state change: The state remains modified, shared, or exclusive.

WRITE MISS When a write miss occurs in the local cache, the processor initiates a memory read to read the line of main memory containing the missing address. For this purpose, the processor issues a signal on the bus that means *read-with-intent-to-modify* (RWITM). When the line is loaded, it is immediately marked modified. With respect to other caches, two possible scenarios precede the loading of the line of data.

First, some other cache may have a modified copy of this line (state = modify). In this case, the alerted processor signals the initiating processor that another processor has a modified copy of the line. The initiating processor surrenders the bus and waits. The other processor gains access to the bus, writes the modified cache

---

[1] In some implementations, the cache with the modified line signals the initiating processor to retry. Meanwhile, the processor with the modified copy seizes the bus, writes the modified line back to main memory, and transitions the line in its cache from modified to shared. Subsequently, the requesting processor tries again and finds that one or more processors have a clean copy of the line in the shared state, as described in the preceding point.

line back to main memory, and transitions the state of the cache line to invalid (because the initiating processor is going to modify this line). Subsequently, the initiating processor will again issue a signal to the bus of RWITM and then read the line from main memory, modify the line in the cache, and mark the line in the modified state.

The second scenario is that no other cache has a modified copy of the requested line. In this case, no signal is returned, and the initiating processor proceeds to read in the line and modify it. Meanwhile, if one or more caches have a clean copy of the line in the shared state, each cache invalidates its copy of the line, and if one cache has a clean copy of the line in the exclusive state, it invalidates its copy of the line.

WRITE HIT When a write hit occurs on a line currently in the local cache, the effect depends on the current state of that line in the local cache:

- **Shared:** Before performing the update, the processor must gain exclusive ownership of the line. The processor signals its intent on the bus. Each processor that has a shared copy of the line in its cache transitions the sector from shared to invalid. The initiating processor then performs the update and transitions its copy of the line from shared to modified.

- **Exclusive:** The processor already has exclusive control of this line, and so it simply performs the update and transitions its copy of the line from exclusive to modified.

- **Modified:** The processor already has exclusive control of this line and has the line marked as modified, and so it simply performs the update.

L1-L2 CACHE CONSISTENCY We have so far described cache coherency protocols in terms of the cooperate activity among caches connected to the same bus or other SMP interconnection facility. Typically, these caches are L2 caches, and each processor also has an L1 cache that does not connect directly to the bus and that therefore cannot engage in a snoopy protocol. Thus, some scheme is needed to maintain data integrity across both levels of cache and across all caches in the SMP configuration.

The strategy is to extend the MESI protocol (or any cache coherence protocol) to the L1 caches. Thus, each line in the L1 cache includes bits to indicate the state. In essence, the objective is the following: for any line that is present in both an L2 cache and its corresponding L1 cache, the L1 line state should track the state of the L2 line. A simple means of doing this is to adopt the write-through policy in the L1 cache; in this case the write through is to the L2 cache and not to the memory. The L1 write-through policy forces any modification to an L1 line out to the L2 cache and therefore makes it visible to other L2 caches. The use of the L1 write-through policy requires that the L1 content must be a subset of the L2 content. This in turn suggests that the associativity of the L2 cache should be equal to or greater than that of the L1 associativity. The L1 write-through policy is used in the IBM S/390 SMP.

If the L1 cache has a write-back policy, the relationship between the two caches is more complex. There are several approaches to maintaining coherence. For example, the approach used on the Pentium II is described in detail in [SHAN05].

17.4 MULTITHREADING AND CHIP MULTIPROCESSORS

The most important measure of performance for a processor is the rate at which it executes instructions. This can be expressed as

$$\text{MIPS rate} = f \times IPC$$

where f is the processor clock frequency, in MHz, and IPC (instructions per cycle) is the average number of instructions executed per cycle. Accordingly, designers have pursued the goal of increased performance on two fronts: increasing clock frequency and increasing the number of instructions executed or, more properly, the number of instructions that complete during a processor cycle. As we have seen in earlier chapters, designers have increased IPC by using an instruction pipeline and then by using multiple parallel instruction pipelines in a superscalar architecture. With pipelined and multiple-pipeline designs, the principal problem is to maximize the utilization of each pipeline stage. To improve throughput, designers have created ever more complex mechanisms, such as executing some instructions in a different order from the way they occur in the instruction stream and beginning execution of instructions that may never be needed. But as was discussed in Section 2.2, this approach may be reaching a limit due to complexity and power consumption concerns.

An alternative approach, which allows for a high degree of instruction-level parallelism without increasing circuit complexity or power consumption, is called multithreading. In essence, the instruction stream is divided into several smaller streams, known as threads, such that the threads can be executed in parallel.

The variety of specific multithreading designs, realized in both commercial systems and experimental systems, is vast. In this section, we give a brief survey of the major concepts.

Implicit and Explicit Multithreading

The concept of thread used in discussing multithreaded processors may or may not be the same as the concept of software threads in a multiprogrammed operating system. It will be useful to define terms briefly:

- **Process:** An instance of a program running on a computer. A process embodies two key characteristics:
  - **Resource ownership:** A process includes a virtual address space to hold the process image; the process image is the collection of program, data, stack, and attributes that define the process. From time to time, a process may be allocated control or ownership of resources, such as main memory, I/O channels, I/O devices, and files.
  - **Scheduling/execution:** The execution of a process follows an execution path (trace) through one or more programs. This execution may be interleaved with that of other processes. Thus, a process has an execution state (Running, Ready, etc.) and a dispatching priority and is the entity that is scheduled and dispatched by the operating system.

- **Process switch:** An operation that switches the processor from one process to another, by saving all the process control data, registers, and other information for the first and replacing them with the process information for the second.[2]
- **Thread:** A dispatchable unit of work within a process. It includes a processor context (which includes the program counter and stack pointer) and its own data area for a stack (to enable subroutine branching). A thread executes sequentially and is interruptible so that the processor can turn to another thread.
- **Thread switch:** The act of switching processor control from one thread to another within the same process. Typically, this type of switch is much less costly than a process switch.

Thus, a thread is concerned with scheduling and execution, whereas a process is concerned with both scheduling/execution and resource ownership. The multiple threads within a process share the same resources. This is why a thread switch is much less time consuming than a process switch. Traditional operating systems, such as earlier versions of UNIX, did not support threads. Most modern operating systems, such as Linux, other versions of UNIX, and Windows, do support thread. A distinction is made between user-level threads, which are visible to the application program, and kernel-level threads, which are visible only to the operating system. Both of these may be referred to as explicit threads, defined in software.

All of the commercial processors and most of the experimental processors so far have used explicit multithreading. These systems concurrently execute instructions from different explicit threads, either by interleaving instructions from different threads on shared pipelines or by parallel execution on parallel pipelines. Implicit multithreading refers to the concurrent execution of multiple threads extracted from a single sequential program. These implicit threads may be defined either statically by the compiler or dynamically by the hardware. In the remainder of this section we consider explicit multithreading.

Approaches to Explicit Multithreading

At minimum, a multithreaded processor must provide a separate program counter for each thread of execution to be executed concurrently. The designs differ in the amount and type of additional hardware used to support concurrent thread execution. In general, instruction fetching takes place on a thread basis. The processor treats each thread separately and may use a number of techniques for optimizing single-thread execution, including branch prediction, register renaming, and superscalar techniques. What is achieved is thread-level parallelism, which may provide for greatly improved performance when married to instruction-level parallelism.

Broadly speaking, there are four principal approaches to multithreading:

- **Interleaved multithreading:** This is also known as **fine-grained multithreading**. The processor deals with two or more thread contexts at a time, switching from one thread to another at each clock cycle. If a thread is blocked because

---

[2]The term *context switch* is often found in OS literature and textbooks. Unfortunately, although most of the literature uses this term to mean what is here called a process switch. other sources use it to mean a thread switch. To avoid ambiguity, the term is not used in this book.

of data dependencies or memory latencies, that thread is skipped and a ready thread is executed.

- **Blocked multithreading:** This is also known as **coarse-grained multithreading**. The instructions of a thread are executed successively until an event occurs that may cause delay, such as a cache miss. This event induces a switch to another thread. This approach is effective on an in-order processor that would stall the pipeline for a delay event such as a cache miss.

- **Simultaneous multithreading (SMT):** Instructions are simultaneously issued from multiple threads to the execution units of a superscalar processor. This combines the wide superscalar instruction issue capability with the use of multiple thread contexts.

- **Chip multiprocessing:** In this case, the entire processor is replicated on a single chip and each processor handles separate threads. The advantage of this approach is that the available logic area on a chip is used effectively without depending on ever-increasing complexity in pipeline design. This is referred to as multicore; we examine this topic separately in Chapter 18.

For the first two approaches, instructions from different threads are not executed simultaneously. Instead, the processor is able to rapidly switch from one thread to another, using a different set of registers and other context information. This results in a better utilization of the processor's execution resources and avoids a large penalty due to cache misses and other latency events. The SMT approach involves true simultaneous execution of instructions from different threads, using replicated execution resources. Chip multiprocessing also enables simultaneous execution of instructions from different threads.

Figure 17.7, based on one in [UNGE02], illustrates some of the possible pipeline architectures that involve multithreading and contrasts these with approaches that do not use multithreading. Each horizontal row represents the potential issue slot or slots for a single execution cycle; that is, the width of each row corresponds to the maximum number of instructions that can be issued in a single clock cycle.[3] The vertical dimension represents the time sequence of clock cycles. An empty (shaded) slot represents an unused execution slot in one pipeline. A no-op is indicated by N.

The first three illustrations in Figure 17.7 show different approaches with a scalar (i.e., single-issue) processor:

- **Single-threaded scalar:** This is the simple pipeline found in traditional RISC and CISC machines, with no multithreading.

- **Interleaved multithreaded scalar:** This is the easiest multithreading approach to implement. By switching from one thread to another at each clock cycle, the pipeline stages can be kept fully occupied, or close to fully occupied. The hardware must be capable of switching from one thread context to another between cycles.

---

[3]Issue slots are the position from which instructions can be issued in a given clock cycle. Recall from Chapter 16 that instruction issue is the process of initiating instruction execution in the processor's functional units. This occurs when an instruction moves from the decode stage of the pipeline to the first execute stage of the pipeline.

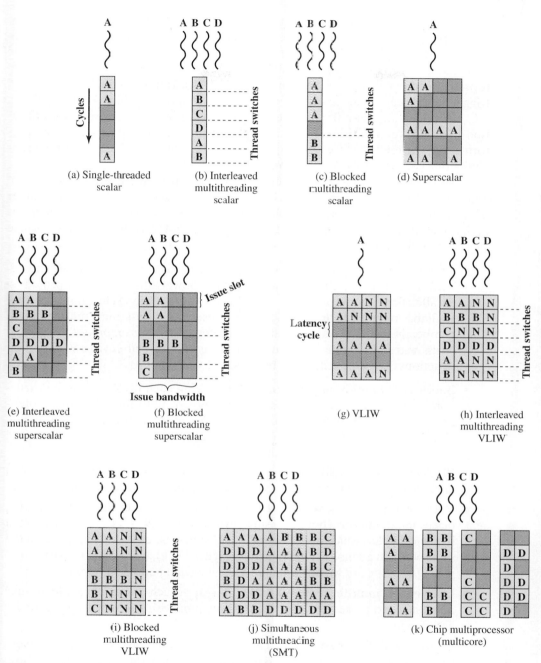

Figure 17.7 Approaches to Executing Multiple Threads

- **Blocked multithreaded scalar:** In this case, a single thread is executed until a latency event occurs that would stop the pipeline, at which time the processor switches to another thread.

Figure 17.7c shows a situation in which the time to perform a thread switch is one cycle, whereas Figure 17.7b shows that thread switching occurs in zero cycles.

In the case of interleaved multithreading, it is assumed that there are no control or data dependencies between threads, which simplifies the pipeline design and therefore should allow a thread switch with no delay. However, depending on the specific design and implementation, block multithreading may require a clock cycle to perform a thread switch, as illustrated in Figure 17.7. This is true if a fetched instruction triggers the thread switch and must be discarded from the pipeline [UNGE03].

Although interleaved multithreading appears to offer better processor utilization than blocked multithreading, it does so at the sacrifice of single-thread performance. The multiple threads compete for cache resources, which raises the probability of a cache miss for a given thread.

More opportunities for parallel execution are available if the processor can issue multiple instructions per cycle. Figures 17.7d through 17.7i illustrate a number of variations among processors that have hardware for issuing four instructions per cycle. In all these cases, only instructions from a single thread are issued in a single cycle. The following alternatives are illustrated:

- **Superscalar:** This is the basic superscalar approach with no multithreading. Until relatively recently, this was the most powerful approach to providing parallelism within a processor. Note that during some cycles, not all of the available issue slots are used. During these cycles, less than the maximum number of instructions is issued; this is referred to as *horizontal loss*. During other instruction cycles, no issue slots are used; these are cycles when no instructions can be issued; this is referred to as *vertical loss*.

- **Interleaved multithreading superscalar:** During each cycle, as many instructions as possible are issued from a single thread. With this technique, potential delays due to thread switches are eliminated, as previously discussed. However, the number of instructions issued in any given cycle is still limited by dependencies that exist within any given thread.

- **Blocked multithreaded superscalar:** Again, instructions from only one thread may be issued during any cycle, and blocked multithreading is used.

- **Very long instruction word (VLIW):** A VLIW architecture, such as IA-64, places multiple instructions in a single word. Typically, a VLIW is constructed by the compiler, which places operations that may be executed in parallel in the same word. In a simple VLIW machine (Figure 17.7g), if it is not possible to completely fill the word with instructions to be issued in parallel, no-ops are used.

- **Interleaved multithreading VLIW:** This approach should provide similar efficiencies to those provided by interleaved multithreading on a superscalar architecture.

- **Blocked multithreaded VLIW:** This approach should provide similar efficiencies to those provided by blocked multithreading on a superscalar architecture.

The final two approaches illustrated in Figure 17.7 enable the parallel, simultaneous execution of multiple threads:

- **Simultaneous multithreading:** Figure 17.7j shows a system capable of issuing 8 instructions at a time. If one thread has a high degree of instruction-level parallelism, it may on some cycles be able fill all of the horizontal slots. On other cycles, instructions from two or more threads may be issued. If sufficient threads are active, it should usually be possible to issue the maximum number of instructions on each cycle, providing a high level of efficiency.

- **Chip multiprocessor (multicore):** Figure 17.7k shows a chip containing four processors, each of which has a two-issue superscalar processor. Each processor is assigned a thread, from which it can issue up to two instructions per cycle. We discuss multicore computers in Chapter 18.

Comparing Figures 17.7j and 17.7k, we see that a chip multiprocessor with the same instruction issue capability as an SMT cannot achieve the same degree of instruction-level parallelism. This is because the chip multiprocessor is not able to hide latencies by issuing instructions from other threads. On the other hand, the chip multiprocessor should outperform a superscalar processor with the same instruction issue capability, because the horizontal losses will be greater for the superscalar processor. In addition, it is possible to use multithreading within each of the processors on a chip multiprocessor, and this is done on some contemporary machines.

Example Systems

PENTIUM 4 More recent models of the Pentium 4 use a multithreading technique that the Intel literature refers to as *hyperthreading* [MARR02]. In essence, the Pentium 4 approach is to use SMT with support for two threads. Thus, the single multithreaded processor is logically two processors.

IBM POWER5 The IBM Power5 chip, which is used in high-end PowerPC products, combines chip multiprocessing with SMT [KALL04]. The chip has two separate processors, each of which is a multithreaded processor capable of supporting two threads concurrently using SMT. Interestingly, the designers simulated various alternatives and found that having two two-way SMT processors on a single chip provided superior performance to a single four-way SMT processor. The simulations showed that additional multithreading beyond the support for two threads might decrease performance because of cache thrashing, as data from one thread displaces data needed by another thread.

Figure 17.8 shows the IBM Power5's instruction flow diagram. Only a few of the elements in the processor need to be replicated, with separate elements dedicated to separate threads. Two program counters are used. The processor alternates fetching instructions, up to eight at a time, between the two threads. All the instructions are stored in a common instruction cache and share an instruction translation facility, which does a partial instruction decode. When a conditional branch is encountered, the branch prediction facility predicts the direction of the branch and, if possible, calculates the target address. For predicting the target of a subroutine return, the processor uses a return stack, one for each thread.

Instructions then move into two separate instruction buffers. Then, on the basis of thread priority, a group of instructions is selected and decoded in parallel. Next, instructions flow through a register-renaming facility in program order. Logical registers are mapped to physical registers. The Power5 has 120 physical general-purpose registers and 120 physical floating-point registers. The instructions are then moved into issue queues. From the issue queues, instructions are issued

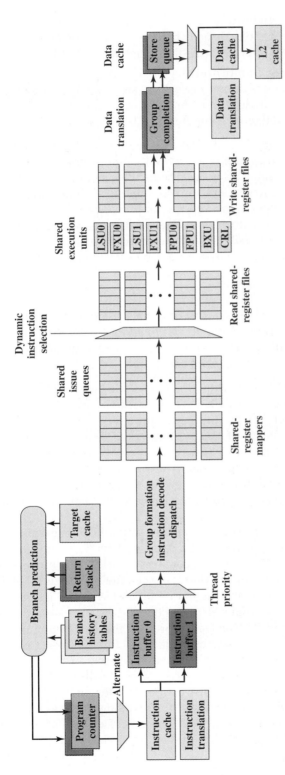

Figure 17.8 Power5 Instruction Data Flow

BXU = Branch execution unit and
CRL = Condition register logical execution unit
FPU = Floating-point execution unit
FXU = Fixed-point execution unit
LSU = Load/store unit

Shared by two threads ▨   Thread 0 resource ▨   Thread 1 resource ▨

using symmetric multithreading. That is, the processor has a superscalar architecture and can issue instructions from one or both threads in parallel. At the end of the pipeline, separate thread resources are needed to commit the instructions.

17.5 CLUSTERS

An important and relatively recent development computer system design is clustering. Clustering is an alternative to symmetric multiprocessing as an approach to providing high performance and high availability and is particularly attractive for server applications. We can define a cluster as a group of interconnected, whole computers working together as a unified computing resource that can create the illusion of being one machine. The term *whole computer* means a system that can run on its own, apart from the cluster; in the literature, each computer in a cluster is typically referred to as a *node*.

[BREW97] lists four benefits that can be achieved with clustering. These can also be thought of as objectives or design requirements:

- **Absolute scalability:** It is possible to create large clusters that far surpass the power of even the largest standalone machines. A cluster can have tens, hundreds, or even thousands of machines, each of which is a multiprocessor.

- **Incremental scalability:** A cluster is configured in such a way that it is possible to add new systems to the cluster in small increments. Thus, a user can start out with a modest system and expand it as needs grow, without having to go through a major upgrade in which an existing small system is replaced with a larger system.

- **High availability:** Because each node in a cluster is a standalone computer, the failure of one node does not mean loss of service. In many products, fault tolerance is handled automatically in software.

- **Superior price/performance:** By using commodity building blocks, it is possible to put together a cluster with equal or greater computing power than a single large machine, at much lower cost.

Cluster Configurations

In the literature, clusters are classified in a number of different ways. Perhaps the simplest classification is based on whether the computers in a cluster share access to the same disks. Figure 17.9a shows a two-node cluster in which the only interconnection is by means of a high-speed link that can be used for message exchange to coordinate cluster activity. The link can be a LAN that is shared with other computers that are not part of the cluster or the link can be a dedicated interconnection facility. In the latter case, one or more of the computers in the cluster will have a link to a LAN or WAN so that there is a connection between the server cluster and remote client systems. Note that in the figure, each computer is depicted as being a multiprocessor. This is not necessary but does enhance both performance and availability.

In the simple classification depicted in Figure 17.9, the other alternative is a shared-disk cluster. In this case, there generally is still a message link between

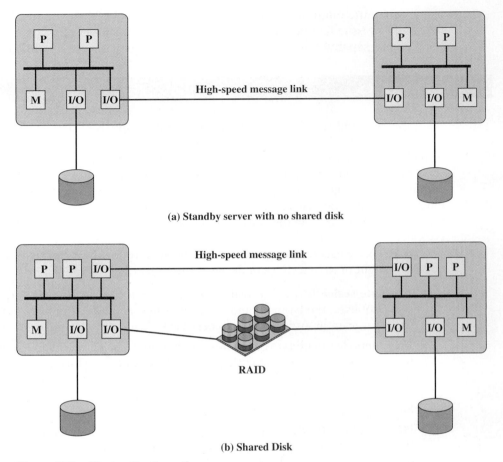

(a) Standby server with no shared disk

(b) Shared Disk

Figure 17.9 Cluster Configurations

nodes. In addition, there is a disk subsystem that is directly linked to multiple computers within the cluster. In this figure, the common disk subsystem is a RAID system. The use of RAID or some similar redundant disk technology is common in clusters so that the high availability achieved by the presence of multiple computers is not compromised by a shared disk that is a single point of failure.

A clearer picture of the range of cluster options can be gained by looking at functional alternatives. Table 17.2 provides a useful classification along functional lines, which we now discuss.

A common, older method, known as **passive standby**, is simply to have one computer handle all of the processing load while the other computer remains inactive, standing by to take over in the event of a failure of the primary. To coordinate the machines, the active, or primary, system periodically sends a "heartbeat" message to the standby machine. Should these messages stop arriving, the standby assumes that the primary server has failed and puts itself into operation. This approach increases availability but does not improve performance. Further, if the only information that is exchanged between the two systems is a heartbeat message,

Table 17.2   Clustering Methods: Benefits and Limitations

Clustering Method	Description	Benefits	Limitations
Passive Standby	A secondary server takes over in case of primary server failure.	Easy to implement.	High cost because the secondary server is unavailable for other processing tasks.
Active Secondary:	The secondary server is also used for processing tasks.	Reduced cost because secondary servers can be used for processing.	Increased complexity.
Separate Servers	Separate servers have their own disks. Data is continuously copied from primary to secondary server.	High availability.	High network and server overhead due to copying operations.
Servers Connected to Disks	Servers are cabled to the same disks, but each server owns its disks. If one server fails, its disks are taken over by the other server.	Reduced network and server overhead due to elimination of copying operations.	Usually requires disk mirroring or RAID technology to compensate for risk of disk failure.
Servers Share Disks	Multiple servers simultaneously share access to disks.	Low network and server overhead. Reduced risk of downtime caused by disk failure.	Requires lock manager software. Usually used with disk mirroring or RAID technology.

and if the two systems do not share common disks, then the standby provides a functional backup but has no access to the databases managed by the primary.

The passive standby is generally not referred to as a cluster. The term *cluster* is reserved for multiple interconnected computers that are all actively doing processing while maintaining the image of a single system to the outside world. The term **active secondary** is often used in referring to this configuration. Three classifications of clustering can be identified: separate servers, shared nothing, and shared memory.

In one approach to clustering, each computer is a **separate server** with its own disks and there are no disks shared between systems (Figure 17.9a). This arrangement provides high performance as well as high availability. In this case, some type of management or scheduling software is needed to assign incoming client requests to servers so that the load is balanced and high utilization is achieved. It is desirable to have a failover capability, which means that if a computer fails while executing an application, another computer in the cluster can pick up and complete the application. For this to happen, data must constantly be copied among systems so that each system has access to the current data of the other systems. The overhead of this data exchange ensures high availability at the cost of a performance penalty.

To reduce the communications overhead, most clusters now consist of servers connected to common disks (Figure 17.9b). In one variation on this approach, called **shared nothing**, the common disks are partitioned into volumes, and each volume is owned by a single computer. If that computer fails, the cluster must be reconfigured so that some other computer has ownership of the volumes of the failed computer.

It is also possible to have multiple computers share the same disks at the same time (called the **shared disk** approach), so that each computer has access to all of the volumes on all of the disks. This approach requires the use of some type of locking facility to ensure that data can only be accessed by one computer at a time.

Operating System Design Issues

Full exploitation of a cluster hardware configuration requires some enhancements to a single-system operating system.

FAILURE MANAGEMENT How failures are managed by a cluster depends on the clustering method used (Table 17.2). In general, two approaches can be taken to dealing with failures: highly available clusters and fault-tolerant clusters. A highly available cluster offers a high probability that all resources will be in service. If a failure occurs, such as a system goes down or a disk volume is lost, then the queries in progress are lost. Any lost query, if retried, will be serviced by a different computer in the cluster. However, the cluster operating system makes no guarantee about the state of partially executed transactions. This would need to be handled at the application level.

A fault-tolerant cluster ensures that all resources are always available. This is achieved by the use of redundant shared disks and mechanisms for backing out uncommitted transactions and committing completed transactions.

The function of switching applications and data resources over from a failed system to an alternative system in the cluster is referred to as **failover**. A related function is the restoration of applications and data resources to the original system once it has been fixed; this is referred to as **failback**. Failback can be automated, but this is desirable only if the problem is truly fixed and unlikely to recur. If not, automatic failback can cause subsequently failed resources to bounce back and forth between computers, resulting in performance and recovery problems.

LOAD BALANCING A cluster requires an effective capability for balancing the load among available computers. This includes the requirement that the cluster be incrementally scalable. When a new computer is added to the cluster, the load-balancing facility should automatically include this computer in scheduling applications. Middleware mechanisms need to recognize that services can appear on different members of the cluster and may migrate from one member to another.

PARALLELIZING COMPUTATION In some cases, effective use of a cluster requires executing software from a single application in parallel. [KAPP00] lists three general approaches to the problem:

- **Parallelizing compiler:** A parallelizing compiler determines, at compile time, which parts of an application can be executed in parallel. These are then split off to be assigned to different computers in the cluster. Performance depends on the nature of the problem and how well the compiler is designed. In general, such compilers are difficult to develop.
- **Parallelized application:** In this approach, the programmer writes the application from the outset to run on a cluster, and uses message passing to move data, as required, between cluster nodes. This places a high burden on the programmer but may be the best approach for exploiting clusters for some applications.

- **Parametric computing:** This approach can be used if the essence of the application is an algorithm or program that must be executed a large number of times, each time with a different set of starting conditions or parameters. A good example is a simulation model, which will run a large number of different scenarios and then develop statistical summaries of the results. For this approach to be effective, parametric processing tools are needed to organize, run, and manage the jobs in an effective manner.

Cluster Computer Architecture

Figure 17.10 shows a typical cluster architecture. The individual computers are connected by some high-speed LAN or switch hardware. Each computer is capable of operating independently. In addition, a middleware layer of software is installed in each computer to enable cluster operation. The cluster middleware provides a unified system image to the user, known as a **single-system image**. The middleware is also responsible for providing high availability, by means of load balancing and responding to failures in individual components. [HWAN99] lists the following as desirable cluster middleware services and functions:

- **Single entry point:** A user logs onto the cluster rather than to an individual computer.
- **Single file hierarchy:** The user sees a single hierarchy of file directories under the same root directory.
- **Single control point:** There is a default workstation used for cluster management and control.
- **Single virtual networking:** Any node can access any other point in the cluster, even though the actual cluster configuration may consist of multiple interconnected networks. There is a single virtual network operation.
- **Single memory space:** Distributed shared memory enables programs to share variables.
- **Single job-management system:** Under a cluster job scheduler, a user can submit a job without specifying the host computer to execute the job.
- **Single user interface:** A common graphic interface supports all users, regardless of the workstation from which they enter the cluster.
- **Single I/O space:** Any node can remotely access any I/O peripheral or disk device without knowledge of its physical location.
- **Single process space:** A uniform process-identification scheme is used. A process on any node can create or communicate with any other process on a remote node.
- **Checkpointing:** This function periodically saves the process state and intermediate computing results, to allow rollback recovery after a failure.
- **Process migration:** This function enables load balancing.

The last four items on the preceding list enhance the availability of the cluster. The remaining items are concerned with providing a single system image.

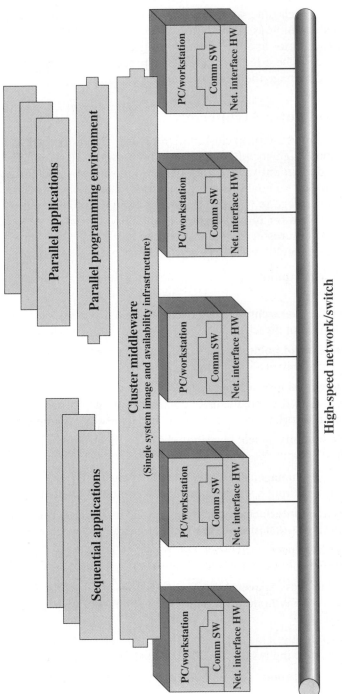

Figure 17.10 Cluster Computer Architecture [BUYY99a]

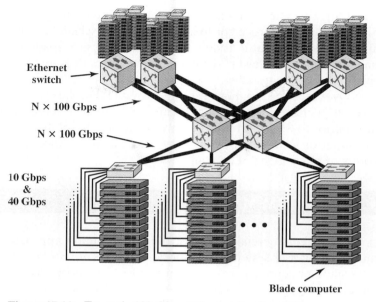

Ethernet switch

N × 100 Gbps

N × 100 Gbps

10 Gbps & 40 Gbps

Blade computer

Figure 17.11 Example 100-Gbps Ethernet Configuration for Massive Blade Server Site

Returning to Figure 17.10, a cluster will also include software tools for enabling the efficient execution of programs that are capable of parallel execution.

Blade Servers

A common implementation of the cluster approach is the blade server. A blade server is a server architecture that houses multiple server modules ("blades") in a single chassis. It is widely used in data centers to save space and improve system management. Either self-standing or rack mounted, the chassis provides the power supply, and each blade has its own processor, memory, and hard disk.

An example of the application is shown in Figure 17.11, taken from [NOWE07]. The trend at large data centers, with substantial banks of blade servers, is the deployment of 10-Gbps ports on individual servers to handle the massive multimedia traffic provided by these servers. Such arrangements are stressing the on-site Ethernet switches needed to interconnect large numbers of servers. A 100-Gbps rate provides the bandwidth required to handle the increased traffic load. The 100-Gbps Ethernet switches are deployed in switch uplinks inside the data center as well as providing interbuilding, intercampus, wide area connections for enterprise networks.

Clusters Compared to SMP

Both clusters and symmetric multiprocessors provide a configuration with multiple processors to support high-demand applications. Both solutions are commercially available, although SMP schemes have been around far longer.

The main strength of the SMP approach is that an SMP is easier to manage and configure than a cluster. The SMP is much closer to the original single-processor model for which nearly all applications are written. The principal change required in going from a uniprocessor to an SMP is to the scheduler function. Another benefit of the SMP is that it usually takes up less physical space and draws less power than a comparable cluster. A final important benefit is that the SMP products are well established and stable.

Over the long run, however, the advantages of the cluster approach are likely to result in clusters dominating the high-performance server market. Clusters are far superior to SMPs in terms of incremental and absolute scalability. Clusters are also superior in terms of availability, because all components of the system can readily be made highly redundant.

17.6 NONUNIFORM MEMORY ACCESS

In terms of commercial products, the two common approaches to providing a multiple-processor system to support applications are SMPs and clusters. For some years, another approach, known as nonuniform memory access (NUMA), has been the subject of research and commercial NUMA products are now available.

Before proceeding, we should define some terms often found in the NUMA literature.

- **Uniform memory access (UMA)**: All processors have access to all parts of main memory using loads and stores. The memory access time of a processor to all regions of memory is the same. The access times experienced by different processors are the same. The SMP organization discussed in Sections 17.2 and 17.3 is UMA.

- **Nonuniform memory access (NUMA):** All processors have access to all parts of main memory using loads and stores. The memory access time of a processor differs depending on which region of main memory is accessed. The last statement is true for all processors; however, for different processors, which memory regions are slower and which are faster differ.

- **Cache-coherent NUMA (CC-NUMA):** A NUMA system in which cache coherence is maintained among the caches of the various processors.

A NUMA system without cache coherence is more or less equivalent to a cluster. The commercial products that have received much attention recently are CC-NUMA systems, which are quite distinct from both SMPs and clusters. Usually, but unfortunately not always, such systems are in fact referred to in the commercial literature as CC-NUMA systems. This section is concerned only with CC-NUMA systems.

Motivation

With an SMP system, there is a practical limit to the number of processors that can be used. An effective cache scheme reduces the bus traffic between any one processor and main memory. As the number of processors increases, this bus traffic also increases. Also, the bus is used to exchange cache-coherence signals, further adding to the burden. At some point, the bus becomes a performance bottleneck. Performance degradation seems to limit the number of processors in an SMP configuration to somewhere between 16 and 64 processors. For example, Silicon Graphics' Power Challenge SMP is limited to 64 R10000 processors in a single system; beyond this number performance degrades substantially.

The processor limit in an SMP is one of the driving motivations behind the development of cluster systems. However, with a cluster, each node has its own private main memory; applications do not see a large global memory. In effect, coherency is maintained in software rather than hardware. This memory granularity affects performance and, to achieve maximum performance, software must be tailored to this environment. One approach to achieving large-scale multiprocessing while retaining the flavor of SMP is NUMA. For example, the Silicon Graphics Origin NUMA system is designed to support up to 1024 MIPS R10000 processors [WHIT97] and the Sequent NUMA-Q system is designed to support up to 252 Pentium II processors [LOVE96].

The objective with NUMA is to maintain a transparent system wide memory while permitting multiple multiprocessor nodes, each with its own bus or other internal interconnect system.

Organization

Figure 17.12 depicts a typical CC-NUMA organization. There are multiple independent nodes, each of which is, in effect, an SMP organization. Thus, each node contains multiple processors, each with its own L1 and L2 caches, plus main memory. The node is the basic building block of the overall CC-NUMA organization. For example, each Silicon Graphics Origin node includes two MIPS R10000 processors; each Sequent NUMA-Q node includes four Pentium II processors. The nodes are interconnected by means of some communications facility, which could be a switching mechanism, a ring, or some other networking facility.

Each node in the CC-NUMA system includes some main memory. From the point of view of the processors, however, there is only a single addressable memory, with each location having a unique system wide address. When a processor initiates a memory access, if the requested memory location is not in that processor's cache, then the L2 cache initiates a fetch operation. If the desired line is in the local portion of the main memory, the line is fetched across the local bus. If the desired line is in a remote portion of the main memory, then an automatic request is sent out to fetch that line across the interconnection network, deliver it to the local bus, and then deliver it to the requesting cache on that bus. All of this activity is automatic and transparent to the processor and its cache.

In this configuration, cache coherence is a central concern. Although implementations differ as to details, in general terms we can say that each node must maintain some sort of directory that gives it an indication of the location of various portions of memory and also cache status information. To see how this scheme works, we give an example taken from [PFIS98]. Suppose that processor 3 on node 2 (P2-3) requests a memory location 798, which is in the memory of node 1. The following sequence occurs:

1. P2-3 issues a read request on the snoopy bus of node 2 for location 798.
2. The directory on node 2 sees the request and recognizes that the location is in node 1.

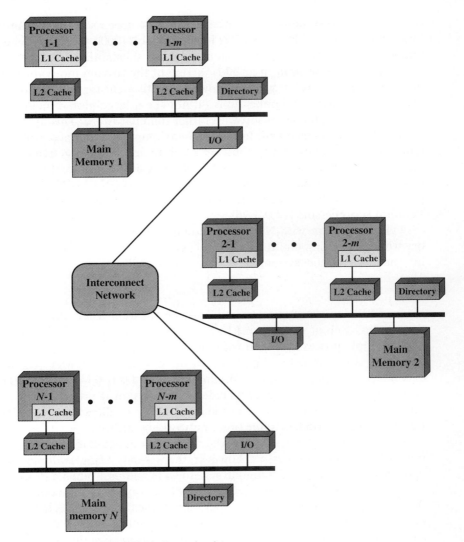

Figure 17.12 CC-NUMA Organization

3. Node 2's directory sends a request to node 1, which is picked up by node 1's directory.

4. Node 1's directory, acting as a surrogate of P2-3, requests the contents of 798, as if it were a processor.

5. Node 1's main memory responds by putting the requested data on the bus.

6. Node 1's directory picks up the data from the bus.

7. The value is transferred back to node 2's directory.

8. Node 2's directory places the data back on node 2's bus, acting as a surrogate for the memory that originally held it.

9. The value is picked up and placed in P2-3's cache and delivered to P2-3.

The preceding sequence explains how data are read from a remote memory using hardware mechanisms that make the transaction transparent to the processor. On top of these mechanisms, some form of cache coherence protocol is needed. Various systems differ on exactly how this is done. We make only a few general remarks here. First, as part of the preceding sequence, node 1's directory keeps a record that some remote cache has a copy of the line containing location 798. Then, there needs to be a cooperative protocol to take care of modifications. For example, if a modification is done in a cache, this fact can be broadcast to other nodes. Each node's directory that receives such a broadcast can then determine if any local cache has that line and, if so, cause it to be purged. If the actual memory location is at the node receiving the broadcast notification, then that node's directory needs to maintain an entry indicating that that line of memory is invalid and remains so until a write back occurs. If another processor (local or remote) requests the invalid line, then the local directory must force a write back to update memory before providing the data.

NUMA Pros and Cons

The main advantage of a CC-NUMA system is that it can deliver effective performance at higher levels of parallelism than SMP, without requiring major software changes. With multiple NUMA nodes, the bus traffic on any individual node is limited to a demand that the bus can handle. However, if many of the memory accesses are to remote nodes, performance begins to break down. There is reason to believe that this performance breakdown can be avoided. First, the use of L1 and L2 caches is designed to minimize all memory accesses, including remote ones. If much of the software has good temporal locality, then remote memory accesses should not be excessive. Second, if the software has good spatial locality, and if virtual memory is in use, then the data needed for an application will reside on a limited number of frequently used pages that can be initially loaded into the memory local to the running application. The Sequent designers report that such spatial locality does appear in representative applications [LOVE96]. Finally, the virtual memory scheme can be enhanced by including in the operating system a page migration mechanism that will move a virtual memory page to a node that is frequently using it; the Silicon Graphics designers report success with this approach [WHIT97].

Even if the performance breakdown due to remote access is addressed, there are two other disadvantages for the CC-NUMA approach [PFIS98]. First, a CC-NUMA does not transparently look like an SMP; software changes will be required to move an operating system and applications from an SMP to a CC-NUMA system. These include page allocation, already mentioned, process allocation, and load balancing by the operating system. A second concern is that of availability. This is a rather complex issue and depends on the exact implementation of the CC-NUMA system; the interested reader is referred to [PFIS98].

Vector Processor Simulator

17.7 VECTOR COMPUTATION

Although the performance of mainframe general-purpose computers continues to improve relentlessly, there continue to be applications that are beyond the reach of the contemporary mainframe. There is a need for computers to solve mathematical problems of physical processes, such as occur in disciplines including aerodynamics, seismology, meteorology, and atomic, nuclear, and plasma physics.

Typically, these problems are characterized by the need for high precision and a program that repetitively performs floating-point arithmetic operations on large arrays of numbers. Most of these problems fall into the category known as *continuous-field simulation*. In essence, a physical situation can be described by a surface or region in three dimensions (e.g., the flow of air adjacent to the surface of a rocket). This surface is approximated by a grid of points. A set of differential equations defines the physical behavior of the surface at each point. The equations are represented as an array of values and coefficients, and the solution involves repeated arithmetic operations on the arrays of data.

Supercomputers were developed to handle these types of problems. These machines are typically capable of billions of floating-point operations per second. In contrast to mainframes, which are designed for multiprogramming and intensive I/O, the supercomputer is optimized for the type of numerical calculation just described.

The supercomputer has limited use and, because of its price tag, a limited market. Comparatively few of these machines are operational, mostly at research centers and some government agencies with scientific or engineering functions. As with other areas of computer technology, there is a constant demand to increase the performance of the supercomputer. Thus, the technology and performance of the supercomputer continues to evolve.

There is another type of system that has been designed to address the need for vector computation, referred to as the *array processor*. Although a supercomputer is optimized for vector computation, it is a general-purpose computer, capable of handling scalar processing and general data processing tasks. Array processors do not include scalar processing; they are configured as peripheral devices by both mainframe and minicomputer users to run the vectorized portions of programs.

Approaches to Vector Computation

The key to the design of a supercomputer or array processor is to recognize that the main task is to perform arithmetic operations on arrays or vectors of floating-point numbers. In a general-purpose computer, this will require iteration through each element of the array. For example, consider two vectors (one-dimensional arrays) of numbers, A and B. We would like to add these and place the result in C. In the example of Figure 17.13, this requires six separate additions. How could we speed up this computation? The answer is to introduce some form of parallelism.

Several approaches have been taken to achieving parallelism in vector computation. We illustrate this with an example. Consider the vector multiplication $C = A \times B$, where A, B, and C are $N \times N$ matrices. The formula for each element of C is

$$c_{i,j} = \sum_{k=1}^{N} a_{i,k} \times b_{k,j}$$

$$\begin{bmatrix} 1.5 \\ 7.1 \\ 6.9 \\ 100.5 \\ 0 \\ 59.7 \end{bmatrix} + \begin{bmatrix} 2.0 \\ 39.7 \\ 1000.003 \\ 11 \\ 21.1 \\ 19.7 \end{bmatrix} = \begin{bmatrix} 3.5 \\ 46.8 \\ 1006.093 \\ 111.5 \\ 21.1 \\ 79.4 \end{bmatrix}$$

$$A \quad + \quad B \quad = \quad C$$

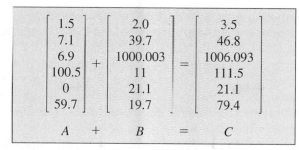

Figure 17.13 Example of Vector Addition

where A, B, and C have elements $a_{i,j}$, $b_{i,j}$, and $c_{i,j}$ respectively. Figure 17.14a shows a FORTRAN program for this computation that can be run on an ordinary scalar processor.

One approach to improving performance can be referred to as *vector processing*. This assumes that it is possible to operate on a one-dimensional vector of data. Figure 17.14b is a FORTRAN program with a new form of instruction that allows

```
      DO 100 I = 1, N
      DO 100 J = 1, N
      C(I, J) = 0.0
      DO 100 K = 1, N
      C(I, J) = C(I, J) + A(I, K) + B(K, J)
100   CONTINUE
```

(a) Scalar processing

```
      DO 100 I = 1, N
      C(I, J) = 0.0 (J = 1, N)
      DO 100 K = 1, N
      C(I, J) = C(I, J) + A(I, K) + B(K, J) (J = 1, N)
100   CONTINUE
```

(b) Vector processing

```
      DO 50 J = 1, N - 1
      FORK 100
50    CONTINUE
      J = N
100   DO 200 I = 1, N
      C(I, J) = 0.0
      DO 200 K = 1, N
      C(I, J) = C(I, J) + A(I, K) + B(K, J)
200   CONTINUE
      JOIN N
```

(c) Parallel processing

Figure 17.14 Matrix Multiplication (C = A × B)

vector computation to be specified. The notation ($J = 1$, N) indicates that operations on all indices J in the given interval are to be carried out as a single operation. How this can be achieved is addressed shortly.

The program in Figure 17.14b indicates that all the elements of the ith row are to be computed in parallel. Each element in the row is a summation, and the summations (across K) are done serially rather than in parallel. Even so, only N^2 vector multiplications are required for this algorithm as compared with N^3 scalar multiplications for the scalar algorithm.

Another approach, *parallel processing,* is illustrated in Figure 17.14c. This approach assumes that we have N independent processors that can function in parallel. To utilize processors effectively, we must somehow parcel out the computation to the various processors. Two primitives are used. The primitive FORK n causes an independent process to be started at location n. In the meantime, the original process continues execution at the instruction immediately following the FORK. Every execution of a FORK spawns a new process. The JOIN instruction is essentially the inverse of the FORK. The statement JOIN N causes N independent processes to be merged into one that continues execution at the instruction following the JOIN. The operating system must coordinate this merger, and so the execution does not continue until all N processes have reached the JOIN instruction.

The program in Figure 17.15c is written to mimic the behavior of the vector-processing program. In the parallel processing program, each column of C is computed by a separate process. Thus, the elements in a given row of C are computed in parallel.

The preceding discussion describes approaches to vector computation in logical or architectural terms. Let us turn now to a consideration of types of processor organization that can be used to implement these approaches. A wide variety of organizations have been and are being pursued. Three main categories stand out:

- Pipelined ALU
- Parallel ALUs
- Parallel processors

Figure 17.15 illustrates the first two of these approaches. We have already discussed pipelining in Chapter 14. Here the concept is extended to the operation of the ALU. Because floating-point operations are rather complex, there is opportunity for decomposing a floating-point operation into stages, so that different stages can operate on different sets of data concurrently. This is illustrated in Figure 17.16a. Floating-point addition is broken up into four stages (see Figure 10.22): compare, shift, add, and normalize. A vector of numbers is presented sequentially to the first stage. As the processing proceeds, four different sets of numbers will be operated on concurrently in the pipeline.

It should be clear that this organization is suitable for vector processing. To see this, consider the instruction pipelining described in Chapter 14. The processor goes through a repetitive cycle of fetching and processing instructions. In the absence of branches, the processor is continuously fetching instructions from sequential locations. Consequently, the pipeline is kept full and a savings in time is achieved. Similarly, a pipelined ALU will save time only if it is fed a stream of data from

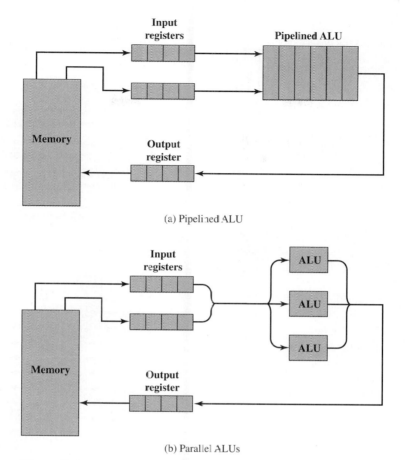

(a) Pipelined ALU

(b) Parallel ALUs

Figure 17.15 Approaches to Vector Computation

sequential locations. A single, isolated floating-point operation is not speeded up by a pipeline. The speedup is achieved when a vector of operands is presented to the ALU. The control unit cycles the data through the ALU until the entire vector is processed.

The pipeline operation can be further enhanced if the vector elements are available in registers rather than from main memory. This is in fact suggested by Figure 17.15a. The elements of each vector operand are loaded as a block into a vector register, which is simply a large bank of identical registers. The result is also placed in a vector register. Thus, most operations involve only the use of registers, and only load and store operations and the beginning and end of a vector operation require access to memory.

The mechanism illustrated in Figure 17.16 could be referred to as *pipelining within an operation*. That is, we have a single arithmetic operation (e.g., $C = A + B$) that is to be applied to vector operands, and pipelining allows multiple vector elements to be processed in parallel. This mechanism can be augmented with *pipelining across operations*. In this latter case, there is a sequence of arithmetic vector operations, and instruction pipelining is used to speed up processing. One approach

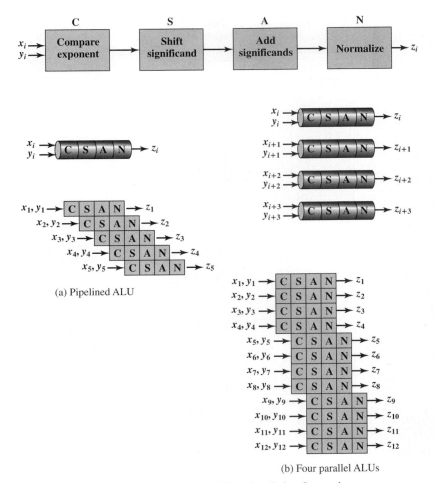

(a) Pipelined ALU

(b) Four parallel ALUs

Figure 17.16 Pipelined Processing of Floating-Point Operations

to this, referred to as **chaining**, is found on the Cray supercomputers. The basic rule for chaining is this: A vector operation may start as soon as the first element of the operand vector(s) is available and the functional unit (e.g., add, subtract, multiply, divide) is free. Essentially, chaining causes results issuing from one functional unit to be fed immediately into another functional unit and so on. If vector registers are used, intermediate results do not have to be stored into memory and can be used even before the vector operation that created them runs to completion.

For example, when computing $C = (s \times A) + B$, where A, B, and C are vectors and s is a scalar, the Cray may execute three instructions at once. Elements fetched for a load immediately enter a pipelined multiplier, the products are sent to a pipelined adder, and the sums are placed in a vector register as soon as the adder completes them:

1. Vector load $A \rightarrow$ Vector Register (VR1)
2. Vector load $B \rightarrow$ VR2

3. Vector multiply $s \times VR1 \rightarrow VR3$

4. Vector add $VR3 + VR2 \rightarrow VR4$

5. Vector store $VR4 \rightarrow C$

Instructions 2 and 3 can be chained (pipelined) because they involve different memory locations and registers. Instruction 4 needs the results of instructions 2 and 3, but it can be chained with them as well. As soon as the first elements of vector registers 2 and 3 are available, the operation in instruction 4 can begin.

Another way to achieve vector processing is by the use of multiple ALUs in a single processor, under the control of a single control unit. In this case, the control unit routes data to ALUs so that they can function in parallel. It is also possible to use pipelining on each of the parallel ALUs. This is illustrated in Figure 17.16b. The example shows a case in which four ALUs operate in parallel.

As with pipelined organization, a parallel ALU organization is suitable for vector processing. The control unit routes vector elements to ALUs in a round-robin fashion until all elements are processed. This type of organization is more complex than a single-ALU CPI.

Finally, vector processing can be achieved by using multiple parallel processors. In this case, it is necessary to break the task up into multiple processes to be executed in parallel. This organization is effective only if the software and hardware for effective coordination of parallel processors is available.

We can expand our taxonomy of Section 17.1 to reflect these new structures, as shown in Figure 17.17. Computer organizations can be distinguished by the presence of one or more control units. Multiple control units imply multiple processors. Following our previous discussion, if the multiple processors can function cooperatively on a given task, they are termed *parallel processors*.

The reader should be aware of some unfortunate terminology likely to be encountered in the literature. The term *vector processor* is often equated with a pipelined ALU organization, although a parallel ALU organization is also designed for vector processing, and, as we have discussed, a parallel processor organization may also be designed for vector processing. *Array processing* is sometimes used to refer to a parallel ALU, although, again, any of the three organizations is optimized for the processing of arrays. To make matters worse, *array processor* usually refers to an auxiliary processor attached to a general-purpose processor and used to perform vector computation. An array processor may use either the pipelined or parallel ALU approach.

At present, the pipelined ALU organization dominates the marketplace. Pipelined systems are less complex than the other two approaches. Their control

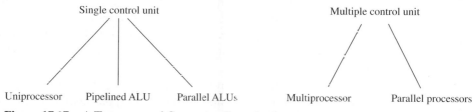

Figure 17.17 A Taxonomy of Computer Organizations

unit and operating system design are well developed to achieve efficient resource allocation and high performance. The remainder of this section is devoted to a more detailed examination of this approach, using a specific example.

IBM 3090 Vector Facility

A good example of a pipelined ALU organization for vector processing is the vector facility developed for the IBM 370 architecture and implemented on the high-end 3090 series [PADE88, TUCK87]. This facility is an optional add-on to the basic system but is highly integrated with it. It resembles vector facilities found on super-computers, such as the Cray family.

The IBM facility makes use of a number of vector registers. Each register is actually a bank of scalar registers. To compute the vector sum $C = A + B$, the vectors A and B are loaded into two vector registers. The data from these registers are passed through the ALU as fast as possible, and the results are stored in a third vector register. The computation overlap, and the loading of the input data into the registers in a block, results in a significant speeding up over an ordinary ALU operation.

ORGANIZATION The IBM vector architecture, and similar pipelined vector ALUs, provides increased performance over loops of scalar arithmetic instructions in three ways:

- The fixed and predetermined structure of vector data permits housekeeping instructions inside the loop to be replaced by faster internal (hardware or microcoded) machine operations.
- Data-access and arithmetic operations on several successive vector elements can proceed concurrently by overlapping such operations in a pipelined design or by performing multiple-element operations in parallel.
- The use of vector registers for intermediate results avoids additional storage reference.

Figure 17.18 shows the general organization of the vector facility. Although the vector facility is seen to be a physically separate add-on to the processor, its architecture is an extension of the System/370 architecture and is compatible with it. The vector facility is integrated into the System/370 architecture in the following ways:

- Existing System/370 instructions are used for all scalar operations.
- Arithmetic operations on individual vector elements produce exactly the same result as do corresponding System/370 scalar instructions. For example, one design decision concerned the definition of the result in a floating-point DIVIDE operation. Should the result be exact, as it is for scalar floating-point division, or should an approximation be allowed that would permit higher-speed implementation but could sometimes introduce an error in one or more low-order bit positions? The decision was made to uphold complete compatibility with the System/370 architecture at the expense of a minor performance degradation.
- Vector instructions are interruptible, and their execution can be resumed from the point of interruption after appropriate action has been taken, in a manner compatible with the System/370 program-interruption scheme.

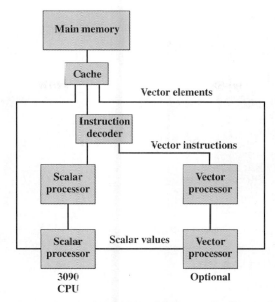

Figure 17.18 IBM 3090 with Vector Facility

- Arithmetic exceptions are the same as, or extensions of, exceptions for the scalar arithmetic instructions of the System/370, and similar fix-up routines can be used. To accommodate this, a vector interruption index is employed that indicates the location in a vector register that is affected by an exception (e.g., overflow). Thus, when execution of the vector instruction resumes, the proper place in a vector register is accessed.

- Vector data reside in virtual storage, with page faults being handled in a standard manner.

This level of integration provides a number of benefits. Existing operating systems can support the vector facility with minor extensions. Existing application programs, language compilers, and other software can be run unchanged. Software that could take advantage of the vector facility can be modified as desired.

REGISTERS A key issue in the design of a vector facility is whether operands are located in registers or memory. The IBM organization is referred to as *register to register,* because the vector operands, both input and output, can be staged in vector registers. This approach is also used on the Cray supercomputer. An alternative approach, used on Control Data machines, is to obtain operands directly from memory. The main disadvantage of the use of vector registers is that the programmer or compiler must take them into account for good performance. For example, suppose that the length of the vector registers is K and the length of the vectors to be processed is $N > K$. In this case, a vector loop must be performed, in which the operation is performed on K elements at a time and the loop is repeated N/K times. The main advantage of the vector register approach is that the operation is decoupled from slower main memory and instead takes place primarily with registers.

FORTRAN ROUTINE:

```
        DO 100 J = 1, 50
        CR(J) = AR(J) * BR(J) − AI(J) * BI(J)
100     CI(J) = AR(J) * BI(J) + AI(J) * BR(J)
```

Operation	Cycles
AR(J) * BR(J) → T1(J)	3
AI(J) * BI(J) → T2(J)	3
T1(J) − T2(J) → CR(J)	3
AR(J) * BI(J) → T3(J)	3
AI(J) * BR(J) → T4(J)	3
T3(J) + T4(J) → CI(J)	3
TOTAL	18

(a) Storage to storage

Operation	Cycles
AR(J) → V1(J)	1
V1(J) * BR(J) → V2(J)	1
AI(J) → V3(J)	1
V3(J) * BI(J) → V4(J)	1
V2(J) − V4(J) → V5(J)	1
V5(J) → CR(J)	1
V1(J) * BI(J) → V6(J)	1
V4(J) * BR(J) → V7(J)	1
V6(J) + V7(J) → V8(J)	1
V8(J) → CI(J)	1
TOTAL	10

(c) Storage to register

Vi = Vector registers
AR, BR, AI, BI = Operands in memory
Ti = Temporary locations in memory

Operation	Cycles
AR(J) → V1(J)	1
BR(J) → V2(J)	1
V1(J) * V2(J) → V3(J)	1
AI(J) → V4(J)	1
BI(J) → V5(J)	1
V4(J) * V5(J) → V6(J)	1
V3(J) − V6(J) → V7(J)	1
V7(J) → CR(J)	1
V1(J) * V5(J) → V8(J)	1
V4(J) * V2(J) → V9(J)	1
V8(J) + V9(J) → V0(J)	1
V0(J) → CI(J)	1
TOTAL	12

(b) Register to register

Operation	Cycles
AR(J) → V1(J)	1
V1(J) * BR(J) → V2(J)	1
AI(J) → V3(J)	1
V2(J) − V3(J) * BI(J) → V2(J)	1
V2(J) → CR(J)	1
V1(J) * BI(J) → V4(J)	1
V4(J) + V3(J) * BR(J) → V5(J)	1
V5(J) → CI(J)	1
TOTAL	8

(d) Compound instruction

Figure 17.19   Alternative Programs for Vector Calculation

The speedup that can be achieved using registers is demonstrated in Figure 17.19. The FORTRAN routine multiplies vector A by vector B to produce vector C, where each vector has a real part (AR, BR, CR) and an imaginary part (AI, BI, CI). The 3090 can perform one main-storage access per processor, or clock, cycle (either read or write); has registers that can sustain two accesses for reading and one for writing per cycle; and produces one result per cycle in its arithmetic unit. Let us assume the use of instructions that can specify two source operands and a result.[4] Part (a) of the figure shows that, with memory-to-memory instructions, each iteration of the computation requires a total of 18 cycles. With a pure register-to-register

---

[4]For the 370/390 architecture, the only three-operand instructions (register and storage instructions, RS) specify two operands in registers and one in memory. In part (a) of the example, we assume the existence of three-operand instructions in which all operands are in main memory. This is done for purposes of comparison and, in fact, such an instruction format could have been chosen for the vector architecture.

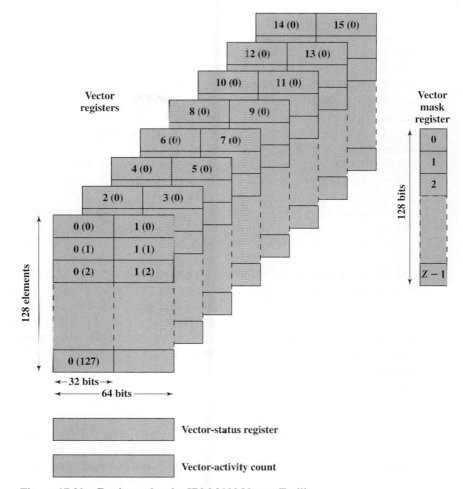

Figure 17.20   Registers for the IBM 3090 Vector Facility

architecture (part (b)), this time is reduced to 12 cycles. Of course, with register-to-register operation, the vector quantities must be loaded into the vector registers prior to computation and stored in memory afterward. For large vectors, this fixed penalty is relatively small. Figure 17.19c shows that the ability to specify both storage and register operands in one instruction further reduces the time to 10 cycles per iteration. This latter type of instruction is included in the vector architecture.[5]

Figure 17.20 illustrates the registers that are part of the IBM 3090 vector facility. There are sixteen 32-bit vector registers. The vector registers can also be coupled to form eight 64-bit vector registers. Any register element can hold an integer or floating-point value. Thus, the vector registers may be used for 32-bit and 64-bit integer values, and 32-bit and 64-bit floating-point values.

---

[5]Compound instructions, discussed subsequently, afford a further reduction.

The architecture specifies that each register contains from 8 to 512 scalar elements. The choice of actual length involves a design trade-off. The time to do a vector operation consists essentially of the overhead for pipeline startup and register filling plus one cycle per vector element. Thus, the use of a large number of register elements reduces the relative startup time for a computation. However, this efficiency must be balanced against the added time required for saving and restoring vector registers on a process switch and the practical cost and space limits. These considerations led to the use of 128 elements per register in later 3090 implementations.

Three additional registers are needed by the vector facility. The vector-mask register contains mask bits that may be used to select which elements in the vector registers are to be processed for a particular operation. The vector-status register contains control fields, such as the vector count, that determine how many elements in the vector registers are to be processed. The vector-activity count keeps track of the time spent executing vector instructions.

COMPOUND INSTRUCTIONS As was discussed previously, instruction execution can be overlapped using chaining to improve performance. The designers of the IBM vector facility chose not to include this capability for several reasons. The System/370 architecture would have to be extended to handle complex interrupts (including their effect on virtual memory management), and corresponding changes would be needed in the software. A more basic issue was the cost of including the additional controls and register access paths in the vector facility for generalized chaining.

Instead, three operations are provided that combine into one instruction (one opcode) the most common sequences in vector computation, namely multiplication followed by addition, subtraction, or summation. The storage-to-register MULTIPLY-AND-ADD instruction, for example, fetches a vector from storage, multiplies it by a vector from a register, and adds the product to a third vector in a register. By use of the compound instructions MULTIPLY-AND-ADD and MULTIPLY-AND-SUBTRACT in the example of Figure 17.19, the total time for the iteration is reduced from 10 to 8 cycles.

Unlike chaining, compound instructions do not require the use of additional registers for temporary storage of intermediate results, and they require one less register access. For example, consider the following chain:

$$A \rightarrow VR1$$

$$VR1 + VR2 \rightarrow VR1$$

In this case, two stores to the vector register VR1 are required. In the IBM architecture there is a storage-to-register ADD instruction. With this instruction, only the sum is placed in VR1. The compound instruction also avoids the need to reflect in the machine-state description the concurrent execution of a number of instructions, which simplifies status saving and restoring by the operating system and the handling of interrupts.

THE INSTRUCTION SET Table 17.3 summarizes the arithmetic and logical operations that are defined for the vector architecture. In addition, there are memory-to-register

Table 17.3 IBM 3090 Vector Facility: Arithmetic and Logical Instructions

Operation	Data Types — Floating-Point: Long	Short	Binary or Logical	Operand Locations			
Add	FL	FS	BI	V + V → V	V + S → V	Q + V → V	Q + S → V
Subtract	FL	FS	BI	V − V → V	V − S → V	Q − V → V	Q − S → V
Multiply	FL	FS	BI	V × V → V	V × V → V	Q × V → V	Q × S → V
Divide	FL	FS	—	V/V → V	V/S → V	Q/V → V	Q/S → V
Compare	FL	FS	BI	V · V → V	V · S → V	Q · V → V	Q · S → V
Multiply and Add	FL	FS	—		V + V × S → V	V + Q × V → V	V + Q × S → V
Multiply and Subtract	FL	FS	—		V − V × S → V	V − Q × V → V	V − Q × S → V
Multiply and Accumulate	FL	FS	—	P + · V → V	P + · S → V		
Complement	FL	FS	BI	− V → V			
Positive Absolute	FL	FS	BI	|V| → V			
Negative Absolute	FL	FS	BI	−|V| → V			
Maximum	FL	FS	—	· V → Q		Q · V → Q	
Maximum Absolute	FL	FS	—	· V → Q		Q · V → Q	
Minimum	FL	FS	—	· V → Q		Q · V → Q	
Shift Left Logical	—	—	LO				
Shift Right Logical	—	—	LO				
And	—	—	LO	V & V → V	V & S → V	Q & V → V	Q & S → V
OR	—	—	LO	V/V → V	V/S → V	Q/V → V	Q/S → V
Exclusive-OR	—	—	LO	V ⊕ V → V	V ⊕ S → V	Q ⊕ V → V	Q ⊕ S → V

Explanation

Data types
FL Long floating point
FS Short floating point
BI Binary integer
LO Logical

Operand locations
V Vector register
S Storager
Q Scalar (general or floating-point register)
P Partial sums in vector register
· Special operation

655

load and register-to-memory store instructions. Note that many of the instructions use a three-operand format. Also, many instructions have a number of variants, depending on the location of the operands. A source operand may be a vector register (V), storage (S), or a scalar register (Q). The target is always a vector register, except for comparison, the result of which goes into the vector-mask register. With all these variants, the total number of opcodes (distinct instructions) is 171. This rather large number, however, is not as expensive to implement as might be imagined. Once the machine provides the arithmetic units and the data paths to feed operands from storage, scalar registers, and vector registers to the vector pipelines, the major hardware cost has been incurred. The architecture can, with little difference in cost, provide a rich set of variants on the use of those registers and pipelines.

Most of the instructions in Table 17.3 are self-explanatory. The two summation instructions warrant further explanation. The accumulate operation adds together the elements of a single vector (ACCUMULATE) or the elements of the product of two vectors (MULTIPLY-AND-ACCUMULATE). These instructions present an interesting design problem. We would like to perform this operation as rapidly as possible, taking full advantage of the ALU pipeline. The difficulty is that the sum of two numbers put into the pipeline is not available until several cycles later. Thus, the third element in the vector cannot be added to the sum of the first two elements until those two elements have gone through the entire pipeline. To overcome this problem, the elements of the vector are added in such a way as to produce four partial sums. In particular, elements 0, 4, 8, 12, . . . , 124 are added in that order to produce partial sum 0; elements 1, 5, 9, 13, . . . , 125 to partial sum 1; elements 2, 6, 10, 14, . . . , 126 to partial sum 2; and elements 3, 7, 11, 15, . . . , 127 to partial sum 4. Each of these partial sums can proceed through the pipeline at top speed, because the delay in the pipeline is roughly four cycles. A separate vector register is used to hold the partial sums. When all elements of the original vector have been processed, the four partial sums are added together to produce the final result. The performance of this second phase is not critical, because only four vector elements are involved.

17.8 RECOMMENDED READING

[MILE00] is an overview of cache coherence algorithms and techniques for multiprocessors, with an emphasis on performance issues. Another survey of the issues relating to cache coherence in multiprocessors is [LILJ93]. [TOMA93] contains reprints of many of the key papers on the subject.

[UNGE02] is an excellent survey of the concepts of multithreaded processors and chip multiprocessors. [UNGE03] is a lengthy survey of both proposed and current multithreaded processors that use explicit multithreading.

A thorough treatment of clusters can be found in [BUYY99a] and [BUYY99b]. [WEYG01] is a less technical survey of clusters, with good commentary on various commercial products. [DESA05] describes IBM's blade server architecture.

Good discussions of vector computation can be found in [STON93] and [HWAN93].

BUYY99a Buyya, R. *High-Performance Cluster Computing: Architectures and Systems.* Upper Saddle River, NJ: Prentice Hall, 1999.

BUYY99b Buyya, R. *High-Performance Cluster Computing: Programming and Applications.* Upper Saddle River, NJ: Prentice Hall, 1999.

DESA05 Desai, D., et al. "BladeCenter System Overview." *IBM Journal of Research and Development,* November 2005.

LILJ93 Lilja, D. "Cache Coherence in Large-Scale Shared-Memory Multiprocessors: Issues and Comparisons." *ACM Computing Surveys,* September 1993.

MILE00 Milenkovic, A. "Achieving High Performance in Bus-Based Shared-Memory Multiprocessors." *IEEE Concurrency,* July-September 2000.

TOMA93 Tomasevic, M., and Milutinovic. V. *The Cache Coherence Problem in Shared-Memory Multiprocessors: Hardware Solutions.* Los Alamitos, CA: IEEE Computer Society Press, 1993.

UNGE02 Ungerer, T.; Rubic, B.; and Silc, J. "Multithreaded Processors." *The Computer Journal,* No. 3, 2002.

UNGE03 Ungerer, T.; Rubic, B.; and Silc, J. "A Survey of Processors with Explicit Multithreading." *ACM Computing Surveys,* March, 2003.

WEYG01 Weygant, P. *Clusters for High Availability.* Upper Saddle River, NJ: Prentice Hall, 2001.

17.9 KEY TERMS, REVIEW QUESTIONS, AND PROBLEMS

Key Terms

active standby	MESI protocol	symmetric multiprocessor
cache coherence	multiprocessor	(SMP)
cluster	nonuniform memory access	uniform memory access
directory protocol	(NUMA)	(UMA)
failback	passive standby	uniprocessor
failover	snoopy protocol	vector facility

Review Questions

17.1 List and briefly define three types of computer system organization.

17.2 What are the chief characteristics of an SMP?

17.3 What are some of the potential advantages of an SMP compared with a uniprocessor?

17.4 What are some of the key OS design issues for an SMP?

17.5 What is the difference between software and hardware cache coherent schemes?

17.6 What is the meaning of each of the four states in the MESI protocol?

17.7 What are some of the key benefits of clustering?

17.8 What is the difference between failover and failback?

17.9 What are the differences among UMA. NUMA, and CC-NUMA?

Problems

17.1 Let α be the percentage of program code that can be executed simultaneously by n processors in a computer system. Assume that the remaining code must be executed sequentially by a single processor. Each processor has an execution rate of x MIPS.

    a. Derive an expression for the effective MIPS rate when using the system for exclusive execution of this program, in terms of n, α, and x.

    b. If $n = 16$ and $x = 4$ MIPS, determine the value of α that will yield a system performance of 40 MIPS.

17.2 A multiprocessor with eight processors has 20 attached tape drives. There are a large number of jobs submitted to the system that each require a maximum of four tape drives to complete execution. Assume that each job starts running with only three tape drives for a long period before requiring the fourth tape drive for a short period toward the end of its operation. Also assume an endless supply of such jobs.

    a. Assume the scheduler in the OS will not start a job unless there are four tape drives available. When a job is started, four drives are assigned immediately and are not released until the job finishes. What is the maximum number of jobs that can be in progress at once? What are the maximum and minimum number of tape drives that may be left idle as a result of this policy?

    b. Suggest an alternative policy to improve tape drive utilization and at the same time avoid system deadlock. What is the maximum number of jobs that can be in progress at once? What are the bounds on the number of idling tape drives?

17.3 Can you foresee any problem with the write-once cache approach on bus-based multiprocessors? If so, suggest a solution.

17.4 Consider a situation in which two processors in an SMP configuration, over time, require access to the same line of data from main memory. Both processors have a cache and use the MESI protocol. Initially, both caches have an invalid copy of the line. Figure 17.21 depicts the consequence of a read of line x by Processor P1. If this is the start of a sequence of accesses, draw the subsequent figures for the following sequence:

    1. P2 reads x.

    2. P1 writes to x (for clarity, label the line in P1's cache x').

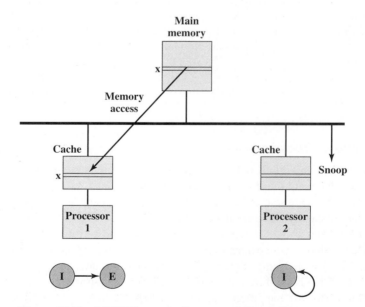

Figure 17.21 MESI Example: Processor 1 Reads Line x

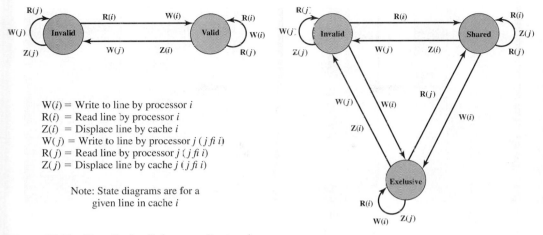

$W(i)$ = Write to line by processor i
$R(i)$ = Read line by processor i
$Z(i)$ = Displace line by cache i
$W(j)$ = Write to line by processor j ($j \neq i$)
$R(j)$ = Read line by processor j ($j \neq i$)
$Z(j)$ = Displace line by cache j ($j \neq i$)

Note: State diagrams are for a
given line in cache i

Figure 17.22 Two Cache Coherence Protocols

3. P1 writes to x (label the line in P1's cache x").
4. P2 reads x.

17.5 Figure 17.22 shows the state diagrams of two possible cache coherence protocols. Deduce and explain each protocol, and compare each to MESI.

17.6 Consider an SMP with both L1 and L2 caches using the MESI protocol. As explained in Section 17.3, one of four states is associated with each line in the L2 cache. Are all four states also needed for each line in the L1 cache? If so, why? If not, explain which state or states can be eliminated.

17.7 An earlier version of the IBM mainframe, the S/390 G4, used three levels of cache. As with the z990, only the first level was on the processor chip [called the processor unit (PU)]. The L2 cache was also similar to the z990. An L3 cache was on a separate chip that acted as a memory controller, and was interposed between the L2 caches and the memory cards. Table 17.4 shows the performance of a three-level cache arrangement for the IBM S/390. The purpose of this problem is to determine whether the inclusion of the third level of cache seems worthwhile. Determine the access penalty (average number of PU cycles) for a system with only an L1 cache, and normalize that value to 1.0. Then determine the normalized access penalty when both an L1 and L2 cache are used, and the access penalty when all three caches are used. Note the amount of improvement in each case and state your opinion on the value of the L3 cache.

17.8 **a.** Consider a uniprocessor with separate data and instruction caches, with hit ratios of H_d and H_i, respectively. Access time from processor to cache is c clock cycles, and transfer time for a block between memory and cache is b clock cycles. Let f_i

Table 17.4 Typical Cache Hit Rate on S/390 SMP Configuration [MAK97]

Memory Subsystem	Access Penalty (PU cycles)	Cache Size	Hit Rate (%)
L1 cache	1	32 KB	89
L2 cache	5	256 KB	5
L3 cache	14	2 MB	3
Memory	32	8 GB	3

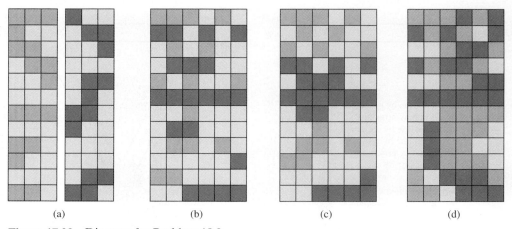

(a)   (b)   (c)   (d)

Figure 17.23   Diagram for Problem 18.9

be the fraction of memory accesses that are for instructions, and f_d is the fraction of dirty lines in the data cache among lines replaced. Assume a write-back policy and determine the effective memory access time in terms of the parameters just defined.

b. Now assume a bus-based SMP in which each processor has the characteristics of part (a). Every processor must handle cache invalidation in addition to memory reads and writes. This affects effective memory access time. Let f_{inv} be the fraction of data references that cause invalidation signals to be sent to other data caches. The processor sending the signal requires t clock cycles to complete the invalidation operation. Other processors are not involved in the invalidation operation. Determine the effective memory access time.

17.9   What organizational alternative is suggested by each of the illustrations in Figure 17.23?

17.10   In Figure 17.7, some of the diagrams show horizontal rows that are partially filled. In other cases, there are rows that are completely blank. These represent two different types of loss of efficiency. Explain.

17.11   Consider the pipeline depiction in Figure 14.13b, which is redrawn in Figure 17.24a, with the fetch and decode stages ignored, to represent the execution of thread A. Figure 17.24b illustrates the execution of a separate thread B. In both cases, a simple pipelined processor is used.

a. Show an instruction issue diagram, similar to Figure 17.7a, for each of the two threads.

b. Assume that the two threads are to be executed in parallel on a chip multiprocessor, with each of the two processors on the chip using a simple pipeline. Show an instruction issue diagram similar to Figure 17.7k. Also show a pipeline execution diagram in the style of Figure 17.24.

c. Assume a two-issue superscalar architecture. Repeat part (b) for an interleaved multithreading superscalar implementation, assuming no data dependencies. *Note:* There is no unique answer; you need to make assumptions about latency and priority.

d. Repeat part (c) for a blocked multithreading superscalar implementation.

e. Repeat for a four-issue SMT architecture.

17.12   The following code segment needs to be executed 64 times for the evaluation of the vector arithmetic expression: $D(I) = A(I) + B(I) \times C(I)$ for $0 \le I \le 63$.

     Load R1, B(I)   /R1 ← Memory $(\alpha + I)$/
     Load R2, C(I)   /R2 ← Memory $(\beta + I)$/

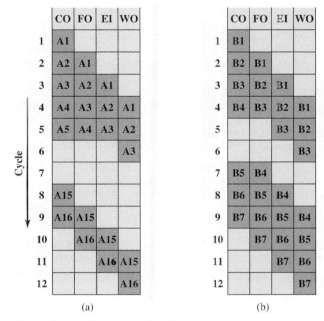

Figure 17.24 Two Threads of Execution

$$
\begin{array}{ll}
\text{Multiply R1, R2} & /R1 \leftarrow (R1) \times (R2)/ \\
\text{Load R3, A(I)} & /R3 \leftarrow \text{Memory } (\gamma + I)/ \\
\text{Add R3, R1} & /R3 \leftarrow (R3) + (R1)/ \\
\text{Store D1, R3} & /\text{Memory } (\theta + I) \leftarrow (R3)/
\end{array}
$$

where R1, R2, and R3 are processor registers, and $\alpha, \beta, \gamma, \theta$ are the starting main memory addresses of arrays B(I), C(I), A(I), and D(I), respectively. Assume four clock cycles for each Load or Store, two cycles for the Add, and eight cycles for the Multiplier on either a uniprocessor or a single processor in an SIMD machine.

a. Calculate the total number of processor cycles needed to execute this code segment repeatedly 64 times on a SISD uniprocessor computer sequentially, ignoring all other time delays.

b. Consider the use of an SIMD computer with 64 processing elements to execute the vector operations in six synchronized vector instructions over 64-component vector data and both driven by the same-speed clock. Calculate the total execution time on the SIMD machine, ignoring instruction broadcast and other delays.

c. What is the speedup gain of the SIMD computer over the SISD computer?

17.13 Produce a vectorized version of the following program:

```
       DO 20 I = 1, N
       B(I, 1) = 0
       DO 10 J = 1, M
       A(I) = A(I) + B(I, J) × C(I, J)
10     CONTINUE
       D(I) = E(I) + A(I)
20     CONTINUE
```

17.14 An application program is executed on a nine-computer cluster. A benchmark program took time T on this cluster. Further, it was found that 25% of T was time in which the application was running simultaneously on all nine computers. The remaining time, the application had to run on a single computer.

    a. Calculate the effective speedup under the aforementioned condition as compared to executing the program on a single computer. Also calculate α, the percentage of code that has been parallelized (programmed or compiled so as to use the cluster mode) in the preceding program.

    b. Suppose that we are able to effectively use 17 computers rather than 9 computers on the parallelized portion of the code. Calculate the effective speedup that is achieved.

17.15 The following FORTRAN program is to be executed on a computer, and a parallel version is to be executed on a 32-computer cluster.

```
L1:        DO 10 I = 1, 1024
L2:            SUM(I) = 0
L3:            DO 20 J = 1, I
L4:   20          SUM(I) = SUM(I) + I
L5:   10   CONTINUE
```

Suppose lines 2 and 4 each take two machine cycle times, including all processor and memory-access activities. Ignore the overhead caused by the software loop control statements (lines 1, 3, 5) and all other system overhead and resource conflicts.

    a. What is the total execution time (in machine cycle times) of the program on a single computer?

    b. Divide the I-loop iterations among the 32 computers as follows: Computer 1 executes the first 32 iterations (I = 1 to 32), processor 2 executes the next 32 iterations, and so on. What are the execution time and speedup factor compared with part (a)? (Note that the computational workload, dictated by the J-loop, is unbalanced among the computers.)

    c. Explain how to modify the parallelizing to facilitate a balanced parallel execution of all the computational workload over 32 computers. By a balanced load is meant an equal number of additions assigned to each computer with respect to both loops.

    d. What is the minimum execution time resulting from the parallel execution on 32 computers? What is the resulting speedup over a single computer?

17.16 Consider the following two versions of a program to add two vectors:

L1: **DO** 10 I = 1, N	**DOALL** K = 1, M
L2: A(I) = B(I) + C(I)	**DO** 10 I = L(K − 1) + 1, KL
L3: 10 **CONTINUE**	A(I) = B(I) + C(I)
L4: SUM = 0	10 **CONTINUE**
L5: **DO** 20 J = 1, N	SUM(K) = 0
L6: SUM = SUM + A(J)	**DO** 20 J = 1, L
L7: 20 **CONTINUE**	SUM(K) = SUM(K) + A(L(K − 1) + J)
	20 **CONTINUE**
	ENDALL

    a. The program on the left executes on a uniprocessor. Suppose each line of code L2, L4, and L6 takes one processor clock cycle to execute. For simplicity, ignore the time required for the other lines of code. Initially all arrays are already loaded in main memory and the short program fragment is in the instruction cache. How many clock cycles are required to execute this program?

b. The program on the right is written to execute on a multiprocessor with M processors. We partition the looping operations into M sections with $L = N/M$ elements per section. DOALL declares that all M sections are executed in parallel. The result of this program is to produce M partial sums. Assume that k clock cycles are needed for each interprocessor communication operation via the shared memory and that therefore the addition of each partial sum requires k cycles. An l-level binary adder tree can merge all the partial sums, where $l = \log_2 M$. How many cycles are needed to produce the final sum?

c. Suppose $N = 2^{20}$ elements in the array and $M = 256$. What is the speedup achieved by using the multiprocessor? Assume $k = 200$. What percentage is this of the theoretical speedup of a factor of 256?

MULTICORE COMPUTERS

LEARNING OBJECTIVES

After studying this chapter, you should be able to:

◆ Understand the hardware performance issues that have driven the move to multicore computers.

◆ Understand the software performance issues posed by the use of multithreaded multicore computers.

◆ Have an appreciation of the use of multicore organization on embedded systems, PCs and servers, and mainframes.

A **multicore** computer, also known as a **chip multiprocessor**, combines two or more processors (called cores) on a single piece of silicon (called a die). Typically, each core consists of all of the components of an independent processor, such as registers, ALU, pipeline hardware, and control unit, plus L1 instruction and data caches. In addition to the multiple cores, contemporary multicore chips also include L2 cache and, increasingly, L3 cache.

This chapter provides an overview of multicore systems. We begin with a look at the hardware performance factors that led to the development of multicore computers and the software challenges of exploiting the power of a multicore system. Next, we look at multicore organization. Finally, we examine three examples of multicore products, covering personal computer and workstation systems (Intel), embedded systems (ARM), and mainframes (IBM).

18.1 HARDWARE PERFORMANCE ISSUES

As we discuss in Chapter 2, microprocessor systems have experienced a steady, exponential increase in execution performance for decades. Figure 2.12 shows that this increase is due partly to refinements in the organization of the processor on the chip, and partly to the increase in the clock frequency.

Increase in Parallelism and Complexity

The organizational changes in processor design have primarily been focused on increasing instruction-level parallelism, so that more work could be done in each clock cycle. These changes include, in chronological order (Figure 18.1):

- **Pipelining:** Individual instructions are executed through a pipeline of stages so that while one instruction is executing in one stage of the pipeline, another instruction is executing in another stage of the pipeline.

- **Superscalar:** Multiple pipelines are constructed by replicating execution resources. This enables parallel execution of instructions in parallel pipelines, so long as hazards are avoided.

- **Simultaneous multithreading (SMT):** Register banks are replicated so that multiple threads can share the use of pipeline resources.

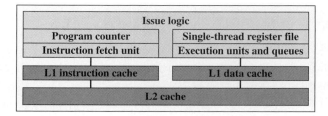

(a) Superscalar

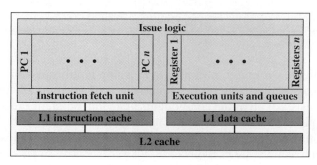

(b) Simultaneous multithreading

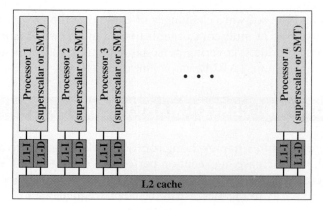

(c) Multicore

Figure 18.1 Alternative Chip Organizations

For each of these innovations, designers have over the years attempted to increase the performance of the system by adding complexity. In the case of pipelining, simple three-stage pipelines were replaced by pipelines with five stages, and then many more stages, with some implementations having over a dozen stages. There is a practical limit to how far this trend can be taken, because with more stages, there is the need for more logic, more interconnections, and more control signals. With superscalar organization, increased performance can be achieved by increasing the number of parallel pipelines. Again, there are diminishing returns as the number of pipelines increases. More logic is required to manage hazards and to stage instruction resources. Eventually, a single thread of execution reaches the point where hazards and resource dependencies prevent the full use of the multiple

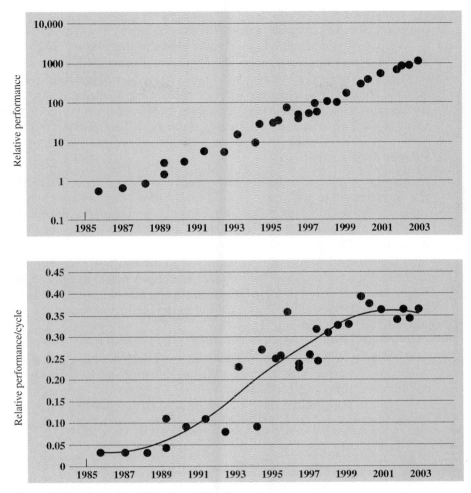

Figure 18.2 Some Intel Hardware Trends

pipelines available. This same point of diminishing returns is reached with SMT, as the complexity of managing multiple threads over a set of pipelines limits the number of threads and number of pipelines that can be effectively utilized.

Figure 18.2, from [OLUK05], is instructive in this context. The upper graph shows the exponential increase in Intel processor performance over the years.[1] The lower graph is calculated by combining Intel's published SPEC CPU figures and processor clock frequencies to give a measure of the extent to which performance improvement is due to increased exploitation of instruction-level parallelism. There is a flat region in the late 1980s before parallelism was exploited extensively. This is followed by a steep rise as designers were able to increasingly exploit pipelining, superscalar techniques, and SMT. But, beginning about 2000, a new flat region of the curve appears, as the limits of effective exploitation of instruction-level parallelism are reached.

---

[1]The data are based on published SPEC CPU figures from Intel, normalized across varying suites.

There is a related set of problems dealing with the design and fabrication of the computer chip. The increase in complexity to deal with all of the logical issues related to very long pipelines, multiple superscalar pipelines, and multiple SMT register banks means that increasing amounts of the chip area are occupied with coordinating and signal transfer logic. This increases the difficulty of designing, fabricating, and debugging the chips. The increasingly difficult engineering challenge related to processor logic is one of the reasons that an increasing fraction of the processor chip is devoted to the simpler memory logic. Power issues, discussed next, provide another reason.

Power Consumption

To maintain the trend of higher performance as the number of transistors per chip rise, designers have resorted to more elaborate processor designs (pipelining, superscalar, SMT) and to high clock frequencies. Unfortunately, power requirements have grown exponentially as chip density and clock frequency have risen. This is shown in the Figure 18.3, which repeats Figure 2.11.

One way to control power density is to use more of the chip area for cache memory. Memory transistors are smaller and have a power density an order of magnitude lower than that of logic (see Figure 18.4). Further, as chip transistor density has increased, the percentage of chip area devoted to memory has grown, and is now well over half the chip area.

By 2015, we can expect to see microprocessor chips with about 100 billion transistors on a 300 mm^2 die. Assuming about 50–60% of the chip area is devoted to memory, the chip will support cache memory of about 100 MB and leave over 1 billion transistors available for logic.

How to use all those logic transistors is a key design issue. As discussed earlier in this section, there are limits to the effective use of such techniques as superscalar

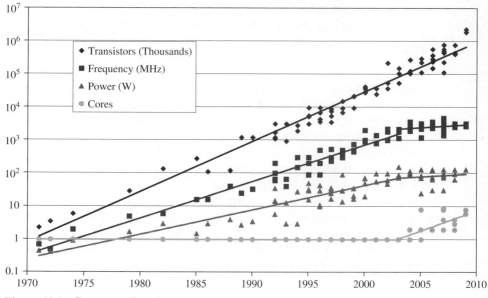

Figure 18.3 Processor Trends

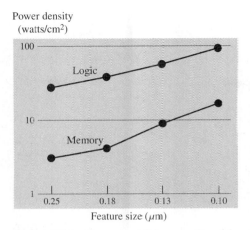

Power density
(watts/cm²)

Figure 18.4 Power and Memory Considerations

and SMT. In general terms, the experience of recent decades has been encapsulated in a rule of thumb known as **Pollack's rule** [POLL99], which states that performance increase is roughly proportional to square root of increase in complexity. In other words, if you double the logic in a processor core, then it delivers only 40% more performance. In principle, the use of multiple cores has the potential to provide near-linear performance improvement with the increase in the number of cores.

Power considerations provide another motive for moving toward a multicore organization. Because the chip has such a huge amount of cache memory, it becomes unlikely that any one thread of execution can effectively use all that memory. Even with SMT, you are multithreading in a relatively limited fashion and cannot therefore fully exploit a gigantic cache, whereas a number of relatively independent threads or processes has a greater opportunity to take full advantage of the cache memory.

18.2 SOFTWARE PERFORMANCE ISSUES

A detailed examination of the software performance issues related to multicore organization is beyond our scope. In this section, we first provide an overview of these issues, and then look at an example of an application designed to exploit multicore capabilities.

Software on Multicore

The potential performance benefits of a multicore organization depend on the ability to effectively exploit the parallel resources available to the application. Let us focus first on a single application running on a multicore system. Recall from Chapter 2 that Amdahl's law states that:

$$\text{Speed up} = \frac{\text{time to execute program on a single processor}}{\text{time to execute program on } N \text{ parallel processors}}$$

$$= \frac{1}{(1 - f) + \dfrac{f}{N}} \tag{18.1}$$

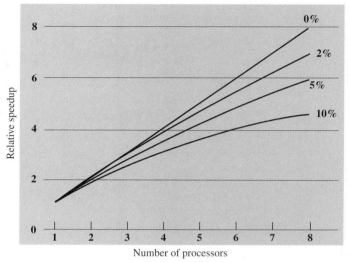

(a) Speedup with 0%, 2%, 5%, and 10% sequential portions

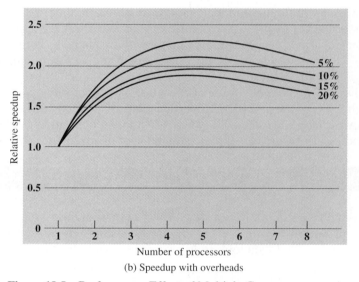

(b) Speedup with overheads

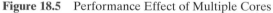

Figure 18.5 Performance Effect of Multiple Cores

The law assumes a program in which a fraction $(1 - f)$ of the execution time involves code that is inherently serial and a fraction f that involves code that is infinitely parallelizable with no scheduling overhead.

This law appears to make the prospect of a multicore organization attractive. But as Figure 18.5a shows, even a small amount of serial code has a noticeable impact. If only 10% of the code is inherently serial ($f = 0.9$), running the program on a multicore system with 8 processors yields a performance gain of only a factor of 4.7. In addition, software typically incurs overhead as a result of communication and distribution of work among multiple processors and as a result of cache coherence overhead. This results in a curve where performance peaks and then begins to degrade because of the increased burden of the overhead of using multiple processors (e.g., coordination and OS management). Figure 18.5b, from [MCDO05], is a representative example.

However, software engineers have been addressing this problem and there are numerous applications in which it is possible to effectively exploit a multicore system. [MCDO05] analyzes the effectiveness of multicore systems on a set of database applications, in which great attention was paid to reducing the serial fraction within hardware architectures, operating systems, middleware, and the database application software. Figure 18.6 shows the result. As this example shows, database management systems and database applications are one area in which multicore systems can be used effectively. Many kinds of servers can also effectively use the parallel multicore organization, because servers typically handle numerous relatively independent transactions in parallel.

In addition to general-purpose server software, a number of classes of applications benefit directly from the ability to scale throughput with the number of cores. [MCDO06] lists the following examples:

- **Multithreaded native applications:** Multithreaded applications are characterized by having a small number of highly threaded processes. Examples of threaded applications include Lotus Domino or Siebel CRM (Customer Relationship Manager).

- **Multiprocess applications:** Multiprocess applications are characterized by the presence of many single-threaded processes. Examples of multi-process applications include the Oracle database, SAP, and PeopleSoft.

- **Java applications:** Java applications embrace threading in a fundamental way. Not only does the Java language greatly facilitate multithreaded applications, but the Java Virtual Machine is a multithreaded process that

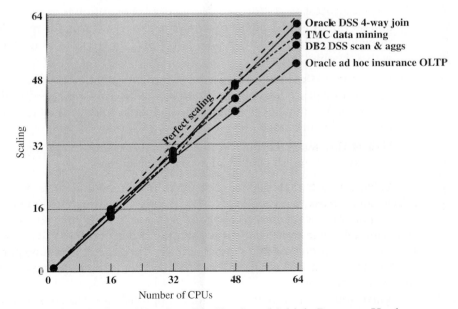

Figure 18.6   Scaling of Database Workloads on Multiple-Processor Hardware

provides scheduling and memory management for Java applications. Java applications that can benefit directly from multicore resources include application servers such as Sun's Java Application Server, BEA's Weblogic, IBM's Websphere, and the open-source Tomcat application server. All applications that use a Java 2 Platform, Enterprise Edition (J2EE platform) application server can immediately benefit from multicore technology.

- **Multi-instance applications:** Even if an individual application does not scale to take advantage of a large number of threads, it is still possible to gain from multicore architecture by running multiple instances of the application in parallel. If multiple application instances require some degree of isolation, virtualization technology (for the hardware of the operating system) can be used to provide each of them with its own separate and secure environment.

Application Example: Valve Game Software

Valve is an entertainment and technology company that has developed a number of popular games, as well as the Source engine, one of the most widely played game engines available. Source is an animation engine used by Valve for its games and licensed for other game developers.

In recent years, Valve has reprogrammed the Source engine software to use multithreading to exploit the power of multicore processor chips from Intel and AMD [REIM06]. The revised Source engine code provides more powerful support for Valve games such as Half Life 2.

From Valve's perspective, threading granularity options are defined as follows [HARR06]:

- **Coarse threading:** Individual modules, called systems, are assigned to individual processors. In the Source engine case, this would mean putting rendering on one processor, AI (artificial intelligence) on another, physics on another, and so on. This is straightforward. In essence, each major module is single threaded and the principal coordination involves synchronizing all the threads with a timeline thread.

- **Fine-grained threading:** Many similar or identical tasks are spread across multiple processors. For example, a loop that iterates over an array of data can be split up into a number of smaller parallel loops in individual threads that can be scheduled in parallel.

- **Hybrid threading:** This involves the selective use of fine-grain threading for some systems and single threading for other systems.

Valve found that through coarse threading, it could achieve up to twice the performance across two processors compared to executing on a single processor. But this performance gain could only be achieved with contrived cases. For real-world gameplay, the improvement was on the order of a factor of 1.2. Valve also found that effective use of fine-grain threading was difficult. The time per work unit can be variable, and managing the timeline of outcomes and consequences involved complex programming.

Valve found that a hybrid threading approach was the most promising and would scale the best as multicore systems with eight or sixteen processors became

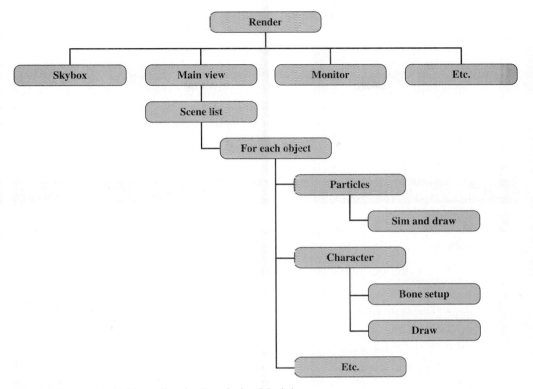

Figure 18.7   Hybrid Threading for Rendering Module

available. Valve identified systems that operate very effectively when assigned to a single processor permanently. An example is sound mixing, which has little user interaction, is not constrained by the frame configuration of windows, and works on its own set of data. Other modules, such as scene rendering, can be organized into a number of threads so that the module can execute on a single processor but achieve greater performance as it is spread out over more and more processors.

Figure 18.7 illustrates the thread structure for the rendering module. In this hierarchical structure, higher-level threads spawn lower-level threads as needed. The rendering module relies on a critical part of the Source engine, the world list, which is a database representation of the visual elements in the game's world. The first task is to determine what are the areas of the world that need to be rendered. The next task is to determine what objects are in the scene as viewed from multiple angles. Then comes the processor-intensive work. The rendering module has to work out the rendering of each object from multiple points of view, such as the player's view, the view of TV monitors, and the point of view of reflections in water.

Some of the key elements of the threading strategy for the rendering module are listed in [LEON07] and include the following:

- Construct scene-rendering lists for multiple scenes in parallel (e.g., the world and its reflection in water).
- Overlap graphics simulation.

- Compute character bone transformations for all characters in all scenes in parallel.
- Allow multiple threads to draw in parallel.

The designers found that simply locking key databases, such as the world list, for a thread was too inefficient. Over 95% of the time, a thread is trying to read from a data set, and only 5% of the time at most is spent in writing to a data set. Thus, a concurrency mechanism known as the single-writer-multiple-readers model works effectively.

18.3 MULTICORE ORGANIZATION

At a top level of description, the main variables in a multicore organization are as follows:

- The number of core processors on the chip
- The number of levels of cache memory
- The amount of cache memory that is shared

Figure 18.8 shows four general organizations for multicore systems. Figure 18.8a is an organization found in some of the earlier multicore computer chips and is still seen in embedded chips. In this organization, the only on-chip cache is L1 cache, with each core having its own dedicated L1 cache. Almost invariably, the L1 cache is divided into instruction and data caches. An example of this organization is the ARM11 MPCore.

The organization of Figure 18.8b is also one in which there is no on-chip cache sharing. In this, there is enough area available on the chip to allow for L2 cache. An example of this organization is the AMD Opteron. Figure 18.8c shows a similar allocation of chip space to memory, but with the use of a shared L2 cache. The Intel Core Duo has this organization. Finally, as the amount of cache memory available on the chip continues to grow, performance considerations dictate splitting off a separate, shared L3 cache, with dedicated L1 and L2 caches for each core processor. The Intel Core i7 is an example of this organization.

The use of a shared L2 cache on the chip has several advantages over exclusive reliance on dedicated caches:

1. Constructive interference can reduce overall miss rates. That is, if a thread on one core accesses a main memory location, this brings the frame containing the referenced location into the shared cache. If a thread on another core soon thereafter accesses the same memory block, the memory locations will already be available in the shared on-chip cache.

2. A related advantage is that data shared by multiple cores is not replicated at the shared cache level.

3. With proper frame replacement algorithms, the amount of shared cache allocated to each core is dynamic, so that threads that have a less locality can employ more cache.

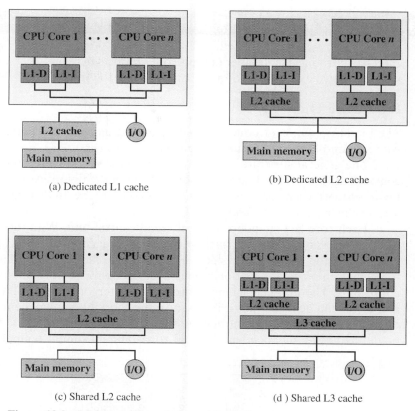

Figure 18.8 Multicore Organization Alternatives

4. Interprocessor communication is easy to implement, via shared memory locations.

5. The use of a shared L2 cache confines the cache coherency problem to the L1 cache level, which may provide some additional performance advantage.

A potential advantage to having only dedicated L2 caches on the chip is that each core enjoys more rapid access to its private L2 cache. This is advantageous for threads that exhibit strong locality.

As both the amount of memory available and the number of cores grow, the use of a shared L3 cache combined with either a shared L2 cache or dedicated per-core L2 caches seems likely to provide better performance than simply a massive shared L2 cache.

Another organizational design decision in a multicore system is whether the individual cores will be superscalar or will implement simultaneous multithreading (SMT). For example, the Intel Core Duo uses superscalar cores, whereas the Intel Core i7 uses SMT cores. SMT has the effect of scaling up the number of hardware-level threads that the multicore system supports. Thus, a multicore system with four cores and SMT that supports four simultaneous threads in each core appears the same to the application level as a multicore system with 16 cores. As software is developed to more fully exploit parallel resources, an SMT approach appears to be more attractive than a superscalar approach.

18.4 INTEL x86 MULTICORE ORGANIZATION

Intel has introduced a number of multicore products in recent years. In this section, we look at two examples: the Intel Core Duo and the Intel Core i7-990X.

Intel Core Duo

The Intel Core Duo, introduced in 2006, implements two x86 superscalar processors with a shared L2 cache (Figure 18.8c).

The general structure of the Intel Core Duo is shown in Figure 18.9. Let us consider the key elements starting from the top of the figure. As is common in multicore systems, each core has its own dedicated **L1 cache**. In this case, each core has a 32-kB instruction cache and a 32-kB data cache.

Each core has an independent **thermal control unit**. With the high transistor density of today's chips, thermal management is a fundamental capability, especially for laptop and mobile systems. The Core Duo thermal control unit is designed to manage chip heat dissipation to maximize processor performance within thermal constraints. Thermal management also improves ergonomics with a cooler system and lower fan acoustic noise. In essence, the thermal management unit monitors digital sensors for high-accuracy die temperature measurements. Each core can be defined as an independent thermal zone. The maximum temperature for each

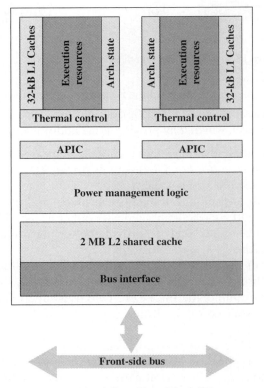

Figure 18.9 Intel Core Duo Block Diagram

thermal zone is reported separately via dedicated registers that can be polled by software. If the temperature in a core exceeds a threshold, the thermal control unit reduces the clock rate for that core to reduce heat generation.

The next key element of the Core Duo organization is the **Advanced Programmable Interrupt Controller** (APIC). The APIC performs a number of functions, including the following:

1. The APIC can provide interprocessor interrupts, which allow any process to interrupt any other processor or set of processors. In the case of the Core Duo, a thread in one core can generate an interrupt, which is accepted by the local APIC, routed to the APIC of the other core, and communicated as an interrupt to the other core.

2. The APIC accepts I/O interrupts and routes these to the appropriate core.

3. Each APIC includes a timer, which can be set by the OS to generate an interrupt to the local core.

The **power management logic** is responsible for reducing power consumption when possible, thus increasing battery life for mobile platforms, such as laptops. In essence, the power management logic monitors thermal conditions and CPU activity and adjusts voltage levels and power consumption appropriately. It includes an advanced power-gating capability that allows for an ultra fine-grained logic control that turns on individual processor logic subsystems only if and when they are needed.

The Core Duo chip includes a shared 2-MB **L2 cache**. The cache logic allows for a dynamic allocation of cache space based on current core needs, so that one core can be assigned up to 100% of the L2 cache. The L2 cache includes logic to support the MESI cache coherence protocol for the attached L1 caches. The key point to consider is when a cache write is done at the L1 level. A cache line gets the M state when a processor writes to it; if the line is not in E or M-state prior to writing it, the cache sends a Read-For-Ownership (RFO) request that ensures that the line exists in the L1 cache and is in the I state in the other L1 cache. The Intel Core Duo extends this protocol to take into account the case when there are multiple Core Duo chips organized as a symmetric multiprocessor (SMP) system. The L2 cache controller allow the system to distinguish between a situation in which data are shared by the two local cores, but not with the rest of the world, and a situation in which the data are shared by one or more caches on the die as well as by an agent on the external bus (can be another processor). When a core issues an RFO, if the line is shared only by the other cache within the local die, we can resolve the RFO internally very fast, without going to the external bus at all. Only if the line is shared with another agent on the external bus do we need to issue the RFO externally.

The **bus interface** connects to the external bus, known as the Front Side Bus, which connects to main memory, I/O controllers, and other processor chips.

Intel Core i7-990X

The Intel Core i7-990X, introduced in November of 2008, implements four x86 SMT processors, each with a dedicated L2 cache, and with a shared L3 cache (Figure 18.8d).

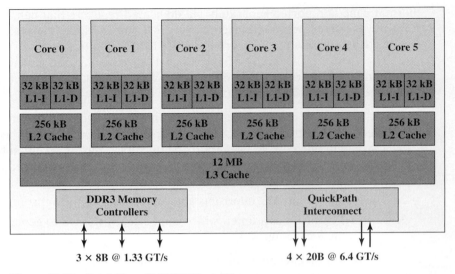

Figure 18.10   Intel Core i7-990X Block Diagram

The general structure of the Intel Core i7-990X is shown in Figure 18.10. Each core has its own **dedicated L2 cache** and the four cores share a 12-MB **L3 cache**. One mechanism Intel uses to make its caches more effective is prefetching, in which the hardware examines memory access patterns and attempts to fill the caches speculatively with data that's likely to be requested soon. It is interesting to compare the performance of this three-level on chip cache organization with a comparable two-level organization from Intel. Table 18.1 shows the cache access latency, in terms of clock cycles for two Intel multicore systems running at the same clock frequency. The Core 2 Quad has a shared L2 cache, similar to the Core Duo. The Core i7 improves on L2 cache performance with the use of the dedicated L2 caches, and provides a relatively high-speed access to the L3 cache.

The Core i7-990X chip supports two forms of external communications to other chips. The **DDR3 memory controller** brings the memory controller for the DDR main memory[2] onto the chip. The interface supports three channels that are 8 bytes wide for a total bus width of 192 bits, for an aggregate data rate of up to 32 GB/s. With the memory controller on the chip, the Front Side Bus is eliminated.

Table 18.1   Cache Latency (in clock cycles)

CPU	Clock Frequency	L1 Cache	L2 Cache	L3 Cache
Core 2 Quad	2.66 GHz	3 cycles	15 cycles	—
Core i7	2.66 GHz	4 cycles	11 cycles	39 cycles

---

[2]The DDR synchronous RAM memory is discussed in Chapter 5.

The **QuickPath Interconnect** (QPI) is a cache-coherent, point-to-point link based electrical interconnect specification for Intel processors and chipsets. It enables high-speed communications among connected processor chips. The QPI link operates at 6.4 GT/s (transfers per second). At 16 bits per transfer, that adds up to 12.8 GB/s, and since QPI links involve dedicated bidirectional pairs, the total bandwidth is 25.6 GB/s. Section 3.5 covers QPI in some detail.

18.5 ARM11 MPCORE

The ARM11 MPCore is a multicore product based on the ARM11 processor family. The ARM11 MPCore can be configured with up to four processors, each with its own L1 instruction and data caches, per chip. Table 18.2 lists the configurable options for the system, including the default values.

Figure 18.11 presents a block diagram of the ARM11 MPCore. The key elements of the system are as follows:

- **Distributed interrupt controller (DIC):** Handles interrupt detection and interrupt prioritization. The DIC distributes interrupts to individual processors.
- **Timer:** Each CPU has its own private timer that can generate interrupts.
- **Watchdog:** Issues warning alerts in the event of software failures. If the watchdog is enabled, it is set to a predetermined value and counts down to 0. It is periodically reset. If the watchdog value reaches zero, an alert is issued.
- **CPU interface:** Handles interrupt acknowledgment, interrupt masking, and interrupt completion acknowledgement.
- **CPU:** A single ARM11 processor. Individual CPUs are referred to as **MP11 CPUs**.
- **Vector floating-point (VFP) unit:** A coprocessor that implements floating-point operations in hardware.
- **L1 cache:** Each CPU has its own dedicated L1 data cache and L1 instruction cache.
- **Snoop control unit (SCU):** Responsible for maintaining coherency among L1 data caches.

Table 18.2 ARM11 MPCore Configurable Options

Feature	Range of Options	Default Value
Processors	1 to 4	4
Instruction cache size per processor	16 kB, 32 kB, or 64 kB	32 kB
Data cache size per processor	16 kB, 32 kB, or 64 kB	32 kB
Master ports	1 or 2	2
Width of interrupt bus	0 to 224 by increments of 32 pins	32 pins
Vector floating point (VFP) coprocessor per processor	Included or not	Included

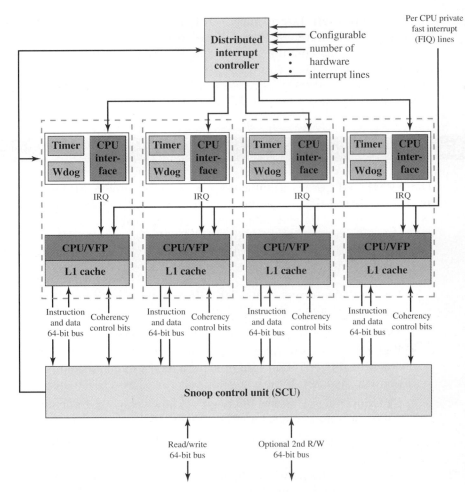

Figure 18.11 ARM11 MPCore Processor Block Diagram

Interrupt Handling

The Distributed Interrupt Controller (DIC) collates interrupts from a large number of sources. It provides

- Masking of interrupts
- Prioritization of the interrupts
- Distribution of the interrupts to the target MP11 CPUs
- Tracking the status of interrupts
- Generation of interrupts by software

The DIC is a single functional unit that is placed in the system alongside MP11 CPUs. This enables the number of interrupts supported in the system to be independent of the MP11 CPU design. The DIC is memory mapped; that is, control registers for the DIC are defined relative to a main memory base address. The DIC is accessed by the MP11 CPUs using a private interface through the SCU.

The DIC is designed to satisfy two functional requirements:

- Provide a means of routing an interrupt request to a single CPU or multiple CPUs, as required.
- Provide a means of interprocessor communication so that a thread on one CPU can cause activity by a thread on another CPU.

As an example that makes use of both requirements, consider a multithreaded application that has threads running on multiple processors. Suppose the application allocates some virtual memory. To maintain consistency, the operating system must update memory translation tables on all processors. The OS could update the tables on the processor where the virtual memory allocation took place, and then issue an interrupt to all the other processors running this application. The other processors could then use this interrupt's ID to determine that they need to update their memory translation tables.

The DIC can route an interrupt to one or more CPUs in the following three ways:

- An interrupt can be directed to a specific processor only.
- An interrupt can be directed to a defined group of processors. The MPCore views the first processor to accept the interrupt, typically the least loaded, as being best positioned to handle the interrupt.
- An interrupt can be directed to all processors.

From the point of view of software running on a particular CPU, the OS can generate an interrupt to all but self, to self, or to specific other CPUs. For communication between threads running on different CPUs, the interrupt mechanism is typically combined with shared memory for message passing. Thus, when a thread is interrupted by an interprocessor communication interrupt, it reads from the appropriate block of shared memory to retrieve a message from the thread that triggered the interrupt. A total of 16 interrupt IDs per CPU are available for interprocessor communication.

From the point of view of an MP11 CPU, an interrupt can be

- **Inactive:** An Inactive interrupt is one that is nonasserted, or which in a multiprocessing environment has been completely processed by that CPU but can still be either Pending or Active in some of the CPUs to which it is targeted, and so might not have been cleared at the interrupt source.
- **Pending:** A Pending interrupt is one that has been asserted, and for which processing has not started on that CPU.
- **Active:** An Active interrupt is one that has been started on that CPU, but processing is not complete. An Active interrupt can be pre-empted when a new interrupt of higher priority interrupts MP11 CPU interrupt processing.

Interrupts come from the following sources:

- **Interprocessor interrupts (IPIs):** Each CPU has private interrupts, ID0-ID15, that can only be triggered by software. The priority of an IPI depends on the receiving CPU, not the sending CPU.
- **Private timer and/or watchdog interrupts:** These use interrupt IDs 29 and 30.
- **Legacy FIQ line:** In legacy IRQ mode, the legacy FIQ pin, on a per CPU basis, bypasses the Interrupt Distributor logic and directly drives interrupt requests into the CPU.
- **Hardware interrupts:** Hardware interrupts are triggered by programmable events on associated interrupt input lines. CPUs can support up to 224 interrupt input lines. Hardware interrupts start at ID32.

Figure 18.12 is a block diagram of the DIC. The DIC is configurable to support between 0 and 255 hardware interrupt inputs. The DIC maintains a list of interrupts, showing their priority and status. The Interrupt Distributor transmits to each CPU Interface the highest Pending interrupt for that interface. It receives back the

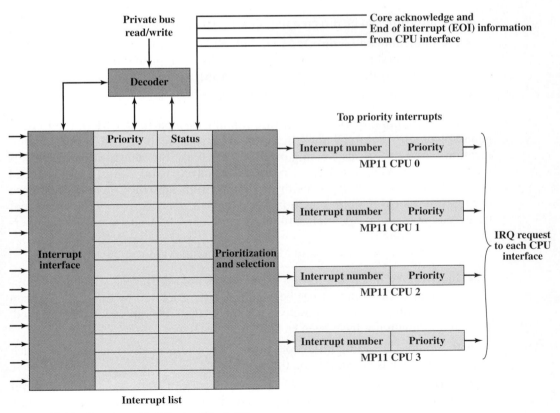

Figure 18.12 Interrupt Distributor Block Diagram

information that the interrupt has been acknowledged, and can then change the status of the corresponding interrupt. The CPU Interface also transmits End of Interrupt Information (EOI), which enables the Interrupt Distributor to update the status of this interrupt from Active to Inactive.

Cache Coherency

The MPCore's Snoop Control Unit (SCU) is designed to resolve most of the traditional bottlenecks related to access to shared data and the scalability limitation introduced by coherence traffic.

The L1 cache coherency scheme is based on the MESI protocol described in Chapter 17. The SCU monitors operations with shared data to optimize MESI state migration. The SCU introduces three types of optimization: direct data intervention, duplicated tag RAMs, and migratory lines.

Direct data intervention (DDI) enables copying clean data from one CPU L1 data cache to another CPU L1 data cache without accessing external memory. This reduces read after read activity from the Level 1 cache to the Level 2 cache. Thus, a local L1 cache miss is resolved in a remote L1 cache rather than from access to the shared L2 cache.

Recall that main memory location of each line within a cache is identified by a tag for that line. The tags can be implemented as a separate block of RAM of the same length as the number of lines in the cache. In the SCU, **duplicated tag RAMs** are duplicated versions of L1 tag RAMs used by the SCU to check for data availability before sending coherency commands to the relevant CPUs. Coherency commands are sent only to CPUs that must update their coherent data cache. This reduces the power consumption and performance impact from snooping into and manipulating each processor's cache on each memory update. Having tag data available locally lets the SCU limit cache manipulations to processors that have cache lines in common.

The **migratory lines** feature enables moving dirty data from one CPU to another without writing to L2 and reading the data back in from external memory. The operation can be described as follows. In a typical MESI protocol, one processor has a modified line and another processor attempts to read that line, the following actions occur:

1. The line contents are transferred from the modified line to the processor that initiated the read.
2. The line contents are written back to main memory.
3. The line is put in the shared state in both caches.

The MPCore SCU handles this situation differently. The SCU monitors the system for a migratory line. If one processor has a modified line, and another processor reads then writes to it, the SCU assumes such a location will experience this same operation in the future. As this operation starts again, the SCU will automatically move the cache line directly to an invalid state rather than expending energy moving it first into the shared state. This optimization also causes the processor to transfer the cache line directly to the other processor without intervening external memory operations.

18.6 IBM zENTERPRISE 196 MAINFRAME

In this section, we look at a mainframe computer organization that uses multicore processor chips. The example we use is the IBM zEnterprise 196 mainframe computer [CURR11, WHIT11], which began shipping in late 2010. Section 7.8 provides a general overview of the z196, together with a discussion of its I/O structure.

Organization

The principal building block of the mainframe is the multichip module (MCM), a glass ceramic module that houses 8 chips. The key components of the configuration are shown in Figure 18.13:

- **Processor unit (PU):** There are six 5.2-GHz processor PU chips, each containing four processor cores plus three levels of cache. The PUs have external

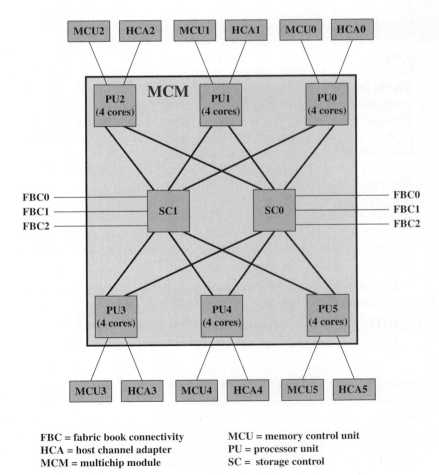

FBC = fabric book connectivity   MCU = memory control unit
HCA = host channel adapter   PU = processor unit
MCM = multichip module   SC = storage control

Figure 18.13   IBM z196 Processor Node Structure

connections to main memory via memory control units and to I/O via host channel adapters. Thus, each MCM includes 24 core processors.

- **Storage control (SC):** The two SC chips contain an additional level of cache plus interconnection logic for connecting to three other MCMs.

The microprocessor core features a wide superscalar, out-of-order pipeline that can decode three z/Architecture CISC instructions per clock cycle and execute up to five operations per cycle. The instruction execution path is predicted by branch direction and target prediction logic. Each core has six execution units: two integer units, one floating-point unit, two load/store units, and one decimal unit.

Cache Structure

The z196 incorporates a four-level cache structure, which IBM states is the industry's first four-level cache. We look at each level in turn (Figure 18.14).

Each core has a dedicated 192-kB **level 1 cache**, divided into a 128-kB data cache and a 64-kB instruction cache. The L1 cache is designed as a store-through cache to L2, that is, altered data are also stored to the next level of memory. These caches are 8-way set associative.

Each core also has a dedicated 1.5-MB **level 2 cache**, which is also a store-through to L3. The L2 cache is 12-way set associative.

Each 4-core processor unit chip includes a 24-MB **level 3 cache** shared by all four processors. Because L1 and L2 caches are store-through, the L3 cache must process every store generated by the four cores on its chip. This feature maintains data availability during a core failure. The L3 cache is 12-way set associative. The z196 implements embedded DRAM (eDRAM) as L3 cache memory on the chip.

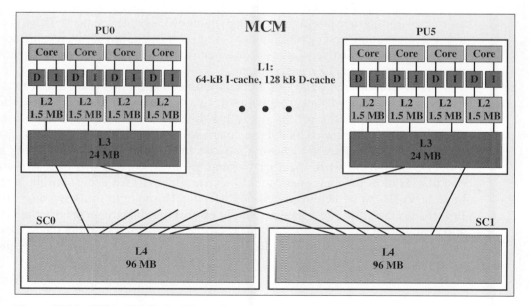

Figure 18.14   IBM z196 Cache Hierarchy

While this eDRAM memory is slower than static RAM (SRAM) normally used to implement cache memory, you can put a lot of it onto a given area. For many workloads, having more memory closer to the chip is more important than having fast memory.

Finally, all 6 PUs on an MCM share a 192-MB **level 4 cache**, which is split into one 96-MB cache on each SC. The principal motivation for incorporating a level 4 cache is that the very high clock speed of the core processors results in a significant mismatch with main memory speed. The fourth cache layer is needed to keep the cores running efficiently. The large shared L3 and L4 caches are suited to transaction-processing workloads exhibiting a high degree of data sharing and task swapping. The L4 cache is 24-way set associative. The SC chip, which houses the L4 cache, also acts as an L4 cache cross-point switch for L4-to-L4 traffic to up to three remote books[3] by three bidirectional data buses. L4 is the coherence manager, meaning that all memory fetches must be in the L4 cache before that data can be used by the processor.

All four caches use a line size of 256 bytes.

The z196 is an interesting study in design trade-offs and the difficulty in exploiting the increasingly powerful processors available with current technology. The large L4 cache is intended to drive the need for access to main memory down to the bare minimum. However, the distance to the off-chip L4 cache costs a number of instruction cycles. Thus, the on-chip area devoted to cache is as large as possible, even to the point of having fewer cores than possible on the chip. The L1 caches are small, to minimize distance from the processor and ensure that access can occur in one cycle. The L2 cache is dedicated to a single core, in an attempt to maximize the amount of access that can occur without resort to a shared cache. The L3 cache is shared by all four processors on a chip and is as large as possible, to minimize the need to go to the L4 cache.

Because all of the books of the zEnterprise 196 share the workload, the four L4 caches on the four books form a single pool of L4 cache memory. Thus, access to L4 means not only going off-chip but perhaps off-book, further increasing access delay. This means relatively large distances exist between the higher-level caches in the processors and the L4 cache content.

To overcome the delays that are inherent to the book design and to save cycles to access the off-book L4 content, the designers try to keep instructions and data as close to the processors as possible by directing as much work of a given logical partition workload on the processors located in the same book as the L4 cache. This is achieved by having the system resource manager/scheduler and the z/OS dispatcher work together to keep as much work as possible within the boundaries of as few processors and L4 cache space (which is best within a book boundary) as can be achieved without affecting throughput and response times. Preventing the resource manager/scheduler and the dispatcher from scheduling and dispatching a workload on any processor available, and keeping the workload in as small a portion, contributes to overcoming latency in a high-frequency processor design such as the z196.

---

[3]Recall from Chapter 7 that a z196 book consists of an MCM, memory cards, and I/O cage connections.

18.7 RECOMMENDED READING

Two books that provide good coverage of the issues in this chapter are [OLUK07] and [BAER10]. [GOCH06] and [MEND06] describe the Intel Core Duo. [FOG08b] provides a detailed description of the Core Duo pipeline architecture.

[ARM08b] provides thorough coverage of the ARM Cortex-A8 pipeline. [HIRA07] and [GOOD05] are good overview articles.

ARM08b ARM Limited. *ARM11 MPCore Processor Technical Reference Manual.* ARM DDI 0360E, 2008. www.arm.com

BAER10 Baer, J. *Microprocessor Architecture: From Simple Pipelines to Chip Multiprocessors.* New York: Cambridge University Press, 2010.

FOG08b Fog, A. *The Microarchitecture of Intel and AMD CPUs.* Copenhagen University College of Engineering, 2008. http://www.agner.org/optimize/

GOCH06 Gochman, S., et al. "Introduction to Intel Core Duo Processor Architecture." *Intel Technology Journal,* May 2006.

GOOD05 Goodacre, J., and Sloss, A. "Parallelism and the ARM Instruction Set Architecture." *Computer,* July 2005.

HIRA07 Hirata, K., and Goodacre, J. "ARM MPCore: The Streamlined and Scalable ARM11 processor core." *Proceedings, 2007 Conference on Asia South Pacific Design Automation,* 2007.

MEND06 Mendelson, A., et al. "CMP Implementation in Systems Based on the Intel Core Duo Processor." *Intel Technology Journal,* May 2006.

OLUK07 Olukotun, K.; Hammond, L.; and Laudon, J. *Chip Multiprocessor Architecture: Techniques to Improve Throughput and Latency.* San Rafael, CA: Morgan & Claypool, 2007.

18.8 KEY TERMS, REVIEW QUESTIONS, AND PROBLEMS

Key Terms

Amdahl's law	multicore	superscalar
chip multiprocessor	simultaneous multithreading (SMT)	

Review Questions

18.1 Summarize the differences among simple instruction pipelining, superscalar, and simultaneous multithreading.

18.2 Give several reasons for the choice by designers to move to a multicore organization rather than increase parallelism within a single processor.

18.3 Why is there a trend toward giving an increasing fraction of chip area to cache memory?

18.4 List some examples of applications that benefit directly from the ability to scale throughput with the number of cores.

18.5 At a top level, what are the main design variables in a multicore organization?

18.6 List some advantages of a shared L2 cache among cores compared to separate dedicated L2 caches for each core.

Problems

18.1 Consider the following problem. A designer has a chip available and must decide what fraction of the chip will be devoted to cache memory (L1, L2, L3). The remainder of the chip can be devoted to a single complex superscalar and/or SMT core or multiple somewhat simpler cores. Define the following parameters:

n = maximum number of cores that can be contained on the chip
k = actual number of cores implemented ($1 \leq k \leq n$, where $r = n/k$ is an integer)
$perf(r)$ = sequential performance gain by using the resources equivalent to r cores to form a single processor, where $perf(1) = 1$.
f = fraction of software that is parallelizable across multiple cores.

Thus, if we construct a chip with n cores, we expect each core to provide sequential performance of 1 and for the n cores to be able to exploit parallelism up to a degree of n parallel threads. Similarly, if the chip has k cores, then each core should exhibit a performance of $perf(r)$ and the chip is able to exploit parallelism up to a degree of k parallel threads. We can modify Amdhal's law (Equation 18.1) to reflect this situation as follows:

$$\text{Speedup} = \frac{1}{\dfrac{1-f}{perf(r)} + \dfrac{f \times r}{perf(r) \times n}}$$

a. Justify this modification of Amdahl's law.
b. Using Pollack's rule, we set $perf(r) = \sqrt{r}$. Let $n = 16$. We want to plot speedup as a function of r for $f = 0.5; f = 0.9; f = 0.975; f = 0.99; f = 0.999$. The results are available in a document at this book's Premium Content site (multicore-performance.pdf). What conclusions can you draw?
c. Repeat part (b) for $n = 256$.

18.2 The technical reference manual for the ARM11 MPCore says that the Distributed Interrupt Controller is memory mapped. That is, the core processors use memory mapped I/O to communicate with the DIC. Recall from Chapter 7 that with memory-mapped I/O, there is a single address space for memory locations and I/O devices. The processor treats the status and data registers of I/O modules as memory locations and uses the same machine instructions to access both memory and I/O devices. Based on this information, what path through the block diagram of Figure 18.11 is used for the core processors to communicate with the DIC?

18.3 In this question we analyze the performance of the following C program on a multi-threaded architecture. You should assume that arrays A, B, and C do not overlap in memory.

```
for (i=0; i<328; i++) {
        A[i] = A[i]*B[i];
        C[i] = C[i]+A[i];
        }
```

Our machine is a single-issue, in-order processor. It switches to a different thread every cycle using fixed round robin scheduling. Each of the N threads executes one instruction every N cycles. We allocate the code to the threads such that every thread executes every Nth iteration of the original C code.

Integer instructions take 1 cycle to execute, floating-point instructions take 4 cycles and memory instructions take 3 cycles. All execution units are fully pipelined. If an instruction cannot issue because its data is not yet available, it inserts a bubble into the pipeline, and retries after I cycles.

Below is our program in assembly code for this machine for a single thread executing the entire loop.

```
loop:   ld f1, 0 (r1)       ;f1 = A[i]
        ld f2, 0 (r2)       ;f2 = B[i]
        fmul f4, f2, f1     ;f4 = f1*f2
        st f4 0(r1)         ;A[i] = f4
        ld f3, 0(r3)        ;f3 = C[i]
        fadd f5, f4, f3     ;f5 = f4 + f3
        st f5 0(r3)         ;C[i] = f5
        add r1, r1, 4       ;i++
        add r2, r2, 4
        add r3, r3, 4
        add r4, r4, -1
        bnez r4, loop       ;loop
```

a. We allocate the assembly code of the loop to N threads such that every thread executes every Nth iteration of the original loop. Write the assembly code that one of the N threads would execute on this multithreaded machine.

b. What is the minimum number of threads this machine needs to remain fully utilized issuing an instruction every cycle for our program?

c. Could we reach peak performance running this program using fewer threads by rearranging the instructions? Explain briefly.

d. What will be the peak performance in flops/cycle for this program?

APPENDIX A

PROJECTS FOR TEACHING COMPUTER ORGANIZATION AND ARCHITECTURE

A.1 Interactive Simulations

A.2 Research Projects

A.3 Simulation Projects
SimpleScalar
SMPCache

A.4 Assembly Language Projects

A.5 Reading/Report Assignments

A.6 Writing Assignments

A.7 Test Bank

Many instructors believe that research or implementation projects are crucial to the clear understanding of the concepts of computer organization and architecture. Without projects, it may be difficult for students to grasp some of the basic concepts and interactions among components. Projects reinforce the concepts introduced in the book, give students a greater appreciation of the inner workings of processors and computer systems, and can motivate students and give them confidence that they have mastered the material.

In this text, I have tried to present the concepts of computer organization and architecture as clearly as possible and have provided numerous homework problems to reinforce those concepts. Many instructors will wish to supplement this material with projects. This appendix provides some guidance in that regard and describes support material available in the **Instructor's Resource Center (IRC)** for this book, accessible by instructors online from Prentice Hall. The support material covers six types of projects and other student exercises:

- Interactive simulations
- Research projects
- Simulation projects
- Assembly language projects
- Reading/report assignments
- Writing assignments
- Test bank

A.1 INTERACTIVE SIMULATIONS

Interactive simulations provide a powerful tool for understanding the complex design features of a modern computer system. Today's students want to be able to visualize the various complex computer systems mechanisms on their own computer screen. A total of 20 simulations are used to illustrate key functions and algorithms in computer organization and architecture design. Table A.1 lists the simulations by chapter. At the relevant point in the book, an icon indicates that a relevant interactive simulation is available online for student use.

Because the simulations enable the user to set initial conditions, they can serve as the basis for student assignments. The IRC for this book includes a set of assignments, one set for each of the interactive simulations. Each assignment includes a several specific problems that can be assigned to students.

The interactive simulations were developed under the direction of Professor Israel Koren, at the University of Massachusetts Department of Electrical and Computer Engineering. Aswin Sreedhar of the University of Massachusetts developed the interactive simulation assignments. For access to the animations, click on the rotating globe at this book's web site at http://williamstallings.com/ComputerOrganization.

Table A.1 Computer Organization and Architecture—Interactive Simulations by Chapter

Chapter 4—Cache Memory	
Cache Simulator	Emulates small-sized caches based on a user-input cache model and displays the cache contents at the end of the simulation cycle based on an input sequence which is entered by the user, or randomly generated if so selected.
Cache Time Analysis	Demonstrates Average Memory Access Time analysis for the cache parameters you specify.
Multitask Cache Demonstrator	Models cache on a system that supports multitasking.
Selective Victim Cache Simulator	Compares three different cache policies.
Chapter 5—Internal Memory	
Interleaved Memory Simulator	Demonstrates the effect of interleaving memory.
Chapter 6—External Memory	
RAID	Determine storage efficiency and reliability.
Chapter 7—Input/Output	
I/O System Design Tool	Evaluates comparative cost and performance of different I/O systems.
Chapter 8—OS Support	
Page Replacement Algorithms	Compares LRU, FIFO, and Optimal.
More Page Replacement Algorithms	Compares a number of policies.
Chapter 14—CPU Structure and Function	
Reservation Table Analyzer	Evaluates reservation tables. which are a way of representing the task flow pattern of a pipelined system.
Branch Prediction	Demonstrates three different branch prediction schemes.
Branch Target Buffer	Combined branch predictor/branch target buffer simulator.
Chapter 15—Reduced Instruction Set Computers	
MIPS 5-Stage Pipeline	Simulates the pipeline.
Loop Unrolling	Simulates the loop unrolling software technique for exploiting instruction-level parallelism.
Chapter 16—Instruction-Level Parallelism and Superscalar Processors	
Pipeline with Static vs. Dynamic Scheduling	A more complex simulation of the MIPS pipeline.
Reorder Buffer Simulator	Simulates instruction reordering in a RISC pipeline.
Scoreboarding Technique for Dynamic Scheduling	Simulation of an instruction scheduling technique used in a number of processors.
Tomasulo's Algorithm	Simulation of another instruction scheduling technique.
Alternative Simulation of Tomasulo's Algorithm	Another simulation of Tomasulo's algorithm.
Chapter 17—Parallel Processing	
Vector Processor Simulation	Demonstrates execution of vector processing instructions.

A.2 RESEARCH PROJECTS

An effective way of reinforcing basic concepts from the course and for teaching students research skills is to assign a research project. Such a project could involve a literature search as well as a Web search of vendor products, research lab activities, and standardization efforts. Projects could be assigned to teams or, for smaller projects, to individuals. In any case, it is best to require some sort of project proposal early in the term, giving the instructor time to evaluate the proposal for appropriate topic and appropriate level of effort. Student handouts for research projects should include

- A format for the proposal
- A format for the final report
- A schedule with intermediate and final deadlines
- A list of possible project topics

The students can select one of the listed topics or devise their own comparable project. The IRC includes a suggested format for the proposal and final report as well as a list of possible research topics.

A.3 SIMULATION PROJECTS

An excellent way to obtain a grasp of the internal operation of a processor and to study and appreciate some of the design trade-offs and performance implications is by simulating key elements of the processor. Two useful tools that are useful for this purpose are SimpleScalar and SMPCache.

Compared with actual hardware implementation, simulation provides two advantages for both research and educational use:

- With simulation, it is easy to modify various elements of an organization, to vary the performance characteristics of various components, and then to analyze the effects of such modifications.
- Simulation provides for detailed performance statistics collection, which can be used to understand performance trade-offs.

SimpleScalar

SimpleScalar [BURG97, MANJ01a, MANJ01b] is a set of tools that can be used to simulate real programs on a range of modern processors and systems. The tool set includes compiler, assembler, linker, and simulation and visualization tools. SimpleScalar provides processor simulators that range from an extremely fast functional simulator to a detailed out-of-order issue, superscalar processor simulator that supports nonblocking caches and speculative execution. The instruction set architecture and organizational parameters may be modified to create a variety of experiments.

The IRC for this book includes a concise introduction to SimpleScalar for students, with instructions on how to load and get started with SimpleScalar. The manual also includes some suggested project assignments.

SimpleScalar is a portable software package the runs on most UNIX platforms. The SimpleScalar software can be downloaded from the SimpleScalar Web site. It is available at no cost for noncommercial use.

SMPCache

SMPCache is a trace-driven simulator for the analysis and teaching of cache memory systems on symmetric multiprocessors [RODR01]. The simulation is based on a model built according to the architectural basic principles of these systems. The simulator has a full graphic and friendly interface. Some of the parameters that they can be studied with the simulator are: program locality; influence of the number of processors, cache coherence protocols, schemes for bus arbitration, mapping, replacement policies, cache size (blocks in cache), number of cache sets (for set associative caches), number of words by block (memory block size).

The IRC for this book includes a concise introduction to SMPCache for students, with instructions on how to load and get started with SMPCache. The manual also includes some suggested project assignments.

SMPCache is a portable software package the runs on PC systems with Windows. The SMPCache software can be downloaded from the SMPCache Web site. It is available at no cost for noncommercial use.

A.4 ASSEMBLY LANGUAGE PROJECTS

Assembly language programming is often used to teach students low-level hardware components and computer architecture basics. CodeBlue is a simplified assembly language program developed at the U. S. Air Force Academy. The goal of the work was to develop and teach assembly language concepts using a visual simulator that students can learn in a single class. The developers also wanted students to find the language motivational and fun to use. The CodeBlue language is much simpler than most simplified architecture instruction sets such as the SC123. Still it allows students to develop interesting assembly level programs that compete in tournaments, similar to the far more complex SPIMbot simulator. Most important, through CodeBlue programming, students learn fundamental computer architecture concepts such as instructions and data co-residence in memory, control structure implementation, and addressing modes.

To provide a basis for projects, the developers have built a visual development environment that allows students to create a program, see its representation in memory, step through the program's execution, and simulate a battle of competing programs in a visual memory environment.

Projects can be built around the concept of a Core War tournament. Core War is a programming game introduced to the public in the early 1980s, which was popular for a period of 15 years or so. Core War has four main components: a memory array of 8000 addresses, a simplified assembly language Redcode, an executive program called MARS (an acronym for Memory Array Redcode Simulator) and the set of contending battle programs. Two battle programs are entered into the memory array at randomly chosen positions; neither program knows where the other one is. MARS executes the programs in a simple version of time-sharing. The two programs take turns: a single instruction of the first program is executed, then a single instruction of the second, and so on. What a battle program does during the execution cycles allotted to it is entirely up to the programmer. The aim is to destroy the other program by ruining its instructions. The CodeBlue environment substitutes CodeBlue for Redcode and provides its own interactive execution interface.

The IRC includes the CodeBlue environment, a user's manual for students, other supporting material, and suggested assignments.

A.5 READING/REPORT ASSIGNMENTS

Another excellent way to reinforce concepts from the course and to give students research experience is to assign papers from the literature to be read and analyzed. The IRC includes a suggested list of papers to be assigned, organized by chapter. The Premium Content Web site provides a copy of each of the papers. The IRC also includes a suggested assignment wording.

A.6 WRITING ASSIGNMENTS

Writing assignments can have a powerful multiplier effect in the learning process in a technical discipline such as computer organization and architecture. Adherents of the Writing Across the Curriculum (WAC) movement (**http://wac.colostate.edu/**) report substantial benefits of writing assignments in facilitating learning. Writing assignments lead to more detailed and complete thinking about a particular topic. In addition, writing assignments help to overcome the tendency of students to pursue a subject with a minimum of personal engagement, just learning facts and problem-solving techniques without obtaining a deep understanding of the subject matter.

The IRC contains a number of suggested writing assignments, organized by chapter. Instructors may ultimately find that this is the most important part of their approach to teaching the material. I would greatly appreciate any feedback on this area and any suggestions for additional writing assignments.

A.7 TEST BANK

A test bank for the book is available at the IRC site for this book. For each chapter, the test bank includes true/false, multiple choice, and fill-in-the-blank questions. The test bank is an effective way to assess student comprehension of the material.

APPENDIX B

ASSEMBLY LANGUAGE AND RELATED TOPICS

The topic of assembly language was briefly introduced in Chapter 13. This appendix provides more detail and also covers a number of related topics. There are a number of reasons why it is worthwhile to study assembly language programming (as compared with programming in a higher-level language), including the following:

1. It clarifies the execution of instructions.
2. It shows how data is represented in memory.
3. It shows how a program interacts with the operating system, processor, and the I/O system.
4. It clarifies how a program accesses external devices.
5. Understanding assembly language programmers makes students better high-level language (HLL) programmers, by giving them a better idea of the target language that the HLL must be translated into.

We begin this chapter with a study of the basic elements of an assembly language, using the x86 architecture for our examples.[1] Next, we look at the operation of the assembler. This is followed by a discussion of linkers and loaders.

Table B.1 defines some of the key terms used in this appendix.

B.1   ASSEMBLY LANGUAGE

Assembly language is a programming language that is one step away from machine language. Typically, each assembly language instruction is translated into one machine instruction by the assembler. Assembly language is hardware dependent, with a different assembly language for each type of processor. In particular, assembly language instructions can make reference to specific registers in the processor, include all of the opcodes of the processor, and reflect the bit length of the various registers of the processor and operands of the machine language. An assembly language programmer must therefore understand the computer's architecture.

Programmers rarely use assembly language for applications or even systems programs. HLLs provide an expressive power and conciseness that greatly eases the programmer's tasks. The disadvantages of using an assembly language rather than an HLL include the following [FOG08a]:

1. **Development time.** Writing code in assembly language takes much longer than writing in a high-level language.
2. **Reliability and security.** It is easy to make errors in assembly code. The assembler is not checking if the calling conventions and register save conventions are obeyed. Nobody is checking for you if the number of PUSH and POP instructions is the same in all possible branches and paths. There are so many possibilities for hidden errors in assembly code that it affects the reliability and security of the project unless you have a very systematic approach to testing and verifying.

---

[1]There are a number of assemblers for the x86 architecture. Our examples use NASM (Netwide Assembler), an open source assembler. A copy of the NASM manual is at this book's Premium Content site.

Table B.1   Key Terms for this Appendix

Assembler

A program that translates assembly language into machine code.

Assembly Language

A symbolic representation of the machine language of a specific processor, augmented by additional types of statements that facilitate program writing and that provide instructions to the assembler.

Compiler

A program that converts another program from some source language (or programming language) to machine language (object code). Some compilers output assembly language which is then converted to machine language by a separate assembler. A compiler is distinguished from an assembler by the fact that each input statement does not, in general, correspond to a single machine instruction or fixed sequence of instructions. A compiler may support such features as automatic allocation of variables, arbitrary arithmetic expressions, control structures such as FOR and WHILE loops, variable scope, input/output operations, higher-order functions and portability of source code.

Executable Code

The machine code generated by a source code language processor such as an assembler or compiler. This is software in a form that can be run in the computer.

Instruction Set

The collection of all possible instructions for a particular computer; that is, the collection of machine language instructions that a particular processor understands.

Linker

A utility program that combines one or more files containing object code from separately compiled program modules into a single file containing loadable or executable code.

Loader

A program routine that copies an executable program into memory for execution.

Machine Language, or Machine Code

The binary representation of a computer program which is actually read and interpreted by the computer. A program in machine code consists of a sequence of machine instructions (possibly interspersed with data). Instructions are binary strings which may be either all the same size (e.g., one 32-bit word for many modern RISC microprocessors) or of different sizes.

Object Code

The machine language representation of programming source code. Object code is created by a compiler or assembler and is then turned into executable code by the linker.

---

3. **Debugging and verifying.** Assembly code is more difficult to debug and verify because there are more possibilities for errors than in high-level code.

4. **Maintainability.** Assembly code is more difficult to modify and maintain because the language allows unstructured spaghetti code and all kinds of tricks that are difficult for others to understand. Thorough documentation and a consistent programming style are needed.

5. **Portability.** Assembly code is platform-specific. Porting to a different platform is difficult.

6. **System code can use intrinsic functions instead of assembly.** The best modern C++ compilers have intrinsic functions for accessing system control registers and other system instructions. Assembly code is no longer needed for device drivers and other system code when intrinsic functions are available.

7. **Application code can use intrinsic functions or vector classes instead of assembly.** The best modern C++ compilers have intrinsic functions for vector operations and other special instructions that previously required assembly programming.

8. **Compilers have been improved a lot in recent years.** The best compilers are now quite good. It takes a lot of expertise and experience to optimize better than the best C++ compiler.

Yet there are still some advantages to the occasional use of assembly language, including the following [FOG08a]:

1. **Debugging and verifying.** Looking at compiler-generated assembly code or the disassembly window in a debugger is useful for finding errors and for checking how well a compiler optimizes a particular piece of code.

2. **Making compilers.** Understanding assembly coding techniques is necessary for making compilers, debuggers and other development tools.

3. **Embedded systems.** Small embedded systems have fewer resources than PCs and mainframes. Assembly programming can be necessary for optimizing code for speed or size in small embedded systems.

4. **Hardware drivers and system code.** Accessing hardware, system control registers, and so on may sometimes be difficult or impossible with high level code.

5. **Accessing instructions that are not accessible from high-level language.** Certain assembly instructions have no high-level language equivalent.

6. **Self-modifying code.** Self-modifying code is generally not profitable because it interferes with efficient code caching. It may, however, be advantageous, for example, to include a small compiler in math programs where a user-defined function has to be calculated many times.

7. **Optimizing code for size.** Storage space and memory is so cheap nowadays that it is not worth the effort to use assembly language for reducing code size. However, cache size is still such a critical resource that it may be useful in some cases to optimize a critical piece of code for size in order to make it fit into the code cache.

8. **Optimizing code for speed.** Modern C++ compilers generally optimize code quite well in most cases. But there are still cases where compilers perform poorly and where dramatic increases in speed can be achieved by careful assembly programming.

9. **Function libraries.** The total benefit of optimizing code is higher in function libraries that are used by many programmers.

10. **Making function libraries compatible with multiple compilers and operating systems.** It is possible to make library functions with multiple entries that are compatible with different compilers and different operating systems. This requires assembly programming.

The terms *assembly language* and *machine language* are sometimes, erroneously, used synonymously. Machine language consists of instructions directly executable by the processor. Each machine language instruction is a binary string containing an opcode, operand references, and perhaps other bits related to execution, such as flags. For convenience, instead of writing an instruction as a bit string, it can be written symbolically, with names for opcodes and registers. An assembly language makes much greater use of symbolic names, including assigning names to specific main memory locations and specific instruction locations. Assembly language also includes statements that are not directly executable but serve as instructions to the assembler that produces machine code from an assembly language program.

Assembly Language Elements

A statement in a typical assembly language has the form shown in Figure B.1. It consists of four elements: label, mnemonic, operand, and comment.

LABEL If a label is present, the assembler defines the label as equivalent to the address into which the first byte of the object code generated for that instruction will be loaded. The programmer may subsequently use the label as an address or as data in another instruction's address field. The assembler replaces the label with the assigned value when creating an object program. Labels are most frequently used in branch instructions.

As an example, here is a program fragment:

```
L2: SUB  EAX, EDX   ;subtract contents of register EDX from
                    ;contents of EAX and store result in EAX
    JG   L2         ;jump to L2 if result of subtraction is
                    ;positive
```

The program will continue to loop back to location L2 until the result is zero or negative. Thus, when the jg instruction is executed, if the result is positive, the processor places the address equivalent to the label L2 in the program counter.

Reasons for using a label include the following;

1. A label makes a program location easier to find and remember.
2. The label can easily be moved to correct a program. The assembler will automatically change the address in all instructions that use the label when the program is reassembled.
3. The programmer does not have to calculate relative or absolute memory addresses, but just uses labels as needed.

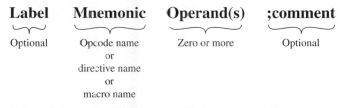

Label	**Mnemonic**	**Operand(s)**	**;comment**
Optional	Opcode name or directive name or macro name	Zero or more	Optional

Figure B.1   Assembly-Language Statement Structure

MNEMONIC The mnemonic is the name of the operation or function of the assembly language statement. As discussed subsequently, a statement can correspond to a machine instruction, an assembler directive, or a macro. In the case of a machine instruction, a mnemonic is the symbolic name associated with a particular opcode.

Table 12.8 lists the mnemonic, or instruction name, of many of the x86 instructions. Appendix A of [CART06] lists the x86 instructions, together with the operands for each and the effect of the instruction on the condition codes. Appendix B of the NASM manual provides a more detailed description of each x86 instruction. Both documents are available at this book's Premium Content site.

OPERAND(S) An assembly language statement includes zero or more operands. Each operand identifies an immediate value, a register value, or a memory location. Typically, the assembly language provides conventions for distinguishing among the three types of operand references, as well as conventions for indicating addressing mode.

For the x86 architecture, an assembly language statement may refer to a register operand by name. Figure B.2 illustrates the general-purpose x86 registers, with their symbolic name and their bit encoding. The assembler will translate the symbolic name into the binary identifier for the register.

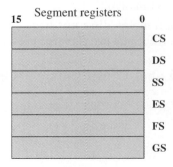

Figure B.2 Intel x86 Program Execution Registers

As discussed in Section 11.2, the x86 architecture has a rich set of addressing modes, each of which must be expressed symbolically in the assembly language. Here we cite a few of the common examples. For **register addressing**, the name of the register is used in the instruction. For example, MOV ECX, EBX copies the contents of register EBX into register ECX. Immediate addressing indicates that the value is encoded in the instruction. For example, MOV EAX, 100H copies the hexadecimal value 100 into register EAX. The immediate value can be expressed as a binary number with the suffix B or a decimal number with no suffix. Thus, equivalent statements to the preceding one are MOV EAX, 100000000B and MOV EAX, 256. **Direct addressing** refers to a memory location and is expressed as a displacement from the DS segment register. This is best explained by example. Assume that the 16-bit data segment register DS contains the value 1000H. Then the following sequence occurs:

```
MOV AX, 1234H
MOV [3518H], AX
```

First the 16-bit register AX is initialized to 1234H. Then, in line two, the contents of AX are moved to the logical address DS:3518H. This address is formed by shifting the contents of DS left 4 bits and adding 3518H to form the 32-bit logical address 13518H.

COMMENT All assembly languages allow the placement of comments in the program. A comment can either occur at the right-hand end of an assembly statement or can occupy an entire text line. In either case, the comment begins with a special character that signals to the assembler that the rest of the line is a comment and is to be ignored by the assembler. Typically, assembly languages for the x86 architecture use a semicolon (;) for the special character.

Type of Assembly Language Statements

Assembly language statements are one of four types: instruction, directive, macro definition, and comment. A comment statement is simply a statement that consists entirely of a comment. The remaining types are briefly described in this section.

INSTRUCTIONS The bulk of the noncomment statements in an assembly language program are symbolic representations of machine language instructions. Almost invariably, there is a one-to-one relationship between an assembly language instruction and a machine instruction. The assembler resolves any symbolic references and translates the assembly language instruction into the binary string that comprises the machine instruction.

DIRECTIVES Directives, also called **pseudo-instructions**, are assembly language statements that are not directly translated into machine language instructions. Instead, directives are instruction to the assembler to perform specified actions doing the assembly process. Examples include the following:

- Define constants
- Designate areas of memory for data storage
- Initialize areas of memory

- Place tables or other fixed data in memory
- Allow references to other programs

Table B.2 lists some of the NASM directives. As an example, consider the following sequence of statements:

Table B.2 Some NASM Assembly-Language Directives

(a) Letters for RES*x* and D*x* Directives

Unit	Letter
byte	B
word (2 bytes)	W
double word (4 bytes)	D
quad word (8 bytes)	Q
ten bytes	T

(b) Directives

Name	Description	Example
DB, DW, DD, DQ, DT	Initialize locations	`L6 DD 1A92H` `;doubleword at L6 initialized to 1A92H`
RESB, RESW, RESD, RESQ, REST	Reserve uninitialized locations	`BUFFER RESB 64` `;reserve 64 bytes starting at BUFFER`
INCBIN	Include binary file in output	`INCBIN "file.dat" ; include this file`
EQU	Define a symbol to a given constant value	`MSGLEN EQU 25` `;the constant MSGLEN equals decimal 25`
TIMES	Repeat instruction multiple times	`ZEROBUF TIMES 64 DB 0` `;initialize 64-byte buffer to all zeros`

```
L2 DB   "A"       ;byte initialized to ASCII code for A (65)
   MOV  AL, [L1]  ;copy byte at L1 into AL
   MOV  EAX, L1   ;store address of byte at L1 in EAX
   MOV  [L1], AH  ;copy contents of AH into byte at L1
```

If a plain label is used, it is interpreted as the address (or offset) of the data. If the label is placed inside square brackets, it is interpreted as the data at the address.

MACRO DEFINITIONS A macro definition is similar to a subroutine in several ways. A subroutine is a section of a program that is written once, and can be used multiple times by calling the subroutine from any point in the program. When a program is compiled or assembled, the subroutine is loaded only once. A call to the subroutine transfers control to the subroutine and a return instruction in the subroutine returns control to the point of the call. Similarly, a macro definition is a section of code that the programmer writes once, and then can use many times. The main difference is that when the assembler encounters a macro call, it replaces the macro call with the macro itself. This process is called **macro expansion**. So, if a macro is defined in an assembly language program and invoked 10 times, then 10 instances of the macro will appear in the assembled code. In essence, subroutines are handled by the hardware at run time, whereas macros are handled by the assembler at assembly time. Macros provide the same advantage as subroutines in terms of modular programming, but without the runtime overhead of a subroutine call and return. The tradeoff is that the macro approach uses more space in the object code.

In NASM and many other assemblers, a distinction is made between a single-line macro and a multi-line macro. In NASM, single-line macros are defined using the %DEFINE directive. Here is an example in which multiple single-line macros are expanded. First, we define two macros:

```
%DEFINE B(X) = 2*X
%DEFINE A(X) = 1 + B(X)
```

At some point in the assembly language program, the following statement appears:

```
MOV AX, A(8)
```

The assembler expands this statement to:

```
MOV AX, 1+2*8
```

which assembles to a machine instruction to move the immediate value 17 to register AX.

Multiline macros are defined using the mnemonic &MACRO. Here is an example of a multiline macro definition:

```
%MACRO PROLOGUE 1
        PUSH EBP       ;push contents of EBP onto stack
                       ;pointed to by ESP and
                       ;decrement contents of ESP by 4
        MOV EBP, ESP ;copy contents of ESP to EBP
        SUB ESP, %1  ;subtract first parameter value from ESP
```

The number 1 after the macro name in the %MACRO line defines the number of parameters the macro expects to receive. The use of %1 inside the macro definition refers to the first parameter to the macro call.

The macro call

```
MYFUNC: PROLOGUE 12
```

expands to the following lines of code:

```
MYFUNC: PUSH    EBP
        MOV     EBP, ESP
        SUB     ESP, 12
```

Example: Greatest Common Divisor Program

As an example of the use of assembly language, we look at a program to compute the greatest common divisor of two integers. We define the greatest common divisor of the integers a and b as follows:

$$\gcd(a,b) = \max[k, \text{such that } k \text{ divides } a \text{ and } k \text{ divides } b]$$

where we say that k divides a if there is no remainder. Euclid's algorithm for the greatest common divisor is based on the following theorem. For any nonnegative integers a and b,

$$\gcd(a, b) = \gcd(b, a \bmod b)$$

Here is a C language program that implements Euclid's algorithm:

```
unsigned int gcd (unsigned int a, unsigned int b)
{
    if (a == 0 && b == 0)
        b = 1;
    else if (b == 0)
        b = a;
    else if (a != 0)
        while (a != b)
            if (a <b)
                b -= a;
            else
                a -= b;
    return b;
}
```

Figure B.3 shows two assembly language versions of the preceding program. The program on the left was done by a C compiler; the program on the right was programmed by hand. The latter program uses a number of programmer's tricks to produce a tighter, more efficient implementation.

B.2 ASSEMBLERS

The assembler is a software utility that takes an assembly program as input and produces object code as output. The object code is a binary file. The assembler views this file as a block of memory starting at relative location 0.

There are two general approaches to assemblers: the two-pass assembler and the one-pass assembler.

Two-Pass Assembler

We look first at the two-pass assembler, which is more common and somewhat easier to understand. The assembler makes two passes through the source code (Figure B.4):

```
gcd:        mov     ebx,eax         gcd:        neg     eax
            mov     eax,edx                     je      L3
            test    ebx,ebx         L1:         neg     eax
            jne     L1                          xchg    eax,edx
            test    edx,edx         L2:         sub     eax,edx
            jne     L1                          jg      L2
            mov     eax,1                       jne     L1
            ret                     L3:         add     eax,edx
L1:         test    eax,eax                     jne     L4
            jne     L2                          inc     eax
            mov     eax,ebx         L4:         ret
            ret
L2:         test    ebx,ebx
            je      L5
L3:         cmp     ebx,eax
            je      L5
            jae     L4
            sub     eax,ebx
            jmp     L3
L4:         sub     ebx,eax
            jmp     L3
L5:         ret
```

    (a) Compiled program   (b) Written directly in assembly language

Figure B.3 Assembly Programs for Greatest Common Divisor

FIRST PASS In the first pass, the assembler is only concerned with label definitions. The first pass is used to construct a **symbol table** that contains a list of all labels and their associated **location counter** (LC) values. The first byte of the object code will have the LC value of 0. The first pass examines each assembly statement. Although the assembler is not yet ready to translate instructions, it must examine each instruction sufficiently to determine the length of the corresponding machine instruction and therefore how much to increment the LC. This may require not only examining the opcode but also looking at the operands and the addressing modes.

Directives such as DQ and REST (see Table B.2) cause the location counter to be adjusted according to how much storage is specified.

When assembler encounters a statement with a label, it places the label into the symbol table, along with the current LC value. The assembler continues until it has read all of the assembly language statements.

SECOND PASS The second pass reads the program again from the beginning. Each instruction is translated into the appropriate binary machine code. Translation includes the following operations:

1. Translate the mnemonic into a binary opcode.
2. Use the opcode to determine the format of the instruction and the location and length of the various fields in the instruction.
3. Translate each operand name into the appropriate register or memory code.

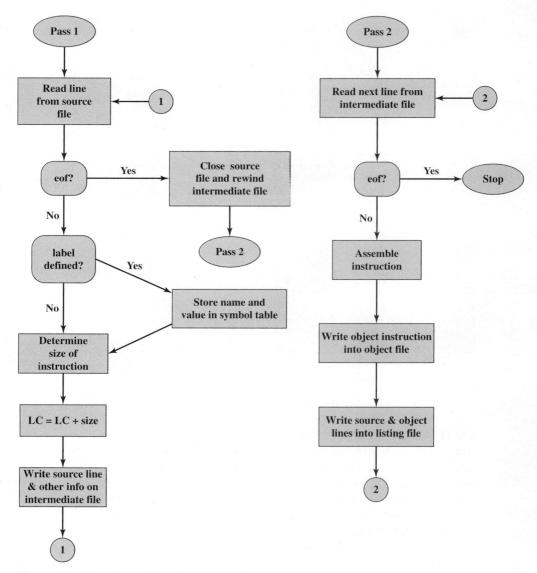

Figure B.4 Flowchart of Two-Pass Assembler

4. Translate each immediate value into a binary string.
5. Translate any references to labels into the appropriate LC value using the symbol table.
6. Set any other bits in the instruction that are needed, including addressing mode indicators, condition code bits, and so on.

A simple example, using the ARM assembly language, is shown in Figure B.5. The ARM assembly language instruction ADDS r3, r3, #19 is translated in to the binary machine instruction 1110 0010 0101 0011 0011 0000 0001 0011.

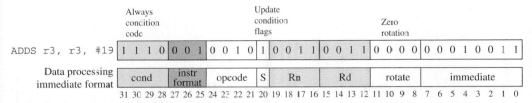

Figure B.5 Translating an ARM Assembly Instruction into a Binary Machine Instruction

ZEROTH PASS Most assembly language includes the ability to define macros. When macros are present there is an additional pass that the assembler must make before the first pass. Typically, the assembly language requires that all macro definitions must appear at the beginning of the program.

The assembler begins this "zeroth pass" by reading all macro definitions. Once all the macros are recognized, the assembler goes through the source code and expands the macros with their associated parameters whenever a macro call is encountered. The macro processing pass generates a new version of the source code with all of the macro expansions in place and all of the macro definitions removed.

One-Pass Assembler

It is possible to implement an assembler that makes only a single pass through the source code (not counting the macro processing pass). The main difficulty in trying to assemble a program in one pass involves forward references to labels. Instruction operands may be symbols that have not yet been defined in the source program. Therefore, the assembler does not know what relative address to insert in the translated instruction.

In essence, the process of resolving forward references works as follows. When the assembler encounters an instruction operand that is a symbol that is not yet defined, the assembler does the following:

1. It leaves the instruction operand field empty (all zeros) in the assembled binary instruction.
2. The symbol used as an operand is entered in the symbol table. The table entry is flagged to indicate that the symbol is undefined.
3. The address of the operand field in the instruction that refers to the undefined symbol is added to a list of forward references associated with the symbol table entry.

When the symbol definition is encountered so that a LC value can be associated with it, the assembler inserts the LC value in the appropriate entry in the symbol table. If there is a forward reference list associated with the symbol, then the assembler inserts the proper address into any instruction previously generated that is on the forward reference list.

Example: Prime Number Program

We now look at an example that includes directives. This example looks at a program that finds prime numbers. Recall that prime numbers are evenly divisible by only 1

```
unsigned guess;                          /* current guess for prime */
unsigned factor;                         /* possible factor of guess */
unsigned limit;                          /* find primes up to this value */

printf ("Find primes up to : ");
scanf("%u", &limit);
printf ("2\n");                          /* treat first two primes as */
printf ("3\n");                          /* special case */
guess = 5;                               /* initial guess */
while (guess < = limit) {                /* look for a factor of guess */
    factor = 3;
    while (factor * factor < guess && guess% factor != 0)
    factor + = 2;
    if (guess % factor != 0)
        printf ("%d\n", guess);
    guess += 2;                          /* only look at odd numbers */
}
```

Figure B.6   C Program for Testing Primality

and themselves. There is no formula for doing this. The basic method this program uses is to find the factors of all odd numbers below a given limit. If no factor can be found for an odd number, it is prime. Figure B.6 shows the basic algorithm written in C. Figure B.7 shows the same algorithm written in NASM assembly language.

B.3 LOADING AND LINKING

The first step in the creation of an active process is to load a program into main memory and create a process image (Figure B.8). Figure B.9 depicts a scenario typical for most systems. The application consists of a number of compiled or assembled modules in object-code form. These are linked to resolve any references between modules. At the same time, references to library routines are resolved. The library routines themselves may be incorporated into the program or referenced as shared code that must be supplied by the operating system at run time. In this section, we summarize the key features of linkers and loaders. First, we discuss the concept of relocation. Then, for clarity in the presentation, we describe the loading task when a single program module is involved; no linking is required. We can then look at the linking and loading functions as a whole.

Relocation

In a multiprogramming system, the available main memory is generally shared among a number of processes. Typically, it is not possible for the programmer to know in advance which other programs will be resident in main memory at the time of execution of his or her program. In addition, we would like to be able to swap active processes in and out of main memory to maximize processor utilization by providing a large pool of ready processes to execute. Once a program has been swapped out to disk, it would be quite limiting to declare that when it is next

```
%include "asm_io.inc"
segment .data
Message db "Find primes up to: ", 0

segment .bss
Limit resd 1                            ; find primes up to this limit
Guess resd 1                            ; the current guess for prime

segment .text
    global _asm_main
_asm_main:
    enter 0,0                           ; setup routine
    pusha

    mov eax, Message
    call print_string
    call read_int                       ; scanf("%u", & limit);
    mov [Limit], eax
    mov eax, 2                          ; printf("2\n");
    call print_int
    call print_nl
    mov eax, 3                          ; printf("3\n");
    call print_int
    call print_nl

    mov dword [Guess], 5                ; Guess = 5;
while_limit:                            ; while (Guess <= Limit)
    mov eax, [Guess]
    cmp eax, [Limit]
    jnbe end_while_limit                ; use jnbe since numbers are unsigned

    mov ebx, 3                          ; ebx is factor = 3;
while_factor:
    mov eax,ebx
    mul eax                             ; edx:eax = eax*eax
    jo end_while_factor                 ; if answer won't fit in eax alone
    cmp eax, [Guess]
    jnb end_while_factor                ; if !(factor*factor < guess)
    mov eax,[Guess]
    mov edx,0
    div ebx                             ; edx = edx:eax% ebx
    cmp edx, 0                          ; if !(guess% factor != 0)
    je end_while_factor

    add ebx,2; factor += 2;
    jmp while_factor
end_while_factor:
    je end_if                           ; if !(guess% factor != 0)
    mov eax, [Guess]                    ; printf("%u\n");
    call print_int
    call print_nl
end_if:
    add dword [Guess], 2                ; guess += 2
    jmp while_limit
end_while_limit:

    popa
    mov eax, 0                          ; return back to C
    leave
    ret
```

Figure B.7 Assembly Program for Testing Primality

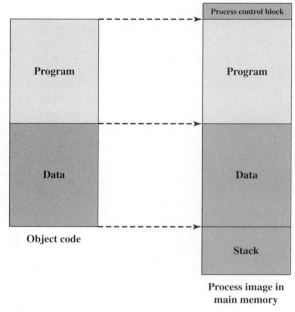

Figure B.8   The Loading Function

swapped back in, it must be placed in the same main memory region as before. Instead, we may need to **relocate** the process to a different area of memory.

Thus, we cannot know ahead of time where a program will be placed, and we must allow that the program may be moved about in main memory due to swapping.

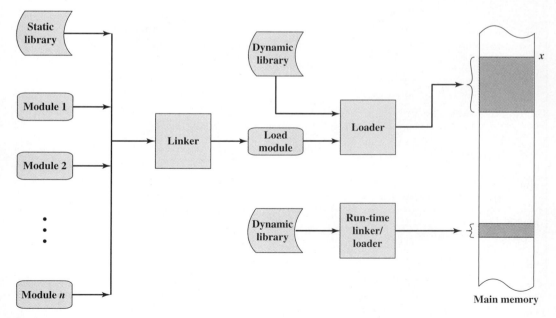

Figure B.9   A Linking and Loading Scenario

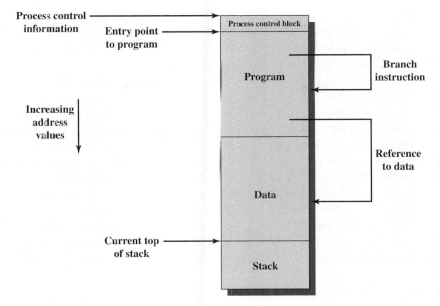

Figure B.10   Addressing Requirements for a Process

These facts raise some technical concerns related to addressing, as illustrated in Figure B.10. The figure depicts a process image. For simplicity, let us assume that the process image occupies a contiguous region of main memory. Clearly, the operating system will need to know the location of process control information and of the execution stack, as well as the entry point to begin execution of the program for this process. Because the operating system is managing memory and is responsible for bringing this process into main memory, these addresses are easy to come by. In addition, however, the processor must deal with memory references within the program. Branch instructions contain an address to reference the instruction to be executed next. Data reference instructions contain the address of the byte or word of data referenced. Somehow, the processor hardware and operating system software must be able to translate the memory references found in the code of the program into actual physical memory addresses, reflecting the current location of the program in main memory.

Loading

In Figure B.9, the loader places the load module in main memory starting at location x. In loading the program, the addressing requirement illustrated in Figure B.10 must be satisfied. In general, three approaches can be taken:

- Absolute loading
- Relocatable loading
- Dynamic run-time loading

ABSOLUTE LOADING An absolute loader requires that a given load module always be loaded into the same location in main memory. Thus, in the load module presented to the loader, all address references must be to specific, or absolute, main memory addresses. For example, if x in Figure B.9 is location 1024, then the first word in a load module destined for that region of memory has address 1024.

The assignment of specific address values to memory references within a program can be done either by the programmer or at compile or assembly time (Table B.3a). There are several disadvantages to the former approach. First, every programmer would have to know the intended assignment strategy for placing modules into main memory. Second, if any modifications are made to the program that involve insertions or deletions in the body of the module, then all of the addresses will have to be altered. Accordingly, it is preferable to allow memory references within programs to be expressed symbolically and then resolve those symbolic references at the time of compilation or assembly. This is illustrated in Figure B.11. Every reference to an instruction or item of data is initially represented by a symbol. In preparing the module for input to an absolute loader, the assembler or compiler will convert all of these references to specific addresses (in this example, for a module to be loaded starting at location 1024), as shown in Figure B.11b.

Table B.3 Address Binding

(a) Loader

Binding Time	Function
Programming time	All actual physical addresses are directly specified by the programmer in the program itself.
Compile or assembly time	The program contains symbolic address references, and these are converted to actual physical addresses by the compiler or assembler.
Load time	The compiler or assembler produces relative addresses. The loader translates these to absolute addresses at the time of program loading.
Run time	The loaded program retains relative addresses. These are converted dynamically to absolute addresses by processor hardware.

(b) Linker

Linkage Time	Function
Programming time	No external program or data references are allowed. The programmer must place into the program the source code for all subprograms that are referenced.
Compile or assembly time	The assembler must fetch the source code of every subroutine that is referenced and assemble them as a unit.
Load module creation	All object modules have been assembled using relative addresses. These modules are linked together and all references are restated relative to the origin of the final load module.
Load time	External references are not resolved until the load module is to be loaded into main memory. At that time, referenced dynamic link modules are appended to the load module, and the entire package is loaded into main or virtual memory.
Run time	External references are not resolved until the external call is executed by the processor. At that time, the process is interrupted and the desired module is linked to the calling program.

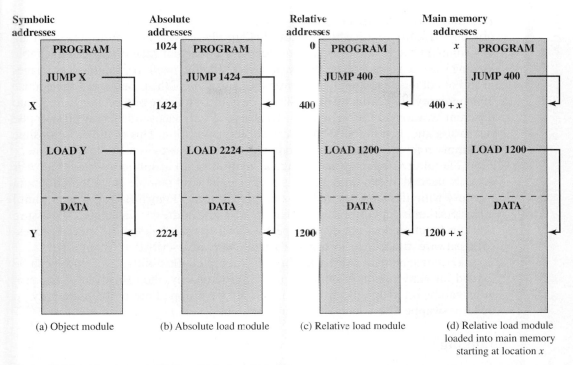

Figure B.11   Absolute and Relocatable Load Modules

RELOCATABLE LOADING The disadvantage of binding memory references to specific addresses prior to loading is that the resulting load module can only be placed in one region of main memory. However, when many programs share main memory, it may not be desirable to decide ahead of time into which region of memory a particular module should be loaded. It is better to make that decision at load time. Thus we need a load module that can be located anywhere in main memory.

To satisfy this new requirement, the assembler or compiler produces not actual main memory addresses (absolute addresses) but addresses that are relative to some known point, such as the start of the program. This technique is illustrated in Figure B.11c. The start of the load module is assigned the relative address 0, and all other memory references within the module are expressed relative to the beginning of the module.

With all memory references expressed in relative format, it becomes a simple task for the loader to place the module in the desired location. If the module is to be loaded beginning at location x, then the loader must simply add x to each memory reference as it loads the module into memory. To assist in this task, the load module must include information that tells the loader where the address references are and how they are to be interpreted (usually relative to the program origin, but also possibly relative to some other point in the program, such as the current location). This set of information is prepared by the compiler or assembler and is usually referred to as the relocation dictionary.

DYNAMIC RUN-TIME LOADING Relocatable loaders are common and provide obvious benefits relative to absolute loaders. However, in a multiprogramming environment, even one that does not depend on virtual memory, the relocatable loading scheme is inadequate. We have referred to the need to swap process images in and out of main memory to maximize the utilization of the processor. To maximize main memory utilization, we would like to be able to swap the process image back into different locations at different times. Thus, a program, once loaded, may be swapped out to disk and then swapped back in at a different location. This would be impossible if memory references had been bound to absolute addresses at the initial load time.

The alternative is to defer the calculation of an absolute address until it is actually needed at run time. For this purpose, the load module is loaded into main memory with all memory references in relative form (Figure B.11c). It is not until an instruction is actually executed that the absolute address is calculated. To assure that this function does not degrade performance, it must be done by special processor hardware rather than software. This hardware is described in Chapter 8.

Dynamic address calculation provides complete flexibility. A program can be loaded into any region of main memory. Subsequently, the execution of the program can be interrupted and the program can be swapped out of main memory, to be later swapped back in at a different location.

Linking

The function of a linker is to take as input a collection of object modules and produce a load module, consisting of an integrated set of program and data modules, to be passed to the loader. In each object module, there may be address references to locations in other modules. Each such reference can only be expressed symbolically in an unlinked object module. The linker creates a single load module that is the contiguous joining of all of the object modules. Each intramodule reference must be changed from a symbolic address to a reference to a location within the overall load module. For example, module A in Figure B.12a contains a procedure invocation of module B. When these modules are combined in the load module, this symbolic reference to module B is changed to a specific reference to the location of the entry point of B within the load module.

LINKAGE EDITOR The nature of this address linkage will depend on the type of load module to be created and when the linkage occurs (Table B.3b). If, as is usually the case, a relocatable load module is desired, then linkage is usually done in the following fashion. Each compiled or assembled object module is created with references relative to the beginning of the object module. All of these modules are put together into a single relocatable load module with all references relative to the origin of the load module. This module can be used as input for relocatable loading or dynamic run-time loading.

A linker that produces a relocatable load module is often referred to as a linkage editor. Figure B.12 illustrates the linkage editor function.

DYNAMIC LINKER As with loading, it is possible to defer some linkage functions. The term *dynamic linking* is used to refer to the practice of deferring the linkage of some external modules until after the load module has been created. Thus, the load

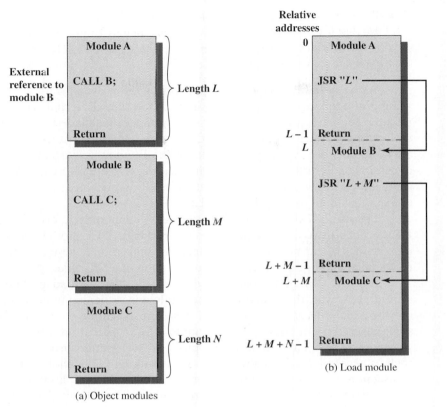

Figure B.12   The Linking Function

module contains unresolved references to other programs. These references can be resolved either at load time or run time.

For **load-time dynamic linking** (involving upper dynamic library in Figure B.9), the following steps occur. The load module (application module) to be loaded is read into memory. Any reference to an external module (target module) causes the loader to find the target module, load it, and alter the reference to a relative address in memory from the beginning of the application module. There are several advantages to this approach over what might be called static linking:

- It becomes easier to incorporate changed or upgraded versions of the target module, which may be an operating system utility or some other general-purpose routine. With static linking, a change to such a supporting module would require the relinking of the entire application module. Not only is this inefficient, but it may be impossible in some circumstances. For example, in the personal computer field, most commercial software is released in load module form; source and object versions are not released.

- Having target code in a dynamic link file paves the way for automatic code sharing. The operating system can recognize that more than one application is using the same target code because it loaded and linked that code. It can use that information to load a single copy of the target code and link it to both applications, rather than having to load one copy for each application.

- It becomes easier for independent software developers to extend the functionality of a widely used operating system such as Linux. A developer can come up with a new function that may be useful to a variety of applications and package it as a dynamic link module.

With **run-time dynamic linking** (involving lower dynamic library in Figure B.9), some of the linking is postponed until execution time. External references to target modules remain in the loaded program. When a call is made to the absent module, the operating system locates the module, loads it, and links it to the calling module. Such modules are typically shareable. In the Windows environment, these are call dynamic-link libraries (DLLs) Thus, if one process is already making use of a dynamically linked shared module, then that module is in main memory and a new process can simply link to the already-loaded module.

The use of DLLs can lead to a problem commonly referred to as **DLL hell**. DLL occurs if two or more processes are sharing a DLL module but expect different versions of the module. For example, an application or system function might be re-installed and bring in with it an older version of a DLL file.

We have seen that dynamic loading allows an entire load module to be moved around; however, the structure of the module is static, being unchanged throughout the execution of the process and from one execution to the next. However, in some cases, it is not possible to determine prior to execution which object modules will be required. This situation is typified by transaction-processing applications, such as an airline reservation system or a banking application. The nature of the transaction dictates which program modules are required, and they are loaded as appropriate and linked with the main program. The advantage of the use of such a dynamic linker is that it is not necessary to allocate memory for program units unless those units are referenced. This capability is used in support of segmentation systems.

One additional refinement is possible: An application need not know the names of all the modules or entry points that may be called. For example, a charting program may be written to work with a variety of plotters, each of which is driven by a different driver package. The application can learn the name of the plotter that is currently installed on the system from another process or by looking it up in a configuration file. This allows the user of the application to install a new plotter that did not exist at the time the application was written.

B.4 RECOMMENDED READING

[SALO93] covers the design and implementation of assemblers and loaders.

The topics of linking and loading are covered in many books on program development, computer architecture, and operating systems. A particularly detailed treatment is [BECK97]. [CLAR98] also contains a good discussion. A thorough practical discussion of this topic, with numerous OS examples, is [LEVI00].

[BART03] is an excellent treatment for learning assembly language for x86 processors; suitable for self-study. [CART06] covers assembly language for x86 machines. For the serious x86 programmer, [FOG08a] is highly useful. [KNAG04] is a thorough treatment of ARM assembly language.

BART03   Bartlett, J. *Programming from the Ground Up.* 2003. Available at this book's Premium Content site.

BECK97   Beck, L. *System Software.* Reading, MA: Addison-Wesley, 1997.

CART06   Carter, P. *PC Assembly Language.* July 23, 2006. Available at this book's Web site.

CLAR98   Clarke, D., and Merusi, D. *System Software Programming: The Way Things Work.* Upper Saddle River, NJ: Prentice Hall, 1998.

FOG08a   Fog, A. *Optimizing Subroutines in Assembly Language: An Optimization Guide for x86 Platforms.* Copenhagen University College of Engineering, 2008. http:// www.agner.org/optimize/

KNAG04   Knaggs, P., and Welsh, S. *ARM: Assembly Language Programming.* Bournemouth University School of Design, Engineering & Computing. August 31, 2004. Available at this book's Premium Content site.

LEVI00   Levine, J. *Linkers and Loaders.* San Francisco: Morgan Kaufmann, 2000.

SALO93   Salomon, D. *Assemblers and Loaders.* Ellis Horwood Ltd, 1993. Available at this book's Premium Content site.

B.5 KEY TERMS, REVIEW QUESTIONS, AND PROBLEMS

Key Terms

assembler	label	mnemonic
assembly language	linkage editor	one-pass assembler
comment	linking	operand
directive	load-time dynamic linking	relocation
dynamic linker	loading	run-time dynamic linking
instruction	macro	two-pass assembler

Review Questions

B.1   List some reasons why it is worthwhile to study assembly language programming.

B.2   What is an assembly language?

B.3   List some disadvantages of assembly language compared to high-level languages.

B.4   List some advantages of assembly language compared to high-level languages.

B.5   What are the typical elements of an assembly language statement.

B.6   List and briefly define four different kinds of assembly language statements.

B.7   What is the difference between a one-pass assembler and a two-pass assembler?

Problems

B.1   Core War is a programming game introduced to the public in the early 1980s [DEWD84], which was popular for a period of 15 years or so. Core War has four main components: a memory array of 8000 addresses, a simplified assembly language Redcode, an executive program called MARS (an acronym for Memory Array Redcode

Simulator) and the set of contending battle programs. Two battle programs are entered into the memory array at randomly chosen positions; neither program knows where the other one is. MARS executes the programs in a simple version of time-sharing. The two programs take turns: a single instruction of the first program is executed, then a single instruction of the second, and so on. What a battle program does during the execution cycles allotted to it is entirely up to the programmer. The aim is to destroy the other program by ruining its instructions. In this problem and the next several, we use an even simpler language, called CodeBlue, to explore some Core War concepts.

CodeBlue contains only five assembly language statements and uses three addressing modes (Table B.4). Addresses wrap around, so that for the last location in memory, the relative address of +1 refers to the first location in memory. For example, ADD #4, 6 adds 4 to the contents of relative location 6 and stores the results in location 6; JUMP @5 transfers execution to the memory address contained in the location five slots past the location of the current JUMP instruction.

a. The program Imp is the single instruction COPY 0, 1. What does it do?
b. The program Dwarf is the following sequence of instructions:

```
ADD #4, 3
COPY 2, @2
JUMP -2
DATA 0
```

What does it do?
c. Rewrite Dwarf using symbols, so that it looks more like a typical assembly language program.

B.2 What happens if we pit Imp against Dwarf?

B.3 Write a "carpet bombing" program in CodeBlue that zeros out all of memory (with the possible exception of the program locations).

B.4 How would the following program fare against Imp?

Table B.4 CodeBlue Assembly Language

(a) Instruction Set

Format		Meaning
DATA	\<value\>	\<value\> set at current location
COPY	A, B	copies source A to destination B
ADD	A, B	adds A to B, putting result in B
JUMP	A	transfer execution to A
JUMPZ	A, B	if B = 0, transfer to A

(b) Addressing Modes

Mode	Format	Meaning
Literal	# followed by value	This is an immediate mode, the operand value is in the instruction.
Relative	Value	The value represents an offset from the current location, which contains the operand.
Indirect	@ followed by value	The value represents an offset from the current location; the offset location contains the relative address of the location that contains the operand.

```
Loop   COPY #0, −1
       JUMP −1
```

Hint: Remember that instruction execution alternates between the two opposing programs.

B.5   **a.** What is the value of the C status flag after the following sequence:

```
mov al, 3
add al, 4
```

b. What is the value of the C status flag after the following sequence:

```
mov al, 3
sub al, 4
```

B.6   Consider the following NAMS instruction:

```
cmp vleft, vright
```

For signed integers, there are three status flags that are relevant. If vleft = vright, then ZF is set. If vleft > vright, ZF is unset (set to 0) and SF = OF. If vleft < vright, ZF is unset and SF $\neq$ OF. Why does SF = OF if vleft > vright?

B.7   Consider the following NASM code fragment:

```
mov  al, 0
cmp  al, al
je next
```

Write an equivalent program consisting of a single instruction.

B.8   Consider the following C program:

```
/* a simple C program to average 3 integers */
main ()
{  int avg;
   int i1 = 20;
   int i2 = 13;
   int i3 = 82;
   avg = (i1 + i2 + i3)/3;
}
```

Write an NASM version of this program.

B.9   Consider the following C code fragment:

```
if (EAX == 0) EBX = 1;
else EBX = 2;
```

Write an equivalent NASM code fragment.

B.10   The initialize data directives can be used to initialize multiple locations. For example,

```
db 0x55,0x56,0x57
```

reserves three bytes and initializes their values.

NASM supports the special token $ to allow calculations to involve the current assembly position. That is, $ evaluates to the assembly position at the beginning of the line containing the expression. With the preceding two facts in mind, consider the following sequence of directives:

```
message db 'hello, world'
msglen equ $-message
```

What value is assigned to the symbol msglen?

B.11 Assume the three symbolic variables V1, V2, V3 contain integer values. Write an NASM code fragment that moves the smallest value into integer ax. Use only the instructions mov, cmp, and jbe.

B.12 Describe the effect of this instruction: cmp eax, 1

Assume that the immediately preceding instruction updated the contents of eax.

B.13 The xchg instruction can be used to exchange the contents of two registers. Suppose that the x86 instruction set did not support this instruction.

a. Implement xchg ax, bx using only push and pop instructions.

b. Implement xchg ax, bx using only the xor instruction (do not involve other registers).

B.14 In the following program, assume that a, b, x, y are symbols for main memory locations. What does the program do? You can answer the question by writing the equivalent logic in C.

```
        mov     eax,a
        mov     ebx,b
        xor     eax,x
        xor     ebx,y
        or      eax,ebx
        jnz     L2
L1:                     ;sequence of instructions...
        jmp     L3
L2:                     ;another sequence of instructions...
L3:
```

B.15 Section B.1 includes a C program that calculates the greatest common divisor of two integers.

a. Describe the algorithm in words and show how the program does implement the Euclid algorithm approach to calculating the greatest common divisor.

b. Add comments to the assembly program of Figure B.3a to clarify that it implements the same logic as the C program.

c. Repeat part (b) for the program of Figure B.3b.

B.16 **a.** A 2-pass assembler can handle future symbols and an instruction can therefore use a future symbol as an operand. This is not always true for directives. The EQU directive, for example, cannot use a future symbol. The directive "A EQU B+1" is easy to execute if B is previously defined, but impossible if B is a future symbol. What's the reason for this?

b. Suggest a way for the assembler to eliminate this limitation such that any source line could use future symbols.

B.17 Consider a symbol directive MAX of the following form:

symbol MAX list of expressions

The label is mandatory and is assigned the value of the largest expression in the operand field. Example:

```
    MSGLEN MAX A, B, C ;where A, B, C are defined symbols
```

How is MAX executed by the Assembler and in what pass?

GLOSSARY

absolute address　An address in a computer language that identifies a storage location or a device without the use of any intermediate reference.

accumulator　The name of the CPU register in a single-address instruction format. The accumulator, or AC, is implicitly one of the two operands for the instruction.

address bus　That portion of a system bus used for the transfer of an address. Typically, the address identifies a main memory location or an I/O device.

address space　The range of addresses (memory, I/O) that can be referenced.

arithmetic and logic unit (ALU)　A part of a computer that performs arithmetic operations, logic operations, and related operations.

ASCII　American Standard Code for Information Interchange. ASCII is a 7-bit code used to represent numeric, alphabetic, and special printable characters. It also includes codes for *control characters*, which are not printed or displayed but specify some control function.

assembly language　A computer-oriented language whose instructions are usually in one-to-one correspondence with computer instructions and that may provide facilities such as the use of macroinstructions. Synonymous with *computer-dependent language*.

associative memory　A memory whose storage locations are identified by their contents, or by a part of their contents, rather than by their names or positions.

asynchronous timing　A technique in which the occurrence of one event on a bus follows and depends on the occurrence of a previous event.

autoindexing　A form of indexed addressing in which the index register is automatically incremented or decremented with each memory reference.

base　In the numeration system commonly used in scientific papers, the number that is raised to the power denoted by the exponent and then multiplied by the mantissa to determine the real number represented (e.g., the number 10 in the expression $2.7' \; 10^2 = 270$).

base address　A numeric value that is used as a reference in the calculation of addresses in the execution of a computer program.

binary operator　An operator that represents an operation on two and only two operands.

bit　In the pure binary numeration system, either of the digits 0 and 1.

block multiplexor channel　A multiplexer channel that interleaves blocks of data. See also *byte multiplexor channel*. Contrast with *selector channel*.

branch prediction　A mechanism used by the processor to predict the outcome of a program branch prior to its execution.

buffer　Storage used to compensate for a difference in rate of flow of data, or time of occurrence of events, when transferring data from one device to another.

bus   A shared communications path consisting of one or a collection of lines. In some computer systems, CPU, memory, and I/O components are connected by a common bus. Since the lines are shared by all components, only one component at a time can successfully transmit.

bus arbitration   The process of determining which competing bus master will be permitted access to the bus.

bus master   A device attached to a bus that is capable of initiating and controlling communication on the bus.

byte   A sequence of eight bits. Also referred to as an *octet*.

byte multiplexor channel   A multiplexer channel that interleaves bytes of data. See also *block multiplexor channel*. Contrast with *selector channel*.

cache   A relatively small fast memory interposed between a larger, slower memory and the logic that accesses the larger memory. The cache holds recently accessed data, and is designed to speed up subsequent access to the same data.

cache coherence protocol   A mechanism to maintain data validity among multiple caches so that every data access will always acquire the most recent version of the contents of a main memory word.

cache line   A block of data associated with a cache tag and the unit of transfer between cache and memory.

cache memory   A special buffer storage, smaller and faster than main storage, that is used to hold a copy of instructions and data in main storage that are likely to be needed next by the processor and that have been obtained automatically from main storage.

CD-ROM   Compact Disk Read-Only Memory. A nonerasable disk used for storing computer data. The standard system uses 12-cm disks and can hold more than 550 Mbytes.

central processing unit (CPU)   That portion of a computer that fetches and executes instructions. It consists of an Arithmetic and Logic Unit (ALU), a control unit, and registers. Often simply referred to as a *processor*.

cluster   A group of interconnected, whole computers working together as a unified computing resource that can create the illusion of being one machine. The term *whole computer* means a system that can run on its own, apart from the cluster.

combinational circuit   A logic device whose output values, at any given instant, depend only upon the input values at that time. A combinational circuit is a special case of a sequential circuit that does not have a storage capability. Synonymous with *combinatorial circuit*.

compact disk (CD)   A nonerasable disk that stores digitized audio information.

computer architecture   Those attributes of a system visible to a programmer or, put another way, those attributes that have a direct impact on the logical execution of a program. Examples of architectural attributes include the instruction set, the number of bits used to represent various data types (e.g., numbers, characters), I/O mechanisms, and techniques for addressing memory.

computer instruction   An instruction that can be recognized by the processing unit of the computer for which it is designed. Synonymous with *machine instruction*.

computer instruction set A complete set of the operators of the instructions of a computer together with a description of the types of meanings that can be attributed to their operands. Synonymous with *machine instruction set*.

computer organization Refers to the operational units and their interconnections that realize the architectural specifications. Organizational attributes include those hardware details transparent to the programmer, such as control signals; interfaces between the computer and peripherals; and the memory technology used.

conditional jump A jump that takes place only when the instruction that specifies it is executed and specified conditions are satisfied. Contrast with *unconditional jump*.

condition code A code that reflects the result of a previous operation (e.g., arithmetic). A CPU may include one or more condition codes, which may be stored separately within the CPU or as part of a larger control register. Also known as a *flag*.

control bus That portion of a system bus used for the transfer of control signals.

control registers CPU registers employed to control CPU operation. Most of these registers are not user visible.

control storage A portion of storage that contains microcode.

control unit That part of the CPU that controls CPU operations, including ALU operations, the movement of data within the CPU, and the exchange of data and control signals across external interfaces (e.g., the system bus).

daisy chain A method of device interconnection for determining interrupt priority by connecting the interrupt sources serially.

data bus That portion of a system bus used for the transfer of data.

data communication Data transfer between devices. The term generally excludes I/O.

decoder A device that has a number of input lines of which any number may carry signals and a number of output lines of which not more than one may carry a signal, there being a one-to-one correspondence between the outputs and the combinations of input signals.

demand paging The transfer of a page from auxiliary storage to real storage at the moment of need.

direct access The capability to obtain data from a storage device or to enter data into a storage device in a sequence independent of their relative position, by means of addresses that indicate the physical location of the data.

direct address An address that designates the storage location of an item of data to be treated as operand. Synonymous with *one-level address*.

direct memory access (DMA) A form of I/O in which a special module, called a *DMA module*, controls the exchange of data between main memory and an I/O module. The CPU sends a request for the transfer of a block of data to the DMA module and is interrupted only after the entire block has been transferred.

disabled interrupt A condition, usually created by the CPU, during which the CPU will ignore interrupt request signals of a specified class.

diskette A flexible magnetic disk enclosed in a protective container. Synonymous with *flexible disk*.

disk pack   An assembly of magnetic disks that can be removed as a whole from a disk drive, together with a container from which the assembly must be separated when operating.

disk stripping   A type of disk array mapping in which logically contiguous blocks of data, or strips, are mapped round-robin to consecutive array members. A set of logically consecutive strips that maps exactly one strip to each array member is referred to as a stripe.

dynamic RAM   A RAM whose cells are implemented using capacitors. A dynamic RAM will gradually lose its data unless it is periodically refreshed.

emulation   The imitation of all or part of one system by another, primarily by hardware, so that the imitating system accepts the same data, executes the same programs, and achieves the same results as the imitated system.

enabled interrupt   A condition, usually created by the CPU, during which the CPU will respond to interrupt request signals of a specified class.

erasable optical disk   A disk that uses optical technology but that can be easily erased and rewritten. Both 3.25-inch and 5.25-inch disks are in use. A typical capacity is 650 Mbytes.

error-correcting code   A code in which each character or signal conforms to specific rules of construction so that deviations from these rules indicate the presence of an error and in which some or all of the detected errors can be corrected automatically.

error-detecting code   A code in which each character or signal conforms to specific rules of construction so that deviations from these rules indicate the presence of an error.

execute cycle   That portion of the instruction cycle during which the CPU performs the operation specified by the instruction opcode.

fetch cycle   That portion of the instruction cycle during which the CPU fetches from memory the instruction to be executed.

firmware   Microcode stored in read-only memory.

fixed-point representation system   A radix numeration system in which the radix point is implicitly fixed in the series of digit places by some convention upon which agreement has been reached.

flip-flop   A circuit or device containing active elements, capable of assuming either one of two stable states at a given time. Synonymous with *bistable circuit, toggle.*

floating-point representation system   A numeration system in which a real number is represented by a pair of distinct numerals, the real number being the product of the fixed-point part, one of the numerals, and a value obtained by raising the implicit floating-point base to a power denoted by the exponent in the floating-point representation, indicated by the second numeral.

G   Prefix meaning 2^{30}.

gate   An electronic circuit that produces an output signal that is a simple Boolean operation on its input signals.

general-purpose register   A register, usually explicitly addressable, within a set of registers, that can be used for different purposes, for example, as an accumulator, as an index register, or as a special handler of data.

global variable A variable defined in one portion of a computer program and used in at least one other portion of that computer program.

high-performance computing (HPC) A research area dealing with supercomputers and the software that runs on supercomputers. The emphasis is on scientific applications, which may involve heavy use of vector and matrix computation, and parallel algorithms.

immediate address The contents of an address part that contains the value of an operand rather than an address. Synonymous with *zero-level address*.

indexed address An address that is modified by the content of an index register prior to or during the execution of a computer instruction.

indexing A technique of address modification by means of index registers.

index register A register whose contents can be used to modify an operand address during the execution of computer instructions; it can also be used as a counter. An index register may be used to control the execution of a loop, to control the use of an array, as a switch, for table lookup, or as a pointer.

indirect address An address of a storage location that contains an address.

indirect cycle That portion of the instruction cycle during which the CPU performs a memory access to convert an indirect address into a direct address.

input-output (I/O) Pertaining to either input or output, or both. Refers to the movement of data between a computer and a directly attached peripheral.

instruction address register A special-purpose register used to hold the address of the next instruction to be executed.

instruction cycle The processing performed by a CPU to execute a single instruction.

instruction format The layout of a computer instruction as a sequence of bits. The format divides the instruction into fields, corresponding to the constituent elements of the instruction (e.g., opcode, operands).

instruction issue The process of initiating instruction execution in the processor's functional units. This occurs when an instruction moves from the decode stage of the pipeline to the first execute stage of the pipeline

instruction register A register that is used to hold an instruction for interpretation.

integrated circuit (IC) A tiny piece of solid material, such as silicon, upon which is etched or imprinted a collection of electronic components and their interconnections.

interrupt A suspension of a process, such as the execution of a computer program, caused by an event external to that process, and performed in such a way that the process can be resumed. Synonymous with *interruption*.

interrupt cycle That portion of the instruction cycle during which the CPU checks for interrupts. If an enabled interrupt is pending, the CPU saves the current program state and resumes processing at an interrupt-handler routine.

interrupt-driven I/O A form of I/O. The CPU issues an I/O command, continues to execute subsequent instructions, and is interrupted by the I/O module when the latter has completed its work.

I/O channel   A relatively complex I/O module that relieves the CPU of the details of I/O operations. An I/O channel will execute a sequence of I/O commands from main memory without the need for CPU involvement.

I/O controller   A relatively simple I/O module that requires detailed control from the CPU or an I/O channel. Synonymous with *device controller*.

I/O module   One of the major component types of a computer. It is responsible for the control of one or more external devices (peripherals) and for the exchange of data between those devices and main memory and/or CPU registers.

I/O processor   An I/O module with its own processor, capable of executing its own specialized I/O instructions or, in some cases, general-purpose machine instructions.

isolated I/O   A method of addressing I/O modules and external devices. The I/O address space is treated separately from main memory address space. Specific I/O machine instructions must be used. Compare *memory-mapped* I/O.

k   Prefix meaning $2^{10} = 1024$. Thus, 2 kb = 2048 bits.

local variable   A variable that is defined and used only in one specified portion of a computer program.

locality of reference   The tendency of a processor to access the same set of memory locations repetitively over a short period of time.

M   Prefix meaning $2^{20} = 1,048,576$. Thus, 2 Mb = 2,097,152 bits.

magnetic disk   A flat circular plate with a magnetizable surface layer, on one or both sides of which data can be stored.

magnetic tape   A tape with a magnetizable surface layer on which data can be stored by magnetic recording.

mainframe   A term originally referring to the cabinet containing the central processor unit or "main frame" of a large batch machine. After the emergence of smaller minicomputer designs in the early 1970s, the traditional larger machines were described as mainframe computers, mainframes. Typical characteristics of a mainframe are that it supports a large database, has elaborate I/O hardware, and is used in a central data processing facility.

main memory   Program-addressable storage from which instructions and other data can be loaded directly into registers for subsequent execution or processing.

memory address register (MAR)   A register, in a processing unit, that contains the address of the storage location being accessed.

memory buffer register (MBR)   A register that contains data read from memory or data to be written to memory.

memory cycle time   The inverse of the rate at which memory can be accessed. It is the minimum time between the response to one access request (read or write) and the response to the next access request.

memory-mapped I/O   A method of addressing I/O modules and external devices. A single address space is used for both main memory and I/O addresses, and the same machine instructions are used both for memory read/write and for I/O.

microcomputer   A computer system whose processing unit is a microprocessor. A basic microcomputer includes a microprocessor, storage, and an input/output facility, which may or may not be on one chip.

microinstruction   An instruction that controls data flow and sequencing in a processor at a more fundamental level than machine instructions. Individual machine instructions and perhaps other functions may be implemented by microprograms.

micro-operation   An elementary CPU operation, performed during one clock pulse.

microprocessor   A processor whose elements have been miniaturized into one or a few integrated circuits.

microprogram   A sequence of microinstructions that are in special storage where they can be dynamically accessed to perform various functions.

microprogrammed CPU   A CPU whose control unit is implemented using microprogramming.

microprogramming language   An instruction set used to specify microprograms.

multiplexer   A combinational circuit that connects multiple inputs to a single output. At any time, only one of the inputs is selected to be passed to the output.

multiplexor channel   A channel designed to operate with a number of I/O devices simultaneously. Several I/O devices can transfer records at the same time by interleaving items of data. See also *byte multiplexor channel, block multiplexor channel.*

multiprocessor   A computer that has two or more processors that have common access to a main storage.

multiprogramming   A mode of operation that provides for the interleaved execution of two or more computer programs by a single processor.

multitasking   A mode of operation that provides for the concurrent performance or interleaved execution of two or more computer tasks. The same as multiprogramming, using different terminology.

nonuniform memory access (NUMA) multiprocessor   A shared-memory multiprocessor in which the access time from a given processor to a word in memory varies with the location of the memory word.

nonvolatile memory   Memory whose contents are stable and do not require a constant power source.

nucleus   That portion of an operating system that contains its basic and most frequently used functions. Often, the nucleus remains resident in main memory.

ones complement representation   Used to represent binary integers. A positive integer is represented as in sign magnitude. A negative integer is represented by reversing each bit in the representation of a positive integer of the same magnitude.

opcode   Abbreviated form for *operation code.*

operand   An entity on which an operation is performed.

operating system   Software that controls the execution of programs and that provides services such as resource allocation, scheduling, input/output control, and data management.

operation code   A code used to represent the operations of a computer. Usually abbreviated to opcode.

orthogonality A principle by which two variables or dimensions are independent of one another. In the context of an instruction set, the term is generally used to indicate that other elements of an instruction (address mode, number of operands, length of operand) are independent of (not determined by) opcode.

page In a virtual storage system, a fixed-length block that has a virtual address and that is transferred as a unit between real storage and auxiliary storage.

page fault Occurs when the page containing a referenced word is not in main memory. This causes an interrupt and requires the operating system to bring in the needed page.

page frame An area of main storage used to hold a page.

parity Bit A binary digit appended to a group of binary digits to make the sum of all the digits either always odd (odd parity) or always even (even parity).

peripheral equipment In a computer system, with respect to a particular processing unit, any equipment that provides the processing unit with outside communication. Synonymous with *peripheral device.*

pipeline A processor organization in which the processor consists of a number of stages, allowing multiple instructions to be executed concurrently.

predicated execution A mechanism that supports the conditional execution of individual instructions. This makes it possible to execute speculatively both branches of a branch instruction and retain the results of the branch that is ultimately taken.

process A program in execution. A process is controlled and scheduled by the operating system.

process control block The manifestation of a process in an operating system. It is a data structure containing information about the characteristics and state of the process.

processor In a computer, a functional unit that interprets and executes instructions. A processor consists of at least an instruction control unit and an arithmetic unit.

processor cycle time The time required for the shortest well-defined CPU micro-operation. It is the basic unit of time for measuring all CPU actions. Synonymous with *machine cycle time.*

program counter Instruction address register.

programmable logic array (PLA) An array of gates whose interconnections can be programmed to perform a specific logical function.

programmable read-only memory (PROM) Semiconductor memory whose contents may be set only once. The writing process is performed electrically and may be performed by the user at a time later than original chip fabrication.

programmed I/O A form of I/O in which the CPU issues an I/O command to an I/O module and must then wait for the operation to be complete before proceeding.

program status word (PSW) An area in storage used to indicate the order in which instructions are executed, and to hold and indicate the status of the computer system. Synonymous with *processor status word.*

random-access memory (RAM) Memory in which each addressable location has a unique addressing mechanism. The time to access a given location is independent of the sequence of prior access.

read-only memory (ROM)   Semiconductor memory whose contents cannot be altered, except by destroying the storage unit. Nonerasable memory.

redundant array of independent disks (RAID)   A disk array in which part of the physical storage capacity is used to store redundant information about user data stored on the remainder of the storage capacity. The redundant information enables regeneration of user data in the event that one of the array's member disks or the access path to it fails.

registers   High-speed memory internal to the CPU. Some registers are user visible; that is, available to the programmer via the machine instruction set. Other registers are used only by the CPU, for control purposes.

scalar   A quantity characterized by a single value.

secondary memory   Memory located outside the computer system itself; that is, it cannot be processed directly by the processor. It must first be copied into main memory. Examples include disk and tape.

selector channel   An I/O channel designed to operate with only one I/O device at a time. Once the I/O device is selected, a complete record is transferred one byte at a time. Contrast with *block multiplexor channel, multiplexor channel*.

semiconductor   A solid crystalline substance, such as silicon or germanium, whose electrical conductivity is intermediate between insulators and good conductors. Used to fabricate transistors and solid-state components.

sequential circuit   A digital logic circuit whose output depends on the current input plus the state of the circuit. Sequential circuits thus possess the attribute of memory.

sign–magnitude representation   Used to represent binary integers. In an N-bit word, the leftmost bit is the sign ($0 =$ positive, $1 =$ negative) and the remaining $N - 1$ bits comprise the magnitude of the number.

solid-state component   A component whose operation depends on the control of electric or magnetic phenomena in solids (e.g., transistor crystal diode, ferrite core).

speculative execution   The execution of instructions along one path of a branch. If it later turns out that this branch was not taken, then the results of the speculative execution are discarded.

stack   An ordered list in which items are appended to and deleted from the same end of the list, known as the top. That is, the next item appended to the list is put on the top, and the next item to be removed from the list is the item that has been in the list the shortest time. This method is characterized as last-in-first-out.

static RAM   A RAM whose cells are implemented using flip-flops. A static RAM will hold its data as long as power is supplied to it; no periodic refresh is required.

superpipelined processor   A processor design in which the instruction pipeline consists of many very small stages, so that more than one pipeline stage can be executed during one clock cycle and so that a large number of instructions may be in the pipeline at the same time.

superscalar processor   A processor design that includes multiple-instruction pipelines, so that more than one instruction can be executing in the same pipeline stage simultaneously.

symmetric multiprocessing (SMP)   A form of multiprocessing that allows the operating system to execute on any available processor or on several available processors simultaneously.

synchronous timing A technique in which the occurrence of events on a bus is determined by a clock. The clock defines equal-width time slots, and events begin only at the beginning of a time slot.

system bus A bus used to interconnect major computer components (CPU, memory, I/O).

truth table A table that describes a logic function by listing all possible combinations of input values and indicating, for each combination, the output value.

twos complement representation Used to represent binary integers. A positive integer is represented as in sign magnitude. A negative number is represented by taking the Boolean complement of each bit of the corresponding positive number, then adding 1 to the resulting bit pattern viewed as an unsigned integer.

unary operator An operator that represents an operation on one and only one operand.

unconditional jump A jump that takes place whenever the instruction that specified it is executed.

uniprocessing Sequential execution of instructions by a processing unit, or independent use of a processing unit in a multiprocessing system.

user-visible registers CPU registers that may be referenced by the programmer. The instruction-set format allows one or more registers to be specified as operands or addresses of operands.

vector A quantity usually characterized by an ordered set of scalars.

very long instruction word (VLIW) Refers to the use of instructions that contain multiple operations. In effect, multiple instructions are contained in a single word. Typically, a VLIW is constructed by the compiler, which places operations that may be executed in parallel in the same word.

virtual storage The storage space that may be regarded as addressable main storage by the user of a computer system in which virtual addresses are mapped into real addresses. The size of virtual storage is limited by the addressing scheme of the computer system and by the amount of auxiliary storage available, and not by the actual number of main storage locations.

volatile memory A memory in which a constant electrical power source is required to maintain the contents of memory. If the power is switched off, the stored information is lost.

word An ordered set of bytes or bits that is the normal unit in which information may be stored, transmitted, or operated on within a given computer. Typically, if a processor has a fixed-length instruction set, then the instruction length equals the word length.

REFERENCES

ABBREVIATIONS

ACM   Association for Computing Machinery
IBM   International Business Machines Corporation
IEEE   Institute of Electrical and Electronics Engineers

ACOS86   Acosta, R.; Kjelstrup, J.; and Torng, H. "An Instruction Issuing Approach to Enhancing Performance in Multiple Functional Unit Processors." *IEEE Transactions on Computers*, September 1986.

ADAM91   Adamek, J. *Foundations of Coding*. New York: Wiley, 1991.

AGAR89   Agarwal, A. *Analysis of Cache Performance for Operating Systems and Multiprogramming* Boston: Kluwer Academic Publishers, 1989.

AGER87   Agerwala, T., and Cocke, J. *High Performance Reduced Instruction Set Processors*. Technical Report RC12434 (#55845). Yorktown, NY: IBM Thomas J. Watson Research Center, January 1987.

AMDA67   Amdahl, G. "Validity of the Single-Processor Approach to Achieving Large-Scale Computing Capability." *Proceedings, of the AFIPS Conference*, 1967.

ANDE67a   Anderson, D.; Sparacio, F.; and Tomasulo, F. "The IBM System/360 Model 91: Machine Philosophy and Instruction Handling." *IBM Journal of Research and Development*, January 1967.

ANDE67b   Anderson, S., et al. "The IBM System/360 Model 91: Floating-Point Execution Unit." *IBM Journal of Research and Development*, January 1967. Reprinted in [SWAR90, Volume 1].

ANTH08   Anthes, G. "What's Next for the x86?" *ComputerWorld*, June 16, 2008.

ARM08a   ARM Limited. *Cortex-A8 Technical Reference Manual*. ARM DDI 0344E, 2008, www.arm.com

ARM08b   ARM Limited. *ARM11 MPCore Processor Technical Reference Manual*. ARM DDI 0360E, 2008, www.arm.com

ASH90   Ash. R. *Information Theory*. New York: Dover, 1990.

ATKI96   Atkins, M. "PC Software Performance Tuning." *IEEE Computer*, August 1996.

AZIM92   Azimi, M.; Prasad, B.; and Bhat, K. "Two Level Cache Architectures." *Proceedings COMPCON '92*, February 1992.

BACO94   Bacon, F.; Graham, S.; and Sharp, O. "Compiler Transformations for High-Performance Computing." *ACM Computing Surveys*, December 1994.

BAER10   Baer, J. *Microprocessor Architecture: From Simple Pipelines to Chip Multiprocessors*. New York: Cambridge University Press, 2010.

BAIL93   Bailey, D. "RISC Microprocessors and Scientific Computing." *Proceedings, Supercomputing '93*, 1993.

BASH81   Bashe, C.; Bucholtz, W.; Hawkins, G.; Ingram, J.; and Rochester, N. "The Architecture of IBM's Early Computers." *IBM Journal of Research and Development*, September 1981.

BASH91   Bashteen, A.; Lui, I.; and Mullan, J. "A Superpipeline Approach to the MIPS Architecture." *Proceedings, COMPCON Spring '91*, February 1991.

BELL70   Bell, C.; Cady, R.; McFarland, H.; Delagi, B.; O'Loughlin, J.; and Noonan, R. "A New Architecture for Minicomputers—The DEC PDP-11." *Proceedings, Spring Joint Computer Conference*, 1970.

BELL71   Bell, C., and Newell, A. *Computer Structures: Readings and Examples*. New York: McGraw-Hill, 1971.

BELL74 Bell, J.; Casasent, D.; and Bell, C. "An Investigation into Alternative Cache Organizations." *IEEE Transactions on Computers*, April 1974.

BELL78a Bell, C.; Mudge, J.; and McNamara, J. *Computer Engineering: A DEC View of Hardware Systems Design.* Bedford, MA: Digital Press, 1978.

BELL78b Bell, C.; Newell, A.; and Siewiorek, D. "Structural Levels of the PDP-8." In [BELL78a].

BELL78c Bell, C.; Kotok, A.; Hastings, T.; and Hill, R. "The Evolution of the DEC System-10." *Communications of the ACM*, January 1978.

BENH92 Benham, J. "A Geometric Approach to Presenting Computer Representations of Integers." *SIGCSE Bulletin*, December 1992.

BETK97 Betker, M.; Fernando, J.; and Whalen, S. "The History of the Microprocessor." *Bell Labs Technical Journal*, Autumn 1997.

BEZ03 Bez, R., et al. "Introduction to Flash Memory." *Proceedings of the IEEE*, April 2003.

BLAA97 Blaauw, G., and Brooks, F. *Computer Architecture: Concepts and Evolution.* Reading, MA: Addison-Wesley, 1997.

BLAH83 Blahut, R. *Theory and Practice of Error Control Codes.* Reading, MA: Addison-Wesley, 1983.

BOHR98 Bohr, M. "Silicon Trends and Limits for Advanced Microprocessors." *Communications of the ACM*, March 1998.

BORK03 Borkar, S. "Getting Gigascale Chips: Challenges and Opportunities in Continuing Moore's Law." *ACM Queue*, October 2003.

BORK07 Borkar, S. "Thousand Core Chips—A Technology Perspective." *Proceedings, ACM/IEEE Design Automation Conference*, 2007.

BRAD91a Bradlee, D.; Eggers, S.; and Henry, R. "The Effect on RISC Performance of Register Set Size and Structure Versus Code Generation Strategy." *Proceedings, 18th Annual International Symposium on Computer Architecture*, May 1991.

BRAD91b Bradlee, D.; Eggers, S.; and Henry, R. "Integrating Register Allocation and Instruction Scheduling for RISCs." *Proceedings, Fourth International Conference on Architectural Support for Programming Languages and Operating Systems,* April 1991.

BREW97 Brewer, E. "Clustering: Multiply and Conquer." *Data Communications*, July 1997.

BREY09 Brey, B. *The Intel Microprocessors: 8086/8066, 80186/80188, 80286, 80386, 80486, Pentium, Pentium Pro Processor, Pentium II, Pentium III, Pentium 4 and Core2 with 64-bit Extensions.* Upper Saddle River, NJ: Prentice Hall, 2009.

BROW96 Brown, S., and Rose, S. "Architecture of FPGAs and CPLDs: A Tutorial." *IEEE Design and Test of Computers*, Vol. 13, No. 2, 1996.

BURK46 Burks, A.; Goldstine, H.; and von Neumann, J. *Preliminary Discussion of the Logical Design of an Electronic Computer Instrument.* Report prepared for U.S. Army Ordnance Department, 1946, reprinted in [BELL71].

BUYY99a Buyya, R. *High Performance Cluster Computing: Architectures and Systems.* Upper Saddle River, NJ: Prentice Hall, 1999.

BUYY99b Buyya, R. *High Performance Cluster Computing: Programming and Applications.* Upper Saddle River, NJ: Prentice Hall, 1999.

CANT01 Cantin, J., and Hill, H. "Cache Performance for Selected SPEC CPU2000 Benchmarks." *Computer Architecture News*, September 2001.

CART06 Carter, P. *PC Assembly Language*, July 23, 2006. Available at this book's Web site.

CEKL97 Cekleov, M., and Dubois, M. "Virtual-Address Caches, Part 1: Problems and Solutions in Uniprocessors." *IEEE Micro*, September/October 1997.

CHAI82 Chaitin, G. "Register Allocation and Spilling via Graph Coloring." *Proceedings, SIGPLAN Symposium on Compiler Construction*, June 1982.

CHEN94 Chen, P.; Lee, E.; Gibson, G.; Katz, R.; and Patterson, D. "RAID: High-Performance, Reliable Secondary Storage." *ACM Computing Surveys*, June 1994.

CHEN96   Chen, S., and Towsley, D. "A Performance Evaluation of RAID Architectures." *IEEE Transactions on Computers*, October 1996.

CHOW86   Chow, F.; Himmelstein, M.; Killian, E.; and Weber, L. "Engineering a RISC Compiler System." *Proceedings, COMPCON Spring '86*, March 1986.

CHOW87   Chow, F.; Correll, S.; Himmelstein, M.; Killian, E.; and Weber, L. "How Many Addressing Modes Are Enough?" *Proceedings, Second International Conference on Architectural Support for Programming Languages and Operating Systems*. October 1987.

CHOW90   Chow, F., and Hennessy, J. "The Priority-Based Coloring Approach to Register Allocation." *ACM Transactions on Programming Languages*, October 1990.

CLAR85   Clark, D., and Emer, J. "Performance of the VAX-11/780 Translation Buffer: Simulation and Measurement." *ACM Transactions on Computer Systems*, February 1985.

CLEM00   Clemenwts, A. "The Undergraduate Curriculum in Computer Architecture." *IEEE Micro*, May/June 2000.

COHE81   Cohen, D. "On Holy Wars and a Plea for Peace." *Computer*, October 1981.

COLW85a   Colwell, R.; Hitchcock, C.; Jensen, E.; Brinkley-Sprunt, H.; and Kollar, C. "Computers, Complexity, and Controversy." *Computer*, September 1985.

COLW85b   Colwell, R.; Hitchcock, C.; Jensen, E.; and Sprunt, H. "More Controversy About 'Computers, Complexity, and Controversy.'" *Computer*, December 1985.

COOK82   Cook, R., and Dande, N. "An Experiment to Improve Operand Addressing." *Proceedings, Symposium on Architecture Support for Programming Languages and Operating Systems*, March 1982.

COON81   Coonen J. "Underflow and Denormalized Numbers." *IEEE Computer*, March 1981.

COUT86   Coutant, D.; Hammond, C.; and Kelley, J. "Compilers for the New Generation of Hewlett-Packard Computers." *Proceedings, COMPCON Spring '86*, March 1986.

CRAG79   Cragon, H. "An Evaluation of Code Space Requirements and Performance of Various Architectures." *Computer Architecture News*, February 1979.

CRAG92   Cragon, H. *Branch Strategy Taxonomy and Performance Models*. Los Alamitos, CA: IEEE Computer Society Press, 1992.

CRAW90   Crawford, J. "The i486 CPU: Executing Instructions in One Clock Cycle." *IEEE Micro*, February 1990.

CRIS97   Crisp, R. "Direct RAMBUS Technology: The New Main Memory Standard." *IEEE Micro*, November/December 1997.

CUPP01   Cuppu, V., et al. "High Performance DRAMS in Workstation Environments." *IEEE Transactions on Computers*, November 2001.

CURR11   Curran, B., et al. "The zEnterprise 196 System and Microprocessor." *IEEE Micro*, March/April 2011.

DATT93   Dattatreya, G. "A Systematic Approach to Teaching Binary Arithmetic in a First Course." *IEEE Transactions on Education*, February 1993.

DAVI87   Davidson, J., and Vaughan, R. "The Effect of Instruction Set Complexity on Program Size and Memory Performance." *Proceedings, Second International Conference on Architectural Support for Programming Languages and Operating Systems*, October 1987.

DENN68   Denning, P. "The Working Set Model for Program Behavior." *Communications of the ACM*, May 1968.

DERO87   DeRosa, J., and Levy, H. "An Evaluation of Branch Architectures." *Proceedings, Fourteenth Annual International Symposium on Computer Architecture*, 1987.

DESA05   Desai, D., et al. "BladeCenter System Overview." *IBM Journal of Research and Development*, November 2005.

DEWA90   Dewar, R., and Smosna, M. *Microprocessors: A Programmer's View*. New York: McGraw-Hill, 1990.

DOWD98   Dowd, K., and Severance, C. *High Performance Computing*. Sebastopol, CA: O'Reilly, 1998.

DUBE91   Dubey, P., and Flynn, M. "Branch Strategies: Modeling and Optimization." *IEEE Transactions on Computers*, October 1991.

ECKE90   Eckert, R. "Communication Between Computers and Peripheral Devices—An Analogy." *ACM SIGCSE Bulletin*, September 1990.

EISC07   Eischen, C. "RAID 6 Covers More Bases." *Network World*, April 9, 2007.

ELAY85   El-Ayat, K., and Agarwal, R. "The Intel 80386—Architecture and Implementation." *IEEE Micro*, December 1985.

ERCE04   Ercegovac, M., and Lang, T. *Digital Arithmetic.* San Francisco: Morgan Kaufmann, 2004.

EVEN00a Even, G., and Paul, W. "On the Design of IEEE Compliant Floating-Point Units." *IEEE Transactions on Computers*, May 2000.

EVEN00b Even, G., and Seidel, P. "A Comparison of Three Rounding Algorithms for IEEE Floating-Point Multiplication." *IEEE Transactions on Computers*, July 2000.

EVER98   Evers, M., et al. "An Analysis of Correlation and Predictability: What Makes Two-Level Branch Predictors Work." *Proceedings, 25th Annual International Symposium on Microarchitecture*, July 1998.

EVER01   Evers, M., and Yeh, T. "Understanding Branches and Designing Branch Predictors for High-Performance Microprocessors." *Proceedings of the IEEE*, November 2001.

FARH04   Farhat, H. *Digital Design and Computer Organization.* Boca Raton, FL: CRC Press, 2004.

FARM92   Farmwald, M., and Mooring, D. "A Fast Path to One Memory." *IEEE Spectrum*, October 1992.

FATA08   Fatahalian, K., and Houston, M. "A Closer Look at GPUs." *Communications of the ACM*, October 2008.

FLEM86   Fleming, P., and Wallace, J. "How Not to Lie with Statistics: The Correct Way to Summarize Benchmark Results." *Communications of the ACM*, March 1986.

FLYN72   Flynn, M. "Some Computer Organizations and Their Effectiveness." *IEEE Transactions on Computers*, September 1972.

FLYN85   Flynn, M.; Johnson, J.; and Wakefield, S. "On Instruction Sets and Their Formats." *IEEE Transactions on Computers*, March 1985.

FLYN87   Flynn, M.; Mitchell, C.; and Mulder, J. "And Now a Case for More Complex Instruction Sets." *Computer*, September 1987.

FLYN01   Flynn, M., and Oberman, S. *Advanced Computer Arithmetic Design.* New York: Wiley, 2001.

FOG08a   Fog, A. *Optimizing Subroutines in Assembly Language: An Optimization Guide for x86 Platforms.* Copenhagen University College of Engineering, 2008, http://www.agner.org/optimize/

FOG08b   Fog, A. *The Microarchitecture of Intel and AMD CPUs.* Copenhagen University College of Engineering, 2008, http://www.agner.org/optimize/

FRAI83   Frailey, D. "Word Length of a Computer Architecture: Definitions and Applications." *Computer Architecture News*, June 1983.

FRIE96   Friedman, M. "RAID Keeps Going and Going and…" *IEEE Spectrum*, April 1996.

FULL11   Fuller, S., and Millet, L., eds. *The Future of Computing Performance: Game Over or Next Level?* Washington, DC: National Academies Press, 2011, www.nap.edu

FURB00   Furber, S. *ARM System-on-Chip Architecture.* Reading, MA: Addison-Wesley, 2000.

FUTR01   Futral, W. *InfiniBand Architecture: Development and Deployment.* Hillsboro, OR: Intel Press, 2001.

GENU04   Genu, P. *A Cache Primer.* Application Note AN2663. Freescale Semiconductor, Inc., 2004 (available in Premium Content Document section).

GHAI98   Ghai, S.; Joyner, J.; and John, L. *Investigating the Effectiveness of a Third Level Cache.* Technical Report TR-980501-01, Laboratory for Computer Architecture, University of Texas at Austin, 1998, http://lca.ece.utexas.edu/pubs-by-type.html

GIBB04 Gibbs, W. "A Split at the Core." *Scientific American*, November 2004.

GIFF87 Gifford, D., and Spector, A. "Case Study: IBM's System/360-370 Architecture." *Communications of the ACM*, April 1987.

GOCH06 Gochman, S., et al. "Introduction to Intel Core Duo Processor Architecture." *Intel Technology Journal*, May 2006.

GOLD54 Goldstine, H.; Pomerene, J.; and Smith, C. *Final Progress Report on the Physical Realization of an Electronic Computing Instrument.* Princeton: The Institute for Advanced Study Electronic Computer Project, 1954.

GOLD91 Goldberg, D. "What Every Computer Scientist Should Know About Floating-Point Arithmetic." *ACM Computing Surveys*, March 1991.

GOOD83 Goodman, J. "Using Cache Memory to Reduce Processor-Memory Bandwidth." *Proceedings, 10th Annual International Symposium on Computer Architecture*, 1983. Reprinted in [HILL00].

GOOD05 Goodacre, J., and Sloss, A. "Parallelism and the ARM Instruction Set Architecture." *Computer*, July 2005.

GREG98 Gregg, J. *Ones and Zeros: Understanding Boolean Algebra, Digital Circuits, and the Logic of Sets.* New York: Wiley, 1998.

GRIM05 Grimheden, M., and Torngren, M. "What Is Embedded Systems and How Should It Be Taught?—Results from a Didactic Analysis." *ACM Transactions on Embedded Computing Systems*, August 2005.

GSOE08 Gsoedl, J. "Solid State: New Frontier in Storage." *Storage*, July 2008.

GUST88 Gustafson, J. "Reevaluating Amdahl's Law." *Communications of the ACM*, May 1988.

HAMM97 Hammond, L.; Nayfay, B.; and Olukotun, K. "A Single-Chip Multiprocessor." *Computer*, September 1997.

HAND98 Handy, J. *The Cache Memory Book.* San Diego: Academic Press, 1998.

HARR06 Harris, W. "Multi-Core in the Source Engine." *bit-tech.net technical paper*, November 2, 2006, bit-tech.net/gaming/2006/11/02/Multi_core_in_the_Source_Engin/1

HAYE98 Hayes, J. *Computer Architecture and Organization.* New York: McGraw-Hill, 1998.

HEAT84 Heath, J. "Re-Evaluation of RISC 1." *Computer Architecture News*, March 1984.

HENN82 Hennessy, J., et al. "Hardware/Software Tradeoffs for Increased Performance." *Proceedings, Symposium on Architectural Support for Programming Languages and Operating Systems*, March 1982.

HENN84 Hennessy, J. "VLSI Processor Architecture." *IEEE Transactions on Computers*, December 1984

HENN91 Hennessy, J., and Jouppi, N. "Computer Technology and Architecture: An Evolving Interaction." *Computer*, September 1991.

HENN06 Henning, J. "SPEC CPU2006 Benchmark Descriptions." *Computer Architecture News*, September 2006.

HENN07 Henning, J. "SPEC CPU Suite Growth: An Historical Perspective." *Computer Architecture News*, March 2007.

HIDA90 Hidaka, H.; Matsuda, Y.; Asakura, M.; and Kazuyasu, F. "The Cache DRAM Architecture: A DRAM with an on-Chip Cache Memory." *IEEE Micro*, April 1990.

HIGB90 Higbie, L. "Quick and Easy Cache Performance Analysis." *Computer Architecture News*, June 1990.

HILL89 Hill, M. "Evaluating Associativity in CPU Caches." *IEEE Transactions on Computers*, December 1989.

HILL00 Hill, M.; Jouppi, N.; and Sohi, G. *Readings in Computer Architecture.* San Francisco: Morgan Kaufmann, 2000.

HINT01 Hinton, G., et al. "The Microarchitecture of the Pentium 4 Processor." *Intel Technology Journal*, Q1, 2001, http://developer.intel.com/technology/itj/

HIRA07 Hirata, K., and Goodacre, J. "ARM MPCore: The Streamlined and Scalable ARM11 Processor Core." *Proceedings, 2007 Conference on Asia South Pacific Design Automation*, 2007.

HUCK83 Huck, T. *Comparative Analysis of Computer Architectures*. Stanford University Technical Report No. 83-243, May 1983.

HUGU91 Huguet, M., and Lang, T. "Architectural Support for Reduced Register Saving/Restoring in Single-Window Register Files." *ACM Transactions on Computer Systems*, February 1991.

HUTC96 Hutcheson, G., and Hutcheson, J. "Technology and Economics in the Semiconductor Industry." *Scientific American*, January 1996.

HWAN93 Hwang, K. *Advanced Computer Architecture*. New York: McGraw-Hill, 1993.

HWAN99 Hwang, K, et al. "Designing SSI Clusters with Hierarchical Checkpointing and Single I/O Space." *IEEE Concurrency*, January–March 1999.

IBM01 International Business Machines, Inc. *64 Mb Synchronous DRAM*. IBM Data Sheet 364164, January 2001.

INTE98 Intel Corp. *Pentium Pro and Pentium II Processors and Related Products*. Aurora, CO, 1998.

INTE01a Intel Corp. *Intel Pentium 4 Processor Optimization Reference Manual*. Document 248966-04, 2001, http://developer.intel.com/design/Pentium4/documentation.htm

INTE01b Intel Corp. *Desktop Performance and Optimization for Intel Pentium 4 Processor*. Document 248966-04, 2001, http://developer.intel.com/design/Pentium4/documentation.htm

INTE04a Intel Corp. *IA-32 Intel Architecture Software Developer's Manual (4 volumes)*. Document 253665 through 253668. 2004, http://developer.intel.com/design/Pentium4/documentation.htm

INTE04b Intel Research and Development. *Architecting the Era of Tera*. Intel White Paper, February 2004, http://www.intel.com/labs/teraera/index.htm

INTE04c Intel Corp. *Endianness White Paper*, November 15, 2004.

INTE11 Intel Corp. *Intel® 64 and IA-32 Intel Architectures Software Developer's Manual (3 volumes)*. Denver, CO, 2011.

JACO08 Jacob, B.; Ng, S.; and Wang, D. *Memory Systems: Cache, DRAM, Disk*. Boston: Morgan Kaufmann, 2008.

JAME90 James, D. "Multiplexed Buses: The Endian Wars Continue." *IEEE Micro*, June 1990.

JOHN91 Johnson, M. *Superscalar Microprocessor Design*. Englewood Cliffs, NJ: Prentice Hall, 1991.

JOHN08 John, E., and Rubio, J. *Unique Chips and Systems*. Boca Raton, FL: CRC Press, 2008.

JOUP88 Jouppi, N. "Superscalar versus Superpipelined Machines." *Computer Architecture News*, June 1988.

JOUP89a Jouppi, N., and Wall, D. "Available Instruction-Level Parallelism for Superscalar and Superpipelined Machines." *Proceedings, Third International Conference on Architectural Support for Programming Languages and Operating Systems*, April 1989.

JOUP89b Jouppi, N. "The Nonuniform Distribution of Instruction-Level and Machine Parallelism and Its Effect on Performance." *IEEE Transactions on Computers*, December 1989.

KAEL91 Kaeli, D., and Emma, P. "Branch History Table Prediction of Moving Target Branches Due to Subroutine Returns." *Proceedings, 18th Annual International Symposium on Computer Architecture*, May 1991.

KAGA01 Kagan, M. "InfiniBand: Thinking Outside the Box Design." *Communications System Design*, September 2001, www.csdmag.com

KALL04 Kalla, R.; Sinharoy, B.; and Tendler, J. "IBM Power5 Chip: A Dual-Core Multithreaded Processor." *IEEE Micro*, March–April 2004.

KANE92 Kane, G., and Heinrich, J. *MIPS RISC Architecture*. Englewood Cliffs, NJ: Prentice Hall, 1992.

KAPP00 Kapp. C. "Managing Cluster Computers." *Dr. Dobb's Journal*, July 2000.

KATE83 Katevenis, M. *Reduced Instruction Set Computer Architectures for VLSI.* PhD dissertation, Computer Science Department. University of California at Berkeley, October 1983. Reprinted by MIT Press, Cambridge, MA, 1985.

KATZ89 Katz, R.; Gibson, G.; and Patterson, D. "Disk System Architecture for High Performance Computing." *Proceedings of the IEEE*, December 1989.

KEET01 Keeth, B., and Baker, R. *DRAM Circuit Design: A Tutorial.* Piscataway, NJ: IEEE Press, 2001.

KNAG04 Knaggs, P., and Welsh, S. *ARM: Assembly Language Programming.* Bournemouth University, School of Design, Engineering, and Computing, August 31, 2004, www.freetechbooks.com/arm-assembly-language-programming-t729.html

KNUT71 Knuth, D. "An Empirical Study of FORTRAN Programs." *Software Practice and Experience*, Vol. 1, 1971.

KNUT98 Knuth, D. *The Art of Computer Programming, Volume 2: Seminumerical Algorithms.* Reading, MA: Addison-Wesley, 1998.

KOLB05 Kolbehdari, M., et al. "The Emergence of PCI Express* in the Next Generation of Mobile Platforms." *Intel Technology Journal*, February 2005.

KOOP96 Koopman, P. "Embedded System Design Issues (the Rest of the Story). *Proceedings, 1996 International Conference on Computer Design*, 1996.

KUCK77 Kuck, D.; Parker, D.; and Sameh, A. "An Analysis of Rounding Methods in Floating-Point Arithmetic." *IEEE Transactions on Computers*, July 1977.

KUGA91 Kuga, M.; Murakami, K.; and Tomita, S. "DSNS (Dynamically-hazard resolved, Statically-code-scheduled, Nonuniform Superscalar): Yet Another Superscalar Processor Architecture." *Computer Architecture News*, June 1991.

LEE91 Lee, R.; Kwok, A.; and Briggs, F. "The Floating Point Performance of a Superscalar SPARC Processor." *Proceedings, Fourth International Conference on Architectural Support for Programming Languages and Operating Systems*, April 1991.

LEON07 Leonard, T. "Dragged Kicking and Screaming: Source Multicore." *Proceedings, Game Developers Conference 2007*, March 2007.

LEON08 Leong, P. "Recent Trends in FPGA Architectures and Applications." *Proceedings, 4th IEEE International symposium on Electronic Design, Test. and Applications*, 2008.

LILJ88 Lilja. D. "Reducing the Branch Penalty in Pipelined Processors." *Computer*, July 1988.

LILJ93 Lilja, D. "Cache Coherence in Large-Scale Shared-Memory Multiprocessors: Issues and Comparisons." *ACM Computing Surveys*, September 1993.

LITT61 Little, J. "A Proof for the Queuing Formula: $L = \lambda W$." *Operations Research*, May–June, 1961.

LITT11 Little, J. "Little's Law as Viewed on Its 50th Anniversary." *Operations Research*, May–June, 2011.

LOVE96 Lovett, T., and Clapp, R. "Implementation and Performance of a CC-NUMA System." *Proceedings, 23rd Annual International Symposium on Computer Architecture*, May 1996.

LUND77 Lunde, A. "Empirical Evaluation of Some Features of Instruction Set Processor Architectures." *Communications of the ACM*. March 1977.

MACD84 MacDougall, M. "Instruction-level Program and Process Modeling." *IEEE Computer*, July 1984.

MADD09 Maddox, R., et al. *Weaving High Performance Multiprocessor Fabric: Architectural Insights to the Intel QuickPath Interconnect.* Hillsboro, OR: Intel Press, 2009.

MAK04 Mak, P., et al. "Processor Subsystem Interconnect for a Large Symmetric Multiprocessing System." *IBM Journal of Research and Development*, May/July 2004.

MAK97 Mak, P., et al. "Shared-Cache Clusters in a System with a Fully Shared Memory." *IBM Journal of Research and Development*, July/September 1997.

MANO08 Mano, M., and Kime, C. *Logic and Computer Design Fundamentals.* Upper Saddle River, NJ: Prentice Hall, 2008.

MANS97 Mansuripur, M., and Sincerbox, G. "Principles and Techniques of Optical Data Storage." *Proceedings of the IEEE*, November 1997.

MARR02 Marr, D., et al. "Hyper-Threading Technology Architecture and Microarchitecture." *Intel Technology Journal*, First Quarter, 2002.

MASH95 Mashey, J. "CISC vs. RISC (or what is RISC really)." *USENET comp.arch newsgroup, article 46782*, February 1995.

MAYB84 Mayberry, W., and Efland, G. "Cache Boosts Multiprocessor Performance." *Computer Design*, November 1984.

MAZI10 Mazidi, M.; Mazidi, J.; and Causey, D. *The x86 PC: Assembly Language, Design and Interfacing.* Upper Saddle River, NJ: Prentice Hall, 2010.

MCDO05 McDougall, R. "Extreme Software Scaling." *ACM Queue*, September 2005.

MCDO06 McDougall, R., and Laudon, J. "Multi-Core Microprocessors Are Here." *;login*, October 2006.

MCEL85 McEliece, R. "The Reliability of Computer Memories." *Scientific American*, January 1985.

MEND06 Mendelson, A., et al. "CMP Implementation in Systems Based on the Intel Core Duo Processor." *Intel Technology Journal*, May 2006.

MILE00 Milenkovic, A. "Achieving High Performance in Bus-Based Shared-Memory Multiprocessors." *IEEE Concurrency*, July–September 2000.

MIRA92 Mirapuri, S.; Woodacre, M.; and Vasseghi, N. "The MIPS R4000 Processor." *IEEE Micro*, April 1992.

MOOR65 Moore, G. "Cramming More Components Onto Integrated Circuits." *Electronics Magazine*, April 19, 1965.

MORS78 Morse, S.; Pohlman, W.; and Ravenel, B. "The Intel 8086 Microprocessor: A 16-bit Evolution of the 8080." *Computer*, June 1978.

MOSH01 Moshovos, A., and Sohi, G. "Microarchitectural Innovations: Boosting Microprocessor Performance Beyond Semiconductor Technology Scaling." *Proceedings of the IEEE*, November 2001.

MULL10 Muller, J., et al. *Handbook of Floating-Point Arithmetic.* Boston: Birkhauser, 2010.

MYER78 Myers, G. "The Evaluation of Expressions in a Storage-to-Storage Architecture." *Computer Architecture News*, June 1978.

NOVI93 Novitsky, J.; Azimi, M.; and Ghaznavi, R. "Optimizing Systems Performance Based on Pentium Processors." *Proceedings COMPCON '92*, February 1993.

NOWE07 Nowell, M.; Vusirikala, V.; and Hays, R. "Overview of Requirements and Applications for 40 Gigabit and 100 Gigabit Ethernet." *Ethernet Alliance White Paper*, August 2007.

OBER97a Oberman, S., and Flynn, M. "Design Issues in Division and Other Floating-Point Operations." *IEEE Transactions on Computers*, February 1997.

OBER97b Oberman, S., and Flynn, M. "Division Algorithms and Implementations." *IEEE Transactions on Computers*, August 1997.

OKLO08 Oklobdzija, V., ed. *Digital Design and Fabrication.* Boca Raton, FL: CRC Press, 2008.

OLUK96 Olukotun, K., et al. "The Case for a Single-Chip Multiprocessor." *Proceedings, Seventh International Conference on Architectural Support for Programming Languages and Operating Systems*, 1996.

OLUK05 Olukotun, K., and Hammond, L. "The Future of Microprocessors." *ACM Queue*, September 2005.

OLUK07 Olukotun, K.; Hammond, L.; and Laudon, J. *Chip Multiprocessor Architecture: Techniques to Improve Throughput and Latency.* San Rafael, CA: Morgan & Claypool, 2007.

OMON99 Omondi, A. *The Microarchitecture of Pipelined and Superscalar Computers.* Boston: Kluwer, 1999.

OSUN11   Osuna, A., et al. *IBM System Storage Tape Library Guide for Open Systems.* IBM Redbook SG24-5946-07, June 2011.

PADE81   Padegs, A. "System/360 and Beyond." *IBM Journal of Research and Development,* September 1981.

PADE88   Padegs, A.; Moore, B.; Smith, R.; and Buchholz, W. "The IBM System/370 Vector Architecture: Design Considerations." *IEEE Transactions on Communications,* May 1988.

PARH10   Parhami, B. *Computer Arithmetic: Algorithms and Hardware Design.* Oxford: Oxford University Press, 2010.

PATT82a   Patterson, D., and Sequin, C. "A VLSI RISC." *Computer,* September 1982.

PATT82b   Patterson, D., and Piepho, R. "Assessing RISCs in High-Level Language Support." *IEEE Micro,* November 1982.

PATT84   Patterson, D. "RISC Watch." *Computer Architecture News,* March 1984.

PATT85a   Patterson, D. "Reduced Instruction Set Computers." *Communications of the ACM,* January 1985.

PATT85b   Patterson, D., and Hennessy, J. "Response to 'Computers, Complexity, and Controversy.'" *Computer,* November 1985.

PATT88   Patterson, D.; Gibson, G.; and Katz, R. "A Case for Redundant Arrays of Inexpensive Disks (RAID)." *Proceedings, ACM SIGMOD Conference of Management of Data,* June 1988.

PATT01   Patt, Y. "Requirements, Bottlenecks, and Good Fortune: Agents for Microprocessor Evolution." *Proceedings of the IEEE,* November 2001.

PAVA97   Pavan, P., et al. "Flash Memory Cells—An Overview." *Proceedings of the IEEE,* August 1997.

PEIR99   Peir, J.; Hsu, W.; and Smith, A. "Functional Implementation Techniques for CPU Cache Memories." *IEEE Transactions on Computers,* February 1999.

PELE97   Peleg, A.; Wilkie, S.; and Weiser, U. "Intel MMX for Multimedia PCs." *Communications of the ACM,* January 1997.

PFIS98   Pfister, G. *In Search of Clusters.* Upper Saddle River, NJ: Prentice Hall, 1998.

POLL99   Pollack, F. "New Microarchitecture Challenges in the Coming Generations of CMOS Process Technologies (keynote address)." *Proceedings of the 32nd Annual ACM/IEEE International Symposium on Microarchitecture,* 1999.

POPE91   Popescu, V., et al. "The Metaflow Architecture." *IEEE Micro,* June 1991.

PRES01   Pressel, D. "Fundamental Limitations on the Use of Prefetching and Stream Buffers for Scientific Applications." *Proceedings, ACM Symposium on Applied Computing,* March 2001.

PRIN97   Prince, B. *Semiconductor Memories.* New York: Wiley, 1997.

PRIN02   Prince, B. *Emerging Memories: Technologies and Trends.* Norwell, MA: Kluwer, 2002.

PROP11   Prophet, G. "Use GPUs to Boost Acceleration." *IDN,* December 2, 2011.

PRZY88   Przybylski, S.; Horowitz, M.; and Hennessy, J. "Performance Trade-Offs in Cache Design." *Proceedings, Fifteenth Annual International Symposium on Computer Architecture,* June 1988.

PRZY90   Przybylski, S. "The Performance Impact of Block Size and Fetch Strategies." *Proceedings, 17th Annual International Symposium on Computer Architecture,* May 1990.

RADI83   Radin, G. "The 801 Minicomputer." *IBM Journal of Research and Development,* May 1983.

RAGA83   Ragan-Kelley, R., and Clark, R. "Applying RISC Theory to a Large Computer." *Computer Design,* November 1983.

RAMA77   Ramamoorthy, C. "Pipeline Architecture." *Computing Surveys,* March 1977.

RECH98   Reches, S., and Weiss, S. "Implementation and Analysis of Path History in Dynamic Branch Prediction Schemes." *IEEE Transactions on Computers,* August 1998.

REDD76   Reddi, S., and Feustel, E. "A Conceptual Framework for Computer Architecture." *Computing Surveys*, June 1976.

REIM06   Reimer, J. "Valve Goes Multicore." *ars technica*, November 5, 2006, arstechnica.com/articles/paedia/cpu/valve-multicore.ars

RICH07   Riches, S., et al. "A Fully Automated High Performance Implementation of ARM Cortex-A8." *IQ Online*, Vol. 6, No. 3, 2007, www.arm.com/iqonline

SAKA02   Sakai, S. "CMP on SoC: Architect's View." *Proceedings, 15th International Symposium on System Synthesis*, 2002.

SATY81   Satyanarayanan, M., and Bhandarkar, D. "Design Trade-Offs in VAX-11 Translation Buffer Organization." *Computer*, December 1981.

SCHA97   Schaller, R. "Moore's Law: Past, Present, and Future." *IEEE Spectrum*, June 1997.

SCHW99   Schwarz, E., and Krygowski, C. "The S/390 G5 Floating-Point Unit." *IBM Journal of Research and Development*, September/November 1999.

SEAL00   Seal, D., ed. *ARM Architecture Reference Manual.* Reading, MA: Addison-Wesley, 2000.

SERL86   Serlin, O. "MIPS, Dhrystones, and Other Tales." *Datamation*, June 1, 1986.

SHAN38   Shannon, C. "Symbolic Analysis of Relay and Switching Circuits." *AIEE Transactions*, Vol. 57, 1938.

SHAN03   Shanley, T. *InfinBand Network Architecture.* Reading, MA: Addison-Wesley, 2003.

SHAN05   Shanley, T. *Unabridged Pentium 4. The: IA32 Processor Genealogy.* Reading, MA: Addison-Wesley, 2005.

SHAR97   Sharma, A. *Semiconductor Memories: Technology, Testing, and Reliability.* New York: IEEE Press, 1997.

SHAR03   Sharma, A. *Advanced Semiconductor Memories: Architectures, Designs, and Applications.* New York: IEEE Press, 2003.

SHEN05   Shen, J., and Lipasti, M. *Modern Processor Design: Fundamentals of Superscalar Processors.* New York: McGraw-Hill, 2005.

SIEG04   Siegel, T.; Pfeffer, E.; and Magee, A. "The IBM z990 Microprocessor." *IBM Journal of Research and Development*, May/July 2004.

SIEW82   Siewiorek, D.; Bell, C.; and Newell, A. *Computer Structures: Principles and Examples.* New York: McGraw-Hill, 1982.

SIMA97   Sima, D. "Superscalar Instruction Issue." *IEEE Micro*, September/October 1997.

SIMA04   Sima, D. "Decisive Aspects in the Evolution of Microprocessors." *Proceedings of the IEEE*, December 2004.

SIMO96   Simon, H. *The Sciences of the Artificial.* Cambridge, MA: MIT Press, 1996.

SING10   Singh, G., et al. "The Feeding of High-Performance Processor Cores—Quickpath Interconnects and the New I/O Hubs." *Intel Technology Journal*, September 2010.

SING11   Singh, G. "The IBM PC: The Silicon Story." *Computer*, August 2011.

SLOS04   Sloss, A.; Symes, D.; and Wright, C. *ARM System Developer's Guide.* San Francisco: Morgan Kaufmann, 2004.

SMIT82   Smith, A. "Cache Memories." *ACM Computing Surveys*, September 1982.

SMIT87   Smith, A. "Line (Block) Size Choice for CPU Cache Memories." *IEEE Transactions on Communications*, September 1987.

SMIT88   Smith, J. "Characterizing Computer Performance with a Single Number." *Communications of the ACM*, October 1988.

SMIT89   Smith, M.; Johnson, M.; and Horowitz, M. "Limits on Multiple Instruction Issue." *Proceedings, Third International Conference on Architectural Support for Programming Languages and Operating Systems*, April 1989.

SMIT95   Smith, J., and Sohi, G. "The Microarchitecture of Superscalar Processors." *Proceedings of the IEEE*, December 1995.

SMIT08   Smith, B. "ARM and Intel Battle over the Mobile Chip's Future." *Computer*, May 2008.

SODE96   Soderquist, P., and Leeser, M. "Area and Performance Tradeoffs in Floating-Point Divide and Square-Root Implementations." *ACM Computing Surveys*, September 1996.

SOHI90   Sohi, G. "Instruction Issue Logic for High-Performance Interruptable, Multiple Functional Unit, Pipelined Computers." *IEEE Transactions on Computers*, March 1990.

STAL88   Stallings, W. "Reduced Instruction Set Computer Architecture." *Proceedings of the IEEE*, January 1988.

STAL11   Stallings, W. *Data and Computer Communications, Ninth Edition.* Upper Saddle River, NJ: Prentice Hall, 2011.

STAL12   Stallings, W. *Operating Systems, Internals and Design Principles, Seventh Edition.* Upper Saddle River, NJ: Prentice Hall, 2012.

STEN90   Stenstrom, P. "A Survey of Cache Coherence Schemes of Multiprocessors." *Computer*, June 1990.

STEV64   Stevens, W. "The Structure of System/360, Part II: System Implementation." *IBM Systems Journal*, Vol. 3, No. 2, 1964. Reprinted in [SIEW82].

STON93   Stone, H. *High-Performance Computer Architecture.* Reading, MA: Addison-Wesley, 1993.

STON96   Stonham, T. *Digital Logic Techniques.* London: Chapman & Hall, 1996.

STRE78   Strecker, W. "VAX-11/780: A Virtual Address Extension to the DEC PDP-11 Family." *Proceedings, National Computer Conference*, 1978.

STRE83   Strecker, W. "Transient Behavior of Cache Memories." *ACM Transactions on Computer Systems*, November 1983.

STRI79   Stritter, E., and Gunter, T. "A Microprocessor Architecture for a Changing World: The Motorola 68000." *Computer*, February 1979.

SWAR90   Swartzlander, E., ed. *Computer Arithmetic, Volumes I and II.* Los Alamitos, CA: IEEE Computer Society Press, 1990.

TAMI83   Tamir, Y., and Sequin, C. "Strategies for Managing the Register File in RISC." *IEEE Transactions on Computers*, November 1983.

TANE78   Tanenbaum, A. "Implications of Structured Programming for Machine Architecture." *Communications of the ACM*, March 1978.

TJAD70   Tjaden, G., and Flynn, M. "Detection and Parallel Execution of Independent Instructions." *IEEE Transactions on Computers*, October 1970.

TOMA93   Tomasevic, M., and Milutinovic, V. *The Cache Coherence Problem in Shared-Memory Multiprocessors: Hardware Solutions.* Los Alamitos, CA: IEEE Computer Society Press, 1993.

TOON81   Toong, H., and Gupta, A. "An Architectural Comparison of Contemporary 16-Bit Microprocessors." *IEEE Micro*, May 1981.

TUCK87   Tucker, S. "The IBM 3090 System Design with Emphasis on the Vector Facility." *Proceedings, COMPCON Spring '87*, February 1987.

UNGE02   Ungerer, T.; Rubic, B.; and Silc, J. "Multithreaded Processors." *The Computer Journal*, No 3, 2002.

UNGE03   Ungerer, T.; Rubic, B.; and Silc, J. "A Survey of Processors with Explicit Multithreading." *ACM Computing Surveys*, March 2003.

VOGL94   Vogley, B. "800 Megabyte Per Second Systems Via Use of Synchronous DRAM." *Proceedings, COMPCON '94*, March 1994.

VONN45   Von Neumann, J. *First Draft of a Report on the EDVAC.* Moore School, University of Pennsylvania, 1945. Reprinted in *IEEE Annals on the History of Computing*, No. 4, 1993.

VRAN80   Vranesic, Z., and Thurber, K. "Teaching Computer Structures." *Computer*, June 1980.

WALL85   Wallich, P. "Toward Simpler, Faster Computers." *IEEE Spectrum*, August 1985.

WALL91   Wall, D. "Limits of Instruction-Level Parallelism." *Proceedings, Fourth International Conference on Architectural Support for Programming Languages and Operating Systems*, April 1991.

WANG99   Wang, G., and Tafti, D. "Performance Enhancement on Microprocessors with Hierarchical Memory Systems for Solving Large Sparse Linear Systems." *International Journal of Supercomputing Applications*, Vol. 13, 1999.

WEIC90   Weicker, R. "An Overview of Common Benchmarks." *Computer*, December 1990.

WEIN75   Weinberg, G. *An Introduction to General Systems Thinking.* New York: Wiley, 1975.

WEIS84   Weiss, S., and Smith, J. "Instruction Issue Logic in Pipelined Supercomputers." *IEEE Transactions on Computers,* November 1984.

WEYG01   Weygant, P. *Clusters for High Availability.* Upper Saddle River, NJ: Prentice Hall, 2001.

WHIT97   Whitney, S., et al. "The SGI Origin Software Environment and Application Performance." *Proceedings, COMPCON Spring '97,* February 1997.

WHIT11   White, B., et al. *IBM zEnterprise 196 Technical Guide.* IBM Redbook SG24-5946-07, June 2011.

WILE03   Wilen, A.; Schade, J.; and Thronburg, R. *Introduction to PCI Express—A Hardware and Software Developers Guide.* Hillsboro, OR: Intel Press, 2003.

WILK65   Wilkes, M. "Slave Memories and Dynamic Storage Allocation." *IEEE Transactions on Electronic Computers*, April 1965. Reprinted in [HILL00].

WILL90   Williams, F., and Steven, G. "Address and Data Register Separation on the M68000 Family." *Computer Architecture News*, June 1990.

YEH91   Yeh, T., and Patt, N. "Two-Level Adapting Training Branch Prediction." *Proceedings, 24th Annual International Symposium on Microarchitecture*, 1991.

ZHAN01   Zhang, Z.; Zhu, Z.; and Zhang, X. "Cached DRAM for ILP Processor Memory Access Latency Reduction." *IEEE Micro*, July–August 2001.

INDEX